LOOKING FOR INFORMATION: A SURVEY OF RESEARCH ON INFORMATION SEEKING, NEEDS, AND BEHAVIOR

THIRD EDITION

LIBRARY AND INFORMATION SCIENCE

Series Editor: **Amanda Spink**
Faculty of Education at the Queensland
University of Technology, Australia

Recent and Forthcoming Volumes

LIBRARY AND INFORMATION SCIENCE

LOOKING FOR INFORMATION: A SURVEY OF RESEARCH ON INFORMATION SEEKING, NEEDS, AND BEHAVIOR

THIRD EDITION

EDITED BY

DONALD O. CASE
School of Library and Information Science,
College of Communication and Information Studies,
University of Kentucky, Lexington

Series Editor: Amanda Spink

Emerald

United Kingdom • North America • Japan
India • Malaysia • China

PART 2: CONCEPTS RELEVANT TO INFORMATION BEHAVIOR

PART 3: MODELS, PARADIGMS, AND THEORIES IN THE STUDY OF INFORMATION BEHAVIOR

PART 4: METHODS FOR STUDYING INFORMATION BEHAVIOR

PART 5: RESEARCH RESULTS AND REFLECTIONS

List of Figures and Tables

Editorial Advisory Board

Preface

Looking for Information explores human information seeking and use. It provides examples of methods, models, and theories used in information behavior research, and reviews more than four decades of research on the topic. The book will be useful for scholars in related fields, and also for students at the graduate and advanced undergraduate levels. It is intended for use not only in information studies and communication, but also in the disciplines of education, management, business, medicine, nursing, public health, and social work.

The first edition of this book appeared in May of 2002. At the time there was no single, comprehensive text on the general topic of information behavior research even though interest in the topic was growing. Perhaps for that reason, *Looking for Information* was fairly popular, and in October of 2003 it was chosen as the "Best Information Science Book of 2002" by the American Society for Information Science and Technology (ASIS&T). A second edition appeared in 2007 with revised versions of most chapters, and a larger set of references.

This third edition of the book maintains the original structure (of 13 chapters divided into five sections), however every chapter has changed in some way. Most notably the chapters on theories and models have been expanded and reorganized. New concepts and examples (e.g., of collaboration and sharing of information) have been added to other chapters, along with additional recommended readings and questions for discussion. Almost one hundred older references have been removed and about 350 new ones added, for a total of about 1400 citations to relevant works; almost a quarter of these were published within the last six years — between January 2006 and November 2011. I hope that you find these changes useful.

Acknowledgments

It would be awkward to try to thank every one of the dozens of people who have contributed, in some way, to the writing of the latest edition of *Looking for Information*. I will simply mention a few who offered the most advice: Reijo Savolainen, of the University of Tampere; J. David Johnson, of the

University of Kentucky College of Communication and Information Studies; David D. Bartley, of University of Kentucky Health Care; and Wendy A. Miller, of the Lexington Public Library. Thanks also to the editors at Emerald, for their patience and support.

Donald O. Case

PART 1

INTRODUCTIONS AND EXAMPLES

Chapter 1

Information Behavior: An Introduction

What you *don't* know has power over you; knowing it brings it under your control, and makes it subject to your choice. Ignorance makes real choice impossible.

— Abraham Maslow (1963, p. 116)

Beyond obsessions, curiosity, and creativity, lies a host of motivations *not* to seek information.

— David Johnson (1997, p. 70)

Chapter Outline

1.1. Introduction

This volume describes common and essential human behaviors: seeking and using information. Noticing a change in the weather, deciding to visit another city, finding out about travel schedules, choosing a departure date, and buying an airline ticket are examples of a range of activities known as "information behavior." These include accidental encountering, needing, finding, choosing, using, and sometimes even avoiding, information. They are types of behaviors that are basic to human existence.

This introductory chapter describes the scope of the book and its contents. It says briefly what kinds of concepts, questions, and research have been developed regarding information behavior, and why this topic has attracted attention. I make the case that the nature of this research has changed over several decades, away from an emphasis on institutional sources and searches, and toward a focus on how individuals encounter and make sense of their environment.

The Internet could serve as a metaphor for information behavior and the way our view of it has changed. Think back to a time before the World Wide Web was available. All of the information was out there in individual books, journals, radio and TV programs, offices, filing cabinets, minds, and computers. But because it was divided by source, by location, by person, and by channel, it was not always easily located or examined. Making arrangements for *travel* is one comprehensive example: One could hear the weather forecast on the radio, read about a destination in a travel guide, call hotels to make reservations, telephone an airline to learn departure times and fares, visit a travel agent to pick up a ticket, and so on. In terms of research, each of those needs and transactions have needed to be conducted (and studied) separately. But now it is possible to satisfy all travel-related requests on a single website. Not only have the different channels of communication collapsed down to one, but less goal-oriented behaviors, such as browsing, may play a larger role than ever before. Looking for information becomes more holistic.

The contrast between new and old is even greater when we compare tasks in the office and classroom to their counterparts of 20 years ago. Obscure bits of information — the text of a government regulation, the date of an event, the author of a document — are more easily found in a single "place" — the Web. Both work and education have changed as a result.

In a manner similar to the emergence of the World Wide Web, our view of information behavior has become more integrated and less dictated by sources and institutions. As what we know about these behaviors has grown, so has the vocabulary used to describe it.

1.1.1.   A Bit of Vocabulary

In introducing the subject matter of this book I will be using terms like "information," "information need," "information seeking," and "information behavior" without defining them fully until later chapters. For the moment let us assume that there *are* such things as "information" and "information needs" that can be satisfied by "information seeking" or "information behavior." To tide us over until these concepts are fleshed out, here are some brief definitions:

- *Information* can be any *difference* you perceive, in your environment or within yourself. It is any aspect that you notice in the pattern of reality.

- An *information need* is a recognition that your knowledge is inadequate to satisfy a goal that you have.
- *Information seeking* is a conscious effort to acquire information in response to a need or gap in your knowledge.
- *Information behavior* (hereafter, "IB") encompasses information seeking as well as the totality of other *unintentional* or *passive* behaviors (such as glimpsing or encountering information), as well as purposive behaviors that do not involve seeking, such as actively *avoiding* information.
- *Information practices*, a term more popular in Europe and Canada than the United States, may be thought of as a synonym for information behavior — although it maintains some differences that will be explored in a later chapter.

The most commonly discussed of these concepts is *information seeking*. It is a behavior so commonplace that it is generally not an object of concern until time pressure makes it so. If we are making a major decision (e.g., buying a house) or finishing a task by a deadline (e.g., writing a report), we might find ourselves in an earnest information seeking mode: talking to others, searching the Web, reading magazines, watching the news, and so on. We may do everything we can to satisfy our desire for input, until either our need is satisfied or we have run out of time. More commonly, it is the latter, as the demand for "information" is usually elastic — there is always more that one could know. After our need is met (or we give up) we return to a more passive state of information seeking, at least as regards the object of our earlier curiosity.

Consider also cases in which the acquisition of information does *not* concern an immediate task like buying or writing something. Our daily life is peppered with instances in which we become interested in learning more about a topic after accidentally encountering some bit of information about it. This sort of curiosity, unmotivated by an immediate goal, is a common aspect of human life.

The situations described above, no matter how familiar to all of us, are much more complex than they may appear on the surface. Information seeking behavior often escapes observation. It is difficult to generalize about behaviors that vary so much across people, situations, and objects of interest, and which often take place inside a person's head. This book is about the many ways in which information seeking has been defined, explicated, observed, and measured in studies of human behavior.

1.1.2. Emphasizing People Rather Than Systems

Systematic research on information seeking — at least on the use of sources like books or newspapers — dates back nearly a century. In the first three decades of the twentieth century, studies of information "channels" and "systems" — chiefly libraries and the mass media — accumulated slowly. The 1940s saw the first published reviews of this literature. By the 1960s, such investigations, particularly of the specialized information needs and uses of scientists and engineers, were appearing regularly in a variety of journals and reports.

But much of this older literature was really not about information seeking in the sense in which that concept is discussed in current research. Rather, most of the investigations focused on the *artifacts* and *venues* of information seeking: books, journals, newspapers, radio and television broadcasts, schools, universities, libraries, professional conferences, and the like. What was actually studied were the information *sources* and how they were used, rather than the individual users, their needs (as they saw them), where they went for information, and what kind of results they experienced. Surveys of individuals made such strong assumptions about their needs, motivations, habits, and behaviors that the range of responses they could make was severely constrained; what mattered in these early investigations was how *formal information systems* served the serious (e.g., work, health, or political) information needs of the population studied. Typically this literature was called "information needs and uses" research, or sometimes "user studies" or "audience research." Choo and Auster (1993) call this tradition "system-centered" research; Vakkari (1999) refers to it as "system oriented"; a host of other commentators have applied similar labels.

It was not until the 1970s that investigations begin to branch out beyond the focus on formal channels and task-oriented needs. The emphasis shifted away from the structured "information system" and toward the person as a finder, creator, interpreter, and user of information. In mass media research the focus shifted to the "gratifications" that users experienced, rather than focusing on "effects" that messages had on people and how to persuade them to do things. Even studies of formal information systems began to consider a wider range of people, more general needs and problems, and the ways in which those systems often failed to serve their publics. The term "information seeking" — and, later, "sense making" — began to be preferred in describing the kind of phenomena that interested a growing number of scholars.

Some observers (see, e.g., Vakkari, 1999) have stereotyped the concerns of the old versus the new research on information behavior. Table 1.1 contrasts the person and system orientations by posing some examples of research questions that are typical for each.

The right column in Table 1.1 reflects research questions that have motivated thousands of studies — typically institutionally sponsored evaluations of library use, selective dissemination of information (SDI)

Table 1.1: Contrasting examples of information behavior research questions.

	Person oriented	System oriented
Task-oriented studies	• How do lawyers make sense of their tasks and environment?	• What kinds of documents do engineers need for their work, and how might the corporate information center supply them?
	• How does a manager learn about job-related information *outside of* formal organizational channels?	• How satisfied and successful are student searches of a university library's Web-based catalog?
	• What happens when a voter has too much information about a candidate or an issue?	• How much use do medical doctors make of medical databases?
Nontask-oriented studies	• How do the elderly learn about and cope with problems or opportunities that come up in their daily lives?	• How does the public use a library for personal pleasure and growth: what they ask for, borrow, and read?
	• Why do TV viewers choose one program over another, and what satisfactions do they achieve in doing so?	• How do we persuade teenagers to act in healthy and responsible ways? What messages about drug abuse do they attend to, in which medium, and why?
	• Why do people browse in stores when they have no explicit need in or intention to buy?	• Why do people ignore safety warnings on packages and advertisements?

programs, information retrieval systems, interface designs, information campaigns, advertising effectiveness, and the like. A few of these studies will be discussed in this book, almost exclusively the "nontask-oriented" variety. The left column reflects the emphasis of this volume, and hence, the predominate type of examples used within.

1.1.3. Ten Myths About Information and Information Seeking

A key development in the shift toward more user- or person-centered theories and methods were the questions raised in the early 1970s by several researchers, chief among them Professor Brenda Dervin (Ohio State University). A landmark 1976 article by Dervin encapsulated several years of her work by challenging 10 assumptions that had dominated research on communication and information seeking up to that time. In her article she was concerned chiefly with the everyday information needs of the ordinary, urban resident. However, much of what she says also applies to more formalized needs. Here are the 10 "dubious assumptions" that Dervin (1976a) identified in past writings about information seeking.

1. *Only "objective" information is valuable.* People are rational beings who process data from the environment to analyze alternatives and make optimal decisions. Several problems plague this assumption, including our common tendency to rely on easily available sources of information such as our friends. For most tasks and decisions in life, people tend to settle for the first satisfactory solution to a problem, rather than the best solution.

2. *More information is always better.* Yet too much information leads to overload and thence to deliberate ignoring of inputs. "Having information" is not the same as "being informed," so increasing the flow of information does not always result in an informed person. Typically there is not a problem getting enough information but rather with interpreting and understanding what information there is — an internal, rather than an external, locus of control.

3. *Objective information can be transmitted out of context.* But people tend to ignore isolated facts when they cannot form a complete picture of them. Individuals yearn to understand how information connects to other facts, beliefs and emotions they have, and how all these affect one another.

4. *Information can only be acquired through formal sources.* This assumption, often made by those in educational institutions, flies in the face of actual behavior. People use formal sources rarely, instead gathering and applying information from informal sources, often friends and family, throughout their lives.

5. *There is relevant information for every need.* The truth is that mere information cannot satisfy many human needs. People may want information in the sense of learning or understanding or entertainment; more commonly they need the physical and psychological necessities of daily life, such as food, shelter, clothing, money, and love. Information cannot substitute for many human needs, nor even facilitate all of them.

6. *Every need situation has a solution.* Institutions such as libraries, medical clinics, and social service agencies are focused on finding solutions to problems. To do so they attempt to map what the client says — the words they use — onto the resources and responses of their system. But sometimes the client is looking for something — a reassurance, an understanding — that does not come in the shape of a

canned response. Nevertheless, the system will usually provide an answer of some type, in its own language and logic, whether it is useful to the client or not.

7. *It is always possible to make information available or accessible.* Formal information systems are limited in what they can accomplish, at least where the vague, ambiguous, and constantly changing needs of the public are concerned. People will continue to come up with their own answers to their own unique, unpredictable questions without resorting to formal information systems.

8. *Functional units of information, such as books or television programs, always fit the needs of individuals.* Information systems such as libraries or broadcasters define themselves in terms of their units of storage or production: in the case of libraries, these are books, journals, audio-visual materials, or websites; in the case of broadcasters, it is programs, ads, or public service announcements. But the "functional units" of the individual are not often these things; rather, they are responses, solutions, instructions, ideas, friendships, and so forth. Thus, client requests for help, action, or resources tend to be reinterpreted by institutions as information needs that can be fulfilled with the units that they provide: books, programs, and the like. The client cannot always effectively use these units of information.

9. *Time and space — individual situations — can be ignored in addressing information seeking and use.* Yet often it is the individual's definition of the situation that shapes his or her needs as much as the "real" situation itself. If individuals perceive a lack of predictability and control of an outcome, then they worry. The worry itself becomes a need.

10. *People make easy, conflict-free connections between external information and their internal reality.* We tend to assume an ordered universe, in which connections exist between the internal and external. In our research, we tend to ask "what" and "how" rather than "why." We ask what people read or view, rather than why they do so. We lack understanding about how people inform themselves, how they make connections *over time*, the sense they make of their world between significant events. Dervin said that instead of studying what "information does ... for people" we need to focus on "what people do to information" (p. 333).

Dervin argued that all 10 of these assumptions were flawed in the ways indicated. Of course, she made these statements about *everyday* information needs, not in the context of highly specific, task-oriented needs like scientific or business data for decision making. There are indeed times when people act mostly rational and optimal in their information seeking and processing. Those situations, too, will be addressed in this volume.

1.1.4. When, Why, and Where Information Behavior has been Studied

As a subject of scholarly attention, information behavior has been studied in many different contexts, with a variety of people and a broad array of motives and goals. All people seek information, yet for some people and in some situations the stakes are much higher. Higher stakes are more likely to create situations that attract research.

To illustrate the kinds of people and situations that have been investigated over the past five decades, first let us consider several hypothetical cases. The examples below are constrained by several assumptions. These assumptions are valuable because they will help us compare situations by creating a "standard" set of reactions. However, each assumption has limitations, which will be noted. The assumptions are that information seeking behavior is highly *rational* (which is not often true), that such behavior is oriented toward making some kind of *decision* (a common, yet flawed, assumption), and that it is possible to make relatively simple judgments about the *value* of our decisions (itself a value judgment to which some people would object).

Consider the relative importance of three types of situations and information needs, as located on a hypothetical continuum (Figure 1.1). This continuum reflects the number of people ultimately affected by the search for information and subsequent decisions based on it: at one end are trivial decisions affecting few people, whereas at the other are important decisions that may affect millions of human lives.

Now, one could argue that it is anthropocentric to use humans as the sole benchmark for judging the *importance* of a decision. We could easily imagine real-world problems that involved other sentient beings (e.g., animals) or nonsentient things (e.g., tropical rain forests). If we think through the implications of such problems, we may notice that we tend to judge their importance by their ultimate impact on our own feelings or

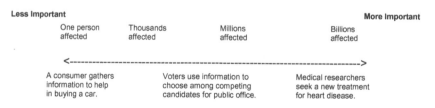

Figure 1.1: A continuum of importance.

well-being as humans. So, while recognizing that we could use other real-world objects as benchmarks, for the purposes of this discussion we will consider "numbers of people affected" as a simple indicator of importance.

First, imagine a person trying to choose between different models of a car that vary by features and price; although there are many publications (both printed and electronic) that offer just such information, the outcome of this search is simply not very consequential. Presumably this situation would fall near the "unimportant" end of our hypothetical continuum because it affects only one consumer.

Second, consider a citizen about to go to the polls, choosing among candidates based on information about their positions and past performance; electing public officials is certainly an important decision, and yet this is just one vote out of many. This situation is more important than the first, but less crucial than others we might imagine.

Third, imagine a biomedical scientist, with years of training and experience, working in an expensive laboratory, developing treatments for heart disease. This scientist must keep abreast of what other researchers are doing in the field, what discoveries have been made, what new equipment and techniques are available, and so forth. (To be more realistic, we could identify just one specific need, such as the answer to the question "What are the effects of dietary fish oil on measures of serum cholesterol?") Surely the information needs of this person are important, as judged by the investment society has made in the scientist and the potential outcomes of the work. The scientist's decisions about which research leads to follow could affect millions of people around the globe.

Laying out these hypothetical situations and judging their importance is a precursor to an explanation of why more research has been conducted on some kinds of information seeking and not on other types. We might all agree that the case of the scientist who is working on treatments for heart disease that might affect millions of lives is worthy of study. By studying the information needs of such scientists, and how they go about satisfying those needs, we just might be able to devise a tool or service that would help them reach their research goals a little sooner. In such situations, the potential for public good (and for private profit) is enormous. This is why many of the investigations the reader will encounter in this volume have focused on high-stakes and high-status occupations: research scientists, medical doctors, aerospace engineers, corporate managers, and the like.

And yet many types of information seeking behavior are worthy of study. Sometimes relatively trivial decisions, such as the automobile purchase described above, are the target of expensive investigations due to the cumulative importance of individual decisions. There is an entire industry, commonly called *market research* that investigates purchase decisions; individual purchases are relatively trivial, yet millions of them add up to significant amounts of money.

We can see a similar logic operating in studies of voting: how a particular individual finds out about issues and candidates may not seem important, but the information-gathering habits of millions of voters may have a crucial impact on a society as a whole. Therefore, there is a sizable literature on political communication, and more specifically on what kinds of information people glean from the mass media. The listening, watching, reading, and learning that takes place in support of buying and voting — and many other daily tasks — is sometimes referred to as "everyday" information seeking. We will learn about that as well in this book.

There is another very important focus of investigation that we have not touched on yet (although the medical study comes close): "basic" research on human information behavior. Ideally, what we would really like to know is how people go about seeking (or avoiding) information in a *generic* way, free of specific contexts like heart disease research or car purchases. Unfortunately, as with other attempts to conduct basic research on human behavior, it is difficult to generalize beyond the specific type of stimulus that prompted the behavior.

There is some doubt as to how deeply researchers can investigate truly basic human behaviors regarding information. Certainly some psychological investigations of perception, human information processing, and pattern recognition are relevant to basic considerations of information seeking. Such studies deal with the fundamental question "What is information?" and are discussed in Chapter 3 of this volume. Suffice to say that, for this book, I am concerned also with a social element: information seeking is *inter*personal as well as *intra*personal.

In the latter sense, perhaps the closest we come to basic research on information seeking are studies of communication in dyads and small groups in laboratory settings. Social scientists conduct these studies to understand how individuals solicit, process, and interpret data and cues they receive from others. Even in closed laboratory settings, the nature of the information itself may intrude. I will say more on this point as we review specific studies.

Finally, one important distinction that is made in the literature on information seeking is between *formal* and *informal* sources of information. The prototypical formal source is a printed one — a textbook, encyclopedia, or daily newspaper — but may also be exemplified by the words of an acknowledged expert on a subject. Informal sources tend to be friends, colleagues, and family, but in the view of some they could encompass what we learn from popular culture as well: TV programs, songs on the radio, Internet discussion lists, Facebook, tweets, and so forth. I will make use of this formal versus informal distinction in reviewing some of the findings on information behavior.

1.1.5. The Contexts in Which Information Behavior Is Investigated

The previous section raised the issue of context with considerations such as individual situations, motives for seeking information, the specific activities and kinds of information, the surrounding environment, the types of people, and the size of the social group involved in the investigations. There is no nice, neat, logical delineation of these factors, as human behavior itself is not completely rational or uniform. The examples used later in this volume have been selected with an eye toward the literature that actually *exists* — that is the patterns of studies that have been conducted, particularly since 1990.

There are a variety of approaches that we could use to consider the vast literature on information seeking and related topics. I could, for example, review studies chronologically, showing how they shifted in focus and method. Or investigations could be selected on the basis of the discipline in which they were published, whether in information studies, communication, management, medicine, and so forth. In fact, both *historical* (in this chapter and the final chapter) and *disciplinary* (in most of the other chapters) categorizations are sometimes invoked in this volume, but they take a back seat to three other ways of considering the literature: by theory, methods, and context.

What is meant by "theory" and "methods" may be obvious to most readers, but "context" warrants some further explanation (see Chapter 10 for more details). For the purposes of organizing this book, *context* will be taken to mean the particular combination of person and situation that served to frame an investigation. In Chapters 11 and 12 I review information seeking investigations under three general categories: the *occupation* studied (e.g., manager, doctor, social scientist, and chemist), the *social role* of the persons under investigation (e.g., consumer, voter, student, patient, and television viewer), and the *demographic* groupings (e.g., by age, gender, race, ethnicity, and geography). Although a respondent could easily represent an occupation, a role, and a demographic group at the same time, as well as illustrating the use of any number of information sources, investigators typically choose to frame their research questions and respondent samples in terms of one of these three ways. In Chapter 12, for example, I will describe a study of the "urban poor" (a demographic group) that approached its topic by sampling janitors (an occupation). The bulk of investigations that fall under the heading of "information seeking" have concerned the information needs and uses of a specific occupation, role, or demographic group.

1.1.6.   The Scope of "Information Behavior"

Information seeking is a topic that has been written about in thousands of documents from several distinct disciplines. Because almost everything to do with humans is potentially relevant to this topic, I have trimmed the scope of this book to highlight aspects of information behavior that have become more important in recent years.

For starters, there are two things that this book primarily is *not* about. I refer to the time-honored topics of "library use" and "information retrieval." Both of these (particularly the first) do indeed have strong connections to human information seeking, but each topic has a voluminous literature of its own that is really more about systems (continuing documents or computer files) than it is about people. One could also say that these have received too much emphasis in the "information needs and uses" literature. Generally speaking, the research described here is *not* well representative of pre-1980 information seeking research, which tended to focus on the use of libraries and paper documents or databases; I say little about such studies here. Relatedly I pass by the many thousands of studies on learning and the education of students, even though they do involve issues of information acquisition.

I have also narrowed my review by time period. Nearly a quarter of the publications discussed herein (over 300 items) date from 2007 or later; most of the rest were published during the 1990s and 2000s. Although I make citations to some earlier, seminal discussions and definitions of the concepts discussed in this volume, those are merely included to ensure proper credit and historical perspective. Most of the examples and references in this book are taken from the past three decades of published literature. As is emphasized here and in the concluding chapter, recent investigations of information seeking focus more on the *seeker* and less on the *sources* or *channels* they use, although it is not possible to ignore the latter entirely.

I have chosen to highlight certain aspects that have received too little attention from mainstream investigators of information seeking; among these less-examined topics are the connection between entertainment and information; passive and accidental information acquisition; sharing of information among peers; and ignoring and avoiding information.

My examples are taken chiefly from the disciplines of information studies, communication, psychology, and professional fields like management, business, medicine, and public health. The investigations used to explain typical findings or methods are taken from a variety of contexts. I am aiming for a multidisciplinary understanding of the concept of information seeking. I hope I have succeeded in reaching that goal.

1.2. How This Book Is Organized, and How to Use It

1.2.1. *Organization of the Chapters*

This book consists of 13 chapters. I like to think of these chapters as grouped into five segments:

One: Introductions and examples (Chapters 1 and 2)
Two: Concepts relevant to information behavior (Chapters 3, 4, and 5)
Three: Models, paradigms, and theories in the study of information behavior (Chapters 6 and 7)
Four: Methods for studying information behavior (Chapters 8 and 9)
Five: Research results and reflections (Chapters 10, 11, 12, and 13)

I have begun by mentioning several basic concepts: *information, information needs, information seeking, information behavior,* and *information practices.* Each will be explored in more depth in Chapters 3 and 4. I have sketched out the history and scope of the literature I intend to review.

Chapter 2 is my attempt to give information behavior a human face by exploring five examples from the individual's point of view. Please do not be misled by the simplistic and everyday nature of these five scenarios. They are here because I believe it is important to recognize that information seeking is something we all do in the course of our everyday existence. It is not a domain of behavior restricted to scientists, engineers, physicians, managers, and the like. We should acknowledge it as a common need before we plunge into the explication of the fuzzy concepts that have tended to plague this research.

Beginning Part Two, Chapter 3 (The Concept of Information) explores the vital notion of *information* and analyzes several problems inherent in its definition. The reader may judge that I say far too much about the definition of information — don't we all know what it is? But I think it is only fair to acknowledge how much commentary this everyday notion has generated. Readers who are new to this literature would be wise to save Chapter 3 for a later time.

Chapters 4 (Information Needs and Information Seeking) and 5 (Related Concepts) continue the review of basic concepts by offering definitions of many other terms frequently invoked in the information seeking literature, such as *decision making, browsing, foraging, encountering, sharing, selective exposure, avoidance, overload, information anxiety, knowledge gap, information poverty, pertinence, relevance, entertainment,* and a variety of spatial metaphors (e.g., *grounds* and *horizons*).

In Part three, Chapter 6 (Models of Information Behavior) and Chapter 7 (Metatheories, Paradigms, and Theories) provide general background about models and theories that have been used to study information seeking. Chapter 8 (The Research Process) contains a brief tutorial about methods of investigation. Then Chapter 9 (Methods: Examples by Type) proceeds to explore methods and techniques commonly used in information seeking studies, providing one or more examples of each approach: laboratory experiment, field experiment, mail survey, e-mail or web-based survey, individual and focus group interview, participant observation, diaries and experience sampling, history, content analysis, meta-analysis, and combinations of these.

In Part four of this book, Chapters 10 through 12 identify 14 commonly researched categories of people, and summarize one or more typical studies for each group. Other relevant studies are mentioned in context. First, Chapter 10 explores the history, size, and structure of the information seeking literature. Chapter 11 then examines findings about *occupations* (e.g., doctors). Chapter 12 also reviews individual studies of information seeking, but this time considering investigations of social *roles* (e.g., consumers) and *demographic groups* (e.g., the elderly). Altogether over 100 investigations are cited in Chapters 10 through 12, and 30 are described in detail.

Finally, Chapter 13 summarizes the approaches and findings of the current literature and suggests avenues for future research. The book concludes with a glossary, a collection of questions for discussion, and a bibliography of almost 1400 works cited in the text.

1.2.2. Which Chapters to Read If...

This book could be used in several different ways, depending on the needs and goals of the reader. For those who simply want a quick review of the recent literature on information seeking, Chapters 10 through 12 could be read on their own.

For methods courses in information behavior, Chapters 6 through 9 (covering theories and methods) could be read together, or in combination with Chapters 10 through 13 (reviewing research results). Methodologists interested in the range of concepts that might be measured in investigations should also read Chapters 4 and 5 on relevant concepts; experienced researchers can skip Chapter 8 on basic methods, as this is intended for neophytes.

Finally, students of information seeking, information behavior, and information needs and uses will want to read the book straight through. This text could also be useful in courses on user-centered design of information systems, information architecture, and the like. The appendixes include several questions for each chapter, which may be used as the basis for classroom discussions or written exercises.

Now let's begin our exploration by looking at some examples of information seeking from the seeker's perspective.

Chapter 2

Common Examples of Information Behavior

Information-seeking must be one of our most fundamental methods for coping with our environment. The strategies we learn to use in gathering information may turn out to be far more important in the long run than specific pieces of knowledge we may pick up in our formal education and then soon forget as we go about wrestling with our day-to-day problems.

— Lewis Donohew, Leonard Tipton, and Roger Haney (1978, p. 31)

Blood donors often ask, "Will I faint?" Cancer patients ask, "Will I die?" citizens facing everyday situations ask, "How long will it take me to handle this?"

— Brenda Dervin (1992, p. 75)

Chapter Outline

In this chapter we will make the case that searching for information is an important part of being human, and it is something that we do on a regular basis. Out of necessity we will encounter concepts and terminology that will be explained fully in later chapters of this book. Consider this chapter to be a preview of what is to come.

Every day of our lives we engage in some activity that might be called information seeking, though we may not think of it that way at the time. From the moment of our birth we are prompted by our environment and our motivations to seek out information that will help us meet our needs.

This chapter will consider six situations in which information seeking behaviors are in full swing. That is, these are scenarios that face millions of people (at least in developed nations) each year, in which decisions and choices are made that require a great deal of data, information, and understanding. Each will underscore the complexity of information seeking and the strategies we use to make it simpler.

All of the stories here involve not only the search for information but the choice of which data to retain and consider. Five of the tales can be characterized as decision making as well, a narrower type of behavior that is studied in its own right and is not always considered in studies of information seeking.

Let's first consider a very familiar type of activity: shopping.

2.1.   Six Information Seeking Scenarios

2.1.1.   Buying Products

Few decisions are more common in developed societies than choosing to purchase a product. In our role as consumer we may buy thousands of items a year, mostly foodstuffs, but also intangibles like services and many hundreds of household items. Of the latter, only a few may be considered major purchase decisions: houses, cars, boats, furniture, and large appliances, among others.

From the consumer's perspective it is the expensive, infrequently purchased items that tend to garner the most thought. However, it is important to recognize that many small purchases over the course of a lifetime — such as toothpaste or soft drinks — also amount to large expenditures. The fact that even our most minor needs eventually amount to a great deal of money accounts for the attention paid to the purchase decision from two different perspectives: market research (intended to aid the producers of goods and services) and product evaluations (intended to aid the consumers of these).

On the production side, a great deal of thought goes into the design and especially the advertising of items for sale. Advertising is intended to present (and sometimes inundate) the consumer with reminders of the product's existence and with persuasive information about it. Hence, the marketing of products attempts to minimize the effort a consumer expends to search for information.

Indeed, from the marketer's perspective, the information that is put out in print, on radio and television, on the Internet, and on billboards would result ideally in an entirely knee-jerk reaction: the consumer sees the ads, then sees the product, and then buys the product. For those who make and sell products, it is better that the consumer does not engage in a lengthy search for information, but simply buys the item as quickly as possible.

Except for those few truly and obviously superior products, the producers are likely to prefer that the consumer does not compare brands at all.

Research on these questions is accomplished by a variety of scientists working in industry and in universities; most have training in psychology or business (or both). When their reports are not proprietary, they may be published in the *Journal of Consumer Research*, the *Journal of Marketing Research*, the *Journal of Advertising Research*, or in more general publications.

Product makers are not the only ones who do research. There are other organizations that, for both profit and public service, provide the research and testing that the consumers do not (and indeed often cannot) do for themselves. In North America an example is the monthly magazine *Consumer Reports*, published by Consumers Union. A nonprofit organization founded in 1936, Consumers Union reviews goods and services and publishes investigative reports intended to help consumers make intelligent purchase decisions. Consumers Union reinforces its independence (unlike some other "consumer guides") by not accepting advertising and not allowing their published opinions to be used in advertising. Other publications of this type include *Consumer Digest* and *Consumers' Research Magazine*, neither of which undertakes the extensive testing programs of *Consumer Reports*.

The publications of *Consumer Reports* offer a prime example of what the consumer needs to know to make an informed purchase. The magazine conducts comparative tests of many brands and styles of a product, presenting the results in simplified tables with accompanying text. No matter whether the cost of the purchase is small (e.g., peanut butter) or large (e.g., a new car), the goal is to reduce the often massive amount of salient information into a few key factors, rated or described in the simplest way possible.

Let's consider a hypothetical review of passenger cars (Table 2.1).

Table 2.1: Comparison of passenger cars test results for sedans.

	Mercedes C-300	Volvo S80	Lexus ES350
Price	**$41,000**	**$37,000**	**$36,000**
Likely reliability	• •	• • •	• • • •
Braking	• • • •	• • •	• • • •
Ride	• • • •	• • •	• • •
Comfort	• • •	• • •	• • • •
Controls/displays	• •	• •	• • •
Acceleration, 0–60 mph	7.0 seconds	8.0 seconds	7.4 seconds
Required fuel type	Premium	Regular	Regular
Fuel economy	21 mpg	20 mpg	23 mpg

Imagine a consumer (we'll call her Julie) is shopping for a new car. Like many consumers, she already has some background information regarding cars: their makes, models, styles, cost, popularity, and perhaps a sense of their mechanical reliability. She has seen the models that interest her driving about town, and she has shared opinions about them with friends and relatives.

Having two children and a husband to transport, Julie wants a car of intermediate size and good quality. Three sedans made by Mercedes, Volvo, and Lexus interest her, because she has had at least one friend who owned each one of these models and was pleased with them.

Of course, to completely evaluate a car, one needs to drive it. However, from past experience Julie is wary of dealerships and salespeople, and has decided to go to them only after doing some background research. In fact, she thinks she might ultimately buy the car through a broker, making the deal over the telephone or the Internet after visiting the dealers to test-drive the models.

Julie starts her quest for facts with a review from a consumer magazine. Like many such publications, it contains color pictures of the various models, charts with dozens of facts on each model (e.g., dimensions, fuel consumption, features, and prices), comparisons of cars by type (e.g., the best luxury vehicles), and subject ratings and recommendations. What draws Julie to this particular publication is its reputation for objectivity and frequency-of-repair charts, based on hundreds of thousands of reports from owners of the vehicles reviewed and unique to this magazine.

Julie learns several facts from the magazine that help her differentiate the three cars. The first thing she notices is that the price range for the Mercedes is several thousand dollars more than the other two, apparently because of the manufacturer's prestige and reputation in North America. Acceleration is considerably slower with the Volvo, as it has a smaller engine than the other two. Fuel economy is similar among the three models, yet the Volvo and Lexus can use lower-octane fuel — making the Mercedes the most costly to operate. The Mercedes and Lexus are rated better for braking ability than the Volvo, while the Lexus and Volvo score better on dashboard design. Turning to the frequency-of-repair charts, Julie sees different patterns among the 14 "trouble spots" (electrical, brakes, transmission, etc.) but concludes that the Lexus may be more reliable than the other two. Julie concludes that, in matters other than the above, the three cars are similar.

Julie is leaning toward the purchase of the Volvo, reasoning that its use of ordinary fuel means a lower cost of operation; compounding those savings over many years of ownership makes the Volvo the least expensive of these higher end sedans. Yet she retains some doubt as to whether the Volvo is truly equivalent in features to the other two. She knows she can get basic price information — dealer costs, sticker price, and the costs of major options — from a variety of sources.

In her office one evening after work, Julie locates the Website for *Kelley Blue Book*. Here she is able to get price quotes for the three cars with similar options; the Mercedes is considerably more expensive than the other two cars in price, yet the engine (3.5 L) is the same as that of the Lexus (3.5 L). Does the engine size really matter so much, Julie asks herself? Probably not, she concludes.

Armed with this information, Julie heads to the Mercedes and Volvo dealers for test-drives, deciding against any further consideration of the Lexus. She likes the Volvo but finds the salespeople at that dealership to be too persistently aggressive. At the Mercedes dealer, in contrast, the salesman subjects her to less talk, and puts her in a positive mood for her spin in the car; she immediately falls in love with the Mercedes she drives, but realizes that it has many more options than the basic version that she has been considering.

As the week goes by, Julie discusses the purchase with several friends and family members. One friend cautions her strongly against the Mercedes on the basis of maintenance problems she encountered with her own Mercedes, an anecdote that Julie finds persuasive. On the other hand, her husband, who up until now has remained silent on the topic, argues strongly for the Mercedes on the basis of its larger engine capacity. "What if we want to tow a trailer some day?" he asks. That is a scenario that Julie had not even thought of, and it causes her to go back to the Internet to find the costs of towing packages for each car. While still convinced that the Volvo would be the more sensible choice, Julie ends up buying a Mercedes through a nationwide car broker. And besides — it came in more attractive colors!

Three common anomalies of information seeking are worth pointing out in this scenario. One, the mysterious influence we call "taste" has a powerful role in the decision process. Two, personal contacts have strong influence, whether they compel agreement (e.g., the advice of a friend or loved one), or disagreement (an overbearing salesperson). Drawing upon basic human emotions, these two influences can overwhelm any collection of facts, no matter how large or persuasive, as noted in the Chapter 1 comments regarding the fallacy of rational decision making. Three, it is useful to keep in mind that affluence and education can make a great difference in both the sources of information available to people and their inclination to pay attention to that information. In this scenario, an affluent (and probably well-educated) shopper both knows about and has easy access to channels of information that a poorer or less-educated person may not be aware of or inclined to use.

2.1.2. Finding Information in a Library

In the widespread literature that could be included under the rubric of information seeking, there is a genre of empirical work that is larger than any other: studies of people finding information in libraries. Most of the publications in this genre focus on "information as a thing" (Buckland, 1991a), that is, use of books, journals, and other "packages" of information.

So let us imagine another information seeker, this one called Leslie. Leslie is writing a paper for her history class on the 1898 war between Spain and the United States. She has gone to the library to gather background data on the role of the United States president, William McKinley, in the decision to declare war on Cuba. Among her questions are these: Had McKinley favored war from the beginnings of his presidential campaign in 1896? Was McKinley reasonably well informed of the facts regarding unrest in Cuba and Spanish military weakness there and on the high seas? Who were McKinley's closest advisors and what was their advice to him regarding intervention? So Leslie has gone to a university library to find answers to these questions. The particular library she has chosen contains roughly 3 million books and subscribes to more than 4000 printed journals and has electronic access to many more.

Before we begin following Leslie's search, let us consider some tendencies of libraries and their users. First, it is important to recognize that all but the smallest libraries can be complex and intimidating. Although libraries make every attempt to place materials on similar topics in close approximation, this goal is elusive. For one thing it is hard to decide what any one document is "about"; for another, library materials are divided into a multitude of forms — books, journals, computer files (typically through a link from the online catalog), video recordings (on DVDs), and loose materials (in file cabinets or archival boxes) to name some major categories.

As if it were not difficult enough to classify the content of these different forms of media, sometimes information on the same topic and medium might still be found in different places; background material on international conflicts could be found on the shelves of the main collection, on nearby shelves reserved for oversized books, in the collection that serves the reference desk, or perhaps in a special collection or archive. For example, biographies of American presidents will be found on the main shelves of a library, but the personal documents to which they refer are likely to be held in the archives of a distant library.

Once one considers the various interactions of (intellectual) content with (physical) form, it can be seen why libraries become difficult places to search systematically, even with experience. Many visitors to a library end their search prematurely when faced with a large building full of millions of items and the imperfect tool of the electronic catalog.

Leslie begins by consulting the electronic catalog, a tool she has used before. Being a regular visitor to this library, she is aware that if she chooses to consider journal articles she will need to consult at least one other electronic index to obtain the titles and full-text of articles that contain relevant information, and that this would entail much more work than a simple search of the library's holdings. She decides to restrict herself to books about the war and McKinley.

This library offers two different interfaces for searching their holdings. The simpler one is a graphical interface that Leslie has not used before but hopes is less cumbersome than the "traditional" catalog. So first Leslie tries typing the words "war cuba mckinley" into the search box of the graphical interface. Immediately she is presented with a screen divided into two kinds of displays. On the left side of the display is a cluster of words, with lines connecting them. In the middle of this network-like diagram are her own search terms (war cuba mckinley) and branching out from them in all directions are other terms: Cuba, Spain, President, United States, History, Novel, Nations, Battle, McKinley, McKinney ... and a variety of other words that appear to be synonyms or alternate spellings (and meanings!) of the words she typed. On the right of the screen is a list of books, a few of which are indeed relevant to her topic.

Not sure what to do with the cluster of words — many of which seem irrelevant — Leslie decides to retreat to the traditional interface for searching the catalog. Selecting the other interface she types "McKinley" into the "Search:" box and chooses "within Title" from the pull-down list to the right of the box. She is rewarded with a listing of 12 books. Looking at the book titles, however, she is dismayed to see that few of them are about the former president; rather, they are books that begin with the name "McKinley," whether that is the name of a county or a mountain or a person. Next she receives a list of four books by typing "William McKinley." Even though that seems like very little material to browse through, she heads for the shelves. Checking the books in the "E711" section of the Library of Congress system, Leslie immediately sees that there are many more books on her topic than were retrieved in her search — dozens more, in fact. Based on the titles alone, Leslie's first insight is that most of these books are about the life and/or presidency of McKinley, and are likely to contain merely brief descriptions of the war with Spain in 1898.

After browsing a while and picking up two books about the McKinley administration and one biography of the president, she heads to the reference department of the library. There she asks why her search of the electronic catalog was so incomplete. The reference librarian shows her that there are such things as subject headings in the catalog records. Returning to a terminal for the online catalog, Leslie this time selects the "within Subject" choice from the pull-down menu, and types in "McKinley, William."

This time, 25 books on McKinley are retrieved, even those that do not have his name in the title (Figure 2.1).

Leslie starts to examine the 25 listings, one at a time. The most promising title appears to be *The Spanish-American War and President McKinley*, a book that she just missed because it was at E715. She makes note of several other McKinley books she missed in her browsing session at the shelf, seeing also that two of the more relevant ones are already checked out.

Now that she knows about subject headings, Leslie sees one that could be useful: "Spanish-American War." Searching that phrase as a subject heading gives her 127 titles. Intimidated by the size of this new list, Leslie slowly pages down through the titles until she just cannot read any more. She has jotted down the call numbers of the most promising books, most of which are in the E711–715 range of the Library of Congress system, and a bibliography at Z8561 on the top floor of the library.

Still carrying her initial three selections, Leslie goes back to the E shelves and an hour later has examined 15 other books, selecting just two highly *relevant* ones to check out from the library and leaving behind all three of the first books she chose. She knows that the bibliography in the Z shelves would help her determine whether she has missed anything — this library does not own everything — but the bibliography is two floors above her and she is tired. "This is enough to finish my paper," Leslie says to herself as she heads to the circulation desk.

In this scenario several lessons about information seeking can be observed. Although perhaps two-thirds of adults in the United States and Canada make some use of libraries in a given year, relatively few (mostly

SearchRequest: S = MCKINLEY, WILLIAM	University Online Catalog
Subject Index	Search Results: 25 Entries Found

MCKINLEY, WILLIAM 1843–1901	
1	COMPLETE LIFE OF WILLIAM MCKINLEY AND STORY OF HIS . . . [1901]
2	DICKEN TROUTMAN BALKE FAMILY PAPERS [1816] archive-mss
3	EDWARD HENRY HOBSON PAPERS [1857] archive-mss
4	FROM MCKINLEY TO HARDING PERSON RECOLLECTIONS OF . . . [1923]
5	ILLUSTRIOUS LIFE OF WILLIAM MCKINLEY OUR MARTYRED . . . [1901]
6	IN THE DAYS OF MCKINLEY [1959]
7	LIFE OF WILLIAM MCKINLEY [1916]
8	LIFE OF WILLIAM MCKINLEY SOLDIER LAWYER STATESMAN [1896]
9	MAN WHO SHOT MCKINLEY [1970]
10	MCKINLEY MEMORIAL IN PHILADELPHIA HISTORY OF THE . . . [1909]
	CONTINUED ON NEXT PAGE

Click on entry to display full record

Figure 2.1: Portion of an online catalog listing.

students and faculty in universities) search library collections in any degree of depth. Leslie is an untypical user in that she knows how to use a librarian and a catalog; the reluctance of even regular users of libraries to consult these resources is well documented (consider, for example, the commentary by Borgman, 1996).

Leslie is, however, typical in her nonlinear search pattern; her search is not a neat one that moves swiftly from catalog to shelf to circulation desk; rather, there is a back-and-forth movement between the catalog and the shelf, with considerable time taken to examine works and reconsider her query. Typical of library users, Leslie takes some shortcuts (choosing to consider only books, not journal articles), reverses some of her early decisions (leaving behind the initial choices of books), and ultimately ends the search process prematurely by not fetching the bibliography and checking that (presumably comprehensive) guide against her search results.

2.1.3. Healing a Patient

Although our usual focus in information behavior research is the individual, it is important to recognize that much information seeking takes place in groups, and that sharing of information with others is very common. In this scenario we consider the many exchanges that might take place among members of a health care team in a hospital. Because the information seeking plays out over several days and involves many individuals, it is possible only to sketch out some of the dozens of actions and interactions that are likely to occur. Also for simplicity's sake we will consider only a single patient, while recognizing that such a team would certainly be caring for multiple patients at any one time, each at different stages of crisis or healing. To further condense the description, we focus on only four key team members: physician (Dan), day nurse (Marta), night nurse (Gary), and pharmacist (Ming).

The story begins without the team, in the emergency entrance to a rural hospital, where a 22-year-old male has been brought in by an ambulance shortly after midnight. The man was in a car accident and is semi-conscious but shows no other injuries other than contusions. Unfortunately, the man carries no identification and the car was registered in a female name out of state. Thus, he must be admitted without access to a medical history.

The patient is first examined by a nurse, and then by an attending physician. Both of these administer the Glasgow Coma Scale (GCS), a 15-point neurological measurement of consciousness. A score of eight is recorded each time, which could indicate severe brain injury. Then he is taken for CT scan of the head and upper body, and a blood test for presence of alcohol and drugs. Afterwards, the patient is taken to the intensive care unit (ICU). Here the night nurse, Gary, supervises the movement of the patient to one of the ICU's 15 beds. The patient is soon fitted with an IV to deliver fluids and medications, and devices to monitor blood pressure, heart rate and oxygen levels of the blood. His temperature is taken, and he is given periodic ice packs to reduce swelling. Gary also gives the patient the coma test again, consulting a "flashcard" he keeps for this purpose, as he has trouble recalling the individual indicators. He records a score of 10 on the chart using the conventional breakdown for the Eye, Verbal, and Motor components of the scale: "GCS 10 = E2 V4 M4 at 01:17." The patient is given no medications at this point, as they might interfere with indicators for the scale.

The patient's hospital room contains a number of potential sources of information, the ultimate origin of which, in some cases, is the patient himself. Among these sources are: the monitors attached to the patient (including blood pressure, heart rate, and oxygen level of blood); the CT scan results, viewable at a nearby workstation; electronic and paper versions of the patient records, including orders for medications administered; and a bedside white board for nurses to record any facts that need to be called to the immediate attention of anyone who enters. On this board Gary has noted the latest coma scale score and the words "Patient Name Unknown." In a nearby alcove outside the room is a nursing station, where a number of medical reference works (e.g., the *AACN Procedure Manual for Critical Care*, *Quick Reference to Critical Care*, and *Micromedex*) are available online, along with medical databases like *MedLine* and *Drug Interaction Checker*.

The fact that the patient's name is not yet known is a serious problem, as nothing is understood about medical problems that might have pre-dated the accident. This situation is resolved early in the morning as the responding police officers report to the hospital switchboard that they were finally able to contact the registered owner of the wrecked vehicle and determine that the patient is her son; now they have a name, which is passed upstairs to Gary where he duly records it on the patient's white board. As the morning shift Gary verbally passes on his recorded observations to the day nurse, Marta: the patient is partly consciousness now, and has vomited twice during the night; temperature has been only slightly elevated, although blood pressure has been high for someone of this age and weight; his GCS is currently 11.

Marta, with the help of other hospital staff, begins a series of inquiries about the patient's medical records and history, and the status of his health insurance. Emergency medical procedures allow for medical records to be transferred electronically to the treating hospital in such cases. The medical records — which are relatively few in number — become part of the data accessible in the ICU. Late in the morning, the attending physician, Dan, shows up to examine the patient and be filled in on the situation. Marta calls his attention to several important facts: the patient is not yet fully consciousness for more than short periods of time; the blood test showed presence of both alcohol and opiates, which makes the accident a legal matter; the patient has a current prescription for Adderall (for attention deficit disorder); and he has no medical insurance.

Among other treatment decisions Dan and Marta decide to consult one of the unit's pharmacists, Ming, about whether the patient should be given an anti-emetic (anti-vomiting medication), and the implications of administering any other medications, given the patient's medical history. A two-way radio call reveals that Ming is unavailable until later, which is agreeable. Meanwhile, Marta consults the *Drug Interaction Checker* for possible interactions with Adderall, although Dan has told her that the patient could well do without this medication, given the circumstances. She learns that Adderall can be addictive and can also raise blood pressure — factors to keep in mind in this case. She notes this in the patient's electronic chart.

Late in the afternoon the patient is more conscious for a longer time, moaning and complaining of a severe headache. Ming and Dan appear for their consult, and are able to ask the patient questions about his current and past condition, and his medication habits. He claims to have been in good health before the accident (which he does not remember), but denies taking any drugs (prescribed or otherwise), including Adderall. He asks for some Oxycodone, an opioid, for his headache. These responses cause some skepticism among the three medical professionals about the patient's truthfulness.

Outside of the room, the three caregivers discuss what to do. Given that the patient shows possible signs of drug abuse, they are unwilling to prescribe strong pain medications. They decide that small doses of acetaminophen are warranted, as the GCS is now at the high end (12) of the moderate injury portion of the scale. Another CT scan would be advisable if the patient worsens, but not if he improves. They decide to continue monitoring him and checking in again during the evening.

The next day the patient appears better in several respects. Apart from evident bruising, other vital signs are good: lower blood pressure and normal body temperature. His GCS is 13. The patient continues to complain about headaches, but not so loudly as the day before; from training and experience Marta and Dan know that headaches are common for concussion victims for several days after injury. The ICU has an interest in moving patients along as quickly as possible, so that they always have beds free for emergency patients. Two days into the patient's stay the ICU has come close to capacity, and Dan and Marta agree that the patient is stable enough to be discharged to his family. This is done, but not before a police officer makes arrangements to take a statement before the patient leaves the state. Through a warrant, the police also obtain the results of the blood test administered at the time of admission, however they are not given any other medical records.

Among the features in this scenario are continuing measures of, and searches for, information, careful recoding of any relevant data, and frequent sharing of information among team members. Given the life-and-death nature of the work, missing or inaccurate information is a constant worry, as there are many opportunities for potential adverse events. There is also a concern for control of patient information, due to privacy and legal issues. The collaboration of multiple skilled workers, equipped with both deep knowledge and extensive physical resources, makes a positive outcome much more likely.

2.1.4.   Betting on Race Horses

As in the previous scenario, for horse races the seeker makes a choice. Despite the prevalence of horse-racing language in politics (e.g., "the dark horse candidate" and "backing the right horse" in an election), there are some differences between choosing a candidate and picking a horse. Rather than choosing one candidate from among two or three, in a typical horse race several choices might be made from among roughly 5 to 12 horses, and the type of bet that might be made on the horse(s) multiplies the number of possibilities many times over.

The complexity of horse racing leads to a common, sheepish admission at the tracks: "I choose horses based on their name." That is, if a name like "Gambling Everything" makes one laugh and seems to capture the moment, why not bet on that horse? Infrequent visitors to the race course, attending more for fun than the hope of profit, freely admit the unscientific basis for their choices; if the name is especially clever, reminds them of a friend or circumstance in their lives, then that is a sign to bet on the horse. It is not the only simplified system for betting. Some bet on an animal's color, with the gray horse in a race likely to create odds more favorable than the horse's reputation deserves. Occasionally the gender of a horse will determine many bets, especially in a race in which a talented filly vies with stallions. Races that draw horses from other countries may elicit bets based on nationality. Some wager not on the horse but on the record, gender, or nationality of the jockey (and so on).

Why is properly picking a horse so complicated that people will resort to simple strategies like the above? First, it must be obvious that no matter how much data are considered, horse racing itself is not a science and offers many unexpected surprises. The most dramatic example of this is when a highly ranked horse stumbles in a race, or bumps an opponent in such a way as to be disqualified. Even in the most mundane race, the horse most favored by the bettors wins only one-third of the time (Ainslie, 1986, p. 49).

Serious bettors who gather and use as much information as possible about the horse, the jockey, the trainer, and the track (among other things) are called "handicappers." Handicappers firmly believe that, given enough information, they can swing the odds to their favor in an enterprise where the average bettor loses about 20 cents on the dollar. Not surprisingly, a large publishing industry has grown to serve the information needs of handicappers.

The publications on horse racing are many. Most people who have been to a track are familiar with the racing program sold at the track itself, important for its listings of information about the horses and races to be held on that day at that track. However, a track's own program is just the tip of the iceberg of information about horses. Whatever data a North American track distributes about its own races, that information is overwhelmed by what can be found in the *Daily Racing Form* (published by Triangle Publications, Inc.), which is published every racing day and distributed internationally. The *Daily Racing Form* is in turn dwarfed by the *American Racing Manual*, an encyclopedic by-product of the *Form* that covers an entire year. In addition, there are several (mostly weekly) magazines devoted to racing. Among them are *American Turf Monthly* (advice for handicappers), *The Blood-Horse* (the inside story on horse breeding), and *Turf and Sport Digest* (news for the horsing industry as well as the frequent bettor).

Just what information could merit so many publications? Considering only information about the horse and jockey, there are many items of data to consider. The key category of information is the horse's recent record of racing (the *Form* usually lists the last nine races) and sometimes one to three workouts (trials that were not races). Regarding each race, there are approximately 25 items of information (all on a single line), including the date, length, type, timing, and top three placers of the race, along with the jockey, odds, and weights carried by the horse, and often ending with a subjective evaluation of the horse's performance (e.g., "tired" or "failed to menace"). Elsewhere on the page are summaries of the horse's lifetime earnings by year, and the names of the sire, dam, owner, breeder, and trainer. Altogether, the *Form* typically offers about 250 discrete data items regarding each horse — and there are typically 5–12 horses in each race! Even without considering the other relevant information contained in the form about the race itself (e.g., what types of horses can race and how much they can win) and the track (top times for each of up to 16 different lengths that races can run), we can see that each race offers the potential for consideration of several thousand data items.

But humans do not want to digest several thousand items of information and often simply do not have the time to do so. Therefore each handicapper relies on a selection system that eliminates most of this information; typically they focus on just a few dozen data items about each race and sometimes considerably fewer. Less successful but a lot less work are the systems described above, such as "Always bet on the prettiest horse!"

Let us consider the case of an occasional bettor who would like to become a regular handicapper, a common enough circumstance. Joe, our bettor, goes to the track and buys a copy of the *Racing Form*, along with a program of the day's races. It is his first time with the *Form*, and he is at first overwhelmed by the scope and depth of information he finds there. With the first race just an hour a way, he settles into a comfortable spot and starts making notes on what he reads.

Joe has a few rules of thumb in mind to guide his reading. Looking at the listing for the first race, he notes the "morning line" (projected) odds for each of the nine horses that will start that day. Joe can see right away that three of the horses are expected to run at much better odds than the other six; horses one and two are likely to pay $3 for every $1 bet (i.e., odds of 3:1), whereas horse three is expected to run at 4:1. All of the other horses have odds of 8:1 or worse, with one poor horse paying 50:1 for a win. For a moment Joe ponders what he could do with $50 for every dollar he bets, then shakes himself back to reality with a reminder that such horses very rarely win; he also reminds himself that he has to check the TV monitors at race time to see how much the odds have changed as bets are wagered; in parimutuel betting the odds are based on the actual pattern of bets made, rather than the estimates of the *Racing Form*'s handicappers.

Joe decides to concentrate on what are clearly the best three horses in the race and on just three types of information: the horse's performance in recent races, the jockey's record, and something called the "speed rating." He notes that horse one, Entropy, won one of his last nine races, and has placed second (i.e., "placed") in three others. Horse two, Uncertainty, has also won one of his last nine races, and has placed second in two others. The number three horse, Signal, has not won a single race, yet has managed to come in second three times, and has come in third (i.e., "showed") two times as well; furthermore, all of Signal's second-places were in the last three races, indicating an improving performance.

Not seeing a clear pattern in these data, Joe decides to look more closely at each race for further clues. He considers an important question: has the horse won *at this distance* before? Joe knows that distance is an important factor and that an earlier win at the same distance is a strong indicator of potential success today. Races can be a variety of different distances, and many horses excel at the shorter or the longer distances, but not both; in addition, some races are run on the turf (i.e., the grass strip inside of the dirt track), and some horses specialize in such a surface. From the top of the *Racing Form* Joe sees that this is a 1-mile race on the dirt track, and recalls that it has not rained this week; a track muddy from recent rains would require consideration of yet other factors, and Joe feels like he has too much to think about already.

Our bettor happily reads that Uncertainty's win and places have all taken place on the turf, and that may well allow him to eliminate that horse from consideration. His comfort is lessened when he realizes that Entropy's victory was in a race of 6 furlongs (three-fourths of a mile) whereas Signal's near-misses have all been in races of 1 mile. So neither horse has won at this race before, but Signal looks better prepared for this long race.

Next Joe considers the speed rating, which is an objective metric that compares the horse's performance with a rating of 100, meaning that the horse's running time (in a particular race) equaled the track record for that particular distance. Entropy, Joe sees, has a speed rating of 80 for his winning race, indicating a performance 4 seconds slower than the track's record; his places earned similar ratings. Although not usually a dirt racer, Uncertainty is undoubtedly a faster horse at an average rating of 84 for his three best races. Signal begins to look worse with speed ratings between 77 and 81.

So now the picture is looking even more muddy. Joe turns to a separate table in the *Racing Form* that lists the performance records of each jockey, over many races and with different horses. Here, at last, is clear-cut information: Entropy's jockey has won 17% of his races, while the other two jockeys hover near 8%. Joe jots this down on a little table he has been sketching on a notepad (Table 2.2). This cinches it: Entropy is to be the horse Joe bets to win.

It is now 32 minutes to race time and Joe remembers that he needs to check out the latest information on the track TV monitors. Up to this moment he has been dealing with information that is at least hours, and in some cases months or years, old. It is with a shock that Joe reads on the monitor that Entropy has been scratched from the race, and that Signal has had a change of jockey. Another look at the table in the racing form tells him that the new jockey has a better record — 11% wins — than Signal's old jockey. Joe looks

Table 2.2: Joe's notes on the three top horses.

Horse	Odds	Wins	Places	Track	Speed	Jockey won (%)
Entropy	3:1	1	3	Dirt	80	17
Uncertainty	3:1	1	2	Dirt	84	8
Signal	4:1	0	3	Turf	79	8

at the latest odds and realizes that the turf horse, Uncertainty, is now the crowd's favorite at even odds (1:1) while Signal has crept up to 5:2. "Do the other bettors know something I don't?" Joe wonders.

Joe considers spending more time with the *Racing Form*. He knows that it contains information on the horse's recent condition, class, parentage, and so forth, but he is feeling undecided and a bit pressed for time; he needs to place a bet within the next 20 minutes. It is then that Joe recollects a potentially valuable source of information that appears in no published document: the horse's condition at this moment. Walking quickly over to the rear of the racing stands, in a few minutes Joe finds himself at the paddock, where the horses for the first race are being paraded for a large number of bettors crowded around the rails. After a few minutes of craning his neck and standing on his toes, Joe manages clear glimpses of both Uncertainty and Signal; the former animal appears nervous while Signal appears calm and strong. With his mind made up, Joe rushes to the nearest betting window where, after 5 minutes of waiting he bets $10 on Signal to win at the latest odds of 2:1.

Ten minutes later the finish line is crossed first by Channel, a horse that Joe had not even considered. Trying to salvage a lesson from this first race, Joe notices that in the last 15 minutes of betting, Channel's odds moved from 6:1 up to 3:1 — a sign that many bettors had begun to favor the horse. "I would have noticed that trend if I had been paying more attention to the monitor," Joe says to himself, and then with a start realizes that he has much less time to do the next analysis: Race Two will begin in only 25 minutes.

We can notice a few principles in this case study: the searcher has much too much data to systematically analyze in the brief time before each race. Hence Joe attempts to simplify the "search space" for a solution by ignoring many categories of information he deems less relevant. Unlike many other search processes that result in some kind of decision, in this case the most important data — the betting odds — keep changing constantly, right up to 2 minutes before the race. Like the opportunity for first-hand observation of additional information (the horse's condition), the need to "monitor the monitor" can be a distraction from further analysis.

2.1.5. Finding the Law

George is spending his Saturday in the law library. A lawyer in a small Kentucky law firm, George has been practicing just 5 months (problem 1) and is overwhelmed by his work (problem 2), which is chiefly tax law (problem 3). Nevertheless, he promised his sister, Edna, to write a legal memorandum on her alimony case even though he feels that he does not have the experience, time, or background to do a perfect job of it. The hard fact is that Edna cannot afford a lawyer, is starting to have trouble paying her rent, and besides, she is his sister. So even though the course George took in family law is only a dull memory now, today he joins dozens of other lawyers and students in a quest to find the law.

George knows the basic facts of the case all too well. Last year when Edna divorced her husband Fred, the court ordered him to make monthly alimony payments. Three months ago Fred took a new job in another town, moved to an apartment, gave up his phone, and stopped making payments. Fred's only direct communication with Edna was a phone message warning that he would have to skip her next payment to afford the deposit on his new place, and that he would "make it up to her later." The first few weeks Edna was annoyed yet somewhat sympathetic, because she was the one who filed for divorce. But after a month went by with neither the next nor the previous alimony payment, Edna felt foolish that she had not acted more quickly; to make matters worse, Fred has proved to be impossible to contact.

Edna knows that she has legal recourse through the court, but also knows that it could be a struggle to document the facts and recover lost payments. So she turned to George first. George is determined to settle this dispute as quickly as possible, even if it means he has to pay another attorney to follow up his work later; unfortunately he has precious little time over the next few weeks to devote to it. Though George believes that Edna's case is a straightforward one, he wants to check two issues in particular: first, whether a recent raise in Edna's modest salary could reduce alimony or impede collection of what is owed to her; and second, whether Edna's hesitancy to act when the first payment never arrived might allow her husband to argue that she had agreed to the stoppage of payments.

George starts with the index to the *Corpus Jurus Secundum* (referred to as the CJS) and locates the section on Divorce in this encyclopedia-like reference tool. He finds, two subheadings down, a section on "arrears"; he spends some time reading this section of the main body of *CJS*, and also in a newer *Supplement*. As well as reminding himself of the key points of the law in this area, he locates a citation to a recent case decided in Kentucky. George jots down the citation to the Kentucky case, a parallel citation, and a frequently cited decision from New York State. Next George turns to the *Quick Index* to the state volumes of the *American Law Reports* and finds an entry (Figure 2.2) to a discussion of "arrearages" under the heading "Alimony — Delinquent or overdue payments." After reading the discussion in *American Law Reports*, and noting references to yet other cases, George decides to read the cases themselves.

George looks up the Kentucky case in *Kentucky Decisions*, which reports cases for his state, and another in the *New York Reports, Second Series*. For his last task of the day, George uses a public terminal and his office's LEXIS

ALIMONY—Cont'd
Delinquent or overdue payments
   debt, right of spouse to set off debt owed
      by other spouse against accrued spousal
      or child support payments, 11 ALR5th 259

   laches or acquiescence as defense, so as

   to bar recovery of arrearages of permanent

   alimony or child support, 5 ALR4th 1015

   visitation, withholding visitation rights for

   failure to make alimony or support payments,

   65 ALR4th 1155

Figure 2.2: Excerpt from the *American Law Reports.*

account number to search the online version of *Shepard's Citations* to check on the continuing validity of the cases he examined; he finds the most relevant cases are still valid.

George has spent 3 hours in the library and is tired. But at least he feels grounded in the relevant law and has checked the case updates. Tomorrow George will draft a memorandum on Edna's situation, and the following week he will discuss it with a colleague who practices family law. He knows that it may be hard to get money out of Fred if he continues to avoid responsibility, but George is certain that, should Fred attempt legal resistance, Edna's case would be most compelling to a court.

Given Brenda Dervin's emphasis on "everyday" information seeking (see Chapter 1), most of her 10 points are not particularly relevant to a highly structured search of formal information sources by an experienced attorney. However, it is worth noting that, although George certainly found "the law" governing his sister's situation, her problems are not over yet! There is much work to be done before the records of law and previous decisions may result in some kind of action in Edna's favor. As Dervin implies, few problems are immediately solved by the discovery of relevant information. And as some psychologists and criminologists have documented, court decisions are not always as rational as we might hope, either.

2.1.6.   *"I Want to Know More about Cancer"*

Let's consider an entirely different kind of desire for information, one in which there is no decision or choice to be made, and in which it is difficult to determine exactly what the "need" is. "Curiosity" is the label that we might apply to the situation described below; according to Webster's *New World Dictionary*, curiosity is a word that is used to indicate a general "desire to know," sometimes "about things that do not necessarily concern one."

It is certainly hard to say what makes us curious about a subject. In a famous article about why and how people ask questions, Robert Taylor (1968) wrote about "visceral needs" of mysterious origins that make themselves known only through a vague uneasiness about not knowing something. The visceral need remains "unarticulated" until we verbalize it to ourselves or someone else. In the process of trying to state what it is we want to know, the information need usually comes out in an imperfect and unsatisfactory statement ("compromised," in Taylor's words). Brenda Dervin's (1983a) investigations into "sense making" employ a similar concept: the information *gap*. That is, until we recognize the existence of a gap in our knowledge — often signaled by a mild anxiety and/or a need to act — we are not motivated to search for information. However, whether we ask questions, read books, or take another kind of action to find something out, it is important to recognize that information often comes to us, fortuitously, in the course of our normal lives. The *serendipity* factor — the seemingly accidental discovery of relevant information — operates more often than we might expect.

Our searcher this time is named Maria. Maria, who is in her early 30s, was never particularly concerned with matters of personal health until a favorite cousin discovered that a firm, red lump on her arm was cancerous. Through several weeks of a successful treatment plan, Maria kept in frequent telephone contact with her worried cousin, who lived in a distant state.

Maria had heard the dreaded word "cancer" her entire life. When she was a teenager her grandfather had died of lung cancer, but other than him, nobody close to her had ever been diagnosed with cancer. She knew that many old people died of cancerous growths. Cancer, like death itself, was something that Maria would rather not think about.

Not long after her cousin's discovery, Maria came down with a sore throat and visited a nearby medical clinic. While in the waiting room she noticed a brochure, "What You Need to Know about Skin Cancer," published by the National Cancer Institute of the National Institutes of Health. She took the brochure home to read and was surprised to learn that almost half of all mature adults are likely to have had skin cancer. She had thought cancers were pretty rare, except among the elderly. At least Maria felt confident now that she knew how to spot skin cancer herself and what to do to avoid it. And, for a time, that was all she wanted to know about cancers.

Some weeks later, coming across the brochure on skin cancer in her living room, Maria found herself curious. What *was* cancer, exactly, and what caused it? The brochure did not say much about the underlying nature and causes of carcinoma, but it listed a toll-free number for further information (1-800-4-CANCER), which she called to request other brochures in the National Cancer Institute series. Later she had coffee with a friend who was a nurse and asked some very basic questions about cancer. Maria did not understand quite everything that she was told by her friend, but understood enough to know that she wanted to know more. *Why* she needed to know more, she was not exactly sure, but maybe it could be useful in defending herself against future illness.

One day Maria bought some skin cream made by the Avon company. With the skin cream came a list of other Avon products, which mentioned that company's "Breast Cancer Awareness Crusade" and listed a Website. Out of curiosity Maria used her home computer to reach Avon's Web page, where she found, along with answers to frequently asked questions about breast cancer, some fascinating narratives by women who had survived the illness. She had never thought about using the Internet for this sort of information; somehow it made it easier for her to read about the scary topic of cancer.

Maria noticed that the Avon site did not refer to any other related sites. She decided to do a search on the word "cancer" and was bewildered by the number of sites (over 200 million) that contained a reference to the word. Obviously, she had to be more specific. Her nurse friend had mentioned the Mayo Clinic as a good source of information; searching for the words "Mayo Clinic" lead to a site called the "Mayo Breast Cancer Center" that included many pages of clearly written material on cancer in its various forms. She printed some pages, and skimmed or read others.

Finding more information on cancer became a kind of challenge. Through the Mayo site she found a link to a page sponsored by the National Institutes of Health. Maria felt like she might be able to trust this information more, because it was provided by a national government. However, she found the site somewhat overwhelming — so much information was about government projects or about research projects — and she did not find the sort of common-language explanations she was looking for. She noticed a link to the National Cancer Institute's Website and there found the same material that she had read in the brochures they had sent her. At this point she decided to call it a day and stop searching.

Maria's interest in cancer did not stop here. At various times she spent hours browsing the personal health sections of a local bookstore and the public library in her town. She talked to her friends about "all this stuff I've learned on the Internet" and became known as somebody who liked to talk about health matters. In turn, Maria learned a great deal listening to the experiences of her friends — their worries about staying healthy, and their stories about relatives who had cancer and heart disease. It seemed like every conversation Maria had with others about health sent her back to the Internet to answer a question, to learn about a disease, or simply to surf.

Maria's case represents two of the softer dimensions of information seeking: a tendency to avoid certain information until one is ready to deal with it, balanced against a curiosity motivated by deeply held feelings. In situations like Maria's, the urge to find facts and hear personal stories may satisfy some emotional need to be reassured, to be comforted, to *connect* with others. In this sense there is no final answer that will end information seeking — it is the project of a lifetime.

2.2. Summary

We have seen, through six fictitious case studies, the playing out of information seeking in different contexts. Common to them all has been the need to deal with (potentially, at least) great volumes of information, much of it complex. In all cases the searchers have attempted to lessen their cognitive load by jettisoning some types of information, taking a shortcut to a state of satisfaction or decision.

The results of most searches, although incomplete and perhaps even resulting in failure (witness Joe's lost bet), were, at the time, *good enough* to satisfy the needs of the seeker, a type of behavior that is called *satisficing*. With the exception of the ICU team (a group of professionals with considerable resources) the seekers of information did *not* make every possible attempt to attain the most complete, accurate, and detailed information available (*optimizing*) but rather gathered just enough data, opinions, and impressions to feel satisfied with the process. When a person reaches such a stage, he or she may end the task with a feeling of closure.

These six scenarios were chosen to provide readers with contrasting elements across different information seeking activities. These contrasts are highlighted in Table 2.3, in which the scenarios are ranked in order of *time pressure*. The primary *motivation* in each of the six scenarios varies widely; two searches are prompted by assignments given to the seeker by other persons, and the rest are personally chosen by the seeker out of self-interest. *Sources of information* used by each person are more homogeneous. Most seekers use a mixture of formal (e.g., printed publications or electronic sources) and informal information (e.g., the opinions of friends); the major exceptions are the three assigned tasks, in which documentation of official sources is important.

Time pressure is determined by how quickly a search for information must be concluded: minutes, hours, days, weeks, or months. The *degree of thoroughness* roughly summarizes the ratio of data-actually-gathered-and-considered to all-data-potentially-relevant in a search. The *time pressure* and

Table 2.3: Comparison of six case studies.

Seeker(s) and situation	Main motivation	Sources of information	Time pressure	Degree of thoroughness
Julie: car purchase	Optimize functionality and value	Friends, Web pages, salespeople	Low (months)	Low
Leslie: library research	Class assignment; earn credit/grade	Online catalogs, books, journals, professional advice (on how to search)	Moderate (weeks)	Moderate
Hospital ICU team members: caring for an accident victim	Work assignment; desire to help others	Observation of patient, paper and electronic records, monitoring devices, medical manuals, hospital employees	Very high (hours or days, based on patient improvement)	High
Joe: horse race wager	Desire for thrill; to win money	Special journals, observation, intuition	Very high (minutes)	High
George: legal research	Work assignment; help relatives	Special databases and publications, professional advice	High (days)	High
Maria: information on cancers	Curiosity; preemptive information search	Web pages, books, brochures, friends, experts	None (lifetime)	Moderate

required degree of thoroughness faced by the seekers of information vary the most, as can be seen by examining the more extreme cases.

Maria's interest in cancer-related information comes out of a personal curiosity that may last a lifetime; in her case there is no identifiable time pressure at present. In an optional purchase such as Julie's, the decision could be postponed indefinitely, making the search for information protracted; as well, the number of variables is large and the importance of subjective judgment (e.g., taste) is so important that a relatively low proportion of potentially relevant data are considered in the final decision. In the case of Joe's racing wager, a decision must be made within minutes, and the amount of information of potential relevance is so large that only selective use of information is possible. Finally, George's legal research requires not only very fast turnaround (days) but absolute accuracy as well; therefore, George must be especially careful to search all of the relevant sources and to do so thoroughly. The other cases lie in between these extremes regarding time and thoroughness.

The cases we have examined represent quite common scenarios: writing a term paper, buying a product, satisfying our curiosity, and so forth. There is one sense in which they are *not* representative, however: most of the academic research conducted on information seeking examines scenarios more like those of George (work in a professional or occupational setting) and Leslie (searching formal sources, particularly in libraries).

In fact, a high percentage of the situations examined in traditional information seeking research have involved either laboratory scientists, engineers in private firms, or university research faculty (in a broad array of disciplines). Because we will be reviewing such cases in future chapters, there is no need to emphasize such complicated research settings at this point in our discussion. The human factors bearing on information seeking are similar with all questions and in all fields of inquiry.

Now that we have grounded the topic in familiar human situations, we will next turn our attention to a basic question: their corresponding definitions and corollary concepts. What is "information?" What is "information seeking?"

Recommended for Further Reading

Aspray, W., & Hayes, B. (Eds.) (1956). *Everyday information: The evolution of information seeking in America.* Cambridge, MA: MIT Press.

    This edited book features examples of how individuals have pursued their daily information needs over several decades, including chapters on car buyers, airline travelers and sports fans.

Connaway, L. S., Dickey, T. J., & Radford, M. L. (2011). "If it is too inconvenient I'm not going after it": Convenience as a critical factor in information-seeking behaviors. *Library & Information Science Research, 33*(3), 179–190.

A review of two recent studies of library users, noting that they frequently cite convenience as a factor in how and where they search for information, however their definition of convenience may change over time, depending on their situation.

MacIntosh-Murray, A. (2001). Scanning and vicarious learning from adverse events in health care. *Information Research, 7*(1). Retrieved from http://InformationR.net/ir/7-1/paper113.html

This review of studies of information failures in medical practice discusses how health care organizations can systematically learn to avoid such problems.

PART 2

CONCEPTS RELEVANT TO INFORMATION BEHAVIOR

Chapter 3

The Concept of Information

Information seems to be everywhere. We talk of its being encoded in the
genes ... Disseminated by media of communication ... Exchanged in conversation ... Contained in all sorts of things .... Libraries are overflowing
with it, institutions are bogged down by it, and people are overloaded with
it ... [yet] no one seems to know exactly what information is.
— Christopher Fox (1983, p. 3)

Information, usually seen as the precondition of debate, is better understood
as its by-product. When we get into arguments that focus and engage our
attention, we become avid seekers of relevant information. Otherwise we take
in information passively — if we take it in at all.
— Christopher Lasch (1995, p. 162)

Chapter Outline

3.1. Searching for a Definition of Information

"Information" is a fairly old English word, making an early appearance in one of Chaucer's tales sometime between 1372 and 1386 (Schement, 1993a, p. 177); Capurro and Hjørland (2002) take its origin back to Latin and Greek terms of the pre-Christian era. One would think that hundreds of years of usage would tend to settle a word and result in a consensus on its meaning. This has not been the case with the term "information." Especially in the last five decades, as the various phenomena that people call information began to be objects of empirical study, meanings of the word have proliferated. Schrader (1983, p. 99) goes so far as to complain about "the multiplicity of vague, contradictory, and sometimes bizarre notions of the nature of the term 'information'."

One of the problems of studying any phenomenon — or merely talking about a thing — is reaching an agreement on what to call it. Words are ambiguous, the same string of characters often having multiple meanings. Each meaning may identify a distinct concept in the way that the noun "port" can refer to a fortified wine, the left side of a ship, or a gateway or opening for passage (a harbor, a modem port, a valve port, etc.). The case of the word "information" is much more complex, as it has been used to denote various overlapping concepts, rather than neatly distinct phenomena as is the situation with "port."

Unless otherwise stipulated, in this book "information" will be taken to mean any difference that makes a difference to a conscious, human mind (Bateson, 1972, p. 453). In other words, information is whatever appears significant to a human being, whether originating from an external environment or a (psychologically) internal world. This definition was chosen by the anthropologist Gregory Bateson, after he had struggled for two decades with the inadequacies of mathematical definitions of information. A perceived difference, according to Bateson, is a basic "unit of mind" that can be inferred through study of both humans and animals.

Other authors have employed definitions of information that are similar to Bateson's. A popular version originated with communication scholar Gerald Miller (1969): information is any stimulus we recognize in our environment. Others (e.g., Bates, 2005b; Dervin, 1976a; Higgins, 1999; Johnson, 1997; Rogers, 1986) have defined information as the recognition of patterns in the world around us.

Obviously, the characterization of information as a difference implies a very broad definition for a common word that has been defined in several distinct ways — with virtually all other definitions implying more restrictions on meaning. That is, many authors have used other words to define a concept that they have called "information," some of them incorporating specific requirements, such as information must always be true or useful, or it must be embodied in a form or object, or it must be intentionally transmitted, and so forth.

The reason for adopting this broad (some would say vague) definition is because this book reviews a great many studies from several disciplines and needs to cover a variety of more restrictive concepts. The reason some other definitions are less appropriate will be made clearer in the remainder of this chapter, which first discusses the nature of conceptual explication and then examines a variety of definitions for "information," each of which identifies a somewhat different concept than the rest.

3.1.1. *Explicating "Information"*

To discuss and study any concept, we first need to define it. In the process, we may identify and define other ideas that are related to (and sometimes derived from) the concept under study. In the case of information, two related concepts include "knowledge" and "data." "Information behavior," "information seeking," "information source," and "information use" are among several other, higher-order concepts that build upon the concept of information.

Social scientists call the process of defining a concept "explication." As discussed by Chaffee (1991), explication is the intellectual process that relates theory to research, which links a focal concept to the ways in which it is studied. For researchers who aspire to direct observation of phenomena, explication eventually results in an operational definition of a concept, a set of procedures used to observe and measure instances of a concept. In this chapter, we deal only with the initial stages of explication — reviewing and analyzing existing definitions — and leave issues of measurement for later chapters. Lambert and Loiselle (2007) offer examples of the later stages of explication.

The process of explication often starts with a word for which we have only a general meaning. At this stage, we have only a nominal, or dictionary, definition for a term — that is, a word is defined by other words. Explication continues by examining what has been written about the concept; we review the publications about it, with an eye toward how different authors have defined and used the concept. In doing this, we may not only find multiple definitions for the term, but discover that some authors have studied the same concept but called it by a different name.

The next step in explication is to analyze the meaning of a term by one or both of two approaches. The first possible approach is a top-down procedure. We distill the discussions of many authors to their abstract core: what is the heart of what they say about the concept? In the case of information, a core idea may be that it is a message expressed in some medium, and/or that it has the potential of altering a person's consciousness. As Chaffee (1991, pp. 26–27) points out, finding a single, central meaning is unusual, particularly when distinct research literatures are examined.

In the second alternative, the bottom-up approach to meaning analysis, we list all of the subsidiary concepts that make up the focal concept. For "information," we might attempt to list exhaustively all the possible forms that information could take — a Web page, a book, a radio broadcast, a conversation, a handwritten note, e-mail, and so on. This is a massive task that would be subject to change over time as new forms of information appear or are identified. Listing all examples of information has been one way that researchers have guided the observation of the concept.

Whichever means of analysis is chosen, the eventual result is a more abstract definition than one defined by near synonyms. The definition may be expressed as a series of critical distinctions between the focal concept and related concepts; for example, what is the difference between information and data? Or, instead, it may simply identify attributes that serve to identify something as an instance of the concept; for example, a book is an instance of information because it contains symbols that can, or are intended to, inform someone.

The remainder of this chapter will consider, through literature review and distillation, the various definitions of information and their key distinctions.

3.1.2. The Concept of Information

Ordinarily, we both use and hear the word "information" without much concern for its definition; we know what we mean when we use the word. At first glance, the *Oxford English Dictionary* definition seems adequate: "(1) The action of informing. The action of telling or fact of being told of something. (2) That of which one is apprised or told; intelligence, news." This nominal definition reveals at least one important distinction: the term may be used to indicate either a process (informing) or a kind of message (news).

Further distinctions lay buried in the nominal definition, as a series of publications have made obvious. One explication of the term (Wellisch, 1972) uncovered eight distinct definitions of information without any common elements. Not long afterward, Wersig and Neveling (1975) identified 17 unique definitions, which they grouped into six broad categories. Summarizing 30 years of commentary, Levitan (1980) declared that 29 different concepts had been associated with the term information. A review by Schement (1993b) includes a selection of 22 definitions written between 1968 and 1989. More recently, Fricke (2009, p. 139) points out a dozen characterizations of information, while allowing that there are "many more." How has the concept of information been used such that so many definitions have resulted? The empirical work of Shenton and Hayter (2006) demonstrate that it is not only scholars who are unclear on the concept, ordinary people are confused about what the word means, too.

The central difficulty is that the word "information" has been used to denote several different concepts. The adoption of the term by multiple disciplines is part, but not all, of the problem. The same term has been used to refer to, among other phenomena, sensory stimuli, mental representations, problem solving, decision making, an aspect of human thinking and learning, states of mind, the process of communication, judgments about the relevance of information to information needs, the content of subject specialties, recorded knowledge, and particular objects that carry information such as documents. It is no surprise that scholars have struggled to come up with a formulation that promises to condense most of these meanings into one universal principle or attribute.

3.1.3. *Typologies of Information Concepts*

Let's first examine four parallel attempts to identify different "families" of information definitions. Two attempts to distinguish types of information concepts, one from 1976 and the other from 1992, illustrate how periodically we revisit the problem of defining information. Two articles by Dervin (1976a, 1977) set the stage for the development of the sense-making school of thought (see Chapters 4 and 7) regarding information seeking. In her articles, Dervin posited three types of information, based on the writings of philosopher Popper (1972):

1. Objective, external information is that which describes reality (but never completely so).
2. Subjective, internal information represents our picture or cognitive map of reality, the structures we impute onto reality.
3. Sense-making information reflects the procedures and behaviors that allow us to "move" between external and internal information to understand the world, and usually to act on that understanding as well.

Dervin argues that to look at information in such a way has several advantages. For example, it acknowledges that legitimate inputs may come from inside us, rather than viewing the only important information as arising from external sources. In a similar way, this view does not privilege formal information systems (e.g., books) over informal sources (e.g., friends, relatives, or coworkers); consulting the latter is a much more common approach to understanding than are the former channels.

In a manner reminiscent of Dervin, Ruben (1992, pp. 22–24) places information conceptualizations into three "orders." The first-order information captures information as "environmental artifacts and representations; environmental data, stimuli, messages, or cues." This environmental sense of information consists of "stimuli, messages, or cues, waiting to be attended to." The second-order information is that which is "internalized, individualized appropriations and representations." Here Ruben identifies information as something that is "transformed and configured for use by a living system," internal representations that include "semantic networks, personal constructs, images, rules or mind." And the third-order information is that which is "socially constructed, negotiated, validated, sanctioned and/or privileged appropriations, representations, and artifacts." The third-order information, then, is the social context of information.

Dervin's and Ruben's types of information are parallel but not identical, especially in the terms and examples they use to describe their third category, which for Dervin is decidedly intrapersonal, abstract, and process-oriented. For Ruben, the social context is external, is socially constructed, and may encompass physical objects like books (which seem to fall under Dervin's objective category).

Two other typologies, both from the 1990s, are also somewhat parallel, but they bear only a modest resemblance to the Dervin and Ruben schemes. Buckland's (1991a) widely cited typology portrays uses of the term "information" as falling into three categories. The first category is information-as-process, which refers to the act of informing, the communication of information, and how a person's state of knowledge is changed. A second sense of information is information-as-knowledge, a usage of the term denoting that the information is perceived in the first category (i.e., the knowledge communicated). The final sense of the term is information-as-thing, in which "objects, such as data and documents ... are referred to as 'information' because they are regarded as being informative."

Buckland takes great pains to explain the difficulties inherent in such a typology, pointing out the intangible nature of the first two categories (which makes them difficult to observe), the issue of intentionality (some definitions of information take for granted an intention to communicate), and the problem that any object in the world might potentially be informative ("if everything is information, then being information is nothing special"). He concludes that it is essential to investigate information-as-process, even though information-as-thing cannot be dismissed as a focus of study.

The second typology is similar to that of Buckland but breaks out his two categories of information-as-thing and information-as-knowledge into three overlapping conceptions of information. Altogether, McCreadie and Rice (1999, pp. 47–58) identify four distinct "conceptualizations," the first of which is information as a resource or commodity. Under this conceptualization, information is something that can be "produced, purchased, replicated, distributed, sold, manipulated, passed along, controlled," such as a message that travels from sender to receiver, with or without some kind of payment in exchange.

The second type of information is characterized as data in the environment, that is, "objects, artifacts, sounds, smells, events" that may be perceived in the environment. This category takes into account the potential for unintentional communication of information, such as when one observes and interprets natural phenomena.

McCreadie and Rice's third type of information concept is that expressed as a representation of knowledge, such as in "documents, books, periodicals." Finally, their fourth type of information is as a part of the communication process. That is, information is meanings that are created as people go about their lives and try to make sense of their world.

While at first glance it may seem that these latter two typologies characterize types of information in similar ways, there are several differences, particularly in the distinctions they make between representation, thing, and (in the case of McCreadie and Rice) resource. McCreadie and Rice use "documents, books, periodicals" among their examples of representations, whereas Buckland uses those as examples of "things." It seems that McCreadie and Rice are trying to make finer distinctions than Buckland regarding possible embodiments of information.

Ultimately, the typologies of Dervin, Ruben, Buckland, and McCreadie and Rice are each distinct from one another in several ways. At least the distinctions these authors make are useful in illustrating the many ways one could parse the attributes of the information concept.

3.2. Definitions of Information and their Problems

The typologies discussed earlier in this chapter fall short of providing specific definitions of "information." Rather, their intention is to show that there are distinct usages of the term rather than a single universal usage.

Nevertheless, many authors have attempted to create a general definition of information that at least would be adequate for some areas of investigation. As we shall see, many scholars have incorporated into their definitions specific and powerful assumptions regarding the nature of information.

We begin our examination with the most influential definition of information, one that developed a half-century ago for the study of signal transmission in broadcasting and telephony. Now it might seem odd that a definition for such a mundane concept as information should come to us from a highly specialized field as telephone engineering. In fact one writer (Tor Nørretranders, 1991; English translation, 1998) jokes that:

> there are plenty of grounds for a conspiracy theory of the most devious kind: that the notion of information was invented and developed by engineers from big private corporations who then made a profitable business out of having the rest of us talk about truth, beauty, meaning and wisdom — on the phone. (p. 96)

In Nørretranders's view, this development was unfortunate because it shifted our attention away from the more important elements involved in information — the senders and receivers of messages — and toward characteristics of the carrier.

3.2.1.   The Influential and Restrictive "Information Theory"

The first widely recognized attempt to define information, the misnamed "Information Theory" (properly called "The Mathematical Theory of Communication"), is still frequently invoked to describe the nature of information. The popularity of information theory cannot be overemphasized: a review of two decades (Zunde, 1984) listed over 400 selected citations to this theory; by now, the number of references to information theory surely runs into thousands.

Fifty years ago, the works of Shannon and Weaver (1949) on communication of messages gave rise to a popular conception of information. Shannon, an engineer at Bell Labs, was concerned with the fidelity of telecommunications signals, such as those sent over radio waves, and the determination of the effective capacities of telecommunication channels. It was Shannon who came up with a model of communication as a process of signal transmission. His model of communication became the basis for applying measures to parts of messages based on the statistical

```
                              Noise
SOURCE --------> TRANSMITTER ------> [ ] ------> RECEIVER ----------> DESTINATION
       Message            Signal sent Signal received    Message
```

Figure 3.1: Shannon's model.

probability of their appearance — a technique that led to improvements in signal transmission because it helped to predict the likelihood of errors and decide how to correct them, such as the sending of redundant portions of a message.

In Shannon's famous diagram (Figure 3.1), the source and destination of a message were seen as being at the opposite ends of a chain, linked by a message converted by a transmitter into a signal sent over some kind of channel to the receiver, which converts the signal back to a message for delivery to the destination. The channel was acted on by sources of noise, which could disrupt or distort the message.

Along with the diagram came both a definition and measure for the concept of information, as it is encoded in a message. Shannon's definition of information was based on the notion of entropy, a measure of the degree of disorganization in a system that reflected a tendency for any state of affairs to lose order and become more random. In signal transmission, noise is the vehicle for the effects of entropy, that is, noise degrades the signal to some degree. Messages are organized exchanges (e.g., grammatical sentences) based on selections from an agreed-upon set of signals (phonemes, words, letters, etc.). The requirement that the message elements are selected from a fixed universe of possible elements has led some scholars to refer to it as a theory of "selective information" to contrast it with theories of "semantic information," that is, theories concerned with the meaning of messages.

The effects of entropy lead to more randomness in messages that, in turn, leads to higher levels of uncertainty. In Shannon's view, these higher levels of uncertainty imply the potential for more information in the message. At the opposite end of the entropy scale would be messages that are highly organized — and thus familiar to the receiver — but which tend to carry little "new" information. Shannon's theorems dealt with statistical probabilities associated with the selection of signals from a well-defined set. However, subsequent applications of Shannon's work tended to interpret the theory in terms of uncertainty reduction for the receiver of the signals — what Ritchie (2003) calls "epistemological probability."

Such a definition of information is somewhat counterintuitive because we tend to associate information with certainty, rather than uncertainty (Miller, 1983a). In fact, Shannon had been advised by computer scientist John von Neumann to call his concept "entropy" rather than "information" (or "uncertainty," another near synonym) because entropy was a term less likely to be confused with everyday meanings associated with the word "information" (Campbell, 1982, p. 32; Machlup & Mansfield, 1983, p. 48). Indeed, these opposite or "negative" forms of Shannon's definition appeared in the writings of physicist Leo Szilard in 1929 and philosopher Charles Pierce in 1878 (Morowitz, 1991).

To demonstrate how easy it is to misunderstand Shannon's notion of uncertainty when we apply it to human communication, Miller (1983a, p. 495) provides the example of the sentences "Rex is a dog" and "Rex is a mammal." The latter sentence contains terms less likely to appear in everyday usage, so according to Shannon's measure it would carry more "information" that is, a rarer, more surprising, message. But the term "dog" is more specific than "mammal" (which could be a dog, a bat, a dolphin, or many other creatures); semantically, therefore, we would judge that "Rex is a dog" carries more information, reversing the logic of Shannon's measure. It is all too easy to misinterpret Shannon's definition of information outside the realm of signal transmission (Losee, 1997).

Common misunderstandings of Shannon's information theory are partly attributable to his coauthors and advocates. Warren Weaver, a physicist, was invited to write an introduction to two journal articles by Shannon that the University of Illinois was publishing under the title "The Mathematical Theory of Communication." In his introduction to Shannon's work, Weaver speculated on how Shannon's model of signal transmission might be applied to human communication. Weaver acknowledged in a later publication that the model could be taken too literally: "Information must not be confused with meaning," Weaver said (1949, p. 8). Thus, he anticipated that some scholars would attempt to extend the theory to the subjective interpretation of signals by humans.

Nevertheless, Weaver's broad-ranging analogies and speculations became conflated with the very limited theorems devised by Shannon, much to the latter's chagrin; according to Ritchie (1986, 1991), it is Weaver's extrapolation of Shannon's model to which most writings refer, not to Shannon's original explanation and theorems. To confuse matters further, Shannon himself was inconsistent in his use of the terms uncertainty and entropy (Cole, 1993).

Despite its flaws, Shannon's simple depiction of signal transmission as linear, one-way process was seen by many scholars as an adequate model of human communication. Additional interpretations (e.g., Berlo, 1960) resulted in inevitable simplification and distortion of the model. David Berlo's famous "Source-Message-Channel-Receiver" model (Rogers, 1986, pp. 86–90) dropped the "signal" component of Shannon's model. Conflating the concepts of message and signal ignored an important distinction between meanings (messages) and their encodings (signals).

For several decades, various simplified versions of Shannon's model became the basis for studying the exchange of messages among people (Rogers, 1994). As Shera and Cleveland (1977) put it:

> Everybody tried to get into the act, hopeful that Shannon's magical formula would unlock countless information secrets and give a

quantitative measure for laying a scientific theoretical foundation for practically every major field lacking one. Unfortunately this overextension was generally an intellectual get-rich-quick scheme and, in the long run, most of the hopefuls fell to the wayside. (p. 261)

A 1974 article by James Watt and Robert Krull can serve as an example of how some researchers applied Shannon's concepts. In a study of television viewing habits, Watt and Krull (1974) noted that other researchers had no classification system in common for program contents. Some would use categorizations like "news, mystery drama, situation comedy, quiz-audience," while others used "documentary, crime-detective, comedy-variety, game shows" to cover the same content. Obviously, these variations posed problems for researchers trying to test for effects of television viewing, given that the results of independent investigations were not directly comparable.

Instead of subjective classifications of content, Watt and Krull argued that "structural or form characteristics of the program may also have an effect on the audience"; therefore, they proposed a "content-free measure of television program form" that applied "information theory entropy terms" to features that appeared on television screens (1974, pp. 44–45). In a study of adolescent viewing, they developed several formulas for measuring various aspects of a broadcast. For instance, "verbal time entropy is defined as the degree of randomness of the time of audible behavior on the part of characters in a program"; a formula measured this in terms of a negative, logarithmic function of the time that a series of television characters produced audible sound. I do not need to reproduce Watt and Krull's various formulas to suggest that although they did indeed carefully measure "nonrandom viewing patterns," their results are difficult to interpret in terms of what normally concerns us about television viewing and its effects. Our judgments about television programs are almost always based on the content of the program, whereas their measures deliberately ignored the content. Nevertheless, Ritchie (1991) describes Watt and Krull's work as among the more successful applications of Shannon's entropy measure, along with Finn's (1985, 1986) studies of unpredictability in news articles.

Eventually, the Shannon and Weaver model came to be seen as inadequate for expressing many of the important features of human communication. As early as 1969, Donald MacKay complained that:

communication engineers have not developed a concept of information at all. They have developed a theory dealing with only one particular feature or aspect of messages "carrying" information — their unexpectedness or surprise value. (pp. 56–57)

Nørretranders (1991/1998, p. 96) observes that Shannon's view of information equated it with "something completely meaningless, something closely related to disorder .... quite unlike what the rest of us understand by the everyday word 'information' — meaning, content, overview, order." It is what Brier (1992) calls a "mechanistic concept of information," which reduces human cognition to the level of computer processing. Shannon's so-called "information theory" simply did not adequately reflect the way in which people interpret and assess the "meaning" of messages. As the Canadian sociologist Klapp (1982) concluded:

> Meaning, being subjective, and referring to synthetic or holistic properties that cannot be reduced to the sum of parts, might be called a higher sort of information that does not come easily, let alone inevitably, from a growing heap of mere information. (p. 58)

3.2.2. Five Problematic Issues in Defining Information

Despite its popularity, Shannon and Weaver's implied definition of information contains several assumptions and requirements that differ from the ways we usually think about and experience similar phenomena in everyday life. Their definition is useful only in a very limited sense.

The Shannon and Weaver definition is not alone in posing such problems. Most information concepts contain assumptions regarding five issues that often turn out to be problematic when we try to apply their definitions. The five types of assumptions are about the following:

Utility: Does information, in order to be information, have to have some kind of effect, some sort of usefulness for humans? If not, what would be the point of talking about it? In particular, must information reduce uncertainty about something? If information does not reduce uncertainty, must it be useful in some other way — for example, in providing entertainment, emotional uplift, or some other kind of useful stimulation?

Physicality: Must information always take on some physical form, such as a book, the sound waves of human speech, or a natural object that embodies some kind of data? Is it even proper to discuss what people know, or believe, as being information? A related, and perhaps distinct, issue is whether information (or at least its effects) must be directly observable. If the effects are not directly observable, then how can it be the subject of scholarly study? This latter question bears on Belkin's seventh and eighth requirements, which he calls methodological, and is addressed in Chapter 6.

Structure/Process: Must information be structured in some way? That is, must it be composed of elements in fixed relations to one another, or in some way consist of a complex "whole," such as an image? Or is information a process, some kind of function, a series of steps — a sort of recipe?

Intentionality: When studying information, is it necessary to assume that someone (or something) intends to communicate it to another entity? Or is some information simply out there in the environment, to be perceived and interpreted by a sentient organism? For instance, we can imagine circumstances in which information is not communicated with a *purpose* (i.e., a utility) in mind; a glance at threatening clouds informs us that rain is imminent, but in this case the generator of the message is an aspect of the natural world and has no intentions.

Truth: Must information, in order to be information, be true? Is it improper to call something information if it is demonstrably false? If so, then we need another term for that which is untrue, such as misinformation.

Let's examine each of these issues in turn and consider what various authors have written about them.

3.2.3. Utility as a Requirement

As Dretske (1990) says (in "Putting Information to Work," his essay in a volume about language and cognition), the concept of information isn't fruitful if it doesn't account for an effect of some kind:

> Information isn't much good if it doesn't do anything. ... a difference that doesn't make a difference isn't really a difference at all. ... I mean a causal difference, a difference in the kinds of effects it has. (p. 112)

Dretske's concern is the relationship of "information" to causation and hence explanation of behavior; he doesn't think that information is the same thing as a "belief" or a "meaning." We can accept Dretske's claim at a superficial level: it is not worth discussing a concept that makes no "difference" in the world. Yet this leaves many questions unanswered: what, how, and when are these effects happening?

First, it is necessary to say something about the relationship between information (or knowledge) and power (see Braman, 1989, 2006, for a fuller discussion of this topic). Suffice it to say that information can have powerful effects on humans, but usually does not. Yes, it is easy to imagine that, if we knew in advance which team would win the world cup or which stock would increase in value, we could easily turn that information into a large sum of money — which in turn could be used in various, powerful ways — but the accurate prediction of future events is rare. Of course, if we know other people's secrets, we may be able to compel them to do our bidding by threatening to disclose the secrets — an unusual and perverted kind of power. And it is true that having specialized knowledge (e.g., of medicine) may grant one certain privileges and enable one to attract money. But such "formal knowledge" is closely bound to issues of performance, competence, and (especially) institutions and social relations. As Friedson (1986) says, knowledge must have agency in order to exercise power. Many discussions in the "information is power" vein tend to underplay the complex social relations (e.g., organizations like universities, governments, and corporations) or material objects (e.g., properties or weapons) typically involved in accumulating, maintaining, and using power.

In contrast, most of the "information" in our possession has little value or effect in and of itself. Most of what we know results only in subtle changes or uses in the real world. Some examples of relatively "powerless" information are the current time and temperature, the names of capitals of the world's nations, or what the person next to me just said. Nevertheless, Kari (2007) offers some evidence that information can have effects of both a psychological and a physical nature.

A more specific utility of information in which there has been more scientific interest and evidence is the ability of information to reduce uncertainty. From the 1950s through the 1970s, definitions of information proliferated, most of them incorporating the uncertainty aspect of Shannon's model. A review by Bouazza (1989) reflects the majority view regarding the role of uncertainty in these definitions: "The most cited and perhaps the most useful definition of information is 'that which reduces uncertainty'" (p. 145).

In the interest of brevity, we ignore definitions that try to preserve major portions of Shannon's definition (e.g., those discussed by Artandi, 1973; Fairthorne, 1975), as they are too narrow to be compatible with common-sense notions of information. The most common drawback of these early attempts is that they insist on defining information in terms of uncertainty reduction — typically in the execution of a choice or decision. For example, Wersig and Neveling (1975) declare:

> The basic term "information" can only be understood if it is defined in relation to ... the information needs of people involved in social labour ... Either as reduction of uncertainty caused by communicated data. Or as data used for reducing uncertainty. (p. 138)

Like many such definitions, Wersig and Neveling's definition implies that information must be useful ("involved in social labour") and intentional ("communicated").

Similarly, Everett Rogers defines information in terms of reducing uncertainty in a decision task, as "patterned matter-energy that affects the probabilities of alternatives available to an individual making a decision" (Rogers, 1986, p. 85). Other writers leave out the assumption that a task is being performed, but they still cling to the uncertainty component, in which information is whatever "removes the doubt, restricts the uncertainty, reduces the ignorance, curtails the variance" (Nauta, 1972, p. 179).

The emphasis on uncertainty continues to current times. For example, one book (Klir, 1996, p. vii) on the nature of information begins with the words: "The concept of information, which is the subject of this book, is intimately connected with the concept of uncertainty ... information in a given context is obtained by a cognitive agent whenever relevant uncertainty is reduced." This is a typical approach for defining information among economists. Hirshleifer (1973), for example, discusses the probability of signals but draws a contrast with the way that probability is applied (p. 31):

> Uncertainty is summarized by the dispersion of individuals' subjective probability [or belief] distributions over possible states of the world. Information, for our purposes, consists of events tending to change these probability distributions. A rather different concept of "information" is employed in communications and statistical theory, according to which a dispersed probability distribution is called less "informative" than a concentrated one. This latter concept uses the term "information" merely as a negative measure of uncertainty.

It is important to note once again that while this writer refers indirectly to Shannon's work, he is actually discussing epistemological probability — likelihood estimates in the "real world" of human communication.

The idea that information must be useful to be information has been undermined in several critiques, most notably by Fox (1983) and Losee (1997). The latter observes that:

> a good definition or theory of information ...should bear some resemblance to the natural language notion of information but need not adhere to it when the natural language definition loses its generality and explanatory power. This happens when the common language definition of information, for example, becomes conflated with the notion of *useful* information, that is, information is understood to be in all cases useful. For those accepting this concept of information, if it is not useful, it is not information.

> Requiring that all information be useful limits the domain of discussions about information to cognitive processes that can "use" something; it excludes the information carried by a subatomic particle which is not sensed by a cognitive process. We try to avoid excluding information phenomena. (p. 257)

Neither must information (intentionally communicated or otherwise) automatically reduce uncertainty. To use an example from Fox (1983), suppose that I tell you something but you do not believe me. I have not reduced your uncertainty. Or suppose I tell you that the stock market crashed this morning. Last you heard, the market was going up, so perhaps I have reduced your uncertainty about the overall direction of the market (assuming you have been wondering about it), and yet I have probably created uncertainty within you regarding collateral knowledge (e.g., the values of your individual stock holdings). As Fox points out, there are other scenarios in which communicating information might actually increase uncertainty, rather than decrease it.

Some other disciplines that initially exploited uncertainty reduction have recently questioned the ubiquity of such a psychological drive. For instance, in the interpersonal communication literature, we have the emergence of problematic integration theory (Babrow, 1992) and uncertainty management theory (Babrow, Kasch, & Ford, 1998). Both of these theories question the assumption that humans always strive to reduce uncertainty. While most discussions emphasize the negative effects of uncertainty, some other scholars (e.g., Brashers, Goldsmith, & Hsieh, 2002; Huber & Sorrentino, 1996; Sorrentino & Roney, 2000) identify positive psychological effects of uncertainty — for instance, it may provide "hope."

Uncertainty management theory, in particular, highlights how people sometimes deliberately increase uncertainty. Uncertainty management theory holds that uncertainty is experienced "not simply as an uncomfortable tension demanding reduction" (Bradac, 2001, p. 463) but as feelings and cognitions that can be managed in other ways as well; these may include "seeking instead ambiguity and even confusion" (Bradac, 2001, p. 471). This is because "individuals may use uncertainty as a tool ... sometimes this cognitive state will be cultivated, rather than eradicated" (Bradac, 2001, p. 464).

Two examples of the deliberate increasing of uncertainty in interpersonal conversation are apparent when a physician must deliver a threatening diagnosis to a patient. One party to the dyad, the physician, might choose to provide an uncertainty-increasing message when he or she believes the patient is certain of bad news (Ford, Babrow, & Stohl, 1996); the patient, in turn, might avoid information in order to maintain uncertainty, or even seek out uncertainty-increasing information (Brashers et al., 2000). In both cases, increased uncertainty might actually provide some increase in comfort for the patient, even though in a way that might compromise his or her treatment. Affifi and Weiner (2004) give other examples in the health care context whereby individuals deliberately "avoid relevant information" (p. 182).

Other scholars have also debated the effects of new information on uncertainty. Lang, Newhagen, and Reeves (1996) imply that cognitive capacity limits may prevent new information from reducing uncertainty. Berlo (1977) notes that information always reduces uncertainty in the "now," but in the long term it may have the opposite effect. Yovits and Foulk (1985) conducted an empirical study in which they tested the assumption that information always reduces uncertainty; they found that sometimes new information made their subjects less sure that their evaluations of a problem were correct. Similar conclusions are reached by Kellermann and Reynolds (1990) and Robertson (1980).

Although uncertainty is not satisfactory as a basis for defining information itself, it is nevertheless an important concept for information seeking. Even though information can be encountered in a passive way, actively acquiring information implies recognition of uncertainty or anomalies at some level. Kuhlthau (1993b) makes good arguments for considering uncertainty as a beginning stage in the process of finding information, and Yoon and Nilan (1999) demonstrate that one cannot study uncertainty without considering what informants already know (i.e., certainty).

What about other effects of information? That is, if information does not always reduce uncertainty, must it have some other utility to be considered "information"? Some authors include in their definitions of information almost any kind of stimulation that humans find useful. Examples of such stimulation could include sound (from music or from a waterfall), sight (the words of a novel, the images of a painting, a photograph, or a film), or touch (the feel of warm sunshine or cool water on skin). Each of these sensations "tells us" something. In Chapter 5, and obliquely below under "Truth," I argue that such stimuli include potentially useful information. Therefore, if information must have an effect, it should extend to outcomes beyond "reducing uncertainty."

3.2.4. Physicality as a Requirement

Everyone acknowledges that information can have a physical form (e.g., see Buckland, 1991a; McCreadie & Rice, 1999), but few explicitly argue that it must. Indeed, many scholars take pains to state that a more useful conceptualization of information is as a phenomenon that exists apart from physical media; that is, that we should not think about information as primarily something found in human-created messages like printed texts.

However, as Krippendorff (1984, 2009) has pointed out, at some level, information must have a physical form. He argues in favor of information defined as "a change in an observer's state of uncertainty caused by some event in his world" (*sic*, 1984, p. 49). This, of course, places Krippendorff's definition in the "uncertainty requirement" camp we have already discussed. But the interesting aspect is how he analogizes information to energy:

> First, neither energy nor information exists in a vacuum. Both are embodied in material processes to which one must refer. Just as one can speak of energy only in conjunction with some specific resource, fuel or storage capacity ... so one can speak of information only in conjunction with a physically identifiable source, a message or a situation as described by an observer, and relative to what he already knows. Second, energy and information are measures of work .... Information is a measure of the (intellectual) work required to distinguish, to a degree better than chance, among a set of initially uncertain possibilities. (1984, pp. 49–50)

Certainly information in the sense of thoughts has a physical dimension: the electrical impulses of a human nervous system. In any event, it does not pose much of a restriction to insist that information must have a physical component, in the sense that energy does. In Krippendorff's case, it is much more of a restriction to require that information reduce uncertainty — as his Shannonesque conceptualization makes clear.

3.2.5. Structure/Process as a Requirement

Other families of definitions avoid the uncertainty concept through use of analogy — typically to a structure or process — and sometimes require intentionality to do so. Frické (2009, p. 139) calls this characterization of information "a state or structure transformer."

Boulding (1956) used the analogy of an image or a "picture in our head" in his popular characterization of messages and meaning. In Boulding's view (1956, p. 7), "the meaning of a message is the change which it produces in the image" — that is, the image of reality (or a portion of it) that exists in someone's mind. This conception of information is similar to the one offered by Bateson (1972, p. 452) at the start of this chapter, defining "change" as "difference which occurs across time."

Expanding on Boulding's analogy, Pratt (1977) defines information as an event: "That which occurs within the mind-upon-absorption-of-a-message"

(p. 215). That is, information (or an "informative event") is what we call a change in one's mental image. For Pratt, then, information is the event that changes someone's image of reality. Like those of Boulding and Bateson, Pratt's definition has ties to the "internal information" described by Dervin and Ruben earlier in this chapter.

The "image" metaphor is evoked by Donohew and Tipton (1973) as well. But, for them, the idea of "image" is not something like a holistic picture, but rather a complex mental structure of parts and subparts:

> An individual's "image of reality" is divided into three parts. First are the goals, beliefs, and knowledges [sic] which an individual has compiled as a result of his lifetime of experiences. These cognitive "objects" are defined as any concepts, issues, material objects, or ideas which exist psychologically for a person ... The second part of an individual's image or reality is the concept of self. This includes an evaluation of his ability to cope with various situations ...The third part of the image of reality is an information-handling "set" developed out of past experiences. The "set" probably controls the selection of information used by the individual to cope with the environment. Here we are talking about an individual's information-seeking and processing "styles." (pp. 246–247)

Similarly, MacKay argued that information must be considered in the contest of a hierarchy of goals (Cornelius, 2002, p. 413).

Other authors have conceptualized information as a structure or organization of experience and sensory data, for example, Thompson (1968) and Belkin and Robertson (1976). Following Thompson's definition, Belkin and Robertson (1976) state that "information is that which is capable of transforming structure" (p. 198) — in other words, it changes the knowledge state of the recipient. A parallel characterization comes from MacKay (1969) in which information is "that which does logical work on the organism's orientation" (p. 95).

Belkin (1978) notes that characterizing information as something that transforms knowledge structures has its problems, but it relates well to information as it has been defined in a variety of disciplines. Given that information-as-process assumes that a process has an effect on some entity — as an alteration of a mental image or the creation of meaning in a human mind — the process and structure views of information are analogically similar. In some definitions of this type, individual authors have added one or more restrictions to serve their purposes. Belkin and Robertson (1976), for example, are concerned with document retrieval systems and therefore assume that messages are intentional and that messages are represented by texts: "a collection of signs purposefully structured by a sender with the intention of changing the image structure of a recipient" (p. 201).

Cole (1994) notes a dilemma that accompanies the assumption that information changes a cognitive structure: if "new" information can modify knowledge structures, then "old" or "expected" information must not modify knowledge structures in the same way, or at least at the same time. New, or "pure," information must be extremely rare because such information is completely unanticipated, and there is a natural tendency not to recognize, see, or perceive that which is unanticipated. Information, then, has the quality of being unexpected and expected, old and new, at the same time. Therefore, for information to be unexpected and expected, old and new, at the same time, information must enter the perceptual system in at least a two-stage process.

More recently, Losee (1997) has advanced a general and coherent definition of information. He attempts to resolve some of the conflicts between definitions of belief, knowledge, information, and misinformation by viewing information generically as processes that produce outputs. The processes, or functions, may be invoked by humans, or machines, or other entities. The inputs into the process can be perceived from the environment or retrieved from human memory. The output of the process (e.g., the value taken on by a variable) is informative about both the original inputs and the process that produced the output from those inputs. Thus, Losee defines information as "the values of characteristics in the processes' output" (p. 256).

In Losee's view, by examining any output we can usually infer something about the process that created it. Examining a tree, for example, informs us about its origins, soil, moisture, and growth process. Or a cake, which is created through a procedure that includes ingredients, instructions, and heating, may be inspected to determine some, but not all, of the ingredients and the process by which it was created.

Defining information in terms of the output of a process, Losee concludes, moves beyond discipline-specific definitions (such as the tendency for decision theorists to define information in terms of uncertainty reduction) and provides a link between various studies of information. Yet, while Losee's definition sidesteps some of the criticisms of Fox regarding information-as-process, it substitutes the vagueness of "process" with a mysterious "function" that takes input and returns a value to be attached to variables (or "characterizations"). This in turn begs the question of how variables emerge in the first place and what determines the nature of the functions. These are not necessarily questions that Losee is responsible for answering, but rather problems to be faced by researchers trying to apply his definition of information. The chapter by Hörz (1996) is yet another commentary on the notion of information as structure or process.

Fox (1983) criticizes all structure-based definitions as failing to provide a clear definition of "structure" itself. Fox also makes compelling arguments that information cannot be considered either an event or a process, although he also provides counterexamples supporting the process view of information.

Fox himself favors defining information as a type of "telling," as represented in propositions. It would be impossible to fairly convey Fox's arguments in any shorthand version, presented as they are in 213 pages. It may suffice to say that his is the most extended dissertation on the subject thus far. Fox summarizes his conclusions in this way:

> Information need not be true, though misinformation must be false; information need not be believed by anyone; information need not originate with a reliable informant, but it must originate with someone in an appropriate position to know. Ontologically, information is propositions [the identification of which] depends on contextual factors. (pp. 212–213)

Fox admits that his conclusions leave several issues unresolved, including the:

> ... crucial notion of the amount of information carried by a set of sentences remains unanalyzed. The notion of informativeness remains unanalyzed. ... The details of how meaning determines propositional content as a function of context is not well understood. (p. 213)

In the intervening years since Fox's book, Nørretranders (1991/1998) has published a text that addresses the relation of context to content. Nørretranders introduces the term exformation to describe the ways in which messages may refer to a "mass of information" that is "not present" and "explicitly discarded" but nevertheless is understood to be relevant by the receiver and is used in construing the meaning of a message (p. 92).

Nørretranders provides two examples to illustrate the concept of exformation, first involving an extremely short message and the second involving no message at all. The first example is Victor Hugo's famous query to his publisher regarding the appearance of his latest novel, *Les Misérables,* in 1862. On vacation and out of touch with news about public reaction to his work, Hugo mailed a letter consisting of a single character: "?" His publisher replied, simply, "!" Without prearrangement, both parties understood these exchanges to mean something like the question "How is my book selling?" and the response, "Surprisingly well!"

Nørretranders's second example corresponds to the saying "no news is good news." When parents do not receive a phone call from their son away at college, they assume that he is OK and that things are fine. Information has been conveyed without sending a message at all. This example echoes Cole's (1994) observation about "new" information versus "old" or "expected" information: can "no news" be viewed as merely preserving the original knowledge structure or does it still modify the structure, but in a different way?

3.2.6. *Intentionality as a Requirement*

The manner in which Fox characterizes information has a critical limitation. His analysis is based, by necessity, on propositions expressed in the form of sentences. ("In this work I deal only with information carried by sentences," Fox, 1983, p. 7). Fox notes that his propositions represent "what is asserted to be the case by (someone who writes or utters)" (p. 77). One problem with this constraint is that it returns us to the assumption of a message intentionally sent by a sender to a receiver.

We could call this type of intentionality the "communication assumption" — that information necessarily involves communication, and hence, intention to communicate. Bowers and Bradac (1982) see the presence of intentionality as a key dividing point among rival definitions of "communication." Their examination of 27 metatheoretical discussions of communication finds that 18 of their authors hold that intentionality is a requirement for communication to exist. Few of those theorists have an unusual definition for "intention"; most mean the concept in its usual sense: a "purposeful activity .... [that] must be explained by 'in order to' as well as 'because' statements" (Bowers & Bradac, 1982, p. 7).

Although the restriction of intentionality may hold true for what is the most important sense of information — the exchange of information between humans (e.g., see Buckland, 1998) — it does not apply to all senses in which we use the word. Information may originate outside natural language propositions, for example, as signs occurring in our environment. Whether we are viewing the natural world (e.g., trees, animals, rocks) or the human-made world (e.g., what people are wearing and doing, or a printed sign that says "exit"), we can take in stimuli that have meaning. The only way to retain the notion of intentionality is to assume that it can refer to either a "sender" ("someone who writes or utters") or a "receiver" (the viewer of the world), but does not necessarily involve both ends of a communication process.

If we believe that people must intend to receive in order to take in information, then information is, in this more limited sense, intentional. Intentionality solely on the part of the receiver was suggested by Westley and Maclean in 1957, and in a discussion of news-seeking behavior by

Westley and Barrow (1959). The latter described "the need of the selecting receiver to be oriented in his extended environment" (p. 431); this assumption would take in the kind of "viewing" that I discussed previously. Theirs was a rather radical conception of communication, because it did not assume that a sender's intentions were involved; hence, Bowers and Bradac count it among the "nonintentional" definitions of communication. However, it is an intentional view of information behavior. This is a different view from that of Stonier (1990, p. 21), who asserts that:

> ... information exists. It does not need to be perceived to exist. It does not need to be understood to exist.

3.2.7. Truth as a Requirement

Losee (1997) also considers the notion of "misinformation." He notes that information can have various flaws, including inaccuracy, incompleteness, lack of justification, and intent to deceive. Do we need a special label for information that is so flawed as to be untrue?

Traditionally, philosophers have made a distinction of this type regarding knowledge, the common stance being that knowledge is "justified true belief." In this definition, belief is taken to be "the most elementary of our opinions ... characterized by two qualities: ... either true or false ... arrived at either rationally or nonrationally" (Cherwitz & Hikins, 1986, p. 31). "Justified" means that the believer has sufficient, relevant evidence that his or her belief is true. The "justified true belief" definition of knowledge (sometimes called "strong knowledge") has been criticized (e.g., Gettier, 1963), leading to the concept of "weak knowledge": beliefs or views that are true, yet lack justification (Frické, 2009). Frické (p. 140) says that "... weak personal or public knowledge, in its recorded form, is suitable as a view of information."

Patrick Wilson's quote at the beginning of the fifth chapter suggests that the truth or falsity of information is something that we can ignore in discussing information in the abstract sense. For one thing, it could be argued that we rarely know for sure if something (a statement or perception) is true or not; even if a "fact" is demonstrated to be true at this moment, it may be possibly proven wrong a few moments later. Fox (1983, p. 212) and Derr (1985, p. 496) also hold that information need not be true, based upon analyses of usage of the term in ordinary discourse. Buckland (1991b) concludes that

> ... the question of whether specific bits of knowledge are true is not central to our concerns. We adopt the position that the process of

becoming informed is a matter of changing beliefs. Whether these beliefs are held or denied by others and whether they are compatible with some a priori or fundamental assertion need not detain us. (p. 43)

Some would disagree with this point of view and instead argue that a true–false distinction is worth keeping in defining "information." Fricke (1997), for example, argues that information should be "truthlike" in order to "fit the world" so that we can "succeed in our interactions with the world" (p. 888). Dretske (1981, 1983) also states that information must tell us truly about a state of affairs, such that we can learn from it; he concludes that false information and misinformation cannot be considered to be varieties of information, but rather distinct concepts. These points of view is shared by Floridi (2005), who argues that for semantic information to be meaningful, it must be at least "contingently truthful," otherwise it is mere "pseudo-information." Finally, Budd (2011, p. 56) suggests that information "cannot be defined unless within the context of meaning and truth" and that information consists of "meaningful communicative action that aims at truth claims and conditions" (p. 70).

However, we are concerned here with a broad view of information phenomena that fits both real life and empirical studies of real life, not with establishing a philosophical distinction. Studies of information seeking provide many examples in which people value information that they know not to be entirely true. For purposes of this text, then, we will generally ignore any distinction between the truth or falsity of information, unless such is the focus or finding of a given investigation.

3.3.   Must there be a Universal Definition of Information?

All the definitions we have examined have taken a stance on one or more of these issues. The distinctions and disagreements among reviewers of definitions are too many to resolve; in short, there is as yet no single, widely accepted definition for the concept of information, even among the few thousand scholars who have written about information seeking. At least among recent reviews, however, there has been some agreement on the types of definitions of information that exist.

To summarize the chapter thus far, we can see that there have been many attempts to characterize information, some of them quite broad (e.g., the image/event/structure/process definitions), whereas others have been very narrowly focused (e.g., the view of information as a selection of signals from a well-defined set of symbols, the reception of which may reduce uncertainty for the receiver of the signals).

Narrow definitions assume one or more of the restrictions discussed earlier in the chapter. They hold that information must be useful, that its transmission is intentional, or that it must be represented in a recordable medium (in written or spoken language, or images), and/or that information must be true (or at least easily verifiable). Shannon's model contains examples of all of these assumptions. The vast majority of the early definitions and investigations of information seeking include at least the first three of these assumptions.

Before we go any further, it is important to note that defining information in an absolute and final sense is not entirely necessary for the study of information phenomena to proceed. As Artandi (1973) and others have pointed out, all we need are useful conceptualizations of information. Belkin (1978) makes this point most effectively when he says:

> ... we are not concerned with definitions of information, but rather with concepts of information. The distinction is that a definition presumably says what the phenomenon defined is, whereas a concept is a way of looking at, or interpreting, the phenomenon ... by accepting the idea of a concept one becomes free to look for a useful concept, rather than a universally true definition of information. (p. 58)

If we wish to keep talking about "information," we may have to give up on a universal definition. Hempel (1952) notes that there are some terms in any conceptual scheme that are so basic that they need not be fully explicated. Hempel calls these basic concepts "primitive terms." Primitive terms are simply accepted as they are commonly understood. Chaffee (1991, p. 7) provides the example of the concept of a "person," or a "human." Perhaps there are some fields in which what we mean by "human" needs to be carefully defined and is subject to debate — in zoology, for example. But, for most purposes of study, we do not need to explain that particular notion. It is when we deal with concepts that build upon the notion of humans — family, community, society — that we are in need of careful definitions for those concepts.

Information can be, and has been, treated as a primitive term as well. Some writers believe this approach is problematic — see Frohmann (2004, p. 86) and Nunberg (1996, p. 110). Yet it has been a common practice in the IB literature; commenting on a variety of recent studies, Vakkari (1997) notes that:

> ... one of the striking features in many studies was the use of the central concepts, like information, knowledge, information need, seeking, and use as primitive concepts, i.e., without definition. (p. 460)

Can we reconcile the various definitions of "information" with one another? It does not seem so, and perhaps it is not necessary. Although there is scholarly disagreement over the "most rigorous," or "most easily quantifiable,"or "most productive," or "most parsimonious" meaning of "information," these debates have done little to promote a fuller understanding of the concept among a community of scholars. In fact, if anything such discourse has resulted in a fracturing of scholarly effort in studying the phenomenon of information, it has resulted in too many definitions that defy comparison and that provide no common basis for understanding. Allen (1969) and Dervin (1977) discussed using the concept of "communication" instead (see the insightful discussion by Frohmann, 2004, pp. 53–67). Similarly, Furner (2004) argues that there are so many productive substitutes for the concept of "information" that we could do without it all together:

> ... philosophers of language have modeled the phenomena fundamental to human communication in ways that do not require us to commit to a separate concept of "information." Indeed, we can conclude that such a concept is unnecessary for information studies. Once the concepts of interest have been labeled with conventional names such as "data," "meaning," "communication," "relevance," etc., there is nothing left (so it may be argued) to which to apply the term "information." (p. 428)

Instead, let us treat "information" as a primitive term, as a phenomenon that we all recognize when we see it in its various forms (Fox, 1983, p. 16). Information would then be treated as "anything that exists psychologically for a person" (Carter, 1965; Chaffee, 1991, p. 9). We have only to look around us to establish the fact that information exists in the form of physical objects (what Buckland (1991a) calls "information-as-thing"), and hundreds of studies have documented that people believe that information exists as a psychological object as well — a disembodied result of "becoming informed."

Fox (1983) observes that the "ordinary notion of information" is one through which "information scientists apparently do succeed in communicating with one another quite effectively regarding information and related concepts" (p. 5). Nunberg (1996, p. 110), as well, notes, "'Information' is able to perform the work it does precisely because it fuzzes the boundaries between several genetically distinct categories of experience."

Allowing a broad definition of information poses problems for operationalization and measurement of concepts, as shall be seen as individual studies are reviewed in later chapters. Yet to argue for any tighter definition of information would be to limit the scope of this book, which is intended to review a broad spectrum of investigations having to do with information seeking and sense-making. Therefore, in this text, I allow for any definition of information, however, vague or difficult to study. Where more restricted definitions of information apply in the review of individual theories, methods, or studies, they will be made explicit.

It should be noted that the definition "any difference that makes a difference" places at least one important restriction on the scope of information: it rules out the possibility of information existing independently of a knowing mind. For the purpose of this chapter, we assume that a conscious brain must be engaged at some point for information to be said to exist. Otherwise, we are back to the unhelpful stance that "everything is information."

Two examples, the first suggested by Fox and the second by Buckland, will help to make the restriction clear. First, Fox provides the example of someone who keeps a secret diary that no one else is ever allowed to read. Some definitions of information would imply that, since the content of the diary was never communicated, it cannot be considered information. (Fox uses this straw man to defeat the requirement that a message must be transferred — i.e., received — to qualify as information.) Of course, a diary is a clear example of information-as-thing, and the symbols written in the diary are an expression of a human mind — it is some kind of message, even if never received by any other than its creator. So, yes, a secret diary (an unviewed, human-created record) can safely be considered information.

In the second example, trees could be viewed as carrying information in the form of their growth pattern of rings, which among other things tell us about the amount of rain that fell in a past season. Even if no person has viewed that information, is it not still information? For our purposes, the answer is "no." It is nothing more than wood until someone both encounters and makes some sense of it. So, if a tree falls in the forest and there is no one there to see it, then it conveys no information.

To conclude this portion of the chapter, it bears emphasizing that in this text we will consider only human information behavior, and the making or meaning or sense, and therefore we interpret information as requiring the involvement of a human mind. (It could be easily argued that animals use information, but they are simply outside the scope of this book; see Bates (2005b) for a distinction between animal and human use of information.) As will be seen in later chapters, a broad conceptualization of information is in keeping with the way the term has been employed in studies of information needs, uses, seeking, and sense-making.

3.4.   Distinctions among Information, Knowledge, and Data

A side issue as regards information seeking research is worth noting. Much attention has also been granted to defining the concepts of "data" and "knowledge." Machlup (1983) examines the issue of whether information is synonymous with data and knowledge, noting that there has been a tradition to treat the three as a hierarchy, with data at the bottom and knowledge at the top. Raber (2003) raises a troubling question about such an arrangement when he says: "But at what moment and how does information become knowledge?"

Machlup (1983) holds that historical usage of the three terms does not fully justify the notion that information is data that has been processed and/or organized. The origins of the term in the Latin *dare*, "to give," along with the history of its usage, imply that the word data ("the givens") can be assumptions, facts, measurements, and so forth, expressed in either words or numbers. As Machlup points out (p. 647), many writers claim that data are a "raw" type of information, whereas a few others see information as a type of data. Machlup concludes that there is neither precedent nor need to establish a hierarchy between the two words.

The common notion that knowledge is information that has been sifted, organized, and understood by a human brain is on firmer ground. Brown and Duguid (2000) complain that the two concepts are unfortunately conflated:

> People are increasingly eager that their perfectly respectable cache of information be given the cachet of knowledge. Such redefinitions surreptitiously extend the overlapping area where knowledge and information appear as interchangeable terms. Nevertheless ... there do appear to be some generally accepted distinctions between knowledge and information ... . For example, it sounds right to ask, "Where is that information?" but odd to ask, "Where's that knowledge?" (p. 2)

Machlup (1983) makes the useful point that "information is acquired by being told, whereas knowledge can be acquired by thinking" (p. 644). Through our inner experience of thought, we can form new knowledge without taking in new information from the external environment. Information implies transfer, says Machlup, while knowledge is a state ("knowing"). Knowledge and information are therefore not usually the same, except that "information in the sense of that which is being told may be the same as knowledge in the sense of that which is known, but need not be the same" (p. 644). Hayes (1993) makes a somewhat different point when he says that "knowledge is internal; it cannot be received but must be internally created" (p. 5). Savolainen (2009a) discusses similar issues in distinguishing between knowing and acting in practice.

Other authors sometimes raise the issue of truth, discussed earlier, in the knowledge-information distinction back to the truth issue discussed earlier. Raber (2003, p. 8) notes: "The relationship between knowledge and truth is especially problematic," whereas Frické (2009) points out that data can be flawed and thus untrue. Yet Dretske (1981, p. 45) makes no distinction between the two in regards to a truth requirement: "Information is what is capable of yielding knowledge, and since knowledge requires truth, information requires it also."

Decades of arguments about distinctions among the words data, information, and knowledge (and sometimes "wisdom," too) have not prevented the continued use of terminological hierarchies. Frické (2009) and Rowley (2007) each examine examples of the commonly used DIKW (data-information-knowledge-wisdom) pyramid in which wisdom appears at the top, with knowledge beneath, supported by information and then data lying at the base. Both authors find the underlying assumptions of this structure to be problematic. Echoing arguments made above, Frické (p. 140) advocates a view that "... makes knowledge and information synonymous. Knowledge and information collapse into each other." Saab and Riss (2011) also demonstrate that different levels in the hierarchy are intertwined in the process of making meaning (or sense) of patterns of stimuli.

In this book, the usage of the terms data, information, and knowledge will generally be used synonymously, because they are usually not clearly delineated in studies of information behavior. Knowledge, however, is strictly a phenomenon of the human mind, whereas data and information are often represented by tangible, physical objects. That information usually has a physical manifestation has often been the key consideration in past studies of information seeking. The way that information seeking is typically approached under the new paradigm, although, is in the sense of knowledge — something in someone's mind — not primarily as a physical object.

The usage of data, information, and knowledge outlined above represents a necessary simplification of the many definitions and examples that have been discussed in dozens of scholarly works. However, the fine distinctions made among data, information, and knowledge are of little value in most studies of information seeking. This book will treat information as a broad concept, encompassing instances that would be considered unusual by some scholars.

3.5. Summary

This chapter has explored the central concept employed in studying information seeking: information. We have seen that there are widespread disagreements about what would constitute a general definition of information. Most of these disagreements concern the issues of truth, physicality, intentionality, uncertainty, and utility. The most common types of definitions that have emerged assume that information is something that either reduces uncertainty or changes one's image of reality. In this chapter, I provide examples that suggest that a truly universal concept of information would need to fulfill at least the following requirements:

1. allow for common-sense notions of information used in everyday discourse;
2. allow for unintentional origins of information (e.g., observations of the natural world) as well as for purposeful communication among people;
3. allow for internally generated information (e.g., memories, constructions) as well as externally generated information (e.g., reading a text);
4. allow for types of information beyond that needed for "solving a problem" or "making a decision";
5. admit the importance of informal sources (e.g., friends) as well as formal sources (e.g., data or documents); and
6. involve the human mind, either in the creation, perception, or interpretation of information; to leave out such a requirement is to declare that anything is information and that would leave us with no focus for our investigations.

I have considered numerous distinctions made over the years, but I argue in favor of treating information as a primitive concept that is so basic to human understanding that it does not require a tight definition. To the extent that information needs a definition, it must be a broad one, such as "any difference that makes a difference" (implying a change to the structure of a human mind), or Bates' (2005b) second definition of information as "some pattern of organization of matter and energy that has been given meaning by a living being"). Such characterizations, vague although they are, would allow us to consider what many authors have said about information seeking without having to worry about whether they restricted their observations to phenomenon that must be true, observable, physical, intentional, and so forth.

In the next chapter, I will build on the initial discussion of information to define information needs. Following that, Chapter 5 ventures farther afield to consider more peripheral concepts and behaviors related to information seeking. A review of these other concepts is important in addressing several vexing questions about information-related behavior:

- Why do people seek information?
- What makes information relevant?
- Can information be found without intentionally searching for it?
- Is it possible to have too much information?

- Why do people sometimes avoid information?
- How does information differ from entertainment?

These and other issues are taken up in Chapters 4 and 5.

Recommended for Further Reading

Boulding, K. (1956). *The image: Knowledge in life and society*. Ann Arbor, MI: University of Michigan Press.
   An oft-cited book by the unconventional thinker Kenneth Boulding. Boulding uses the analogy of an "image" to discuss how we come to know our world.

Capurro, R., & Hjørland, B. (2002). The concept of information. In B. Cronin (Ed.), *Annual review of information science and technology* (Vol. 37, pp. 343–411). Medford, NJ: Information Today.
   A comprehensive discussion of the history of definitions of information.

Frické, M. (2009). The knowledge pyramid: A critique of the DIKW hierarchy. *Journal of Information Science, 35*(2), 131–142.
   A highly readable discussion, from the standpoint of philosophy, of definitions and relations among the concepts of data, information, knowledge, and wisdom, touching on the issues of truth, physicality, utility, and structure.

Frohmann, B. (2004). *Deflating information: From science studies to documentation*. Toronto: University of Toronto Press.
   While focused on the discourse surrounding the concept of "scientific information," the initial chapters of Frohmann's book give a fascinating account of how information seeking, use, and other behaviors have been studied over several decades.

Schement, J. R. (1993). Communication and information. In J. R. Schement & B. Ruben (Eds.), *Information and behavior* (Vol. 4, pp. 3–33). New Brunswick, NJ: Transaction Books.
   Jorge Schement examines a variety of definitions of information. A companion article in the same volume supplies the history of the word itself.

Thayer, L. (1987). How does information "'inform"? In B. D. Ruben (Ed.), *Information and behavior* (Vol. 2, pp. 13–26). New Brunswick, NJ: Transaction Books.
   Lee Thayer's amusing essay considers several problematic aspects of information as the term is commonly used. He convincingly makes the point that information is always "from the perspective of some observer."

Chapter 4

Information Needs and Information Seeking

Need for information consists of the process of perceiving a difference between an ideal state of knowledge and the actual state of knowledge.
— Lidwien van de Wijngaert (1999, p. 463)

Information seeking is the behavior that is the directly observable evidence of information needs and the only basis upon which to judge both the nature of the need and its satisfaction.
— Bryce Allen (1996, p. 56)

Chapter Outline

4.1. The Motivational Puzzle

Not only has a definition of "information" proved difficult to establish, describing exactly how it influences human behavior has also been controversial. Krikelas (1983) suggests that there are at least as many definitions of subsidiary concepts — including *information need* — as there are for information itself.

What do we mean when we say that people "need" information? This concept is the next most fundamental, building on a primitive notion of "information." In this chapter I will consider how various scholars have defined the concept of *need* and *information need*.

4.1.1.   What Is a "Need?"

It is fitting to begin with a definition of what we mean by a human "need," because it is upon this hook that most writers hang the motivations for information seeking. "Needs" are typically characterized as an "inner motivational state" (Grunig, 1989, p. 209) that brings about thought and action. Other "inner states" may include, for example, wanting, believing, doubting, fearing, or expecting (Liebnau & Backhouse, 1990; Searle, 1983).

The distinctions made among varieties of "need" can be bewildering. An essay by Andrew Green (1990) describes debates over the nature of "needs" that have taken place among political philosophers and social policy advocates. Green identifies four general conclusions about the concept of need (pp. 65–67). First, a need is always *instrumental*: it involves reaching a desired goal. If I "need to know" the chemical composition of heroin, it is typically because I desire to accomplish something with that information. That "something" may be to answer a test question, to write about narcotics for a class assignment, or simply to satisfy my curiosity. It is also the case that my need in those examples is based on some preexisting need: to pass a class, to get a degree, to be a knowledgeable person, and so forth. The key factor is that knowing it will put me at, or closer to, an end state that I want to achieve.

Second, according to Green, "needs are usually contestable. In this they differ from wants." That is, if I say that I *want* to know the chemical formula for heroin, you could hardly argue with me about this odd desire. However, if I say I *need* to know what heroin consists of, you might ask me why; if I replied that I need it to write an essay on drug addiction for an English course, you could perhaps reasonably argue that I do not really "need" to know that fact to write a good essay on addiction (or to demonstrate writing skills, either). A good exploration of Green's first two points are found in Beautyman and Shenton (2009).

Third, need is related to the concept of *necessity* in such a way as to carry, at times, more moral weight. That is, we use phrases like "human need" or "basic need" to refer to goal states (e.g., to be safe or to be loved, in the view of Abraham Maslow) that everyone agrees are good. Doyal and Gough (1984) say that basic human needs include "health, autonomy, learning, production, reproduction, communication and political authority"; Lederer, Galtung, and Antal (1980) suggest that hypothesizing any needs beyond "primary" ones like food and shelter is problematic. Distinctions among primary versus secondary needs have led some information seeking scholars (e.g., Wilson, 1981) to argue that information is clearly a secondary, rather than a basic, need.

On the other hand, for a half-century the psychological literature has treated "the need for cognition," as though it were a basic, rather than a secondary need (e.g., Cacioppo & Petty, 1982; Cohen, Stotland, & Wolfe, 1955; Henning & Vorderer, 2001). Experiments with sensory deprivation point to pathologies that can result from lack of stimuli (Zubek, 1969). Psychologists like Henry Murray (1938) and Abraham Maslow (1963), as well as economist Manfred Max-Neef (1992), believed that people have a need to understand, and perhaps even to share, what their senses tell them. For example, among the basic needs identified by Murray (1938) were three involving information: "exposition" (the need to provide information to, and educate, others); "harm avoidance" (the need to avoid pain, whether physical or mental); and "infavoidance" (the need to conceal weakness and failure). Max-Neef's (1992) needs include those for learning and curiosity, and for leisure and imagination.

To *deny* a life-sustaining need (e.g., for medical care) would be morally wrong. Yet even regarding such a basic need we might make distinctions; if I said to you that I *needed* narcotics, that statement may be true in the sense that drugs are *necessary* to accomplish my goal — to satisfy my addiction. But it would probably not motivate you to help me satisfy those needs. You might judge my felt need to imply such a "bad" purpose that, even while acknowledging the truth of my need, you would feel comfortable in denying me your help. Perhaps you would rationalize by saying that I really need something else such as a drug treatment program.

This line of thinking leads to Green's fourth point: that need is not necessarily a state of mind, and it is possible to be unaware of one's *true* needs. For example, I may *think* I need to scan every psychology journal in the library to find information about recovered memory syndrome. But an experienced librarian might judge that what I *really* need to do is to search *Psychology Abstracts* on the Internet. Thus, a need may be unrecognized or unacknowledged, undesired, or simply misunderstood, by the individual who has it (Derr, 1983).

So this leads us back to the distinction between needs and wants. Others have needs that we may judge to be "merely" desires, not needs. Obviously it is more difficult to find evidence of needs than it is of wants, because wants more typically result in observable behaviors. We can also ask people what they want, but people may not be able to articulate their needs so easily — this is certainly true if they are not even aware of their needs.

Green suggests that, within the study of information behavior, most attempts to define "need" faded away after some initial attempts made during the 1960s and 1970s. According to his view, most subsequent writers have taken for granted whatever definitions had been proposed up to the

1970s, such as those discussed by Brittain (1970), Line (1974), Menzel (1966a), and Roberts (1975). One notable exception is Richard Derr (1983, 1985) who made worthwhile attempts to define both information and information need during the 1980s. A new book by Charles Cole (2012) promises to bring attention back to the important issue of need, as have recent investigations like those of Lundh (2010) and Lu and Yuan (2011).

4.1.2. Needs versus Demands

So what then is an "information need?" Forsythe, Buchanan, Osheroff, and Miller (1992) point out that

> no explicit consensus exists in the literature regarding the meaning of the central concept of "information need."... In effect, "information need," has been defined according to the particular interests and expertise of various authors. (p. 182)

"Information need" is often described simply, and somewhat circularly, as a cause of information seeking. Ikoja-Odongo and Mostert (2006, p. 147), for example, say that "an information need is a requirement that drives people into information seeking." It is problematic, however, to simply assume that actions one takes are solely caused by an earlier, internal "need." Thus, the relationship between the initial need, and what we do about it (e.g., make a demand of an information source), is critical.

Brittain's (1970) book ventures into the realm of need by first noting that most research up to that point had instead concerned *demand* — the requests made of an information system, such as a library or database. Data regarding demands were readily available from (or at least easily collectible in) information agencies that supported studies of their users. Demands are relatively easy to measure. Investigations of information demands supported the goals of libraries and vendors to improve their services. So, according to Brittain, "most studies which have purported to be of information needs have in fact been of information uses or, at best, demands" (1970, p. 3).

Another writer, John O'Connor (1968), has suggested three "possible meanings" of information need: (1) a "negotiated" (and thus, refined) version of the *initial* question or demand stated by the inquirer; (2) whatever information provided that actually "helps" the work of the inquirer; or (3) giving the inquirer documents that he or she judges to be "pertinent" on the basis of a comparison with their internal need. O'Connor finds problems with all of these possible meanings, as they may involve differing standards of judgment. That is, different people (e.g., the inquirer, the provider, and groups of colleagues) use varying criteria, at different points in time (e.g., immediate vs. long-term effects). O'Connor's concern with the relativity of judgment was echoed by Line (1974, p. 87), who ponders, "who is to say what is 'necessary' for himself or others?" Or, as Michael Ignatieff put it:

> there are few presumptions in human relations more dangerous than the idea that one knows what another human being needs better than they do themselves. (1984, p. 11)

Few investigations of information seeking delve very deeply into the issue of what human "needs" really are. Not many even question the notion of "information needs." Rather, most writers assume that information needs exist and are relatively unproblematic. When information seeking researchers *do* refer to more fundamental discussions of how information needs arise, they typically cite one or more of four authors in doing so: Robert Taylor, Nicholas Belkin, Carol Kuhlthau, and Brenda Dervin.

4.2. Four Scholars Ponder Information Needs

4.2.1. Seeking Answers

The earliest of the popular depictions of how information needs arise is that of information scientist Robert Taylor. Taylor discussed the origins of information needs in 1962, and his 1968 article holds the distinction of being one of the most frequently cited items in the information seeking literature (Edwards, 2005; Palmquist, 2005). Taylor's characterization of the origins of information needs provides a particularly useful frame of reference for the concepts discussed in the next chapter.

Taylor focuses on how and why people come to ask questions at library reference desks. He describes a series of four stages or levels that began with a "conscious or even unconscious need for information ... a vague sort of dissatisfaction ... probably inexpressible in linguistic terms" (1968, p. 182). Taylor calls this unexpressed need for information the *visceral* need. The next level a person reaches is "a *conscious* mental description ... an ambiguous and rambling statement" which sometimes results in talking to another person about it.

At this point the inquirer may be able to construct a *formalized* ("qualified and rational") statement of the need. However, the person is not aware whether the need could be answered in that form by any available person or information system. In the fourth and final stage, "the question is recast in anticipation of what the files can deliver." This *compromised* need may be a question asked of a librarian, or a search statement entered into an

Visceral need ---> Conscious need ---> Formalized need ---> Compromised need

Figure 4.1: Taylor's typology of information needs.

information retrieval system. At this point the question also reflects the kinds and forms of data that may be available (such as books, images, or tabular data) and the ways in which they are organized or indexed. Essentially, the final stage is a *compromise* between how the requester originally envisions the query and how the query must be restated to match the language used by the source.

In summary, Taylor says that our chain of cognition and communication often proceeds as shown in Figure 4.1.

The implications of this conceptualization of information need are several. A perception of need may differ greatly from its ultimate expression in words. There may be "unconscious needs." Recognition of uncertainty does not always lead to action. And central to the entire process is the ability to communicate one's thoughts, to "negotiate" questions and answers.

Let's look at an example of how this typology can relate to a real-life situation. A patron asks a librarian, "Do you have books on philosophy?" It may be that the inquirer in this case actually wants to understand the traditional distinction philosophers have made between "truth" and "truthfulness." She may start with a broader request that she hopes will orient the librarian to what is coming: a more specific statement about her needs. A helpful response to such a question would not be one of the obvious ones ("yes," "no," or "I don't know") but rather a request for clarification ("What is it you'd like to find out?"). The inquirer might then follow with a more specific request ("I need a dictionary that would explain the difference between…"), or instead might settle for directions to the philosophy section of a library. Thus, Taylor's typology helps to explain why people seeking help in libraries may ask questions that are overly general.

4.2.2. Reducing Uncertainty

The notion of *information as uncertainty reduction* is one that dates back to at least to the nineteenth century, according to Morowitz (1991). In the late 1940s Shannon and Weaver popularized this connection between information and uncertainty, although in a counterintuitive way (see Chapter 3). By the 1970s, reducing uncertainty was firmly cemented in scholarly dialogue about motivations for information seeking.

For example, in 1973 Charles Atkin (1973) offered a definition of *information need* as "a function of extrinsic uncertainty produced by a perceived discrepancy between the individual's current level of certainty about important environmental objects and a criterion state that he seeks to achieve" (p. 206). The "environmental objects" in his definition refer to people, things, events, or ideas that possess psychological importance for the individual. In Atkin's view, humans sense differences between what they know and what they want to know as regards a salient "thing" in their mental universe. Thus, they constantly compare current levels of knowledge against goal states that they wish to reach (presumably "perfect knowledge" of all those things that concern us), and react by seeking information whenever they sense uncertainty.

Most of Atkin's work was aimed at understanding use of the mass media. A more sustained research project concerning uncertainty reduction evolved in the field of interpersonal communication. For over 30 years, Charles Berger (1987, 1997, 2002), Berger and Calabrese (1975), James Bradac (2001), and Berger and Bradac (1982) have investigated the role of uncertainty in interpersonal relations, demonstrating how people seek information strategically when faced with uncertainty in conversation and social situations. Dale Brashers (2001) and Brashers et al. (2002) have portrayed information seeking as one of several strategies that one may use to "manage uncertainty" in one's environment. Uncertainty reduction continues to be fruitfully explored as a goal in face-to-face interactions.

More central to information behavior (IB) research is the work of Nicholas Belkin (1978, 2005) and his collaborators (Belkin & Robertson, 1976; Belkin, Oddy & Brooks, 1982; Belkin & Vickery, 1985), and Carol Kuhlthau (1988a, 1988b, 1991, 1993a, 1993b, 1997, 2004a, 2004b, 2005) and her co-authors (Kuhlthau & Tama, 2001; Cole & Kuhlthau, 2000) in advancing a view of information as tied to uncertainty.

In terms of its vocabulary and sources, Belkin's writings most reflect Taylor's concept of "visceral need." To Belkin the basic motivator of information seeking is an "anomalous state of knowledge" (ASK). An ASK exists when a person recognizes that there is an anomaly (i.e., a gap or uncertainty) in their state of knowledge regarding a situation or topic. Faced with an ASK, individuals may attempt to address their uncertainty by requesting or consulting information. The person will then judge whether the anomaly has been resolved; if it is not resolved, another ASK may be generated, or the motivation to address it may be exhausted.

To illustrate these last two stages of ASK, consider our earlier request for philosophy books. If indeed the hypothetical inquirer is directed to shelves filled with hundreds of philosophy texts, she may very well decide to give up and ignore her anomalous state of knowledge. Alternatively, she might be handed a dictionary of philosophy that contains a discussion of the concept of "truth";

reading what the dictionary says, she decides whether the text resolves her uncertainty, or whether she needs further explanation. Her anomaly might well change in the process of seeking: now she realizes that it is the nature of "belief" that she does not understand. Again she must decide whether to continue until her information needs are met, or be satisfied with what she knows now. In a sense, an inquirer always "gives up" eventually, because there is always more that could be known regarding a topic. The question of "when" is determined by available resources and the inquirer's level of motivation.

Much of Carol Kuhlthau's research is based on psychologist George Kelly's (1963) theory of learning as a process of testing constructs. Uncertainty is a beginning stage in any search, and this is often accompanied by feelings of anxiety — which is a powerful motivator to either get on with the work, or to give up entirely. Kuhlthau's work was pioneering in several ways, particularly in its attention to the role of affect in information behavior. Like Taylor, she was concerned with stages (or phases) of a search process; her research on students demonstrates how they reach a state of closure as regards their information needs — the final level of Taylor's typology. Uncertainty reduction is a key component in all of Kuhlthau's research. A recent application of her model is found in Hyldegard (2009).

4.2.3. Making Sense

While Artandi (1973) saw uncertainty reduction as one approach to defining "information," she also saw a second framework: semiotics. Semiotics deals with the study of cultural products (such as language) as a system of signs that convey meaning by way of established conventions. So Artandi's second approach to understanding information stressed the production of meaning, or "sense."

The most ambitious attempt to explain the origins of information needs lies in the work of Brenda Dervin and her colleagues (see Dervin, Foreman-Wernet, & Lauterbach, 2003; Tidline, 2005) on "sense-making." This line of inquiry has been applied widely in the context of what Savolainen (1995) calls "everyday life information seeking," rather than traditional research on the use of factual information from libraries, television, newspapers, or other sources. Perhaps for that reason, sense-making tends to emphasize the *feelings* rather than cognitions "in situations where humans reached out for something they called information" (Dervin, 1992, p. 68).

Brenda Dervin believes that we have a need to "make sense" of the world. Dervin believes that it is safe to assume that need

> implies a state that arises within a person, suggesting some kind of gap that requires filling. When applied to the word information, as in

information need, what is suggested is a gap that can be filled by something that the needing person calls "information." (1983b, p. 156)

Dervin prefers to define information need as a compulsion to *make sense* of a current situation, when faced with problems or worries, or the need to understand or make a choice:

> The individual, in her time and place, needs to make sense.... She needs to inform herself constantly. Her head is filled with questions. These questions can be seen as her "information needs." (p. 170)

In the sense-making characterization, a search for information starts with questions directed at making sense of the situation; communication is central to the process of "bridging the gap" to reach some kind of information or help desired. The strategies employed are shaped by the searcher's conceptualization of both the gap and the bridge, and by the answers, ideas, and resources obtained along the way. They are engaged in a search for meaning (Cornelius, 1996; Wilson, 1984). As others have noted (Kuhlthau, 1991, 2004a; Mellon, 1986), emotions are at least as important as cognitions in "gappy" situations: searchers may be intent upon reducing their anxiety as much as their uncertainty. And one need for information may easily lead to another, in a kind of chain, as Shenton and Dixon (2004b) have demonstrated in their research.

4.2.4.   *The Spectrum of Motivations*

That people have information needs is a fundamental assumption regarding information seeking. Taylor, Belkin, Kuhlthau, and Dervin all provide frameworks to discuss a phenomenon that remains beyond our observation: the activity in human minds that leads to an individual recognizing an information need.

The work of all four scholars has been widely applied and continues to be cited. Robert Taylor's writings have been used in the training of public service workers such as reference librarians. The work of Nicholas Belkin has been widely applied in the development of information systems, in which the emphasis is on the way that queries evolve as the answers they generate are evaluated. Carol Kuhlthau's research is used a great deal in educational settings, at both K-12 and university levels.

Dervin's work has been, like Taylor's, used to understand what takes place in question-answering arenas like the library reference desk. Dervin's "neutral questioning approach to the reference interview"

Figure 4.2: The spectrum of views regarding motivations.

(Dervin & Dewdney, 1986) advocates asking open-ended questions (e.g., "What are you trying to understand?" or "How are you planning to use this information?") to better understand the questioner's situation and needs. Because of sense-making's emphasis on emotions as well as cognitions, it has also inspired a broader audience of professionals involved in human services, such as specialists in health care and in social welfare.

What scholars say about information needs can be illustrated on a continuum that reflects their assumptions about the nature of information, *why* people seek it, and what they *use* it for. We might call one end of the spectrum the *Objective* pole and the other the *Subjective* pole (Figure 4.2).

At the Objective end of the continuum are those who view information as reflecting an objective reality, and information seeking as driven primarily by a rational judgment that some uncertainty exists that would be resolved by specific information; emotional motivations of the search process, such as anxiety, tend to be set aside. The prototypical search from the Objective point of view is one in which there is a well-defined need to retrieve a specific fact to make a decision or solve a problem. From this perspective, information needs are thought to be relatively fixed. The early writings of communication scholar Charles Atkin (1972, 1973) best illustrate this view; he acknowledges "noninstrumental" information seeking motives, but he defines them as out of his scope (1973, p. 205).

In contrast, the Subjective pole represents the idealized view that many (and perhaps even the majority of) searches for information are prompted by a vague feeling of unease, a sense of having a gap in knowledge, or simply by *anxiety* about a current situation. This view does not deny that purposeful thought leads to information seeking, but rather emphasizes that humans are often driven to "make sense" of an entire situation, not merely its component "data," and that rational goals are often overstated. Under such a view, information needs are highly dynamic. Brenda Dervin's work is an exemplar of the Subjective view, although most IB researchers tend toward that end of the spectrum.

Of course, saying that there are two views of information needs makes an artificial distinction. The differences between the Objective and Subjective camps are not all that great; there are many examples of overlap and agreement. But proposing these stereotypes helps to explain why different approaches to studying searches and sense-making have evolved. The Objective school tends to focus on the psychological aspects of processing information; it tends to view some types of information seeking as trivial or irrational — particularly in cases in which people do not use the most authoritative sources of information or in which they ignore seemingly relevant information. The Subjective camp holds that an understanding of the receiver as "making sense" of the world leads to more accurate picture of when and how messages are "received" — and when they are not.

In ending this section I must note two facts. First, that in labeling the work of these four authors as being about "answers," "uncertainty," and "gaps" I am grossly oversimplifying their respective works. My stereotypes are simply meant to make their ideas both more digestible and more comparable. The reader is urged to follow up with the "Recommended for Further Reading" suggestions for this chapter.

Second, neither do I mean to suggest that these characterizations of information needs — as answers, as uncertainty reduction, or as gaps — belong exclusively to the four authors mentioned. Rather, it is merely that these four authors are frequently cited in discussions of how information needs arise and are attended to in certain kinds of information seeking.

Connections between information acquisition and the concepts of uncertainty, ambiguity, and curiosity, in particular, were widely explored by psychologists from the 1940s through the 1960s such as Allport and Postman (1947), Berlyne (1960), Driscoll and Lanzetta (1965), and Miller, Galanter, and Pribram (1960). Many other authors in the last half-century have invoked the idea of uncertainty reduction as a prime motivator for information seeking. The notion of "making sense" also has roots in the work of sociologists like Cicourel (1964), Garfinkel (1967), and Schutz (1962, 1964, 1967).

4.3. The Trouble with Information Needs

Wilson (1981, 1997) says that, while researchers fret over a definition of information *need*, much of the time they are really studying information seeking *behaviors*. Belkin and Vickery (1985) point out that observing an information need is problematic, because it exists inside someone's head and must be inferred by any interested observer while a search is in process, or after it has taken place:

> Less tractable is the issue of why people look for information at all; that is, what is the status of the concept or category of *information need?*... [I]s there such a thing as a need for information, which can be considered on its own ... or is information-seeking behaviour contingent upon the desire to satisfy other types of needs, or to resolve situations which are not in themselves information-dependent? (p. 6)

Indeed, other scholars (e.g., Wilson, 1981; Poole, 1985) believe that the notion of an information need is an unrealistic concept, as most information needs could be said to be accounted for by more general needs, and in any event they cannot be observed. An example of their first type of objection would be that our need to know the prices of items (e.g., bread) may be driven by our need to eat (surely a more basic human need), or our need to conserve our resources (less basic, but compelling to most humans). That needs and motivations may be hierarchical in this way is also a central assumption of Terror Management Theory (Pyszczynksi, Greenberg, & Solomon, 1999), discussed in Chapter 7. Others suggest that information may indeed be a basic human need, but deny that needs are hierarchical (Max-Neef, 1992).

Bosman and Renckstorf (1996) point out the circular nature of assumptions about information needs as a distinct motivator:

> it is in fact an *ad hoc* notion created for practical purposes in order to predict information-seeking behaviour and information consumption. It is rather obvious that people who consume much information on a certain subject will also state that they have a certain need for this information.... However, if one wants to explain why some people do and others do not consume certain information, the information needs concept is as elucidating as, for instance, explaining criminal behaviour on the basis of hypothetical "criminality needs." (p. 43)

In reviewing issues surrounding human motivations, Hirschman and Holbrook (1986) say that "action theorists" (e.g., Goldman, 1970; Hampshire, 1982) generally argue that wants and desires — when coupled with beliefs about the relationship between means and ends — provide *reasons* for actions. However, these theorists are divided about whether such reasons could be said to *cause* actions.

In the case of information, Bosman and Renckstorf see three overlapping motivations that determine a need for it:

> social utility (e.g., in order to have topics of conversation), instrumental utility (e.g., in order to decide whether to buy something) and intrinsic utility (e.g., the entertainment value of the information offered). (p. 46)

The first (social) and last (intrinsic) of these "utilities" are not always counted as "real" information needs. Bryce Allen (1996) points this out when he says

> there may be a variety of gratifications that are provided by the information-seeking process that cannot be considered meeting a

specific information need or solving a particular problem. Another way of looking at these information activities is that they meet needs (such as the need for entertainment or companionship) that are not classified as information needs. (p. 56)

Given the multidimensional nature of such needs, how are we to describe them? Harter (1992) argues that to talk about an individual's "information need" is virtually the same as describing his or her "current psychological state," because needs shift stochastically as each relevant piece of information is encountered. One bit of knowledge may raise questions, lead to another fact or to a new conclusion, and so forth, which changes one's knowledge state and hence what one finds relevant and worth seeking. At least Wilson, Pool, Bosman and Renckstorf, and Harter would agree that, however information needs are characterized, they are not something fixed and long-lasting. Kari's (2010) exploration of possible meanings of "information use" takes a similar view in that "use" may involve the construction of knowledge in response to an evolving need.

Most of what I have said (and quoted) thus far has downplayed the idea that having information is a "basic" human need. Many psychologists would disagree. George Miller (1983b), for example, described information gathering in instinctual terms. Another psychologist, Abraham Maslow (1963), said "I am convinced that man *does* have a need to know," describing it as "instinct-like," even though he admitted that he could not prove its existence (p. 111). Wendell Garner, who wrote extensively on the role of information in forming cognitive structures, believed that "the search for structure is inherent in behavior.... People in any situation will search for meaningful relations between the variables existing in the situation" (1962, p. 339). Milton Rokeach's view was that "we are all motivated by the desire, which is sometimes strong and sometimes weak, to see reality as it actually is" (1960, p. 400). To "see reality," we *need* information about it.

4.4. Information Seeking and Information Behavior

We come, at last, to information seeking. It may seem counterintuitive, but researchers have had less to say about seeking and use (Savaolainen, 2009b) than they have about needs. Perhaps the meaning of the term is thought to be obvious. Most accounts of empirical investigations do not bother to provide a definition of information seeking, taking it for granted as what people do in response to a need for information. It could be said that information seeking is more closely tied to the concept of "need" than it is to the notion of "information" itself. For instance, Tom Wilson has said that information seeking is "the purposive seeking for information as a consequence of a need to satisfy some goal" (1999b).

The few authors who state an explicit definition of information seeking typically describe a process of either *discovering patterns* or *filling in gaps* in patterns previously recognized. Garner (1962), for example, implies that it is the search for relationships among stimuli. Likewise, Zerbinos (1990) says that

> information seeking takes place when a person has knowledge stored in long term memory that precipitates an interest in related information as well as the motivation to acquire it. It can also take place when a person recognizes a gap in their knowledge that may motivate that person to acquire new information. (p. 922)

The basic notions behind what Garner and Zerbinos describe date back to John Dewey's (1910/1933) characterizations; Dewey saw *inquiry* as motivated by recognition of a problem — of something lacking in a situation. Gary Marchionini's definition of information seeking is problem oriented: "a process in which humans purposefully engage in order to change their state of knowledge" and which is "closely related to learning and problem solving" (1995, pp. 5–6). Also relevant is the way that Brenda Dervin defines sense-making in terms of confronting problematic situations; indeed, for some investigators information seeking has come to be synonymous with sense-making.

Johnson offers one of a few definitions that are more restrictive than those above: "Information seeking can be defined as the purposive acquisition of information from selected information carriers" (1997, p. 26). In this case there is no reference to the "purpose" itself, or to what motivates a person to select a "carrier" and acquire information from it. Krikelas (1983) describes information seeking in like terms, saying that it starts with a "need-creating event/environment" — a characterization also echoed by Julien and Michels (2004, pp. 547–548) and Westbrook (2008, p. 24).

The reader may have noticed that the definitions of information seeking quoted above emphasize *purposive activity*. There is a broader term that encompasses information seeking yet also includes behaviors that are passive: "information behavior." Tom Wilson (1999b) defines this term as:

> the totality of human behaviour in relation to sources and channels of information, including both active and passive information seeking, and information use. Thus, it includes face-to-face communication with others, as well as the passive reception of information as in, for example, watching television advertisements, without any intention to act on the information given.

In recent years the label of "information behavior" has firmly established itself as a covering term for a broader range of information-related phenomena, many of which topics are receiving fresh attention (see Chapters 10–12 for examples). It is a term whose time has come.

In conclusion, information seeking is a taken-for-granted concept, a catchall phrase that encompasses a variety of behaviors seemingly motivated by the recognition of "missing" information. Although it is the most common term in use, information seeking is typically defined strictly in terms of active and intentional behavior, which limits its applicability to the broad range of research currently being conducted on human use of information.

4.5. Summary

In this chapter I have explored the notion of information need. I have pointed out, as have many others before me, that "need" is an awkward concept, particularly in that it is not easily observable. Rather, needs are more typically inferred *post hoc*, after some action or request has been made manifest.

The notion of an information need is rooted in more basic human needs. The extent to which humans have a "need to know" is disputed, with most scholars identifying it as a secondary need that is much less important than the need for food, shelter, or companionship.

I described four oft-cited conceptions of how information needs arise: models by Taylor, Belkin, Kuhlthau, and Dervin. Each of these is similar in that they all point toward feelings of uncertainty, ambiguity, or uneasiness as the root cause of information needs. You will read more about these authors — particularly the work of Brenda Dervin — in future chapters. For now, here is a brief comparison of what they say about the origins of information needs.

Robert Taylor talks about a series of stages in which "vague sort of dissatisfaction" may (or may not) become "an ambiguous and rambling statement" that in turn may (or may not) become an articulated question. Taylor's examples suggest that his main focus is the situations in which one person asks another person a question, as occurs at a library reference desk. Taylor's work helps us to understand the nature of human questioning or, as Taylor calls it, "question negotiation."

Nicholas Belkin emphasizes the notion of anomaly and the uncertainty that accompanies it. He also invokes the idea of a "state of knowledge" that is being constantly updated and compared with earlier states to judge whether or not an anomaly has been resolved. Although Belkin's concepts are very general, his work lends itself to the modeling of information retrieval systems. In such systems the results retrieved are evaluated and may result in additional query statements if the results are judged to be inadequate, or if the retrieved information results in a "shifting" of the focus and vocabulary of the question. Belkin's writings are often cited in some combination with those of Taylor and Kuhlthau (e.g., see Attfield & Dowell, 2003; Bruce, 2005; Cole, Leide, Beheshti, Large & Brooks, 2005; Ford, 2004a).

Carol Kuhlthau uses psychological theories of learning to advance the idea of uncertainty as a starting point in library research. She has also emphasized the importance of emotions in information behavior. Like Taylor, she suggests that information seeking is expressed in stages.

Brenda Dervin freely acknowledges the overlap between her ideas and those of Taylor, Belkin, and Kuhlthau. Like Belkin she invokes the idea of a "gap" in life's experience as a motivating stimulus for seeking information. However, Dervin is concerned with a broader issue than simply getting answers to questions. Her writings emphasize basic issues in human welfare, such as the goals of feeling secure and self-actualized. For Dervin, looking for "information" is only *one* response to a "gap"; other responses could include seeking reassurance, expressing feelings, connecting with another human being, and so forth.

Many writers on the topic of information needs suggest that it is not a basic human need, comparable to those for food, shelter, security, or companionship. Information needs are said to change constantly with new, relevant sensory inputs. In other words, new questions emerge as old ones are answered or even partially satisfied. Yet some psychologists with existential leanings see information processing as a basic aspect of being human; they are inclined to see information as a basic human need after all.

Finally, I addressed the concept of "information seeking" itself, pointing out that researchers rarely bother to define it explicitly. When it is defined at all, it is described as a reaction to the recognition of an information need — a somewhat circular definition. I make a case for use of the term "information behavior" as better suited to characterizing a broad range of relevant human behaviors dealing with information.

Information needs and information seeking are related to a host of other notions, some of them tightly coupled and others more peripheral. In the next chapter we will explore these related concepts and see where and how they fit in.

Recommended for Further Reading

Allen, B. (1996). *Information tasks: Toward a user-centered approach to information systems.* San Diego, CA: Academic Press.

Although directed at the design of information systems, Allen discusses many aspects of information seeking, including the concept of "need." His book contains many examples of how social relations and context influence the seeking of information.

Beautyman, W., & Shenton, A. (2009). When does an academic information need stimulate a school-inspired information want? *Journal of Librarianship and Information Science, 41*, 67–80.

Beautyman and Shenton review the concept of information need and apply the ideas of Brenda Dervin to a participant observation study of primary school children. They found that children often seek information on topics related to those they studied in class, based on a variety of motives.

Bradac, J. J. (2001). Theory comparison: Uncertainty reduction, problematic integration, uncertainty management, and other curious constructs. *Journal of Communication, 51*, 456–476.

A comprehensive introduction to the ways in which uncertainty has been dealt within research on interpersonal communication.

Dervin, B. (1983). Information as a user construct: The relevance of perceived information needs to synthesis and interpretation. In S. A. Ward, & L. J. Reed (Eds.), *Knowledge structure and use: Implications for synthesis and interpretation* (pp. 153–184). Philadelphia, PA: Temple University Press.

A well-written explanation of Dervin's earliest views on the subjective nature of information.

Green, A. (1990). What do we mean by user needs? *British Journal of Academic Librarianship, 5*, 65–78.

Green's article is broader in scope than either its title or journal of publication would imply. His topic is human "need" and how it has been defined by political philosophers and social theorists. The concept of need is a slippery one, and even more so when we discuss the need for information, which is even more subjective than needs for physical things and states.

Taylor, R. S. (1968). Question-negotiation and information seeking in libraries. *College and Research Libraries, 29*, 178–194.

Taylor's observations about how a reference question is negotiated between librarian and client still seem fresh after many years. In this piece he suggests how information needs arise and are satisfied.

Chapter 5

Related Concepts

> Though we speak of knowledge, it is to be remembered that we are not distinguishing among knowledge, belief, opinion and information. We are not concerned with whether a man's image of the world is correct, whether his beliefs are true, whether his information is information or misinformation.
> — Patrick Wilson (1973, p. 462)

> We are not, can not, be moved by the "truth" of information. We can only be moved by its *relevance*.
> — Lee Thayer (1987, p. 18)

Chapter Outline

We will now consider some other concepts that are closely related to information seeking. Among these highly relevant notions are *decision making, relevance, pertinence, salience, selective exposure, browsing, serendipity, knowledge gaps, information poverty, information overload, information avoidance*, *information encountering*, *information anxiety*, *entertainment*, and *collaborative information sharing*. This chapter will explore these concepts in the context of what people think and do when they are looking for that thing we call "information."

5.1. Decision Making

Donohew and Tipton (1973, p. 251) point out that "much information seeking research is intertwined with decision making." A great deal of the information-seeking literature indeed refers to decision making and problem solving. Although they are not universal aspects of information seeking, solving problems and making decisions and judgments are undoubtedly important in life. Herbert Simon and his associates go so far as to say that:

> the work of managers, of scientists, of engineers, of lawyers — the work that steers the course of society and its economic and governmental organizations — is largely work of making decisions and solving problems. (Simon, 1992, p. 32)

Because so many information-seeking studies are concerned with the first three of the professions mentioned by Simon, it is no surprise that seeking of information has often been characterized in terms of the problems and decisions seekers face.

5.1.1. Making Decisions

Reviews of the extensive decision making literature by Goldstein and Hogarth (1997), March and Shapira (1992), March (1994), and Zey (1992) point out that decision making research has a long history and a considerable number of dimensions, applications, and offshoots. Two major distinctions are whether the decisions are made by individuals or by groups, and whether these are one-time decisions versus repeated choices. For example, some investigations focus on *one-time* decisions by *individuals*, acting on the basis of *preferences*.

Most reviewers exclude use of the term "decision," when it refers solely to an experimental subject identifying the presence or absence of an attribute (e.g., a musical tone) in a stimulus (e.g., a sound). Goldstein and Hogarth (1997) refer to this latter branch of investigation as research on *judgment*, to distinguish it from research that focuses on choice and decisions.

Some areas of decision making research are unlikely to hold much relevance for information behavior that takes place in real-world contexts.

For example, many normative models (how people *should* choose among alternatives) seem invalid outside highly specialized contexts (such as games of chance in which exact probabilities can be calculated). Descriptive models, focusing on how people *actually* choose, have been examined in both highly structured and ill-defined problem situations. It is the latter that more closely resemble most circumstances studied under the rubric of information behavior.

Normative models and highly structured problems have been extensively studied by economists and psychologists operating under well-defined paradigms of experimentation and mathematical modeling. In contrast, poorly structured problems (e.g., management decisions about strategy) typically involve information that is lacking or unreliable, unclear goals, inadequate measures of success, and short supplies of time, money, and attention. Poorly defined problem situations have attracted attention from a number of disciplines, including management, sociology, and psychology, using both experiments and more qualitative methods like protocol analysis.

"Decisions" are typically characterized as choices made from among alternatives; that is, at least two options are available, and the decision maker may select only one of them. Faced with such a situation, the decision maker must gather information that allows each potential choice to be evaluated and compared to the alternative(s). A typical example of such decision making is the car-buying scenario discussed in Chapter 2, in which a consumer gathers information to make a purchase decision. Whether the decisions are purchases or other kinds of choices, they can be looked at as comparisons of alternatives (e.g., a particular model of car, an information source) across their attributes (e.g., price, accessibility).

Uncertainty is a key concept in decision making research, as it has been in information seeking (e.g., Belkin, 1978, 2005; Ford, 2004a; Kuhlthau, 1993b, 2004a; Spink & Cole, 2004) and communication (e.g., Berger, 1987, 1997, 2002; Brashers, 2001). It is usually assumed that, whether we are reading or conversing, we are at least partially engaged in an attempt to reduce uncertainty. Decision making research also assumes uncertainty reduction as a key process, even though it cannot be assumed that possessing more information always reduces uncertainty (Bradac, 2001; Yovits & Foulk, 1985).

A frequent concern in decision making research is the degree to which our rationality is bounded. It is obvious that we have limits to both our attention and our ability to process information. For example, there are fairly consistent experimental findings about information overload. Cognitive load may be measured as the number of alternatives that need to be examined, multiplied by the number of their attributes; attributes are ways that things can differ from one another, such as the important features of a car.

We tend to be more sensitive to increases in the number of attributes than we are to increases in the number of alternatives we must examine. Once the number of alternatives and attributes rises above 10 each, individuals are likely to experience overload. As the number of information items increase — or as the amount of available time decreases — people resort to simpler and less reliable rules for making choices to shorten their search time (e.g., Brucks, 1985; Ozanne, Brucks, & Grewal, 1992; Urbany, Dickson, & Wilkie, 1989). Psychological research on decision making typically focuses on examining the *rules* that people use to make choices. For example, in applying the lexicographic rule, a person would decide which attribute is most important (say, a car's fuel economy) and choose an alternative only on that basis; in the event of a "tie," they would consider the next most important attribute to resolve their choice.

Whatever rule is used to reduce search time, we know that people are prone to "satisficing" — choosing the first "acceptable" answer to a question or solution to a problem. In other words, at some point we decide we have "enough" information and decide to stop searching and make a decision (Berryman, 2008; Katopol, 2007; Prabha, Connaway, Olszewski, & Jenkins, 2007; Warwick, Rimmer, Blandford, Gow, & Buchanan, 2009).

Most information behavior literature considers essentially unique searches, deciding how to address a health problem or finding relevant articles for a paper. However, much of our everyday activity involves *repeated* behavior. Long ago, Cyert, Simon, and Trow (1956) discussed why routine (programmed) choices are much easier to make than novel (nonprogrammed) decisions. Klein (2009) refers to the former as "cybernetic" decisions. Klein provides examples of how common such decisions are in everyday life, for example, in feeding oneself or walking to work. The notion of cybernetic decisions — in which "standard operating procedures" are established by prior experience and altered only in the event of negative feedback — is highly relevant to everyday information seeking. This concept of feedback and its importance in information behavior has been reviewed by Kelly (2005), Newhagen (1997), and Spink (1997).

For instance, Savolainen (1995, p. 262) describes his everyday life information seeking (ELIS) model as reflecting Bourdieu's concept of *habitus*, "a relatively stable system of dispositions by which individuals ... evaluate the importance of different choices". While Savolainen's investigation was aimed at examining "nontrivial issues such as unemployment or health problems," there is much about his framework that captures routine choices regarding many types of actions and the information on which they are based. One category of life experiences has to do with "consumption of goods and services" (Bianchi, 1997b; Case, 2000; Hirschman & Holbrook, 1986; see also Savolainen (1995, p. 263). Therefore, some of the many approaches to decision making are surely relevant to this, even though some maintain that "consumers ... are not merely decision makers" but rather people "emerging into being" (Hirschman & Holbrook, pp. 215–217).

5.1.2. Solving Problems

Simon (1992, p. 32) makes a distinction between problem solving and decision making when he says that *problem solving* has to do with identifying issues worthy of attention, setting goals, and designing suitable courses of action. In contrast, *decision making* is the activity of evaluating and choosing among alternative actions to take in response to a problem. Together, the two activities form a sequence that begins with focusing on a problem and ends with selecting from among various choices.

March (1994) agrees that decision making is a separate and narrower activity than problem solving, and he further emphasizes that the *search* for alternatives and the choice of which to pay *attention* to are the key components of decision making. According to March (1994, p. 23), "The study of decision making is, in many ways, the study of search and attention."

However, definitions by organizational theorists like Simon and March may not be universally held; some authors from other fields collapse together goal-setting and searching and call it all "problem solving." This is because the solving of problems has been investigated primarily by psychologists, while decision making has been studied mostly by economists, operations researchers, and organizational theorists. Interestingly, the organizational theorist's view, with its emphasis on attention and search, is readily congruent with the usual focus of information-seeking studies. Therefore, in this review I set aside the usual preoccupation of problem-solving studies with problem identification and the setting of goals; instead, I focus on decision making, which is to say attention management and search processes.

Some writers assume that information seeking is always motivated by a need to solve a problem. Yet Sperber and Wilson (1995) point out that problem solving does not fit all situations in which humans are "informed":

> Most discussions of information processing ... have been concerned with the realisation of absolute goals. "Problem solving" has become the paradigm of information processing. The problems considered have a fixed solution; the goal of the information-processing device is to find this solution; efficiency consists in finding it at the minimal cost. However, not all cognitive tasks fit this description; many tasks consist not in reaching an absolute goal, but in improving on an existing state of affairs. (pp. 46–47)

In other words, information seeking is not always motivated by the need to "solve a problem" or "make a decision" — activities that have a clear-cut and short-term end. Sometimes it is a desire simply to have *more or less* of some quality: more information, stimulation, or assurance; or less uncertainty, boredom, overload, or anxiety.

5.2. Browsing, Etc.

5.2.1. *Browsing, Scanning, Encountering, and Serendipity*

As shown in the scenarios presented in the second chapter of this book, information does not always result in either a decision or the reduction of uncertainty. Sometimes the receipt of information causes us to reassess the state of our ignorance (thereby increasing uncertainty), as one thinks "I know so little about this!" At other times, we can be so overloaded with information that further progress toward a goal becomes (cognitively or emotionally) impossible to make. Information may be sought merely for stimulation or entertainment value. And sometimes information is encountered without being sought.

Some writers on information seeking assume it to be an *intentional* action; that is, for information seeking to take place, the individual must be consciously and actively looking for information. Most other scholars (e.g., see the review by Chang & Rice, 1993) allow for the possibility of "unintentional communication," such as when we notice data in the environment (objects or events, whether of human or nonhuman origin). Such accidental or incidental encounters with information (Williamson, 1998) may either trigger a preexisting interest or cause a new interest to arise. The most common terms used to describe such phenomena are "browsing" and "scanning." A closely related concept is "serendipity."

Browsing is certainly the central (and oldest) concept among a variety of terms used to denote informal or unplanned search behaviors. As an English word, "browsing" itself derives from old French and refers to the way that animals feed upon vegetation. Since at least 1823, the word has been applied to reading habits, and thus *Webster's Third New International Dictionary* includes among its meanings "to look over casually (as a book) ... . To skim through a book reading at random passages ... . To look over books (as in a store or library) ... ." (Chang & Rice, 1993).

Browsing has come to refer to a wide range of information behaviors, ranging from aimless scanning to goal-directed searching. Chang and Rice (1993) note the bifurcated nature of the concept as it is commonly used: it may refer to purposive, goal-directed actions, or it may imply nonpurposive, unplanned behavior. Perhaps the very vagueness of the term has encouraged the proliferation of alternate terminology during recent years.

Long a consideration among librarians, the use of browsing by scientists as a topic of empirical investigation was first discussed by Saul Herner in 1954. Since at least the mid-1960s, the concept has appeared regularly in the general literature (e.g., Gerstberger & Allen, 1968; Herner, 1970; Levine, 1969; Overhage & Harman, 1965). An allied notion, *scanning*, has been employed in studies about as long (e.g., Aguilar, 1967; Duncan, 1972). Enough publications on browsing had accrued by 1985 to occasion a 112-page report (Ayris, 1986). The most recent comprehensive review of the literature (Chang & Rice, 1993, which featured 164 references) states that "we do not have a good vocabulary to describe and discuss various forms or degrees of browsing" (p. 233). Since then, the vocabulary to describe browsing has expanded to include terms like scanning and encountering.

Many authors consider browsing to be a type of information seeking, even though the browser may be seeking nothing in particular. Apted (1971) makes the point that accidental discovery of information is a special case of browsing that we should distinguish as *serendipity*. Although most studies of information seeking have chosen to ignore instances of encountering information by serendipity, it is obvious that such circumstances are fairly common. The role and value of serendipity in scientific investigation has been much discussed (e.g., Roberts, 1989; Shapiro, 1986).

Boyce, Meadow, and Kraft (1994) link serendipity and browsing when they say that:

> people find valuable information on subject B when searching for subject A, a phenomenon often called *serendipity*. The very act of browsing allows a user to recognize information of value in other contexts than that in mind when the search was started. (p. 177)

At times individuals simply engage in scanning their field of vision without a particular goal in mind (e.g., when we browse a magazine rack). A childhood fascination with certain objects in the environment — such as coins — may result in a perusal of magazines about coins in a bookstore; the browser may admire photographs of coins, glance at articles about specific types of coins, and so on. Only later might this half-formed interest lead to a complex of learning and actions that we call a "hobby," a work-like activity that is done for pleasure, without external rewards (Case, 2009a; Hartel, 2003; Stebbins, 2001). Similarly, an adult's curiosity about a social issue such as drug abuse may result in sustained reading on the topic without any particular plan of action.

Yet we can also "encounter" information without premeditated action (i.e., without conscious browsing), as when we glance at an advertising billboard that pictures an attractive product — say, a new car that we now learn is a Lexus. Therefore, it is safe to claim that at least the *absorption* of information may not be overtly intentional. An early review of the concept of browsing (Herner, 1970) described it as a mechanism that we could not stop even if we wished to:

> Continually, awake or asleep, consciously or unconsciously, we rummage through our minds, reviewing the data we have collected and stored within them … . [W]e know, or our minds store memories of, what interests us, and we match the contents of what we sense, regardless of where it occurs, against what interests us. (p. 408)

During the 1990s, two empirical studies of browsing shed further light on the process. The first, by Kwasnik (1992), focused on the notion of a "view," a span of attention regarding what one could see at a single time. Kwasnik (1992) then identified six activities involved in browsing. The second investigation, by Toms (1999), contains an extensive review of what psychologists have had to say about our *motivations* for exploration, curiosity, and the like. She reviews theories (e.g., uses and gratifications theory, play theory, and expectancy-value theory, as described in Chapter 7 of this book) that have been used to explain browsing behavior. Toms's own results suggest that browsing is more closely "connected to satisfying human curiosity than to resolving a predetermined information gap or need" (p. 204).

The most recent word on the topic comes from veteran information scientist Marcia Bates (Bates, 2007) who believes that browsing is composed of four stages: glimpsing, selecting, examining, and acquiring. She argues against indiscriminate use of the word "scanning" (which has two almost opposite dictionary definitions, and which she insists is "not browsing" in the fullest sense). The definition Bates arrives at is:

> Browsing is the activity of engaging in a series of glimpses, each of which may or may not lead to closer examination of a (physical or represented) object, which may or may not lead to (physical or conceptual) acquisition of the object.

5.2.2.   *Additional Distinctions*

Distinctions among degrees of browsing — some of which go back many years — have led to a proliferation of terminology to describe individual behaviors. The most distinctive (Choo, 1998, 2001a, 2001b; Saunders & Jones, 1990) consider *scanning of the environment* to have four modes, the lowest effort of which is the sort of "undirected viewing" that results in the serendipitous discovery (or "sensing") of what information exists in the environment. This seems to correspond to Erdelez's (1997, 1999, 2004, 2005) concept of "information encountering," which she equates with "accidental discovery," "serendipity," and "incidental learning." Awamura (2006) analyzes various aspects of encountering and suggests how they are related, particularly in regards to discovery of information on the Web. Kormos (2005) argues that libraries should find more ways to promote accidental discovery and incidental learning.

In Choo's typology, "conditioned viewing" or *browsing* results from a higher level of effort, the goal of which is to increase understanding and to make sense of the environment. It is only with still greater effort that focused "searches" are evident, according to Choo, and this level of seeking can be either informal or formal. Informal searches are those that examine relatively few sources and aim to increase knowledge within narrow limits,

Table 5.1: Examples of browsing goals by domain of interest, goal type, and terminology.

Example domains	Distinction made, with associated terms			
	Well-defined (formal search and retrieval)	**Semidefined (browse, forage, scan)**	**Poorly defined (browse, graze, navigate, scan)**	**Undefined (encounter, serendipity)**
Library or bookstore	Find material by a particular author or on a specific subject	Find books, tapes, or articles on a general subject	Find any material of potential interest	Discover previously unknown interests
Electronic information resources	Find specific pages or records using controlled terms or attributes	Find records or pages matching general, natural language terms	Follow links to pages that pique interest	Accidentally encounter pages of interest
TV/radio	Locate specific program, e.g., *Cheers*, on a specific channel, e.g., WTBS	Choose a specific TV channel (4) or radio frequency (FM 88.4)	Watch or listen to whatever catches attention, purposefully	Serendipitous viewing or listening, unintentionally
Shopping	Find an item of a particular brand in a category, e.g., Kellogg's Cornflakes	Find items in a category, e.g., breakfast cereals	Find something to eat, e.g., packaged foods	Pass by/see items for sale without intent to buy

Source: Adapted from Figure 3 on page 262 of Chang and Rice (1993). With permission of Information Today, Inc., www.infotoday.com

with the goal of simply learning; formal searches involve both more effort and more sources and are tied to an impending decision or action.

To make the vocabulary issue even more complicated, additional terminology is used in specific domains in which browsing phenomena are studied. Studies of organizational information seeking favor the descriptor *environmental scanning* (e.g., Correia & Wilson, 2001). The concept of browsing is widely employed in investigations of the interface for electronic information systems, where the word *navigation* is sometimes used to indicate a movement through search space in graphic interfaces (e.g., Thompson & Croft, 1989). Proper and Bruza (1999) use the phrase *information discovery* to apply solely to the identification and retrieval of relevant content from electronic sources. In usage studies of both television and the Internet, the term *surfing* may be used for the frequent scanning of multiple channels that is enabled by the remote control, or for browsing of Web sites (e.g., Ferguson & Perse, 2000).

Another extensive literature uses a "foraging" metaphor (Cronin & Hert, 1995; Jacoby, 2005; O'Connor, Copeland, & Kearns, 2003; Pirolli, 2009; Sandstrom, 1994, 2001; Spink & Cole, 2006), which sometimes corresponds more closely to the formal searches described by Choo (1998), yet draws examples from many other arenas (e.g., the search for food). Some investigations of document retrieval also invoke an analogy to "grazing" (e.g., Bates, 1989, 2005c).

In only two contexts does the primary term, browsing, still seem to suffice on its own: *shopping* (e.g., Bloch, Ridgway, & Sherrell, 1989; Lan, 2010; Salomon & Koppelman, 1992; Schmidt & Spreng, 1996) and *book usage within libraries* (e.g., Baker, 1986; Hemminger, Lu, Vaughan, & Adams, 2007). Chang and Rice (1993) tease out the origins and research usages of these terms in their comprehensive review of browsing concepts. Table 5.1 combines and adapts distinctions made by Saunders and Jones (1990), Chang (2005), Chang and Rice (1993), and Choo (1998) to illustrate browsing terminology.

5.3. Relevance, Pertinence, and Salience

5.3.1. Relevance and Pertinence

The topic of browsing provokes us to consider how one recognizes something of interest, and, by extension, the general problem of *relevance*. Relevance is a concept that extends well beyond browsing. A great deal has been written about it in the information science literature and most of that concerned with technical measures of document retrieval. The latter topic is of minor interest to this discussion; of greater importance is the general issue of what we *mean* when we say that information is relevant to a person.

Much commentary and some empirical investigations regarding relevance — and the related terms of *pertinence* and *salience* — are to be found in literature on perception, attention, memory, attitude and belief formation, and persuasion. Psychological investigations of these phenomena have been extended in the direction of speech, mass media studies, and information retrieval. Besides their import to basic research on human psychology, mechanisms of attention and attitude have great practical applications in everything from learning and healing to publicity and advertising.

The dictionary informs us that "relevance" means to have a close, logical relationship to a matter, topic, thought, remark, or question. Ritchie (1991), striving for a definition consistent with those for the term "information," says that:

> relevance has to do with meaning and describes the relationship of patterns and whatever patterns indicate to the cognitive environments of the originator and perceiver of a message. Patterns with communicative potential are data, and data with relevance are information. (p. 20)

In their book on the concept of relevance in communication, Sperber and Wilson (1995) imply that any pattern (e.g., a message in a conventional form) that attracts our attention calls for interpretation by us. Our interpretation must take into account the *context* of the message — the background of time, place, persons, and recent ideas, statements, and events. "Relevance" is the interpretive connection that is made between the observed pattern and the context of the observation (Ritchie, 1991, pp. 16–20). Furner (2004) goes so far as to suggest that the study of relevance may be the most productive approach to understanding what is meant by the term "information" (see Chapter 3).

Sperber and Wilson see relevance as a key aspect of efficiency in human information processing. Our long-term goal is to improve "one's knowledge of the world as much as possible given the available resources" (Sperber and Wilson, 1995, p. 47). We always face two problems in processing information efficiently: First, the environment contains much more information than our senses can process; second, we have "plenty of unfinished business" in our minds. The unfinished business may run the gamut of time and importance from "Is there a God?" to "What should I have for dinner tonight?" — plus a few thousand other questions and concerns.

In information science, relevance is used in a different sense than the characterization of Sperber and Wilson; that is, relevance is equated with *aboutness* and *topicality*. A document is relevant to an information need if it is judged to be "on the topic" (Harter, 1992). Topicality serves as the basis for measures — the most common ones being precision and recall — of the effectiveness of a document retrieval system.

We will take a short detour to consider briefly the substantial literature on relevance in the context of information retrieval.

5.3.2. Relevance in Information Retrieval

In its most common form, relevance measures are operationalized as a document retrieval system user (or some other judge) declaring a document to be either "relevant" or "not relevant" to a specific request for information. Thus, relevance measures are based on the relationship between an information request and the content of a collection of document records — or more usually document *surrogates* (e.g., author-title-keywords) rather than the complete text (Belkin & Vickery, 1985). Investigators have sought an *objective* measure of relevance for this particular situation of information transfer.

Even though a narrow definition of relevance enjoyed wide acceptance during the 1950s and 1960s, there was a growing recognition that it left out important aspects of information seekers and their situation. Rees and Saracevic (1966) were among the earliest critics of objective definitions of relevance, and by the mid-1970s the criticisms were widespread.

The main problem facing an objective operationalization of relevance is the contextual nature of human judgment. Even when the terminology of the request maps neatly onto the terms of a document index, there may be reasons why such a match may not be judged truly relevant. Setting aside the obvious problem that words can have multiple meanings and varying interpretations, it has been effectively demonstrated that relevance assessments can shift, depending on the order in which retrieved documents are presented to a judge. There is considerable variation among judges as to the point at which a document starts being relevant and ceases to be nonrelevant (Eisenberg, 1988; Janes & McKinney, 1992).

Harter (1992) describes a number of examples in which relevance is clearly not judged on the basis of topicality. A common case is one in which a user judges information to be relevant even though it is not strictly "about" the stated information need; such judgments are in tune with the everyday, dictionary sense of relevancy as "bearing on or relating to the matter in hand." For example, when searching for information on the Peruvian economy, we may encounter an article about the global effects of El Niño, which may lead us to wonder what effects that weather phenomenon will have on the fishing and farming sectors of the Peruvian economy; the article is not "about" the topic of our interest, but nevertheless we see it as relevant to our information need. Harter (1992) goes so far as to suggest that *"references on the topic may be less important than relevant references not on the topic* — references that allow the making of new intellectual connections" (p. 612).

Accordingly, since the 1970s, the information science literature has shifted toward a definition of relevance that is based on the knowledge state and intentions of the user rather than a logical match of terminology by the information system — toward a *subjective* view (Ingwersen & Järvelin, 2005; Mizzaro, 1998). The subjective characterization of relevance is most commonly called *situational* relevance (Barry, 1994; Bruce, 1994; Dervin & Nilan, 1986; Wilson, 1973) or sometimes *pertinence* (Belkin & Vickery, 1985; Howard, 1994; Kemp, 1974) or *psychological* relevance (Harter, 1992). Belkin and Vickery (1985) make a neat distinction between objective relevance and situational relevance (i.e., pertinence) by saying that "relevance is the property that assigns an answer to a question and pertinence is the property that assigns an answer to [an] information need" (p. 46).

Froehlich (1994), in fact, points out that what most people mean when they use the word "relevance" is actually "pertinence": "bearing on or connected to" an information *need*, rather than a stated *question*. In other words, they mean subjective relevance. In Froehlich's view, this meaning of relevance forms a "natural category from cultural experience," in reference to Eleanor Rosch's theory of prototypes and basic-level categories (Rosch & Lloyd, 1978). Rosch demonstrated that people divide up (categorize) their perceptual world according to certain principles. Basic-level categories (such as "bird") are usually the first learned by children, and they gradually come to organize the contents of this category around the most "typical" example (which functions as a prototype) of the category. Thus, in North America either the sparrow or American robin comes to be the central example to which are all other birds are compared. Not surprisingly, birds like pelicans and storks are regarded as peripheral examples of the bird category, as not being "typical" enough even though they have the logical, defining characteristics of "birdness": feathers, wings, beaks, and the ability to fly. Flightless birds, like the penguin or ostrich, may be judged as even poorer examples of birds, depending on one's origins.

Froehlich is saying, then, that subjective relevance (pertinence) is the core meaning of a cluster of related concepts. Other concepts include germane, material, apposite, and apropos (Froehlich, 1991). The cluster of overlapping meanings has, at its center, the everyday sense of "relevance," while at the periphery is the technical sense of relevance as answers (or documents) that logically match a formal, stated query — the technical view of relevance.

Whatever we call it, the subjective view of relevance argues for the importance of the user's knowledge state and intentions at the time of encountering information. For example, a document might be retrieved by a system on the basis of a logical match between words in a query and words in a title. However, it may be that the user has previously read that document. The mere fact that the information is *not novel* is likely to cause users to judge it as *not relevant* to their needs; presumably, the information in the document is already a part of the context of their information seeking. In keeping with this view, some psychologists note that pertinence (situational relevance) is determined by *context* and guides selective attention to information (Lachman, Lachman, & Butterfield, 1979, pp. 194–197).

5.3.3.   Salience

A related term less frequently discussed in information studies is *salience*. Something that is salient "stands out," and is vivid, unexpected, notable, conspicuous, prominent, or "unpleasant, deviant, extreme, intense, unusual, sudden, brightly lit, colorful, alone" (Kiesler & Sproull, 1982, p. 556). Salience evokes the figure/ground distinction in gestalt psychology, in which certain principles (e.g., proximity, similarity, closure) tend to account for which elements in an image stand out from the others. What is it that grabs our attention when we look at a scene? What stands out as the "figure" and what is perceived as mere background? Salient items of information are more easily recalled later, perhaps because they are coded more effectively in memory (Glass, Holyoak, & Santa, 1979).

A salient stimulus is not necessarily relevant to one's current information needs. Witnessing a car accident as a pedestrian certainly raises one's interest and potential for taking action. ("Should I call for an ambulance? Should I help the victims exit their vehicles? Should I offer to serve as a witness? Should I get out of the street?") Yet, if the scenario does not map on to preexisting interests, sympathies, intentions, or plans, no action may be taken and the incident may pass from the mind of the witness minutes later. ("I must be on my way. I don't want to get involved.")

Correspondingly, potentially relevant sources of information may not appear particularly salient at the time an information need begins to emerge. Our need for the exact address of a new movie theater may not occur to us as we pass by the phone directory on our way to the front door, or as we drive by the neighbor who first told us about it. It is only later, when we can't find the theater, that our cell phone suddenly becomes more salient. ("I'll call directory assistance, or my neighbor!") Sometimes we pass over the easy sources of information because we do not see them in that context at the time; later, those sources may be highly salient and we may be willing to be much more active in our search for information.

Johnson (1997) sees both salience and beliefs as a part of "personal relevance factors" that are antecedent to any information-seeking activity.

That is, before one begins to consider the characteristics of an information source and its usefulness, an interaction occurs between a gap in knowledge, beliefs about that topic of knowledge, and the import or "standoutedness" of it. We pay attention and render action to those things that are salient to us. Later, we will examine Johnson's model that describes the sequence of events and factors that lead to information seeking. For now, the cluster of concepts we call relevance, pertinence, and salience give rise to another question: When do we decide *not* to pay attention to information? This is a phenomenon known as "selective exposure."

5.4. Avoiding Information

5.4.1. Selective Exposure and Information Avoidance

It is widely believed that humans tend to seek information that is congruent with their prior knowledge, beliefs, and opinions, and to avoid exposure to information that conflicts with those internal states. In contrast, a high level of interest regarding a certain topic will tend to increase exposure — interested people are motivated to acquire more information about a topic that fascinates them.

An early look at selective exposure to information was that of Hyman and Sheatsley (1947), who invoked selectivity as a reason why attempts to use the mass media to change attitudes or behavior (e.g., in political campaigns) often fail. In addition to the general tendency to reinforce preexisting knowledge, beliefs, and attitudes, Hyman and Sheatsley observed several other tendencies. First, some people are chronically ignorant in relation to the topic of the information campaign and there is something about the uninformed that makes them harder to reach.

Schramm (1973) believed that selective exposure was "due to a complex set of causes," and he identified five of them: (1) availability of the stimulus (i.e., how easily at hand it is), (2) contrast of the stimulus with its background, (3) mindset of the receiver (i.e., a history of previous experiences that guide our attention to particular cues, and not to others), (4) estimated usefulness of the stimulus, and (5) individual qualities of the receiver (especially education and social status). Regarding this final cause, Schramm noted that degree of education predicted the choice of medium (e.g., print) in information seeking and was a function of "an appetite for information." He was uncertain if we would ever understand the underlying process that results in such individual frames of reference for interpreting information.

People who are interested in a topic tend to acquire more information about it (Chew & Palmer, 1994; Reagan, 1996). There are also differences in the ways that people interpret the same information: their perceptions and memory are distorted by their individual motives and attitudes. Finally, receiving information does not necessarily change attitudes or behavior. For all these reasons, simply increasing the flow of information does not automatically attain the desired result.

Twenty years after Hyman and Sheatsley published their observations, a critical review by Sears and Freedman (1967) raised questions about the phenomenon of selective exposure and clarified its nature. Sears and Freedman noted that experimental evidence showed that people do not always prefer information that agrees with their opinions. In cases in which discrepant information might be highly useful, or where an individual already had a great deal of information on the topic, a person was open to dissonant (i.e., contradictory) information; and the tendency to openness was more common among educated individuals. Later experiments (e.g., Frey, 1982; Frey & Rosch, 1984) using better measures of information seeking and avoidance showed that we often seek dissonant information in cases where it might improve future decisions we make, and even in some cases where it might not. Yet, in general, such research still demonstrates a preference for supportive information in most cases.

More to the point, Sears and Freedman also noted a sense in which selective exposure is common: while there are *instances* in which we may welcome contradictory statements, *in the long term* we drift toward information that supports our point of view. In other words, we tend toward a usual diet of information that is *mostly* congruent with our beliefs and opinions.

Over the five decades that selective information seeking has been discussed, many others have pondered the implications of selective perception and attention for the next step: using information. Thayer (1987), for example, notes that knowledge often does not result in changes of behavior. We tend to think that acquiring information obligates one to think, feel, or do something about it. But *informed behavior* does not always result from exposure to information. Not only are people *told* that taking drugs and smoking are ultimately bad for their health, they can observe this fact in the world around them; those observations, however, often do not result in less consumption of harmful substances. As Sears and Freedman pointed out, failure to act on information is often due less to selective exposure than to a *rejection* of information with which we disagree: "Perhaps resistance to influence is accomplished most often and most successfully at the level of information evaluation, rather than at the level of selective seeking and avoiding of information" (p. 213).

Zillman and Bryant (1985) observe that we tend to think of preference for entertainment content, for example, as fairly stable, a matter of a deeply ingrained "taste" of unknown origin. These authors, however, believe that "the choice behavior in question grows from a situational context [in which] affective and emotional states and reactions play a key role" (p. 157). Atkin (1985) agrees to the extent that selection (and sometimes, avoidance) of entertainment seems to be motivated by both affective and utilitarian concerns — that is, seeking both emotional gratification and the means to reach some goal.

Reviewing a number of studies in which individuals were placed in either boring or stressful conditions, then allowed to select entertainment programming, Zillman and Bryant (1985) found support for "therapeutic" uses of media. That is, one of the ways people cope with negative affect is to choose materials that may diffuse such feelings: arousing programming (if bored), calming music (if stressed), or simply messages that comfort or distract. Zillman and Bryant regard this "selective behavior to be intelligent in that messages are exploited for their therapeutic value" (p. 186), even though such selections offer only short-term relief to emotional problems. This tendency to use various media — especially television — to ameliorate stress has been noted for many decades (e.g., Bryant & Vorderer, 2006; Pearlin, 1959; Vorderer, Klimmt & Ritterfeld, 2004).

The notion of *selecting* inputs can also be applied to *avoiding* them. Noted Yale sociologist Charles Perrow, in his essay "On Not Using Libraries", discusses the *avoidance* of information (Perrow, 1989). Perrow reverses the typical view of libraries when he says that:

> I require libraries to *hide* most of the literature so that I will not become delirious from the want of time and wit to pursue it all. There is just too much material. The problem is not access, it is the reverse, containment … . Were I now to browse the stacks … I would drown, or panic, and certainly lose my way." (pp. 29–30)

Perrow says that, as most of what he reads is determined by the demands of others (students, colleagues, journal editors) and he has adequate ways of keeping up with the literature in his field, he is rarely motivated to seek library materials. When he *does* need a book, article, or chapter from the library, his way of coping is to send an assistant to get it so that he will not be distracted by adjacent materials. Perrow's strategy is an extreme example of *filtering*, justified by his belief that most of the literature in his area is redundant and of low quality.

Wilson (1995) points out that filtering behavior (or "nonuse," as he calls it) is both efficient and perfectly rational if it is a matter of conscious *policy*:

> being presented with more information than one could absorb …
> being burdened by a large supply of relevant information, that is

forced to spend more time and energy on assimilating new information than one would like to do ... information one thinks to be probably relevant but does not use because of lack of time. (pp. 45–46)

In a later publication, Wilson (1996) provides a scenario of how a nonuse policy might be implemented for interdisciplinary researchers, faced as they are by many documents from the multiple literatures they monitor:

Large literatures may be cut down drastically: one may ignore the past, ignore "foreign" contributions, ignore contributions from identifiable schools and traditions of thought (e.g., no Marxists, no deconstructionists, no positivists, etc.), ignore work done with certain techniques or in particular styles or with particular approaches. (p. 199)

Case, Johnson, Andrews, and Allard (2005) review the history of commentaries about avoiding information, tracing it back to various psychological concepts from the early 20th century and before. Closely related terms include selective attention, selective exposure, cognitive dissonance, coping, monitoring and blunting, escape, distraction, unrealistic optimism, and willful blindness, among others. Additional explanations and examples of avoiding information are found in Baker (2005), Ek and Heinström (2011), Heinström (2010), Miller (1987), Savolainen (2007b), and Sweeny, Melnyk, Miller, and Shepperd (2010). In addition, many scholars have reconciled avoidance behaviors with the more typical tendency to seek out information in order to reduce uncertainty (see Affifi & Weiner, 2004; Bradac, 2001; Brashers, 2001; Brashers et al., 2002; Sairanen & Savolainen, 2010). At times it seems that we strive to know both more and less at the same time.

Yet, most of the time, information is not avoided but rather simply not *used*. This applies to the average person as well as the scholar. Dervin (1983b), for example, criticizes the tendency for studies of information usage to blame the public for not taking more advantage of authoritative information — typically in the form of documents or expert advice. Dervin takes the counterview that most "canned" information is not relevant to the needs of most individuals in the general public:

When you listen to people's reasons for not using or rejecting information ... what you hear them say most often is, "It didn't fit my circumstances," or "It arrived too late," or "I couldn't make it work for me." (p. 170)

Of course, not using relevant information also has its consequences, and most of the time these are not very severe. Yet the Anglo-American legal system has a long history (going back to at least 1861) of punishing those who engaged in "willful blindness," "purposeful avoidance," or "deliberate indifference" (among other terms), in cases in which their failure to act on information caused harm to others (Heffernan, 2011).

When, for whatever reason, entire groups of people do not get the same information as other groups, we speak of them as having a "knowledge gap" or as being "information poor" — the subject of Section 5.4.2.

5.4.2. *Knowledge Gaps and Information Poverty*

Earlier when we considered the concept of a "gap," it referred to an *individual's* encounter with a discrepancy or lack of "sense" in their environment. When such gaps are differential and persistent, they are called "knowledge gaps" (Chatman & Pendleton, 1995; Chew & Palmer, 1994; Kwak, 1999; Tichenor, Donohue, & Olien, 1970). That is, when one human group (whether defined by income, education, location, or other variable) persistently differs from another human group in *what they know*, a knowledge gap is said to exist.

Knowledge gaps are often discussed in the context of public information campaigns (Rice & Atkin, 1989, 1994), which are attempts to inform mass audiences of some facts or practices. Information campaigns are often conducted with the intention of improving health practices, such as publicity aimed at encouraging people to avoid illegal drugs, stop smoking, eat less fat, get more exercise, and so forth. Public information efforts can also attempt to inform people about matters of fact, such as public television programming (typically aimed at children) intended to increase literacy or knowledge of language, science, history, and geography. In the United States, programs like *Sesame Street* and *3-2-1-Contact* are of this type.

One of the problems with such well-intentioned programming is that some segment of the intended audience may not watch at all or may watch but learn less than other audience segments. When that happens, disparities in knowledge may actually be created among groups by a program intended to reduce them. A particular concern is when an already disadvantaged group such as lower income persons ("the poor") do not get the message at all, either through nonexposure or through exposure without learning. Niederdeppe (2008) provides an example of this: when celebrities contract cancer, this is often widely reported in the mass media; such news tends to prompt only those with more education, health knowledge, and community involvement to seek further information. This differential effect, of course, is not a new phenomenon, but merely an extension of an old observation as rephrased by Dervin (1989, p. 219): "the informationally rich get richer, the poor get poorer."

A basic example of "the poor get poorer" mechanism is *literacy*. If one never learns to read, the potential for learning is greatly diminished and others who can read will more steadily increase the amount of knowledge they possess. Recently, this concern has been extended to those who never learn to use computers and telecommunications networks. People who do know how to use computers (and have access to them — a separate issue) have both additional means of learning and more stores of information available to them.

The tendency of information campaigns to perform poorly, or to fail altogether, was noted by Hyman and Sheatsley as early as 1947. Later scholars outlined how such attempts to inform and persuade could be successful (McCombs, 1972; Mendelsohn, 1973), and recent reviews of decades of campaign evaluations outline the circumstances that can lead to persuasion and change (Friestad & Wright, 1994; Noar, Benac & Harris, 2007; Viswanath & Finnegan, 1996).

Cecile Gaziano's (1997) review of 97 knowledge gap studies claims that inequalities are increasing, especially in public affairs and health knowledge. Her analysis points out the many "barriers to knowledge acquisition" that have been blamed for gaps among both individuals and groups: attitudes, beliefs; values; domain, accuracy, and/or breadth of knowledge; family socialization; community identity and connectedness; socioeconomic status (SES); ethnic or racial group stratification; behaviors; media use; and media exposure. It is these latter two variables — media use and media exposure — that seem to explain the largest effects in most studies of knowledge gaps. She concludes that information sources are often linked to socioeconomic status:

> If knowledge is distributed equally within a social subsystem, equal knowledge acquisition within the system is not assured. Exposure to information sources, especially to print media, frequently correlates with SES and having a greater number of information sources often correlates with knowledge gaps ... .[G]reater access [by the most advantaged] to an array of economic and financial information sources, especially in newspapers, subscription newsletters, and computerized databases, greatly increases their ability to maintain and increase their privileged position, relative to that of the less advantaged. (p. 254)

When some segment of a population seems to be permanently ignorant, their state is labeled *information poverty*. Childers and Post (1975) define information poverty as a "culture" marked by three characteristics: (1) a low level of processing skills, marked by reading, language, hearing, or eyesight deficiencies; (2) social isolation in a subculture, leading to unawareness of information known to a larger public, reliance upon rumor and folklore, and dependence on entertainment-oriented media like television; and (3) a tendency to feel fatalistic and helpless, which in turn reduces the likelihood of active information seeking. According to Childers and Post, the prototypical member of the information poor ...:

> does not know which formal channels to tap in order to solve his problems ... watches many hours of television daily, seldom reads

newspapers and magazines and never reads books ... does not see his problems as information needs ... is not a very active information seeker ... [and] is locked into an informal information network that is deficient in the information that is ordinarily available to the rest of society. (pp. 42–43)

Wilson (1983) says that:

information poverty is a typical soft concept, and there is no way of saying what its incidence is; but certainly there are many for whom the world is a tiny place and the supply of second-hand knowledge a very small one. Information poverty can be a self-selected condition freely entered into and willingly endured. (p. 151)

We might question the validity of the information poverty concept as described by Childers and Wilson, because it seems to encompass such a broad swath of human groups and behaviors, most of which could be described more parsimoniously by the word "ignorance." To a degree, Dervin (1989) clarifies the concept in discussing "how research categories perpetuate inequities" in society by defining "users" in terms of *systems they are supposed to use*; that is, if the "have-nots" do not use the information sources designed for the "haves," it is their own damn fault. Haider and Bawden (2007) take a similar view, suggesting that information poverty is defined by elites to justify the sorts of information services that they provide.

Whatever the applicability of the term "information poverty," the basic concept underlying it has been invoked and enlarged in a number of books and articles on the information society and the digital divide (e.g., Goulding, 2001; Jaeger & Thompson, 2004; Norris, 2001; Schiller, 1996; Wilson, 2010b).

As Goulding (2001) suggests, the underlying reasons for selection, rejecting or avoiding information, may have to do with "information overload" and the feelings of anxiety to which a flood of stimuli give rise. These are the topics of Section 5.4.3.

5.4.3. *Information Overload and Anxiety*

In contrast to a state of ignorance about something, it is also possible to have too much information. According to Rogers (1986, p. 181), *information overload* "is the state of an individual or system in which excessive communication inputs cannot be processed, leading to breakdown." Sociologists and political scientists (e.g., Karl Deutsch, 1963) tend to discuss overload in the "systemic" (or global) sense, in which such a flood of messages proliferate in the urban environment that many are ignored.

In contrast, the psychological viewpoints on overload (as represented in the writings of James Grier Miller and Henry Mintzberg, for example) are prone to characterizing it as an *individual* factor. Miller (1960, 1978), a psychiatrist, attributed some aspects of schizophrenia to information overload. Similarly, management theorist Mintzberg (1975) explored the problems created by overload in decision making, noting that:

> brains have difficulty processing all the relevant information — there
> is too much, it may not fit with expectations and previous patterns,
> and some of it may simply be too threatening to accept. (p. 17)

When too much information confronts us, we cease to pay prompt and careful attention to some of it. It would be wrong to characterize this "editing" of reality as *always* problematic, because we naturally treat information selectively, choosing only a small portion of all possible inputs for our attention. We mark the difference between what we "need to know" versus what would be merely "nice to know" (Paisley, 1993). Such selective attention to environmental inputs is called "filtering" by psychologists Miller et al.(1960), who point out that it is common for humans to filter their experience. Indeed, the elderly may be forced to do so more often due to cognitive decline (Mata & Nunes, 2010).

Miller (1960) classified possible responses to overload into seven categories:

1. Omission — failing to process some of the inputs
2. Error — processing the information incorrectly in some way
3. Queuing — delaying processing of some information with the intention of catching up later
4. Filtering — processing only that information identified as having "high priority"
5. Approximation — lowering standards of discrimination by being less precise in categorizing inputs and responses
6. Multiple channels — splitting up the incoming information in order to decentralize the response
7. Escaping — giving up the burden of attending to inputs entirely

A review of voter reasoning by Popkin (1993) points out that voters in the United States presidential elections commonly:

> ... use shortcuts in obtaining information, shortcuts in evaluating
> information, and shortcuts in storing and recalling information
> about parties, candidates, and issues. (1993, p. 19)

Yet we employ these filtering strategies at our peril. Katz and Kahn's (1978) analysis of Miller's strategies points out that most of them have the potential to be maladaptive. Omission, error, and escape are by definition dysfunctional, they point out, whereas queuing, filtering, and approximating *can* be maladaptive if not based on well-considered priorities. In other words, people who use these strategies in their jobs or personal life are likely to make serious errors.

One is reminded of Abraham Maslow's connection between knowledge and avoidance of responsibility (Maslow, 1963, p. 122): "we can seek knowledge in order to reduce anxiety and we can also *avoid* knowing in order to reduce anxiety." Sometimes we would rather not know that we are at high risk for a disease or natural disaster. Public health campaigns that attempt to encourage safe practices by emphasizing potentially harmful effects are often "tuned out" by readers, viewers, and listeners who simply would rather not know. We often think of information as *reducing* anxiety, but such is not always the case. A study of the effects of a consumer health information service (Pifalo, Hollander, Henderson, DeSalvo, & Gill, 1997) found that 52% of the people who received information said that it reduced their anxiety about a health concern; yet for another 10%, having the medical information *increased* their anxiety.

George Miller's categories reflect the ways that people *adjust* to having too much information. When adjustment is not possible — where the mechanisms above do not work, and when a person does not have the freedom to abandon a task (such as is the case with students and school assignments) — the result is stress and *anxiety*. If one cannot address the anxiety by taking action, a typical result of anxiety is lowered performance and less enjoyment, whether on the job or in one's personal life. We often feel that way about information because we do not control its production and dissemination, and the environment bombards us with plenty of it. The psychologist Garner (1962) believed that finding a pattern in information was necessary to maintain peace of mind:

> The search for structure is inherent in behavior .... People in any situation will search for meaningful relations between the variables existing in the situation, and if no such relations exist or can be perceived, considerable discomfort occurs. (pp. 339–340)

Graphic designer and architect Wurman (1989) coined the term *information anxiety* and devoted an entire book to the notion. He defined it as a condition "produced by the ever-widening gap between what we understand and what we think we should understand. *Information anxiety* is the black hole between data and knowledge" (p. 34). His definition does not emphasize information overload as a cause of anxiety, but portions of his book do so. It is not merely the huge amount of information that we perceive in our environment, Wurman implies, but also an accompanying feeling of being unable to keep up, no matter what strategies we employ.

The idea that information can cause anxiety and dysfunction is an old one, particularly among scholars of management and human factors. Organizational theorist Weick (1970, 1995) considered information *load* to be one of the crucial properties of the work environment that determine how well people perform on the job. It is not surprising, then, that several studies of information behavior have focused on information overload, including that of Farhoomand and Drury (2002). Their survey asked 124 managers across various companies and government agencies in four English-speaking countries to define "information overload," and identify its frequency, sources, effects, and the actions they take in response. Most described overload in terms of excessive or irrelevant volume or in terms of an inability to manage or understand information. Over half of the respondents said that they experienced the feeling often, and most said they "filtered" information to combat overload. Savolainen (2007b) in a study of environmental activists in Finland, found that they reduced information flows both by filtering less useful material and by reducing the number of information sources they monitored. Allen and Wilson (2003), Bawden and Robinson (2009), and Eppler and Mengis (2004) have provided other examples of definitions and measures of information overload.

Of course, libraries are prime sites for overload. Meier (1963) documented a case in which psychological stress and service failures resulted when requests for service exceeded the capacity of a library staff to accommodate them. But more commonly it is students, rather than staff, who experience information overload in libraries. Mellon (1986, p. 162) describes how university students are sometimes stymied in their library research by feelings they described as "scary, overpowering, lost, helpless, confused." Mellon studied 6,000 students and found that about 80% of them associated their first experiences with academic libraries with anxiety. Jiao and Onwuegbuzie (1997) have demonstrated that negative perceptions of the library, library staff, library devices, and one's own abilities predict less library usage, as do certain demographic variables. Kuhlthau (1988a) sees the ubiquity of confusion and anxiety among novice library users as confirming psychologist George Kelly's view of behavior as the *testing of constructs*, in which encounters with new situations frequently begin with negative feelings (Kelly, 1963). It is not surprising that both Ford (2003) and Katopol (2005) point to overload and attendant anxiety as key issues that need to be addressed in designing educational support systems. And Morrison (2002) says that new employees are often anxious and thus afraid to ask too many questions of oldtimers in an organization.

Not surprisingly, Batson, Coke, Chard, Smith, and Taliaferro (1979), and other psychological studies, have found that people are more prone to seeking information when they are in a good mood. We would naturally expect information seeking to be less likely when conducted under a cloud of negative feelings.

How often do searches for information end in failure due to heightened anxiety? Probably a great many. It is easy to imagine calling a halt to research when one is faced with an overwhelming number of information sources and an uncertainty about their relative quality. "Giving up" evokes both the remarks of Charles Perrow and the predictions of cost–benefit analysis: when the effort of gathering information seems too great, we make do with what little information we have. And yet when one stops searching before one has found much of anything, the result may be a complete failure to meet task goals. For this reason, encouraging success in task-related information seeking has been a major concern of information literacy advocates (e.g., Lowe & Eisenberg, 2005; Thompson, 2007; Walker, 2009).

In some ways the phenomenon of overload is paradoxical because humans also seem to have a need for stimulation. Kuhlthau (1993a) notes that while the arrival of new information may cause anxiety, the failure of new information to appear may cause boredom. Zillman and Bryant (1985, p. 158) observed the same pattern in their experiments, writing that "extreme understimulation (boredom) and extreme overstimulation (stress) constitute aversive states." Both understimulation and overstimulation are uncomfortable, but the latter is surely harder on our mental health.

Overload can appear in a number of contexts, work settings being the most common (Eppler & Mengis, 2004). In studies of office workers, O'Reilly (1980) discovered that too much information appeared to degrade the job performance of these workers while it *increased* their satisfaction; in contrast, white collar workers reporting "underload" (too little information to perform their task optimally) also reported lower levels of satisfaction than those workers with too much information. Allen and Wilson's (2003) multiple case studies of business organizations point to some of the causes and consequences of information overload.

But everyday tasks also present overloads. Almost 40 years ago, Jacoby, Speller, and Berning (1974) pointed out that the typical American supermarket displayed more than 8,000 unique items — a number that has surely grown much larger in the intervening years. Experiments with hundreds of consumers have confirmed that they use only a limited amount of information — typically just three or four product attributes — in making purchase decisions. Since the early investigations that established overload effects in shopping, market researchers have been studying how this phenomenon differs among subpopulations (e.g., the elderly, children, the poor), whether there is an optimal information load, and which kinds of information should be provided for a given product type (Owen, 1992).

Newspapers contain much more information than readers care to digest; two-thirds of the stories they contain are ignored by the public (Graber, 1984). Television stimuli may overload the viewer, at times intentionally in the case of ads and entertainment programming. Yet even watching the news on television may burden the processing powers of the viewer when:

> the brevity of information-heavy presentations, and the lack of stopping points to allow reflection and internalization of the story make it almost impossible for average viewers to process more than a fraction of this overload of information (Graber, 1989, p. 148).

Given the proliferation of media in our time, with the World Wide Web now competing with television in the degree to which it juxtaposes strange images on a screen, it is inevitable that overload will become an ever more present distraction in making sense of the world. A January 1999 feature in *Inc.* magazine claimed that there had been over 3,000 newspaper and magazine articles on "information overload" published in the previous 2 years; as of 2011, there are 3.7 million Web sites that mention the phrase. What irony: even our awareness of overload is overloaded!

In addition to the sheer amount of information in the world, Donnelly (1986) complains that overload has a *qualitative* dimension as well:

> What the rhetoric, fantasy, unrootedness, and unrelatedness of much of our communications images have in common is not what is put into them, but what is left out. They are as light as confetti ... the problem with this type of information overload is not simply quantity, but the unconnected, excited nature of the images that package and distribute this information, whether it be news of the world or stories of human interest. (p. 186)

Donnelly's complaint is an old one, advanced by critics of television over several decades. The paradox is that at times *we cause our own overload* by choosing to attend to many messages or other stimuli (Neill, 1992). Our need for stimulation highlights the close link between the concepts of information and *entertainment*.

5.5. Information versus Entertainment

One of the less discussed topics in the study of information seeking is the artificial distinction between "entertainment" and "information." The literature of information behavior treats these two concepts as if they had nothing to do with one another. And yet they exist on a continuum, with some sensory input being "purely" enjoyable, other input being "purely" informative, and much of what we encounter in everyday life falling somewhere between the two extremes. Cermak (1996, p. 116) hits the nail on the head when he says:

> Although information and entertainment may be conceptually distinct, from a practical point of view they are hopelessly entangled. One would be hard pressed to name a vehicle for delivering information that is not also used for delivering entertainment.

Part of this bias against entertainment undoubtedly comes from our tendency to overrationalize human behavior. We prefer to see people primarily as *thinking* beings. Hence, we emphasize cognitive factors in behavior rather than affective influences. As will be seen in the review of literature on decision making that follows, it is tempting to overemphasize (and even reify) rationality in human behavior.

Zillman and Bryant (1986, p. 303) define entertainment as "any activity designed to delight," observing further that "no culture of which we have an adequate accounting has been entirely without it." In their historical overview of the topic, Zillman and Bryant (1994) note that early Western philosophy (beginning with Plato), as well as religion, tended to disparage entertainment as morally unfit or stemming from human failings. For example, in his work *Pensées*, Pascal (1670/1940, p. 50) stated that humans have an "instinct which impels them to seek amusement ... [arising] from the sense of their constant unhappiness." It was not until the 19th and early 20th centuries that amusement began to be studied in a serious, nonmoralistic fashion (e.g., Freud, 1905/1960).

Zillman and Bryant (1986, p. 321) conclude that "media idealists" believe that only "serious" uses of information channels are worthy of study, leading to an unfortunate state of affairs in which "effects of entertainment, presumably because of the ready condemnation of entertainment as cheap escapism, have received very little attention from researchers." Intellectual snobbery may be partly to blame. Davis (1986) claims that one predictor of a successful social theory is its invocation of "high-status" explanatory factors, such as "rationality" or "the division of labor." Those that invoke other factors, such as the influence of communication media or information sources, tend to fail:

> few would rank McLuhan in the same league as Marx, Durkheim, Weber, Simmel or Freud ... the factor [McLuhan invokes] is anathema to many intellectuals and social scientists who regard television as merely kitsch. (p. 299)

Serious investigation of the utility of print and electronic entertainments (e.g., Radway, 1985; Rosengren, 1974) are less than three decades old. It was not until a 1981 essay by William Safire (cited in Bogart, 1983) popularized the term "infotainment" that closer attention began to be paid to the ways in which fact and fiction, news and dramatic programming, influence one another.

University of Denver professor Mendelsohn (1966) wrote an entire book on the use of the mass media for entertainment. Early in the volume, he rails against the cultural bias against the use of entertaining materials:

> the investigator of entertainment is immediately struck by the ascriptive language that is used by layman and scientists alike, by theologian and social critic, by educator and moralist, by legislator and social commentator. For the most part, the language about entertainment emanating from these sources is equally highly negative, disparaging, and admonishing. In short, entertainment is relegated to those rubrics that are ordinarily reserved for the "evils of society." (p. 18)

It is not merely popular society but scholarly discourse that tends to shove entertainment under the rug. In the case of information-seeking research, any content that is potentially diverting has often been defined as "out of scope." The information scientist Allen (1996) argues that the human "need for entertainment" is not even "classified as an information need" because it is commonly assumed that a:

> ... search for information is purposive and thus can be analyzed as a kind of problem solving. These narrow assumptions exclude a range of information behaviors that are not associated with information needs and do not appear to fit the problem-solving perspective. It is quite possible for someone to search for information, not because of an information need, but for some other motivation. People who watch television programs may do so because they need to know what is going on in the world, or they may just want to be entertained and diverted. (p. 55)

Brenda Dervin, too, challenges the artificiality of the information–entertainment distinction made by "experts":

> Experts make judgments as to how their "information" will help. They deem some observations as "information," others as "entertainment," some as "factual," others as "opinion." (Dervin, 1983a, p. 27)

In other words, we have a tendency to dichotomize (fact versus opinion, information versus entertainment) phenomena that are not really that discrete. Making information and entertainment into distinct categories inevitably results in a focus on utilitarian behaviors — as anything labeled as "entertainment" by definition cannot inform anyone and is thus not worthy of our attention. Another scholar, Wilson (1983), points out the folly of reifying this view of information when he observes that:

> ... for many of us, a good deal of time is spent gathering information in the activity best described as simply watching the world go by. The world is a spectacle, a great show, and watching it is an endless source of entertainment and instruction. We can do it seated in a café, watching television programs, looking out the window, reading newspapers, or traveling. It is a frequent complaint by critics of the mass media that television news is treated by its producers as a form of entertainment, not as a serious instructional form. The charge is correct but the blame is undeserved. (p. 142)

The tendency to treat news as entertainment has received much attention in studies of journalism, whether in print or electronic formats. For instance, Levy and Windahl (1984) found that television viewers actively seek news (for specific information and general surveillance of the environment), but that they did not actively seek entertainment programming. Rather, entertainment seeking is more of a *ritualized* behavior that is less goal-directed and more habitual than instrumental use of media (Dozier & Rice, 1984). Television is sometimes viewed more for the process than the content, and may spark interaction with others. People differ widely in the degree to which they actively seek involvement with media, and that their degree of effort is partly related to the information versus entertainment dichotomy.

In the print realm, Donohew, Nair, and Finn (1984, pp. 279–280) suggest that news reading is preceded by a desire for entertainment seeking; that is, readers have a need for novel stimuli that first draws them to certain articles, and it is only later that what they read is integrated into their personal cognitive structure. The irony in this is that readers may be drawn toward novel (i.e., entertaining) information that, upon reading, becomes threatening to their belief structure, resulting in increased uncertainty and anxiety, and possibly more seeking of information as a further outcome.

Holmöv (1982) goes even further, claiming that the amount of news reading is largely unrelated to actual knowledge of particular news topics, and that readers of serious news may be reading entirely for the fun of it. An alternative explanation, according to Holmöv, is that readers are programmed to read for the sake of "learning," even though they may not absorb or remember what they read. In any event, it is clear that the desire to be stimulated plays a prominent role in the seeking of "news" (Finn, 1985, 1986). In fact, Ekström (2000, p. 474) characterizes journalism as a form of storytelling in which "Reality, *au naturel*, is seldom exciting enough; embellishment and exaggeration are common." Ekström (2000, p. 488) also notes, "Many viewers do not look to television primarily for information, but rather for entertainment, diversion and escape. Good stories and attractions serve these purposes well."

Dervin's (1983b) view of the mass media as information sources resembles that of Wilson:

> The picture that emerges is one that shows most citizens, educated or otherwise, essentially relying on close friends and relatives for their information. Media, primarily so-called entertainment television, make up the major portion of the information day. Use of books, newspapers, and magazines is typically low. People seek formal information sources only in a small subset of situations — when all else has failed in coping with a situation or when outside factors force them to. And current efforts to make the information more palatable evidently do not override this essential picture of a "law of least effort" operating. (p. 158)

One has only to consider what actually happens in publishing and broadcasting to realize how artificial and unfair is the sharp distinction between information and entertainment. Most books published are fiction, and one genre alone, "romances," accounts for 36% of all mass market fiction sales (Kremer, 2011). Communications researcher Reeves (1989) points out the difficulty of dichotomizing the content of information, whether in print or broadcast media:

> New information cannot be prejudged just because we are aware of the message genre it represents. It is still reasonable to assume that people judge some information as factual, some as lies, and some as fantasy; however, it is likely that these evaluations do not exactly overlap content genre. There is fact in fiction and vice versa. (p. 195)

An Associated Press (2007) poll found that, apart from the Bible, Americans read more types of fiction books than nonfiction books. So it is not surprising that most of what public libraries circulate is fiction. Richard Rubin (2010, p. 412) explains why when he says that:

> the public good recognizes people's right to enjoy life, and that the library has a role in promoting entertainment and pleasure. Certainly the presence of copious fiction, romance, travel, and popularized science and history attests to ... strong feelings about this dimension of library service.

Public libraries provide fiction because that is what their clients want, despite some ambivalence about devoting scarce resources to nonfactual materials (Rubin, 2010). Whether library clients use fiction to complete an educational assignment or for personal growth, entertainment, or escape from an unpleasant reality is not a part of the library's consideration. Fiction plays a key role in attracting people to many libraries in the first place, and that effect in itself has value.

One might imagine that university libraries eschew entertainment materials, and this is largely true. Yet consider that, at least in North American higher education, students choose academic majors based on a mix of practical ("work") and gratifying ("play") considerations. Students who choose to major in the literature of their native language do not always do so to prepare for a particular career. The minority who hope to become a faculty member in, say, English literature face intense competition for a very few positions. Most students major in literature because the subject matter is interesting, is personally satisfying, may provide an insight into human affairs, and so forth — more for reasons of personal satisfaction than for strictly utilitarian purposes.

Clearly, we learn from fiction. Experiments by psychologists Gerrig and Prentice (1991) demonstrate that "facts" in fictional readings are quickly incorporated into existing world knowledge. "Fiction may be twice as true as fact," according to Oatley (1999, p. 101) in terms of its joint effects on thinking and feeling. The emotional component in narrative is particularly compelling. Spacks (1985) points out, "Fictional characters and actions, comprehended, may teach us to understand better ... characters and actions that comprise our real-life experience" (p. 23). Ross's (1999) extended interviews with 194 heavy readers uncovered a variety of motivations having to do with personal growth: awakening to new possibilities, finding a role model, confirming self-worth, connecting with the experience of others, accepting one's self and situation, getting the courage to make a change, and so forth. Most of the motivations for reading fiction are affective, rather than cognitive, according to Ross; relevant information tends to be encountered in the text by accident, rather than design.

Although the university library provides many materials that are of an obviously factual nature — most science and mathematics fall into this realm — some portion of academic "information" certainly has "entertainment" content. Popular novels, for instance, might be useful for their literary or social content. Even a work of dubious literary value might be acquired if it becomes controversial. For example, novels by Bret Ellis, such as *Less Than Zero* (1985), *American Psycho* (1991), and *Imperial Bedrooms* (2010) are often found in university library collections. Yet reviews of these novels have variously described them as "ghastly," "impoverished," "pointless," "sensationalist," "juvenile," "boring," "mediocre," "lame," "misogynistic," and "cheesy." On the other hand, some critics have come to their defense, including Norman Mailer. Were the Ellis novels selected for research collections based on their literary value, their controversial history, their entertainment potential, their popularity, or what? Or, more likely, was it related to some combination of those factors? Curry (1994), in fact, uses Ellis's second novel as a vehicle for exploring how public libraries deal with the issue of adding controversial books to their collections, noting the interplay among the deciding factors of publicity, popular demand, and reviewers' opinions. These are also factors in university library collection decisions. We might erroneously assume that loftier educational criteria trump all of them, but they *do not*. It is too difficult to judge where information ends and entertainment begins.

Perhaps more obvious instances of the mixing of information and entertainment are media *forms* that deliberately do so to capture audience attention. Film documentaries strive to be interesting and provocative as well as informative. Educational television programming for children (e.g., *Sesame Street*) strives for visual variety to keep the young viewers' attention long enough for the *content* to be absorbed by them. Public health advocates (e.g., Brown & Childers, 2002) advocate "edutainment" approaches to health information campaigns; embedding persuasive messages in dramas, soap operas, and music videos is more likely to capture the attention of the intended audiences and to hold them long enough for the message to have an effect (Moyer-Gusé, 2008). The question for information campaigns is "What is the proper mix of education and entertainment?" (Rice & Atkin, 1994). Another example is the increasingly ubiquitous "infomercial" that tries (or at least pretends) to teach us something while selling us a related product or service.

The newspaper *USA Today* has been nicknamed "McPaper" on the grounds that, analogous to fast food, it is popular but not as nourishing as we would hope. Among the criticized aspects of *USA Today* are its colorful graphs, which often convey surprisingly little data; many of these charts use the shape of objects rather than a conventional line to represent trends in data; thus, the upward slope of a whale's back might represent increases in whale populations. The use of such graphics in the business world has provoked Tufte (1983) to condemn them as "chart junk." Tufte even attributes the loss of the *Challenger* space shuttle to a "cute" but misleading chart and a faulty graph that were influential in the decision to launch the shuttle at a low temperature.

It is not merely reading or viewing in which a mix of information and entertainment is to be found. Consider this quotation from a *Wall Street Journal* article in which various financial experts explained to the reporter why money from small investors left mutual funds and went into individual stocks during the dot-com boom:

> And don't forget the entertainment value. For many, trading stocks is a source of both pleasure and profits. "The press has played up the dot-com stocks," says Scott Greenbaum, a financial planner in Purchase, N.Y. "People want to participate. Mutual funds are pretty boring by contrast." (Clements, 1999, p. c1)

We would think that investing money and saving for retirement are behaviors too important to approach with anything less than cold-blooded rationality — but, apparently, they are not. Other types of purchasing behavior are also regarded as providing "psychological gratification" by those who study them (e.g., Belk, 1995; Bianchi, 1997b).

The converging media that comprise the Internet are following the model of the old forms we have considered above. For example, Tewksbury's (2003) analysis of World Wide Web usage suggests that the most popular WWW content for North Americans is "sports" — another category that blurs the line between "news" and "entertainment," according to Luhmann (2000). And a study by Spink, Ozmutlu, & Lorence (2004) notes that searching for sexual images is not only very common, but accounts for more time and effort on the part of users than other types of searches; is this strictly for "entertainment" or more driven by an "information need"?

This confluence of information and entertainment is so ubiquitous that we hardly notice it. The conceptual overlap is not new, but rather it is something we have typically chosen to ignore in studying information seeking. It is hard to disentangle the two concepts of information and entertainment, or even to say which comes first, as Cermak (1996, pp. 116–117) argues:

> One might argue that the concept of entertainment is broader than the concept of information in that humans can derive enjoyment from activities that have little obvious information content: playing softball or dancing. Alternatively, one can view "information" as the broader category as in cases such as seeing crossing signals at an intersection or hearing the directions to a retail store. However, often entertainment becomes a consequence of information transmission as in reading a book or listening to music where information and entertainment are inseparable.

One conclusion to take away from this discussion is this: perhaps the "most authoritative source" is not what many people prefer when seeking information; maybe they would rather have the most entertaining one. Of course, when "hard facts" are presented in an entertaining manner, we have the best of both worlds.

5.6. Sharing and Collaboration

Most of the discussion in this book takes an individual perspective: information seeking is typically the work of one person at a time. However, we know that people often work in groups, and that they actively share information among themselves even when not working toward a common goal. In fact, as will be discussed in Chapter 7, some theories (e.g., Lave and Wenger, 1991) take the group or organization as the unit of analysis and examine how communities develop practices around information gathering and dissemination.

"Sharing information" is the broadest category under consideration here. Sharing most commonly takes place between two individuals, as in a telephone conversation or an e-mail exchange. As a number of studies have shown, networks of individuals operating outside of work environments may exchange information frequently (e.g., Erdelez & Rioux, 2000; Fisher, Naumer, Durrance, Stromski, & Christiansen, 2005; McKenzie, 2003a; Pettigrew, 1999; Veinot, 2010); these are particularly present in the communities that form around leisure pursuits, such as hobbies (e.g., Case, 2010; Fulton, 2009a; Lee & Trace, 2009). However, most of the research involving sharing takes place in work environments, and focuses on collaboration in the pursuit of some common task or project. Indeed, Fidel, Pejtersen, Cleal, and Bruce (2004) point out that information seeking by multiple persons should only be labeled "collaborative" if the individuals involved *do* share a common goal, whether or not it involves employment.

As Talja and Hansen (2006) discuss, collaboration has been studied in many work contexts (see Chapter 11 for details of some of these studies). They emphasize that collaboration involves people interacting with a task or situation, and that this takes place within a social context, such as an organization. As might be imagined, prime locations for collaborative information sharing occur in knowledge-intensive work, such as health care (e.g., Nicholas, Williams, Smith, & Longbottom, 2005; Reddy & Jansen, 2008; Reddy & Spence, 2008), interdisciplinary academic research (e.g., Palmer, 1999; Palmer & Neumann, 2002), software design (e.g., Bruce et al., 2003; Fidel et al., 2004), or military command and control (e.g., Prekop, 2002; Sonnenwald, 2006; Sonnenwald & Pierce, 2000).

Several other labels are relevant to this category of studies. "Computer-Supported Cooperative Work" (CSCW) is a characterization long used by those involved in the design of information systems, and even this term has an antecedent in the 1980s development of "office automation." Yet, because sharing information does not entirely depend on using computers, other characterizations of it have come into use among information behavior researchers, including "collaborative information seeking," "distributed cognition," and "knowledge management." It is also obvious that sharing of information plays a key role in "scientific and scholarly communication" as well.

Among the many other writers discussing collaborative information seeking and sharing are Brown (2010), Choo (2007), Davenport and Hall (2002), Finholt (2002), Foster (2009), Hall (2003), Hall and Widén (2008), Hertzum (2008), Hertzum and Pejtersen (2000), Hyldegard (2009), Ipe (2003), Jaeger and Burnett (2010), Kim and Grunig (2011), Shah (2010),

Talja (2002), Whittaker (2011), Widén-Wulff (2007), Widén-Wulff and Davenport (2007), Widén-Wulff and Ginman (2004), and Wilson (2010a).

5.7. Summary

In this chapter, we have explored several peripheral concepts and behaviors, including decision making, browsing, relevance, information anxiety, information overload, knowledge gaps, information poverty, entertainment seeking, and sharing of information.

I first discussed the relationship of the decision making and problem-solving literature to information seeking, finding some parts of it relevant. Then, I moved on to consider the burgeoning number of discussions of browsing and its sibling topics, foraging and encountering.

Whenever information is actively sought, issues of relevance, pertinence, and salience arise. "Context" — a person's situation, background, and environment — partly determines one's perceptions during information seeking. Context will affect the choice of sources that are attended to and meanings that are derived.

Conditions or distractions may also emerge in the information-seeking process. There is, for example, a tendency for uncertainty to make us anxious; a feeling of uncertainty comes not only from having too little information, but from having too much information as well. In a behavior possibly related to anxiety (as a relief mechanism), or possibly unrelated (as a result of a human need for play and creativity), people tend to seek out entertainment as well as information. Often they prefer to mix fact and fiction to some degree. The desire to be entertained in turn strongly affects the type of sources to which people turn for their information.

Finally, information sharing, and especially collaborative work arrangements and the information exchanges they engender, has been an increasing focus of attention in recent years.

Now that we have been introduced to the principal notions that come into play in discussions of information seeking, we can turn to the theories and models that make use of them. The following chapters consider the models, paradigms, and theories under which information seeking has been investigated.

Recommended for Further Reading

Bryant, J. & Miron, D. (2002). Entertainment as media effect. In J. Bryant & D. Zillman (Eds), *Media effects: Advances in theory and research* (pp. 549–582). Hillsdale, NJ: Erlbaum.

Bryant and Miron provide a brief history of opinions about the role of entertainment in human affairs, and its treatment as a research topic in recent decades. They describe how the concept has been, and might be, approached by investigators of this characteristically human activity.

March, J. (1994). A primer on decision making: How decisions happen. New York, NY: Free Press.

An interesting summary of several decades worth of research on decision making, with special emphasis on the seemingly subjective and irrational aspects of decisions.

Sairanen, A. & Savolainen, R. (2010). Avoiding health information in the context of uncertainty management. *Information Research 15*(4). Retrieved from http://InformationR.net/ir/15-4/paper443.html

An example of an empirical investigation of the concepts of avoidance and uncertainty management. The authors found four strategies that were used to avoid information, including selective exposure, withdrawal from social situations where undesired information might be encountered, avoiding health care professionals, and simply not thinking about health issues.

Schwartz, B. (2004). *The paradox of choice: Why more is less.* New York, NY: ECCO.

Barry Schwartz is a professor of social theory and social action at Swarthmore College. His book is an exceptionally readable and practical summary of research on decision making — how people choose among various options.

Schwartz points out that while everyone believes that more choice is always better, empirical studies continue to show that once options go beyond a certain point, the more choices there are the more frustrated people are, the poorer decisions they make (because they skip options or get confused), and the less happy they are with the choices they make (no matter what those choices were). He includes many examples related to information behaviors.

Wurman, R. S. (1989). *Information anxiety.* New York, NY: Doubleday.

The influential graphics designer Richard Saul Wurman is noted most commonly for his Access series of travel guides. Those guides emphasize certain principles that Wurman has identified as making information easier to find and digest. For instance, the guides exploit the human preference for spatial analogies and also make highly effective use of color-coding in presenting information. In this book, Wurman explains how "data glut" and the confusions and anxiety it provokes within us have made his philosophy of design necessary.

PART 3

MODELS, PARADIGMS, AND THEORIES IN THE STUDY OF INFORMATION BEHAVIOR

Chapter 6

Models of Information Behavior

Theoretical models of information seeking must address three key issues. First, models should provide a sound theoretical basis for predicting changes in information-seeking behaviors ... Second, models should provide guidance for designing effective strategies for enhancing information seeking ... Third, models should explicitly conceptualize information seeking behavior, developing rich descriptions of it. Finally, models should answer the "why" question, they should explicitly address the underlying forces that impel particular types of information seeking.

— Johnson (1997, p. 104)

It is a widely shared notion that the aim of INS studies is to build models of information behavior which show how different factors or variables influence information seeking.

— Talja, Keso, and Pietiläinen (1999, p. 753)

Chapter Outline

6.1.   Models

Models are often said to precede the development of formal theory, which is one reason for discussing them before I address theories used to explain information behavior. As they are typically depicted in diagrams, models are also somewhat easier to grasp than formal theories for those who are new to the subject matter under investigation. However, I recognize that a good argument could be made for explaining theories first, then models; models are usually more specific than theories, dealing with the particulars of a chosen context. In some cases, models may explicitly refer to one or more theories, as is the case in the Wilson model below. Nevertheless, we will start by discussing nine of the most-cited, general models of information seeking. Each of them resembles a conventional flowchart and suggests sequences of events. They all aim to describe and explain circumstances that predict actions by individuals to find information of some kind. Following a bit of background information regarding models, each of the nine models will be depicted and explained.

6.1.1.   What is a Model?

Models typically focus on more specific problems than do theories. An example of a limited model would be one that depicts how research subjects typically navigate through a series of Web pages; such a model may not address how *all* people find information on the World Wide Web (much less how humans find information in multiple circumstances), and yet it might eventually *lead* to a theory of electronic information seeking. An instance of a limited model is Claude Shannon's depiction of signal transmission (see Chapter 3); it led to both explicit theories of the information content of messages and to vague theories about how mass media had effects on its viewers (so-called hypodermic needle theories; Klapper, 1960).

Models are often defined in relation to theories. For instance, methods text by Simon and Burstein (1985, p. 53) calls models "minitheories." More will be said about theory in the next chapter; for now let us say that a theory is a set of related statements that explain, describe, or predict phenomena in a given context. Both theories and models are simplified versions of reality, yet models typically make their content more concrete through a diagram of some sort. By illustrating casual processes, models make it easier to see if hypotheses are consistent with what we observe in real life (Reynolds, 1971). Like a theory, a model describes relationships among concepts but is tied more closely to the real world: one changes a model only after first comparing it against the real world and confirming that modifications are warranted (Cappella, 1977).

Models range from the purely pragmatic and descriptive (e.g., a flowchart of how a document moves through a bureaucratic process), to formal models that combine mathematical and pictorial logics (as found in statistical path analyses, such as that used by Sin (2011) to model the effect of socio-structural and individual factors on information behavior). Simulations, such as the use of algorithms in artificial intelligence to model certain behaviors (e.g., the perception of shapes in studies of computer vision), are also models (Cappella, 1977). Some disciplines have made extensive use of complex models; the study of consumer behavior, which is of some relevance to information seeking, developed and tested four distinct models of consumer information search and decision processes within an eight-year period (Walters, 1974).

As a means of representing and organizing complex processes, models have strengths and weaknesses (Johnson, 1997, pp. 112–113). On the positive side, the depiction of key elements makes clear the investigator's approach and selection of explanatory factors. The strength of a model to simplify one phenomenon can become a weakness when it is overgeneralized to another, dissimilar phenomenon. Shannon's model is again an apt example, as it has been applied much more broadly than was intended by its creator.

6.1.2. Models of Information Seeking

Wilson (1999a, p. 250) points out that models of information seeking typically do not embody fully formed theories:

> A model may be described as a framework for thinking about a problem and may evolve into a statement of the relationships among theoretical propositions. Most models in the general field of information behaviour are of the former variety: they are statements, often in the form of diagrams, that attempt to describe an information-seeking activity, the causes and consequences of that activity, or the relationships among stages in information-seeking behaviour.

Dozens of information seeking models have been published over the past four decades. These models vary as to their assumptions, structure, purposes, scope, and intended uses. An initial consideration is whether the model is intended to be general, or rather context-specific. More is said, below, about the portrayal of context in some models.

An initial division among models is whether they emphasis *exposure* (typically to mass media or Internet messages) rather than a proactive *seeking* of information (voluntary action based on an emerging situation or need). This is correlated with the recurring nature of needs and uses: we always need good health (although we may not pay much attention to information about maintaining it), we frequently use job-related information, yet we infrequently need many other types of information that apply only in specific situations and tasks. Thus, the models that emphasize exposure are typically those that have to do with health, and sometimes shopping – topics in which other parties try to influence our behavior. An example of such an "exposure" model for the health domain is found in Longo (2005).

Another way that models vary is in their structure. Several of the most general models resemble flowcharts, and indeed some of them use flow-charting symbols, such as the yes–no decision diamond (e.g., Donohew & Tipton, 1973; Freimuth, Stein, & Kean, 1989). Flowchart models tend to be focused on information processing and decision-making, and give less attention to contextual and personal variables and types of sources and actions. They also tend to be unambiguous, with a deterministic sequence of actions from which any deviation is not depicted. Because they deal with repeated comparisons, decisions and actions, they may incorporate feedback loops to show the need to repeat certain sequences.

The degree to which models specify actions and channels or sources that might be used in information seeking, and outcomes that follow from that seeking (or avoiding), is another dimension of variation. That is, some models simply "end" with a box or circle that says "information seeking" or "search" (or "stop" if current information is considered adequate); the aforementioned Donohew and Freimuth models are examples of this feature, as well as the health-related models of Afifi and Weiner (2006), Griffin, Dunwoody, and Neuwrith (1999), ter Huurne, Griffen, and Gutteling (2009), and Kahlor (2010). In contrast, other models suggest how that search might occur, or at least what kinds of channels and sources it might involve (Longo, 2005; Miller & Jablin, 1991; Niedwiedzka, 2003). And some models go further to describe outcomes of that seeking, such as states of physical and psychological health (e.g., Czaja, Manfredi, & Price, 2003; Longo, 2005).

A third dividing point among the information seeking models is whether they are truly "testable" (e.g., through quantitative measures and statistical correlational techniques such as path analysis, or via systematic gathering and analysis of qualitative data). How do we know that the model reflects reality for at least some people, and is not simply the idiosyncratic view of one author? What evidence could we gather to decide whether the model is valid?

Some of the models, particularly in the health arena, are intended to be the basis for measures that would lend themselves to statistical testing or modeling; see, for example, Afifi and Weiner (2006), Czaja, Manfredi, and Price (2003), and Johnson and Meischke (1993). In contrast, other models are more of a picture of potential factors to consider in qualitative studies of information seeking; these may, or may not, be testable is some fashion. A two-part (e.g., quantitative–qualitative) division among these models is not quite that clear cut (e.g., Sin's, 2011 chapter about students' use of public libraries uses statistical testing in an unusual combination of quantitative and qualitative data). Yet one can see that some authors have very specific types of measures or observations in mind, while others simply suggest that certain types of factors should be studied in some way.

There are undoubtedly other ways that models could be characterized, e.g., by degree of parsimony. The main point of this introduction is that models vary along several dimensions, not the least of which is the terminology they employ, and at times it is even difficult to compare them.

This chapter will feature nine models, roughly in chronological order: Wilson (1981), Krikelas (1983), Ellis (1989, 1993), Kuhlthau (1991, 2004a), Byström and Järvelin (1995), Leckie, Pettigrew, and Sylvain (1996), Savolainen (1995), Johnson (1997), and Wilson (1999a). Wilson has published several versions of his model, of which I will use the earliest (1981) and latest (1999a; originally published 1996) to show how his thinking has developed. Some of these models are also discussed by Järvelin and Wilson (2003), Godbold (2006), and Ikoja-Odongo and Mostert (2006).

These models chosen for discussion are more fully developed and/or more widely used than most others. The major criterion for inclusion here is that the model *attempts to depict and explain a sequence of behavior* by referring to relevant variables, rather than merely indicates a sequence of events. For instance, the "flow model of information seeking, avoiding, and processing" by Donohew and Tipton (1973) – perhaps the earliest attempt to model information seeking – depicts sequences of events but does not identify important influences (e.g., demographic, task, contextual, or psychological variables). The authors explicitly say that their model was not intended to be used for designing investigations of information seeking.

The models depicted are of a middle-level of generality, as well. This has to do with how specific they are: they suggest enough potential processes and variables to guide the design of an investigation; on the other hand, they are still *simplified* versions of reality, and do not attempt to depict every possible influence or process.

A few examples of each side of this divide will help to explain what I mean by middle-level of generality – although it is clear that recent authors have been much more tempted to complicate rather than simplify. On the ultra-simplified end we have Foster's (2004) "nonlinear model of information seeking behavior," for example, which consists of a triangle of "core processes" (Opening, Orientation, and Consolidation) encompassed by two squares, the inner representing "intrinsic context" surrounded by "extrinsic context." While this makes sense in the context of Foster's original study, it is too general to guide research without further explanation and specification. Foster's model has undergone at least two revisions, the latest being an extension by Foster, Urquhart, and Turner (2008).

There are many examples of the overly complex variety, and these are often the result of attempts to combine and align the various other models mentioned here – a melding which never quite works, because it mixes together different levels of abstraction and varieties of observable concepts, often ignoring the intent of the original authors. Some examples include: Godbold's (2006) series of figures that combine, in various combinations, diagrams by Dervin, Wilson, Ellis, Kuhlthau, and others; and Niedwiedzka's (2003) recasting of Wilson's model to include "context" (in the form of personal, role-related, and environmental intervening variables) cascading in from the top to influence the other 11 features of the model. Niedzwiedzka's is one of the better attempts to reflect "context" by placing it outside the rest of the model and indicating that it consists of certain intervening variables. Most other authors of models really do not specify what they mean by context, and how it affects the other processes and variables in the model. That makes for difficulties in implementing and testing the suitability of the underlying model in an actual study.

I have included two models (by Ellis, and by Leckie et al.) that have been extended by others beyond their original, limited audiences of study. Otherwise these are mostly *general* models, in terms of the breadth of populations, roles and tasks they are meant to apply to. It is often the case that information seeking models are narrowly focused along some dimension – usually by task, discipline, or job. For example, the models proposed by Ingwersen (1996) and Marchionini (1995, p. 59) are meant to apply to a particular *task*, typically searching electronic information in databases or online library catalogs. The models of Voigt (1961), Menzel (1964), Paisley (1968), and Orr (1970) were intended specifically to portray the information seeking of scientists. The "addressing information needs" model of Hernon (1984) was been used to study social scientists. The model of Baldwin and Rice (1997) was meant to apply to security analysts – surely a tiny population. Miller and Jablin's model applies to new employees of (apparently large) organizations. These are all worthwhile models for the audiences they examine.

Similarly there are many models that focus only on health information, usually related to "risks" (e.g., cancer or HIV/AIDS, and behaviors that might contribute to developing those diseases). Among the more general of these are Kahlor's "Planned Risk Information Seeking Model" (2010) and Longo's "Expanded Conceptual Model of Health Information Seeking Behaviors" (2005), which applies to the "information seeking of patients and consumers." The latter model is useful in identifying 5 contextual factors and 10 types of personal variables that influence the seeking of health information, and illustrating the contingent nature of exposure to information (i.e., we can be aware without attending to information, or access information but choose not to use it). McKenzie's (2003a) four-mode by two-phase table of information practices was developed in the context of studying women with multiple pregnancies. While applicable to nonhealth contexts, the "interacting" phase seems to imply only to situations in which interpersonal sources are used.

There are many other models specifically geared toward health information and behaviors. Some are mentioned in Section 6.2.9. All of them refer to a risk assessment or health problem, rather than general information seeking.

6.2.   Examples of Information Seeking Models

6.2.1.   The First Wilson Model

A series of models by Wilson (1981, 1994, 1997, 1999a) reflects trends in the theory and practice of information seeking research. Their evolution makes them particularly interesting to analyze and compare with those of other researchers.

The Wilson models examined here have appeared in their current forms fairly recently, even though they are based on diagrams originally published in 1981. The first model (Figure 6.1) identifies 12 components, starting with the "information user" – although Wilson makes clear that he is interested in much more than "use" itself.

Wilson's information user has a need, which may (or may not) stem from his or her level of satisfaction (or dissatisfaction) with previously acquired information. Wilson suggests that the perceived need then leads the user into a cluster of activities, the most straightforward of which is to make direct demands on sources or systems of information. The results of these demands lead either to success (in which case the information is "used") or to failure, which is presumed to be a dead end, as information that is not "found" cannot be used. It is odd, however, that "failure" of "demands on other information sources" are not depicted as directly feeding back to "need" by way of another arrow.

An important aspect of Wilson's model is the recognition that information is exchanged with other people (a process he calls information transfer) in the course of information use and seeking behaviors. As he points out, relatively little attention has been paid to informal transfer of

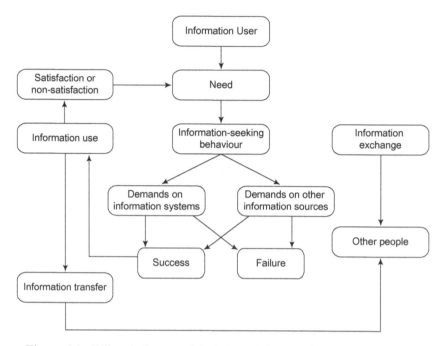

Figure 6.1: Wilson's first model. Adapted from: Wilson, T. D. (1999). Models in information behaviour research. *Journal of Documentation, 55*(3), 249–270.

information among individuals. But other people are an important source of information in many circumstances, even during direct interaction with a formal system such as a library.

In describing his model, Wilson acknowledges its limits:

> [I]t does little more than provide a map of the area and draw attention to gaps in research; it provides no suggestion of causative factors in information behaviour and, consequently, it does not directly suggest hypotheses to be tested. (1981, pp. 251–252)

6.2.2.   The Krikelas Model

Provided here partly for its historical value is the early and widely cited model of James Krikelas (1983). In addition to being one of the first explicit depictions of information seeking, Krikelas' model was prescient in emphasizing both the importance of uncertainty as a motivating factor, and of the potential for an information seeker to retrieve an answer from their own memory or those of nearby persons. The Krikelas model contains 13 components. The causal process generally flows downward, with some provision for feedback loops. In describing his model, Krikelas asks us to ...

> imagine a situation in which a person becomes aware of a state of uncertainty about a problem (question, issue) and attempts to reduce that state of uncertainty to an acceptable level. The cause of that uncertainty may be a specific event or simply an ongoing process associated with work, ordinary life, or both. Naturally, for many issues much of the information required would already exist in the individual's memory; only a small part of a person's ongoing needs would produce an outward behavior that we might identify as information seeking. Furthermore the level of "urgency" and the perceived importance of the problem ... would influence the pattern of information seeking.

The Krikelas model (Figure 6.2) thus claims to be a general one that would apply to "ordinary life." At the top of the model (implying a beginning) are the twin actions of "information gathering" and "information giving." The activities of information gathering come about in response to deferred needs, which in turn have been stimulated by an event or the general environment of the seeker.

Krikelas sees any attempt to isolate individual elements of the environment as "hopeless." The results of information gathering are directed to memory or, in physical form, to some kind of personal file or other storage mechanism. Thus, information gathering is the acceptance and holding of "stimuli ... in storage to be recalled on demand. Such efforts may have a purpose (directed but not problem-specific)" (p. 9).

Yet, as revealed in his discussion, what Krikelas mainly has in mind are efforts to keep up with literature relevant to one's work – which is a more specific, occupation-oriented version of information seeking than we would prefer to see. But his model at least does not restrict itself to one type of occupation. For Krikelas, information gathering *does* have a more general and less formal purpose too, which he describes as "an attempt to continually construct a cognitive environmental 'map' to facilitate the need to cope with uncertainty" (p. 9). Hence, Krikelas identifies uncertainty as a key concept.

Information giving is defined as "the act of disseminating messages [which] may be communicated in written (graphic), verbal, visual, or tactile forms" (p. 13). About *information giving* Krikelas says little, except to point out that individuals are typically both senders and receivers of information, and that neither role is independent of the other.

As aforementioned, information gathering comes about because of an environment or event that creates needs. Some of these needs can be

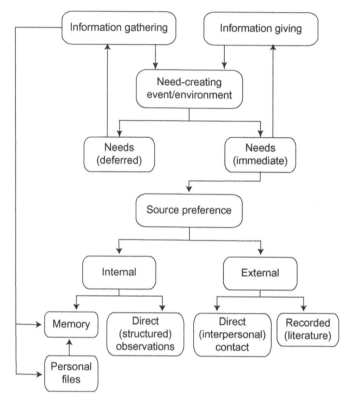

Figure 6.2: The Krikelas model. Adapted from page 13 of Krikelas, J. (1983). Information seeking behavior: Patterns and concepts. *Drexel Library Quarterly, 19,* 5–20. Used with permission of the College of Information Science and Technology, Drexel University, Philadelphia, PA.

deferred, which leads to storage in memory and/or physical media, while other needs are immediate, or at least are dealt with as though they were urgent. To meet an information need, the searcher is assumed to consciously select a source. As Krikelas describes in his scenario, the source could be *internal* (i.e., oneself) or *external* (other people – communicated with through some kind of medium).

Although Krikelas makes a hard distinction between "direct (interpersonal) contact" and "recorded (literature)," it is important to realize that today's expanded media environment blurs such boundaries. Although the main and preferred source of information for people is still likely to be face-to-face conversation, "direct contact" could occur over a telephone or a videophone, or by way of e-mail, voicemail, or a videotape as well. Krikelas undoubtedly had in mind the main kind of "recorded" material one found in libraries two decades ago (books and journals), but the increased ease of asynchronous interpersonal communication makes the distinction between "recorded" and "live" difficult. Even the issue of what kind of human communication is truly interactive is a complex one (Durlak, 1987).

One appealing aspect of the Krikelas model is its simplicity. The model is a simple, one-dimensional flowchart in which all of the arrows travel in one direction (i.e., there are no two-way influences among the boxes) and no one part of the process encompasses another.

Of course, simplicity implies oversimplification, and leads us to some comments and questions about the model (see also Henefer & Fulton, 2005). The environment could be depicted as surrounding the other factors, rather than appearing as a box in the middle of them. The manner in which "information giving" is depicted as separate from "sources" seems odd. Would not those persons and objects that impart information be considered sources? Likewise, it is unclear whether "personal files" can also include "recorded literature" as well as notes made by oneself – one would assume so. Therefore, it seems like a distinction is being made between a formal information system (such as a library) and an informal one (such as the contents of an individual's home or office). It is also notable that *characteristics of the seeker* are not considered in the model. Demographic variables such as age or education might affect information seeking; perhaps these could be considered to be a part of the "need-creating environment."

Although the Krikelas model could be applied to ordinary life, it nevertheless retains the flavor of a "library search model" in the way it seems to depict the decision points along the path to either the reference desk (Immediate Need-External Source-Librarian) or the library collection (Immediate Need-External Source-Stacks). Perhaps it is more applicable to the information seeking of students or professionals in some work-oriented context. The Krikelas model *does* have the virtues of simplicity and comprehensiveness: it emphasizes the important roles of one's own memory and of information received from others, along with the formal sources typically emphasized in such models. It continues to be cited in the information behavior literature, for example by Baker, Wilson, Nordstrom, and Legwand (2007), Godbold (2006), and Ikoja-Odongo and Mostert (2006).

6.2.3. The Ellis Model

Ellis (1989) did not depict his model as a diagram, but rather described it in a series of paragraphs. He has been careful to point out that it is not meant to indicate a fixed sequence of events, but instead, the order of actions might vary and be iterative as well. Developed using a grounded theory approach, the model first appeared in a study of university-based social scientists. Later it was used in an investigation of physicists and chemists (Ellis, Cox, & Hall, 1993), and later applied to engineers and scientist in industry (Ellis & Haugan, 1997). Others have used in studies of humanities scholars (e.g., Bronstein, 2007). As it has been applied in different contexts, it has come to be associated with Wilson's (1999) figure depicted here.

Ellis' model initially featured six types of activities and later added the two final actions described below (Figure 6.3):

- Starting: the initial search for information in which potentially relevant sources are identified.
- Chaining: following (backwards or forwards) chains of citations or other types of connections among materials.
- Browsing: semi-directed search in areas of potential interest, such as scanning tables of contents, indices, and subject headings.
- Differentiating: assessing and filtering sources by examining differences in nature and quality.
- Monitoring: maintaining awareness of developments in a given subject area by regular checking of key sources.
- Extracting: systematic examination of a particular source to extract material of interest.
- Verifying: checking that information (e.g., data and citations) is correct.
- Ending: additional seeking at the end of a project, e.g., a final search of literature.

In various publications (e.g., Ellis, 2005) Ellis and his colleagues provide many specific examples of what they mean by these actions. The model has been extended by Meho and Tibbo (2003) in another study of social scientists, and by Bronstein (2007) in an investigation of Jewish Studies scholars. Thivant (2005) also makes use of portions of the model in studying economists and business analysts.

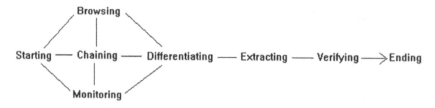

Figure 6.3: The Ellis model. Adapted from: Wilson, T. D. (1999). Models of information behaviour research. *Journal of Documentation, 55*(3), 249–270.

Järvelin and Wilson (2003) point out the applicability of the Ellis model to many empirical situations, and imply that using it in multiple studies across different domains might reveal contrasting patterns that could be further investigated; however, they fault it for not suggesting more explicit causative factors that might directly explain seeking behaviors.

6.2.4. The Kuhlthau Model

The model of "Information Search Process" by Carol Kuhlthau (1991) is universally applicable to any domain. Based on theories of learning, it depicts a series of cognitive and affective stages or behaviors through which people are thought to move as they find and evaluate information. As Wilson (1999a, p. 254) points out, Kuhlthau's model attempts a different level of analysis than the other models in focus here. Her model does not consider some factors and variables generally considered in information seeking research (e.g., the type of need and what sort of information or other "help" might satisfy it); or the availability of sources and their characteristics. Her focus is on the feelings, thoughts, and actions that follow as a person becomes aware of a gap in their knowledge. Kuhlthau's model has been cited nearly a thousand times in the academic literature.

The Kuhlthau model (Figure 6.4) includes seven stages, moving from left to right as a time sequence. At the extreme left of the model (the beginning) is the stage of "initiation," in which a person becomes aware of uncertainty or lack of knowledge about something. This is the birth of an information need, as the person identifies what is missing in their knowledge. The stage that follows is "selection," in which we select the topic we are pursuing and how to

Model of the Information Search Process						
	Initiation	Selection	Exploration	Formulation	Collection	Presentation	Assessment
Feelings (Affective)	Uncertainty	Optimism	Confusion Frustration Doubt	Clarity	Sense of direction / Confidence	Satisfaction or Disappointment	Sense of accomplishment
Thoughts (Cognitive)	vague ⟶			focused	increased	interest	Increased self-awareness
Actions (Physical)	seeking	relevant Exploring	information ⟶	seeking	pertinent Documenting	information	

Figure 6.4: The Kuhlthau model. Adapted from: Kuhlthau, C. (1993b). A principle of uncertainty for information seeking. *Journal of Documentation, 49*, 339–355.

approach it. At this point one assesses one's own degree of interest, necessary tasks, and available resources (time, relevant information), and tends to be optimistic about the process and outcome. In the third stage, "exploration," feelings of doubt and confusion may arise, as sources are explored and the information search becomes difficult to frame or express to information systems or other persons. At this point some seekers may abandon their effort to expand their understanding. The fourth stage is "formulation," a time when focus is sharpened and clarity of purpose may be achieved. At this point the search may narrow and confidence in the outcome tends to return. Stage five is "collection," when effort is focused on gathering, digesting, and recording the most relevant information on the topic. At the sixth stage, "presentation," one is able to use the retrieved information to answer the initial question or complete the task (e.g., a report for school or work). Any further searching at this stage is likely to turn up redundant information. Finally, a seventh stage may be "assessment" of what one has accomplished, leading to improved self-awareness and esteem (Figure 6.4).

Kuhlthau's model is based on many years of research, mainly with students. She identifies uncertainty as a key concept, and emphasizes the role that emotions (such as frustration or doubt) play in motivating the search for information. It is distinct from the other models shown here in that it focuses on actions, cognitions, and emotions that take place during a search, while not offering a general explanation of the "before" and "after" of the sequence. That is, the model does not depict any contextual factors leading to the recognition of an information need (e.g., school or work or everyday life demands and curiosities), nor does it follow the actions out to their specifics (e.g., types of sources considered and pursued). While general in its statements, the model has been applied mostly in education, and mostly with imposed queries (see Gross, 2001).

6.2.5.   The Leckie Model

The model by Leckie et al. (1996) resembles the Krikelas model in its limitation to a range of people – in this case, "professionals." It features six factors connected by arrows, all but one of them unidirectional (i.e., "outcomes" and "characteristics of information needs" influence each other in mutual fashion). The Leckie model is depicted as flowing from top to bottom (Figure 6.5). The causal process begins on the top with "work roles," which in turn influence "tasks."

The meaning of some of the terms is not explained in very much depth in the accompanying text, although some of their significance can be inferred from the authors' review of other studies (seemingly the main objective of their article) and their discussion of commonalities among those studies.

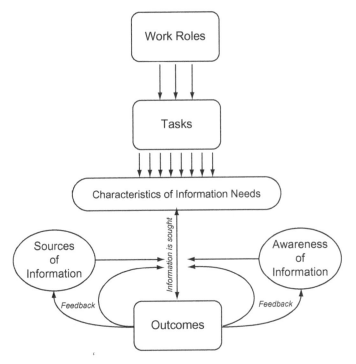

Figure 6.5: The Leckie, Pettigrew, and Sylvain model. Adapted from
Leckie, G., Pettigrew, K., & Sylvain, C. (1996). Modeling the information
seeking of professionals: A general model derived from research on engineers,
health care professionals and lawyers. *Library Quarterly, 66,* 161–193.

Given that the Leckie model is restricted to "professionals" (such as
doctors, lawyers, and engineers), it is not surprising that "work roles" and
"tasks" are thought to be the prime motivators for seeking. Although
individual demographics (age, profession, specialization, career stage, and
geographic location) are not depicted in the model itself, they are said to be
"variables that influence or shape the information needs," along with certain
aspects of the need itself. The latter include the context, frequency, predictability, importance, and complexity of the need situation. Because
the emphasis is on the facts of working life, *beliefs* or *attitudes* are seemingly
less relevant than they are in the Johnson model (which considers health
information among the general population), so their role is not discussed
(Figure 6.5).

In the Leckie et al. model, needs create an awareness of information
sources and/or content, and thus motivate a person to examine those. Here,
the most important variables are thought to be the familiarity and prior

success with the source (or the search strategy employed), along with the trustworthiness, packaging, timeliness, cost, quality, and accessibility of the source(s).

The Leckie et al. model depicts information seeking behavior itself as a two-way arrow labeled "information is sought." The end results of information seeking, labeled "outcomes," affect most other aspects of the model through feedback loops to "sources," "awareness," and "information is sought."

The diagram by Leckie, Pettigrew, and Sylvain is clearly intended to feature *work-related* processes. Thus, it has somewhat limited applicability to everyday life information seeking.

6.2.6. The Byström and Järvelin Model

The Byström and Järvelin model (Figure 6.6) has been cited in the information retrieval literature as a useful way of thinking about the way in which information users operate (see, e.g., Byström, 2005; Ingwersen & Järvelin, 2005; Vakkari, 1999). Their model was based on earlier work by Colin Mick and others (e.g., Mick, Lindsey, & Callahan, 1980). Byström and Järvelin's use of their model in an empirical study drew attention to the importance of "task complexity" in information seeking; that is, that how an information seeker proceeds depends on the degree to which they see the task as complicated. Complex tasks are those for which a person lacks an adequate "mental model" that would enable them to judge exactly what needs to be done, or to evaluate information efficiently; such tasks are quite distinct from those of a routine variety. Byström and Järvelin's painstaking study of 14 civil servants demonstrated that as the complexity of a task increases, needs grow for more complex information, for more information about the problem domain and problem solving; the successfulness of information seeking tends to decrease with complexity.

The model is structured as a feedback loop. It begins with the task as perceived by the user, and the personal factors (e.g., education, experience, attitude, motivation, and mood) and situational factors (e.g., time available for performing the task) affecting the user. These factors affect how the user determines what information is needed, and then what actions (such as selection of a source) he or she takes to satisfy the need. Once a course of action has been chosen and implemented, the results are evaluated for sufficiency and pertinancy; the evaluation tends to fall into one of the three categories: roughly "the search is done," "the search is impossible," or "I need to continue searching." This evaluation feeds back into the determination of needs, yet is mediated by the user's personal style of seeking, which also affects the user's choice of actions to implement before results are obtained and evaluated. As with the personal factors, seeking

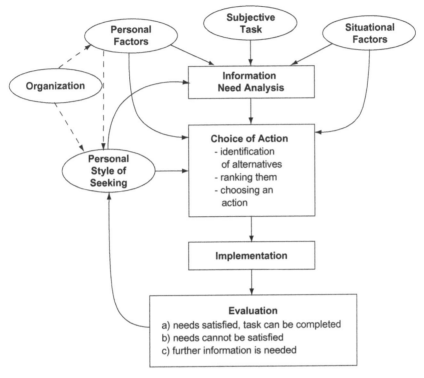

Figure 6.6: The Byström and Järvelin model. Adapted from: Byström, K., & Järvelin, K. (1995). Task complexity affects information seeking and use. *Information Processing & Management, 31*, 191–213.

style is also affected by the organization in which the user works. Järvelin and Wilson (2003) point out that the model ignores any characteristics of the person, other than level of expertise.

6.2.7. The Savolainen Model

Savolainen's model of Everyday Life Information Seeking (ELIS) was developed in the course of his interviews with ordinary citizens pursuing "nonwork" activities. The typical emphasis on work-related actions in information behavior research has tended to neglect the kinds of things that we do in our daily lives, such as shopping, taking care of our homes, and pursuing our hobbies and other personal interests. As Savolainen points out, working and nonworking information seeking are not exclusive of one another, but rather are often complementary.

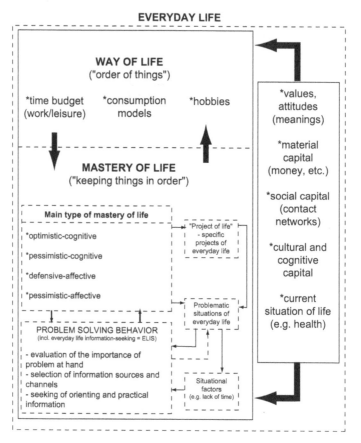

Figure 6.7: The Savolainen model. Adapted from: Savolainen, R. (1995). Everyday life information seeking: Approaching information seeking in the context of 'way of life.' *Library and Information Science Research, 17,* 259–294.

   This ELIS model (Figure 6.7) emphasizes, as Savolainen says, "the role of social and cultural factors that affect people's way of preferring and using information sources" (2005, p. 143). In this respect Savolainen's model is more sociological than the others, as it incorporates concepts such as social capital and cognitive capital, and considers economic factors such as one's wealth. Thus, Savolainen's empirical studies have considered how socio-economic class affects one's media consumption. It might also be said to consider a longer time frame in human lives, as Savolainen is ultimately concerned with what he calls the "mastery of life" – the ways in which we identify projects, budget our time, "keep order" in, and make sense of, our lives. In this latter factor it is quite different from the typical model that is meant to be applied to a series of actions in a more limited time frame, e.g., research on a particular topic, or work on a special project. While several information behavior studies have drawn on the ELIS model (e.g., Fisher, Durrance, & Hinton, 2004), its emphasis on the broad scope of human lives and values is more reminiscent of work outside of our field by scholars such as Csikszentmihalyi (1990) and Mick and Buhl (1992).

While less like a conventional flowchart than the other models, the ELIS components nevertheless are similar to those in earlier examples. It includes, for example, personal facts such as values, attitudes, and psychological orientation toward life (optimistic versus pessimistic, cognitive versus affect), and a variety of situational factors like available time and current state of health. The model is less of a depiction of a casual process than a list of important concepts that must be explored in an in-depth interview.

6.2.8. *The Johnson Model*

Johnson's model contains seven factors under three headings. It is pictured as a causal process that flows from left to right (Figure 6.8), beginning with four "antecedent" factors under two categories. The significance of Johnson's model components is not obvious in its depiction, but rather is explained in depth in his writings (e.g., 1997). Therefore, I will need to say somewhat more about this model than the others.

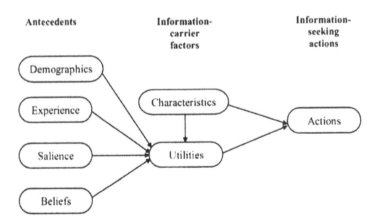

Figure 6.8: The Johnson model. Adapted from: Johnson, J. D., & Meischke, H. (1993). A comprehensive model of cancer-related information seeking applied to magazines. *Human Communication Research, 19*, 343–367.

In Johnson's model, it is the antecedent factors that motivate a person to seek information. The first two are grouped together under the label of *background* factors. One factor is *demographics*: one's age, gender, and ethnicity, along with socioeconomic variables like education, occupation, and wealth. Historically, such demographic variables are the mainstay of social research, which tries to find patterns among the behaviors, beliefs, and attitudes of populations based on correlations with such demographic variables. In any consumer-oriented research, dividing a population by such variables is referred to as *audience segmentation*.

In certain contexts such information may be useful in characterizing and predicting information use, such as gender differences in the context of health information. However, Johnson points out that characterizing information usage on the basis of ethnicity is problematic, because of both overlapping group membership and within-group differences. Dervin's (1989) arguments also cast some doubt on the usefulness of any demographic categories in stereotyping the search for information.

A background factor far more difficult to characterize is one's *direct experience* in relation to the domain of interest. The concept of experience brings us into issues of knowledge representation and memory that are too complex to consider here; suffice it to say that typically one starts out knowing *something* – perhaps little or a great deal – about the phenomenon of interest, as well as about the ways in which one can find out information about it. Thus, a key concept under the heading of experience is the *social network* of the individual with an information need: who do I know who might know the answer to my questions, or know how to find out? For example, Johnson focuses on information about cancer, and thus a prime determinant of knowledge is "who do I know who has had cancer?" A majority of families are touched by the disease in some way, and the occurrence of cancer in one member of the family often motivates other family members to seek information about treatment, so cancer information has high levels of social significance.

Just as the first and second factors are grouped together, the third and fourth fall under the heading of *personal relevance*. These include *beliefs* about the topic and the *salience* of information about the topic. Both are dependent on a person's degree of knowledge – or, conversely, on their state of ignorance – about the topic.

Johnson makes an important distinction about ignorance when he asserts that it is different from "ignoring, which often happens when an individual consciously knows that a problem exists, but chooses not to confront it" (p. 56). This is because ignorance by itself is not typically a motivator for information seeking. People are only motivated to seek information when they both know that they are ignorant *and* the missing information becomes salient. As noted earlier, sometimes people prefer to be ignorant, particularly in matters of health. A confounding problem is that we often believe information that turns out to be flawed; these kind of *false truths* can suppress or distort information seeking.

The concept of *salience* implies that information is not only perceived to be relevant to a need, but that it is also applicable. In Dervin's terms, information that is salient is that which could be used to bridge a gap, solve a problem, or resolve a troublesome ambiguity. Thus salience is the key motivator in deciding to look for information (Johnson, 1997, p. 72).

Beliefs are important in information seeking because they constrain the individual's thinking and level of motivation regarding information seeking. The beliefs that people have about the world and themselves determine the answers to questions like: "Is there is a problem?" "Is there a solution?" and "Can I change my situation?" Beliefs are not only about facts, but also about our relation to the current situation: our degree of control over events, our self-efficacy. If we do not believe that knowing more about a topic will allow us to affect a change, then we are not likely to seek information. Conversely, feeling that we can solve a problem will motive us to find the means to do so – which includes gathering information.

The second column of Johnson's model, *information carrier factors*, encompasses the factors that have preoccupied many older studies of information seeking: the *characteristics* and *utility* of the information channels selected and used by seekers. As Johnson highlights (p. 101), what information seekers are concerned about is the content of the information, not the channel through which it arrives. So the academic preoccupation with the nature of sources and why people select them has been criticized by Dervin (1989) and others as distracting attention from the user of information and their particular needs, which typically do not map neatly onto individual channels or sources. In addition, channels have proliferated greatly due to the development of new media.

The literature that defines a "channel" is often confusing. The primary distinction usually made among the older typologies is between interpersonal (face-to-face interactions with other people) and mediated (print and mass media). Where something like e-mail would fall within such a dichotomy is debatable: it is mediated by a technology, yet can be very much like a personal conversation. In a similar vein is the telephone, which Johnson discusses as a "hybrid" of interpersonal and mediated channels. We will examine the channel classification problem further in other chapters.

For now it is important to note that in almost any information seeking context there is a strong preference for information that comes directly from other people. Use of other channels tends to be predicted by the *social presence* they offer, that is, how much they are perceived as being like a face-to-face conversation with another person, or as Johnson puts it "the extent to which they reveal the presence of other human interactants and can capture the human, feeling side of relationships" (Johnson, 1997, p. 92).

Johnson says relatively little about the *utility* of channels. His main point is that channels are selected on the basis of their match with the seeker's needs, and with expectations regarding likely satisfactions to be obtained. For research on the choice of print media, potential utility is equated with "interest, usefulness and importance for achieving one's goals" (p. 100). One might choose to read a book for advice on health, for example, because it is expected to offer information that friends are unlikely to have. Johnson cites studies suggesting, however, that ease of accessibility often wins out over authoritativeness (the latter implying, apparently, better utility); the public still receives much of their health information in watered-down form from the mass media, despite the availability of health professionals to answer their questions and despite the general preference (noted earlier) for interpersonal channels.

The final component of Johnson's model is *information seeking actions.* Searches for information involve conscious choices among channels and sources, but also imply processes, feelings and a whole host of other behavioral and cognitive elements. Even simple choices among channels and sources may be characterized by the number chosen and the depth to which they were examined. Thus, the study of actions taken by any one individual in quest of information is likely to be involved and result in a unique case study from which generalization is difficult.

Johnson seems to adopt a sense-making perspective when discussing information seeking. He describes, for example, how all information seeking takes places within a context and must be understood as influenced by context. He also notes the fuzziness of the concept of *context* itself. Following Dervin, Johnson asserts that information seeking begins only when a person perceives a gap in his or her existing knowledge. At that point, seeking actions begin and the factors in the model begin to apply.

Johnson's empirical tests of his model (e.g., Johnson & Meischke, 1993) for both health and decision-making, point out both the importance of context and the difficulty of modeling information seeking. With some audiences and tasks, for example, the antecedent variables had little influence on actions taken; in others their effects were significant. Data gathered on channel selection suggest that in many cases one channel may substitute for another; thus the characteristics of channels may be less important than scholars have previously thought. Among a group of engineers the motivational issues are perhaps less driven by problem than by role: information seeking is an end in itself because it is an activity expected of certain individuals in a social system.

Johnson also notes that among the more general difficulties inherent in studying the actions people take when they look for information is a distinction between *active* and *passive* acquisition. It is difficult, if not impossible, to know whether someone has found information in their environment (active acquisition) or, instead, has retrieved it from memory (passive acquisition).

Johnson concludes that his model might possibly be improved through the inclusion of feedback loops between actions and antecedents. Antecedent factors continue to shape the searching actions as they proceed, while actions may simultaneously modify the nondemographic antecedent factors of experience, belief, and salience. That is, "information seeking is clearly a dynamic process, with an individual's level of knowledge changing as it goes on," along with the perception of the gap.

An important consideration in Johnson's model is that it has been the basis for empirical research, and has been tested in health communication studies funded by the United States National Institutes of Health. It has also been applied in other health-related contexts, such as cancer genetics. Although it is a very general model intended to apply to adult populations, it is less applicable to *work* situations. However, another book by Johnson (1996) discusses information seeking research within work organizations and suggests ways that his model can be used in such settings.

6.2.9. The Second Wilson Model

The second of Wilson's models (1999, pp. 256–257), presented below, is based on another of his diagrams from 1981, this time emphasizing the complex *context* of information seeking (a la Dervin). Wilson identified the factors in this model in research from other fields, including "decision making, psychology, innovation, health communication and consumer research" (p. 256).

Wilson's second model is a complex one (Figure 6.9). It invokes explicit theories at points to explain the following three aspects of information seeking:

- Why some needs prompt information seeking more so than others (stress/coping theory, from psychology).
- Why some sources of information are used more than others (risk/reward theory, from consumer research).
- Why people may, or may not, pursue a goal successfully, based on their perceptions of their own efficacy (social learning theory, from psychology).

We might think of Wilson's "activating mechanisms" as motivators: What motivates a person to search for information, and how and to what extent? These motivators are affected by intervening variables of six types: psychological predispositions (e.g., tending to be curious, or averse to risk);

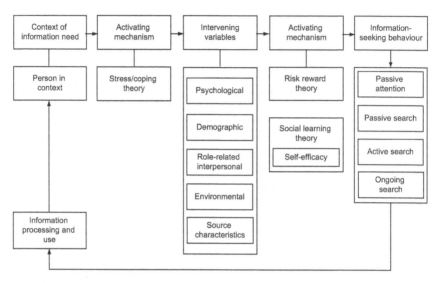

Figure 6.9: Wilson's second model. Adapted from: Wilson, T. D. (1999).
Models in information behaviour research. *Journal of Documentation,*
55(3), 249–270.

demographic background (e.g., age or education); factors related to one's social role (e.g., whether one is acting as a manager or a mother); environmental variables (e.g., the resources available); and characteristics of the sources (e.g., accessibility and credibility).

An important aspect of Wilson's new model is that it recognizes that there are different types of search behaviors: passive attention, passive search, active search, and ongoing search. These differentiations parallel comments made earlier in the book regarding different modes of information seeking: simply being exposed to relevant information versus actively looking for it. By "information processing and use" Wilson implies that the information is evaluated as to its effect on need, and forms part of a feedback loop that may start the process of seeking all over again if the need is not satisfied.

Niedwiedzka (2003) offers a detailed analysis and criticism of Wilson's second model, and proposes several modifications. Among other problems, Niedwiedzka points out that Wilson's graphic separation of "the context" from the person, the intervening variables and features of the information sources, does not make complete sense – as those things form part of the context – and that the activating mechanisms are in operation not only at the point in which a decision is made to seek information, but also at all the other stages. As Niedwiedzka points out, it would be better to name the activating mechanisms like "stress" or "perception of risk" rather than refer to theories about those mechanisms. Yet, as with the other figures, it is difficult to depict the complexities of such realities in a two-dimensional drawing, and attempts to incorporate "context" into models are not always helpful (see the discussion in Section 6.2.11).

6.2.10. Comparing the Models

Given their differences in vocabulary, emphasis, and age, the nine models we have reviewed are difficult to compare in great detail. Obviously they differ in many respects from one another. To start with, eight of them (Ellis, Krikelas, Kuhlthau, Leckie et al., Savolainen, Byström, and Järvelin, and the two by Wilson) come from the literature of information studies, whereas the other one (Johnson) originates from the discipline of communication. There are other differences that stem from the intended applications of the models.

The Krikelas model is simple, straightforward, and widely recognized, yet also somewhat limited in its emphasis on documents (literature and personal files). It shows its age in that it privileges document and/or library usage ("recorded literature"). One of the model's contributions was placing the use of literature in the context of other sources of information, such as other people and one's own observations and memories.

The first Wilson model, in contrast, does not explicitly refer to documents as sources but rather refers to "systems," "sources," and "people" – making it more general than that of Krikelas. The Wilson model was intended to illustrate the broad scope of information behavior, and is thus more useful as a heuristic diagram for designing empirical studies of information seeking; the model itself was an outcome of several years of field research. Beyond those notions emphasized by Krikelas, Wilson's, (1981) model introduces the concepts of the results of seeking (i.e., success or failure), and the degree of satisfaction of a need. It ignores questions of source characteristics and personal preferences among them.

Kuhlthau's model has been by far the most-cited among all of these, perhaps because of the huge number of studies conducted with students and/or about education. Kuhlthau's focus is on feelings, thoughts and actions following recognition of uncertainty, rather than on contextual factors, characteristics of the seeker, or types of sources.

The various evolutions of the Ellis model have been popular in studies of professional workers. While it is phrased in general terms the model retains the flavor of earlier research, in that most of the examples concern documentary sources of information. Nevertheless it has been successfully used with scientists who deal with other kinds of data. It does not appear to be an appropriate model for use with the general public and nonwork contexts (i.e., everyday life).

The Leckie et al. (1996) model is deliberately limited in scope to "professionals." It features six general factors, most notably "work roles" and "tasks." Given its emphasis on tasks, the model emphasizes *work-related* information seeking and so is limited in its applicability to the behaviors of a general population in everyday activities. The explanations in their article are somewhat brief; however, it concisely reviews many relevant studies that invoke some of the variables included in the model.

The Byström and Järvelin model focuses on work-related tasks, with similar limitations to the previous model. Järvelin and Wilson (2003) judge this model to be a good example of how models can guide empirical research and explanation.

In contrast to the models by Leckie et al., and Byström and Järvelin, Savolainen's ELIS model applies to nonwork settings, and all sorts of people. It includes both psychological and social factors, and considers a much longer time frame – conceivably, the entire length of a human life.

The Johnson model is also a more general one. Like that of Krikelas, this model has the virtue of simplicity: it moves in a chain-like sequence in one direction, with only one of the factors possessing more than one arrow (suggesting direct causation). The diagram lumps together potential intervening variables as "antecedent" factors, emphasizes source characteristics, and does not attempt to spell out the various forms that "actions" might take. Among all nine, Johnson's model has the most extended (book-length) explanation and by far the most references to theories and empirical studies on the affects of certain variables in information seeking.

Wilson's second model is much more complex than his first one. It introduces factors that his first model ignored. It identifies not only potential personal variables and modes of seeking, but also suggests relevant theories of motivations behind search behaviors.

All nine models suggest useful insights for analyzing the studies described in the following chapters. Table 6.1 compares surface-level aspects of the nine models.

6.2.11.   Additional Models

There are many other models of information seeking, sometimes meant to apply generally, but usually much more limited in their applicability. Examples of general models include those by Niedwiedzka (2003, mentioned earlier), Godbold (2006), and Lakshminarayanan (2010). Each of these takes a somewhat different path in their modification of earlier models. Niedzweidzka suggests that "context" affects a standard information

Table 6.1: Comparing the nine models[a].

Author(s) outcomes of model	Number of factors or stages	Main antecedent	Main factors or variables	Main or behaviors
Wilson (1981)	12	Need	Seeking or purchase	Demands; success; failure; use; transfer; satisfaction; or nonsatisfaction
Krikelas (1983)	13	Need-creating event or environment	Internal and external sources	Observations; interpersonal contact; use of literature, memory, or personal files; giving; gathering
Ellis (1989, 1993)	8	Research project	Activities: starting, browsing, chaining, monitoring, differentiating, extracting, verifying, ending	Success gathering of information, completion of project
Kuhlthau (1993b)	21: 3 dimensions by 7 stages	A gap in knowledge, or uncertainty. Examples often feature school assignments	Feelings, thoughts and actions, over 7 stages: initiation, selection, exploration, formulation, collection, presentation, assessment	Feelings: uncertainty, optimism, confusion, clarity, satisfaction. Thoughts: interest, self-awareness. Actions: seeking, exploring, documenting.
Leckie et al. (1996)	6	Work roles; tasks	Needs; sources; awareness	"Outcomes"
Byström and Järvelin (1995)	9	Subjective task	Personal and situational factors; personal style of seeking	Information needs analysis; choice of action; implementation; evaluation
Savolainen (1995, 2005)	15+	Desire to master life, keep order	Types of mastery; way of life; projects; situations	"Keeping things in order"; problem-solving behaviors
Johnson (1997)	7	Demographics; direct experience; salience; beliefs	Information carrier utilities and characteristics	"Actions"
Wilson (1996, 1999a)	14–20	Context; person-in-context	Psychological; demographic; role-related; environmental; source characteristics	Passive attention; passive search; active search; ongoing search; seeking, use and processing

[a]The final two columns compare the vocabulary used in the model, not necessarily the meaning of the terms.

seeking sequence (identify need – > decide to seek information, etc.) through three types of "intervening variables" (personal, role-related, and environmental), which act upon various stages of the sequence. These three contextual influences come from "off-stage" as it were, like a meteor shower. The resulting model has many paths and influences, yet without specifying enough to suggest how these might interact and be studied. Goldbold's approach is to attempt to merge together various aspects of the Dervin, Wilson, Ellis, and Kuhlthau models and extend them. Again, the result makes for quite complicated figures that are hard to translate into a study design or even into an explanation of how and why people behave as they do. Finally, Lakshminarayanan (2010) based her model on exhaustive analyses of 34 diaries, each kept for 14 days, and accounting for 15 types of information behaviors. She integrates her findings into a complex, two-figure model of at least two dozen elements.

Many of the more focused models are found in the health domain. For example, there are several that deal with the issue of what people do when they encounter information about health risks: Do they ignore it? Absorb it but take no action? Seek additional information? Change their behavior in response to what they have learned? Such models are used by public health specialists to both study health information seeking and to design ways to encourage people to improve their health-related behaviors. A typical example is Kahlor's (2010) "Planned Risk Information Seeking Model" (PRISM), which is itself an extension of the earlier "Risk Information Seeking and Processing" model. Other models in this vein include the "Health Information Acquisition" model of Freimuth, Stein, and Keen (1989), and the theory of motivated information management by Afifi and Weiner (2004). A typical feature among many of these health-related models is that they terminate in a box that says simply "Information Seeking" (as in the Afifi and Weiner model) or perhaps simply "Action," as they are trying to predict whether such behavior will occur, but are less concerned about how or where seeking might take place (i.e., what sources of information will be consulted). That limits their applicability to the sorts of research questions typically explored by information behavior researchers.

Additional health information models include Czaja, Manfredi, and Price's (2003) "Conceptual Model of Patient Information Seeking," Longo's (2005) "Expanded Conceptual Model of Information Seeking Behaviors," ter Huurne, Griffen and Gutteling's (2009) "Risk Information Seeking and Processing" model, and Veinot's (2010) "Multilevel Model of HIV/AIDS Information/Help Network Development." The latter model stands out in the way that it considers information or advice as just one among several "resources" (or "helps" in Brenda Dervin's terms) that might be sought by a patient; other types of resources sought would include physical treatment and emotional support (e.g., Veinot, 2010).

Where these health-related models most frequently overlap is in the concepts they invoke. The concept of self-efficacy is frequently incorporated in these models, especially those that focus on behavior change. Sometimes coping theory, or monitoring and blunting, are mentioned. Both of these concepts (self-efficacy and coping mechanisms) are mentioned in some mainstream information seeking models. Wilson's (1999) information behavior model and Schwarzer's (2011) "Health Action Process Approach" each invoke both of these concepts, for example.

Bates (2005a) notes that models sometimes lead to theories. In other instances a model illustrates a particular instance of a theory. In the next chapter we will consider what explicit theories have been invoked in information seeking studies.

Recommended for Further Reading

Järvelin, K., & Wilson, T. D. (2003). On conceptual models for information seeking and retrieval research. *Information Research, 9*(1). Retrieved from http://InformationR.net/ir/9-1/infres91.html

Järvelin and Wilson critique several models of information behavior, distinguishing conceptual models from analytic ones. In particular they comment on two of the models described here, by Ellis and by Byström and Järvelin.

Johnson, J. D. (1997). *Cancer-related information seeking.* Cresskill, NJ: Hampton Press.

This 239-page volume examines the information seeking literature from the perspective of health communication. With over 600 references, many of them to more general literature on the topic, Johnson's book makes a useful reference resource.

Leckie, G. J., Pettigrew, K. E., & Sylvain, C. (1996). Modeling the information seeking of professionals: A general model derived from research on engineers, health care professionals and lawyers. *Library Quarterly, 66,* 161–193.

The authors review dozens of studies of the information needs, uses, and habits of medical doctors, nurses, other health professionals, engineers, lawyers, and other professionals.

McQuail, D., & Windahl, S. (1993). *Communication models for the study of mass communication* (2nd ed.). New York, NY: Longman.

As the title implies, this book focuses on models used in research on mass communication. It contains several models relevant to information behavior as well as a wide range of other examples and explications of models.

Savolainen, R. (2005). Everyday life information seeking. In K. E. Fisher, S. Erdelez, & E. F. McKechnie (Eds.), *Theories of information behavior* (pp. 143–148). Medford, NJ: Information Today, Inc.

A cogent explanation of Savolainen's model, its key concepts, and its relationship to other research.

Wilson, T. D. (1999). Models in information behaviour research. *Journal of Documentation, 55*(3), 249–270.

Wilson explains the evolution of models of information retrieval and seeking research, with many cogent examples.

Wilson, T. D. (2005). Evolution in information behaviour modeling: Wilson's model. *Journal of Documentation, 55*(3), 249–270.

A briefer and recent synopsis of how Wilson's thinking has evolved over more than three decades of research.

Chapter 7

Metatheories, Paradigms, and Theories

> The word "theory" threatens to become meaningless. Because its referents are so diverse — including everything from minor working hypotheses, through comprehensive but vague and unordered speculations, to axiomatic systems of thought — use of the word often obscures rather than creates understanding.
>
> — Robert Merton (1968, p. 39)

> Unfortunately, so much work has been done without reference to any theoretical framework that it must either be ignored completely or the "miscellaneous" category would be very large indeed.
>
> — Tom Wilson (1994, p. 17)

Chapter Outline

Just as a pyramid depends on its foundation to provide stability for the rest of the structure, scholars rely on basic assumptions regarding the nature of reality and the purposes and methods of investigation. This chapter introduces the basic building blocks of inquiry and examines their relationship to specific traditions of research.

Obviously, the topics in this chapter could constitute a book in itself. I hope this brief overview of metatheories, perspectives, paradigms, and theories will enable those readers unfamiliar with such issues to better grasp the concepts associated with information seeking and how they have been studied.

7.1. Metatheories, Perspectives, and Paradigms

7.1.1. *Metatheories and the Great Divide*

Metatheory is theory about theory. It addresses the underlying philosophical assumptions about the nature of reality, and of knowledge, that stand behind a particular theory and the other theories and concepts most closely related to it. These kind of distinctions concern the basic *assumptions* that researchers hold about the world and how to investigate it. These include assumptions regarding ontology (the nature of *reality*), axiology (the nature of *values*), epistemology (how we *know*), and methodology (how we *find out*). Metatheory is the usual name for such considerations, although there are overlapping terms, discussed below.

We live in a time of intellectual ferment. Sixty years ago there was little diversity in most social scientific and humanistic investigations of human behavior and cognition. North American psychology, for example, adhered to a behaviorist paradigm of research that strongly restricted what could be taken as evidence regarding the mind (Gardner, 1985). Most disciplines in the "human sciences" (Foucault, 1972) had a fairly restrictive range of theories and methods that were widely accepted by research practitioners, particularly those influential in determining the publication of study results.

The good news is that we now have a much more diverse array of assumptions, approaches, and theories from which to choose. However, that can also be bad news, because there is disagreement on what kinds of perspectives or actions are most appropriate when doing research that involves people. Questions about the purpose and meaning of research abound.

For example, there are those who argue that people (e.g., their observable behaviors) should be the object of our study; others say that we can be more objective by observing only the artifacts of human behavior (e.g., the traces or records that people leave behind); yet other researchers say that there is no such thing as "objectivity," because the investigator is inextricably bound to the object of their study, and the best we can do is collect contextualized narratives or discourses in the domain of our interest.

A key issue (usually called philosophical realism) behind these considerations about objectivity is the degree to which there is a reality separate from the human mind, such that we can study its contents as objects completely separate from ourselves. On one extreme might be the view that we can be totally "objective" about studying other people, because they are more or less like other objects in the world; in this view our own consciousness, experience, and perceptions will have no effect on our ability to gain accurate knowledge of the actions and cognitions of others. At the other extreme of the spectrum could be the assumption that there is no reality "out there" at all, that what we perceive of the world exists entirely in our own minds; this would make it pointless to study the contents of the world as if they were separate objects from our own consciousness. Obviously, there are many possible positions along this imaginary continuum regarding the nature of reality and the potential for knowledge. A related issue has to do with the nature of "truth" — the degree to which it can be established, and the criteria for doing so. There are competing philosophical theories (correspondence, coherence, constructivist, consensus, and pragmatic) regarding truth that are beyond the scope of this chapter, yet which separate several of the theories discussed below.

It is important to note that it is common practice when discussing theory and metatheory to refer to "positivist" (or "post-positivist" or "objectivist") versus "interpretivist" (or "antipositivist") assumptions in research. There are many alternative characterizations and labels for this dichotomy: "positivistic" versus "naturalistic" (Lincoln & Guba, 1985), "empirical" versus "interpretive" (Pavitt, 1999), "subjective" versus "objective" (Abbott, 2004; Ford, 2004b; Hjørland, 2004; Ritzer, 2008), "objectivist" versus "subjectivist" Manicas (1998), "quantitative" versus "qualitative" (Glaser & Strauss, 1967), or "explanation" versus "understanding" (Stewart, 1997). As Creswell and Clark (2011) suggests, some of these dichotomies conflate philosophical views with strategies of inquiry and research designs.

These dichotomies refer to a variety of differences in philosophical assumptions, goals, and methods and not simply the debate over objectivity described above. For instance, the goals (and limits) of research are important as well: is our investigation intended to explain, predict, and perhaps control behavior (objectivist), or rather to describe, understand, and reflect upon behavior (including our own as researcher), and perhaps even to emancipate others (interpretivist)? Most of these simple dichotomies are problematic, especially the alleged sharp division between "quantitative" and "qualitative" methods, as these do not fall neatly underneath the other philosophical distinctions, either logically or historically. Yet, I will make some use of the objectivist/interpretivist divide in identifying schools of theory, as it functions well enough to demarcate the older traditions from some that have become more popular in LIS over the last 30 years. I have two reasons for choosing these terms rather than what might seem more logical dichotomies like "positivist/antipositivist" or "objectivist/subjectivist." The first reason is that I do not want to imply that these are simple, black versus white, oppositions; they in fact interrelate in various ways. Second, some of these terms are value-laden: some would object to having their research labeled "subjective," while "positivist" has become a pejorative term in and of itself.

Deeper background on the issues raised above may be found in the essays by Dick (1999), Hjørland (2004), the concise summary in Bates (2005a), and an entire special issue of the *Journal of Documentation* edited by Hjørland (2005a, 2005b, 2005c). Other worthwhile commentaries on the philosophical underpinnings of research on human behavior include Budd (1995), Dervin (1997), Guba and Lincoln (2005), Sandstrom and Sandstrom (1995), and Slife and Williams (1995).

7.1.2. Perspectives and Paradigms

In addition to calling them "metatheories," there are additional ways of characterizing groups of theories and their underlying assumptions. In an introductory chapter to a volume of studies of information behavior, Dervin (1997) chose the words "perspectives" and "methodologies" to illustrate the broad array of choices available to investigators in this area of study:

> symbolic interaction, pragmatics, system theory, qualitative studies, cultural studies, hermeneutics, political economy, phenomenology, constructivism, interpretive anthropology, transactionism, contextual psychology, ethnography, perspectivism, situationalism and postmodernism. (p. 15)

Dervin's list consists of a mix of labels for different metatheories, research traditions, disciplines, and methods. Only in one case is something explicitly labeled as "theory," and only two or three might be considered methodologies; so perhaps this list is best labeled "perspectives." Hjørland (2002b) also uses this term. Creswell and Clark (2011) prefers the term "worldview." Other authors (e.g., Bates, 2005a; Tuominen, 2004) use the more popular term "paradigm" to mean much the same thing (leaving aside, however, specific methodologies).

One of the difficulties in discussing the concept of theory is that it has layers of meaning. That is, there are not only different *levels* of theory but there are also overarching concepts like "paradigm" that are sometimes conflated with the notion of theory. I will discuss paradigm and theory in the context of a hierarchy that places paradigm in the most global and encompassing position, and "observations" at the bottom — the most limited and narrowest context of theory (see Figure 7.1).

"Paradigm" is a term popularized by the work of the historian of science Thomas Kuhn, who wrote the influential book *The Structure of Scientific Revolutions* (1962). Kuhn has been criticized for using "paradigm" in as many as 21 different ways (Masterman, 1970). Nevertheless, the term has become immensely popular as a way of describing (among other things) the various points of view that researchers take in their search for explanations. Kuhn's most common characterization of a paradigm was that of cluster of concepts, variables, and problems, along with related methodologies.

We might, for example, speak of a "conflict" paradigm that theorizes that conflicts among individuals or groups underlie much of social interaction; many social theories, such as that of Karl Marx, share this view. Alternatively, the "exchange" paradigm says that much of life is based on individual calculations of the costs and benefits of undertaking a certain action, whether the action is speaking to a stranger or getting married. Or we might speak of a "sense-making" paradigm that stresses how people create both meaning and social structure in their lives through their interactions with others. Thus, asking another person for help in solving a personal problem may reveal a solution merely by sharing views of the problem; it may also create friendship or dependency.

However vague the definition of a paradigm, it is an essential concept for describing research on information behavior. First, it is difficult to talk about competing theories, or schools of theories, in information-seeking research. The field is very diverse in its approaches, and formal theories are not always identified in individual investigations. Second, the notion of paradigm highlights the connections between research and the purposes and beliefs of the investigator. For example, a distinction has been made between so-called "critical" and "administrative" research traditions (Livingstone, 2006) that parallels longstanding debates concerning the nature of both theory and research. Administrative research aims to support and improve existing systems, while critical research tends to question them. Livingstone

Paradigm

Grand Theory

Formal Theory

Substantive Theory

Observations

Figure 7.1: A hierarchy of ideas about theory.

quotes critical theorist Theodor Adorno as saying that his role was "to *interpret* phenomena — not to ascertain, sift, classify facts, and make them available as information."

Let us consider two different cases. One researcher's worldview may be that it is not up to her to question the nature of power relationships in the world, but rather to investigate practical problems that face the institution for which she works. Perhaps the researcher's focus is why more people do not make use of a social service agency, and her goal is to explain such behavior and perhaps improve the operations and services of her employer.

In contrast, another investigator may feel compelled to challenge and expose what he judges to be an unfair social relationship — the failure of a government agency to provide the kind of services that most people need — with the intention of raising public awareness of an injustice and perhaps, in so doing, to change the world. Although these two researchers might choose similar methodologies to address the research problem as they have defined it, they would be using dissimilar theories and operating under quite different paradigms.

Some researchers prefer to avoid the term "paradigm" as much as possible. Giddens (1989) prefers the word "perspectives," Gadamer (1976) "traditions," and Dervin (1991) "analytics," when referring to strategies that guide research. Yet others may use the term "approach" to describe both assumptions and the range of methodologies employed in investigations.

I will employ the word *paradigm* in the Kuhnian sense of a "tradition" for the practice of research (Masterman, 1970); "perspective" will be taken to mean the same thing. Traditions, perspectives, and paradigms then subsume models and theories.

7.2. Theories

7.2.1. What Is a Theory?

Theories are explanations. They are generalizations. Theories are statements that try to explain relationships among various phenomena (Baker, 1999) and from which one can make inferences and deductions. Theory results from an interplay among ideas, evidence, and inference (Chaffee, 1991, p. 14).

Beyond these simple statements, more formal definitions of "theory" show wide variance in usage among researchers. Kerlinger (1973, p. 9), for example, defines theory as:

> a set of interrelated constructs (concepts), definitions, and propositions that present a systematic view of phenomena by specifying

relations among variables, with the purpose of explaining and predicting the phenomena.

Simon and Burstein (1985, p. 52) adhere to Kerlinger's complex definition when writing of disciplines like physics and economics, pointing out that "there is no theory unless it is a *body of theory*," a set of well-established definitions, assumptions, and systematically organized propositions. Nearly all explanations of theory invoke the idea that it must be systematic, relying on more than just a single, simple statement. Yet Simon and Burstein also note (as did Merton, quoted at the beginning of this chapter) that theory:

> has a looser meaning; it often refers to a loosely organized collection
> of hypotheses ... and sometimes is even used to refer to almost any
> speculative thinking offered as an explanation ... .

Many examples of this "looser" invocation of theory can be found in everyday life, such as when a friend asks "What's your theory about the Kennedy assassination?" But such vague use of the term also abounds in scholarly discourse. Without passing judgment on whether the author's usage met formal definitions of theory, Pettigrew and McKechnie (2001) examined 1,160 information science articles that invoked theories, hypotheses, frameworks, principles, approaches, conceptualizations, or models as explanations. The results ranged from single concepts (e.g., "relevance" and "information needs") attributed to particular authors to formal theories identified with major figures like Dewey, Freud, Giddens, Habermas, and Merton. Only a minority would probably meet the formal criteria for "theory."

Reynolds (1971) points out that the term theory is commonly used in at least four different senses: (1) a set of "laws" that are "well-supported empirical generalizations"; (2) an "interrelated set of definitions, axioms, and propositions"; (3) "descriptions of causal processes"; or (4) vague concepts, untested hypotheses, or prescriptions of desirable social behaviors (pp. 10–11).

Each of these descriptions has its place, and for this chapter I will mainly assume Reynolds' second definition, which is the *vade mecum* (received or "handbook") view of theory more typical of social research: as an "interrelated set of definitions, axioms, and propositions." Human behavior is seen as complex and requiring a special vocabulary to describe it. Statements about phenomena (e.g., propositions and hypotheses) are used to guide observation and the development of theories. Claims about human behavior are recognized as being probabilistic or conditional (e.g., time and context bound), rather than deterministic.

The first notion — that of theory as a set of laws — is not very satisfactory for the study of human behavior, in which relatively few absolute regularities have been found to exist. That the social sciences see themselves as uncovering universal and absolute laws regarding people is a claim that few, if any, contemporary social researchers would make.

The third conceptualization of theory — as causal processes — will only be used in the limited sense of a *model*, as discussed in the previous chapter. It is difficult to establish causation in human behavior, especially a phenomenon such as information seeking in which many important aspects cannot be observed. However, it is certainly possible to identify key factors and their likely sequences and interactions in the process of information seeking. Models make these aspects explicit and thus guide research design and theory development.

7.2.2. Levels of Theory

A theory is something more specific than a paradigm; the question is, How specific? In a quotation at the beginning of this chapter, the eminent sociologist Robert Merton complains that social scientists do not always share the same definition for *theory*, much less the same goals regarding the kinds of theory to construct. He was particularly concerned about continued attempts to create "grand" theories that tried to explain large segments of human behavior in a universal way. In their emulation of major social theorists like Karl Marx, Herbert Spencer, and Talcott Parsons (Merton, 1968, p. 44), other scholars have tried (and failed) to predict actions and tendencies across too many individuals, contexts, cultures, and societies. Skinner (1985) has pointed to a "return of grand theory" in the work of still-living scholars like Jürgen Habermas and Anthony Giddens, who refuse to restrict theory to limited questions, methods, and evidence.

Davis (1986) describes how "successful" (i.e., both famous and widely applied) social theories addressed major problems (e.g., economic change) and also overturned previous assumptions about the topic (e.g., that religion is largely unrelated to economic activity, a view challenged by Max Weber). Davis examines the grand theories of Karl Marx, Emile Durkheim, and Max Weber, among others, to show how broadly they were applied to explanations of behavior. For example, Durkheim's theory that the division of labor played a primary role in social organization has been used to study phenomena in government, law, religion, science, and the arts, as well as to explain the very notion of individuality among humans. His notion that intermediate social groups, such as occupations, helped to hold society together in the face of declining community and family ties could be considered a "grand theory."

Rather than trying to reinvent or replace the broad theories that emerged during the 19th century, Merton (1968) argued that we should concentrate on the development of limited, "middle-range" theories; such theories function at a higher level than a testable hypothesis, but deal with limited settings, remain close to the level of observable phenomena, and offer the potential for aggregating findings.

To illustrate the middle-range, Merton offered the example of "reference group theory," the idea that individuals judge themselves by referring to the standards of significant people in their lives, rather than to some absolute criteria that apply to all humans. For example, you probably judge how financially "well off" you are by considering the wealth of your friends, relatives, coworkers, and acquaintances — rather than consulting United Nations statistics on average annual incomes around the world, or even those of your own nation. Referential judgments constitute a phenomenon that can be readily observed in many social settings and across cultures, such that results can be compared and related to other sociological concepts, such as class. Some examples of middle-range theory in a professional field (rather than an academic discipline) are found in Liehr and Smith's (1999) discussion of 22 middle-range theories in nursing. For example, one theory concerns how the entry of an elderly person into a nursing home signals an important change of status in life.

Glaser and Strauss (1967) further subdivide middle-range theory into two categories: "formal" and "substantive," as indicated in Figure 7.1 by italics. Formal theory is what we think of as typical social or psychological theory, conceptual statements meant to apply to a general domain like socialization or learning. Formal theory plays a role in developing and marking the boundaries of a discipline; for example, certain theories of socialization are used widely in sociology, and little used elsewhere. Substantive theory concerns a more limited domain, such as a theory of browsing in libraries, or of Web searching behaviors. Substantive theory is more focused on real-world applications.

Whether theories are substantive or formal, Glaser and Strauss argue that they are best developed through induction. This involves building "upwards" from observation, through a process of coding and analysis, leading to the identification of categories of phenomena from which propositions can be developed. In this way, theory is "grounded" in observation rather than derived from abstract ideas. This is why they call it "grounded theory." The grounded theory process does not rely exclusively on *induction* (reasoning from particulars to generalizations), but rather moves back and forth from data gathering to *deduction* (reasoning from generalizations to particular cases) to test the theory.

An example of grounded theory from information seeking is Kuhlthau's (1993a) model of the search process. Kuhlthau's model was developed through close observation of the ways that information seekers construct knowledge by tying it to what they already know as they pass through various stages of uncertainty and understanding. Itself derived from a general, psychological theory (i.e., Kelly, 1963), Kuhlthau's model could be expanded into a more general theory of information seeking through further observation and development. To see how these ideas evolve, let's begin by looking at the foundations of information-seeking theories.

7.3.   Sources of Theory in Information Seeking

Chatman (1996, p. 193) laments that:

> we have no central theory or body of interrelated theories we can view as "middle range." ... it would appear we are currently focused on the application of conceptual frameworks rather than on the generation of specific theories.

Many early studies of information seeking or use made no explicit claims to theory. In the early days of information behavior research, most of the investigations were administrative in nature, concerned with collecting data for the purpose of improving operations in information agencies such as libraries. However, there has never been a shortage of applicable theory from various disciplines that might be applied to the search for, and use of, information. In recent years, investigators have become much more eclectic in finding and applying theory in information behavior research as well as developing their own theoretical constructs.

Over thirty years ago, Zweizig (1977) observed that theories applied in information-seeking studies tended to come from three disciplinary sources: sociology, mass communication, and psychology. Zweizig did not provide examples, but we can still readily identify those first two sources in the work of scholars like Elfreda Chatman, Tom Wilson, and Brenda Dervin. Chatman (1990) invokes Durkheim's sociological grand theory of the division of labor, particularly the concept of *alienation* as it was articulated by Durkheim and related social theorists (e.g., Weber and Merton). Chatman studied the flow, expression, and use of information among janitors, relating their responses to indicators of alienation such as anomie (i.e., normlessness), powerlessness, meaninglessness, isolation, and self-estrangement. She has used various theories in other works; Chatman (1986) used Rogers's (2003) diffusion of innovation theory, stemming from both sociology and communication, to describe the diffusion of job information among workers; and Chatman (1991) employed uses and gratifications theory (e.g., Katz, Blumler, & Gurevitch, 1974), also from mass communication, to explore how janitors used the mass media, and other sources, for information and entertainment. Chatman (2000) cites other sociological theorists, such as Erving Goffman, Alfred Schutz, and Harold Garfinkel. Wilson (1997, 2002) cites psychologists Albert Bandura, Leon Festinger, Susan Folkman, Richard Lazrus, and Susan

Miller, and sociologists Everett Rogers and Alfred Schutz, among many others from those disciplines. Brenda Dervin cites a wide array of theoretical influences, not only from sociology, mass communication, and psychology, but from other fields as well, such as theorists Pierre Bourdieu, Michel Foucault, Anthony Giddens, Erving Goffman, and Jürgen Habermas.

Some kind of psychological theory is implicit in much of information behavior research. Many of the studies of individual use of information retrieval systems and libraries assume a psychological (or cognitive) perspective, whether or not they cite a specific theory or theorist. Indeed, much of information-seeking research could be said to relate to, if not descend directly from, a single psychologist: Sigmund Freud.

Freud's (1922) "pleasure principle" encapsulates the view that both social and psychological activities stem from a need to reduce emotional tension — a type of "drive reduction." People seek pleasure to alleviate unpleasant internal states — painful feelings or felt desires — and thus reduce tension (McQuail & Windahl, 1993, pp. 288–289). Donohew et al. (1984), for example, believe that acquiring information is an automatic human behavior, and typically brings pleasure. Because information seeking implies that people take action in response to some disquieting internal state (e.g., an "anomalous state of knowledge," "uncertainty," or "visceral need"), the pleasure principle could be said to apply universally to information seeking. Indeed, in recent years, there has been renewed interest in viewing information behaviors as driven by uncertainty (see Cole, 1993; Kuhlthau, 1993b, 1997, 1999; Wilson, Ford, Ellis, Foster, & Spink, 2002).

Perhaps because it is common sense that people seek pleasure and avoid pain, Freud is rarely cited in information behavior research. Among those psychologists who are cited at times are Bandura (1977, 1986), Bruner (1973, 1990), Fishbein and Ajzen (1975), Kelly (1963), Leont'ev (1978), Miller (1968, 1983a, 1983b), Piaget (1952), and Vygotsky (1978). Some of the work of John Dewey (e.g., *How We Think*, 1933; *On Experience,* 1960) could be counted among the psychologists, even though Dewey is more noted for his contributions to philosophy and education. Similarly, Foucault (1972, 1980) started his career as a psychologist, although many readers think of his work as more concerned with language and culture.

Besides sociology, psychology, and communication, there are other disciplines that either build on that above (e.g., management and business, especially consumer research) or that have closely related theories (e.g., economics and linguistics). In short, there are a number of academic fields that serve as sources of paradigms and theories for the study of information seeking, and some of their theories have been actively used in such research.

In the way of theory "native" to the study of information seeking, the volume by Fisher, Erdelez, and McKechnie (2005) has allowed information behavior researchers to advance their own theoretical concepts, and to identify applicable theories from other fields. Perhaps the most prolific IB researcher in this regard has been the late Elfreda Chatman, whose admirers have written two chapters in the Fisher et al. book devoted to her theorizing: the "theory of information poverty" (Hersberger, 2005), based on Chatman's experiences in studying aging women in a retirement community (Chatman, 1992); and her theory of "life in the round" (Chatman, 1999; Fulton, 2005a), which explores the influence of social norms and worldviews on information behavior. Both of Chatman's theories suggest researchable propositions that can be tested in field research.

It would be nice if theories and their paradigms could be sorted into neat typologies so that we can compare them. Some typologies have been devised, particularly in sociology — see, for example, Burrell and Morgan (1988), Littlejohn (1983), Ritzer (2008), and Rosengren (1989) — but without much agreement. A number of philosophical examinations (e.g., Hacking, 1999; Rosenberg, 1995; Slife & Williams, 1995) make it clear that both the assumptions and the history of various metatheories (especially schools of thought regarding social action and social construction) are interwoven and difficult to tease apart.

Where information behavior is concerned, the sheer diversity of theoretical borrowings makes a single, comprehensive comparison difficult. In the next section, I use the common distinction between the objectivist ontological position and others (here labeled "interpretivist"). Within the latter, I have adapted some of the categories used by Bates (2005a). I recognize that these two broad groupings are open to dispute. For example, Trochim and Donnelly (2007) refer to constructivists as post-positivists (i.e., objectivists), and other scholars would place some critical theorists there as well.

The remainder of this chapter describes this selection of paradigms and their accompanying theories that have been applied to the investigation of information behavior.

7.4. Objectivist Research Paradigms

There are a number of paradigms used in information behavior research that might fall under the general label of "objectivist." They are discussed under the following headings:

- Zipf's Principle of Least Effort and Cost-Benefit
- Uses and Gratifications and Expectancy Theory
- Uncertainty Management Theory, etc.
- Other Objectivist Theories

7.4.1.   Zipf's Principle of Least Effort and Cost-Benefit

Many authors (e.g., Bierbaum, 1990; Case, 2005; Gratch, 1990; Hardy, 1982; Jansen & Rieh, 2010; Mann, 1993; Poole, 1985) have pointed out that a body of work by philologist Zipf (1949) functions as a paradigm or grand theory for studies of information seeking. Poole's (1985) analysis of the information-seeking literature found that 40 of the 51 studies he sampled lent their support to Zipf's Principle of Least Effort. Although Zipf did not claim that his principle was a formal theory, Poole demonstrates that it has the earmarks of a general theory, and that propositions may be derived from it. Zipf's principle is considered to be a "power law" like Pareto's distribution in economics, and Lotka's regarding author productivity.

According to Zipf (1949), each individual will adopt a course of action that will involve the expenditure of the *probable least average* of his work — in other words, the least effort. Zipf supports his theory with evidence from various aspects of human behavior, most of it based on studies of language usage. For example, the statistical distribution of words in the text of James Joyce's *Ulysses* follows the kind of pattern on which Zipf based his theory. Ranked by frequency of appearance, the tenth most common word in *Ulysses* appears 2653 times; the 100th most common word, 265 times; and the 1000th, 26 times. The result is a distribution of data in which the number 26 appears as a constant.

Zipf called such relationships "harmonic distributions" and posited that any human allocation of resources (words in documents, documents in files, or people in cities) tends to fall into such arrangements. The reason has to do with economy of effort; humans tend to use short, common words whenever they can (leading to highly frequent usage of just a few words) rather than longer words that take more effort. Zipf used the analogy of an artisan seated at a desk; while working, the artisan would tend to pick up tools and lay them down in order of how frequently they were used, with the most frequently used ones kept closest at hand (Kenner, 1986).

A corollary is found in both libraries and office filing systems, in which people tend to use, borrow, or cite the same documents again and again; this has become known as the "80–20" (or sometimes "70–30") rule: 20% of the documents account for 80% of the use. Communication media (e.g., phones, e-mail) exhibit a similar phenomenon: a minority of the population of users (20–30%) tends to account for the majority of messages sent (70–80%). Studies of prominent scientists by Robert Merton and others (summarized in Merton, 1973) found that just a few of them received a disproportionate amount of citations, funding, and other resources (the so-called "Matthew Effect"). And to echo the first example, in Henry James's novel *The Ambassadors*, 75% of the text is composed of 27% of its vocabulary (i.e., 176 of the 665 unique words that make up the entire novel) — again, an approximation to 70–30.

Internet Web sites exhibit harmonic relationships in two ways. First, Broder et al. (2000) have found that about 28% of all Web sites are more "central" in terms of the strengths of their links to other Web sites — approximating the 70–30 ratio. Second, it is clear that just a few sites have vastly larger numbers of visitors, while the rest taper off in a harmonic distribution (Huberman, Pirollis, Pitkow, & Lukose, 1998).

Evidence for the Principle of Least Effort can be found in other realms of information behavior. Like links to Web sites, requests made in libraries also seem to exhibit harmonic relationships: Dorsch and Pifalo (1997) demonstrate that just 25% of medical journals accounted for 74% of the requests in their state of Illinois. The same is apparently true of citations among authors. White (2001) has invoked Zipf's principle to explain patterns of citations that authors make to the works of other authors, based on the notion that supportive (i.e., positive, agreeing) references require more explanation (i.e., effort) than citations that are critical of the works of others. That would explain the relative rarity of critical (i.e., negative) citations.

In the practical realm, the human tendency toward economy of effort is often exploited by system designers. Indexers of documents, whether working by instinct or with term rankings, may establish cutoff points to determine which words are indexed and which are not. Very common words like "and" and "the" are not indexed; rarely occurring words like "onomatopoeia" or "calliope" or "sesquicentennial" will not be indexed either, unless they have some central relationship to the theme of the text. What are indexed are the words in between the common and the rare — the so-called "middle-frequency" terms (Salton & McGill, 1983) — identified by a derivative of Zipf's research, the rank-frequency law of document vocabulary. Similarly, some office managers arrange files by frequency of use so that the most frequently used files are at the front of each drawer, rather than filing them alphabetically or in some subject arrangement. System designers sometimes refer to "Mooer's Law," (1960), which suggests that no one will use an information system if using it is more troublesome than it is worth.

An oft-cited example of least effort at work is when a professional asks the nearest coworker whether any new reports have been published on a topic, rather than conducting a thorough search of the literature in question. As Durrance (1988) put it:

> Research on information seeking has consistently shown that people prefer interpersonal over print sources. That finding came as a surprise to researchers 30 years ago when they looked at information seeking among scientists. An appropriate research question might

be: "Why do information seekers choose oral channels first?" People may simply take the path of least resistance. (p. 161)

Another example is when the professional consults last year's handbook simply because it is in her office, when the latest version exists just down the hall. Allen's (1977) study of 19 research and development engineers found that they operated on a least effort basis when selecting information channels, and easy accessibility was more highly related to the frequency of use than was the quality of the information. Rosenberg (1967) and Orr (1970) made comparable observations about industry workers and scientists. Connaway, Dickey, and Radford say that students are highly influenced by the convenience of information sources. And decades of reviews and studies (see, e.g., Chen & Hernon, 1982) document a strong preference among information seekers for interpersonal sources, who are typically easier and more readily accessible than the most authoritative printed sources. Similarly, Dervin (1983b, p. 158) refers to the tendency of people in "relying on close friends and relatives for their information" as demonstrating a "law of least effort."

However, here we are concerned with theory rather than practice. Zipf notes that the importance of his Principle of Least Effort lies in its universality in regards to human behavior. Over the long haul, humans tend toward a surprising efficiency in their allocation of effort. This tendency has enormous implications for studying the use of information.

A related approach has been called the *cost–benefit paradigm*. This perspective attempts to explain behavior in terms of a trade-off between the effort required to employ a particular type of strategy (e.g., eliminating choices by looking at their worst possible outcomes) and the quality of the resulting action. The notion of a cost–benefit trade-off in information seeking is similar enough to the Principle of Least Effort that the two paradigms are sometimes conflated. There are differences between the two, however, not the least of which is that least effort claims to be a *descriptive* principle that applies across many aspects of human behavior, whether goal-oriented or not. The cost–benefit approach is more *normative* in its assumptions and is applied toward conscious decisions regarding the expenditure of effort to achieve some goal.

According to Hardy (1982), the cost–benefit paradigm (e.g., Dupuit, 1952) proposes that as people seek information they select information channels based on their expected benefits weighed against likely costs. Under this paradigm, information seeking is highly rational and emphasizes a calculation of the benefits to be gained from obtaining the most complete and accurate information. An example is the doctor who considers whether she can render an immediate diagnosis based on the symptoms that are presented by the patient, or whether it is worth the time and money (assuming the patient must pay expenses) to run further laboratory tests before deciding on a treatment plan. The doctor must estimate the likely value of the information yielded by the tests versus the monetary cost and any potential dangers due to a delay in treatment.

In contrast, the Principle of Least Effort, which is chiefly pragmatic and not at all optimal, predicts that seekers will minimize the effort required to obtain information, even if it means accepting a lower quality or quantity of information. Hardy's study of 968 U.S. Forest Service professionals found that they were oversensitive to the costs involved in acquiring information and undersensitive to issues of information quality. On average, Hardy found, the Forest Service workers held acquisition costs twice as important in their decisions as they did the quality of the outcome (i.e., the benefits to be derived from reliable information).

Recent investigations and reviews alluding to Zipf's principle (and related concepts like cost-benefit, convenience, and satisfying) include Agarwal, Xu, and Poo (2011), de Alwis, Majid, and Chaudhry (2006), Bronstein and Baruchson-Arbib (2008), Connaway, Dickey and Radford (2011), Houston (2011), Jansen and Rieh (2010), Lu (2007), O'Connor (2011), and Xu, Tan and Yang (2006).

7.4.2. Uses and Gratifications and Expectancy Theory

Elihu Katz, Jay Blumler, and Mickael Gurevitch, in their preface to 1974 collection *The Uses of Mass Communication,* describe a "perspective," "approach," or "model" that has come to be known as "Uses and Gratifications." This paradigm is concerned with

- the social and psychological origins of *needs*;
- the way in which needs generate *expectations* regarding *sources* of information and entertainment;
- the resulting manner in which people *expose themselves to media*; and
- the resulting *gratifications* of needs, along with other *consequences*, many of which may be unintended.

The uses and gratifications approach to research has several characteristics that distinguish it from other approaches to the study of media usage (see Levy & Windahl, 1984; Palmgreen, 1984). First, it is assumed that the media audience plays an *active* role in the selection of sources to attend to, rather than being the passive target of messages. Second, it is the person who uses the medium, rather than the medium that uses the person. That is, if media have "effects," it is at least partly because people choose to be affected by them. Third, the various media are merely a portion of the range of options individuals may have for fulfilling needs, in a universe dominated by interpersonal contacts and intrapersonal activity. Thus, if one has a need for "entertainment" one could just as well play a card game — whether by oneself or with another individual — rather than watch television, surf the Internet, or read. Fourth, media use can be studied by asking people directly about their interests and motives, rather than collecting data surreptitiously and/or inferring motives to observed behavior. Finally, it is best to suspend value judgments about the significance of various media and their content until the users of the media are studied on their own terms; dismissive judgments about the value of certain kinds of magazine, books, films, television programs, or Internet content do not lead to a better understanding of what those sources *do* for people, and why they choose one source over another.

Livingstone (2006) points out that Elihu Katz was influenced by the work of critical theorists like Theodor Adorno, yet spent most of his effort on "administrative" investigations, hoping to merge these two, often conflicting, views of the purpose of research. For this reason, the uses and gratifications approach has multiple flavors. McQuail and Gurevitch (1974) explain that this perspective can be approached via three research traditions: functional, structural–cultural, or action–motivation. In keeping with theories of drive reduction (like Freud's pleasure principle, discussed previously), the seeking of gratifications clearly has a functionalist flavor: audiences choose among media and content to accomplish the goal of gratification. People actively use media — usage doesn't just "happen" to them.

The structural–cultural tradition emphasizes the media environment that a culture has created, and how those media limit choice and invoke trade-offs in uses and gratifications. For example, Williams (1987, p. 224) suggested that differences in gratifications found in two national studies of political news is due to "structural differences in the ownership, operation, programming, or content of newspapers and television in Great Britain as compared to the United States."

The action–motivation tradition is found in the application of expectancy models such as that of Fishbein and Ajzen (1975). In fact, Rayburn and Palmgreen (1984) say that these two research traditions have enough in common to be merged (as they are in Table 7.1). Expectancy models assume that beliefs and evaluations partly determine the gratifications sought, which in turn influence how media content is chosen and consumed. Williams (1987, p. 225) characterized the expectancy model as saying that:

> either behavior, behavioral intentions, or attitudes [are] a function of (1) expectancy — the perception of an object's possession of a particular attribute or that a certain behavior will lead to certain consequences — and (2) evaluation — that is, the degree of "effect, positive or negative, toward an attribute or behavioral outcome."
> (Palmgreen, 1984)

Table 7.1: Theorists, theories, and theory groups often cited in IB research.

Theorist(s)	Theory or concept(s)	Selected publications citing the theory or theorist
Afifi 06, 09; Babrow 92, 96; Brashers 01, 02	Motivated Information Management; Problematic Integration; Uncertainty Management	Case 05; Heinström 10; Houston 10; Johnson 12; Knauper 09; Sairanen 10; Veinot 09; Weiring 05
Bandura 77, 86	Social Cognitive (Learning) Theory, Self-Efficacy	Afifi 06; Case 04; Ford 03; Heinström 10; Hepworth 04; Miwa 05; Nahl 05; Pálsdóttir, 2008; Savolainen 02; Wiering 05; Wilson 99, 05
Bakhtin 81; Foucault 72, 80; Garfinkel 84; Harré 84, 94; Potter 96	Discursive Action, Discourse Analysis, Ethnomethodology, Positioning Theory	Budd 96; Chatman 91; Day 05; Dervin 99; Given 02, 05; Haider 07; Houston 11; Jaeger 10; Joyce 05; McKenzie 02, 03, 04, 05, 06, 10; Nahl 05, 07; Olsson 05, 09, 10; Pettigrew 01; Radford 01; Savolainen 04, 08; Talja 97, 05; Tuominen 97, 05
Berger 67; Knorr-Cetina 81; Latour 81;	Social Construction of Reality, Social Construction of Knowledge	Bates 05; Case 98; Chatman 91, 96; Houston 11; Leckie 05; Pettigrew 01; Savolainen 93, 09; Sundin 02; Tuominen 97, 05; Williamson 02, 05; Wilson 02
Bourdieu 84, 90	Theory of Taste/Distinction, Symbolic Violence	Dervin 99, 03; Houston 11; Hussey 10; Joyce 05; Laplante 11; Leckie 05; Olsson 05; Pettigrew 01; Savolainen 95, 99, 08; Seldén 01; Thomas 01; Van Snippenburg 96
Csikszentmihalyi 90	Flow Theory	Baker 05; Case 00; Cox 08; Heinström 10; Houston 11; Mick 92; Naumer 05
de Certeau 84; Lave and Wenger 91; Wenger 98	Everyday Practice Communities of Practice	Aspray 11; Davenport 00, 02; Davies 04; Finholt 02; Harris 10; Hemmig 09; Houston 11; Joyce 05; Lueg 08; Ross 05 09; Rothbauer 05, 10; Savolainen 07, 08; Sundin 02; Talja 10
Fish 87; Suleiman 80; Iser 78; Rosenblatt 94;	Reader Response Theory	Massey 05, 07; Mick 92; Radway 85; Reuter 07; Ross 99, 05; Scott 94; Stern 92
Fishbein 75; Katz 74; Palmgreen 84	Theory of Reasoned Action, Uses and Gratifications	Chatman 91; Connaway 11; Dimmick 00; Levy 84; Leung 99; Toms 99; Johnson J 97; Wise 10; Yoo 11; Zerbinos 90

Folkman 84; Miller 87	Stress and Coping Theory, Monitoring and Blunting	Baker 96, 99, 04, 05; Campbell 06; Case 05; Heinström 10; Houston 11; Josefsson 06; Lu 10; Perttilä 10; Pettigrew 01; Rees 00; Sairanen 10; Savolainen 07, 08; Wellstead 11; Wiering 05; Wilson 99, 05
Giddens 84	Structuration Theory	Dervin 92; Leckie 05; Pettigrew 01; Rosenbaum 93, 10; Savolainen 93, 95, 07, 08, 09; Williamson 02
Goffman 59, 75, 83	Presentation of Self (Face)	Case 04; Chatman 96, 00; Chelton 01; Dervin 82; Fisher 07; Houston 11; Mokros 95; Mon 05; Nahl 05; Radford 01; Thivant 05; Tuominen 97
Granovetter 73, 82	Social Network Theory/Strength of Weak Ties	Chatman 91; Dixon 05; Erdelez 00; Desouza 06; Fisher 07; Haythornthwaite 96; Hersberger 01, 03, 05; Huotari 01; Lu 07; Morey 07; Pettigrew 99, 00, 01; Savolainen 01, 08; Veinot 09, 11; Wicks 99
Habermas 84, 87	Theory of Communicative Action	Benoit 00, 05; Burnett 08; Cornelius 96; Dervin 82, 89, 92, 99; Jaeger 10; Newhagen 97; Mehra 07; Pettigrew 01; Savolainen 08; Timpka 90; Wersig 85
Kelly 63	Personal Construct Theory	Bates 05; Cole 00; Julien 04; Kuhlthau 91,93.99,04.05; Mehra 07; Pettigrew 01; Williamson 05; Wilson 02
Lin 02; Coleman 88	Social Capital	Haythornthwaite 96; Hersberger 01, 03, 05; Houston 11; Johnson C 05, 07; Lu 07; Savolainen 08; Veinot 09, 10, 11; Widén-Wulff 04, 07
Merton 68, 72	Reference Group Theory (Insiders/Outsiders)	Chatman 90, 91, 96; Dawson 01; Huotari 01; Lu 07; Pettigrew 01; Sligo 00
Rogers 03	Diffusion of Innovation	Brown 01; Case 87; Chatman 86, 96; Crowley 05; Desouza 06; Houston 11; Johnson J 97; Lajoie-Paquette 05; Pettigrew 01; Savolainen 01
Schutz 62, 64, 67	Phenomenology, Life World	Bates 05; Chatman 96, 00; Hayter 07; Jaeger 10; Kari 03; Marcella 00, 05; Olsson 05; Savolainen 95, 07, 08, 09; Sonnenwald 06; Wilson 99, 02, 03

Table 7.1: (*Continued*)

Theorist(s)	Theory or concept(s)	Selected publications citing the theory or theorist
Smith 92; Stephens 86; Pirolli 99, 09	Optimal Foraging Theory	Jacoby 05; Pirolli 09; Sandstrom 94, 01; Spink 06; Williamson 97, 98; Xu 06
Vygotsky 78; Leont'ev 78	Activity Theory	Allen 08, 11; Bilal 07; Hjørland 02; Meyers 07; Nardi 96; Pettigrew 01; Savolainen 08; Spasser 99; von Thaden 07; Widén-Wulff 07; Wilson 06, 08
Zipf 49; Dupuit 52	Principle of Least Effort Cost–Benefit Analysis	Agarwal 11; Bierbaum 90; Bronstein 08; Case 05; Connaway 11; de Alwis 06; Gratch 90; Hardy 82; Houston 11; Jansen 10; Lu 07; Mann 93; O'Connor 11; Pool 85; Xu 06

Note: Studies are listed by first author only, plus year. See the references section for clarification.

The uses and gratifications perspective has been criticized on several grounds. Most fundamentally, concepts like needs, uses, motives, and gratifications lack some clarity, and may be used somewhat differently across investigators (Rubin, 1994; Ruggiero, 2000). The uses and gratifications approach is not well connected to other theories of beliefs, attitudes, motivations, and behavior, many of which are surely relevant and could serve to ground these central concepts. The uses and gratifications approach offers a rather simplistic explanation of why we choose certain media and content, namely "we use X because X gratifies us" (Williams, 1987). The studies themselves tend to be very individualistic, making it difficult to explain more than the behaviors and reports of those persons studied. Another difficulty with the uses and gratifications approach lies in its assumption of a universally *active* audience. Experience sampling studies by Csikszentmihalyi (1990; see Chapter 9) find little evidence to support the notion of an active television audience, finding instead that television viewers report feeling relaxed and relatively inattentive.

Despite these possible shortcomings, the uses and gratifications approach is highly relevant to the study of information seeking. Chatman (1991) offers an example of an application of this approach. Chatman conducted interviews with janitors to test six propositions about the activities and gratifications of the working-class poor, including their use of the media. She concluded that a theory of gratification was applicable to the study of information seeking. In particular, Chatman found that a focus on gratifications helps us to understand how the poor define and deal with problems in their lives, and why it is that they are not more active in seeking information. Two important reasons for this seeming passivity were that (1) respondents tended to see problems as being resolved by "luck" rather than their own efforts and (2) they failed to see external sources of information, including libraries, as relevant to their everyday problems.

Investigations conducted under the uses and gratifications perspective tend to be compartmentalized by audience and/or medium, without many syntheses across studies. For example, Leung and Wei (1999a, 1999b) focused on use of pagers. Rubin's (1983) study of the uses of television found five common motivations: information, entertainment, escape, habitual passing of time, and companionship. Would these uses apply equally to fiction reading? "Companionship" would seem to be less plausible, as nearby television viewers are more open to interaction than nearby readers.

A few studies make comparisons among such behaviors, or across media. Zerbinos (1990), for example, invokes the uses and gratifications perspective in her study of the uses of newspapers versus videotext, finding more specific information seeking and better recall of facts from the electronic news, but she discusses only the surveillance functions of these media. Yoo (2011) used a more comprehensive list of gratifications and motivations in his study of reading online news, but it is still restricted to one type of Web site, as was an experimental study of emotional responses to social information seeking on Facebook (Wise, Alhabash, & Park, 2010). The gratifications achieved from browsing were described in the latter study, and also by Toms (1999). In a study comparing channels of communication, Dimmick, Kline, and Stafford (2000) compare gratifications one receives from information over the telephone versus e-mail. Williamson (1997, 1998) employs the theory to study a wide range of personal, institutional, and mass media sources used by the elderly. Finally, the framework is also mentioned in a recent study by Connaway et al. (2011).

7.4.3. Uncertainty Management Theory, etc.

A cluster of related theories combines the twin notions of a drive to reduce uncertainty, with the opposing human tendency to avoid distressing information. The basic idea is that we must carefully "manage" or "integrate" information, hence these theories are variously called Problematic Integration Theory (Babrow, 1992; Bradac 2001; Ford et al., 1996), Uncertainty Management Theory (Brashers, 2001; Brashers et al., 2002), and Motivated Information Management (Afifi & Afifi 2009; Afifi & Weiner, 2006). Based largely on observation of human conversation, this line of thinking assumes that people do not always strive to reduce uncertainty. For strategic psychological or social reasons, there are occasions when it makes sense to avoid acknowledging information, or even to deliberately increase uncertainty. An example is being less than fully truthful with a friend when we know that frankness will cause hurt feelings or friction; the friend in turn may understand that some information has been withheld, yet not ask for clarification. As Bradac (2001, p. 464) states, "Individuals may use uncertainty as a tool."

These theories have been applied most frequently in the health arena (e.g., Rosen & Knäuper, 2009; Thompson & O'Hair, 2008; Veinot, 2009; Wiering, 2005). Brashers (2001) cites various findings from health-related studies that point to differential short-term and long-term effects: patients react negatively to short-term uncertainties (e.g., about the effectiveness of the immediate treatment) yet positively to uncertainty about their long-term prognosis, because the latter vagueness supports a feeling of optimism.

Perhaps because of their emphasis on interpersonal communication, these theories have not yet been widely applied to other topics in information behavior. Case, Johnson, Andrews, Case, and Allard (2005), Ek and Heinström (2011), Heinström (2010), Houston (2011), Johnson and Case (2012), and Sairanen and Savolainen (2010) are among the literature reviews discussing these theories.

7.4.4. Other Objectivist Theories

Among the older objectivist theorists and theories, several have been especially influential in IB research. Many of these originated in the disciplines of psychology and sociology during the 1960s and 1970s. In some cases, it might be debatable as to the degree to which they have incorporated interpretivist elements; however, certainly all of these have their roots in much earlier theories.

Rogers' (2003) Diffusion of Innovation Theory explains the reasons for, and rates of, the spread of ideas, practices, and technologies through a social system. According to this sociological theory (which has predecessor and parallel theories in other disciplines), new ideas, behaviors, and artifacts exhibit a process of diffusion as they are communicated through varying channels and differentially adopted by individuals and organizations. Rogers posits five stages in the process of adoption: knowledge, persuasion, decision, implementation, and confirmation. These first two stages involve information seeking. Diffusion (or adoption) of innovations is cited relatively infrequently in the information behavior, perhaps because of its popularity for the study of objects rather than ideas. Chatman (1986) was an early user of the theory. Case and Rogers (1987) used it in an investigation of American farmers' use of information sources and technologies, Savolainen (2001) in discussing a study of Internet newsgroup usage, and Desouza, Awazu, and Wan (2006) made it the basis for an investigation of knowledge use among software engineers and related employees. Reviews citing the potential usefulness of diffusion theory in information behavior include Crowley (2005), Houston (2011), Johnson (1997), Lajoie-Paquette (2005), and McKechnie and Pettigrew (2002).

The concepts of social capital and social networks are employed in a number of theories, including some of the interpretivist paradigms. Lin (2002) and Coleman (1988) were among the first to discuss social capital, and their work has been cited in studies and commentaries by Haythornthwaite (1996), Hersberger (2001, 2003, 2005), Houston (2011), Johnson (2005, 2007), Lu (2007), Veinot (2009, 2010), and Veinot and Williams (2011). Mark Granovetter's (1973, 1982) related construct of the "strength of weak ties" (within general Social Network Theory) is much more popular, having been cited by Chatman (1991), Dixon (2005), Erdelez and Rioux (2000), Fisher and Landry (2007), Haythornthwaite (1996), Hersberger (2001, 2005), Houston (2011), Huotari and Wilson (2001), Lu (2007), Morey (2007), Pettigrew (2000) and Pettigrew and McKechnie (2001), Savolainen (2001, 2008c), Veinot (2009), Veinot and Williams (2011), and Wicks (1999). Granovetter's finding that secondary and tertiary contacts (those people whom our friends and *their* friends know, yet whom we do not) is naturally relevant to those studying human sources of information.

Albert Bandura's Social Cognitive Theory (Bandura, 2001) and Social Learning Theory (1977), and especially his central concept of self-efficacy, continue to influence a number of researchers. Among the examples are a survey about seeking of genetics information (Case, Johnson, Andrews, Allard, & Kelly, 2004), Ford's (2003) model of learning, Hepworth's (2004) study of informal information sources, Pálsdóttir's investigation of health information seeking in Iceland, and models proposed by Wiering (2005) and Wilson (1999).

Merton's (1968, 1972) Reference Group Theory and his conception of insiders versus outsiders have not been cited much in information behavior research since the passing of Elfreda Chatman, who referred to it several times in her various publications (1990, 1991, 1996), and in co-authored pieces: Burnett, Besant, and Chatman (2001), Huotari and Chatman (2001), and Dawson and Chatman (2001). Sligo and Jameson (2000) also used it in their study of health information seeking. Lu (2007) cites several of Merton's works in the context of gatekeeping. It is worth remembering that Merton also pioneered other concepts (e.g., social roles and role models) and methods (e.g., focus groups) sometimes used in information behavior research, but he is usually not cited in those contexts.

Stress and Coping Theory (Folkman, 1984) and the related concepts and measures of monitoring and blunting (Miller, 1987) have been employed by those researchers writing about information overload, uncertainty, avoidance, and related topics. Among the many authors who have used them (see Table 7.1), the most frequent citers have included Lynda Baker (Baker, 1996, 2004b, 2005; Baker & Pettigrew, 1999), Reijo Savolainen (Savolainen, 2007b, 2008a), and Tom Wilson (Wilson, 1999a, 2005). As one example of how researchers have employed this theory, Ya-Ling Lu (2010) uses the coping literature extensively in her examination of how children deal with problems in their daily lives. She concludes that the children she observed seek information to solve problems, to escape, to transition to a new mental state, to change their mood, or to completely avoid confronting what bothers them. Other researchers citing the blunting/avoidance literature are cited in Table 7.1.

Stephens and Krebs (1986), Smith and Winterhalder (1992), and Pirolli and Card (1999) all have written fundamental texts on optimal foraging theory. This theory first emerged in ecological studies to explain the way that organisms optimized the amount of energy they could take in through foraging of food resources. It has since been adapted to the study of information search. Thus, these theorists have been cited extensively in information retrieval research, and also in a number of more mainstream information behavior investigations and commentaries, including Jacoby (2005), Sandstrom (Sandstrom, 1994; Sandstrom & Sandstrom, 1995), Spink and Cole (2006), Williamson (1997, 1998), and Xu et al. (2006).

Csikszentmihalyi's (1990) Flow Theory originated in the positive psychology movement in studies of "optimal" experiences. Flow is a mental state in which one is completely absorbed in one's present activity to the extent that one loses track of time. Although an unobservable state, flow has been studied using conventional psychological methods, such as surveys and experience sampling. The theory is relevant to a number of information behaviors, such as learning or leisure-related activities. Flow is featured in a recent book by Heinström (2010) on personality and interaction with information. Other information behavior scholars who cite flow theory have been (Case, 2000), Cox, Clough, and Marlow (2008), Houston (2011), and Naumer (2005).

Perhaps because of the origins of objectivist theory in the sciences, it is noteworthy that many of the investigations of information seeking in health contexts continue to use methods of observation and analysis (particularly multivariate statistical analysis), and sometimes theories that originate in the objectivist tradition. I say "sometimes" because a certain amount of this research is atheoretical — what we might call "administrative" research that focuses on variables like patient use of information sources. Examples of health research based on this older theory tradition include Afifi and Weiner (2006), Ankem (2007), Case (2009b), Gorman (1999), Harris, Wathen, and Fear (2006), Kwon and Kim (2009), Pálsdóttir (2008), and Wiering (2005). Ankem (2006b) reviews a number of studies of cancer information seeking that also demonstrate this pattern.

7.5. Interpretivist Research Paradigms

Several clusters of theories are often cited in information behavior investigations that clearly break from the earlier, "objectivist" research traditions described above. What these paradigms have in common is the belief that one cannot study the social world in the same way as the natural world, as the former contains agents who have intentions and make meanings. For lack of a better overarching term, I will call these "interpretivist" paradigms. Sometimes they are identified by some variation on the terms listed under the first three labels:

- Constructivist, Activity Theory, and Sense-making
- Social Constructionism and Discourse Analysis
- Phenomenology
- Other Interpretivist Paradigms

7.5.1. *Constructivist, Activity Theory, and Sense-making*

Included under this heading are both "narrow" and "broad" programs of research, both with their core ideas from similar sources. What has been labeled a *constructivist* school of thought (the narrower program) came out of education (Dewey, 1933, 1960) and psychology (Bruner, 1973; Kelly, 1963; Vygotsky, 1978). The core of the constructivist metatheory could be said to derive from the philosophy and learning theory of Dewey (1960). Dewey's philosophy of instrumentalism emphasized pragmatic problem-solving through actions carried out in the real world. He saw both science and individuals as cycling through five phases of reflective operations: suggestion, intellectualization, hypothesis, reasoning, and then testing a solution by action. Conscious connection and interaction with objects and ideas led on the collective level to productive science, and on the individual level to thinking and learning.

Kelly (1963) advocated similar views in his theory of personal construct formation, a key component in his Theory of Personality. Kelly saw a person's behavior as strongly shaped by his or her mental constructs of the world and how it operates; constructs are knowledge structures that "enable us to anticipate events and predict outcomes" (Kuhlthau, 1988a, p. 233). Kelly's construction of knowledge also hypothesized five phases in thinking: encountering a new experience; initial feelings of confusion that result; the formation of a working hypothesis; taking actions that result in either reconstruing a (faulty) hypothesis or validating a (true) one; and, finally, assimilation of the findings with previous knowledge, resulting in changes of behavior. Kelly's work has been particularly influential in the works of Carol Kuhlthau. Bruner's (1990) phases of interpretation and perception parallel, to a large degree, those of Dewey and Kelly.

Prime examples of constructivist thinking are found in Kuhlthau's (1991, 1993a, 2005) research. Other scholars who have drawn upon these ideas include Cole and Kuhlthau (2000), Julien (2004), Williamson (2005), and Wilson (2002).

A related paradigm that builds on the work of Vygotsky (1978) as extended by Leont'ev (1978), Activity Theory has been less used in information behavior research, however seems to have found a home in studies of the workplace and computer usage. The theory is concerned with human reasoning (internalization) and actions upon objects (externalization) that create new artifacts. Key to this paradigm are notions of *activities* (which address needs) and *actions*, which work toward some transformation of reality. In this way, activity has an important role in forming consciousness. Nardi (1996) and Spasser (1999) were among the earlier writers to point out the relevance of Activity Theory to information behavior, and Wilson (2006, 2008b) along with Allen, Karanasios, and Slavova (2011) have written extensive explanations of how it might be used in that arena. The theory has been applied more in task analysis for information system development than in information behavior holistically, but see Hjørland and Christensen (2002) and Widén-Wulff (2007) for counter-examples to that generalization. Wilson sees great potential for Activity Theory for topics such as information literacy and task analysis; however, he points out that it has been infrequently used, as yet.

Sense-making constitutes the wider (theoretically sprawling) outgrowth of constructivist thought. Sense-making has incorporated Dewey, Kelly, and Bruner's notions of life as an encounter with problems and discontinuities in knowledge, and also the view that information is something we create through our interactions with the obstacles in our progress through life. It is an active, process-oriented view of learning and being. The end-product of the process — sense — is equated with knowledge, but also with opinions, intuitions, evaluations, and (effective) responses.

Whether sense-making constitutes a metatheory or a methodology is open to question. Brenda Dervin, the primary proponent of this approach to information seeking and use, notes that "some people call sense-making a theory, others a set of methods, others a methodology, others a body of findings" (Dervin, 1992, p. 61). In one explanation, Dervin (2005) describes her "sense-making methodology" as a "theory for methodology" (p. 26) that builds a bridge between substantive theory (i.e., systematic propositional statements about phenomena) and metatheory ("assumptions about the phenomena and how to study it," p. 25). In contrast to these two senses of "theory," Dervin aims to create a third type of theory that connects the two.

This text will treat sense-making primarily as a metatheory emphasizing naturalistic methods (Dervin & Nilan, 1986; Park, 1994) and that has theoretical grounding in the constructivist learning theories of John Dewey and Jerome Bruner. Yet Dervin acknowledges additional intellectual debts to many other scholars, including Carter (1965, 1973), Geertz (1973), Giddens (1984, 1989), Habermas (1979, 1984, 1987), and Taylor (1962, 1968), among others. Some of these scholars (Giddens and Habermas, especially) trace their intellectual roots in sociological, rather than psychological, directions. A comprehensive overview of Dervin's work is found in the collection by Dervin, Foreman-Wernet, and Lauterbach (2003).

A main tenet of sense-making is that information is not "something that exists apart from human behavioral activity." Rather, information is "created at a specific moment in time-space by one or more humans" (Dervin, 1992, p. 63). Unlike other approaches to information seeking that see information as something "out there" that is transmitted to people (as Dervin says, an information "brick" that is put into a human "bucket"), sense-making sees information as something that is constructed internally in order to address discontinuities in life (see the earlier discussion in Chapter 3 of "gaps"). This approach uncovers the problems that people experience in life and how they face those obstructions.

An early example of sense-making research is reported in Dervin, Jacobson, and Nilan (1982) and Dervin et al. (1982). Donors of blood were asked to describe the process of donating: what happened, what questions they had, and how they hoped the answers to their questions would help them. By documenting a timeline of the steps in the process and analyzing responses to the interview questions, the researchers were able to demonstrate that each step in the process had a distinctive pattern of questions and information usage. The results were used to create a touch-activated, question-answering computer screen that would address donors' information needs at each stage in the process. The answers given included not only the perspectives and responses of the medical personnel, but also those of previous donors, another useful outcome of the research.

The sense-making research agenda produces detailed evidence of the strategies by which individuals cope with problematic situations of all sorts. In doing so, sense-making research places a high value on the insights gained by the persons under study, as they reconstruct their solutions to past problems. In contrast, the constructivist approach is more narrowly focused on learning in specific tasks, such as researching a term paper in a library or testing a solution to a problem.

The constructivist metatheory continues to be used regularly in empirical investigations, although not quite a popular as it was a decade ago. Turner (2010) employs it in her study of oral information practices, as do Meyers, Fisher, and Marcoux (2009) in their investigation of preteens, Olsson (2010a) in his study of theater professionals, and du Preez and Fourie (2009) in an investigation of engineers. In the health arena, McCaughan and McKenna (2007) apply sense-making to the actions of newly diagnosed cancer patients.

7.5.2. Social Constructionism and Discourse Analysis

Although the roots of "social constructionist" (or "discourse-analytic") research stem from different theorists and disciplines, the root theorists share a common emphasis on the importance of language and social interaction in knowledge formation and in establishing social/power relationships. Within the information behavior literature, these streams of thought are often cited together and so will be discussed jointly.

According to Tuominen, Talja, and Savolainen (2002, 2005), construction-ism focuses on talk and language, as they emerge from interaction among members of a community. It is a "bundle of theoretical frameworks" (p. 329) with origins in sociology and in structuralism (Lechte, 1994). Construction-ism emphasizes the ways in which individuals construct understandings, meanings, and identities through dialogue and discourse. It is a framework that emphasizes "what people do with their talk and writing and also with different sorts of cultural resources that people draw on" (Tuominen &

Savolainen, 1997, p. 85). Among the functions that discourse serves is to define the nature of reality — what is real what is true, who is responsible, and to explain our own motivations and behaviors. Savolainen (2007a) sees constructionism as allied with the study of "practices" and standing in contrast to a "cognitive" (or "information processing") viewpoint that influences most other information-seeking research.

The constructionist tradition builds on the discourse analysis work of Bakhtin (1981) and Foucault (1972, 1980); other contributors to this project have been Garfinkel (1967), Harré (1984, 1994), and Potter (1996) — although there are many others (see Tuominen & Savolainen, 1997). Some theorists often cited in this vein include Berger and Luckmann (1967; on the social construction of reality). Closely related to this theory group are works on the social construction of scientific knowledge, such as Karin Knorr-Cetina (1981) and Bruno Latour and Stephen Woolgar (1979), and on the social construction of technology (SCOT; Bijker, Hughes, & Pinch, 1984).

An example of information behavior research in this realm is that of Pettigrew (1999, 2000; now Karen Fisher). Fisher has used the social-discursive framework in several studies to examine information exchange in everyday settings. Her ethnographic study of the flow of information among nurses and elderly patients at a foot clinic led her to develop the concept of an "information ground" — a place in which people come together to perform some task but which temporarily becomes a rich environment for exchanging information on many subjects. Fisher and her colleagues (e.g., Fisher et al., 2004; Fisher, Marcoux, Miller, Sánchez, & Cunningham, 2004) have also studied everyday information flows among immigrants in various community settings.

There have been various other IB studies conducted under the constructionist banner. For example, Given (2002a, 2002b) investigated how undergraduates gave accounts of their information practices, emphasizing the ways in which the students' everyday information needs informed their academic work, and the role of cultural capital in information seeking. Julien and Given (2003) showed how academic librarians construct the identities of the faculty members with whom they work on information literacy activities. McKenzie (2003a, 2003b) used Harré's notion of "positioning" to show how discourse is used to construct identities for self and others, and she has continued with this theoretical frame in her many publications since that time (e.g., 2005, 2006, 2009, 2010). Nahl (2007) applies discourse analysis to three domains in education and psychology, in what she calls "ecological constructionist." A short summary of social positioning theory is provided by Given (2005). While more concerned with information technology than with information seeking, I made use of the SCOT approach in my analysis of policy rhetoric surrounding the development of videotext (a precursor to the World Wide Web; Case, 1994).

7.5.3. Phenomenology

Phenomenological approaches are paramount among information behavior researchers, yet it is difficult to separate this worldview from some others. Ritzer (2008) offers a three-part classification of social theory, one of which he calls "social definitionist." Included in the definitionist camp are action theory, symbolic interactionism, phenomenology, and existentialism. Manicas (1998, p. 267), on the other hand, refers to a divide between "objectivist" and "subjectivist" traditions, with the latter including phenomenology (the key figure being Alfred Schutz), ethnomethodology (pioneered by Harold Garfinkel), and "versions of hermeneutics and critical theory" (e.g., Gadamer, Habermas, and Ricoeur). Ritzer (2008) also describes Schutz and Garfinkel as several others as representing "sociologies of everyday life," overlapping in membership with the social constructionist thinkers. From these we can see that there is wide variation in how theorists are categorized; hence, Table 7.1 lumps together several theorists who are discussed separately below. Under this heading I discuss the broad label of "phenomenology."

Schutz (1967) is an oft-cited figure regarding the *use* of phenomenology in social research, although its philosophical roots are in the work of Edmund Husserl. Schutz's focus is on intersubjectivity among human actors and their subjective interpretations of meaning (including the behavior of others and self). Such interpretations — our definition of the situation — are among the intentional actions we take in the course of our life "projects." The full explanation is found in Schutz (1962, 1964, 1967), and Wilson (2002) offers an introduction to the relevance of Schutz's work for research on information behavior.

As frequently cited as phenomenology and Schutz are in current information behavior literature, it is interesting that neither was cited in Pettigrew and McKechnie's (2001) extensive analysis of 1990s information science literature. Phenomenology is identified as the basis for investigations by Chatman (1996), Hayter (2007), Kari and Savolainen (2003), Marcella and Baxter (2000, 2005), and Savolainen (2008a). It is also invoked in reviews by Chatman (2000), Olsson (2005), Savolainen (1995, 2007c), and Wilson (1981, 1999, 2002, 2003).

7.5.4. Other Interpretivist Paradigms

While "critical theory" is sometimes mentioned in information behavior discourse as a source of theory, the only theorist regularly cited in that tradition is Jürgen Habermas. Critical theory was a later development of Marxism taken up by the Institute of Social Research in Frankfurt, from the 1920s through the 1970s. Affiliated with this "Frankfurt School" were the scholars Max Horkheimer, Theodor Adorno, Herbert Marcuse, and others (Held, 1980). Their critiques of capitalism and culture, along with contributions to epistemology, are still influential. In the 1970s, Habermas took up many of the same themes of these earlier scholars, but with some marked differences in assumptions, especially as regards the role of scientific research. Habermas' "Theory of Communicative Action" is usually identified as the most recent development in this long stream of thought. His notion of a "public sphere" is certainly relevant to many aspects of information exchange, especially to publishing and libraries. Habermas' theory has been regularly cited in relation to information seeking since the early 1980s, including these scholars: Benoit (2000, 2005), Burnett and Jaeger (2008), Cornelius (1996), Dervin (1989, 1992, 1999), Dervin et al. (1982), Newhagen (1997), Mehra (2007), Pettigrew and McKechnie (2001), Savolainen (2008a), Timpka and Arborelius (1990), and Wersig and Windel (1985).

Giddens (1984), although certainly influenced by Habermas, is not normally included among the critical theorists. Giddens' theorizing about the nature and evolution of social structures ("structuration") are helpful in understanding both the constraints under which human agents operate in society, and how this enables them to accomplish certain tasks, through an interaction of norms, meanings, practices, and power relations. Giddens' citers among information behavior scholars include Dervin (1992), Leckie (2005), Pettigrew and McKechnie (2001), Rosenbaum (1993, 2010), Savolainen (1993, 1995, 2009a), and Williamson and Manaszewicz (2002).

Goffman's (1959, 1974, 1983) "Face Theory" is associated with his symbolic interactionist research on how we present ourselves to others — an emphasis on interpersonal interaction. Goffman's "Frame Analysis" is concerned with how we organize our experiences, using a conceptual "frame" (structure) to guide our actions. His work has been invoked in the following information behavior publications: Case et al. (2004), Chatman (1996, 2000), Chelton (2001), Dervin et al. (1982), Fisher and Landry (2007), Houston (2011), Mokros, Mullins, and Saracevic (1995), Mon (2005), Nahl (2005), Radford (2001), Thivant (2005), and Tuominen and Savolainen (1997).

Bourdieu (1984, 1990) is noted for his "Theory of Taste" or "Distinction," along with the concept of "symbolic violence" (i.e., the legitimation of social order via the imposition of symbolic systems, such that world structures are "taken for granted"). These theories have special relevance for studies of everyday life information seeking (ELIS, e.g., Savolainen, 1995, 1999, 2008a). Other information behavior scholars citing Bourdieu include Dervin (1999, 2003), Houston (2011), Hussey (2010), Joyce (2005), Laplante and Downie (2011), Leckie (2005), Olsson (2005), Pettigrew and McKechnie (2001), Seldén (2001), Thomas and Nyce (2001), and Van Snippenburg (1996).

Relevant to Bourdieu's work, Lave and Wenger (1991) and Wenger (1998) describe a "community of practice" as a group of people who share some kind of work or interests, and thus knowledge. They share information and thus learn from one another, forming meanings and identity. Lave and Wenger's theoretical work is cited by Aspray and Hayes (2011), Davenport and Hall (2002), Davies and McKenzie (2004), Finholt (2002), Harris, Veinot, and Bella (2010), Hemmig (2009), Houston (2011), Lueg (2008), Savolainen (2007a, 2008a), Sundin (2002), and Talja (2010), among others. As Talja explains, the community of practice approach is distinct from Michel de Certeau's "The Practice of Everyday Life" (1984); however, the two theories are clearly related. Rather than a focus on the community, de Certeau's work operates on the individual level, describing how we do not passively consume the world's objects and ideas, but rather actively alter them to make them our own. De Certeau's work is cited by Davenport, Higgins, and Somerville (2000), Houston (2011), Joyce (2005), Ross (2005, 2009), Rothbauer (2005), and Savolainen (2008a).

Reader Response Theory is closely related to de Certeau's notion of modifying our lived experiences. The theory focuses on the way that readers actively experience and create meaning during the act of reading. This emphasis naturally aligns with other theories used in information behavior emphasizing the creation of meaning. Many scholars have been involved in building Reader Response Theory, including Fish (1987), Iser (1978), Suleiman and Crosman (1980), and Rosenblatt (1994) and others. Among the scholars who have used or mentioned the theory are Massey, Weeks, and Druin (2005), Massey, Druin, and Weeks (2007), Mick and Buhl (1992), Radway (1985), Reuter (2007), Ross (1999, 2005), Scott (1994), and Stern (1992).

Sometimes mentioned in information behavior commentaries, yet left out of this chapter, is the general category of "pragmatism." According to Creswell and Clark (2011), pragmatism does not advocate for any fixed ontology, philosophy, or method, but rather emphasizes a practical concern with addressing a research problem and using any worldview or technique that enables useful research to take place. Hence, it is a good basis for the mixed methods approach discussed in Chapter 9.

Undoubtedly, other theoretical influences could be tracked in this manner. Other theorists cited multiple times in information behavior research include Bhaskar, Deleuze, Derrida, Freire, Gadamer, Gramsci, Lacan, and Marcuse. The volume by Leckie, Given, and Buschman (2010) may help the reader understand their relevance.

7.6. Mapping the Theoretical Influences on Authors

As mentioned in the introductory discussion, I have taken a fairly narrow definition of what qualifies as a theory. That is, I have not included solitary concepts for which only a few pages of explanation have yet appeared. Many theories or principles have been invoked in information-seeking research, although some of them appear in relatively few studies. Depending on what passes for theory, and how many uses of it must occur before we take it to be generally applicable, there are many other candidates that could be discussed as theories relevant to information seeking.

Fisher et al. (2005), Pettigrew, Fidel, and Bruce (2001), and Pettigrew and McKechnie (2001) offer a number of examples of potentially relevant theories, paradigms, frameworks, and concepts in their analyses, some of which have not been described earlier in this book. Table 7.1 includes examples of theories and concepts invoked in discussions of information behavior, for which I found at least six examples in the literature over the last three decades. This list is meant to be illustrative, rather than exhaustive, of theories used in information behavior research; it is based on what has actually been cited, rather than an intellectual history of who *should* be given credit for a particular theory.

Table 7.1 lists theorists in alphabetical order, except in a few cases in which citations to theorists are so highly correlated that it would be difficult to disentangle them. A prime example is the close connection between Susan Folkman's theory of ways of coping with stress, and Susan Miller's notions of monitoring and blunting as means of emotional control. Many of the other theorists are cited in a more isolated fashion, and so are listed separately. All the theories or paradigms listed in Table 7.1 have been mentioned earlier.

Most of the publications cited are empirical investigations; however, some merely discuss how the theory might be applied to study information behavior. As documented by Rosenbaum (2010), at times theories are cited in a superficial manner. He examined 72 citations to Anthony Giddens' Structuration Theory across 13 LIS journals and found that in 54% of these articles the citation appeared to be "ceremonial" rather than substantive. That is, in each case there was no specific page number, content, or quotation provided, simply a citation to a major work of Giddens. This tendency for some citations to be made in a perfunctory fashion has long been discussed in studies of citation practices (see, e.g., the literature review in Case and Higgins (2000)).

As can be seen from the table, it remains the case that much of the formal theory has been borrowed from other disciplines — although there has been an increase in theorizing by information behavior scholars. In particular, the volume by Fisher et al. (2005) features a number of established scholars who provide synopses of theories or concepts they have found useful in the study of information behavior. Many of the 72 entries in the Fisher et al. (2005) volume (prepared with the help of members of the ASIST Special Interest Group on Information Needs, Seeking, and Use) are concepts, hypotheses, or models developed to explain information-related phenomena, rather than "theories" in the most formal sense used in the social sciences (i.e., an articulated set of constructs, definitions, and propositions). However, many of the entries reflect constructs and theories adopted from other disciplines and are reflected in Table 7.1.

The table illustrates the popularity of certain theories and sensitizing concepts, as well as the broad influences on some prominent information behavior scholars. Regarding the latter point, we can see that some investigators have cited between 6 and 11 theories, or groups of theories, in pursuit of their research programs. In this respect, the table might also be indicative of a theoretical sprawl that makes it difficult to relate individual investigations to one another, as they derive from distinct assumptions and methods.

Certain theories have become more popular over the most recent decade, while others have declined somewhat in the degree to which they are cited. Activity Theory, Communities of Practice, and the various discourse-analytic theorists have been gaining the most adherents. Those theories having a bearing on health behaviors, such as Stress and Coping Theory, and the various Uncertainty Management theories, continue to be applied frequently in recent investigations. On the other hand, Reference Group Theory, Personal Construct Theory, and the Diffusion of Innovations are no longer cited very often in the information behavior literature.

Bates (2002, 2005a) has persuasively argued that there is room for multiple approaches in information behavior research. Empirical research on the *use* of theory and metatheory in information seeking, for example, Pettigrew et al. (2001), Pettigrew and McKechnie (2001), McKechnie and Pettigrew (2002), Julien and Duggan (2000), and McKechnie, Baker, Greenwood, and Julien (2002), have documented the evolution of theories, metatheories, and paradigms in the discipline. The collection of theory summaries by Fisher et al. (2005) point out how many additional choices there are among the various "lenses" used to view information seeking and related topics.

7.7. Summary

I began this chapter by discussing the nature of paradigms adopted by researchers. These are difficult to place in a single framework, both because they overlap and because they operate at different levels of generality. I noted that various words may be used to describe much the same thing regarding research: perspectives, traditions, or approaches. I use the word "paradigm" interchangeably with these.

.

I discussed the nature of theory, describing it as a generalized explanation of the relationships among various phenomena. I described the confusions that arise with varying usage of the term "theory." One implication of that confusion is that theories also vary in the degree to which they attempt to generalize; theorists and epistemologists refer to this as the issue of "levels of theory." In this chapter, a "theory" is assumed to be a closely related *set* of definitions and propositions, rather than a simple statement like "people seek information when they are uncertain." The latter declaration, although perhaps true, needs to have a supporting set of concepts and hypotheses to result in a useful series of investigations of which we can all make sense.

Next, I explored a number of theories that have been applied in information-seeking research. These included Activity Theory, Zipf's Principle of Least Effort, the Uses and Gratifications tradition, Constructivism, Social Constructionism, Social Learning/Cognitive Theory, Theory of Taste, Theory of Reasoned Action, Theory of Communicative Action, Personal Construct Theory, Diffusion of Innovations, Optimal Foraging Theory, Social Network Theory/Strength of Weak Ties, Reader Response Theory, Social Capital Theory, and Uncertainty Management Theory, among others.

Most of these theories have origins that are decades old. Most are likely to continue to attract adherents, as no comprehensive theory of information behavior has emerged. Theories originating in education, psychology, and sociology continue to provide most of the theoretical basis for empirical work on information needs and uses.

Finally, I pointed out that some uses of theory appear to be ceremonial or perfunctory, rather than deeply engaged. This type of usage must decline if we are to make meaningful contributions to the communities of discourse that surround each of these theories.

Recommended for Further Reading

Bates, M. J. (2005a). An introduction to metatheories, theories, and models. In K. E. Fisher, S. Erdelez, & E. F. McKechnie (Eds.), *Theories of information behavior* (pp. 1–24). Medford, NJ: Information Today.
  A synopsis of the various paradigms for studying information behavior.

Chatman, E. A. (1990). Alienation theory: Application of a conceptual framework to a study of information among janitors. *RQ, 29,* 355–368.
  Chatman's study is a fine example of the use of theory in information seeking research, and it makes fascinating reading, too.

Dervin, B. (1992). From the mind's eye of the user: The sense-making qualitative-quantitative methodology. In J. Glazier & R. Powell (Eds.),

Qualitative research in information management (pp. 61–84). Englewood, CO: Libraries Unlimited.

Dervin, a prolific author, has published several explanations of sense-making research. This is one of the most accessible.

Hacking, I. (1999). *The social construction of what?* Cambridge, MA: Harvard University Press.

Philosopher Ian Hacking has made a career of bringing philosophy to bear on issues of social importance. In this book he discusses the origins of "social constructionism" and how it has been applied to social issues.

Rosengren, K. (1989). Paradigms lost and regained. In B. Dervin, L. Grossberg, B. O'Keefe, & E. Wartella (Eds.), *Rethinking communication: Paradigm issues* (Vol. 1, pp. 21–39). Newbury Park, CA: Sage.

Rosengren discusses the ways in which communication scholars — and other social scientists — have been divided by different philosophical and epistemological assumptions. This chapter contains a version of Burrell and Morgan's thoughtful typology of sociological schools.

Savolainen, R. (2006). Spatial factors as contextual qualifiers of information seeking. *Information Research, 11*(4). Retrieved from http://InformationR. net/ir/11-4/paper261.html

An example of how metaphors (in this case, space) can function as a kind of theory. Savolainen examines many examples of how information behavior researchers have employed spatial factors or analogies as influences on information seeking and use. Among them are information grounds (Fisher), information horizons (Sonnenwald), foraging (Sandstrom) and fields/pathways (Pescosolido; Johnson). The article also contains simple examples of metatheoretical paradigms such as perspectivism, pragmaticism, and objectivism.

Weick, K. E. (1995). *Sensemaking in organizations.* Thousand Oaks, CA: Sage.

Weick takes a different perspective from the usual information-seeking authors — who tend to focus on individuals. Here the emphasis is on the responses that social groups and institutions make in the face of ambiguous situations. Weick's fascinating explanations range from the reasons that battered child syndrome took decades to be recognized to why it is that soldiers in battle often fail to fire their guns.

PART 4

METHODS FOR STUDYING
INFORMATION BEHAVIOR

Chapter 8

The Research Process

> What do I want to know in this study? This is a critical beginning point. Regardless of point of view, and quite often because of our point of view, we construct and frame a question for inquiry. After this question is clear, we select the most appropriate methodology to proceed with the research project.
>
> — Valerie Janesick (1998, p. 37)

> The sharp distinction between theory and method implied by many discussions is based on a vastly oversimplified picture of how research operates! what we can know is determined by the available methods for knowing.
>
> — M. Scott Poole and Robert McPhee (1994, p. 43)

Chapter Outline

8.1. Relating Theory to Methodology

The previous chapter discussed some paradigms and various theories that have been, or could be, applied to information behavior. Both paradigms and theories are intertwined with one another and with the research methods chosen by the investigator. M. Scott Poole and Robert McPhee (1994) say that the "domains" of theory and methodology overlap in significant ways; what theories we use tend to indicate what methods are available to us. The overlap occurs because *both* theory and method must be concerned with our type of *explanation* (e.g., is our goal to demonstrate that one variable influences another?) and our approach to *inquiry* (e.g., whether we use a theory to guide observation, or whether we start making observations to build a theory, as discussed in the section on induction and deduction; see also Dervin, 2005, on this topic).

It is important to understand where theory and methodology do *not* overlap, too. Methodology is *not* concerned with *substantive assumptions* about what is being studied, which is a matter for theory (or, more specifically, for metatheory). Only theory addresses the basic assumptions that we make about the nature of reality — whether, for instance, we can ever be objective in our observations of other people. It is the theory that assumes, for example, that the *meaning* of a word is a matter of *agreement* between people (i.e., socially constructed), rather than an objective reality.

Likewise, our *techniques of observation* are *not* a part of theory but rather are of prime concern in methodology. These techniques and tools are what we call "methods" and will be an important focus in this chapter, which considers the process of designing and implementing research. Our choices of design and method have profound implications for what we can know about the phenomena we observe.

The purpose of this chapter is to highlight some basic considerations in *designing* investigations, and to point out different methods commonly used for studying information seeking, needs, and uses. Specific examples of methods will be provided in the chapter that follows this one. We must consider *how* information seeking has been studied to assess what we know about it. This is where methodology enters the picture.

8.1.1.   Why We Need Methods

Methodology concerns how we can *find out*. What kind of principles, logic, and evidence would best advance our goal of learning (and most likely, recording) knowledge about an area or object of study? The specific ways, tools, and techniques of observation and measurement are what we call "methods." As Poole and McPhee (1994, p. 43) emphasize, "method is one's point of contact with the world." We need to have methods to control for human error, which is always present when we are thinking and making observations about reality. Many methodologists (e.g., Babbie, 2009; Katzer, Cook, & Crouch, 1998; Schutt, 2008) have pointed out common sources of human error, including the following:

1. People are by nature poor observers. We make errors of both omission (not seeing what is there) and admission (seeing things that are not there)

in the process. Unless we employ a conscious method, we tend to observe only a fraction of what we actually "see." The fact that you cannot recall much of what you passed the last time you drove to work is not merely a function of memory; you "saw" thousands of details but few were important to you at that time so you did not really "notice" them.

2. People tend to *overgeneralize* from small samples of evidence or opinion. If three friends claim that a local politician is corrupt, we tend to assume that they are right without investigating any further.

3. We tend to notice those things that support our beliefs and ignore evidence that does not. Akin to the "selective exposure" discussed in Chapter 4, this tendency is called *selective perception*.

4. We sometimes *make up information* to support our beliefs, no matter how illogical it might appear to another person. A common example is the so-called "gambler's fallacy": the belief that a run of bad luck (e.g., six tails in a row in coin-tossing) makes it even more likely that a good outcome will follow (i.e., "the next toss is sure to come up heads").

5. Our *ego* is often involved in what we "know" and profess to be true. We are prone to be defensive when several others challenge our point of view. We may go so far as to suspect that their disagreement is based on some personal bias against us, rather than a simple attempt to state their own opinions or evidence.

6. In the extreme case that we call "prejudice," we may simply *close our minds* to any new evidence about an issue. In such a case, no further observations or arguments will ever change our beliefs or opinions.

7. People are prone to *mystify* anything they do not understand. If an issue is too complex, the easy way out is to say that it is something that simply cannot be understood. Many observers would say the same thing regarding the use of information.

Research methods are intended to be a partial corrective for these human failings. By agreeing to guidelines for identifying research problems and gathering and interpreting evidence, scholars and scientists intend to establish communities of discourse regarding their topics of investigation. The point of epistemology and methodology is thus to provide a basis of agreement for debating and assessing knowledge claims in given areas. The resulting communities of discourse are loosely coupled and often disagree about the appropriateness of particular assumptions or techniques — but that is also the nature of science and scholarship.

Research methods are conscious attempts to (collectively) overcome some human shortcomings, while promoting dialogue among researchers. To that end we employ techniques that guard us against the errors described previously. For instance, we might use instruments (notes, photographs, tape recordings, and computer logs) to be more certain that we do not "miss" any information. We make lots of observations to have plenty of evidence on which to base our findings. To keep ourselves honest, we decide in advance which specific things we are going to observe. We state, again in advance, what we think our conclusions are likely to be. As scholars, we make a professional commitment to be methodical and rigorous in our studies and to be open to criticisms from our colleagues. We agree to a continuing dialogue about our research, and agree not to cling so strongly to our conclusions that no one can persuade us with compelling counterevidence. Finally, we agree that certain criteria must be met for findings to be widely accepted: they must make logical sense and agree with our observations.

In summary, methods (and the philosophical assumptions that underlie them) are about how best to explore reality through structured, personal experience (i.e., *inquiry*). Methods offer us a choice of plans for asking questions and finding answers to them.

8.1.2.   Techniques of Measurement and Analysis

It is important to realize that the term "methods" often refers to two types of technique: *measurement* (i.e., observation and data collection) and *analysis*. Various authors (e.g., Poole & McPhee, 1994; Sonnenwald & Iivonen, 1999) have tried to tease apart the interactions of these two dimensions. A list of what I mean by techniques of measurement versus analysis is found in Table 8.1.

Table 8.1: Techniques of measurement and analysis.

Techniques of measurement
- Observation of experimental conditions
- Surveys (self-administered questionnaires or interview schedules)
- Intensive interviews (e.g., focus group interviews)
- Participant observation (including ethnography)
- Diaries (i.e., self-reports of experience, recorded electronically or on paper)
- Collection of other behavioral artifacts (e.g., paper or electronic documents)
- Mixed/multiple methods.

Techniques of analysis
- Case study
- Theory testing
- Model building
- Content analysis
- Discourse analysis
- Network analysis
- Historical analysis
- Statistical (e.g., analysis of variance and significance testing)
- Meta-analysis (of multiple quantitative studies).

Obviously, one first *measures* something, and then one *analyzes* those measurements. So the choices of techniques are intertwined. It is because of this interdependence that we often refer to investigations as if they were solely the technique of measurement or analysis: experiments, surveys, case studies, and so forth. Some methods of measurement require certain kinds of analysis: experiments that gather quantitative data necessitate some kind of statistical analysis; collection of diaries probably dictates content analysis of the entries. In other cases, multiple types of analysis might be used with one type of evidence; for example, a study of book circulation records might use either statistical analysis or content analysis, or both.

Table 8.1 is a primer for the types of investigations that will be covered in the next chapter, with the exception of model building, which we discussed in the previous chapter. Chapter 9 includes explanations of each technique, along with examples how such methods have been used to study information behavior. Readers who are thoroughly familiar with general concepts like validity and with data gathering techniques such as surveys might wish to skip directly to the next chapter for descriptions and examples of specific types of methods.

This chapter will review the basic stages, concepts, and issues in social research; the terminology will be useful in critiquing the study examples that follow.

8.2. Basic Considerations in Research

8.2.1. *Stages of Research*

The classic view of the research process is often portrayed in five stages. These include: (1) imagining a research question; (2) determining what data are needed and designing a specific study to collect it; (3) choosing and implementing research methods; (4) analyzing and interpreting observations; and (5) considering the overall results. Although in practice it is rarely as simple as all that, it is worth briefly considering these five typical steps in the research process. Then we will consider some of the basic issues that lead researchers to choose one type of design or method over another.

The first stage is the one in which an investigation is conceptualized. A theory (or, as Herbert Blumer, 1986, says, a "prior picture" of the world) may come into play, as well as personal motivation. Investigators are drawn to a particular topic, issue, or problem for some reason. Sometimes researchers pursue topics simply because they are paid to do so. For instance, a market researcher or a chemist may work on an agenda strictly defined by their employer. In research involving people, more often the researcher has some personal connection to the object of investigation. Perhaps a scholar is drawn to research on primary education because he sees a need for improvement there, because he has been observing his own children as they learn, or because he feels some aspect of education offers a concrete place to study an abstract concept (e.g., self-efficacy) — or because all three of these reasons apply. As a result, research questions are formed and their answers pursued.

In the second stage, a specific study is designed. Blumer (1986, p. 25) calls this "determination of the data to be sought." Some kind of phenomena and/or venue is selected for observation, which can be as complex as a statistical sample of people or objects, or as simple as selecting a location from which to "watch life go by." A plan is derived for what goal is to be achieved in the study and how to go about achieving it. Again, a theory (if employed) may dictate the goal of the research project and what kinds of designs and data are necessary to achieve it. Key considerations here are the resources available in terms of time and personnel.

The third step is to choose methods and specific procedures for observation, and to carry them out. Multiple sources of evidence contribute to more compelling conclusions and are thus to be preferred — see, for example, Creswell and Clark (2011) and Fidel (2008) on the advantages of mixed methods. (Much more will be said about methods later.)

Once evidence is gathered, it is analyzed and interpreted — in many cases, observations are being interpreted *while* they are made. Classification is the key to many analyses — how many instances of that type versus this type were observed? In survey and experimental research, for example, the measurement and analysis may be primarily quantitative, yet most data gathering involves some degree of interpretation and classification. Consider the common practice of allowing survey respondents to supply an "other" response not anticipated on the questionnaire — all of these responses must be categorized and coded in some way for convenient summary and interpretation. Computer software packages have made it increasingly easy to record, interpret, and analyze data of types both qualitative (e.g., The Ethnograph and QSR NUD*IST) and quantitative (e.g., SPSS); there are also more specialized programs for conducting social network analysis (e.g., UCINET; Borgatti, Mehra, Brass & Labianca, 2009).

In a final and often underemphasized stage, researchers summarize and consider their findings. The investigators write and talk about what they have found, and in some cases they share their conclusions not merely with other researchers but also with the communities or individuals they have studied. Ideally this step leads to an evaluation and reconceptualization of the research — whether it "worked," contributed to theory, was worth the effort, or could be improved upon.

8.2.2. Induction and Deduction

Most investigators have previously established assumptions and preferences that lead them to choose certain designs and techniques. A key consideration is whether they are to proceed inductively or deductively in their research. Taking an inductive approach means that the research will examine particular instances and reason toward generalization. That is, you are gathering, analyzing, and interpreting data in such a way that it may lead to general principles, such as theories. *Grounded theory* is a research goal that attempts to build theory from concrete observations and to keep any generalizations relatively close to the contexts in which they originated, rather than attempting to build an abstract theory that strives (and typically fails) to apply in all situations. Similarly, most "qualitative" methods tend to be inductive in nature, mainly because they assume that generalizations are difficult to make when one is studying people or their creations.

The deductive approach proceeds in the opposite fashion, reasoning from the general to the particular. This is typically the way science is portrayed, as applying a theory to a particular case in an attempt to test the theory. Presumably the theory is either supported or revised, based on the results. However, the number of formal tests of theory are relatively sparse when it comes to studying information seeking. Rather, much of the research has been merely descriptive of a unique situation (i.e., a given information user or organization), or an inductive attempt to generalize about certain types of persons, sources, or effects.

Few investigators or studies stick solely to induction or deduction. Rather, they tend to move back and forth between those modes: collecting information that allows them to state a principle or tendency, then testing that generalization through further research, in an endless chain of logic. Even strong advocates of induction like Glaser and Strauss (1967) point out that the deductive approach can be useful in exploratory stages of research. Seldén (2005) does a good job of explaining the tensions inherent between these two modes of research.

Particularly for those researchers who are testing theory, it is common to state a *research problem*. A research problem is a question that asks about the relationship between two or more variables. A problem might be stated as "What effect does an increase in the number of available information sources have upon the use of an individual source?" Problem statements typically express relations between *variables* and suggest ways in which they might be tested empirically. However, many interesting questions cannot be stated in such a manner because their phenomena are difficult to define and measure and are not amenable to formal testing. That is why we have a diversity of assumptions and methods in social research.

For research problems that test a preexisting theory, *hypotheses* are derived. A hypothesis is a conjectural statement about the relation between two or more variables. Most typically this formal approach to knowledge is used in experimental studies in which the researcher is able to manipulate (or at least anticipate) a change in the environment that might produce some kind of measurable effect among the people present. For example, a hypothesis such as "the introduction of a new information source into a previously stable set of sources will cause a decline in the use of the earlier sources" predicts that a new source will appear and that it will affect use of other information sources. Such concepts as "information use" must be defined so as to be measurable in some way. Once stated in a proper form, hypotheses can be tested through further research and shown to be "probably true" or "probably false." In this way, hypothetical statements can be used to build theory.

Early in the research process, the object(s) of observation must be identified and defined for measurement. This process is called *operationalization*. After explicating a concept of interest (e.g., the explication of "information" in Chapter 3), we must lay out the procedures or operations we will use to measure that concept. We must specify the conditions under which an instance of the concept might be produced and observed. For example, where would we look to find an instance of "information?" How will we recognize it when we see it? What would indicate that "information" is present? How will we measure an instance of "information" once it is observed?

The resulting *operational definition* guides our *observation* of the phenomena. We discover ways to classify or quantify the things we observe: *attributes* (characteristics or qualities that describe something) of people (e.g., female vs. male) or their behavior (e.g., asking a question vs. not asking a question) are grouped together in logical sets called *variables* (e.g., gender = male or female). We develop a strategy for observing those variables in a particular context. Our method might involve watching or interviewing people, examining artifacts that people create (e.g., a log of their television watching or a record of what they have read), or any of a number of different observational possibilities.

8.2.3. Validity and Reliability

The twin concepts of validity and reliability determine how compelling the results of our study will be, and so are important considerations in the choice of methods and construction of measures. *Validity* is the extent that the measurement procedures accurately reflect the concept we are studying. Asking someone if she "knows a lot about world events" is not a particularly valid way of studying "news consumption." Asking the respondent if she subscribes to a newspaper would be more valid, as it gets closer to the heart of the matter. However, an answer to that question does not tell you whether she actually *reads* the newspaper; questions about her newspaper *reading habits* would have even more validity. Perhaps the most valid measures might be some questions — whether administered through an interview or on paper — that would tell us if she can identify the top news stories of the day or week, and so forth.

Reliability is demonstrated when measures are *repeated under the same conditions* and yield highly similar measurements each time. We expect a bathroom scale to give us the same weight from one minute to the next, because we have not had enough time to gain or lose significant weight in such a short period. We would not necessarily expect the scale to register the same weight 20 years later, because the conditions have changed, and we may have gained or lost weight. In contrast, asking several observers to *guess* our weight (and then taking the average of their guesses) would likely be an unreliable measure, as human perceptions vary considerably across observers and even within the same person across time.

There can be a trade-off between validity and reliability. Measures that are highly reliable may not be high on validity, whereas highly valid measures sometimes have problems with reliability. Although it is easily possible to develop measures that are both invalid and unreliable (asking "Is the sky blue today?" would not be a valid measure of color perception, and is likely to draw unreliable answers as well), it is difficult to come up with measures that are both highly valid and highly reliable.

Consider a situation in which we wish to study the use of materials in a library. One basic question would be how many people actually have an opportunity to use the library materials — by entering the building. To answer that simple question, we could station an observer at the door and have him or her count people. However, such a measurement will not be completely reliable; a second observer watching the crowd enter the library might come up with a slightly different count. A superior method would be to install a turnstile in the entrance; we could then assume that one "rotation" of the turnstile equals one "user" of the library. Now we have a reliable count of the persons entering the building.

But what does that simple count tell us about the actual use of the informational materials or services found in the library — the kinds of activities that people more commonly think of as constituting "use?" Virtually nothing: people might have entered merely to use the bathroom or the pay phone.

To capture a more valid measure of the use of materials and services we could distribute a questionnaire at the doorway with specific questions about such uses. Users would fill them out and we would have data about the use of materials by a large number of users. However, we would find that the more, and more detailed, questions we ask, the fewer the users who will complete the survey. The fewer the number of respondents, the less confident we are that we can generalize from our results to the entire population of users. In other words, we might encounter a trade-off between the depth and the breadth of the information we gather.

If we are searching for a really detailed picture of the information usage, we might consider close observations of a small number of users. Perhaps we could follow them around the library and they could talk to us in detail about their internal experience of searching and finding information. Obviously these methods (observation and interview) would require the consent of the participants and have various implications for our study, particularly in the obtrusive way they interfere in the activities of the library user.

Making these detailed observations, we would get closer to the phenomenon of concern: what people actually *do* when they use the library. So these data potentially have a great deal of validity. Pursuing this approach also has drawbacks, though. Some aspects of our methods may lower validity; gathering data from a smaller number of respondents than the earlier approaches will lead to a lack of generalizability. Also we are introducing an artificial element by having the respondent talk out loud, which also may lower the validity of our findings.

Other problems have serious implications for reliability. Reporting on our own thoughts and behaviors can be problematic, particularly due to the unreliability of memories. If we ask three witnesses to a crime what they saw and remember, do they say the same things? Because of both selective perception and variability of memory, typically the witnesses do not say *exactly* the same things, but multiple accounts are often close enough to draw some conclusions. Eyewitness testimony is not completely reliable, but it is often the best evidence we have. If eyewitnesses *always* gave radically different accounts of the same events, courts would have to abandon the use of such information, as it would be inherently unreliable. Likewise, reliability is absolutely basic to the conduct of research.

We can imagine many variations on the design and methods of the hypothetical study of library use, involving changes in the questions asked, the number of respondents studied, the type and manner of questions asked, the time frame for the investigation, and so forth. The point is that, as we move from crude but highly reliable measures toward measures that better reflect the concept under study, we encounter some trade-offs between validity and reliability.

Such trade-offs are partly behind the long-standing disputes over quantitative versus qualitative methods (an unhelpful argument, in most respects). Research designs that intend to produce highly quantitative and reliable measures, such as laboratory experiments, suffer from validity problems because they invoke an artificial situation that may not reflect how people think and behave in the real world. A qualitative approach such as participant observation, however it may be grounded in the real world, raises issues about the reliability of what is observed and measured, because the specific contexts and measurements are difficult (and sometimes impossible) to replicate. There are also issues of interpretation of observations, which tend to be highly individual. By extension, then, we can talk about entire study designs as offering trade-offs in reliability and validity.

One way to conduct research that is both valid and reliable is to be found in the use of multiple methods and multiple sources of data. This will be brought out in the discussions of methods and the examples that follow in the next chapter. Another possibility is to use measures or instruments that have been developed and tested by other researchers. One example is the "scales for information-seeking behavior" questionnaire described by Timmers and Glas (2008). While their items apply mainly to information literacy studies, they are a good example of how standardized instruments may be developed that would improve reliability of responses as well as allowing comparisons across studies.

8.2.4. *Purpose, Units, and Time*

Before selecting a particular method, there are several other considerations that come into play. Among these considerations are the *purpose* of our study, the type of things we intend to observe (typically called *units of analysis*), and the *time* dimension of the investigation.

Research may vary as regards its purpose. Particularly regarding topics that have not yet been widely studied, the goal is simply to *explore* the phenomenon to gain a basic understanding of it. For example, when new media appear, such as the World Wide Web (WWW), the first research questions that emerge may be: "What is this thing called the WWW?" "What does it do?" and "How do people use it?" When the object of study is novel, some aspects of it may not yet be defined well enough for precise measurement. Because new information sources and new variations on existing channels emerge with some frequency, exploratory studies are fairly common in information-seeking research.

When a phenomenon is well established, the focus of investigation is likely to be on documenting its characteristics. *Descriptive* studies are intended to measure well-defined variables regarding the people or objects involved with the phenomenon. To use the WWW as an example once more, descriptive research questions might be: "How many searches are being conducted on the WWW?" "How many Web sites are in existence?" "Which are the most popular sites?" "How many people are using the WWW, and with what frequency?" and "What are the demographic characteristics of WWW users?" Much of the information-seeking literature, particularly the early studies that focused on channels, sources, and audiences for information, are chiefly descriptive in nature.

The ideal type of investigation is that which offers an *explanation* for the phenomenon observed. An explanatory study attempts to answer "why" questions about phenomena, particularly regarding the motives and actions of people. Where the WWW is concerned, such questions might include "Why do people use the WWW, rather than other sources of information?" "Why are companies spending so much money on Web site development and advertising?" and "Why is free speech such an issue for WWW content?" As studying and measuring human intentions is difficult, fewer investigations have attempted to offer explanations for information-seeking behaviors. Constructing explanations for events brings into play the concept of causation: when does one thing cause another to happen? It is this in turn which requires rigorous evidence and logic to establish.

When designing a study we must be clear about what is our primary *unit of analysis*. Studies of information seeking, by definition, involve humans; therefore, individual *people* are most commonly observed and analyzed in such investigations. Yet there are also cases in which our main focus is on aggregates of individuals, as in a comparative study of organizations (e.g., companies or universities); in such cases our unit of analysis is actually a group, rather than the individual. In addition, any kind of human artifact — *objects*, such as books or TV programs, or social *events*, such as a conference or conversation — may also be a unit of observation and analysis. In other words, the design of a study is partly determined by what kind of thing we wish to discuss in our findings. Are we trying to reach a conclusion about the opinions of individuals, for example, or about the usage of a book? Deciding what we are observing and reasoning about will determine how our measures are developed and implemented.

The *time* dimension of the investigation is especially important, particularly when we wish to reason about causes and effects. Time is also important because people and their environments change constantly, so we are always faced with the issue of whether results from a decade ago are still applicable to the world of today. A typical distinction made in methodology is between studies that are conducted solely at *one point in time*, versus those in which multiple measures are taken over *several points in time*. These two approaches are called, respectively, *cross-sectional* versus *longitudinal* studies.

One could look at the time dimension as a question of sampling, just as we must do when we consider human populations: Is it enough to sample one person/time, or should we sample many people/times? The considerable increase in effort required to study phenomenon over time has meant that relatively few studies in information seeking have incorporated a long time frame in their design. However, in the "quasi-experimental" design described in the next chapter, it is typical for some measurements to be repeated twice, at intervals of some weeks or months, to determine whether a change in the environment has had the expected effect. It is also not uncommon for some survey designs to ask the same questions several months or years apart to address the question of change over time.

8.2.5. Ethics in Research

Given human failings and motivations, it should come as no surprise that ethical considerations loom large in social research. Researchers are people, people have values and attitudes, and those predispositions inevitably creep into their investigations of other people. Investigators also have a strong desire to achieve interesting results. Competent researchers strive to keep their values from influencing the results of their studies — a difficult thing to do when one cares deeply about the topic — and to be candid with themselves and others regarding their own potential biases.

Ethics reflect our beliefs about what is just and right behavior versus what we judge to be unjust and wrong. Individuals often disagree about the ultimate bases for judgments of right and wrong, so ethics tend to be based on consensual group norms, sometimes called "standards of conduct." Social researchers have worked out a number of such standards through years of challenging experiences with investigations that have crossed into gray areas of behavior. Therese Baker (1999) reprints excerpts from the American Sociological Association's Code of Ethics, which are indicative of many common ethical problems faced in social research.

Four general ethical guidelines have evolved that are commonly followed in investigations involving humans: we must not harm participants, we must not deceive them, we must make participation voluntary, and we must make data confidential or anonymous. In many public agencies, entities sometimes called "institutional review boards" or "human subject committees" serve as watchdogs to see that such principles are observed in research by their employees. In the text that follows, each of these four principles is discussed in turn, and the implications of each are identified.

No Harm Should Come to Participants in a Study
Although it may seem obvious that causing *physical* harm to a study participant is forbidden, the more challenging issue is preventing potential

psychological discomfort. Who can say for certain when and how mental discomfort might occur? Such harm could be something as subtle as embarrassment that might occur when certain information is revealed about an individual or even an identifiable group of persons — say, the fact that they read a particular magazine, enjoy a certain television series, or made a public comment on a controversial issue. This kind of concern makes it difficult to correlate, for example, individual reading habits as recorded in library circulation records with demographic data about those individuals. In fact, many libraries expressly forbid the release of borrowers' records as a matter of principle, to preserve the privacy of their clients.

Study Participants Should Not Be Deceived or Misled in Any Way
Respondents and informants should be fully informed about the purpose of the study and the nature of questions and observations that might be involved. In most investigations of information-related behavior, this is not an issue. Survey respondents might fully understand that they are going to be asked about what sources of information they turn to, and how they perceive the value of those sources.

However, imagine the potential difficulty in situations in which what the investigator is really interested in is something deeper and more psychological than the questions or observations that are made on the surface. For example, in Chapter 11, I discuss commentaries on journalists that suggest that they rely upon stereotypes, plot devices, or mental models of situations to understand news events and turn them into interesting stories. If one were to say bluntly to a participating journalist that "I'm going to ask you questions about how you report the news, so that I can see whether you perceive events according to stereotypical formulas," that could only lead to self-consciousness on the part of the respondent, and likely to diminished honesty in answering the questions as well. So the investigator may tread a fine line in disclosing fully what is of interest in the study. In many cases, they may not know in advance what themes and findings may emerge from the answers, and they cannot disclose their possible interpretations of what they have not yet heard from the participants.

Participation in Any Investigation Should Be Voluntary
In the early days of social research and even up to the mid-twentieth century, it was not unusual for institutions (e.g., schools, government agencies, and the military) to require that certain individuals participate in studies and/or provide personal information to investigators. For several decades now, the norm in most developed countries has been that individuals have the right to refuse to be the subject of any social or psychological investigation, even if little harm could come from it. If the

individual is under the legal age, a parent or guardian may be required to give permission as well. Even if participants are adults, investigators must take special care with any who are subordinate in status to the researchers, such as students who may imagine dire consequences if they refuse to cooperate.

The norm of voluntary participation presents a particular challenge to investigators in educational settings, who strive to obtain complete information about all of the students in a given class or age group, to give just one example. In such situations the refusal of some people to participate will make the conclusions less valid, because it is difficult to know if there is not something systematically different about those people who declined to be studied.

Any Data Collected About Individuals Should Be Confidential
Ideally, information should be anonymous. If maintaining anonymity is impossible, it should remain at least confidential. A completed postal survey questionnaire that does not contain any name or identifying number is an example of anonymous data. In contrast, data collected in e-mail surveys or face-to-face interviews cannot be anonymous, but the investigator can agree to treat it confidentially; that is, the researcher would not reveal to others the connection between the data and any particular individual. Thus, in reporting the results of a study, care should be taken to see that individual responses are not identifiable in any way. Nevertheless, in some investigations of small organizations it is sometimes possible to make informed guesses about the origin of some quotations or opinions, if one knows the particular group studied. In such cases the investigator must exercise caution in reporting any expression that might be controversial or potentially embarrassing so that it cannot come back to haunt the participant. Imagine, for example, a report that quotes, without attribution, a controversial contribution to a mailing list discussion; it may not be difficult for a reader to search the archives of the forum in question and identify the e-mail address and its owner, making a mockery of confidentiality.

None of these four ethical principles has yet been a major problem in past research on information behaviors. At least according to what has been reported in the literature, past investigators have treated participants with sensitivity and care. Many investigators adhere to what Diener and Crandall (1978, p. 52), quoting Margaret Mead, hold up as an ideal way of treating research participants: "Anthropological research does not have subjects. We work with informants in an atmosphere of trust and mutual respect."

The Ethics of Internet Research
New ethical issues continue to arise. The ubiquity of information exchange on the Internet, for example, has led to discussion among researchers

regarding the ethics of collecting public submissions to mailing lists, discussion boards, and Websites (e.g., Jones, 1999), as well as in using the Internet to conduct survey research (e.g., Cho & LaRose, 1999). Although chat rooms and individual e-mail exchanges are considered to be "private," some researchers maintain that postings to public channels like Usenet and open mailing lists are fair game for analysis and reporting (e.g., Kitchin, 2003). Yet the increasingly common practice of collecting electronic discussions, particularly on controversial topics, raises the issue of whether the contributors are "fully informed" that they are subjects of study. Whatever individual investigators think about the ethics of studying public discussions, institutional review boards typically ask for evidence that research subjects are informed of possible observation and its consequences. If the investigator is taking an active role in the discussion — posing questions to the list, for example — the issue becomes even more complex.

As computer and biomedical technology provide increased monitoring capability of overt behavior and physical responses, we can expect more challenges to the boundaries of acceptable research. Witness the increased awareness of privacy brought about by use of the Internet. Many users gradually became aware that commercial entities were not only tracking the most obvious data — their demographic background (such as they were willing to supply voluntarily) and electronic purchases — but were even recording their visits to Websites in which transactions were *not* conducted. The pervasive use of tracking cookies and of online forms and questionnaires, coupled with the ability to aggregate and cross-reference data by individual computer user, has led to massive collections of data on electronic information seeking. That much of this has been collected without the full consent and understanding of Internet users is an example of how far things can go if ethical data-collection principles are not observed.

8.3. Summary

This chapter has described some basic aspects of methodology and the process of designing a research investigation. My comments about induction versus deduction, validity and reliability, and the design of studies may seem abstract to readers who are relatively new to social research methods. However, I think this brief background will be necessary as we move into the heart of this book: examining a few dozen studies that are representative of the bulk of research on information seeking.

I hope the reader will recognize that, although some investigations may be more compelling than others, there is no single way to approach this subject matter and therefore no "perfect" study design by which to judge the overall quality of all studies. The ultimate subject matter of information-seeking studies is diverse, and therefore so are its methods. *All* investigations are forced to make trade-offs, and therefore have weaknesses. Yet it remains true that some studies have more than others.

For example, consider the issue of how choice of observational method interacts with the amount of data collected. A sample of 30 respondents may be entirely appropriate for a small population study that uses lengthy, face-to-face interviews as its primary method of collecting data. Gathering open-ended responses dictates a limited number of respondents. The focus of the investigation and the size of particular population studied (e.g., a case study of one organization) may do so as well.

But 30 respondents is not a convincing sample for an e-mail survey of a large population, such as "Canadians," "students," or even "IBM employees." Self-administered questionnaires lend themselves to collecting large numbers of relatively "shallow" responses to limited-choice questions; they should not be used to collect data from small samples if their intent is to reach conclusions worthy of broader notice.

Postal and e-mail surveys are so easy to throw together that they are often overused. This is particularly true of e-mail surveys, which have even more weaknesses than paper-based questionnaires (Kaplowitz, Hadlock, & Levine, 2004). Unfortunately, the results of some of these faulty Internet surveys still manage to get published. In selecting examples for the next chapter I was tempted to include a few obviously "weak" investigations for the purpose of contrast. Ultimately, I decided against it, as there is little to be gained by pointing out that flawed studies are still conducted under the rubric of information behavior.

To serve as a template of what topics I include under the rubric of "methods," a distinction was made between techniques of measurement versus techniques of analysis. The listing of common ways that information behavior has been measured and analyzed will guide the choice of examples in Chapter 9.

I concluded by discussing ethical issues that arrive in studying information behaviors. Investigators of information behavior have avoided most of the problems that arise in studying humans, but increasing capabilities for electronic monitoring present new challenges for the ethical collection of data in that area.

The examples of investigations in the next chapter reflect a variety of designs. The purpose of most of them is to describe or explore, rather than to explain, the phenomena they investigate. In virtually all of the studies the unit of analysis is individuals — their characteristics (e.g., age or education), their orientations (e.g., attitudes or opinions), and most of all, their actions (e.g., the use of a particular information source). Some of the studies have taken multiple measures over time, while in other cases the time dimension is ignored. Together they represent a fair sampling of the types of research designs and methods common to information-seeking research.

Recommended for Further Reading

Babbie, E. (2009). *The practice of social research* (12th ed.). Belmont, CA: Wadsworth.

Babbie's work is perhaps the most popular introduction to social science methods ever written. It emphasizes quantitative approaches (especially surveys, experiments, and field experiments), but it also includes discussions of participant observation and case studies. The many earlier editions are just as useful.

Israel, M., & Hay, I. (2006). *Research ethics for social scientists: Between ethical conduct and regulatory compliance.* London: Sage Publications.

Offers an ethical framework for thinking about ethical practices in social research. They include examples of research from multiple nations, and advice and commentary from multiple scholars.

Dillman, D., Smyth, J., & Christian, L. (2008). *Internet, mail and mixed-mode surveys: The tailored design method* (3rd ed.). New York, NY: Wiley.

Dillman and his colleagues have updated this classic guide to conducting surveys. He emphasizes that investigators still need to use techniques similar to those employed in postal surveys in order to improve response rates and reduce response bias.

Glaser, B., & Strauss, A. (1967). *The discovery of grounded theory: Strategies for qualitative research.* Chicago, IL: Aldine.

This classic work on the inductive approach to conducting investigations and building theory continues to be widely cited in investigations of information seeking. A recent book by Strauss and Corbin (2007) provides a broader view of qualitative methods.

Katzer, J., Cook, K., & Crouch, W. (1998). *Evaluating information: A guide for users of social science research* (4th ed.). Boston, MA: McGraw-Hill.

A brief guide, in layman's language, to critical thinking and social scientific methods, this book intends to make its readers knowledgeable and competent consumers of research reports. It succeeds well beyond that, providing a basic background on quantitative methods, spiced with interesting examples, quotations, cartoons, and recommended readings.

Seldén, L. (2005). On grounded theory – With some malice. *Journal of Documentation, 61,* 114–129.

Seldén points out the weaknesses of the grounded theory-based approach and the problems that can occur when researchers are careless.

Yin, R. K. (2011). *Applications of case study research* (3rd ed.). Thousand Oaks, CA: Sage Publications.

Yin provides 21 examples of the case study method in action, along with discussion of related methodological issues.

Chapter 9

Methods: Examples by Type

One can classify these studies in various ways ... by research methodology (survey, observation, bibliometrics); by research purpose (system design improvement, evaluation, planning, hypothesis testing); by unit of analysis (individual, group, question or problem, information need, use made of information).

— Jana Varlejs (1987, pp. 67–68)

Like Agatha Christie's fictional detective Hercule Poirot, the social detective must have an effective method because method is one's contact point with the world. The types of constructs and propositions in our theories, as well as the degree of certainty attached to them, are all dependent on our methodological repertoire.

— M. Scott Poole and Robert McPhee (1994, p. 43)

Chapter Outline

9.1. Types and Examples of Methods

This chapter describes methodologies that have been used in studies of information needs, uses, seeking, and sense-making. The methods identified for discussion are not exhaustive of all possible methodologies, but rather reflect those that have been *used* with some regularity — in some cases frequently and in other cases rarely.

One particular approach is very common: surveys. Whether the data is collected on a paper questionnaire, through a Web site, or by way of personal interview, survey methods have been a dominant means of investigation in this area as they have been in most of the human sciences. An analysis by McKechnie et al. (2002) shows that over a third of all IB investigations use some form of survey methods. They conducted a content analysis of IB articles published during 1993–2000 in seven major information studies journals and conference proceedings. McKechnie et al. identified 14% (247 of 1739 articles) as being information behavior research. Over half of these studies used more than one method (although this was not always well described): 35% were interviews, 20% were questionnaire surveys, 14% observations, 11.6% content or document analysis, and 4.5% diaries; all other methods were in less than 4% of the studies, and most accounted for only 1% of the sample.

Some methods are used rather sparingly in investigations of information seeking, such as experimentation and discourse analysis (each used in about 1% of the studies examined by McKechnie et al.). Other methods that were not so common 30 years ago, such as ethnography, have become increasingly popular for studying information seeking.

With a few exceptions, the following examples have been chosen for their overall quality and representativeness of both the methods and the topics pursued in information seeking studies. Beyond the overall assessments of quality and representativeness, the selection bias has been in the direction of investigations that, first, study larger samples of individuals, and second, are recent. A few older and smaller investigations are mentioned to make particular points and comparisons. Table 9.1 includes most of the studies cited in this chapter.

9.1.1.   The Case Study: Analyzing an Analyst

We begin by considering the *case study*, as it is regarded as a point of comparison for the more elaborate methods to follow. The notion of a case study evolves from the legal profession in which the main unit of analysis is the single instance: a complaint or dispute brought to a court for judgment. In trying a case, the court elicits all of the relevant facts of the situation and

Table 9.1: Works reviewed, and related works cited, for methods.

Method(s)	Works reviewed to illustrate findings	Some other relevant works cited
Case studies	Kuhlthau 99	Campbell 63; Schutt 08; Stake 08; Yin 11; Zach 06
Experiments:		
Formal	Hauser 93	Cook 79; Erdelez 04; Wise 10
Quasi/field	Cole 93	Knaus 00
Postal surveys	Chew 94	Babbie 09; Dillman 08; Pálsdóttir 08, 10
E-mail, Web surveys	Zhang 00	Bruce 98; Huvila 10; Kaplowitz 04; Westbrook 03
Interviews, brief:		
Face-to-face	Atwood 82; Marcella 00, 01; Palmour 79	Attfield 03; 03; Bates 04; Cobbledick 96; du Preez 09; Hersberger 03; Huvila 08, 09; Fisher, 04, 05; JohnsonC 07; Laplante 11; Lu 10; McCaughan 07; Nicholas 05; Olsson 10; Pettigrew 02; Savolainen 07, 08, 10; Urquhart 03; Walker 09; Wellstead 11; Xie 08; Yeh 08; Zhao 09
Phone	Gantz 91	Abrahamson 08; Baxter 10; Cox 08; Fisher 05; Fulton 05, 09; Harris 06; Kelly 09; McKenzie 03; Newhagen 94; Robinson 10; Palmer 02
Interviews, long:		
Focus group	Mullaly 94	Haras 11; Krueger 00; Kuruppu 06; Praba 07; Lunt 96; Meyers 09; Rees 00; White 08
Participant observation	Chatman 90	Beautyman 09; McKnight 06, 07; Miranda 08; Prigoda 07; Shenton 03; Sonnewald 00, 06; Warwick 09
Phenomenological	Mick 92	O'Meara 89, Stooke 05; Thomas 01; Csikszentmihalyi 90; Scott 94; Radway 85
Network analysis	Mackenzie 03; JohnsonC 07	Björneborn 05; Chatman 92; Courtright 05; Dixon 05; Granovetter 73; Haythornthwaite 96; Hersberger 03; Lin 02; Pettigrew 00; Scott 00
Discourse analysis	McKenzie 02; Savolainen 04	Budd 96; Case, 98; Davies 04; Foster 09; Frohmann 04; Johannisson 07; McKenzie 03, 04, 10; Nahl 07; Olsson 09, 10; Tuominen 04
Diaries	Reneker 93	Csikszentmihalyi 90; Elsweiler 11; Kubey 96; Lakshminarayanan 10; Robinson 10; Spencer 71; Toms 02
Unobtrusive:		
Historical	Richmond 88	Darnton 00; Little 11; Ziman 76
Content analysis	White 00	Julien 00; Krippendorff 80; Mokros 95; White 06; Urquhart 11
Multiple or mixed methods	Solomon 97	Chang 06; Creswell 11; Davies 04; Fabritius 99; Fidel 08; Hyldegard 09; Kwon 08; Miranda 08; Mnubi-Mchombu 09; Onwuegbuzie 09; Williamson 10
Meta-analysis	Haug 97	Ankem 05, 06; Covell 85

Note: Studies are listed by first author only, plus year. See the references.

seeks precedent in earlier cases that share characteristics with the case under consideration. Because of its simplicity and groundedness in the real world, the analysis of cases has become a popular method of instruction in law schools and in other professions such as medicine and business. Sigmund Freud made great use of the case study method in his early studies of psychopathology.

Sometimes referred to as "case analysis" or "the case method," this research approach emphasizes *single* entities — a person, an organization, or a nation, for example. Only a single one of these entities may be sampled, or several individual cases may be examined for comparison. The case approach emphasizes the *context* of what is being studied — e.g., the individual in her social world, or the competitive environment in which an organization must make decisions — with as many of the key actors, connections, interactions, situations, processes, and information as can be identified.

The case study method is, then, a research *strategy* in which varied *types of evidence* may be collected (ranging from archival records to first-hand and second-hand accounts of thoughts and actions) by *various methods* (e.g., interviewing and analysis of documents). The type of evidence gathered may be highly quantitative (e.g., sales records of a company or circulation statistics of a library) but is more likely to be highly qualitative (notes or transcripts of an interview).

The noted methodologists Donald Campbell and Julian Stanley (1963) identify the case study as a reference point in assessing how much confidence we can have in our findings in contrast with what we would achieve using experimental methods. Campbell and Stanley compare the case method to various types of experiments, and conclude that case studies do not tell us very much in comparison. There are at least two reasons why findings from the case method can be difficult to establish, generalize, and rely upon.

First, case studies are typically limited in terms of the number of entities and variables that are investigated. Considering only one case is an obvious weakness, although more rigor can be achieved by including multiple cases. In addition, case analyses tend to focus on a single phenomenon (i.e., a change or event, such as the introduction of a new technology into an organization), and naturally tend to deemphasize other factors that might explain the resulting changes (e.g., external developments in the economy or culture).

A second weakness of the case method involves the *length* and *timing* of the investigation. Campbell and Stanley characterize the worst type of case study as a "one-shot" design in which measurements (e.g., observations, interviews) are conducted at only *one point in time*, sometimes after the occurrence of an event that is presumed to be important. In such a case we will know little about what the object of our study was like before we started investigating it; not knowing that, it is impossible to judge whether any real change has occurred at all. Even studying a person or organization both before and after a development can be inadequate if it is in the form of, for example, a single day of observations at two points in time. Such a before-and-after design, which resembles a simple experiment, may still ignore important events that might explain what is observed in the object of study. For example, a sharp raise in interest rates might have a greater effect on the activities of a for-profit organization than would some other factor (a new CEO) we are investigating at the time.

Yin (2011), Stake (2008), and others point out that case studies can be made more rigorous than Campbell and Stanley seem to imply. The case method is improved when it includes diverse sources of evidence (e.g., written records, field observations, verbal reports, etc.), multiple times of observation, and a holistic and process-oriented emphasis. In general, the same techniques that make for good case studies also make for good historical research (see Schutt, 2008, pp. 386–387).

A good example of a case study — and of a longitudinal investigation and intensive interviews as well — comes to us from Carol Kuhlthau (1999). Kuhlthau conducted a five-year study of a securities analyst as he progressed from a beginner to an experienced worker. Keeping in touch with respondents over a five-year period is, in itself, relatively uncommon in information seeking studies. One of the features that makes Kuhlthau's study remarkable is that she actually began following her subject in 1983 when he was a high school student, 15 years before the completion of her investigation. Earlier observations on this single case study were published by Kuhlthau in 1997, and this subject was included along with other case studies published in 1991 and 1988 (a and b).

Kuhlthau's case study was motivated by several basic questions regarding the development of expertise among people who work in information-intensive jobs. In this particular case, an analyst locates and absorbs a great deal of information regarding securities and the general economic environment, processes these, and then provides an analysis in the form of a report to his firm. In addition to understanding how this process happens, Kuhlthau was interested more specifically in *how such expertise develops over time*, hence the longitudinal element to her investigation.

Kuhlthau characterizes her research problem as one involving the concepts of uncertainty, decision making, and task complexity. Several earlier studies have noted that more complex tasks resulted in a greater variety of information sought and in more varied approaches to information seeking. Unlike some past studies, however, Kuhlthau is much more interested in *the process of identifying and interpreting* the information sources that are used by an analyst than in *the type and nature of the sources* themselves.

In a fashion typical of case studies, Kuhlthau identifies both a fruitful environment for such studies (the financial services industry) and a willing respondent (about whom she already had some background data). In case studies, the purposeful selection of participants has the advantage of matching for characteristics useful to the study (e.g., a respondent who has the right kind of position and experience to be subject to the stimuli of interest to the study, and who is articulate); to that end, case studies can reinforce validity. Purposive sampling, however, can also introduce biases into a study, particularly a lack of variety in viewpoints and experience; for that reason, the reliability of the results can suffer. Quite appropriately, Kuhlthau places limits on her results by observing that "the findings from this study cannot be considered as describing information workers' process of information seeking in general, or even that of securities analysts in particular" (1999, p. 411).

She initially interviewed her respondent in 1983, when he participated in a study of searching for materials in a library. Since then, the investigator has conducted lengthy interviews with him every four to five years. In 1990 and 1995 (the last five-year period of the study), Kuhlthau used eight questions to focus the respondent's comments on his search for, and use of, information on the job. Such questions concerned, for example, what uncertainties exist in various aspects of his job, the degree of complexity present in different tasks, how he goes about interpreting information, and the degree to which he uses certain kinds of information sources (e.g., trade journals or company reports).

Kuhlthau extracts and interprets the responses from transcripts of the two taped interviews. This allows her to contrast the respondent's perceptions as a "novice" (in 1990) versus his responses as an "expert" (in 1995). In doing so she focuses on the key issues she has raised — for example, the relationship of uncertainty to information seeking and the complexity of the analyst's task, and the relation of both of those concepts to the analyst's use of particular sources.

She draws a number of specific conclusions from her study, too many to discuss here in great depth. Among her more general findings are that feelings of uncertainty are closely associated with heightened anxiety; that the sense of uncertainty may be more affected by *perceptions* of complexity than by the *actual* complexity of a looming task; and that the analyst comes to see his job as the construction of a narrative, in which the chief objective is to "add value" to the information reported rather than merely to gather facts and deliver "true" conclusions.

Kuhlthau concludes that case studies of this type are a means of adding depth to wider-scale investigations (such as surveys) and that further research needs to go "beyond studying what categories of sources are used by information workers, to studying how and why these sources are used to accomplish a wide range of projects and tasks" (1999, p. 411).

Probably the most critical comment one can make in regard to a case study applies to this example as well: How much can we really learn from the details of one person's experience? This is the age-old question that divides the ideographic and monothetic modes of research, and, some would say, forms the boundary line between the humanities and social sciences.

A constant concern in case studies is whether the unit observed (in this case, a particular securities analyst) is representative of others in the population (i.e., all securities analysts). Whenever we have a sample of one, we have to ask, "Why that person?" It is possible that he might be unusual when compared to other securities analysts; for one thing, he is younger than most, and for another, he is aware of being a subject in an investigation, which might affect both his behavior and responses to questions.

Kuhlthau offers good reasons for the selection of the person she studies, but the more important point is that she is not trying to generalize her findings to the entire population of securities analysts. Rather, she is exploring a basic aspect of human information behavior. We do not have a strong reason to think that this particular person is radically different from all other human beings. In addition, case studies can have a cumulative effect; as further cases are investigated, we can compare findings and hope that they lead us in the direction of generalization.

Kuhlthau is certainly correct in implying that her findings can be applied in two ways. First, it makes an attempt at explaining *why* a person seeks information in particular forms and ways; other research strategies, such as experiments and surveys, usually do not address "why" questions very well. Second, the results of her study can lead to the implementation of further case studies, or to the design of complementary investigations that use entirely different research strategies.

Another case study example is Zach's (2006) investigation of information seeking of arts administrators. This is an example of a multiple case comparison, in which Zach sampled managers of art museums and symphony orchestras in order to make comparisons among their various responses to interview questions, as well as the circumstances of their employment. The complex issues of access to, and sampling of, such a group are discussed in Wildemuth (2009, p. 134).

9.1.2. Laboratory Experiments: Shopping for Cars

Experiments carry a great deal of baggage for both the researchers who use them and those who do not. Long considered to be the "queen of methodologies" by those social researchers studying a small set of well-defined variables, experiments offer the means of controlling for alternate influences and explanations in an investigation. However, laboratory experiments accomplish their control by eliminating so many real-world factors to such a degree that they are frequently criticized for being artificial and having results that may not apply to the world outside the laboratory.

The kind of controls that scientists use to investigate physical phenomena is not often applicable to studying human behavior, because people are aware. They know what experiments are, and may even intuit the possible motivations of experimenters. Humans are constantly learning, both from the world at large and from any experimental situation in which they might find themselves. In addition, experiments involving people have *ethical concerns*. Various laws, regulations, codes, and moral concerns prevent us from creating situations that might harm experimental subjects in any way, to any degree, physically or mentally. No matter how compelling might be the evidence generated by a certain experimental design, if it involves mental stress or severe deception, it cannot be implemented. I say *severe* deception because most experimentation concerning human mental or social phenomena cannot be carried out without some degree of omission or deception regarding the purpose of the experiment, as merely being aware of the purpose may alter the responses of the experimental subjects.

Chiefly for these reasons, it is best not to picture human experiments as taking place in isolated "laboratory" settings (even though many do). For the purposes of investigating information seeking and other human cognitions and behaviors, experimental designs may fall on a continuum stretching from the ideal to the realistic. On the ideal end of the spectrum is found the classic experiment, conducted in a special setting in which many extraneous factors are controlled for, and in which the experiment is conducted as swiftly as possible so as to rule out the confusing events ("history effects") of the real world. The realistic position on the continuum is harder to define, but involves the study of cause and effect in uncontrolled social settings; in this case, the experimental "treatment" (i.e., a development thought to cause change in the human subjects) may be one that is not even introduced by the experimenter but rather by some external event: for example, the availability of a new source of information (e.g., a Web page).

Two decades ago the methodologists Thomas Cook and Donald Campbell (1979) popularized the notion of "quasi-experiments" — investigations that took place in real-world ("field") settings to study intentional changes and their effects on people. Cook and Campbell addressed the needs of educators and policy analysts for research strategies to use in evaluating the effects of educational innovations and social programs. Their work showed how experimental designs could be used outside the laboratory to help us understand, for example, whether programs like *Sesame Street* really made a lasting difference in the rate at which children learned language and other content. Moreover, the notion of quasi-experimental designs gave investigators a way of talking about trade-offs between the design of a study and the generalizability of the results, and served as a guide for assessing the reliability of specific measures and their outcomes. One could also argue that, where people are concerned, there are *only* quasi-experiments; people are simply too clever, and the real world is simply too obtrusive, for "pure" experiments using human subjects.

In the remainder of this section, we will examine two contrasting examples of experimentation. Unless we define information seeking very broadly, we find relatively few laboratory experiments that shed meaningful light on such behavior (although one exception is a study by Erdelez, 2004). Of course there is basic research into the psychology of memory and cognition that might apply, but this is so far removed from the usual concern of information behaviors as to be unhelpful. Fortunately, research into *consumer behavior* includes a great number of attempts at using experiments to understand how people search for, and use, information when they are faced with a purchase decision. What is purchased may be as trivial as laundry detergent or as major as a new car. As foreshadowed in a scenario from Chapter 2, we will consider a laboratory experiment concerned with how people search for information when they are shopping for a car.

Hauser, Urban, and Weinberg (1993), in an article titled "How Consumers Allocate Their Time When Searching for Information," offer an example of an experiment in a highly controlled setting. Their eventual goal was to identify and predict the order in which consumers would choose types of information sources, and how much time they were likely to spend with each source. Hauser et al. chose new car purchases as a domain of interest, assuming that findings from such a study would prove useful to automobile makers (one of which funded the study), as well as provide insight into basic human information behavior in any domain.

In studying this topic, Hauser et al. assumed that consumers make relatively rational decisions based on the cost–benefit principle discussed in Chapter 5. One obvious assumption of cost–benefit approaches is that the value of any information must be weighed against the cost of obtaining it. In an ideal situation, we would spend as much time as we want to pursue as many sources of information as we desire. However, such a "hyperrational" search is not practical; our time is always limited and thus must be budgeted, based on our expectations of what we will gain from an allocation of time.

Researchers studying purchase decisions can use a variety of strategies, including observations of shoppers, interviews with them, and/or analysis of the artifacts that shopping leaves behind such as sales records. As it is difficult to observe how people both think about information sources and use them, a laboratory simulation makes a great deal of sense. It would be extremely difficult to identify and follow actual car buyers through their daily lives as they locate and read printed reviews of cars, talk to friends, visit automobile showrooms, examine cars, bargain with sales representatives, and so forth. Simulating a real-life search process is undoubtedly artificial, but it affords a way to restrict the information sources in such a way as to make them comparable and measurable across the experimental subjects who use them. It also means that a process that might take months in the real world is collapsed into perhaps an hour in the laboratory setting — another means of screening out stray events and influences that are not of interest in the investigation.

To make the information sources as uniform as possible, Hauser et al. tried to replicate all of them on a computer workstation in a laboratory setting, a refinement of an older practice of using physical media such as "story boards" on which information (e.g., photos and text) could be placed as needed. The computer monitor displayed magazine and television advertisements, video of interviews with actual car buyers, articles from consumer reviews and car magazines, videos that depicted a car's interior and exterior, and simulated interactions with a salesperson in which the buyer chose questions from a menu and then viewed film clips of the salesperson answering each question. Users of the workstation could view any of these information sources, in any order, for a total search time of up to 13 minutes.

The experiment involved 177 volunteers, from a list of nearly a thousand car shoppers. Before and after using the workstation to search for information, the subjects indicated on an 11-point scale how likely they were to purchase a particular model based on what they knew at that time. This "purchase intent" measurement was recorded by the computer, which also kept track of the sources used, the sequence of sources, and how much time a subject spent with each one.

Hauser et al. freely acknowledge the artificiality of these procedures and discuss at some length the advantages and disadvantages of studying consumer behavior in this way. For instance, it is impossible to build into the experiment the actual costs involved for different sources: it may take me a half-hour to drive to a car dealer but merely a few minutes to call a dealer (or a friend) for information. Hauser et al. refer to other sources of data (interviews) that they used both to design the experiment and to supplement what they learned from conducting it. For example, they learned from their interviews that buyers typically consulted between two and three sources before an actual purchase. Therefore, the experimenters imposed time constraints on subjects using the workstation to insure that they did not view an unusually large number of sources.

What was learned from the experiment? Consumers showed a clear preference for visiting the virtual showroom to see the car and ask questions about it. Within the limited time they had to choose sources, 81% used the showroom visit and 48% made it their first choice. They spent the most time with this source and it was the most influential source by far. This is not surprising, given the nature of purchasing objects in general and cars in particular — we want to see them, and touch them if possible. We also want to get verbal answers to our questions, as high usage of the salesperson tapes demonstrated. The fact that the laboratory behavior mirrored what consumers tend to do in actual car purchases lends validity to the use of the experimental method to study such behavior.

The articles from magazines were the next most popular source, used by 65% of the subjects and the first choice for 24%. Close behind the articles were the taped interviews with car purchasers, used by 61% of the subjects, and a first choice for 19% of them. Few subjects (9%) chose to look at ads first, even though 38% examined them at some point. Most subjects went back to view the most popular sources a second time.

What can we learn from this example that might extend beyond its domain of car buying? Such an approach to understanding research strategies has value outside consumer research. For example, we could design experiments to examine differential usage of electronic sources of information. When, and under what conditions, do we choose to use Amazon.com rather than an online library catalog to find information on a current book? Given the access to both printed information and people through the Internet, how do seekers allocate their time between those two types of sources? When (and why) might they ask questions of correspondents via e-mail rather than reading text files? Among the many pages of information found on the World Wide Web on a given topic, which are chosen most often and why? Answers to these broad questions can be approached in a number of ways, one of which would be to conduct experiments with a narrowed set of sources in a laboratory setting. Complementary approaches could include analysis of computer transaction logs (Rice & Borgman, 1983) and content analysis of e-mail messages exchanged by peers on an electronic discussion list (e.g., White, 2000).

Interestingly, the Hauser et al. study sidesteps the issue of "cognitive costs" (e.g., the effort it takes to read and understand a comparison of several car models). However, it may well be the case that the mental (and undoubtedly emotional) effort required to use different sources may prove to be the more compelling predictor of use — if we can measure it. The issue of "the cost of thinking" has been long discussed among consumer researchers (see Shugan, 1980), but it is usually considered in terms of formal decision rules and the potential cost of poor choices made by deviating from a rule, rather than as a factor in itself. Apprehension about the mental and emotional effort required to find and understand task-related information may be a key factor in how people go about information seeking, as Kuhlthau (1988a), Mellon (1986), Jiao and Onwuegbuzie (1997), and others have demonstrated.

Aside from a lesson regarding methodology, there is also a substantive finding from this study: people often prefer getting information from other people, even when that information might be less authoritative or reliable. Information about cars is an extreme case of potential unreliability, as salespeople are naturally inclined to present information selectively and in a manner that presents the models they sell as superior.

Erdelez (2004) reports an experiment that attempted to evoke an opportunistic encounter with information. The subjects in the experiment were recruited from a class that was required to write a report on the Web analytics industry. A document relevant to this topic was embedded as a "false drop" that each subject retrieved in the course of the experimental task. Would they interrupt their assigned tasks to explore and make note of this potentially useful information? While the experiment failed to produce the expected effects, it is a useful example of the difficulties encountered in research design.

Finally, Wise et al. (2010) applied uses and gratifications theory to usage of Facebook by 36 experimental subjects. Their literature review and findings suggest two main utilities for Facebook: passive social browsing (e.g., reading the newsfeeds from others), and extractive social searching (actively retrieving the profiles of friends. While this is a fringe topic in the context of information behavior research, I include it because of an unusual feature: they used skin conductance and facial EMG measures. These indicated that participants enjoyed the social searching more than the browsing, even though they spent more time on the latter. Although physiological measures seem very "scientific," they have their own problems related to interpretation and analysis. Nevertheless, the equipment for this sort of research is becoming more widespread and will no doubt be used in future experiments of this type.

9.1.3.   Field Experiments: Reading the Label

The point was made earlier that laboratory experiments, for all their advantages in terms of control, can suffer from artificiality. How can we trust the results when a situation is so staged? For this reason, and because some situations and variables cannot be adequately represented in the laboratory, many experiments take place in real-world settings. So-called "field experiments" trade-off degrees of control in exchange for more realism (Cook & Campbell, 1979).

A good example of the use of field experimentation, and of how it contrasts with corresponding laboratory manipulations, is found in another study that examined shopping behavior. Cole and Balasubramanian (1993) investigated how consumers used information to select breakfast cereals in both the laboratory and the supermarket to compare results from the two different approaches. In this case, the experimenters' motives and funding source are quite different from those of Hauser et al.: Cole and Balasubramanian address the public policy issue of what information should be provided to consumers for them to make an informed choice regarding the nutritional content of the foods they buy. Specifically, they were interested in whether elderly consumers did more poorly than younger buyers when faced with such decisions. A variety of evidence from other studies shows that the degraded memory capacity of older adults influences them toward considering fewer factors when making decisions. Because it is more of a struggle to remember things, the elderly have less cognitive capacity available for processing information. Cole and Balasubramanian hypothesized that this would result in poorer decisions regarding the processed foods they purchase, based on what is known about the products' nutritional value.

Let's look at Cole and Balasubramanian's field experiment first and then consider the laboratory version. Their procedure began with the recruitment of 79 shoppers in three grocery stores. One at a time, each shopper was randomly given one of the two tasks. Half of the consumers were asked to buy a box of cereal, using a $1 coupon they were given as an incentive to participate. The other consumers were asked to do the same, except they were required to use a *decision rule* in selecting the cereal: it must have less than 200 mg of sodium and at least 2 g of fiber in a serving. The investigators showed the shoppers how to locate nutritional information on a box of cereal and confirmed that all subjects were able to locate and read it. All the experimental subjects were observed as they shopped; the numbers of boxes and nutritional panels they examined were noted. Afterward, each participant was interviewed to gather background information (e.g., age and education) and data relevant to the experiment (e.g., knowledge and use of cereal).

The results mostly conformed to the expectations of the researchers, as put forward in their hypotheses. That is, the elderly shoppers (who had an average age of 68) did less searching than the younger consumers (who averaged 36 years of age). Younger shoppers were much less likely to be "satisficers" — choosing to buy the very first box of cereal they examined. The elderly examined fewer boxes and nutritional information; based on the criteria of the decision rule (low sodium and high fiber), the final choices they made were not as good as those of younger shoppers. Furse, Punj, and Stewart (1984) showed parallel results regarding the tendency of the elderly to satisfice when shopping for cars.

Cole and Balasubramanian's field experiment seems to correspond fairly closely to life in the real world. We can even imagine their experimental condition as having a parallel in everyday life: many elderly have been told by their physicians to "buy food that is high in fiber but low in salt." Yet field experiments have gaps in their results that leave them open to alternative explanations. In this case, Cole and Balasubramanian were not able to tell if the elderly shoppers were influenced by their *past shopping experience*. Did they search less because they already knew the sodium and fiber content of some cereals? If they had been previously encouraged to buy healthy cereals, then such a counterexplanation is highly plausible.

To strengthen their findings, Cole and Balasubramanian conducted a second experiment in a laboratory setting with the same task: select a cereal with low sodium and high fiber. This time they used five artificial brands of cereal (labeled A through E) rather than the actual brands found in stores; this eliminated the possibility that previous shopping experience influenced the results. They also introduced a condition aimed at testing whether degraded memory was the cause of less searching among the elderly. Half the experimental subjects were encouraged to write down information given to them about the five cereals; the others simply had to remember the nutritional data they read.

The laboratory experiment included many careful design features and specific conclusions that we need not consider here. Suffice it to say that the basic results of the field experiment were confirmed, while the rival explanation about prior knowledge was ruled out. The elderly participants continued to search less and make poorer choices than the younger consumers. Being able to write down the nutritional information encouraged some of the elderly to examine more information but it did not improve the quality of their choices in terms of the decision rule that they were asked to use.

By using two parallel types of experimental design — field and laboratory — Cole and Balasubramanian were able to improve upon the results that either one might have given if used on its own. At a time when recently introduced regulations required more nutritional information to appear on packaged foods, Cole and Balasubramanian showed that such data were not equally useful to all segments of the population, particularly for the elderly. Based on their results, the experimenters recommended the use of easily recognized symbols that require less capacity to process. Since the time of this research, figures indicating that a food is "heart-healthy" have begun to appear on menus and packages.

Of course, the strengths of experiments also translate into weaknesses of other kinds. The laboratory experiment is highly artificial, and the field procedures (e.g., the decision rule for selecting cereal) are somewhat unnatural as well. In both cases, the stimulus for the study — nutrition panels for breakfast cereal — is a very narrow domain. In the big picture of life, seeking information about breakfast cereals is merely a pixel.

A field experiment by Knaus, Pinkleton, and Austin (2000) examined whether public displays of the AIDS Quilt (a giant tapestry of hundreds of unique cloth panels, each of which was made by the loved one of a person who has died of AIDS) provokes information seeking (and other behaviors) on the part of those who view it. Their results indicate that the AIDS Quilt strongly affected both motivations to seek further information and actual information seeking behavior. Seeing the quilt tended to provoke the viewer to discuss their experience with others and to encourage them to decrease risky sexual behaviors.

9.1.4. Postal Surveys: Information Needs and Issue Relevance

Simply put, the survey is a type of research in which a sample of individuals is asked to respond to questions. As a research strategy the survey approach encompasses a variety of methods of data collection, including individual interviews by phone or in person, the interviewing of people together in small groups, and the increasing use of electronic versions of questionnaires (i.e., by e-mail and Web page). Survey research can make use of a variety of question types and techniques, such as asking the respondent to relate a "critical incident" that illustrates an important type of event or change in the life of the respondent or an organization (see Davenport, 2010; Urquhart et al., 2003, for reviews of this technique).

The printed questionnaire is an exemplar of the survey method, but interviews are harder to categorize. The strength of the survey method is gathering responses from large numbers of individuals — data that can easily be quantified. As interviews become longer and more intensive, we enter a different realm of data collection and research strategy. That is, interviews that require lengthy, unrestricted responses (such as critical incident questions) or that involve more than one respondent (e.g., focus group interviews) are considered to be "qualitative" approaches because responses are gathered verbatim and cannot be easily summarized.

This section will focus on quantifiable examples of survey research, such as large-scale studies using highly structured questionnaires or schedules (the latter being a survey instrument for use in interviews). We will leave the more qualitative uses of interviews for later in this chapter.

A complaint common to reviews of the information seeking literature is that surveys are overused in studying such phenomena. Hewins (1990) even goes so far as to exclude surveys from her otherwise comprehensive review of the 1986–1989 literature. Undoubtedly mail questionnaires have been abused because they require relatively little effort when compared to other methods. However, the popularity of surveys also springs from their other strengths, among which are their economy and standardization of data and their potential for reaching reclusive audiences and encouraging candid responses (Babbie, 2009). Surveys are still an appropriate and valid approach to research problems that require the study of large populations.

The first example of the use of survey techniques in studying information seeking is one that makes use of mail questionnaires. Fiona Chew (1994) explored "The relationship of information needs to issue relevance and media use" in a survey based on the work of Richard Carter (1978). Carter (who was a seminal influence on Brenda Dervin's sense-making research) had hypothesized that information needs are evidenced by three types of "questioning behaviors": Orientation ("What is happening?"; "What do the experts say about it?"), Reorientation ("Do I understand?" and "Am I following this correctly?"), and Construction ("What information can help me develop an opinion?" and "What do I need to reach a solution to the problem?"). Chew, in turn, hypothesized that these distinctions in questioning behavior may lead to differences in individuals' information needs, and subsequently in their use of media to find information, depending on the relevance of the issue.

Chew chose the survey method because she was interested in how members of the public thought about news events. Too much attention, she thought, had been directed at use of media for simple orientation — finding out what is happening, as opposed to finding information and reaching conclusions about events. Chew took advantage of a prominent news development — the 1991 Gulf War — and contrasted it with a more mundane public issue, the U.S. federal budget deficit. These issues had been identified during a nationwide public opinion poll conducted a week before Chew's survey as the two most important problems facing the nation at that time. The Gulf War, a new and shocking development, was regarded as much more important (and thus more relevant) than the budget deficit, which was a more technical and decade-old concern. Thus, the Gulf War became the "high relevance issue" and the deficit the "low relevance issue" for the purposes of the survey. A different survey instrument was devised for each issue, each containing questions about how much attention had been paid to reports about one issue (a great deal, some, little, not much), the degree to which they had certain question types in mind about the issue (e.g., "How does this situation affect me?"), accompanied by questions about type, frequency, and pattern of media use, along with the usual demographic questions.

Chew mailed about 1000 surveys (500 of each type) to randomly selected households within one metropolitan area. It should be noted that Chew only obtained a response rate of 26%, which is considered by some methodologists (e.g., Babbie, 2009) to be dangerously weak for drawing conclusions. Chew could probably have boosted the response rate between 30% and 40% by mailing more than one follow-up reminder. In another survey discussed in Chapter 11, Auster and Choo (1993) mailed up to four questionnaires to their target audience and followed it with a phone call if none of those instruments were returned; they brought their response rate up to 56%, an excellent result for their topic and audience (chief executive officers).

The responses to Chew's questionnaires show a distinct pattern: two-thirds of the respondents paid "a great deal of attention to the Gulf War, with everyone paying at least some attention. In contrast, only a third paid a great deal of attention to the looming deficit, and nearly 11% paid little or no attention to it. Chew is able to relate these responses back to the three types of questioning behavior to show that they differed across the two issues. Regarding the Gulf War, respondents had a higher need to know how the situation would affect them, and what the experts had to say about it (Orientation questions). To a lesser degree they also had more Construction questions, related to identifying different viewpoints on the issue and forming their own opinion about it. The only question regarding the deficit was, again, "How does the situation affect me?" but this was weak compared to the Gulf War.

Chew was also able to demonstrate that the pattern of media usage differed across the two issues, depending on the questioning mode. Information seeking from television was high in all cases, but those respondents who asked only Orientation questions used other media (newspapers, magazines, and radio) less. Those with Construction questions used those media more. Respondents who exhibited all three modes of questioning also reported using media more frequently than anyone else. Chew concludes that "information needs vary by issue relevance" (p. 684) and that "as information needs go beyond orientation, a variety of media are used in a complementary fashion" (p. 686).

Another example of a large sample postal survey is reported by Pálsdóttir (2008, 2010). This was a study of health-related behaviors and beliefs among residents of Iceland. In 2002 and 2007, questionnaires were mailed to a random sample of 1000 residents, about half of whom responded each time. Using statistical methods like cluster analysis, Pálsdóttir demonstrates the tendency of 38% of those sampled to be passive in their learning about health issues and practices. A key factor was the degree to which the respondent felt they could effectively adopt and maintain healthy behaviors. For many, health information tended to be encountered accidentally (e.g., via mass media channels) rather than purposefully sought, calling attention to the need to use multiple channels and methods in order to promote healthy living.

Paper questionnaires can be distributed by other means than postal mail, although this is not often done, due to both logistical and sampling issues. Agarwal, Xu, and Poo (2011) collected a large (346 responses) convenience sample of office workers in Singapore by distributing questionnaires in food courts where they ate their lunch. Undoubtedly the token payment they offered helped to improve the return rate.

9.1.5.   E-mail and Web Surveys: Studying Scholars

A more common application of the survey is the distribution of questionnaires via the Internet: electronic mail, discussion lists, newsgroups, and the Web. Many people now associate surveys with the completion of a form on a Web site — clearly faster and easier than responding on a printed questionnaire, which must be returned through the mail. While Web-based surveys have been a boon to researchers in most senses, it is worth remembering that their response rate is often extremely low — enough to raise questions about the representativeness of the data. And at least some people still prefer to deal with paper instruments, especially for questions that take some thought.

Zhang (2000) used multiple means of collecting survey data, chiefly through having respondents access the questionnaire on a Web page, but also allowing responses by postal mail and fax. Zhang's article contains a good discussion of the strengths and weaknesses of using computers and networks to reach respondents.

Zhang's topic of study — the use of Internet-based scholarly sources by researchers — is not of prime interest here, but her methodological discussion and findings are of great relevance. Zhang points out that the Internet offers the potential of addressing two persistent problems that face postal surveys: low response rates and slow response times. Low response rates are a particularly intractable problem, which is usually an artifact of asking total strangers about topics that they may not care much about. Yet the ease of responding (at least to short lists of questions) offers to lower the effort barrier a bit for those willing to respond, thus potentially upping the response rate. And for those who *do* respond, the speed of the Internet can reduce response times by days, if not weeks (particularly so in international surveys).

Questionnaires can be distributed by e-mail to individuals or through discussion lists to preidentified groups of individuals with known interests. Responding to such surveys can be quite easy, particularly if they do not require much typing. A superior approach, used by Zhang and her colleagues, is to direct the respondent (typically via an e-mail message) to visit a Web site and respond to a precoded questionnaire, which is then submitted for automatic processing. Such a method offers numerous advantages, including interactive checking for valid respondents and responses and automatic tabulation of the responses.

Yet using any computer technology to conduct surveys also presents some difficult challenges to the validity of the research results. This is because of the danger of biasing the original sample (if they must be computer users to respond) and the usable survey returns (if respondents must be comfortable with computers to respond successfully). Respondents with fewer resources and less education, which may translate into less physical and intellectual access to computers, are likely to be left out. The resulting responses tend to suffer from bias by excluding some kinds of potential respondents and favoring the (self-) selection of others who have both access to and interest in computer-related resources.

Zhang in fact discovered that respondents who replied via the Web tended to have a higher perception of their own abilities to use the Internet, tended to use the Internet more, and tended to be younger. Gender and degree of Web access, however, were unrelated to how they chose to respond. Zhang found, as had several earlier studies that she reviews, that some respondents who had ample resources and education preferred not to respond to surveys electronically; about 20% in her study chose to respond by paper or fax rather than via the Web.

There are other problems with electronically delivered surveys. Some respondents view them as even more impersonal than paper questionnaires, for example. The response rate — an important piece of data in determining the generalizability of the findings — may be inflated in electronic surveys (compared to postal surveys), because the researchers typically have better indications of whether the questionnaire was "undeliverable." And use of multiple electronic mailing lists may result in many respondents receiving multiple surveys, creating the potential for multiple responses from the same respondent (which can happen in any case) and exacerbating the problem of determining the sample size and thus the response rate. The additional complexity of an online questionnaire may also result in more failures to complete and submit the instrument successfully — 10% of Zhang's respondents gave up even after accessing and partially completing the form.

Unfortunately, many poorly executed surveys are now conducted over the Internet. Electronic mail may only encourage further use of an overused method. Given the increased ease and lowered costs of conducting surveys electronically, we would at least expect the survey populations to be larger (see Brown, 1999, for an example of an e-mail survey with weaknesses in sampling; Bruce, 1998, for a better example). This is not to conclude that e-mail surveys are necessarily weak, however, particularly when they are coupled with other methods of data gathering. Methodologists who have studied the weaknesses of e-mail surveys suggest that they require the same care and techniques developed in decades of experience with postal surveys. Kaplowitz et al. (2004) found that, in populations with Web access, one still needs to give an advance notification by postal mail in order to achieve a comparable response rate to the same questionnaire delivered by surface mail; even so, there still may be significant age differences in response rates between the mail and Web survey versions. Dillman, Smyth, and Christian (2008) is a good guide to conducting surveys by either method. See Westbrook (2003) for an example of a study that used both postal and e-mail instruments, and Huvila (2010) for an investigation that relied solely on a Web-based survey.

The proliferation of mobile devices is leading to new ways of conducting surveys, at times blurring the distinction between the "dairy method" (discussed below) and longitudinal surveys. In addition to the use of personal digital assistants (PDAs) in this task, some mobile phones are now adequate for hosting short surveys.

In conclusion, while self-administered survey methods have strengths, they also have weaknesses, especially superficiality. Questionnaires cannot easily capture the complexity of information seeking, nor can they observe the influence of context (e.g., place, time, and situation) in the actual use of information. In-depth interviews and participant observation (see the multiple data sources discussion) may be strong on capturing context, but they have their own drawbacks as well.

9.1.6.   Brief Interviews: Studies of Everyday Folks

The interview is a very flexible technique. An interview can last a short time or a long time. Interviews can be accomplished in person (i.e., face-to-face), or over the telephone or computer. Interview questions can be asked just once, or repeated over time with the same respondent. The interviewer can take the formal role of a neutral investigator, or the informal role of a participant in the same activities as the respondent. (The latter type will be considered under the heading of "intensive interviews.") In this section, we consider three examples of "brief" interviews (i.e., typically one time, and much less than an hour in length) used to study information seeking. Along the way I will mention other studies of IB that utilized relatively brief interviews, however interviewing is so commonly used that I cite only a few representatives from many studies that use this method.

Although they are rather rare in the context of information seeking studies, door-to-door (or "doorstep") interviews are still conducted in other realms. The most familiar example in the United States is the visit from the census taker every 10 years. The main advantage of doorstep interviews is that they can survey hundreds of respondents and obtain answers of reasonable depth and reliability.

In a doorstep survey concerning information needs in the United Kingdom, Marcella and Baxter (2000, 2001) discussed the methodology of a random sample of almost 900 members of the public. The Citizenship Information research project was funded by the British Library from 1997 to 1999 to investigate the needs and acquisition of information by or about the government that "may be of value to the citizen either as a part of everyday life or in the participation by the citizen in government" (p. 2). The first stage of the project was a questionnaire survey of almost 1300 citizens, conducted through public libraries and other agencies. The first stage of results was thought to be fairly representative of the British population, but it oversampled library users and thus was complemented with a large sample of doorstep interviews. The interview method could probe more deeply and reach individuals less likely to use the library, such as those lacking in literacy, education, or mobility, than could the distribution of question-naires. But a key problem in door-to-door interviews is getting interviewers to choose a fair sample of residences to approach; if the choice of blocks or of residences within blocks is left to their own judgment, interviewers will be overly influenced by concerns about their safety and a desire to have "comfortable" interactions with others. This will lead them, consciously or unconsciously, to choose nicer blocks and houses — with corner houses tending to be particularly oversampled. However, the "random walk" method (often used in market research surveys) can be used to direct interviewers to a fair sample of households by using a detailed decision algorithm ("if the address is an apartment house, begin with the second apartment on each floor and ..."). In this study, use of the random walk method was found to reach greater proportions of women, elderly, retired, homemakers, and lower social classes, in most cases forming a more representative sample than the questionnaire method (Marcella & Baxter, 2000, 2001, 2005).

Rita Atwood and Brenda Dervin (1982) report results from one of the largest studies of citizen information needs ever conducted (Palmour, Rathbun, Brown, Dervin, & Dowd, 1979). The two researchers were interested in the issue of whether race predicts information seeking behavior. The Palmour et al. study of information needs, in which Dervin was a key investigator, used a multistage probability sample of the 22 million residents of California at that time. One thousand individuals were selected, first by sampling geographic areas (to ensure ethnic diversity), then census blocks within the areas, then dwellings within the blocks. Face-to-face interviews were completed with 646 individuals among the thousand dwellings selected in the random sample.

Atwood and Dervin reanalyzed 205 of the original questionnaires (i.e., schedules) completed by the trained interviewers in the study. They selected matched samples of White, Black, and Hispanic respondents, then chose only those who were able to identify a single "most important question" among those information needs they reported.

The responses of these three similarly sized groups were analyzed to test the hypothesis that a "situated movement state" typology, representing the kinds of gaps that people reported, would be a better predictor than race of the kinds of questions respondents asked in bridging their gaps.

Three kinds of gaps were identified among those reported by the sample of respondents: (1) the need to make a *decision* (e.g., which house to buy); (2) the presence of a *barrier* (e.g., the car is broken and must be fixed); or (3) a *problematic* state over which the respondent has little or no control (e.g., the neighbors keep the respondent awake every night).

The responses to these gaps, as recorded on the interview schedules, were coded as comprising What, Why, How, or When questions that the respondents asked. Fourteen types of sources to which respondents turned to answer these questions were also coded and statistically reduced (using factor analysis) to five; these five factors represent, in effect, strategies used for answering the questions.

Atwood and Dervin's results show that the nature of a gap — as a decision, barrier, or problematic — is a better predictor of subsequent question-asking than is ethnicity. The use of two types of information sources, mass media/business sources and books/libraries, were predicted mainly by interactions (combinations) of the race and situation variables rather than by race or situation alone. In other words, an individual's situation is more influential than his or her race in determining information seeking, at least in terms of the kinds of behaviors (and their measures) examined in this study.

It is more common to use brief, face-to-face interviews in work or school settings. Many information seeking investigations have interviewed respondents, entirely or predominantly, in their place of employment (e.g., Attfield & Dowell, 2003; Brine & Feather, 2010; Cobbledick, 1996; Cole, 1993; Ellis, 1989; Florio & DeMartini, 1993; Gorman & Helfand, 1995; Huvila, 2008a, 2008b, 2009; Lambert, 2010; McCaughan & McKenna, 2007; Nicholas et al., 2005; Wicks, 1999). Another common venue for interviews is the school, as used, for example, by Chang (2006), Erdelez (1997), Julien (1999), Kuhlthau (1988a, 1988b, 1993a), Lu (2010), Seldén (2001), and Walker (2009). Studies by Catherine Johnson (2007), Laplante and Downie (2011), Olsson (2010a), O'Connor (2011), Ooi (2011), Savolainen (2007b, 2007c, 2008b, 2008c, 2010), Wellstead (2011), Xie (2008), and Zhao, Zhang, and Klein (2009) are examples of interviews conducted in the home, or in other locales. Interviews are so commonly used it is not possible to list all of those cited in this book.

An example of telephone survey comes to us from Gantz, Fitzmaurice, and Fink (1991). Gantz et al. were continuing several decades of research on how people learn of news, particularly dramatic events like assassinations, and how they react to such news. Past research had tended to emphasize the passive nature of audiences, and their tendency to wait for information to be presented to them by mass media channels. Gantz et al. wanted to answer three questions:

1. How frequently and for what topics do adults engage in information seeking?
2. What media do they use, and to what extent is their information seeking confined to their usual channels?
3. What is the relationship between interest in specific news topics and information seeking about those topics?

To answer these research questions Gantz et al. conducted a very large number of interviews by telephone. A random sample of 1147 phone numbers was taken from Indianapolis phone directories (a technique that would be seriously flawed today, for reasons described later). Under-graduate students trained for the task made phone calls to each residence, reaching someone at 73% of the dwellings. Another 27% (about a third of the dwellings contacted) of the total sample refused to be interviewed or were otherwise unable to complete the survey. This left 46% of the original sample as respondents to the survey, a fair response rate for this type of survey, although leaving open a question of response bias.

The interviews took about 15 minutes to complete and consisted of structured questions regarding use of the news media, interest in 13 preselected topics (e.g., national politics, the economy, and health), knowledge of a specific recent political event (a U.S.–Soviet summit conference), individual patterns of information seeking, and demographic attributes.

The investigators operationalized the concept of information seeking by asking respondents to state, for each of the topics, how many days of the week they "*actively* turn to the media looking for *more* information about something you've *already* heard about" (p. 633; italicized words were emphasized by the interviewers). Other data were collected by asking the respondent to choose among points on scales, or other predetermined categories.

The results tended to reinforce the stereotype of passivity, at least regarding these general categories. Respondents did *not* turn to the mass media on a daily basis to look for information on any of the 13 topics. The most actively researched topic — on average, about every other day — was the local weather, followed by catastrophic events like earthquakes. Between 24% and 38% of those who participated in the survey *never* looked for additional information on the other topics. And when individuals did attempt to learn more about a topic, it was unusual for them to go beyond the media channels (e.g., newspapers and TV) that they normally used.

Yet when individual information seeking was considered across all of the topics, "one could conclude that most respondents engage in some information-seeking behavior quite regularly" (p. 635) although not daily and not on just one specific topic. The more active viewers tended to be more educated, more wealthy, and more frequent consumers of the news media. More complex patterns were found when the data were examined by age and gender.

Gantz et al. concluded that their overall results showed more activity than earlier studies, possibly because their study included "weather" as a topic when other studies had not. To explain the habitual use of certain media, the investigators invoke the cost–benefit model; that is, seeking involves a rational calculation of the potential reward (the personal, professional, and social value of the information) versus the expenditures (money, time, and effort) required to obtain and process it (see Atkin, 1972, 1973). Therefore, "it would not be worth the effort" for them to try new or rarely used channels of information. For news that does not affect them directly (local weather being one exception), individuals have little incentive to go beyond the normal channels and usual degree of effort. Therefore, information seeking of news amounts to selective attention to specific news items offered by those media that one normally monitors.

In critiquing the Gantz et al. investigation we should first acknowledge that it was a very large-scale study for the topic. Very few surveys of information seeking behaviors (whether by mail, telephone, or in person) have involved samples of over 500 respondents. The research questions arose from a careful review of the literature and the resulting measures (i.e., the interview questions, their response categories and scales) were rigorously constructed. Those are the main strengths of this study.

On the downside, the topic is (necessarily) narrow and the measures artificial. Thirteen very general topics do not very well represent the actual interests that a reader/viewer of the news media would have, even though they may correspond to the formulaic nature of news reporting. Although the investigators attempted to compensate by taking one actual news event, the international summit they chose as a focus turned out to be of only modest interest to the respondents despite their high level of reported awareness; 95% said they knew about the United States–Soviet summit, but fewer than half of those sought any further news about it. The response categories used in survey research (e.g., yes/no, days per week, five-point scales) automatically limit the "realness" (validity) of the data collected. Many of these limitations could be said to be the result of a focus on a narrow range of topics — those covered by the mass media. As the researchers point out, "the news" is almost by definition at some distance from the daily lives of the reader/viewer. Hence, instances of active information seeking are hard to document.

A further limitation that plagues survey research (as noted in other examples, above) is the issue of response bias. Are the people who responded like the people who did not? It is the surveyor's responsibility to make some attempt to answer this question. In the case of attempting a census of a strictly limited population about whom individual information is available (e.g., the faculty of one university) comparing respondents to nonrespondents is fairly easy. In surveying a sample of a very large population, it is not. At the least, however, the investigator can compare the demographics of the respondents with what is known about the entire population (typically using national or local census data). The Atwood and Dervin study made such comparisons (by age, race, and gender) whereas Gantz et al. did not. Could the latter study's nonrespondents have been different from the respondents in age, gender, education, and income level? Gantz et al. did not explore that important question.

There are other strategies that researches can use to assess nonresponse bias. Making additional calls to those households in which the phone was not answered would narrow that group of nonresponses. One can also ask those who answered, but declined to participate in the study, a critical question or two; for example, asking a single question about use of the newspaper would indicate whether those who refused are more likely to be nonreaders (to suggest one likely response bias). Even though many would refuse to answer even *that* single question, those who did would increase our knowledge about nonrespondents. As it is, Gantz et al. report nothing about the majority (54%) of their sample who did not participate; that is, the 27% who could not be reached, plus the 27% who were contacted but declined to participate. Might they have been rather different in their information seeking behaviors than the minority who were interviewed?

Other phone interview studies include those by Abrahamson, Fisher, Turner, Durrance, and Turner (2008), Baxter, Marcella, and Illingworth (2010), Cox, Clough, and Marlow (2008), Fulton (2005b, 2009a, 2009b), Harris et al. (2006), Kelly et al. (2009), and Morey (2007).

Interviews are a ubiquitous method often used in conjunction with other techniques for gathering data, or with certain approaches for its analysis. For example, Woudstra and van den Hooff (2008) used a "think-aloud" technique to elicit thoughts about the selection of human information sources, in order to better understand why a particular person was chosen (which usually had to do with the quality of their knowledge). In their interviews Huvila (2008a, 2009) and Sonnenwald, Wildemuth, and Harmon (2001) used a technique called "information horizon maps," in which respondents sketch out their sources on paper, with distance representing less importance and/or usage. A variation on this technique was employed by Savolainen (2007c). In terms of analysis, an approach called *domain analysis* (Hjørland, 2002a, 2005b; Hjørland & Albrechtsen, 1995; Talja, 2005) may use interviews with members of a discourse community (e.g., scholars in a particular discipline, or practitioners of a certain hobby) in order to understand their culture and knowledge, as well as examine their documents and databases to gather additional information. Talja and Maula's (2003) and Fry's (2006) respective interviews with scholars, Sundin's with nurses (2003), and Hartel's (2003) with hobbyist cooks, are examples of this.

9.1.7.   Intensive Interviews: The Lives of Janitors and Brothers

When interviews strive for in-depth information on the interviewee's feelings, experiences, and perceptions — data that are not very amenable to quantitative analysis — the investigator enters the realm of the *intensive* interview. Such qualitative interview techniques may or may not strive for generalization to individuals and settings beyond those that are observed. For example, intensive interviews are one of many data-gathering methods used by anthropologists to study human groups and their cultures, usually under the assumption that some degree of *objectivity* is possible (O'Meara, 1989; Stooke, 2005). In the hands of other investigators, lengthy and deep interviews may be used to study phenomena that are entirely *subjective* in nature, and the explanations that result may be peculiar to the particular individuals, contexts, places, and times that the investigator observed. In this section we will consider one account of each type: the use of intensive interviews with a small sample of a large social group, in an attempt to understand an entire subculture, and a lengthy study of just three individuals to understand their personal viewpoints.

Elfreda Chatman (1990) used intensive interviews, along with observation, to "discover the social and information worlds of a poor population" (p. 357). We could consider this an example of participant observation or ethnography. This investigator studied a group of 52 janitors — a sample of "the working poor" — over a two-year period. Chatman's goal was to document the meanings, feelings, and language that reflect the social reality of this group, and examine this evidence in the light of theories of social alienation (see Chapter 5).

On repeated occasions over many months, Chatman followed these workers around during their jobs, talking with them and observing their actions. She asked open-ended questions about their lives and work, and asked more structured questions about their sources of information: the mass media, friends, neighbors, and relatives. Some of the evidence she gathered she summarized in six tables listing, for example, the differing types of information they received from radio, TV, newspapers, and magazines.

But most of Chatman's evidence is in the form of verbatim comments, recorded in her field notes, a type of data that are difficult to quantify. In her report of the research, representative samples of respondent comments are categorized by what theme they represent, such as "media channels to the outside world." The most compelling evidence is listed under the five headings — normlessness, powerlessness, meaninglessness, isolation, and self-estrangement — which are indicators of "alienation." For example, under the topic of "isolation" we find a respondent who says, "Workers are out for themselves. There be a lot of misunderstandings about things. Peoples talk about other people." According to Chatman's interpretation of this and related statements, views of this type explain why it is that the janitors typically do not share information with each other. As other respondents say, "I can't trust anybody around here," and "I don't talk to nobody around here." Thus, a number of individual comments and anecdotes support the theory that the janitor's world is one that lacks solidarity and trust, documenting the existence of one of the sources of alienation. Chatman was able to find many instances supporting four of the indicators, but not the fifth, "normlessness."

In her conclusions, Chatman describes how mass media are used both for utilitarian purposes (e.g., learning about trends, such as the spread of AIDS, that might possibly affect them) and for escape (i.e., entertainment programming). She ends her report by emphasizing the importance of studying the information needs and uses of the poor.

Other studies using ethnography or participant observation (typically combining passive observation with interviews) include Beautyman and Shenton (2009), McKnight (2006, 2007), Prigoda and McKenzie (2007), Sonnenwald and Pierce (2000), Shenton and Dixon (2003a, 2003b), Sonnenwald (2006), and Warwick et al. (2009).

Although Chatman left open the possibility that her findings may apply to a larger group (i.e., janitors, or perhaps even "the working poor"), our next example does not attempt generalization. Mick and Buhl's (1992) study of three Danish brothers is an example of *phenomenological* interviewing, intended to uncover the meanings and intentions of the person studied — to see reality in the unique way that the respondent sees it. Mick and Buhl attempt to demonstrate why it is important to study the *meanings* that individual consumers attribute to print advertising. It is Mick and Buhl's contention that most advertising research focuses strictly on the *information* contained in ads, which is assumed to be absorbed by consumers in a relatively uniform way. Even when researchers *do* look beyond the simple content of ads, they tend to project their own interpretations onto the consumers they study. Mick and Buhl believe that a different approach is called for, one that takes into account the recurring themes and projects that characterize an individual's life and make his or her responses to a text different from those that other individuals might have.

Mick and Buhl based their research design on psychological theories regarding personal constructs (Kelly, 1963) and life themes (Csikszentmihalyi, 1990), among other sources. In their view, at an early age individuals begin to structure their goals and actions to create coherence in their lives; they establish one or more life themes (e.g., being for justice, not being taken advantage of). These themes help account for individual differences in the interpretations of objects and events. Therefore, the design of Mick and Buhl's study is intended to discover the individual interpretations and meanings attributed to examples of one type of object: advertisements that appear in magazines.

To achieve the depth they desired, Mick and Buhl chose three brothers already known to them "with a shared sociocultural and family heritage but who were now developing distinct lives." A close personal connection between Buhl and one of the brothers allowed both full cooperation and access to family background details that were useful in their interpretation.

Their study proceeded in two phases. In the first phase, the brothers identified magazines of interest to them and were each interviewed about relevant advertising in those magazines. In the second phase, each brother was interviewed about his life, life themes, and life projects; three months later, each was interviewed about Danish society and its life-styles. Together the brothers generated hundreds of pages of transcripts from three interviews conducted over a four-month period. In addition, the investigators themselves kept diaries throughout the entire project, and recorded their reflections in more than 50 memoranda.

One might think that such narrowly directed and mundane objects as magazine ads would be of little interest to most individuals. But the photos and text in magazine advertising are often carefully crafted to elicit complex responses in the reader, to engage their thoughts and emotions.

In their lengthy journal article reporting the findings from this study, Mick and Buhl demonstrated that each of the three brothers *did* connect some closely held aspect of his life to elements within the ads. For example, their reactions to an ad for a fashionable suit varied widely, from one brother's indication of pride that he had achieved enough in life to be able to wear such a suit, to another's scornful judgment that people only wear such clothing to create a false image of themselves. Each brother's statement could, in turn, be tied to events, values, and choices revealed in his personal history. The significance of such conclusions for the study of information seeking is that seemingly utilitarian messages may have rather different effects, uses, and gratifications across individuals.

Other studies of consumer response are reviewed by Scott (1994), along with the *reader response* research from which some of those studies borrow. Outside the advertising realm, a notable example of the reader response approach is Janice Radway's *Reading the Romance* (1985).

The strengths of the intensive interview lie in the detail that is provided regarding the people studied. The study by Chatman, which samples a fairly large number of people over a long period of time, gives us a good idea of the trade-offs between this type of design and a large-scale survey conducted at one point in time. Chatman cannot interview the larger numbers of respondents that are typically sampled in survey research, but she samples a smaller number over more points in time. It is a group that would be difficult to study by other means, because of the very alienation she highlights in her investigation. The data she collects are rich in detail; some of her evidence can be summarized, but most cannot and must be sampled as it is reported.

Contrasting Chatman's investigation with that by Mick and Buhl (1992), we can see how far one can go to try to capture the viewpoint of the individual. Perhaps the ultimate extension of their method would be a biography of a single person, covering multiple years and focused on certain categories of experience (i.e., significant life events, decisions, and values). Given the limited resources available to most investigators, the desired level of detail for this kind of study is difficult to justify. Mick and Buhl draw on the perceptions of five different people (themselves and the three brothers) to reach their conclusions. They also employed a third investigator to check their translations and interpretations and received comments on their reports from 10 additional reviewers.

Like other methods, the strength of Mick and Buhl's *ideographic* strategy is also its weakness. Granted, the accounts of each individual are vivid and rich, yet they tell us only about one individual's reality. Are the findings applicable beyond that of the individuals studied? Fortunately, in this case there are goals beyond those of the individual findings: first, they want to demonstrate the value of their "life story" method of collecting data; second, they wish to establish that the concepts of *life themes* and *life projects* are valuable in understanding reader responses to texts. It is fair to say that their evidence is compelling as regards the latter goals.

9.1.8.   Focus Group Interviews: Doctors and Nurses Search

The final example of interviews uses the focus group format (see Davenport, 2010 and Lunt & Livingstone, 1996, for histories and critiques of the method). Like the intensive interview, focus group interviews are primarily a qualitative technique, because most (and possibly all) of the data they generate are not amenable to statistical analysis. Rather, the emphasis in a group interview is on capturing spontaneous, verbatim responses using observation, notes, tape recordings, and sometimes videotape. The focus group is particularly useful for uncovering the underlying reasons for opinions, and motivations for actions; emotions and feelings (sometimes captured by facial expressions and body movements as much as spoken words) can also be important data gathered in focus group observations. In addition to the interviewer(s), it is not uncommon to have one or more additional researchers observing the action; in market research, where focus groups are heavily used to evaluate product advertising, it is common to hide the observers behind a one-way mirror.

As the name implies, the interview is conducted with a group of respondents. The group size can vary widely, but most commonly it involves from 8 to 12 participants. Groups smaller than eight do not generate the diversity and critical mass typically needed by the investigators. Groups larger than 12 present difficulties in participation (individuals talk less in larger groups) and observation (it is difficult to observe many individuals at once).

Focus group interviews are typically conducted by a single facilitator, with the assistance of one or more helpers. The participants usually sit around a table or in a circle of chairs in a room that offers as little distraction as possible. Often specially prepared materials are used to provoke response: printed texts, photographs, or videotapes, for example. Flip charts or blackboards are sometimes used to record responses so that group members can remember and react to them.

Krueger and Casey (2000) say that focus groups offer several advantages as a research method. They have relatively high face validity, as they capture real-life data in a setting that is only slightly artificial (i.e., the group discussion); the method is flexible as to topics, number of participants, and specific techniques of questioning and data gathering; and it offers quick results at relatively little cost. Krueger and Casey (2000) also point out that group interviews offer less control than individual interviews, can be difficult to put together, and require both a skilled moderator and a conducive atmosphere to be conducted properly. The resulting data, while gathered quickly, can be difficult to analyze and interpret.

Mullaly-Quijas, Ward, and Woefl (1994) offer a large-scale example of the use of focus groups to study information seeking. In their case the purpose of the group was to gather information from health care professionals about their information seeking in general and their use of particular library and information services available in their hospital and/or community. A total of 14 different groups were conducted, each with between 2 and 12 participants, with a typical group consisting of 10 members. The 121 participants included, in order of their numbers, nurses, pharmacists, doctors, allied health professionals, dentists, medical librarians, hospital administrators, and hospital residents. The interviews lasted about 90 minutes each and participants were paid for their time, a common practice in focus group research.

Information seeking was one of the three topics addressed. Those behaviors were elicited by asking five general questions, several of which had multiple subquestions or "probes" for further information. For example, participants were asked:

- What sources do you use to obtain medical information?
- What factors play a role in your decision to use various sources?
- What are the biggest barriers to gaining access to this information?
- How do you use the information? How do you determine its quality?

Participants not only answered these questions individually, but they reacted to and discussed the responses of other participants. The recorded responses were typed up to form a transcript of more than 800 pages.

The final report on this study undoubtedly contained more information, but the results were summarized very succinctly in the journal article by Mullaly-Quijas et al. For each focus group, responses to some questions are distilled into a few words. For example, in response to the question about barriers to using information sources (many of which are electronic files), a common answer across nearly all groups was "lack of knowledge" about how to use the sources. In contrast, responses about how the information would be used varied widely across groups; physicians not only emphasized "patient care" but also had need of documentation for lawsuits, as did some hospital administrators; pharmacists and allied health professionals were more likely to need information for "patient education"; respondents in academic settings needed information for research and grant-writing; and several other needs and uses were unique to specific locations.

The focus groups in this study were thought to be successful by the investigators, as their results could be used to design a "communication plan" to improve information services. The results indicated problems (e.g., lack of publicity or training) that could be addressed by agencies like the National Library of Medicine or by individual hospitals and librarians. The study also called attention to alternate sources of information, such as contacts with colleagues; pharmacists in particular were often called upon for information by other health professionals.

As acknowledged by the investigators, focus groups have weaknesses as a method when used in isolation and are strengthened when used in combination with other methods. The sociologist Robert Merton (Merton, Fiske, & Kendall, 1956) was noted for his pioneering use of the focus group; Merton not only used group interviews to develop hypotheses and questions for survey research, but also used them in the course of investigations to help interpret the results of his studies.

In this case as in other investigations, focus group results reflect only the opinions of particular participants in a given setting at a particular time. It is risky to generalize the results to a larger population, such as all health professionals. Like other methods that rely upon self-reports, answers to interview questions about specific behaviors can be far off the mark. For example, Covell, Uman, and Manning (1985) observed physicians making six times as many inquiries as they had previously estimated in completing a questionnaire about their information seeking. It always helps to use multiple methods to approach a given research topic.

Other studies utilizing focus groups include Haras (2011), Kuruppu and Gruber (2006), Meyers et al. (2009), Prabha et al. (2007), and White, Matteson, and Abels (2008).

9.1.9. Network Analysis: Mongols and Managers

Sociologists have long been interested in social networks — the array of people with whom one communicates and shares resources. Our pattern of interaction with others not only informs us, it also influences our behavior, opinions, attitudes, and available resources. Our social connections with others determine our "social capital" (Lin, 2002).

Social network analysis is an approach with an affiliated set of analysis techniques. The original method of social network analysis was to use a list or roster of likely names and have informants indicate to whom they talked and how often (or some other indicator of "closeness"). Originally these data were analyzed manually, and in recent decades by computer programs like NEGOPY (Rogers, 1986) or UCINET (Borgatti, Mehra, Brass, & Labianca, 2009). The patterns of interactions form a network in which the actors (individuals or groups) are nodes and their exchange relationships are connectors among the nodes. The analysis could determine a number of features, including cliques of individuals, degree of personal connectedness, and specialized roles such as individuals who provide a "bridge" between two cliques.

Although the technique has been around for decades, an essay by Haythornthwaite (1996) brought network analysis to the attention of more

IB researchers, and a spate of popular nonfiction works (e.g., Watts, 2004) have informed a broader population. For further reading, Dixon (2005) offers a short introduction to some of the concepts and authors behind network analysis, while Scott (2000) contains the full technical details. Two recent examples of studies using this approach are those of Catherine Johnson (2007) and Maureen Mackenzie (2003b).

Johnson (2007) investigated the information seeking of a stratified random sample of 313 Mongolians to see what factors determined which acquaintances, organizations, or media were chosen as information sources. Her lengthy interviews (up to two hours long) made use of matrices of individuals and critical incident-type questions to which the informants responded. She found that informants tended to choose people who had better resources than they did and were not well known by them — an example of a "weak tie" (Granovetter, 1973). Johnson notes that respondents were deliberate in their choices of informants, and therefore they were not indulging in "least effort" behavior when it came to finding information.

An example of a small-scale network analysis is that of Mackenzie (2003b). She conducted brief interviews with 22 line managers in a major U.S. corporation regarding their information sources. Mackenzie asked each of the respondents to name an individual within his or her unit "whom you can depend on as a source of hard-to-get information or whom you may go to because he or she is a credible source or authority." She found that in many cases managers are drawn to a source that represents the best (e.g., trusted or liked) relationship rather than the best information available. Her analysis includes a sociometric map of the connections among the 22 individuals. Mackenzie concludes that "relationship, more than knowledge, is the reason that an individual is sought as an information source" (p. 94).

Four other studies making use of social network analysis or concepts include Chatman's investigation of retired women (1992), Hersberger's (2003) study of networks among homeless parents, Pettigrew's (1999) investigation of foot clinics, and Tardy and Hale's (1998) look at information sharing among "stay-at-home moms." Björneborn (2005) and Courtright (2005) also discuss some aspects of social networks.

9.1.10. *Discourse Analysis: Repertoires and Practices*

Discourse analysis explores conversation and writing for clues to how people envision their world and how it works. There are a wide array of styles using this method, and works using this approach range from fairly short to book-length. Given the extensive use of quotations from the material studied, however, most accounts are rather lengthy. Budd and Raber (1996) is a good introduction to this vein of research, and Olsson

(2009, 2010b) has also written relevant explanations of its utility and theoretical connections. Two examples of its practice are those by Reijo Savolainen (2004) and Pamela McKenzie (2002b, 2003a, 2003b).

Savolainen (2004) was interested in how people talked about the Internet among their other choices of information sources; he wanted to see what kind of accounts individuals gave of their preferences. He interviewed 18 individuals about their everyday-life information seeking, looking for evidence of their "subject positions" as regards the Internet. In his analysis Savolainen identifies three "interpretative repertoires" in what his informants said; he calls them Enthusiastic, Realistic and Critical. The Enthusiastic repertoire sees the Internet as a wonderful tool that enables freedom and a first-choice source of information. In contrast, the Realistic position sees one's choice of sources as strongly dependent on particular situations and contexts. Finally, the Critical repertoire points out the low amount of relevant information available online and its poor organization, which make effective information seeking difficult. The informants did not inhabit these positions absolutely, but rather tended to shift from one repertoire to another within the same conversation. Although not about information seeking, I discovered a similar "Utopian-Dystopian" contrast in discourse regarding the National Information Infrastructure policy debate in the United States (Case, 1998).

In the second example of discourse analysis, McKenzie (2002b, 2003a, 2003b) conducted a long-term study of 19 pregnant women. After initial interviews, she telephoned them twice a week to record recent incidents of everyday-life information seeking. Based on their detailed accounts, she identified four modes of information practices: Active Seeking; Active Scanning of the environment; Everyday (nondirected) Monitoring of the environment; and By Proxy (i.e., via other people seeking on one's behalf). McKenzie's work contains long quotes from informants recounting their information practices. McKenzie (2004, 2009, 2010) and Davies & McKenzie (2004) use a similar approach in analyzing the responses of midwives.

Tuominen (2004) is another analysis of discourse, this time of accounts of information behavior by 20 heart surgery patients and their spouses. Frohmann (2004) is an extended analysis of the discourse surrounding the concept of scientific information. Other examples of discourse analysis include works by Foster (2009), Johannisson and Sundin (2007), and Nahl (2007).

9.1.11. Diaries and Experience Sampling: Incidents and Alarms

Another self-report method tries to use sampling of *time* in the lives of individuals to overcome part of the artificiality problems associated with survey data. The so-called *diary* method takes its name from the common type of daily journal in which we record our personal reflections. Such journals are still used in some investigations, such as the one by Mick and Buhl that was already described.

Diaries have a number of variations. A basic difference lies in whether the respondent chooses when to fill out the diary (as we do when we keep a personal journal), or if the investigator chooses the time (a far more common use of the technique). Another difference is in the form required for reporting, which could be completely "open" but more often involves the use of precoded forms of varying degree of complexity (Wheeler & Reis, 1991).

An example of the use of respondent-controlled diaries is found in Maxine Reneker's (1993) study of "information-seeking among members of an academic community." Renecker recruited 31 informants on the Stanford University campus, giving them tape recorders on which to record incidents of information seeking. The informants were directed to make a recording "whenever they had a question they could not answer 'out of their own heads'" over two one-week time periods. Respondents recorded how they went about addressing their information need and whether or not they were satisfied with the answer they obtained (p. 491). In this way Reneker collected 2050 information seeking incidents, which she transcribed and went over with the informants. She also interviewed the study respondents regarding the potential effect of the method on their behavior, as well as gathering other information from them.

Reneker is not able to convey much of the results that she obtained in the brief article she published on the study, given that the findings are "in the texts of the 2050 incidents" (p. 494). She *does* summarize what she learned from her study by noting (among other things) that

- reasons for seeking information included physiological and affective needs as well as cognitive needs,
- the number of incidents varied widely among informant (from 14 to 245) and in the length that was required to transcribe it (from a few lines to several pages of text),
- the recordings express needs accurately but do not reflect all of the needs that informants may have experienced during that period, and
- she judges the method adequate to have described "the experiences of people in depth and what the experiences and interactions mean to them" (p. 495).

Recent examples of the diary method include Elsweiler, Wilson, and Kirkegaard-Lunn's (2011) study of leisure information needs and television viewing, and Lakshminarayanan's (2010) dissertation, sampling two weeks of the experiences of 34 participants in six countries.

Time-sampling methods have gotten more sophisticated over the years. As a scientific tool, this version of the diary method originated in "work sampling" studies of employees and their tasks. Whereas early "time and motion" studies of factory workers relied upon observations by investigators, white collar tasks were more amenable to self-recording by the worker. In its earlier uses, investigators asked respondents to carry with them a notebook or precoded form and to record what they were doing during certain moments or periods of time. For instance, on a certain day they might be asked to record, at the top and bottom of each hour, what they were doing. Later, investigators, in order to make the method more reliable, sampled recording times randomly; a pager or some other kind of alarm mechanism was used to prompt the respondents, at random times, to record what they had been doing. The random selection of times got around the problem of respondents having to watch the clock, and their tendency to "anticipate" what they would be writing about in their diary entry. Such reports typically were used to calculate costs associated with certain tasks and generally to improve efficiency of operations in organizations, such as in libraries (Spencer, 1971).

Since the 1970s, the random-alarm method has shifted to include what people are *thinking and feeling* (the internal dimension of experience) as well as what they are doing (the external dimension). Depending on the purpose and context of the study, respondents might be asked to record their thoughts and/or behaviors from 3 to 10 times per day, in periods ranging from a few days up to several months. Most of these studies continue to use simple pagers with both audio and vibrating signals, but some devices have been used that allow data entry by the respondent or that simultaneously take physiological measures like respondent blood pressure.

Regarding devices with which the respondent can enter data, Shim (2003) describes the use of handheld devices like PDAs in the collection of information seeking actions and episodes. One example of this technique is Robinson's (2010) survey of 78 design engineers, in which each of them carried a PDA for a 20-day period. Once per hour they were prompted to enter information about their current work task into this handheld computer. This enabled Robinson to draw some conclusions about the amount of time the engineers spent with various sources, and other patterns in their use of information.

Mihaly Csikszentmihalyi (1990) and his colleagues (Kubey & Csikszentmihalyi, 1990; Kubey, Larson, & Csikszentmihalyi 1996) use the phrase "Experience Sampling Method" (ESM) to describe the general technique of random-alarm recordings of thoughts, feelings, and actions. Kubey et al. (1996) report on 20 years of ESM studies of motivations, emotions, and cognitions associated with a variety of activities. The method has been used widely to study how individuals allocate their time within and across cultures. Csikszentmihalyi in particular has used it to study his notion of "flow" — experiences so involving and intrinsically motivating that the passage of time is not noticed.

In a study relevant to some of the modes of information gathering discussed in this book, Kubey and Csikszentmihalyi (1990) report ESM studies of household activities that challenge the "uses and gratifications" view of the "active" television viewer. Their respondents consistently report low concentration and activity but high feelings of relaxation while watching TV programming. In contrast, the highest concentration levels were reported for reading.

9.1.12. Unobtrusive Approaches: Historical Analysis

"Unobtrusive" methods are those that do not intrude into the phenomenon being studied. Participant observation, interviews, questionnaires, and (especially) experiments are all intrusive, because to some degree they alter the way that subjects behave. The people being observed might have behaved differently had an investigation not been conducted.

The notion of unobtrusive social research methods was popularized by Eugene Webb and various colleagues in a 1966 book on "nonreactive measures" (an updated version was published in 1981). The theme of that book was that social researchers were making too much use of experiments, surveys, and other direct observations, and ought to supplement (but not replace) their other sources of evidence with an examination of "traces" of human behavior. What is it that people leave behind (or take away) in the course of their lives? Webb, Campbell, Schwartz, Sechrest, and Grove used the geological analogies of accretion and erosion to discuss possible sources of data about past human behavior. *Accretion* takes place when humans leave something in their wake, such as records of their birth and death, or more mundane indicators of their behavior like the "favorites" pages recorded on their Web browser. *Erosion* is the removal of something, such as the worn bindings on popular library books or the way that the most sought-after films are absent from the shelves of the video rental store. Social researchers are like detectives in finding and interpreting these traces of behavior.

Of course, the interpretation of evidence from the past is an old idea. It forms the basis for the "hermeneutic circle" that underlies the interpretation of religious texts and the writing of history. Examination of national statistics on causes of death formed the basis for the earliest sociological investigations of suicide, by Emile Durkheim (1897/1951). In the twentieth century, examination of one author's citations to the works of other authors became a major method of understanding what those authors had read (i.e., what information they used) and how that had influenced their thinking, as well as understanding larger issues of communication among scientists and scholars (e.g., Cronin, 1984; Leydesdorff, 1998; Zuckerman, 1987). Such studies of the past in no way *affect* the behavior of the persons of interest, and hence they are unobtrusive investigations.

There are two examples of unobtrusive research methods that will be explored here. The first is the traditional approach in history of examining a wide range of historical evidence and reasoning from that to build an explanation of past behavior. The second example will be the content analysis of e-mail.

An example of historical research comes to us from Colin Richmond (1988). Richmond's description of information gathering and use in England in the latter Middle Ages is an ambitious act of narrative and understanding, because relatively little evidence exists of the fifteenth-century phenomenon he seeks to portray. However, one cannot help but be fascinated by what this historian *does* manage to piece together about a rather narrow aspect of information use in that distant time.

To establish his view, Richmond made use of primary documents kept in Oxford's Bodleian Library, and much more extensive use of secondary collections and discussions of fifteenth-century court documents, chronicles, diaries, news bills, news letters, and personal letters — especially the letters of John and Agnes Paston. Such documents cannot tell us much about the "ninety percent of Englishmen" about whom "information ... was collected by their governors, in the main regarding their taxable capacity and their violent habits," but they do tell us *something* about both exchanges of information among "the governing class" and how that information trickled down to the commoner. Richmond proclaims

> what news of great events was gathered by the governed, what their perceptions of such events were, and how they informed one another of them is another story altogether ... All that remains of the story are tantalizing glimpses ... (p. 233)

The news transmitted to "the governed" of England (beginning in the fourteenth century) concerned wars, truces, victories, royal claims and titles, laws, pardons, and significant deaths. An early example is the order of May, 13, 1431, for all sheriffs to proclaim penalties for the possession of seditious or defamatory bills. Sheriffs throughout England told the populace to destroy such bills on sight and to report their writers or distributors (for which they would collect a reward); anyone found in possession of an outlawed bill would be presumed to be the author and faced serious punishment. Such royal proclamations were to be cried and posted in public places such as markets, fairs, or churches.

A particular limitation of these early methods of dissemination lay in their lack of detail and explanation; sometimes, representatives of towns or businesses were required to report to London for a briefing to convey a greater depth of understanding to those they represented. Another general problem with governmental information was that those in power were much less likely to pass on bad news of the sort that might threaten their ability to govern.

For his own glimpse of information use, Richmond carefully limits his essay to the deteriorating state of English governance during the Hundred Years' War and the ways in which a small circle of "soldiers, merchants, bureaucrats, and country gentlemen" exchanged political news to "act in their own and the national interest" (p. 245) to influence the King.

According to Richmond, King Henry V's network of allies and informants enabled him to thwart rebellions against him, and he was also skilled at manipulating public information. In contrast, the impending loss of English territory to the French later presented Henry VI with a political problem he could not overcome: news of compromise with the French led to political moves against the government. Richmond details how persons connected to the Pastons obtained political information and shared it through "newsletters," in some cases dispatching servants to distant places to serve as news correspondents. The Pastons collected and copied letters, both their own and those of others, expressing political news and opinions. This information was collected and disseminated to influence opinion and mobilize political action against a faltering government. Richmond's conclusion — unsurprising to anyone who has worked in any organization — is that "the intricate mesh of patronage which linked king, lords and gentlemen was also an information network, highly personal and highly charged" (p. 245).

Like other studies in history, Richmond's account suffers from both lack of evidence and selective use of what information exists, weaknesses to which the investigator freely admits. From such a distant time only modest amounts of evidence survive, and much of that in the form of biased personal accounts of human motives and actions. In any event, historians must select facts that fit their themes and narratives, especially when writing about more modern times from which a great mountain of evidence survives.

Richmond has carefully limited his research problem (how, where, and why did some citizens obtain government information?) to one he believes he can answer with a surviving body of letters and other documents. Still, he is faced with the task of piecing together a narrative with incomplete evidence, and this involves some guesswork and reasoned imagination. He must, for example, explain how the Duke of Suffolk's letter to his son came into the hands of Paston. He must also conjecture about the motives of the various personages involved in the "network," whether or not they tried to explain their motives in their own letters.

Richmond's study, while not entirely compelling, is nevertheless fascinating. Histories offer many examples of how individuals came into possession of certain facts; Richmond's is one of very few attempts to focus on information exchange among a social circle in a distant time. An essay by Robert Darnton (2000) achieves something similar for eighteenth-century France. A history more in tune with the traditional concerns of information seeking (i.e., of elites) is of communication among scientists during the early years of the Royal Society of London during the seventeenth century, as related by Ziman (1976). Black (2006) describes a few studies in "information history" that have a behavioral angle. An essay by Little, Williams, and Yost (2011) employs a variety of sources to explain how airline passengers found information on flights and destinations, over a period of over 60 years of commercial air travel, and how this has evolved over time.

9.1.13. Unobtrusive Approaches: Content Analysis

A prominent text on content analysis (Krippendorff, 1980) explains how any artifact of communication — newspapers, journal articles, books, speeches, letters, songs, and paintings — might be analyzed to understand themes and orientations. Either the *manifest* content (i.e., surface features such as words) or the *latent* content (underlying themes and meanings) of such artifacts may be recorded and analyzed. Both types of content may be analyzed in the same investigation. The results are sometimes expressed in quantitative terms (e.g., counts of the occurrence of words and/or concepts), although qualitative judgments and interpretation are often involved as well. In fact, David Altheide (1987, 1996) advocates the use of content analysis as an ethnographic technique. White and Marsh (2006) offer other examples of this "flexible methodology."

Brenda Dervin (1976b) reports an early use of content analysis to examine the kinds of needs reflected in letters to newspaper "problem-solver" columns. Marilyn White (2000) has used content analysis to study questions on colon cancer that were submitted to a consumer health electronic mailing list. She wanted to know what kinds of questions were being asked in an electronic environment, what aspects of disease that questioners were most concerned about, how the context of questions were portrayed, and what kind of patterns were manifest in the exchanges (e.g., if there were one or many questions per message).

White and her colleagues sampled 1000 messages gathered from 3000 submitted over nearly three months. Messages to the list came from 152 people (about half of the list) and 58% of these participants asked questions, an average of four per "questioner." The 365 questions that were asked were coded for type, subject, and context using coding schemes developed by other researchers. By far the most popular type (comprising 41% of all questions) were those asking for *verification* of information (e.g., "Do you have to make a special trip just to do gene testing?"), while the remaining 59% were scattered over 17 other categories of question type. Regarding the subject of the questions, about 45% of them were nonmedical (e.g., asking about the address of a new list). Among the medical questions, a third had to do with medication, 22% with diagnosis and 18% with treatment of cancer. The rest of the questions — a few percent each — concerned epidemiology, prognosis, diet, causes, health, and prevention, in that order of frequency. In cross-tabulating type of question by subject, White notes that verification questions dominate each subject category: "The participants were usually verifying information from a variety of sources: a previous message, a physician, or something they had read or heard" (p. 320).

Perhaps the most interesting aspect of this study lies in its discussion of the way that a *context* was established for each question. In 84% of the questions, the participant made an effort to establish the context of the question, either by referring to an earlier message, by "carrying over" part of a previous message, by stating their purpose directly, by describing a journal article or other item, or (most commonly) by telling a story about illness. Given that it usually takes a lot more effort to type one's tale, this is more evidence of the compelling role of narrative in human information seeking.

In her conclusions, White points out that mailing lists serve as "empathetic communities" for their participants. Yet she finds that

> there is little evidence that [lists] figure significantly in the lives of many patients or their family members or caretakers ... the people to whom it may be most important are people who are isolated from others with the condition, who feel more comfortable asking sensitive question in the relatively anonymous environment of an electronic list rather than face-to-face, who simply like the convenience of communicating when the need arises, who prefer to hear many responses to a question (instead of just one), or who want to contact their peers, not necessarily medical professionals.

White's study raises interesting questions about the respective roles of both electronic lists and of question types in information seeking. Will such lists come to be a common vehicle for certain types of information seeking? Is it easier to raise questions about serious illness in an "anonymous environment"? How effective is each type of question in getting the type of response (not necessarily an "answer") that a participant desires? We can expect to see many more studies along these lines in the years to come.

Content analysis has also been used by Mokros et al. (1995) to study transcripts of interactions between librarians and patrons, and by Julien (1996) and Julien and Duggan (2000) to study the content of the information behavior literature itself. Urquhart (2011) calls her analysis of the information behavior literature a "meta-synthesis," however it might also be considered a type of content analysis. White and Marsh (2006) describe other examples.

9.1.14.   Mixed/Multiple Methods

Most studies of human behavior rely strictly on one type of data and data-gathering technique. Investigations that employ multiple types of methods and data are not uncommon, but usually rely on fairly predictable combinations. For example, surveys often combine self-administered questionnaires with interviews of a subsample, as in a 10-participant focus group interview conducted before or after a Web-based survey of several hundred people. Another frequent combination is interviews combined with an examination of human artifacts such as personal documents or social statistics. Creswell and Clark (2011) and Fidel (2008) offer practical advice for going beyond those usual patterns, in an attempt to "triangulate" the evidence, making up for the inadequacies caused by use of a single method. An explanation of how a mixed methods approach connects to epistemology can be found in Onwuegbuzie, Johnson, and Collins (2009).

One investigation of information seeking that used a wide variety of evidence types is that of Paul Solomon (1997a, 1997b). Solomon conducted a three-year study of sense-making and information behavior in the annual work planning phase of a public agency. The agency provided technical assistance on natural resource conservation to external groups, and had been recently merged with a larger agency — a situation featuring a great deal of change and uncertainty. As the researcher himself describes it, "his interest was in discovering how the individuals separately and in consort made sense of their situation and in making sense how they defined, sought, and used information" (p. 1097).

Although the investigator describes his method generally as the *ethnography of communication*, this characterization does not do justice to the many sources of data and means of collecting them. Among the data collected and analyzed in this study were

- first-hand observation and participation in meetings,
- field notes and tape recordings of meetings,
- taped interviews with participants in the meetings,
- special logs kept by the participants regarding their related activities, and
- documents pertinent to the work planning (e.g., memos and reports).

Thus, Solomon's research design combines aspects of several methods, mainly interviews, content analysis, and participant observation. The latter refers to Solomon's participation to some degree in the activities of the group, rather than merely observing. The results, which are reported in three journal articles (consisting of 42 pages of fine print) are difficult to summarize here. Here are a few of the more general findings:

- The participants did not see information, or information seeking or use, as something distinct from their work; rather, it was part and parcel of the tasks that needed doing. They tended to describe what they did as "making sense," rather than "using information."
- The Principle of Least Effort did not adequately explain many observed instances of information seeking. At times the participants went to great lengths to obtain, revisit, and process information to make sense of it before applying the information.
- Sense-making styles varied widely among participants and sometimes clashed.
- Information is embedded in human lives. By focusing on that, rather than the creation of meaning, researchers may be creating an artificial distinction that separates people from the systems and institutions intended to help them.

Solomon's research is to be praised for viewing information behavior from so many different angles. The portrait he paints is a rich one, full of great detail and many examples. Yet, like other ethnographic works, it leaves open to question how well the observations and interpretations may apply to other people and contexts.

More commonly a multiple methods approach takes the form of using just two or three sources of data, some mix of individual interviews, focus groups, observation, questionnaires and document analysis. These have been the dominant designs in a growing number of mixed method investigations, including Chang (2006), Davies and McKenzie (2004), Hyldegard (2009), Kwon (2008), Mnubi-Mchombu, Mostert, and Ocholla (2009), and Williamson and Smith (2010). But some investigations use five or more types of data. A study by Miranda and Tarapanoff (2008) of Brazilian financial managers employs participant observation, individual interviews, focus groups, document analysis, and work process analysis. A similar range of data sources is reflected in an investigation of journalists by Fabritius (1999), discussed in a later chapter. Fabritius' study married participant observations and interviews with talk-aloud protocols, diaries, content analysis of documents, and other observation devices.

9.1.15. Meta-Analysis

As the prefix "meta" implies, meta-analysis takes us one level of abstractness above the methods we have been discussing. Meta-analysis is most commonly used in assessing multiple experiments or surveys, so it could have been discussed under those topics as well. However, given that meta-analysis relies on multiple sources of data, it makes sense to discuss it at this point.

Meta-analyses have been used for a number of years in epidemiology and to a lesser degree in the social sciences. In brief, meta-analysis is a procedure for synthesizing and interpreting the findings of several studies at once. Combining and reanalyzing comparable data from related investigations, meta-analyses extend what we can learn from the individual studies chosen. By combining results from different investigations, meta-analyses can expand the size and scope of the samples of human subjects and increase the generalizability of the findings (Cook & Leviton, 1980; Wolf, 1986).

Meta-analysis can also suggest when quantitative measurements are running out of steam. Morgan and Shanahan (1997), for example, analyzed 20 years of studies on "cultivation" — the way that cumulative exposure to television programming affects our view of reality (e.g., coming to believe that murder is commonplace in society because we see it so frequently on television). Morgan and Shanahan conclude that while some kind of effect is taking place, most of the measured effects in the studies they examined could be attributable to statistical sampling error. Interestingly, they suggest that cultivation research should make more use of ethnography and studies of narrative to search for effects that escape large-scale surveys.

As Ankem (2005) notes, meta-analysis has been used rarely in research on information behavior. One investigator who has used it is Haug (1997). He analyzed 12 studies of physicians' preferences for information sources published between 1978 and 1992. All 12 investigations recorded quantitative data about the frequency of use and/or preferential ranking of various channels and sources of medical information.

As in many such analyses, comparisons among the investigations were limited by dissimilar research questions, instruments, and reports and by the typically small samples. Meta-analyses often combine results of tests of statistical significance, but such a procedure was not possible with these studies due to the differing nature of their data. However, Haug was able to identify nine comparable information sources and, by reinterpreting some of the data, rank the first and second choices of sources of medical information among the many physicians surveyed in the 12 investigations.

Haug notes that doctors in seven of the studies indicated that they consult medical books first, then their medical colleagues. Yet another five studies showed medical journals as a first choice, then colleagues as a second preferred source. Two investigations showed colleagues as a first information source, then journals. Two others indicated meetings, then workshops or courses. The five remaining studies consisted of mixes of colleagues, books, journals, "other sources," and then drug companies. Even though these data were collected over a 14-year period, Haug says there is no apparent trend or change over time. So, we might conclude that, when physicians have an information need, they tend to consult formal sources first (i.e., medical literature — books and journals rank highly in a strong majority of the studies), and as a typical second choice they talk to nearby colleagues.

Haug's results do more to highlight the problems of validity that face survey research than they do to illustrate the advantages of meta-analysis. The problem is that these may be self-reports of idealized behavior, rather than accurate reportings of real actions. This is a problem that survey researchers call a "demand characteristic" of the survey situation: respondents tend to say what they should do, rather than what they actually do. Respondents tend to tell researchers what they think the investigators want to hear as well.

Other studies of physician preferences — but using first-hand observations (e.g., Covell et al., 1985) — find that, although doctors claim to consult medical texts in preference to colleagues, in practice they most often chose colleagues first, and then other sources, before consulting medical books and journals. This is, of course, in keeping with the Principle of Least Effort — asking a colleague tends to be easier and faster. Yet it also reflects something very human about information seeking: it is a social process, and typically it is more enjoyable when it involves interaction with people rather than things.

Ankem's studies (2005, 2006a, 2006b) also offer examples of meta-analysis, in this case of factors affecting information needs and sources among cancer patients.

9.2. Summary

This chapter has offered up at least one example of each major type of research design and data-gathering technique commonly used in information seeking studies. The intention has been twofold. First, I sought to demonstrate the variety of ways in which information seeking may be investigated. Second, I wanted to show that each choice of method offers strengths and weaknesses that must be taken into account when reaching conclusions about the study results.

Most of the investigations described here are of the traditional type. They take an objective view of information, they assume that people are largely rational and that demographic characteristics predict information seeking actions, and they tend to downplay the role of context in the thoughts and actions of those looking for information. The major exceptions to these generalizations among the studies sampled here are the investigations by Kuhlthau (1999) and Mick and Buhl (1992). They reflect the influence of the new paradigm in information studies in their assumptions, as well as their reliance upon qualitative methods and longitudinal designs.

Advocates of the new paradigm point out that experiments and survey methods are often ineffective at uncovering basic aspects of human behavior that relate to information seeking and use, particularly the degree to which it is affected by context. In the worst case, results from such study designs may lead away from actual reality, as in the Covell et al. study demonstrating the unreliability of self-reports of information use by physicians.

The increasingly popular qualitative methods, of course, pose their own trade-offs. They offer a glimpse of more basic and meaningful aspects of information seeking and use. At the same time, they resist easy summary and generalization (indeed, a frequent assumption is that generalization is both impossible and distasteful). From the investigator's standpoint, they require a great deal of effort, particularly in the amount of time one must devote to the design of one's studies.

In the next chapter, we will review information seeking studies in a different framework: by the social *group* (e.g., occupation or demographic category) or social *role* (e.g., consumer, user) that each investigation addresses. By examining studies grouped in this way, we can obtain a better picture of the cumulative results of research: to what extent do the various studies agree, and what do they tell us about information seeking?

Recommended for Further Reading

Creswell, J. W., & Clark, V. (2011). *Designing and conducting mixed methods research*. Los Angeles, CA: Sage.

   Aside from being a good general methods text, this book helps coordinate different ways of collecting and analyzing data.

Dervin, B. (1999). On studying information seeking methodologically: The implications of connecting metatheory to method. *Information Processing & Management, 35,* 727–750.

In this rather abstract essay, Brenda Dervin considers the boundaries between metatheory, methodology, and method. A highlight of this interesting article is her comments regarding how her views regarding constructionism have changed over the years.

Haug, J. D. (1997). Physicians' preferences for information sources: A meta analytic study. *Bulletin of the Medical Library Association, 85*(3), 223–232.
Haug provides a short introduction to the concept of meta-analysis, with an example taken from the information uses of medical doctors. The data used are based on simple rankings of preferred information sources, so the reader does not need to understand statistical significance tests to grasp the basic ideas behind meta-analysis.

Janesick, V. J. (1998). The dance of qualitative research design: Metaphor, methodolatry, and meaning. In N. Denzin, & Y. Lincoln (Eds.), *Strategies of qualitative inquiry* (pp. 35–55). Thousand Oaks, CA: Sage.
A readable introduction to the varieties of qualitative designs, and their commonalities and distinctions. Of particular interest are Janesick's comments on the different ways that studies can be triangulated.

Krueger, R. A., & Casey, M. A. (2000). *Focus groups: A practical guide for applied research.* Newbury Park, CA: Sage.
A basic text on how and why to conduct focused group interviews, and how to analyze and interpret the evidence collected while using them.

Sandstrom, A., & Sandstrom, P. (1995). The use and misuse of anthropological methods in library and information science research. *Library Quarterly, 65,* 161–199.
This husband and wife team reviewed the assumptions behind traditions in anthropology to emphasize how associated methods have been, in some cases, misunderstood by researchers and epistemologists in information studies.

Stake, R. E. (2008). Case studies. In N. Denzin, & Y. Lincoln (Eds.), *Strategies of qualitative inquiry* (3rd ed., pp. 119–150). Thousand Oaks, CA: Sage.
Stake points to specific examples to illustrate the varieties of approaches that case studies have taken.

Watts, D. J. (2004). *Six degrees: The science of a connected age.* New York, NY: W. W. Norton & Company.
The updated edition of a popular treatment of networks and their influence on the world. Examples are taken from a variety of behavioral, medical and physical phenomena. This is perhaps the best of a trio of books that came out in 2002 and 2003 regarding the topic of networks in human life.

PART 5

RESEARCH RESULTS AND REFLECTIONS

Chapter 10

Reviewing the Research: Its History, Size, and Topics

> Several thousand studies have appeared and, clearly, it is impossible to review *all* of this literature.
>
> — Wilson (1994, p. 15)

> In general, the early studies on information seeking (1960–1985) were limited in many ways.
>
> — Ingwersen and Järvelin (2005, p. 56)

Chapter Outline

10.1. Overview of Part Five

The goals of Part Five of the book are, first, to frame the information behavior literature in terms of its size and development, and second, to familiarize the reader with it through examples of studies. Correspondingly, the focus of this chapter is on the history and development of that literature. The objective of the next two chapters will be to provide at least one recent example of each of the most-studied categories of information seekers. In contrast to the chapters concerning methodologies, the emphasis in this segment is on findings from genres of studies, rather than on the methods used in the studies. Also of concern in this part of the volume is the way that different divisions of human populations — by occupation, role, or demographic category — fit together.

As in the last two chapters, this segment of the book will describe highlighted publications in greater depth than found in past reviews of this corpus of literature (e.g., the *Annual Review of Information Science and Technology (ARIST)*). Along with the studies reviewed in some detail, I cite a number of related investigations. Taking into account the distribution of such writings, and the usual groupings that have been employed, I have chosen to focus on the major occupations, social roles, and demographic segments found in the literature. The choices of particular studies under each category are reflected in tables in each of the next two chapters (you may wish to skip ahead to see what I mean). But first, a bit about the history and development of the information-seeking literature.

10.1.1. The History of Studying Information Behavior

The history of research on information-related human behaviors demonstrates that the topic has remained salient for about a century. According to Herbert Poole (1985), the first study of information uses dates back to 1902, when Charles Eliot (1902) wrote about the used and unused portions of a library's collection. Bouazza (1989, p. 144) says that "the history of user studies goes back to the 1920s," and Wilson (1994) credits a 1916 study by Ayres and McKinnie on Cleveland public libraries as the beginning of this genre. Whichever claim is correct, it is clear that the antecedents of information behavior research lie in these early investigations of library use, with some attention paid in the latter study to user characteristics. A turning point in this vein was Berelson's (1949) report on "The library's public," which reviewed two decade's research on the topic of public library use, and raised important questions about who used libraries, and why.

Gradually these early investigations moved beyond single channels (e.g., books, radio, or libraries), to consider multiple channels from among which an individual made active choices in pursuit of particular information. An example of this expansion of breadth and role is found in Westley and Barrow's (1959) study of student use of magazine, newspapers, radio, and television for news — among the first to describe "information seeking" by "information seekers."

The trickle of studies in the first decades of the 20th century became a flood by mid-century. After World War II, with its great burst of energy into the endeavors of basic and applied sciences, attention (and funding) began to turn toward improving dissemination of information from research. Many investigations of "information needs and uses" were conducted during the 1950s and 1960s. Literature reviews of such studies followed soon after: Törnudd (1959), Menzel (1960), Davis and Bailey (1964), Auerbach (1965), Paisley (1965), North American Aviation (1966; updating Auerbach), and

DeWeese (1967; an update of Davis & Bailey). With few exceptions (such as William Paisley's (1965) review of studies in the behavioral sciences), most of the literature concentrated on investigations of science and engineering personnel and materials.

Stand-alone bibliographies of information needs and uses started to decline in number after 1966, when the new *ARIST* began to include comprehensive reviews of this body of publications. For the 45 years, *ARIST* became a main vehicle by which interested scholars kept abreast of research on information behavior (as most have preferred to call it since 1999, e.g., Pettigrew, 1999).

ARIST chapters on information needs and uses appeared in 1966 (Menzel, 1966b), 1967 (Herner & Herner), 1968 (Paisley), 1969 (Allen), 1970 (Lipetz), 1971 (Crane), 1972 (Lin & Garvey), 1974 (Martyn), and 1978 (Crawford). During this same period, Tom and Enid Waldhart (1975) took a different slice of the literature in a bibliography of 1288 publications on "communication research in library and information science." The Waldharts' review covered the period from 1964 to 1973 and emphasized communication among workers in the sciences, technology, and social sciences; consequently, it covered most of the same literature as the *ARIST* reviews published up to 1975.

Perhaps because of the increasing availability of bibliographies on the topic, there was a pause in reviewing information needs and uses publications following Crawford's 1978 *ARIST* chapter. The most significant review and commentary during this lull was Wilson's (1981) article on "user studies and information needs," in the *Journal of Documentation,* which was highly influential in encouraging qualitative research in information behavior. Comprehensive *ARIST* chapters reappeared in 1986 (Dervin & Nilan) and 1990 (Hewins). In the meantime, essays by Hogeweg de Haart (1981), Hernon (1984), and Slater (1988) together reviewed several hundred studies on needs and uses in the social sciences, Stone (1982) described 73 unique items in the humanities, and Rohde (1986) reviewed 52 items concerned with information needs. Gradually, reviews of the information behavior literature grew more specialized and eventually lead to a temporary halt in attempts to review such publications in a general fashion, until the *ARIST* chapters of 2006 (Case) and 2009 (Fisher & Julien).

It is interesting to look back on the patchwork nature of the *ARIST* reviews. The amount of time covered in the general *ARIST* chapters varied from as little as one year's worth of new writings to more than eight years of publications. Authors exercised some latitude in the scope of their reviews, apparently in consideration of their own interests, the amount of material to review, and what earlier *ARIST* chapters had covered. For example, the 1966 and 1967 chapters reviewed only science and technology literature, and the 1990 review purposefully excluded any studies that used survey methodology.

Whatever the chosen time period, each *ARIST* chapter cited earlier reviews and studies in the midst of reviewing recent material from their assigned period. The overlap among chapter references, coupled with the idiosyncratic choices of the authors, makes it difficult to say exactly how many unique publications have been reviewed by *ARIST* alone, much less to come up with an estimate that includes other reviews of this literature.

10.1.2.   *Estimating the Size of the Literature*

It may be helpful to first contemplate the size and rate of growth of the publications relevant to information needs, uses, and seeking. The sheer number of works illustrates the depth and duration of interest in these topics and suggests their importance. The wide range of emphases that these writings encompass have prompted both researchers and reviewers to define boundaries around their interests, however, fuzzy those categories may be. I will build a parallel framework from a selective group of studies that best illustrate key concepts, emphases, and methodologies.

After 1990, *ARIST* did not published any general "information needs and uses" chapters, although several overlapping reviews appeared. A 1991 survey by Helen Tibbo of "Information systems, services, and technology for the humanities" included only a few studies of "actual behavior" (p. 295). Three 1993 *ARIST* chapters, by Choo and Auster ("Environmental Scanning"), Chang and Rice ("Browsing"), and Metoyer-Duran ("Information Gatekeepers") covered some behaviors that have traditionally been considered in the information-seeking literature. In 2001 several reviews appeared in volumes 34 and 35 on more peripheral topics: "The concept of situation in information science" (Cool, 2001); "Using and reading scholarly literature" (King & Tenopir, 2001); "Conceptual frameworks used in information behavior research" (Pettigrew et al., 2001); "Methodologies and methods for user behavioral research" (Wang, 2001); and Solomon (2002) on "Discovering information in context." These reviews cover many topics typically found in the information behavior literature.

In late 2005, a comprehensive review reappeared with my *ARIST* chapter on "Information behavior" (Case, 2006a). That *ARIST* volume (number 40 in the series) also contained a chapter on "Information failures in health care" by Macintosh-Murray and Choo (2006), which reviewed many information behavior-related studies in the medical arena. Volume 41 of *ARIST* contained a chapter on "The problem of context in information behavior research," by Courtright (2007), as well as Downey's (2007) "Human geography and information studies" review. *ARIST* volume 42 included Wilson's (2008b) chapter on "Activity theory and information seeking." The following year included what might be the final comprehensive review of information behavior literature, by Fisher and Julien (2009); their review covered about 230 selected works appearing between 2004 and 2008, plus a few earlier classics and "in press" items. Finally, *ARIST* volume 44 included three reviews with relevance to information behavior, including Caidi, Allard, and Quirke (2010) on "Immigrant information practices," Davenport (2010) on "Confessional methods," and Brown (2010) on "Communication in the sciences."

The decision to discontinue *ARIST* as a stand-alone volume as of 2011, and to fold shorter review essays into the *Journal of the American Society for Information Science and Technology*, suggests that any future reviews of the information behavior literature in that venue will need to be more focused, as they will have a smaller page budget to contend with. Thus, we may see the end of attempts to review the breadth of information behavior publications, except in terms of books like this one, or Spink and Heinström's (2011) new series.

For the purpose of illustrating the size of the information behavior-related corpus of writings, Table 10.1 lists the numbers of documents reviewed in the *ARIST* chapters up to 1990, together with the two largest of the bibliographies that predated the *ARIST* series.

Together, the 11 general *ARIST* chapters published between 1966 and 1990 reviewed about a thousand documents — an average of 67 documents per year of coverage, although this table includes citations redundant with earlier volumes. The 1991 and 1993 thematic chapters, while highly redundant with pre-1993 general reviews, identified additional relevant literature.

Table 10.1: 1964–1990 Reports and *ARIST* reviews.

Author	Number of documents cited
Davis and Bailey (1964)	438
Auerbach (1965)	676
Menzel (1966b, *ARIST*)	26
Herner and Herner (1967, ARIST)	38
Paisley (1968, *ARIST*)	68
Allen (1969, *ARIST*)	58
Lipetz (1970, *ARIST*)	114
Crane (1971, *ARIST*)	109
Lin and Garvey (1972, *ARIST*)	96
Martyn (1974, *ARIST*)	32
Crawford (1978, *ARIST*)	106
Dervin and Nilan (1986, *ARIST*)	136
Hewins (1990, *ARIST*)	101
	1998

The *ARIST* numbers are subject to some overlap, as each reviewer cited earlier "landmark" studies on particular topics. Yet the actual amount published is ultimately underestimated by these counts, because most *ARIST* authors said that there were many more studies potentially relevant to their chosen theme than they chose to review.

The chapter by Hewins (1990) amply illustrates both aspects: redundancy and underdetermination of relevant documents. To start, 20% (20 of 101) of her citations predate the four-year period she intends to review. These include several cited by earlier *ARIST* reviews. Second, Hewins relates in her introduction the necessity of, and criteria for, choosing among potentially relevant studies:

> A search of the literature on information needs and use studies during 1986–89 reveals several hundred citations. Past *ARIST* authors have also found this literature to be large. Some of these studies do not contribute to new knowledge, new methods or theory and model building; many others can be described as site-specific, system-specific, or service-specific.

So if Hewins identified, say, 400 relevant works over that four-year period, then the body of publications was growing by 100 items per year, of which she reviewed about a quarter. In contrast, Dervin and Nilan (1986, p. 3) chose to review 136 of the "more than 300 potentially useful citations since 1978" they uncovered, based on their desire "to focus on issues relating to the conceptualizations that drive the research." Using their criteria, the relevant literature was growing by perhaps 40 items per year and they reviewed about 40% of it.

Empirical support for the recent growth rate of the information behavior literature is found in the study by Julien, Pecoskie, and Reed (2011) that counted only "full-length feature articles" indexed in the database *Library Literature and Information Science (LLIS)* under "information needs" and/ or "information uses." The investigators identified 749 items published between 1999 and 2008, a span of 9 years, or about 83 per year — and their sample does not fully reflect studies published in the mainstream medical literature or other disciplines in which information behavior research is conducted. For example, a PubMed search of "information seeking" results in about 6000 hits from 1971 to 2011, with only a modest number overlapping the coverage of the *LLIS* database (chiefly the medical library/ medical informatics journals). These studies and commentaries are often out of scope for the majority of information behavior researchers less interested in health and medicine. For a review of the literature relevant to health information seeking by patients, see Johnson and Case (2012).

Similar data come from an article by Wilson (2008a, p. 460), which contains a table entitled "Information behavior papers 1990–2006."

The table shows tallies of publications by year curving steadily upward, with fewer than 60 publications published each year previous to 1997, yet 200-plus appearing in 2005 and again in 2006. Although it might be possible that growth of this literature will eventually reach a plateau in northern Europe and North America, it is instructive to see that information behavior research is just getting started in some nations, for example, Spain (González-Teruel & Abad-García, 2007).

While some of these numbers are mere estimates, the overall pattern suggested is that of an escalating growth rate: 30 items per year during the early 1970s, 40 during the early 1980s, 50 by the late 1980s, 60 by the mid-1990s, about 100 per year in the early 2000s, and perhaps 200 items per year by 2010.

Considering those numbers, along with the selectivity applied by *ARIST* authors and the redundancy among chapters, it seems possible that from 1980 through 2011 over 3000 new publications appeared — depending on what we consider "relevant" to that label (e.g., see Wilson, 2008a, p. 462 for his characterization of the subfield of "information searching"). Undoubtedly part of this acceleration has been due to the attention given to personal information seeking since the advent of the World Wide Web, and also to the highly successful "Information Seeking in Context" biennial conferences of 1996–2012.

Therefore, it is easily possible that over 10,000 publications have been published on information needs, uses, seeking, and other aspects of information behavior, even in the stricter senses of those terms, since the early 20th century. Including documents that discuss information seeking in other terms (e.g., as sense making or information practices) could easily make the total higher. This estimate is congruent with searches on bibliographic utilities like OCLC's FirstSearch, which generates thousands of hits on combinations of the term "information" with other keywords (need, use, seeking, etc.), among the literature of the most recent decade.

Obviously it is impossible to be exhaustive in reviewing such a literature. First, it is simply difficult to decide where to draw the boundaries around the topic. And, second, there are issues of specificity and quality that lead one to determine that certain studies are not appropriate for inclusion in a review. The authors of *ARIST* and other reviews of this literature have all faced these problems and made their corresponding choices, resulting in a series of incomplete pictures of the research area. This chapter adds another snapshot to this photo album of research results — one that is similarly selective, yet in greater detail than the others.

10.1.3. Contexts and Categories

An increasingly emphasized generalization is that information behavior takes place in a *context*. Brenda Dervin (1997, p. 14) says that there "is no term more often used, less often defined, and when defined, defined so variously as context." She goes on to complain that

> virtually every possible attribute of a person, culture, situation, behavior, organization, or structure has been defined as context ... context has the potential to be virtually anything that is not defined as the phenomenon of interest.

Dervin provides a few examples that help, at least, to narrow the definition a bit. She quotes John Dewey (1960, p. 90) as saying that "context is ... a selective interest or bias which conditions the subject matter of thinking." To Gregory Bateson (1978, p. 13) context is "the pattern that connects ... without context there is no meaning." Talja, Keso, and Pietiläinen, in an article devoted to how information behavior researchers have dealt with the study of context (1999, p. 752), characterize context as "some kind of a background for something the researcher wishes to understand and explain":

> the site where a phenomenon is constituted as an object to us ... any factors or variables that are seen to affect individuals' information-seeking behavior: socioeconomic conditions, work roles, tasks, problem situations, communities and organizations with their structures and cultures, etc. (p. 754)

A term related to context, but which is sometimes given a narrower meaning, is _situation_. Investigators in information studies and in communication have had much to say about the importance and influence of situation in information behavior. Dervin (1997, p. 14) says that when research is "focused on relationships between people, then factors describing the situation can become context." Savolainen (1993, p. 17) holds that "the term situation refers to the time-space context in which sense is constructed." Vakkari (1997, p. 457) notes that information seeking is "seen as embedded in the actions, tasks and situations they are supporting" in his call for closer attention to the influences of group and society. Donohew and Tipton (1973, p. 248) see a person's "definition of situation as being composed of such things as immediate goals, priorities, and availability of information in the immediate situation."

Both Johnson (2003) and Cool (2001) have written lengthy reviews on how context and situation have been defined and operationalized. Johnson says that context is commonly used in three, progressively complex, senses: As equivalent to the situation in which a process is immersed (a "positivist" orientation, specifying factors that moderate relationships); as contingency aspects of situations that have specific effects (a "post-positivist" view that emphasizes the prediction of outcomes); and as frameworks of meaning (a "post-modern" sense in which the individual is inseparable from the context). He illustrated his essay with examples from two different contexts: studies of organizational communication, compared with cancer-related information seeking. Johnson argued that these two contexts offer useful contrasts in levels of analysis, rationality, and predictability.

Context and situation are important concepts for information behavior research, even if they are ill defined. Information needs do not arise in a vacuum, but rather owe their existence to some history, purpose, and influence. The seeker exists in an environment that partially determines, constrains, and supports the types of needs and inquiries that arise. The seeker also has his or her own memories, predispositions, and motivations — an internal environment of influence. Such is the importance of context that research on it has given rise to a series of conferences, the Information Seeking in Context (ISIC) meetings that have taken place in even-numbered years since 1996. Many of the works cited in this volume were presented at that conference. How context has been defined is an important factor in establishing categories of investigations from which to sample.

As mentioned in earlier chapters, research attention has shifted over the years from a dominant interest in the *use of channels and sources* to an emphasis on the *encountering and seeking of information* and the *interpretation of meaning from that information*. In parallel fashion, this work is devoted to reviewing selected studies and findings that flesh out the aspects of information seeking of more recent interest, not all of them under the banner of "information needs and uses." Investigators have recognized that information seeking does not always boil down to the use of certain sources, an idea that is underscored in a commentary by Choo (1998):

> Our survey suggests that, over the years, information needs and uses studies have progressively broadened their research orientation and research focus.... studies have moved from an orientation that is primarily system-centered (in which information is objective, resides in a document or system, and where the main issue is how to get at this information) to an orientation that is also user-centered (in which information is subjective, resides in the users' minds, and is only useful when meaning has been created by the user). (p. 39)

However, many of the studies reviewed in this work still attempt to make generalizations about sources, groups of people, and the differences among them. Those research conclusions are related here, even though many researchers are skeptical that such generalization is possible. Talja (1997), for example, believes that

> generalizations about differences between individuals or groups are often problematic. Firstly, the diversity of the individual's social roles, tasks and identities is not taken into account.... Secondly, it is impossible to get unmediated knowledge about a person's cognitive skills or even information

seeking behavior, because the ways in which they are accounted for are always mediated by culturally constructed interpretive repertoires. The explanations should not be taken as facts about the permanent attitudes or actual behavioural patterns of individuals or groups. (p. 74)

Despite Talja's reasonable skepticism, there is some value in striving for well-evidenced generalizations about individuals or groups; otherwise, there would be little point in investigating information seeking at all. Talja's comments serve to emphasize the importance of attending to elements of context, particularly those "social roles, tasks and identities," and are a reminder about the dangers of sweeping claims regarding large, diverse populations of subjects. Martzoukou (2005) makes similar points in a critique of Web information-seeking studies.

Other reviewers of this body of publications have seen it in various ways. Most make the same distinction as Choo and Auster between studies that are really investigating information channels (e.g., journals) or systems (e.g., libraries) and those that are studying *people* (the emphasis in this book). Reviewers have used different terminology to reflect the latter type of investigations. For Choo and Auster, they are studies of "work, organizational, and social settings of the users …. users' membership in professional or social groups, their demographic backgrounds" (1993, p. 284). Talja, Keso, and Pietiläinen (1999, p. 752) speak of "socioeconomic conditions, work roles, tasks, problem situations, communities and organizations" as contexts typically examined. Taylor (1991) talks about "information use environments" as consisting of four types: professions, entrepreneurs (including managers), special interest groups, and socioeconomic groups. Dervin (1989) gives 10 examples of "demography" (e.g., age, gender, race, ethnicity, income, and education) as one of the "traditional categories of users" that are studied, along with dozens of alternative ways of grouping people and behaviors.

To form the basis for my own review, I have selected what is common among these various characterizations of the research literature: categories of occupation (profession, work role), demographic background (socioeconomic group, identity, community), and social role (e.g., voter, consumer, student, and patient). Hence, occupations, social roles, and demography — as they relate to information needs and seeking behavior — form the highest-level categories that structure the sample of studies described here.

10.1.4.   Choosing Examples of Studies

I hope to portray both the depth and breadth of the information behavior literature by presenting selected studies that illustrate key topics. Choosing which studies to highlight for this volume has been challenging, and I have employed three heuristics to guide my choices. The first mechanism is the use of the aforementioned framework (see Tables 11.1 and 12.1) to sample one or more studies representing certain *occupations, roles,* and/or *demographic groups* that people may fall into in life. The division between work-related roles and non-work-related roles is not a firm one, because an "occupation" is also a "role" we take in life. Unfortunately, "work" and "nonwork" have been treated rather separately by investigators until recently, as if activities outside the job did not matter. The subtle distinction between job and nonjob corresponds to the notion of the "way of life as 'order of things,'" as articulated by Reijo Savolainen (1995):

> "things" stand for various activities taking place in the daily life world, including not only job but also necessary reproductive tasks such as household care and voluntary activities (hobbies).... in most cases order of things is a relatively well-established constellation of work and nonwork activities .... (pp. 262–265)

Looking at information behavior more holistically, in terms of life projects and roles, represents a shift toward the perspective of the *person* (or, in language more dominant during the 1970s and 1980s, "the user"), and away from the views of the system (e.g., "use of the media," "use of library materials," or "use of the Internet").

The second rule of thumb has been to largely ignore investigations that focus on individual channels, sources, or systems. Most of these excluded studies concern the use of the Internet (or Web), online databases, or library catalogs, and together these constitute a huge literature. Wilson (2008a) also identified these as a separate genre in his reflection on the history of information user research:

> There is also a field of 'information searching,' which has not been dealt with here, but which emerged as separate from information retrieval research ... much of the research deals with approaches to search using Web search engines ...

A few system-oriented studies *are* cited, however, as examples of how the mix of sources may influence everyday information seeking. For further reading on those topics (especially online or Web searching), consider writings by Borgman (2000), Cole (2012), Ingwersen and Järvelin (2005), Marchionini (1995), and Spink and Cole (2005). These works, among many others, emphasize the importance of investigating contextual and individual differences in the choice and use of information systems and sources. Some of them are described in passing below.

The tables depicted in Chapters 11 and 12 do not sample all possible occupations, roles, or demographic categories, but rather those most commonly chosen as a focus of observation. I have exercised my own judgment in choosing studies that I think are unique, well done, illustrative of a particular population or approach, or, in a few cases, make use of especially large samples of respondents.

We have from Julien et al. (2011) empirical evidence of the distribution of "groups studied" over the 749 articles that they analyzed from among 1999–2008 publications. Oddly, 21% of the publications were not specific about who they were studying. Eliminating those "unspecified" studies and recalculating the percentages suggests that 24% of recent studies have concerned "students," 11% were about "scholars," 13% featured "professionals," 10% the general public, and 3% were studies of nonprofessional employees. Yet these categories are somewhat fuzzy as almost half (43%) of those studies that specified an audience were classified as "other" groups. Julien et al. (2011) note (p. 21) that "Those 'others' primarily included nondifferentiated library users and Web users." Thus, it is very likely that the proportions of scholars, the public, and, especially, students are much larger than indicated. These results were similar to a sample of articles from the previous decade (Julien & Duggan, 2000).

The sample of studies discussed in the following chapters loosely reflects this distribution, with one major exception: investigations of *students* will not be emphasized here, as the vast majority of published studies of students focus on their use of single sources, either physical libraries or electronic sources (online catalogs, databases, or the World Wide Web); both of these "information systems" are well covered by other literature reviews.

Finally, the third heuristic I have employed is to favor more recent publications, especially those from 2000 through 2011. In some cases, older items are portrayed to highlight the shifts in assumptions, methods, and findings that have taken place over the last quarter century. By emphasizing works from the most recent decade, I hope to provide an efficient means for reviewing developments in the literature, as well as to reduce it to a more manageable size.

10.2. Summary

This chapter has examined the size and nature of the information-seeking literature. In it I have highlighted several characteristics:

- The literature is quite large, ranging somewhere in the thousands of studies, depending on how one defines the scope of the topic. In recent years, the corpus of studies has been growing by 100 to 200 new publications per year.

- Literature reviews of information behavior publications have grown more specialized over the years as the size of the corpus has grown.
- Recent reviews of the information behavior literature are now more likely to focus on occupations (e.g., physicians and managers), roles (e.g., gatekeepers and consumers), demographic groups (e.g., the elderly and the poor), or explorations of concepts such as "context" or themes like "browsing."

The chapter sets the stage for an examination of recent publications using the latter divisions. In the two chapters that follow, selections of recent studies will consider how the literature has developed along three lines of inquiry: by occupation, by social role, and by demographic group. Decisions of what to review were based on three heuristics:

1. Use of an empirically derived framework representing *occupations, roles,* and *demographic groups.*
2. Elimination of most studies oriented toward general education (e.g., student outcomes), or information systems (e.g., computer, database, or Internet usage). Each of those literatures is massive (the number of information retrieval publications alone is at least three times the size of the core information behavior corpus) and typically are concerned with issues other than "information behavior" *per se.*
3. A preference for more recent investigations (i.e., post-2000).

Recommended for Further Reading

Dervin, B. (1989). Users as research inventions: How research categories perpetuate inequities. *Journal of Communication, 39*(3), 216–232.

The primary topic of Brenda Dervin's article is reification — the tendency for the labels we apply to groups to take on a life of their own. However, it can also serve as a comprehensive inventory of those labels. Dervin lists 12 general groupings under which "users" and their "uses" have traditionally been categorized, and within those provides 57 specific categories of individuals.

Johnson, J. D. (2003). On contexts of information seeking. *Information Processing & Management, 39,* 735–760.

A painstaking analysis of what is meant by the term "context," and how the term has been used by various researchers.

Julien, H., Pecoskie, J. L., & Reed, K. (2011). Trends in information behavior research, 1999–2008: A content analysis. *Library and Information Science Research, 22*, 291–309.
Julien and her colleagues analyze the information behavior literature by proportions, by type of group studied, subject area, etc.

Savolainen, R. (2006). Spatial factors as contextual qualifiers of information seeking. *Information Research, 11*(4). Retrieved from http://InformationR.net/ir/11-4/paper261.html
A novel consideration of space, and spatial metaphors, as contexts that influence information seeking.

Talja, S., Keso, H., & Pietiläinen, T. (1999). The production of "context" in information seeking research: A metatheoretical view. *Information Processing & Management, 35*, 751–763.
Along with more specific tasks and situations, jobs, roles, and personal background have been used to characterize the "context" of individual information seeking. Talja et al. discuss the various ways that concept has been defined and studied.

Chapter 11

Research by Occupation

In practice, context in INS [information needs and seeking] studies usually
refers to ... socioeconomic conditions, work roles, tasks, problem situations,
communities and organizations ... .
— S. Talja, H. Keso, and T. Pietiläinen (1999, p. 752)

Reading the library surveys of the 1960s today, one is struck by how
irrelevant they are for present conditions, and how even less relevant they are
likely to seem within a very short space of time.
— Tom Wilson (1994, p. 42)

Chapter Outline

11.1. By Occupational Category

Occupations have provided the most common structure for the investigation
of information seeking. Julien and Duggan's (2000) examination of this
literature found that almost half of all *identifiable* respondents in such
studies were occupational, and the more recent study of Julien, Pecoskie,
and Reed (2011) pointed to 39% of groups studied definitely being
occupational, with a fair number again unidentified. In a large sample
examined by McKechnie et al. (2002), 32% of the investigations featured

some kind of "worker," most often a type of professional, while another 17% concerned academics or other researchers. In both reviews, then, about half of all studies had an occupational focus. The preponderance of work roles is also obvious from an examination of the *Annual Review of Information Science and Technology* (*ARIST*) or other review documents: the majority of studies are of scientists and engineers (whether employed by universities or industry), scholars, professionals, and workers in general occupational categories like "manager."

The runners-up to occupational investigations are those by role, such as citizen, consumer, patient, or gatekeeper; these make up slightly less than a third of identifiable subjects. Another role, that of "student," accounts for about a quarter of the studies, although they are included sparingly under "roles." (Were I to include general studies of learning, the voluminous education literature would make the role of "student" the most numerous category of all. There are indeed thousands of studies of students, but few studies consider information seeking in more than a peripheral sense.) There are fewer still direct studies of demographic groups, even though demographic variables form a common schema for analyzing the results of these other investigations.

Most of the earliest *ARIST* chapters (1966–1974), along with other reviews of information needs and uses, were concerned primarily with scientists and engineers. Sometime afterward, as researchers gained a firmer view of the pattern of behavior in science and engineering, attention turned first to the social sciences and later to the humanities (Bouazza, 1989, p. 159). As they did so, the academic world began to account for an even larger proportion of the studies than before, as the latter groups were less likely to be found outside of the university. Bates (1996) summarized that progression of attention by researchers in this way:

> In the 1950s and 1960s — in part because of the availability of U.S. Federal grant money — the emphasis was on the needs of scientists and engineers …. Needs in the social sciences were attended to in the 1970s, especially with some major research studies that were performed in Great Britain … attention turned to the arts and humanities in the 1980s and 1990s. (p. 155)

Both the cumulation of studies on some individual disciplines, and the impracticality of studying *all* disciplines in any depth, led to a tendency to aggregate results along the lines of *metadisciplines*, such as science, social science, and the humanities. There are some gray areas (are historians chiefly humanists, or are some of them social scientists?); however, these three basic categories seem to appeal to those attempting to summarize information-seeking results.

Therefore, in discussing these work-related roles, I will proceed in the same fashion in which the research has developed: starting with scientists and engineers, then going on to consider social scientists, then humanities scholars, and then other occupations (see Table 11.1).

11.1.1. Scientists and Engineers

It is fitting to start this review with a description of the information seeking of scientists, because this is where the research in this vein really got started. The "Big Science" (Price, 1963) sparked largely by World War II and afterward by the Cold War resulted in an explosion of research material. There were simply too many findings being published for individual scientists and engineers to monitor effectively. The outcome was frustration and sometimes outright duplication of research efforts, because researchers did not always know that others were gathering or even publishing findings of interest to their work. As a result, money and attention became available to address problems in the dissemination of scientific information and to study communication among scientists and engineers.

A 1984 comment by Tom Wilson accurately characterizes the nature of the literature at that time: "the study of information-seeking behaviour can be said to be the study of *scientists'* information-seeking behaviour" (p. 199). From the 1940s through the 1970s, investigations of scientists (and to some extent, engineers) dominated all others. For better or worse, there seems to have been a relative decline in the number of information-seeking studies of scientists since the mid-1980s. In part this may be because the phenomenon has been well-documented and "played out," and so researchers moved on to less studied groups such as social scientists, humanists, physicians, and others; it may also reflect shifts in funding for such studies. Reviews of the literature on science and/or engineering (e.g., King, Casto, & Jones, 1994; Leckie et al., 1996; Palmer, 1991) may cite classic discussions that are now over 40 years old, such as Nelson and Pollock (1970) or Gerstberger and Allen (1968).

That is not to say that the information behavior of scientists is no longer studied; indeed, there is more interest than ever in the behavior of scientists, especially in areas like scientometrics and bibliometrics (e.g., Borgman, 1990; Borgman & Furner, 2002; Cronin, 1984; Leydesdorff, 1998) and the social construction of scientific problems and communities of discourse (e.g., Knorr-Cetina & Mulkay, 1983; Latour & Woolgar, 1979; Tuominen, Talja, & Savolainen, 2005). It is simply that the investigation of scientists' use of *sources* is less common today than it was in past decades. The methods and samples have not changed much; studies of scientists have tended to employ questionnaires and interviews in studying the reading and

Table 11.1: Works reviewed, and related works cited, for occupation.

Occupation	Works Reviewed to Illustrate Findings	Some Other Relevant Works Cited
Scientists	Bichteler 89; Ellis 93; Palmer 91	Bouazza 89; Brown 99; Case 86; Flaxbart 01; Hallmark 01; Hemminger 07; Herman 04; Jamali 10; Kuruppu 06; Murphy 03; Palmer 96, 99; Tuominen 05
Engineers	Bruce 03, Fidel 04; Holland 95; Pinelli 91; Yitzhaki 04	Allard 09; Allen 69, 77; Case 86; Choo 07, 08; Desouza 06; du Preez 09; Freund 05; Gralewska-Vickery 76; Gerstberger 68; Guo 09; Hertzum 00, 02; Kerins 04; King 94; Kwasitsu 03; Leckie 96, 05; Robinson 10; Shuchman 81; Tenopir 04
Social scientists	Ellis 89, 93; Meho 03; Palmer 02; Ruvane 05; Thivant 05	Bebout 75; Belefant-Miller 01, 03; Brittain 70; Case 86; Herman 04; Hernon 84; Hogeweg de Haart 81; Krampen 11; Paisley 65; Slater 88; White 75
Humanists and interdisciplinary	Bronstein 07; Brown 01, 02; Chu 99; Cole 98; Dalton 04; Foster 04; Meho 01, 03; Palmer 02; Talja 02	Bates 96; Bouazza 89; Caidi 01; Case 86, 91; Duff 02; Gould 88; Hemmig 09; Herman 04; Huvila 08, 09, 10; King 01; Larkin 10; Liew 06; Paisley 86, 90; Rose 03; Sievert 89; Stam 84; Stieg 81; Stone 82; Watson-Boone 94; Westbrook 03; Wiberley 89, 94, 00; Yakel 05; Zach 07
Physicians	Gorman 95, 99; Osheroff 91; Timpka 90; Urquhart 98, 99, 01, 03	Bennett 06; Covell 85; Davies 09; Davis 95; Donat 02; Ely 92; Fourie 08, 09; Haug 97; Nicholas 05; Reddy 08
Nurses	Cogdill 03; 08; Gorman 02; MacIntosh-Murray 01; Sundin 02, 03, 05	Bennett 06; Blythe 93; Corcoran-Perry 90; Haig 93; Johannisson 07; McKnight 06, 07; Mullaly 94; Pettigrew 00; Reddy 08; Strother 86; Turner 08; Wakeham 92
Other medical professionals	Harrison 04; Leckie 96, 05; MacIntosh-Murray 01, 05, 06	Gorman 02; Hepworth 04; Landry 06; Lee 03; Marshall 93; McKenzie 04, 09, 10; Owen 03; Salisan 85; Stefl-Mabry 03, 05
Managers	Auster 93; Choo 01; Correia 01; Hirsh 04; Huotari 01; Mackenzie 03	Baldwin 97; Choo 98, 07; Culnan 83; Daft 86, 88; de Alwis 06; Fahrmoomand 02; Hall 03; Hirsh 04; Kuhlthau 99; Mackenzie 02, 04, 05; Solomon 97; Swanson 87; Widen-Wulf 03; Woudstra 08

Table 11.1: (*Continued*)

Occupation	Works Reviewed to Illustrate Findings	Some Other Relevant Works Cited
Journalists	Attfield 03; Fabritius, 99; Nicholas 99, 00	Ansari 10; Anwar 09; Campbell 97; Dupagne 06; Katz 89; Ross 01; Stocking 89; Zelizer 93
Lawyers and judges	Cole 00; Haruna 01; Kuhlthau 01; Sutton 94; Wilkinson 01	Cheatle 92; Choo 08; Gelder 81; Hainsworth 92; Kerins 04; Leckie 96; Otike 99; Vale 88; Walsh 94
Farmers	Case 87; Leckie 96	Ekoja 04; Meyer 03; Timko 89; Zhao 09
Other occupations: artists, clergy, teachers, actors, etc.	Baker 03, 04; Cobbledick 96; Hemmig 09; Ikoja-Odongo 03, 04; Wicks 99	Agarwal 11; Allen 08; Baldwin 97; Brine 10; Chang 06; Cowan 04; Davies 04; Florio 93; Harrison 04; Lambert 10; Layne 94; Makri 10; Mason 11; Medaille 10; Miranda 08; Olsson 10; Sonnenwald 06; Stam 95; Stefl-Mabry 03, 05; Stilwell 02; von Thaden 08; Westbrook 09; White 08

Note: Studies are listed by first author only, plus year. See the references section for clarification.

gathering habits of samples within a single discipline; Flaxbart's (2001) interviews with six university chemistry faculty and Hallmark's (2001) interviews with 43 academic meteorologists are examples of this approach, each documenting older sources while emphasizing the impact of electronic journals on the habits of these groups. Jamali and Nicholas (2010) surveyed 114 physicists and astronomers, while Hemminger et al. (2007) surveyed 902 academic scientists of all disciplines, each at a single university.

One trend in recent investigations in science has been the usage of more naturalistic observations of information-seeking behaviors. Palmer (1991), for example, opted for in-depth interviews rather than large-scale survey techniques in her study of 67 agriculture researchers (a population studied by Majid, Anwar, & Eisenschitz, 2000, in a more conventional way). Palmer employed a variety of structured (psychometric and personality) inventories and semi-structured personal interviews to elicit patterns of communication, use, and importance of information sources, as well as strategies for locating and organizing information and respondent reflections on the organizational structure of their department.

After coding her questionnaire data, Palmer used statistical cluster analysis to produce classifications of the researchers into five groups reflecting generic "information styles." These styles included the following: "nonseekers" who did little information gathering (predominantly statisticians among the researchers); "lone, wide rangers" who read/scanned a wide variety of literature and tended to work alone; a group of biochemists and entomologists who were shifting their research focus, referred to as "unsettled, self-conscious seekers"; "confident collectors," almost entirely entomologists, who felt on top of their field; and "hunters," composed strictly of biochemists, who paid very close attention to emerging research findings and patterns in their narrow area of investigation.

Interestingly, Palmer made a second categorization of information styles, based this time on her own judgments about the tendencies of the individual researchers as revealed in the interviews. The resulting six subjective stereotypes of information styles — overlords, entrepreneurs, hunters, pragmatists, plodders, and derelicts — grouped the scientists quite differently than the earlier cluster analysis, making clear a strong contrast between categorizations arrived at by personal assessments versus psychometric measures. Palmer discussed the implications of the cluster-derived styles for the management of research environments; she has since published other writings on this topic (Palmer, 1996, 1999).

Ellis et al. (1993) conducted interviews with physicists and chemists to identify aspects of their information seeking. They described eight characteristics of seeking patterns (discussed below under "social scientists"), two of which were unique to the chemists in their sample. The other six characteristics were identified in an earlier investigation of social scientists; in other words, physicists and social scientists were highly similar in the ways they dealt with information in their work.

More traditionally oriented studies of scientists tend to focus strictly on sources of information. An example is Bichteler and Ward's (1989) interviews with a sample of 56 geoscientists across the United States. They found that these scientists spent from 2 to 10 hours per week looking for information, averaging about 4 hours per week. Professional contacts, such as colleagues at work and elsewhere, were the most frequently used sources, followed by journal literature. Another investigation — an e-mail survey with a very limited sample — also focused on the use of sources within a community of astronomers, chemists, mathematicians, and physicists (Brown, 1999). Other examples of old-fashioned, source-oriented studies are those of Noble and Coughlin (1997), who surveyed academic chemists in regards to their use of journals, libraries, and technologies; and Kuruppu and Gruber (2006) who favored a mix of interviews and focus groups in their study of agricultural and biological scientists' use of library services. Murphy's (2003) Internet survey of 149 toxicologists, biochemists, and other scientists working at the U.S. Environmental Protection Agency is another study of information usage by source.

One final comment on studying the information seeking of scientists (as well as anyone else): we cannot necessarily rely on their self-reports. Barry (1995) questioned the reliability of accounts she collected from theoretical physicists regarding their use of electronic sources of information. She suggested that even scientists may exaggerate their use of, and success with, sources of information if that is what they think the researcher wants to hear.

Let us turn now to engineers. In their review of a broad variety of information-seeking literatures, Leckie et al. (1996) described engineering as a highly specialized profession (mechanical, chemical, electrical, etc.) working in a broad range of environments. Engineers are not only engaged in the design, development, testing, and manufacturing of items, but also in research, management, consulting, and sales roles. Their work emphasizes the solving of particular technical problems rather than the production of general conclusions, a fact that separates them from the scientists with whom they are sometimes conflated in studies. As Price (1965, p. 562) once generalized, "the scientist wants to write but not read, and the technologist wants to read but not write." Not surprisingly, engineers are frequent consumers of information; a cross-national (India–United States) study by Allard, Levine, and Tenopir (2009) estimated that engineers spend one-quarter of their time engaged in "information events," while Robinson's investigation (using a novel, handheld computer method of data gathering) suggests that more like 56% of their time is spent in information behaviors.

A consistent finding in examinations of the information seeking of engineers (e.g., Allen, 1977; Case, Borgman, & Meadow, 1986; du Preez & Fourie, 2009; Holland & Powell, 1995; King et al., 1994; Pinelli, 1991; Shuchman, 1981; Tenopir & King, 2004) has been that they make more use of their own knowledge, colleagues, and other within-organization sources of information than they do of the technical literature. What literature they *do* use tends to be from their trade — reports, catalogs, handbooks, and trade journals — more than research publications. This is perfectly in keeping with the context in which most engineers work: in private firms, with specific objectives that are not intended to contribute to the engineering knowledge base but rather to produce a particular thing or service. In such situations, the journal literature may be neither specific nor timely enough for the practical matters at hand, but can be useful at early stages for monitoring the environment that is shared with competitors. The most pertinent information is to be found out from clients and colleagues concerned with the objectives, and so they are typically perceived as the most accessible and familiar sources, which tends to reinforce their usage (Allen, 1977; Gerstberger & Allen, 1968; Gralewska-Vickery, 1973; Hertzum, 2002; Hertzum & Pejtersen, 2000).

One series of investigations of aerospace engineers — one of the first populations to be targeted in information studies of the 1950s and 1960s — was reported by Pinelli, Barclay, Glassman, Kennedy, and Demerath (1991).

A survey jointly sponsored by the United States Department of Defense (DoD) and National Aeronautics and Space Administration (NASA) attempted to ascertain how aerospace knowledge diffuses among engineers and scientists. The first phase of the project sent questionnaires to a random sample of 3298 members of an aeronautics organization; 70% responded. Although the focus of the study was the use of technical reports among other information sources, "the broader purpose of the study is to provide insight regarding the information-seeking habits and practices of ... engineers and scientists" (Pinelli et al., 1991, p. 315).

In a series of questions asking why they used certain information sources, responding engineers and scientists indicated that the relevance of sources was the most compelling reason for their use, followed by accessibility and "technical quality or reliability." Although at first glance the importance of such factors may seem obvious, they represent a subtle shift away from some earlier findings regarding use of information sources by engineers. Earlier studies (e.g., Gerstberger & Allen, 1968; Rosenberg, 1967) had emphasized *accessibility* as the major determinant of whether a source would be used; however, the more recent investigators concluded that "accessibility is simply not the issue that it apparently was 25 years ago" (p. 320) due to an increase in electronic channels of distribution, along with improved indexing, organization, and dissemination. Another difference with Pinelli's respondents was that they were *least* sensitive to the *expense* of sources.

Interestingly, Pinelli et al. refer to measures of "accessibility, ease of use, expense, familiarity, and reliability" as "sociometric" variables. More typically, sociometric data are those indicating "who talks to whom" in a work and/or social environment, thus mapping out a social *network*. The classic sociometric study among engineers was that of Allen and Cohen (1969), whose results pointed to a strong overlap between social and work reasons for communicating with colleagues. Allen and Cohen noted a chicken-and-egg problem in understanding why people in laboratories talk to one person more than another: did an engineer come to prefer communicating with a certain colleague because she works with him frequently, or does she talk with that colleague more simply because she likes him in the first place? Whatever "causes" such behavior patterns, Allen and Cohen documented the way in which the organization charts differ from the actual network of communication in two laboratories, and the important role that informal communication plays in work environments. Their closer examination of "sociometric stars" in the laboratories is a classic example of the role of gatekeepers in organizations (Metoyer-Duran, 1993).

Other investigations of engineers tend to show more depth in their research questions. Holland and Powell (1995), for example, documented the importance of interpersonal information seeking among engineers. They asked very detailed questions of 60 engineers regarding their information sources at work and the relative importance of those sources. The single most highly rated source was "word of mouth," just edging out their own collections of documents and far exceeding any use of libraries or databases. The most highly ranked interpersonal sources were people within the engineer's own work group, followed by others in the company. People outside the company were also well thought of as sources. Interestingly, these engineers reported that the most highly ranked "people" source of information was *intra*personal, that is, their own "personal knowledge" of engineering; to a much lesser degree, they also favored "personal experimentation" as a source of information.

Another study in this vein, by Fidel and Green (2004), chose the accessibility of information sources as perceived by engineers — given that numerous studies have found accessibility to be the factor that mostly influences engineers' selection of information. Fidel and Green found some variation among their respondents, however, in how they interpreted "source accessibility." Saving time was the chief criterion for selecting among documents, while familiarity was the guiding factor in selecting human sources of information. Yitzhaki and Hammershlag (2004) contrasted academic computer scientists with industrial software engineers' use of information and their perceptions of the accessibility of sources. Their mail survey of 233 respondents showed differences among the two groups in age, education, seniority, type of research, and the use of most sources. Within both groups the accessibility of information was only partly correlated with its use; this relationship was stronger among the academics than those in industry. Bruce et al. (2003) and Fidel et al. (2004) used a variety of measures and methods to investigate collaborative information gathering and sharing among members of design teams at Microsoft and Boeing; the investigators illustrate the use of "cognitive work analysis" to explore seven dimensions of the tasks they studied. Freund, Toms, and Waterhouse (2005) take a similar approach. Kwasitsu (2003) studied engineers working on the design and manufacturing of microprocessors, finding that the higher the level of education, the less likely engineers were to depend on their memories, and the more likely they were to rely on libraries. Kerins, Madden, and Fulton (2004) used the critical incident technique (see Chapter 9) in their interviews with 14 undergraduate engineering students about their information seeking; this practice-oriented study is notable in that it explored human sources of information (e.g., faculty and other students) as well as library use. Finally, du Preez and Fourie (2009) sampled 11 consulting engineers (i.e., temporary consultants to a client firm, rather than their full-time employees) in an application of the Leckie et al. model discussed in Chapter 6; du Preez and Fourie discovered a high reliance on personal files and knowledge, and on other people.

Some other studies either include engineers as part of a larger sample of occupations or employ them as a comparison group; these include Choo

(2007), Choo, Bergeron, Detlor, and Heaton (2008), Desouza et al. (2006), and Guo (2009). Choo's work takes a different level of analysis (group, rather than individual), offering insights into the collective mind-set of an occupation or organization.

11.1.2. Social Scientists

The aforementioned tendency to generalize about metadisciplines — science, social science, and the humanities — has typically placed social scientists "between" scientists and humanists in terms of their habits and preferences (e.g., Bebout, Davis, & Oehlerts, 1975; Case, 1986). For example, Wiberley and Jones (1994, p. 503) declare that "... it is useful to look at all scholarship as a continuum from the physical sciences to the quantitative social sciences to the qualitative social sciences to the humanities." There are some gray areas in this typology. For example, are psychologists who are concerned with physiological influences on behavior chiefly scientists or do they belong with the social scientists? Are historians chiefly humanists, or are some of *them* social scientists, too? And where do professions like education or interdisciplinary fields like communication belong?

Nevertheless, the three basic categories of science, social science, and humanities have appealed strongly to many of those who have attempted to review information-seeking results (e.g., the series edited by Constance Gould, 1988; Gould & Handler, 1989; Gould & Pearce, 1991). For instance, many reviewers have concluded that the primary literature of science is in journals, whereas that of the humanist is more likely to be found in books and archives. Brittain (1970) noted that journal literature is highly important to social scientists just as it is to scientists; however, the former also rely on institutional data (e.g., governmental records of births, deaths, education, and taxation) generated for reasons other than social research. Perhaps humanists can be said to have even broader sources of information, once we consider how much they draw upon artifacts of popular culture across the ages. Although different studies have reached varying conclusions about the role of informal channels of communication (with scientists frequently singled out as heaviest users of an "invisible college"), recent consensus seems to be that all kinds of scientists and scholars satisfy much of their information needs through contact with their colleagues in the workplace and at conferences.

Such generalizations about metadisciplines may be true as far as they go, but they do not further our understanding of the important mechanisms of information seeking, nor are they particularly useful in application, as in designing a university information system to serve particular disciplines. The conclusions are far too general for specific application, however interesting they may be. To make matters somewhat more complicated, anyone conducting research *between* disciplines is faced with a more "scattered" array of information sources, and consequently with a higher level of information seeking, as confirmed in a variety of empirical studies (Bates, 1996; Case, 1991; Meho & Haas, 2001; Meho & Tibbo, 2003; Palmer & Neumann, 2002). Hogeweg de Haart (1981) and Paisley (1986, 1990) each proposed matrices that sorted out relationships among individual social sciences and related interdisciplines, such as among academic scholars of management or communication.

There is also the issue of "applied" fields, which proceed from fairly straightforward correspondences between basic science discoveries and their application in related engineering disciplines, to the messier relationships between such pairings as social workers and the social sciences, or between practicing artists and the humanities disciplines. Practitioners make highly variable use of knowledge generated by academic disciplines, with some (e.g., clinical psychologists) more tightly linked to formal channels and others (school teachers and lower level managers as examples) making little use of research findings.

Although generalizations about disciplines and metadisciplines are suspect, the work of Bouazza (1989) is among the best and most recent of such attempts. In reviewing studies about use of information sources by scientists, social scientists, and humanists, Bouazza concluded that:

> ... although physical scientists, social scientists, and humanists tend to rely more on formal sources of information than on informal ones, they do not behave in the same way as far as information use is concerned .... The factors that affect the information use [include] ... (a) The availability, accessibility, quality, cost, and ease of use of information. (b) Seniority, experience, specialty, educational level, professional orientation, and the subjective impressions of the users. (c) The stage of a research project; and the physical, social, political, and economic environments surrounding the user. (p. 159)

The differences that Bouazza cites are taken partly from a review by Bebout et al. (1975). Bouazza's own research, on a sample of 240 scientists, social scientists, and humanists from Carnegie-Mellon University, found that these three groups differed in the way that they used informal sources of information, especially in the data collection stage of research and in course preparation.

The most comprehensive review of social science information needs and uses (with ample comparisons to those in science) is that by Hogeweg de Haart (1981). Emphasizing documentary sources of information, it does an excellent job of summarizing virtually all of the studies conducted up to 1980. A larger but narrower review of social scientists, featuring historians and government publications, appeared in the United States a few years later (Hernon, 1984). A commentary by Cronin (1984) emphasized research on social networks and gatekeepers among social scientists. Finally, Gould and Handler (1989) provided highlights from findings of social science studies, suggesting practical implications for libraries and communication systems.

I will describe a few examples of research on social scientists, some of whom were studied in interdisciplinary samples that included either scientists or humanists. The first is an ambitious investigation of social scientists by Ellis (1989), focusing on the stages and process in their information seeking. He conducted interviews with 47 social scientists: 20 psychologists and the rest from eight other departments. His analysis of the resulting 250 pages of interview transcripts revealed six characteristics of information-seeking patterns in these disciplines, which Ellis called starting, chaining, browsing, differentiating, monitoring, and extracting. Informal contacts were particularly important in the starting phases of projects and were also employed in monitoring developments in a field; the other activities mostly involved published literature. As the labels imply, browsing has to do with semi-directed searches of publications or collections; chaining is the following of references from one document to another; differentiating concerns judgments made about the status, orientation, or quality of sources; and extracting is pulling out from sources specific information of interest.

To improve their understanding of these characteristics, Ellis et al. (1993) compared their earlier findings with new observations of academic physicists and chemists. They found no major differences between the research behaviors of physicists and social scientists. However, in the activities of the chemists, they identified two novel kinds of behaviors, which they labeled "verifying" and "ending." Verifying reflected the efforts of chemists to find errors in their own work, particularly in numerical data but also in equations and citations. Ending referred to the tendency of some chemists to search the literature again following the completion of a project to check on relevant developments that might have taken place since they began their work.

Meho and Tibbo (2003) made further use of Ellis' (1989) model of social science information seeking in order to study 65 faculty members from 14 countries. What the members of the sample had in common was scholarship that focused on some "stateless" population (e.g., Basques, Kurds, Sikhs); this population is a good example of interdisciplinary challenges, due to the ways in which their informants do not fit into standard nation-state cubbyholes. About a third of the scholars they studied were political scientists and almost another third were from departments of sociology or anthropology (18.5% plus 13.8%, respectively); the remaining third were from a broad range of disciplines, including history, geography, and 10 other departments. Meho and Tibbo's method of investigation was novel, involving a series of exchanges via e-mail — a kind of asynchronous interview. Not surprisingly, they found that scholars of stateless people face inadequate academic structures and financial support, difficult research conditions in the field, unavailable or deliberately suppressed information, and a lack of helpful subject indexing. In general, the research of Meho and Tibbo (2003) confirms the robustness of Ellis' model, although the authors identified four additional features not found in that model (accessing, networking, verifying, and information managing); their additional features, they admit, are "not all ... information searching or gathering activities" (p. 583) but proved to be important among this population.

Among other studies, Thivant (2005) used a questionnaire based on a qualitative approach called SICIA (Situation, Complexity, and Information Activity) to investigate the relationship between situations, professional contexts, and strategies in the work of a small sample of economists and financial analysts. He found similarity in information seeking and use strategies used by these two groups, with some differences stemming from their varying contexts of their work. Krampen, Fell, and Schui (2011) analyzed the information seeking of 298 psychologists, along with their demographics and a number of other factors affecting their work.

The most unusual study of a social scientist may be Ruvane's (2005) 2-year observation of a single geographer. Ruvane's sole informant was conducting a lengthy historical investigation of the influence of the Indian Trading Path on settlement patterns in the 18th century and on the subsequent growth of cities in North Carolina. The geographer created digital multimedia maps, based partly on land grant documents, in order to place otherwise isolated facts into a context in which they could be related.

11.1.3. Humanities Scholars

Although Ellis and his colleagues took pains to say that the behaviors they saw among social scientists did not occur in a strict sequence, the existence of "stages" in research projects has long been suggested by studies of various occupations. For example, Bronstein (2007) applied Ellis' model in a qualitative study of 25 Jewish Studies scholars. She interviewed them at length, using a grounded theory approach (see Chapter 7) to develop categories of activities. She found that information-seeking strategies (e.g., browsing, extracting, and citation tracking) varied with the stage or purpose of research, and proposed extensions to the Ellis model in a flow chart. Bronstein concludes that her findings are similar to those of Meho and Tibbo (2003; discussed above) yet in contrast to the findings of Wiberley and Jones (1994) and others who found that humanities scholars work alone; Bronstein's informants developed close contacts with their colleagues.

Chu's (1999) survey of 31 Canadian literary scholars also focused on research stages. Using in-depth interviews and a lengthy questionnaire, Chu collected individual accounts of research projects and scholars' activities; these were used to create a descriptive model of the process of literary criticism. In a second stage of research, she tested her model by surveying a sample of 800 scholars, using an 11-page questionnaire of mostly closed-ended items. Chu confirmed a series of six stages typical of literary scholarship: idea generation, preparation, elaboration, analysis and writing, dissemination, and then "further writing and dissemination." Each of these stages was accompanied by specific activities such as searching for, reading, and annotating materials in the preparation stage, and outlining and discussing ideas for a written work in the elaboration phase. In turn, each stage was seen as having "information functions," such as relating primary materials to different perspectives and themes in the preparation phase, or determining central and peripheral focuses in the elaboration phase. The preparation stage features the highest use of information, according to Chu, whereas the dissemination phase has the least. She was careful to point out that these hypothesized stages do not necessarily occur in a strict sequential order; rather, their sequence is highly susceptible to the newness of the project, competing projects, and personal working style. Chu also found that informal communication among colleagues and other human sources is just as important in literary scholarship as it is in other kinds of work roles.

In comparing her findings with studies of the work stages of other disciplines, Chu noted that her stages are fewer in number than the 11 identified among scientists (Garvey, 1979), more than the three broad phases said to exist among economists (White, 1975), and most like the six stages portrayed by Stone (1980). A contrasting view of research stages is found in Foster (2004). He conducted interviews with a purposive sample of 45 academics (faculty and graduate students), some of whom were from the humanities. Foster identifies a number of activities that happen at initial, middle, and final stages; ultimately, he concludes that seeking is better described as dynamic and holistic rather than sequence-driven and consists of three nonlinear "core processes": opening, orientation, and consolidation.

An investigation of "information acquisition in history Ph.D. students" was conducted by Cole (1998). In interviews with 45 doctoral students from six English universities using the grounded theory approach, Cole tried to understand how it is that historians learn to make inferences from what they read. His discussion is one that is less concerned with seeking than with *thinking*, and is informed by cognitive models of reading comprehension (particularly van Dijk & Kintsch, 1983). Using the analogies of pictures (i.e., background data) and jigsaw puzzles (i.e., the thesis), Cole (1998) concluded that these historians created knowledge structures through a four-stage "information process" that distinguishes "experts" from "novices" in a given knowledge domain. The doctoral students' need to demonstrate their expertise to their thesis committee — the reason why they seek information — determines "how they become informed — that is, the cognition involved in information acquisition" (p. 49).

In a replication of the Stieg (1981) study of historians' information sources, Dalton and Charnigo (2004) surveyed 278 historians, most of whom specialized in either American or European history (although the authors note an "increasing fractionation of the field" in the other ways their respondents described their interests). The pattern of preference for source material was similar to that of the older study, except for increased use of dissertations and electronic sources, and decreased use of newspapers. A study by Duff and Johnson (2002) also focused on the information acquired by historians. Relatedly, Yakel (2005) argues in favor of paying more attention to archives (both physical and electronic) as a place in which both scholars and students seek information. Stam (1984) is a short piece on how art historians locate information. Twenty-five archaeologists were the subjects in Huvila's (2008a, 2008b, 2009) investigation; using interviews and information horizon maps, Huvila depicted sources and interactions with information within seven work roles undertaken by these professionals.

Brown (2001, 2002) has conducted a series of studies of music scholars. Her 2001 publication focuses on communication patterns via e-mail and electronic discussion groups used by such scholars in the United States and Canada to facilitate their research. Employing Diffusion Theory (Rogers, 2003) and using interviews and a survey, she found that music scholars rated e-mail as more helpful than discussion groups. Overall, both modes of communication played marginal roles in music research. In a later work, Brown (2002) proposed a six-stage model of music research, based on interviews with 30 music scholars who described to her their recent research projects. Although focused more narrowly on library use, Liew and Ng's (2006) research on 14 ethnomusicologists adds to what we know about music scholarship.

The world of art received scant attention in information behavior until Rose's (2003) study of the impact of new technologies on the research behaviors of art historians. More recently, several related studies have appeared. Larkin (2010) explored the information behavior of scholars in the visual arts, concluding that this group has needs unique from those of other humanists. Hemmig's (2009) survey was of practicing artists, while Zach (2006) conducted case studies of arts administrators.

As mentioned earlier, many investigations included samples of faculty from multiple disciplines, sometimes with the express purpose of studying the challenges of interdisciplinarity (see the discussions by Caidi, 2001, and Paisley, 1986, 1990, on this theme). An example is Palmer and Neumann's sample of 25 faculty from 13 humanities and social sciences departments.

All these scholars had been affiliated with an interdisciplinary center several years earlier. They used semi-structured interviews to explore a set of questions and analyzed the respondents' publications to determine sources they cited in writing those works.

Palmer and Neumann (2002) identified three categories for which information sources were used: identifying, locating or accessing, and consulting or reading. For example, sources used to locate or access information included libraries, their own collections, colleagues' collections, or electronic resources. They characterize the work of these scholars as composed of "exploration" and "translation," each of which has certain processes, activities, and sources associated with it. For example, translating the work of an unfamiliar discipline is a process of learning, in which consulting particular sources (colleagues, bibliographies, textbooks, etc.) is common. They conclude with suggestions as to how research libraries can better support interdisciplinary work.

A study with similar aims to those of Palmer and Neumann was conducted by Herman (2004a, 2004b). Seven faculty from various departments at one university were interviewed regarding their information needs and processes. As a result, Herman proposes a framework describing information needs, consisting of 11 aspects: subject, function, nature, intellectual level, viewpoint, quantity, quality/authority, date/currency, speed of delivery, place of publication/origin, and processing/packaging. Although it ignores much previous research on the topic, Herman's two-part report makes interesting reading.

Another heterogeneous population is that of Wiberley and Jones (1989) who studied 11 humanities scholars, including two anthropologists and a political scientist who were exploring the humanistic roots of their disciplines. Wiberley and Jones's results, like Sievert and Sievert's (1989) interviews with 27 philosophers, emphasize the solitary nature of such scholarship, with most information acquired through reading. Wiberley and Jones (1994, 2000) revisited these scholars to assess the degree to which they had adopted information technology in their scholarship, finding them somewhat slower to do so than social scientists.

Westbrook (2003) surveyed 215 scholars in women's studies — another group that could be placed in either the social sciences or the humanities. She found women's studies faculty to face six types of information-resource problems: information is hard to find and use; information is of poor quality and coverage; information is of limited quantity; information on the Internet is unsatisfactory; information's interdisciplinarity is difficult; and information is overabundant. These scholars reported three kinds of information-related problems with their own research: doing and keeping up with research, learning how to do and keep up with research, and managing information. The sources they most commonly used fell into eight channels (or formats): books, journals, government documents, people, databases, the Internet, other media, and gray/primary/archival material.

Two other studies described earlier also contained mixed populations of humanists and others. The *ARIST* chapter by King and Tenopir (2001) reviewed the personal and situational factors affecting the use of both print and electronic scholarly literature, as documented by the dozens of empirical studies they cite. King's other studies (Belefant-Miller & King, 2001, 2003; Tenopir, King, Spencer, & Wu, 2009) documented how discipline, age, and productivity of the scholars affect their reading habits. And Foster (2004) conducted interviews with a purposive sample of 45 academics from the humanities, social sciences, engineering, and medicine in order to explore the processes and contexts of their information seeking.

Reviews by Gould (1988), Bouazza (1989), and Watson-Boone (1994) remain good entry points into the pre-1990 humanities information-seeking literature; Palmer and Neumann (2002) cover the relevant literature from the 1990s. There has not been a comprehensive review of more literature; however, many of the other works here offer a segment of that literature.

11.1.4. Health Care Providers

There are a number of reasons why health-related information seeking attracts so much attention. Increasing affluence and life spans in many parts of the world are accompanied by more sophisticated health care, and also other medical problems (obesity, heart disease, drug abuse), along with higher expectations of health care systems (no one wants to suffer or die before their time). Medical research continues to develop expensive drugs and procedures to address health problems and extend life. However, these advances exacerbate the problem of the affordability of health care. In addition, there has been a social movement to promote the active involvement of patients in their own health care (see the next chapter for examples of patient information seeking).

All these factors regarding medicine and health have an important consequence: there is ever more health-related information in existence and an increasing need to stay informed about it. This need applies most strongly to health care providers (physicians, nurses, dentists, and administrators), and also to the public at large. As a result, there has been interest in, and funding for, research related to health information, both for improving dissemination and for usage of information (from the "producer" side). A greater degree of attention is being devoted to how people actually use (or do not use) medical information.

I begin by reviewing studies of physicians, as they constitute the most high-profile community of the health care system, along with nurses.

As befitting their greater numbers in the health care workforce, studies of nurses are becoming more numerous.

What is it that health care providers need to know, and how do they find it out? Nearly every study addresses these questions in terms of formal information sources, and that emphasis is too important to ignore here. On the one hand, practitioners need to know about the world of medical practice and research findings, and on the other, about their patients' conditions. Both aspects receive treatment in the information-seeking literature, but the overwhelming emphasis has been on how providers learn about things like treatment modalities, procedures, equipment, and medication.

There have been several comprehensive reviews of the medical information-seeking literature (see, e.g., Marshall, 1993), Internet-based medical information seeking (Younger, 2010), and various empirical studies also describe previous investigations fairly thoroughly. The best organized entry points into the earlier literature on physicians are found in selective reviews by Gorman (1995, 1999). Gorman (1995) reviewed in depth 11 investigations, conducted between 1979 and 1995, of the "information needs of physicians." The 11 studies consist of a mix of mail survey, interview, ethnographic, and "stimulated recall" methodologies and are used to establish a taxonomy of types of information needed by medical doctors — the lack of which, Gorman says, has hindered comparisons of studies.

The taxonomy that Gorman created is useful in considering the other medical information studies reviewed in this chapter. He divides "information used" into five general types: patient data (on an individual, taken from the patient's medical records, family, friends, and self-reports); population statistics (aggregated data on many patients, recalled from memory or taken from public health reports); medical knowledge (generalizable research and practice, taken from journals and textbooks); logistical information (policies, procedures, and forms used "to get the job done"); and social influences (the patterns of local practice, as learned from talking with colleagues). Gorman emphasizes, though, that a typical clinical question (e.g., "Does Norpace cause fatigue?") contains multiple categories of information.

The "information need" side of the equation is matched to these categories through the 11 studies reviewed. Gorman classified types of needs into four types: *recognized* (obvious needs, articulated by the respondent); *pursued* (needs actually followed up on by the doctor interviewed); *satisfied* (by referring to sources of established medical knowledge or patient data); and *unrecognized* (possibilities not initially recognized by the physician). In each case, the nature of the need is either reported by the respondent in the interview or observed directly by the researcher in the office setting. Much of Gorman's analysis is of "needs," but obviously these also imply actions — seeking and use of information.

Doctors who face patients generate a stream of information needs; what is unclear is how large that stream really is. Osheroff et al. (1991) found that each patient generated five questions, Covell, Uman, and Manning's (1985) study indicated two questions for every three patients, and Ely, Burch, and Vinson (1992) found that it is more like one for every 15 patients. A newer study of clinical librarians (Davies, 2009) suggests that they receive about one question from every four patients — but those are only questions going to librarians. Still, one might well ask how estimates can vary so much. The answer is found in the study designs: each of these is based on very different physician samples and varying criteria for what constitutes a "question." The highest estimate (Osheroff et al., 1991) comes from medical rounds by teams of doctors, residents, and students in an academic setting and included all types of questions; the lowest estimate (Ely et al., 1992) excluded from observation several types of common questions and included a sample of rural physicians, who ask markedly fewer questions than their urban colleagues.

However many questions there are, more than two-thirds of them are probably *not pursued*, according to Covell et al. (1985) and to Gorman and Helfand (1995), although Gorman (1999) says that answers are sought to almost half of the questions that arise if we adopt a broader definition of "information need." Most of the information needs that are pursued are satisfied by textbooks, drug texts, and people (colleagues, consultants, and nonphysicians), with a strong preference for colleagues and other highly familiar sources; relatively little use is made of library or Internet resources. As described in Chapter 6, Haug's (1997) meta-analysis of 12 physician studies also concluded that the most common patterns of sources consulted at that time were local textbooks and colleagues. Given that drug-prescribing questions are the most common type that arise, it is logical that sources of pharmaceutical information are commonly used on a daily (or at least weekly) basis (Connelly, Rich, Curley, & Kelly, 1990; Covell et al., 1985; Ely, Burch, & Vinson, 1992). The migration of medical information to the Internet has shifted use of published information in an electronic direction, at the same time bringing up difficulties with access, convenience, and usability (Bennett, Casebeer, Zheng, & Kristofco, 2006; Younger, 2010), especially for nurses (Nicholas et al., 2005; Turner, Stavri, Revere, & Altamore, 2008).

According to Osheroff et al. (1991), about half of the information that a physician needs to treat a patient can be answered from the medical record; answers to the remaining needs are evenly split between published sources and a synthesis of the physician's existing knowledge and information from the patient. For the physician's practice to actually *improve* (i.e., for doctors to go beyond their education and be innovative), personal reading of journals, textbooks, and the web is typically not enough; interaction with up-to-date colleagues is a more likely avenue for continuing education in medicine (Davis, Thomson, Oxman, & Haynes, 1995; Urquhart, 1998). Bennett et al. (2006) found that colleagues are still a common source of information in practice.

Gorman concluded that the clinical questions that doctors have "tend to be highly complex, embedded in the context of a unique patient's story" (p. 729). There are two related aspects of this conclusion that bear emphasis. The first is a familiar refrain: the primary information comes from humans rather than recorded sources. Stories need to be sifted and interpreted before the information they contain is written down.

The second implication of Gorman's review is that much of the knowledge physicians use in treating patients is a narrative: the story of the patient's history of symptoms and treatments (Tannenbaum, 1994). As Gorman says, "The reliance on stories to communicate information need, because of the complexity and patient specificity, may be one reason for the consistent finding that physicians rely heavily on human sources of information" (p. 734). This kind of knowledge is not merely a list of facts about conditions and implied treatment options that could be pulled from a handbook or database.

One of the studies contained in Gorman's review can serve as a useful example of the investigation of physician information needs and seeking. Timpka and Arborelius (1990) offer an original research approach to physician information seeking. Rather than examining the usual "well-formed questions" and corresponding source preferences, as do most studies in this genre, they investigate "dilemmas" — perplexing situations in which physicians struggle to understand a case that does not make sense. Although the goal of this investigation was to inform the development of decision support systems for doctors, their findings hold more general interest for students of information seeking.

Timpka (a physician) and Arborelius (a psychologist) conducted an in-depth study of 12 general practitioners (GPs), videotaping and analyzing 46 of their consultations with patients. These video recordings were reviewed twice with the GP who was taped. The first time, the physician was asked to stop the tape any time she or he had comments to make (which were recorded for analysis). During the second review, the GP stopped the tape any time he or she had felt uncertain about how to go on.

Timpka and Arborelius sorted the comments made during these sessions into a series of dichotomous categories, such as "spontaneous comments" versus "interviewer-initiated comments," and "stimulated recall" versus "new aspects" of the situation. Those spontaneous comments that identified problems in the consultation session, based on stimulated recall, were dubbed "dilemma situations." Dilemma situations were further broken down into three categories in which knowledge was needed of a medical (32%), personal (19%), or social (49%) type.

Among the 46 consultations, 262 dilemmas were identified. These were cases in which "the GP found it difficult to understand the situation as a whole" (p. 23). An example of a medical dilemma is the case of a patient who presents multiple symptoms for which there is no clear and immediate diagnosis; the diagnosis was the source of 55% of the medical knowledge dilemmas, and the puzzle with most of these was with what kind of treatment to recommend.

The least frequent type of dilemma was of a personal nature, primarily having to do with the competence of the physician in controlling the consultation. These were often cases in which the physician found himself wondering, "What is the right thing to do just now?" An example that Timpka and Arborelius related is of a physician who inadvertently reminds a patient of the death of that person's father, and wonders what he can then say to comfort the patient or address the faux pas.

The situations in which the "knowledge needed" was of the third kind, social, highlighted breakdowns in organizational structure or interpersonal communication. An example of organizational interruption is the misplacing of portions of the patient's medical record. Of particular interest were 99 breakdowns in interpersonal communication, which were analyzed using the universal pragmatics approach of Habermas (1979). These were classified into

> ... situations where the GP did not understand the patient (11%), perceived that the patient violated a social norm (25%), did not trust the patient (42%), did not agree with the patient on the truth of the facts (11%), or was disturbed (11%). (Timpka & Arborelius, 1990, p. 26)

Examples of each type of communication breakdown include not understanding why a patient needed medical attention; perceiving the client as being uncooperative or as trying to control the diagnostic interview; not trusting a patient's statements or understanding of medical terminology; not agreeing with the client's self-diagnosis; and being interrupted by noises or phone calls.

Timpka and Arborelius concluded with an enlightened discussion of "problems in the doctor–patient communication" that suggest difficulties in sense-making on both sides. For instance, they suggest that mistrust is an under-examined issue in medical consultations. Only rarely did Timpka and Arborelius witness confirming kinds of communication strategies, such as the physician asking the patient, "Did you understand what I just explained?"

In the view of Timpka and Arborelius, the GP is faced with the interpretation of narratives, and so is similar to the historian in how he or she reconstructs the truth of a situation. It is only when physicians do not have insights (i.e., "don't get the joke") that they turn to reference sources. Descriptions of disease in the literature are described by Timpka and Arborelius as "iconic" compilations of clinical narratives, which help the doctor to form meaning despite being at times vague and incomplete. They conclude that decision support systems in medicine may have something to learn from multimedia sources in the humanities in the way that those sources support learning and interpretation. Timpka and Arborelius also make a case for their "phenomenological approach with stimulated recall reports" as a superior method to "standard data collection techniques (study of written material, observation, participation, questionnaires, interviewing, and group brainstorming)" in understanding task-based information needs and uses (p. 29).

Another innovative approach to studying physician information seeking has entailed the use of clinical case histories, or "vignettes" (Urquhart, 1998, 1999). In such studies, physicians were presented with several vignettes and asked "a series of questions aimed at eliciting how confident they were in implementing therapy without recourse to additional information ... and which sources would be used if they did seek further information" (Urquhart, 1998, p. 424). Results from such studies indicate a strong preference to consult with a specialist in those cases in which physicians had doubts about proceeding with treatment. A related finding has been that doctors often develop confidence in their knowledge after treating as few as two cases, suggesting that feelings of uncertainty may be extinguished rather quickly by a little practical experience. However, Urquhart (1999) questions whether vignettes are as valid a diagnostic tool in studies of physicians as they have been in studies of other kinds of professionals. A later publication by Urquhart (2001) covers some of the same ground, while Urquhart et al. (2003) discusses use of the critical incident technique and elicitation interviewing for this research.

Given that medical personnel frequently work in teams, it is not surprising that some research concerns collaborative information behavior. In addition to Nicholas et al. (2005), who studied surgical teams, Reddy and Spence (2008) conducted an ethnographic study of an emergency room patient care team. They noted seven types of information needs (as indicated by frequently asked questions); most of these concerned medical information, but some questions were about the team or hospital. Three common triggers of information seeking were found to be lack of expertise, lack of immediately accessible information, and complex information needs. A model developed in this study is also discussed by Reddy and Jansen (2008).

Nurses are much more numerous than physicians but until recently received less attention from researchers. Even more so than doctors, nurses are focused on patient care and so, correspondingly, are their information needs and seeking. Studies by Blythe and Royle (1993), Corcoran-Perry and

Graves (1990), McKnight (2006, 2007), Pettigrew (2000), Turner (2008), and Wakeham (1992), among others, emphasize that nurses consult primarily local sources of information in the context of caring for clients. This includes patient records and laboratory results, coupled with interpersonal sources such as physicians, pharmacists, and other nurses. To this list, Haig (1993) adds nursing journals, if their content is relevant to patient care; Wakeham (1992) notes that these are more often personal subscriptions than publications found in the library.

Urquhart (1998) related several studies of British nurses that used vignettes in their research design. A typical vignette used in the nursing study began by proposing a situation requiring some action from the respondent, such as "Your colleague needs to know about all the ways in which alternative/complementary medicine might be used in your ward ... " (Urquhart, 1998, p. 281). These studies found a wide range of responses to each vignette, with most interviewees suggesting at least one or two sources that could be used to respond to the situation proposed. About 25% of the respondents were characterized as "expert" and "confident" information seekers, who could identify more than two sources of relevant information and had a strategy in mind for approaching the problem. However, 45% of the interviewees were seen as having relatively limited knowledge and skills in information seeking, suggesting the need for further continuing education of nurses.

Sundin (Sundin, 2002, 2003; Sundin & Hedman, 2005) conducted multiple interviews with 20 Swedish nurses to explore the distinctions made between practical and theoretical knowledge and the relationship of that knowledge to the nurse's professional identity; that is, as a legitimate specialty distinct from that of physicians. Sundin argued persuasively for a sociocultural approach to studying information behavior as one aspect of professionalization. His later study (Johannisson & Sundin, 2007) analyzed the discourses of 56 nurses, finding a divide between a science- versus holistically oriented discourse style. Cogdill (2003) studied the information seeking of 300 primary care nurses through a questionnaire and follow-up interviews with 20 of the respondents following episodes with patients. Cogdill found that nurse practitioners most frequently needed information related to drug therapy and diagnosis, and that they most frequently consulted colleagues, drug reference manuals, textbooks, and protocol manuals.

Several studies included samples of nurses along with other persons involved in the situation (e.g., doctors, pharmacists, patients, family members). Gorman, Lavelle, Delcambre, and Maier (2002) used individual and group interviews coupled with participant observation of the information behaviors of a sample of physicians, nurses, and pharmacists in order to design better digital libraries for them. They found that an overabundance of records, coupled with severe time constraints, forced their informants to focus tightly on data related to the patient care problem. Fourie (2008) interviewed eight nurses in a convenience sample that also included five doctors, eight patients, and four family members. As the common condition was a need for palliative care, Fourie's research uncovered evidence of unexpressed needs (e.g., for emotional support) and cases of denial or avoidance. Some of the nurses were especially aware of these psychological issues. Fourie concluded that more research could be done on the perceptions of health care workers about how they (and their employer) envision their role with dying patients and their families. A later publication by Fourie (2009) reviews literature on the role of emotion among health care professionals. Relatedly, Donat and Pettigrew (2002) reviewed literature on both doctors and patients in describing typical information behavior surrounding the dying patient.

MacIntosh-Murray (2001) offered a framework for studying the monitoring of "adverse clinical events." She argued that the incidence and seriousness of medical errors make the scanning behavior of health care workers an important topic for research and suggested variables that will influence the incidence of adverse events. MacIntosh-Murray and Choo (2005) describe the former's dissertation research, which consisted of an ethnographic study in a large tertiary care hospital. Starting with the premise that we know little about how information about patient safety is used for avoiding adverse events, MacIntosh-Murray studied how practices and beliefs influenced how health care providers and their managers make sense of safety risks and adverse events, along with the flow and use of information for improving safety. MacIntosh-Murray found that frontline staff (chiefly nurses) tend to be task driven and must cope with heavy workloads that limit their attention and their recognition of risks. She suggests that nurses can serve as a "change agent" who helps to bridge information gaps and to champion innovation in the hospital. Her subsequent review (MacIntosh-Murray & Choo, 2006) of literature related to "information failures in health care" identifies many other studies and commentaries related to adverse clinical events.

Other health care providers who have been studied include dentists (e.g., Landry, 2006; Mullaly-Quijas, Ward, & Woefl, 1994; Strother, Lancaster, & Gardiner, 1986), mental health care workers (Salasin & Cedar, 1985), hospital social workers (Harrison, Hepworth, & de Chazal, 2004), at-home care providers (Hepworth, 2004), midwives (Davies & McKenzie, 2004; McKenzie, 2004, 2009, 2010), and practitioners of alternative medicine (Owen & Fang, 2003). Several of these are described in other chapters, so only a few will be expanded upon here.

Harrison et al. (2004) studied the information behavior of hospital social workers, using questionnaires, focus groups, and interviews. Their results suggested that these social workers were relatively "information poor," considering their needs versus their lack of access to the Internet and other useful sources; consequently, information seeking tended to be gathered in face-to-face exchanges with other people. Hepworth (2004) interviewed 60 nonprofessionals who provided substantial health care for a relative or other person and suggested a model of information service based on his findings. A review by Fourie (2009) underscores the emotional component of labor by healthcare professionals.

Dentists have been little studied, even though the review by Leckie et al. (1996) says that dentists are most like physicians in their need for information on patient care and changes in the environment regarding techniques, treatments, equipment, and the administration and regulation of their practice. It is apparent from the studies reviewed that health care professionals have a great deal in common in regards to their preferences for information sources. Another study, by Landry (2006), used interviews with 12 dentists to explore the various work roles that these professionals have (provider, administrator, researcher, etc.) and their effect on choice of information sources.

11.1.5. *Managers*

The heterogeneity of this group must be acknowledged right at the start: "managers" *could* be almost anybody. A person who directs the operations of a convenience store with four full-time employees is a manager, as is the chairman of Toyota Motor Corporation. However, as studied in the information-seeking literature, managers are typically higher level employees of large organizations, often described as "executives" or "CEOs." Most literature reviews also assume that "managers" are educated (having at least a bachelor's degree and perhaps a master's in business administration, or a comparable degree in another field), even though higher education was not as prevalent in early studies of managers. For our purposes, "managers" will be assumed to be individuals who have at least some university education and who work in a sizable organization.

A review of managerial information-seeking literature by de Alwis et al. (2006) and a study by Choo and Auster (1993) are good places to start for this occupation. de Alwis, Majid, and Chaudhry focus on source preferences in their extensive survey of past studies. According to them, past studies have examined managerial responses to the accessibility, richness, and quality of information they encounter. Their review identified four dimensions by which these vary, each of which has 12–17 factors: contextual (e.g., roles and tasks), situational (e.g., company, industry, and technology), personal/cultural (e.g., qualifications, years of experience, IT skills), and informational (e.g., awareness, accessibility, and richness of sources).

Choo and Auster focused on "environmental scanning" — a subset of the literature on managers' needs, uses, and seeking — and they offer a useful framework for summarizing findings in this area. Given their focus on scanning, Choo and Auster discuss primarily information that is *external* to the organization (such as what competitors are doing), rather than internal. They highlight findings similar to those among scientists and scholars: informal sources and ease of accessibility of information are even more important to managers than to the other groups. To this they add that people and conversations are the primary way that managers acquire information, and that a defining context of managerial work is the solving of immediate problems. It is the latter characteristic that makes managers most different from scholars and scientists, who may identify research problems and work on them for long periods of time before reaching conclusions; managers, in contrast, rarely have the luxury of extended contemplation, and for that reason are much less likely to spend time reading.

Auster and Choo (1993) were interested in how managers acquire and use information about the external business environment. As described in Chapter 3, this monitoring of the environment is sometimes referred to as "scanning" in the management literature. Auster and Choo studied how managers regarded uncertainty in the environment and how perceived uncertainty affected their use and evaluation of sources. In framing their research problem, the investigators built on earlier work by Aguilar (1967), Rosenberg (1967), Gerstberger and Allen (1968), Culnan (1983), Daft and Lengel (1986), and Daft, Sormunen, and Parks (1988), among others. Their questionnaire was thus able to replicate measures found to be predictive in earlier studies.

To study their research problem, Auster and Choo first picked two information-intensive and fast-moving industries: publishing and telecommunications. They focused their inquiry on Canadian firms with revenues of greater than $5 million and identified the CEOs of the resulting 207 firms. They mailed as many as four questionnaires to their target population, followed by a phone call if none of those instruments was returned. It took that degree of effort to obtain a response rate of 56% (115 respondents of 207 initially contacted); given the nature of the respondents and their lack of direct connection to the investigators, it was remarkable to have attained such a level of response.

Auster and Choo found that CEOs see customers and technological trends as the most strategic portions of the environment to pay attention to; those sectors are also the most uncertain for CEOs. Higher perceptions of uncertainty in the environment were associated with more scanning of the environment. To keep track of environmental change, CEOs relied on multiple sources, both internal and external, both personal and impersonal. Examples of internal sources included the company managers and staff (who were also "personal" sources), while external sources included printed and broadcast media (obviously "impersonal"). A finding that contradicted some earlier studies was that the perceived quality of the source was a better predictor of use than either the accessibility of the source or even the perceived degree of uncertainty in the environment. The two sources that can most be relied upon are subordinate managers and company customers; internal memos, although they were close at hand and used with some frequency, were ranked only in the mid-range in terms of "quality" of information.

Auster and Choo suggest that an increasingly complex and fast-changing business environment prompts CEOs to stress the quality of information over ease of accessibility. Likewise, a study of 186 management report users by Swanson (1987) found that "information value" was more important than accessibility. Thus, both of these studies differ in that respect from the still often-cited findings of Allen (1977), which emphasized accessibility as the most influential variable. Along with Auster and Choo, the studies by Culnan (1983) and Pinelli et al. (1991) argued that a more complex and turbulent environment places a premium on the reliability of information.

The related problem of information overload (see Chapter 5) was addressed by Farhoomand and Drury (2002). In their four-nation survey, 124 managers in companies and government were asked to define "information overload" and to identify its frequency, sources, effects, and the actions they take in response; over half experienced information overload frequently and typically responded by "filtering" information.

Choo (2001a, 2001b) tells about four modes of environmental scanning frequently observed within organizations, claiming that each reflects typical needs, habitual information seeking, and standard uses. Choo's model correlated needs, information seeking, and information uses with managerial traits, organizational strategies, and external situations. It also suggested future research approaches and applications. Choo (2007) extends his work in the direction of how organizational culture influences both information seeking and the formation of beliefs about the outside environment.

Correia and Wilson (2001) interviewed 47 individuals in 19 Portuguese firms of differing sizes to discover factors that influence environmental scanning. Using a case-study approach, coupled with grounded theory, the factors revealed were partly individual: information consciousness (attitude toward information-related activities) and exposure to information (frequency of opportunities of contact with well-informed people and information-rich contexts); and partly organizational: information climate (conditions that determine access to and use of information in an organization) and "outwardness" (links to other organizations). They concluded that the more open the organization is to its environment, the more likely that individuals in the organization will be exposed to relevant information; correspondingly, to the extent that openness occurs, the organization is more likely to develop an information climate that supports the individual.

Huotari and Wilson (2001) focused on "critical success factors" (CSF) in their case studies of the information needs of managers at UK and Finnish universities and business firms; these factors pertain to objectives that, if not achieved, may result in the failure of the organization. Qualitative interviews and social network analysis were combined with a grounded theory approach to identify main themes across the two universities and two companies, confirming the validity of CSF in differing kinds of organizations. Relatedly, Huotari and Chatman (2001) and Savolainen (2009c) explain the constructs of small worlds and social networks often employed in studies such as these.

Mackenzie (2003a) surveyed 50 business managers and 50 nonmanagers, finding significant differences between these two groups in terms of their information behavior and motivations. The results demonstrate that managers tend to gather information they do not need in a quest to simplify their environment and to help make faster decisions. The respondents believed that gathering information gave them the reputation of being well connected and knowledgeable. In addition, her (2003b) interviews with 22 line managers reveal that in some cases they are drawn to a source that represents the best (e.g., most trusted or liked) relationship rather than best information. Other studies by Mackenzie (2002, 2004, 2005) suggested that managers consciously cultivate other individuals as information sources. Hall (2003) took on similar themes to those of Mackenzie, exploring the motives behind the sharing of knowledge in information-intensive organizations.

Widén-Wulff (2003) examined how 15 Finnish insurance companies build their knowledge base. Based on 40 interviews with managers, Widén-Wulff outlined three categories of companies, based on characteristics of their internal environments: "closed businesses" (in which tradition and safety are emphasized), "open companies" (those which are innovative, and which integrate social capital and the individual in their planning process), and the firms "in the middle," which may be transitioning from closed to open.

In a study that encompasses both managers and engineers, Hirsh and Dinkelacker (2004) followed the information seeking of 180 researchers from Hewlett Packard Labs and Compaq Computers during the merger of those two companies. They found heavy use of Web sources, the corporate library, information from standards bodies, and from colleagues outside of the firm. Their results suggested that the factors most influencing selection of sources are time-savings, authoritativeness, and convenience; currency, reliability, and familiarity were relatively less important.

Kuhlthau's (1999) and Baldwin and Rice's (1997) reports contain easily digestible overviews of managerial information usage as background to their respective investigations of security analysts.

11.1.6. Journalists

The communications scholar Elihu Katz once wrote a fascinating essay in the journal *American Behavioral Scientist* (1989) on the topic of "journalists as scientists." Katz's theme was that journalists do not so much resemble professions like doctors and lawyers (who serve individual clients rather than a larger constituency) as much as they are like applied scientists. Journalists, like scientists, have theories and methods, and sometimes make predictions about future events. In the case of journalism, the theories are about people, society, events, and news itself; the methods of inquiry are very rudimentary, however.

The accompanying articles in this issue on journalism are equally interesting. Wolton (1989), for example, mostly agreed with Katz's statements about theory but stressed the different reality of journalists, who "must produce information on a daily basis ... structuring the world as events continue to unfold ... giving form to a world that is rarely rational," unlike scientists, who have "the luxury of standing back from events" (p. 249). In contrast, Goren (1989) flatly disagreed with Katz: journalists do not have explicit theories or methods and are rarely held accountable for the veracity of their pronouncements, as are scientists and professionals. And Roeh (1989) eschewed the comparison with scientists entirely, arguing that no matter how much journalists may deny it, what they actually do is "tell stories" rather than "report facts." A commentary by Zelizer (1993) describes journalists as an "interpretive community" perceived as too insular by some critics. Campbell's (1997) work agrees with these last two, painting news as something that is actively constructed within a variety of constraints imposed by time, the audience, and the news organization.

Whatever is the appropriate way to view the job of news reporting, it is a fascinating profession to study in the context of information behavior (Savolainen, 2009a). In a very concrete way, journalism is *largely* information seeking, along with the prime job of transferring what is found through writing, speaking, and/or filming. Despite the large number of investigations of the audience for news (reader, viewer, or listener studies), until recently there were relatively few focused, empirical studies of what journalists actually do.

One particular investigation stands out for its depth: Fabritius (1999) conducted a qualitative study of journalists using a variety of methods and sources of data. Indeed, a subtheme of her research was how one may triangulate theory, methods, and data to gain a fuller picture of a phenomenon — in this case, the work practices of reporters and their use of electronic sources in that work. Fabritius observed and interviewed a number of journalists in four departments of a Finnish newspaper, including attending editorial meetings and employing talk-aloud protocols to better understand some aspects of journalistic work. In addition, she used a number of other methods and observations. Fabritus had 18 journalists complete "diary" forms after writing a news item, indicating the sources used and their importance; she coupled the resulting 250 diary entries to the actual published items in which they resulted, and in so doing linked process to outcome. She collected documents (such as editorial meeting agendas and press releases) from the newspaper and kept a diary of her fieldwork experience. Fabritus also experimented with yet other observation devices, such as videotape and photographs, as well as critical incident interviews, which turned out to be less productive methods than the others.

Fabritus's findings (which are not easily summarized) establish the influence of the various "cultures" to which journalists belong. The concentric cultures of the profession, a particular medium (such as a newspaper) and the particular news beat within a medium (e.g., foreign news) are manifested in the values, norms, activities, and routines that make up work practice in that context. Together, these determine the criteria by which news is selected and produced, as well as the patterns of information seeking that accompany the processing of stories. Fabritus said that "continuous, proceeding stages" can be discerned in the production of news, "logical steps" that "do not follow each other in a strict chronological order" (p. 411). Searching for and evaluating information (facts and opinions) take place in interaction with a wide variety of sources (e.g., people, documents, firsthand observation). Fabritus concluded that the way journalists learn to process news items, along with "situational factors such as lack of time," is the strongest constraint on the ways that information is sought in journalism (p. 411).

Scholars who make more informal observations of journalistic work practice (e.g., Goren, 1989; Katz, 1989) would agree with Fabritus's emphasis on the culture of journalism and the constraints of time and institutions; indeed, some of them (e.g., Stocking & Gross, 1989) see journalistic work as dominated strongly by predetermined frames of perception and labeling that tend to bias news.

Attfield and Dowell (2003) and Attfield, Blandford, and Dowell (2003) based their conclusions on interviews with reporters for the *London Times*. They examined the role of uncertainty in the work of newspaper reporters in Britain, looking at how they perceived newsworthiness, generated "angles" for stories, exercised creativity, and gathered information in the context of writing. The ideas of Kuhlthau (Kuhlthau & Tama, 2001) and Dervin (Dervin, 2003) figured prominently in this research.

Outside of Europe and North America, studies of journalist information behavior have been infrequent. They seem to be oddly popular in Pakistan, where several students and professors have carried out studies on this topic. The two that have been published are Anwar and Asghar (2009) and Ansari and Zuberi (2010). Both studies tend to focus on source of information; however, latter study contains some interesting comparisons of print with broadcast journalists. For example, according to Ansari and Zuberi, radio professionals do far less searching and reading than either newspaper or television journalists; the latter group reported a great deal of usage of a broad variety of sources.

Other studies of information seeking and use among journalists also tend to be source oriented; a popular focus has been the influence of the Internet on the work of reporters. Nicholas and Williams (1999; Nicholas, Williams, Cole, & Martin, 2000), for example, raised the question of whether the Internet was widely used as a source at that time. In a study of 150 journalists and news librarians in the United Kingdom, they concluded that fewer than 20% were making much use of the Internet for finding information relevant to their reporting. Surprisingly, the heaviest users tended to be midcareer reporters rather than the very youngest (and supposedly most computer literate). Unsurprisingly, the most-used sites were those of online newspapers. Nicholas and Williams categorized the relationships that these news workers have with the Internet as ranging from worship to complete disdain for it as an information source. Perhaps because of the earlier time frame, their study contrasts sharply with online surveys of journalists conducted in the United States (e.g., Dupagne & Garrison, 2006; Ross & Middleberg, 2001), which paint a much more enthusiastic picture of the use of online sources. While more focused on the convergence of print and electronic news gathering and reporting, Dupagne and Garrison (2006) considered the evolution of jobs and roles in the newsroom. The training of reporters and editors in online searching has resulted in less dependence on librarians and other news researchers.

11.1.7. Lawyers

Attorneys share with many scientists an absolute need to stay current with published literature relevant to their work; they cannot afford to miss any new ruling, decision, or regulation that concerns their practice. It may be the case that some areas of the law (e.g., taxation and health and safety regulation) require more research than others, but all lawyers face a rapidly expanding universe of knowledge to which they must attend.

Almost two decades ago, Sutton (1994, p. 199) could say that "there is little known empirically of the information seeking behavior of attorneys" and that we have relied upon anecdotes and legal research primers for what we know about them. The analysis of attorney information seeking by Leckie et al. (1996), for example, rests mainly on texts about the nature and practice of legal research. Those authors said that the primary activities of attorneys — advocacy (with its accompanying legal research), drafting of legal documents, counseling of clients, negotiating outcomes, and managing their practice — all imply a great deal of information seeking of various types. Since those early commentaries, much more has been learned about the information behavior of attorneys.

Sutton's own analysis (1994) theorized about the "mental model" of legal reasoning held by attorneys. The focus of his article is improving information retrieval systems for the law, but it contains a fascinating discussion of the way lawyers think about legal cases, and what this predicts about their search for court decisions that bear on a case. According to Sutton, lawyers rely on their legal education to first identify key cases that define an area of law, then work from those to find cases that apply the relevant legal principle to facts that are similar to the case at hand — a process that Sutton calls "context-sensitive exploration." Ultimately, the search for relevant cases may come down to "tracking" citations from one legal decision to another, which can be a massive and frustrating task. Not only are there many potentially relevant cases, but some of them will have been overruled, criticized, or ignored by more recent decisions, the status of which may not be fully reflected in the indexing systems for case law. Thus, it is a difficult task to identify and analyze all the cases that might be cited by the other side in a legal battle.

Cole and Kuhlthau (2000) studied 15 attorneys, some at the start of their career and the rest at more advanced stages. Drawing on psychological studies of problem solving, Cole and Kuhlthau argued that part of what makes one "expert" in the law is an ability to link the recognition of a problem to potential solutions. Through interviews, they obtained examples of how this comes about, which they expressed in terms of a four-point "value-added arc."

The first of Cole and Kuhlthau's four points is that experts are more efficient at identifying what information is most relevant to a case, for example, knowing what previous cases are most likely to be cited. Second, expert lawyers are able to see the case in terms of how certain information will affect the client; they are able to question witnesses and outline cases in ways "that will benefit the client or jury and judge" (p. 6). The third point in the arc of value is the way that seasoned attorneys are able to package what they know in such a way "so that it is effectively communicated to the client or jury and judge"(p. 6); they have learned to cover all the necessary points in a case to present facts to the court in a concrete way and to prepare effective opening and closing statements. Finally, the fourth "further refinement" occurs when lawyers package their knowledge in such a way that the judge, jury, or client will act on it; this may be accomplished, for example, by working backward from the charges given to the jury in terms of what facts need to be established to decide the case.

Cole and Kuhlthau described their four points as mechanisms for constructing and packaging information, and then using it to persuade others. Legal expertise can be improved, they say, by "simple almost formulaic devices" that stimulate lawyers to think in terms of "how the information will be used" (p. 8). Their future research promises to examine the sources that feed into the four phases of the value-added arc. Another investigation of attorneys by Kuhlthau and Tama (2001) concluded that lawyers desire information services that are highly customized to their needs.

Wilkinson (2001) conducted over 150 interviews with lawyers about how they solved problems in their practice. She concludes that "legal research" is not synonymous with "information seeking." Wilkinson's respondents identified other tasks, such as administration, as constituting both problem-solving and information-seeking activities. In general, they preferred informal and internal sources of information, especially those from larger firms. Haruna and Mabawonku (2001) took a more conventional approach in studying the needs and seeking behaviors of lawyers in Nigeria. They concluded that the most pressing information needs of Nigerian lawyers are recent decisions of superior courts, new legislation, and advice on bettering their knowledge and skills, and that law libraries in their country were not fully meeting the needs of lawyers. Kerins et al. (2004) found the law students they studied in Ireland to be somewhat weak in their information-seeking strategies, at times ignoring what law libraries could offer.

Various other investigations of legal work have been conducted in the United States and England, including several master's and doctoral theses. These include studies by Cheatle (1992), Gelder (1981), Hainsworth (1992), Otike (1999), Vale (1988), and Walsh (1994). Hainsworth has conducted an investigation of the information-seeking behavior of judges. Some of these investigations are difficult to obtain, but fortunately most of that are reviewed briefly in the article by Otike (1999). Finally, Choo et al. (2008) undertook an entirely different type of analysis in their comparative study of three organizations: a law firm, an engineering firm, and a public health agency. One finding specific to the law firm was a higher reliance on informal sources, such as personal networks. Not surprisingly, both the lawyers and engineers were less likely to share information with parties outside their firm than was the health agency.

11.1.8. Farmers

Farmers have been investigated by a relatively small number of studies. Case and Rogers (1987) report a study of 200 farmers who were using an experimental online information system. In the service of explaining how information-intensive farming has become, Case and Rogers characterize one of the farmers as receiving 35 items in the mail on a typical day, including 13 magazines and 3 newspapers. They paraphrase this farmer as saying that hard work and attention to marketing of products are no longer enough; rather "today's agriculture exists in the context of an information society, and so the gathering, processing, and outputting of information is one of the most important roles for a modern farmer" (pp. 57–58). Like the other farmers in this sample, marketing and weather information were particularly important and were typically obtained from radio, television, and word of mouth (e.g., commodity prices from grain elevator operators). Market data is also covered by Timko and Loynes (1989). An investigation by Zhao, Zhang, and Klein (2009) of 167 dairy farmers in Inner Mongolia also highlights the importance of market and policy information. Other investigations stress the utility of customizing information for farmers, particularly in developing countries (Ekoja, 2004; Meyer, 2003).

In a focus on gender, Leckie (1996) interviewed 32 female farmers from Ontario about their experiences growing up on a farm and working as farmers. She found that the typical division of labor on farms tended to exclude women from learning important agricultural information.

11.1.9.   Other Occupations

The occupations discussed above have been the subject of several, or in some cases dozens, of investigations; the occupations mentioned under this heading have been the focus of few empirical studies. To start with, the work of artists has drawn many commentaries in the professional literature (among whom Cowan (2004), Layne (1994), Stam (1995) are the more interesting pieces), yet just three investigations have been published in scholarly journals: Cobbledick (1996), Hemmig (2009), and Mason and Robinson (2011).

Cobbledick (1996) conducted interviews with four artists of different media: a sculptor, a painter, a fiber artist, and a metalsmith. She makes a startling point in her introduction when she discusses how little artists have been studied compared to other occupations. Based on 1995 estimates, there must be almost a million "professional" (i.e., not including part-time or periodic) artists in the United States alone. This was more than the number of lawyers in the United States and also more than the combined number of scientists and social scientists in a country known for an abundance of all three types of professionals. Artists have certainly not enjoyed the kind of attention to information needs and uses that scientists and social scientists have had. Cobbledick argues that this is partly because of a stereotype of artists as "self-contained individuals who create via inspiration" (p. 344). People like that, we might presume, have information needs that are entirely fulfilled through divine intervention.

Cobbledick found that artists do indeed have a need for inspiration — it is one of five types of information needs they have, in fact. The inspiration need is fulfilled in a variety of ways. The sculptor visits the site where the work will be exhibited; the fiber artist surveys nature for interesting patterns; the metalsmith visits churches for inspiration from their structure and content. All of them examine images from published work, although not necessarily works related to their art. A fiber artist, for example, may find the kind of patterns that inspire him or her in pictures of clouds or cell structures.

Artists also have needs for "specific visual information." These are visual elements that appear in their works of art and are more likely to come from printed pictures or from their own experimental drawings. A third kind of information that artists need is technical: "The characteristics and properties of the various techniques and media used to create art" (p. 352). This kind of knowledge is most often found out from other artists and sometimes from books or experimentation. "Current developments in the visual arts," the fourth need, is mainly the province of fine arts journals but also can be gleaned from popular magazines, art exhibits, and colleagues. A fifth type of information about "shows, commissions, and sales" is used for finding work and exhibiting and selling work product; these are learned about through art journals and personal contacts.

Cobbledick discovered that the practices of these four artists were diverse yet included a common reliance on printed material and reading; they do not rely entirely on images to foster creativity, and some of the information they need has nothing to do with "art" per se. Cobbledick also found that people, especially other artists, were very important sources in many contexts. She concludes that the information needs of artists are as broad as human experience itself — needs that are hard to place into the usual categories.

Hemmig's (2009) survey of artists built on some aspects of Cobbledick's work but employed a survey method focused on sources of information. He surveyed 44 practicing artists, most with no academic affiliation. Their top three sources of inspiration were forms occurring in nature, their own personal experience, and art works seen in person; art books and periodicals ranked fifth and sixth among 18 sources mentioned, and some of these apparently came from library usage. Sources of specific visual elements were widely varied and led by "qualities of the medium." Other types of sources examined concerned materials and techniques, and marketing. Hemmig concludes that artists' needs are idiosyncratic, that they like browsing, and that social contacts are important, especially as regards technical and marketing information. While most of Hemmig's sample were over 40 years old, a larger survey (78 respondents) by Mason and Robinson (2011) concentrated on younger, "emerging" artists. Their responses show similarities to those of Hemmig and Cobbledick, except in a greater need for career advice.

Turning to another occupation, Wicks (1999) has studied the "information-seeking behavior of pastoral clergy" making use of social network theory and role theory. Wicks hypothesized that the behavior of clergy was "influenced by the interaction of their work worlds and the work roles" (p. 208). A pastor's worlds are of three types: theological (religious beliefs and positions), denominational (affiliation with an established church), and congregational (the local church in which he or she works). Likewise, there are three roles that clergy undertake: preacher, caregiver, and administrator. Wicks further hypothesized that information seeking among clergy could be characterized as following on a continuum from "open" to "closed," depending on "the particular world in which the pastor is operating and the specific role he or she is performing at the time" (p. 209).

Based on a postal survey of 378 Canadian pastors from six religions, coupled with interviews with 20 clergy members, Wicks was able to demonstrate an interaction between roles that shaped the sources of information to which pastors turned and the degree to which they looked outside their own "small world." A "closed" pattern of information seeking was found in regards to all theological world roles and (unsurprisingly) in the denominational and congregational worlds when acting as an administrator. The clergy were more open to information from outside their social group when providing care to others. The pastor's denomination influenced how open he or she was to outside information in the preaching role, with three affiliations (Anglican, Roman Catholic, and United Church) being more closed than the other three (Baptist, Pentecostal, and Presbyterian). Wicks suggests that this difference is due to size of the denomination, with the larger ones having more internal sources of information (e.g., offices and publications). Wicks compared his findings with other investigations of work roles in other fields and a dozen earlier investigations of the work of clergy. He argues that the fairly large numbers of working clergy, along with their influence over many members of society, make them an important group to study. Another study in this vein is Lambert's (2010) interviews with 10 Baptist ministers; he concluded that ministers shift their information behavior depending on whether they are acting in an administrative role versus a preaching role.

Theater production artists, cast, and crew constitute another topic of studies. Davies and McKenzie (2004) contrasted the practices of a professional theater production company with that of workers in a midwifery clinic. Medaille (2010) surveyed 73 theater artists and interviewed eight others. Thirty-five actors and directors in three nations were interviewed by Olsson (2010a).

Two publications in this category by Ikoja-Odongo and Ocholla (2003, 2004) concern unusual occupations, and both employed the critical incident technique to gather information. For the first study, they interviewed "artisan fisher folk of Uganda," a group that includes a full range of different occupations involving the fishing industry: fish and equipment sales, processing, boat building, net making, fisheries research, government extension, and so forth. Ikoja-Odongo and Ocholla (2004) interviewed 602 entrepreneurs in various businesses in Uganda, including fishermen, metal fabricators, blacksmiths, quarry workers, brick makers, carpenters, builders, mechanics, craftsmen, and various others. Observations of the entrepreneurs' work environments and historical methods were also employed. Their results emphasize the importance of oral traditions and local knowledge in the trades they examined. Information behavior research, Ikoja-Odongo and Ocholla say, must be sensitive to the circumstances of poverty, illiteracy, and lack of infrastructure often found in developing areas, and in doing so could suggest ways of "repackaging" information for use by such entrepreneurs (findings echoed by Serema (2002) in an investigation of communities in Botswana).

The information behavior of sex workers has also been investigated. Baker, Case, and Policicchio (2003) raise the issue of how information professionals might help sex workers cope with health problems. They carried out nonparticipant observation of 75 sex workers, using a social services van in a mid-western U.S. city as a research platform; a similar study was carried out in South Africa by Stilwell (2002).

Other types of occupations studied include army officers (Sonnenwald, 2006), aircraft pilots (von Thaden, 2008), government employees (Woudstra & van den Hooff, 2008), police (Allen, Wilson, Norman, & Knight, 2008; Baker et al., 2003), policymakers (Florio & DeMartini, 1993), architects (Makri & Warwick, 2010), teachers (Chang, 2006; Savolainen, 1995; Stefl-Mabry, 2003, 2005), translators (White et al., 2008), financial professionals (Huvila, 2010; Miranda & Tarapanoff, 2008), securities analysts (Baldwin & Rice, 1997; Kuhlthau, 1999), law enforcement personnel (Baker, 2004a; Stefl-Mabry, 2003, 2005; Westbrook, 2009), theater production cast and crew (Davies & McKenzie, 2004; Medaille, 2010; Olsson, 2010a), directors of shelters for domestic abuse victims (Westbrook, 2009), managers of historic houses (Brine and Feather, 2010), and janitors (Chatman, 1990). Some studies of occupation are nonspecific: Agarwal et al. (2011) studied the source preferences and usage of a variety of professional workers in Singapore, but do not identify the distribution of their job titles, saying only that they all use computers in their work.

11.2. Summary

This chapter has examined the size and nature of the information-seeking literature. Through a selection of recent studies, we have considered how scholars have studied information behaviors within occupations. It can be seen that there is great variety in the kinds of populations and activities that have been examined. In recent years, more attention has been paid to contextual, situational, or role variables than the usual demographic variables. Relatively small populations (e.g., Canadian literary critics, homeless parents, experts on stateless nations) have been sampled for investigation. Yet despite this diversity in the types of social groups studied, investigations concerned with health information seeking have become the dominant genre in terms of numbers, rivaled mainly by the ever-constant attention to students of all types and ages.

One thing that these studies have in common, however, is a concern with sources and channels — typically interpersonal channels versus mass and/or specialized media. A frequent finding is that people still turn to other people for information. Despite an effort to examine the process of information seeking, much of it still comes down to "who or what do people consult for information?" This is an old question within the information needs, uses, and seeking literature that continues to dominate the discussion of findings.

Recommended for Further Reading

Fabritius, H. (1999). Triangulation as a multiperspective strategy in a qualitative study of information seeking behaviour of journalists. In T. D. Wilson & D. K. Allen (Eds.), *Information behaviour: Proceedings of the second international conference on research in information needs, seeking and use in different contexts*, 13/15 August 1998, Sheffield, UK (pp. 406–419). London: Taylor Graham.

Fabritius's study is a fine example of the use of multiple methods and sources of data in studying a single population: participant observation, interviews, diaries kept by participants and the investigator, talk-aloud protocols, videotaping, and photography.

Gorman, P. (1995). Information needs of physicians. *Journal of the American Society for Information Science, 46*, 737–742.

Paul Gorman, a leading figure in the investigation of physician information needs, offers a concise summary of what we know about doctors' information seeking.

MacIntosh-Murray, A., & Choo, C. W. (2006). Information failures in health care. In B. Cronin (Ed.), *Annual Review of Information Science and Technology, 40*, 357–391.

A lengthy review of studies illustrating how easy it is for missing or faulty information in medical practice to lead to adverse outcomes.

Pinelli, T. E. (1991). The information-seeking habits and practices of engineers. *Science & Technology Libraries, 11*(3), 5–25.

A very readable discussion of the difference between science and technology, and how scientists differ from engineers. Pinelli, a scientist with the National Aeronautics and Space Administration (NASA), summarizes six major studies of engineers and their information needs.

Chapter 12

Research by Social Role and Demographic Group

Being a member of a group, such as abused spouses, cancer patients, senior citizens, or janitors, is seen as sufficient to influence individual information-seeking behaviors and patterns.

— Bryce Allen (1996, p. 74)

Information needs and uses need to be examined within the work, organizational, and social settings of the users. Information needs vary according to users' membership in professional or social groups, their demographic backgrounds, and the specific requirements of the task they are performing.

— Chun Choo and Ethel Auster (1993, p. 284)

Chapter Outline

12.1. Two Other Ways of Studying People

The most common approach to studying information seeking has been occupational — sampling a group of people working in a type of job or profession. Yet, sometimes, information-seeking investigations are not based on occupations, but rather on nonwork characteristics of people.

In some investigations (particularly of a psychological nature), what is desired is basic knowledge regarding human capacities, behaviors, and habits, in which case the demographic backgrounds of the people sampled are not so important, and their occupation is virtually irrelevant. At other times, a demographic variable must be considered to ensure that the people studied are comparable; for example, an investigation might select only adults or only children.

Usually, though, some more restrictive elements of the population's background or behavior are introduced to focus the investigation. For example, one might be studying only those people who are eligible to vote in a certain election ("voters"), or only those who buy products ("consumers"), or people facing illness ("patients"), or only those enrolled in formal classes of study ("students"). It is this type of focus that is referred to by the label "role."

Also in this chapter, we consider demographic categorizations of people. The *analysis* of populations by their background characteristics (e.g., age, gender, race, socioeconomic status, and education) is very common in many investigations of humans. However, it is typically not the main *focus* of the study, which is more likely some occupation or role that is practiced by the population under study. Here, we consider a few studies in which demographic background has played a key role in the selection of respondents (Table 12.1).

12.2. By Role

Under the heading of "roles," I review those commonly investigated classifications that we tend to impose upon the general population: citizen (or voter or person-in-the-street), consumer (or shopper), patient, gate-keeper, student, teacher, parent, and so on. McKechnie et al. (2002) pointed out that studies of "ordinary people" make up about 22% of the 1990s information behavior literature; investigations of "students" (a role most people take on for a large portion of their lives) made up another 19% of such studies. A later study (Julien et al., 2011) of the 1999–2008 literature found the same percentage of students (19%) but only 7% of studies of the public, but another 32% were mostly users of libraries and/or the Web, and

Table 12.1: Works reviewed, and related works cited, for role.

Social role	Works reviewed to illustrate findings	Some other relevant works cited
"The public"; citizen; voter	Case, 2004; Chen, 1982; Dervin, 1984; Fisher, 2005; Kari, 2003; Pettigrew, 2002; Savolainen, 1995, 2004, 2005	Baxter, 2010; Beer, 2004; Bowler, 1993; Durrance, 1984; Flanagin, 2001; Hektor, 2003; Julien, 2004; Kalms, 2008; Kaye, 2003; Kitchens, 2003; Palmour, 1979; Popkin, 1993; Savolainen, 2001, 2008; Serema, 2002; Warner, 1973; Williams, 1977
Consumer	Bloch, 1989; Lan, 2010; Laplante, 2011; Savolainen, 2009, 2010	Aspray, 2011; Belk, 1975, 1988, 1995; Bianchi, 1997; Case, 2006; Foxall, 1983; Hauser, 1993; Lehmann, 1999; Mata, 2010; McCracken, 1987; Mick, 1992; Sherry, 1990
Hobbyist; sports fan; club member	Case, 2009; Cox, 2008; Fulton, 2005, 2009; Lee, 2009; O'Connor, 2011	Adams, 2009; Bishop, 2005; Case, 2009, 2010; Chang, 2009; Formanek, 1991; Hartel, 2010, 2011; Otto, 2011; Prigoda, 2007; Stebbins, 2001, 2009; Williamson, 2010
Gatekeeper	Agada, 1999; Baldwin, 1997	Abrahamson, 2008; Barzilai-Nahon, 2005; Donohue, 1989; Lu, 2007; Metoyer-Duran, 1991, 1993; Shoemaker, 1991; Stavri, 2001; Sturges, 2001
Patient	Abrahamson, 2008; Baker, 2004; Box, 2003; Case, 2004; Hepworth, 2003, 2004; Hogan, 2005; Johnson, 2005, 2006; Kwon, 2009; Matthews, 2002; Rees, 2001; Sligo, 2000; Veinot, 2010; Warner, 2004	Andrews, 2005; Ankem, 2006; Anker, 2011; Bates, 2004; Carey, 2001; Davies, 2003; Donat, 2002; Feltwell, 2004; Fourie, 2008; Harris, 2006; Holmes, 2002; Johnson, 1997, 2001; Lion, 2001; Marshall, 1993; Marton, 2003; Mays, 2005; McCaughan, 2007; McKenzie, 2002, 2003, 2004; Muha, 1998; Pálsdóttir, 2008, 2010; Pettigrew, 1999; Pifalo, 1997; Rees, 2000; Taylor, 2001; Tuominen, 2004; Wellstead, 2011; White, 2000; Wikgren, 2001, 2003; Williamson, 2002
Students	Foster, 2003, 2004; Given, 2002, 2005; Gross, 2001, 2004; Heinström, 2003; Jeong, 2004; Toms, 2002; Whitmire, 2003	Alexandersson, 2003; Beautyman, 2009; Bowler, 2010; Chelton, 2004; Cole, 1998, 2005; Connaway, 2011; Heinström, 2006; Hultgren, 2003; Hyldegard, 2009; Jiao, 1997; Julien, 1999; Kerins, 2004; Kuhlthau, 1988, 1991, 2004; Lilley, 2008; Lu, 2010; Mehra, 2007; Mellon, 1986; Seldén, 2001; Thórsteinsdóttir, 2000

Note: Studies are listed by first author only, plus year. See the references for clarification.

yet another 21% were unidentified — so the pattern may be fairly consistent over the last 20 years.

Brenda Dervin says in a 1989 article on "users as research inventions," that role categorizations of people (along with demographic groupings) are often a function of marketing segmentation and the consumer/user mentality that goes with it. Whether the goal is to sell someone something or to study their use of some "system" so that it may be improved, the result is not always positive for those studied. When people are "clustered" into groups and labeled, the resulting categories come to be *reified* — researchers, policymakers, and the general public begin to believe that such categories are *real*, rather than just convenient fictions for the purpose of analysis and planning. The diverse individuals who make up these groups, and their perspectives, tend to be lost in the results. There is also the common situation in which an individual is simultaneously a member of several categories, an issue of "overlap" discussed here further under "Other Demographic Groups."

Unfortunately, it is not the case that such analyses of user categories lead automatically to improvements in services or systems. Indeed, Dervin claims that sometimes they reinforce inequities, finding, for example, that "the poor use the Internet less than the rich" does not suggest a solution to that inequity, but rather may lead to feelings of resignation and blame.

Nevertheless, a common approach in information behavior literature has been to examine large populations in terms of particular, nonwork roles that they play.

12.2.1.   Citizen or Voter

Obviously some investigations can be classified in several different ways. Investigations of "citizens" or "voters" often aspire to improve community and democracy, but they can also cover many other areas of interest to the average citizen. Thus, there is some degree of overlap between this category and some of the others that follow, particularly the demographic emphases that flavor many of these general studies. The emphasis in this particular subsection will be on general investigations of human communities, including their media use. Readers interested specifically in information behavior related to voting and politics are advised to consult Popkin's (1993) review of voter reasoning and "information shortcuts," a study of the "friends and neighbors effect" by Bowler, Donovan, and Snipp (1993), and a survey of undecided voters and their information seeking, by Kitchens, Powell, and Williams (2003).

Voting may be seen as the most common form of political action by the public, but it is not the only one. Baxter, Marcella, and Illingsworth (2010) describe their interviews with representatives of 54 nongovernmental organizations that responded to requests by the Scottish government for input on policies (i.e., "consultation"). These were sampled out of a population of 4168 who responded to issues such as medical care or the environment. Over half of these could be labeled "citizen groups" and the rest were mainly professional associations, business grips, or charities. Most received relevant information through other groups similar to, or connected with, their own (67%), directly from government sources (48%) or via mass media (2%). In preparing a response most consulted at least a portion of their membership; their external sources were fairly evenly divided between the Internet, subject experts and "like-minded groups." Not surprisingly common complaints among respondents concerned lack of feedback about, and low effectiveness of, their input to the policy process. Savolainen (2007d, 2008b) is another investigation examining citizens active in politics, in this case environmental issues. Based on interviews with 18 activists, Savolainen charted sources and pathways, showing that human and Internet sources tended to be consulted first, followed by printed and other sources. Content availability and accessibility were the chief criteria in selecting sources about political issues.

The classic, large-scale investigations of the information behavior of the citizenry are now quite dated: Warner, Murray, and Palmour (1973); Williams, Dordick, and Horstmann (1977); Palmour et al. (1979); Chen and Hernon (1982); and Dervin, Ellyson, Hawkes, Guagnano, and White (1984). Of these, the most widely cited is Chen and Hernon's (1982) study of 2400 New England residents. Among the more important findings of the Chen and Hernon study was the individual (and context-driven) nature of information seeking.

Fifty-two percent of the 3548 "information-seeking situations" recounted by Chen and Hernon's informants were needs for information to solve day-to-day problems; the rest were scattered across 18 different problem situations, with none accounting for more than 6% of the total. Typical "problems" fell into the following categories (roughly in order of importance): having to do with work or jobs in general, or performing specific tasks; consumer issues, such as finding product information; home and housing issues, such as finding, renting, or buying a dwelling, or repairing cars or items around the home; and issues related to education, such as identifying schools and courses, financing a degree, or parenting children.

In each case, interpersonal providers of information were ranked as much more important than institutions or the mass media. In relating who or what they considered consulting to address their problems, 74% of respondents cited their "own experience" as a source of information; this was also rated the "most helpful" source. The other popular sources were "friend, neighbor, or relative" (57%), "newspaper, magazine, or book" and "store, company, or business" (both 45%), "coworker" (43%), and "professional (e.g., doctor or lawyer)" at 41%. Other sources (government, TV/radio, library, telephone book, social service agency, religious leader) were all cited much less frequently (10–27%).

Chen and Hernon's research, along with that by Durrance (1984) and Dervin et al. (1984), highlight a methodological shift in surveys of the general citizenry. These surveys asked more questions about basic human problems and situations and less about the usual institutions that were supposed to address them. Dervin et al., especially, probed deeper into the origins of, and solutions to, personal "gaps" in life. That investigation interviewed 1040 Californians, who reported an average of 8.5 problem situations within the last month. These situations most commonly concerned (in order): family/friends, managing money, shopping/buying, or learning — all of which were reported by over two-thirds of the respondents. Other common gaps involved current events, recreation, health, jobs, children, transportation, or housing, each of which was mentioned by 40% or more of those questioned. As in the Chen and Hernon study, the most common strategy was to turn to one's "own experience" (89% said this), followed by "authorities/professionals" (58%), "family members" (52%), and "friends/neighbors" (48%). Other popular sources of help, ranging in order from 40% down to 30%, were coworkers, media, schools/colleges, business persons, and libraries. By allowing for more specific responses to some questions — such as by breaking down the category of "day to day problems," and separating "family members" from "friends/neighbors" as sources — the California study learned more about the nature of information needs. Other results from Dervin et al. (1984) are mentioned below, in discussing demographic variables.

An emphasis on the problems of everyday life is apparent in a study by Savolainen (1995). He equated "citizen information seeking" with any "nonwork" consumption of media, noting how the degree to which the study of "everyday life" has been "overshadowed by surveys of job-related information needs, seeking, and use" (p. 259). Savolainen urges that greater attention be paid to how people encounter information in the course of activities like leisure and hobbies. His investigation of 22 Finnish citizens — half middle-class and half working class — involved 90-minute interviews on their jobs, consumption habits, leisure time, media use, and the values they attached to information and information seeking. Savolainen also had respondents choose a recent "problematic situation" and relate how they dealt with it (p. 270).

Savolainen describes a pattern of "passive monitoring" of everyday events that take place when life moves along as we expect, versus "active seeking of practically effective information" that happens when the unexpected arises. A person may watch television absentmindedly to "keep an eye on life," and read the daily paper as an aspect of "belonging in the community" (p. 273). Thus, some aspects of media use (and "information seeking" in a broader sense of the term) are not purposeful but rather are simply a part of everyday life practices.

Where problem-oriented information seeking is concerned, Savolainen (1995) had similar findings to earlier, large-scale studies like Chen and Hernon (1982): types of everyday problems were diverse, with employment (7 cases), health (3), and financial worries (3) being mentioned most frequently. Which sources were pursued for problem-solving depended largely on availability and accessibility, with informal sources (e.g., acquaintances) being used much more commonly than formal sources; the middle-class respondents were noted as having more access to experts than the workers. Interestingly, a study by Kalms (2008) suggests that some households, aided by the Internet and various tools and practices, spend a great deal of effort managing information vital to their lives and households; these include information relevant to many of the "problems" descried in earlier studies (financial, medical, educational, political, legal, etc.), as well as about opportunities for improvement and enjoyment (advice, employment, entertainment, travel, social connections, etc.)

Few other large-sample community studies have been performed in recent years. For example, Fisher, Naumer, et al. (2005) conducted a telephone survey of 612 urban residents to discover their "information grounds" — the places where they find useful knowledge in the pursuit of other activities. Among other results, they found the most common information grounds to be places of worship (mentioned by 24%), the workplace (22%), and club, sports team, play group, or hobby (nearly 11%); among nine other common places, libraries were ranked third to last at about a 2% incidence; by far the two strongest "habitual" information sources were individuals with whom they had a strong relationship and the Internet, each identified by over 39% of the sample. From their sources, the respondents obtained general advice (34%) and information about hobbies or travel (22%) or health care (18%). Other large-sample surveys have tended to focus more narrowly on a topic such as health (e.g., Pálsdóttir, 2008, 2010).

Another study involving Fisher and Durrance (Pettigrew, Durrance, & Unruh, 2002) employed a variety of approaches — surveys, observations, interviews, focus groups, and case studies — to assess the use of community information by the general public. Libraries in the states of Illinois, Pennsylvania, and Oregon were sampled to see how the Internet and libraries disseminate local information, answer questions, provide access to governmental services, and connect citizens to one another. The authors conclude that such networks are highly beneficial even while sometimes suffering from deficits in interface design, organization, authority, currency, security, and other factors. A comprehensive review of information seeking conducted in public libraries is found in the chapter by Leckie and Given (2005).

Susan Beer (2004) conducted interviews with representatives of over a hundred community groups, businesses, and information providers in eight remote communities in Shetland and the Western Isles of Scotland. Beer discovered that strong personal ties within the communities enabled residents to find answers from other people. Her informants complained about the lack of relevance of some information from outside (e.g., "urban solutions"), and occasional withholding of information by local parties (sometimes due to journalistic sensitivity within such small communities). Difficulty of travel — even within the islands themselves — was judged to be a key barrier to finding information.

A dramatic change in the information seeking of the public is tied to the emergence of the Internet as an omnibus channel that complements (and, in part, replicates) the usual array of interpersonal and mass media sources of information. Use of the World Wide Web, especially, is often discussed in reports of information-seeking research. For example, Case et al. (2004) argued that patterns of source preferences common in the past (e.g., a preference for information gained in face-to-face or telephone exchanges with friends and family members) have shifted in the light of the widespread availability of email and Web pages. They based their findings on data from a 2002 telephone survey of 882 adults regarding information seeking about the genetic basis of disease. Similarly, in the context of voting-related behavior, Kaye and Johnson (2003) used the results of an online survey of 442 respondents to demonstrate that the Internet is gradually substituting for other media usage — particularly television, radio, and magazines.

While the mechanics of searching the Web (as a single source) falls outside the scope of this review, the investigations that consider Web usage in the context of other sources are considered relevant enough. For example, Hektor (2003) studied 10 Swedish residents, considering the place of Web sources among others available in the respondents' environment, including other people, the TV, and the telephone. Based on interviews and diaries, Hektor noted that the Internet is used broadly for both seeking and giving information, yet it is most often a complement or substitute for other sources, not a unique source in itself (a point also made by Flanagin & Metzger, 2001). The Web is but one channel among many that may be monitored habitually.

Savolainen (2001), Kari and Savolainen (2003), and Savolainen and Kari (2004a, 2004b, 2004c) advanced similar claims concerning the role of the Web among other sources and channels available in daily life. Savolainen (2001) investigated a Finnish newsgroup covering consumer issues; he explored the interaction between information needs, sources, and the social network of newsgroup users; a related article considered the relationship of Bandura's social cognitive theory to the finding of information. Kari and Savolainen (2003) made the case that Web searching needs to be considered within the larger contexts of other sources and the person's "life-world," or everyday reality. A later article by Savolainen and Kari (2004a) extended this thesis by considering the "information source horizon" of the Internet in the context of self-development. Source horizons place information sources and channels in an order of preference, based on attributes like accessibility and quality. Savolainen and Kari's sample of 18 Internet users placed information sources into three categories, by degree of relevance to the respondents' interests and goals; human sources such as friends and colleagues were preferred, followed by print media such as newspapers and books; networked sources were ranked third among six source types. And Savolainen and Kari's (2004b) interviews found that the informants conceptualized the Internet as a space or place, and that they judged what they found there in terms of the quality of other information sources.

Finally, an unusual study by Julien and Michels (2004) focused on a single informant. Julien and Michels were interested in "intra-individual information behavior," by which they meant patterns of need, seeking, context, and source selection across one individual's various daily life situations. Through participant diaries and interviews, they found that time constraints, motivations, context, type of initiating event, location, intended application of the information found, and source type were the most common influences on the information behavior of their one respondent.

12.2.2. Consumer

Information behavior has been frequently studied by marketing researchers over several decades — although their investigations are not always published. Yet, a number of studies of "consumers," "buyers," "shoppers," and the like have been published in journals of advertising or marketing. It is wrong to assume that consumer research is exclusively product oriented, that it says little about basic human behaviors, and that it is of no use to anyone other than profit-oriented companies.

It is worth recalling that the third most common "gap" in Dervin et al. (1984) study was a "shopping/buying" situation, and that the third most common source in Chen and Hernon's (1982) survey was "store, company, or business." Although it is true that the majority of consumer studies are experiments, surveys, and descriptive focus groups aimed at marketing, the breadth of consumer research has widened greatly over the past two decades. More business studies have embraced qualitative methods and pursued more basic questions about human behavior. Many investigations now have less to do with sales and more to do with sense making.

Consumer research has embraced ethnomethodology and phenomenology (e.g., Mick & Buhl, 1992; Sherry, 1990). Some market researchers have turned to unlikely literatures, such as theories of play and classification (Holt, 1995), reader response (Scott, 1994), and poetic explication (Stern, 1989) in attempting to understand individual differences in reaction to objects and advertising. Of particular interest is how consumer research has awakened to the importance of *context* in the understanding of human reactions to things and messages (Foxall, 1983; Mick & DeMoss, 1990). Consumer research relevant to information seeking ranges from experiments on formal information search in making purchases (Hauser et al., 1993; Mata & Nunes, 2010), to browsing in stores (Bloch et al., 1989; Lan, 2010), to making sense of advertising (McCracken, 1987).

In the introduction to a special issue of the *Journal of Marketing* titled "How do Customers and Consumers Really Behave?," Donald Lehmann (1999) declares "for the past 20 years, the dominant paradigm in [consumer behavior] has been information processing ... borrowed from psychology [and] economics ... . In terms of method, the typical approach has used a lab study with controlled manipulation of a few factors" (p. 16). Lehmann predicts that more progress can be made using different approaches. In particular, he advocates less emphasis on psychological and economic theory and more research using biological and historical analogies. The focus must shift, Lehmann says, away from viewing the consumer as a conscious, rational "decision maker" and toward the customer as an emotional, unfocused, learning human. Allegedly "irrational" behavior should not be merely identified as an aberration but should be modeled and explained as much as possible. The microlevel focus on individual judgments of product attributes must give way to the study of how people set goals, make *important* decisions (e.g., where to live and how to allocate their time), and are influenced by other people in their choices. Moving in these directions will require a change in methods, including increased use of qualitative and ethnographic methods, and less use of statistical significance for proving what are often, Lehmann says, trivial hypotheses.

Thus, a chief problem of the old style of consumer research was that it fails to consider the *context* of information seeking. Consumer researchers have not been blind to this deficit. Gordon Foxall (1983), for instance, devotes much of his book *Consumer Choice* to what he calls "situation" and the accompanying problem of intervening variables. Foxall decries the "piecemeal" application of mainstream behavioral methodologies to consumer research and the tendency to treat the consumer as a "black box" about which the main thing to be studied are "attitudes" (beliefs, emotions, and action tendencies). Instead, Foxall argues for an emphasis on the way that situations influence the actions and choices of consumers (1983, pp. 90–93). He identifies the following as "situational characteristics": physical surroundings, social surroundings (other persons present, their characteristics, roles, and interpersonal interactions), temporal perspective (time of day, season of the year, time since/until other relevant action, deadlines, etc.), task definition (e.g., to obtain information about a purchase), and antecedent states and behavior (such as momentary moods and conditions, as distinct from chronic individual traits). These characteristics have found their way into information behavior research. Lan (2010), for example, finds that both the characteristics of the individual consumer and the particular retail environment influence the degree of browsing that takes place. And Laplante and Downie (2011) discuss information gathering about purchases.

The notion of "situational variables" was first advanced by Belk (1975), who has since built upon them an agenda of naturalistic research. Belk, Sherry, and Wallendorf (1988), for example, have documented the "research process" of consumers browsing flea markets and swap meets. One of my own investigations uses a similar approach for interactions at coin shows (Case, 2009a). At least two books (Belk, 1995; Bianchi, 1997b) and many empirical investigations have been devoted to the intersections among consumption, collecting behavior, taste, "flow," and self-concept. One such study from the information behavior tradition is Laplante and Downie's (2011) on music information seeking. Their investigation ties together themes of hedonic consumption, engagement, and taste.

Under this new paradigm, some older marketing topics have been revived and extended. "Consumer search behavior," for example, used to be viewed almost exclusively in the context of learning about products to prepare for a purchase. However, Bloch, Sherrell, and Ridgway (1986, p. 119) argue that "such activities as browsing in an antique shop or subscribing to an automotive magazine by persons not in the market for these products are not addressed by traditional search theories." They have expanded the notion of search behavior to include the everyday, ongoing acquisition of information. In their investigation, which used data from a conventional mail survey but without the usual emphasis on demographic variables as predictors, Bloch et al. found that a significant portion of search behavior was hedonic as well as utilitarian. That is, respondents said that they enjoyed learning about products, even when they did not have an immediate intention to buy; their acquisition of product information was described as a source of fun and pleasure. Lan (2010) and Laplante and Downie (2011) also found that browsing is only partly functional, but rather has strong recreational components.

Savolain's (2009d, 2010) study of house buying is an example of consumer information behavior. Interviews with 16 prospective home buyers resulted in the creation of information source horizon maps.

These depictions allowed Savolainen to tease out the criteria used by these shoppers to screen possible homes for purchase. Internet listings were a prime source of information, yet buyers were particularly sensitive to the timeliness of the information on Web sites. Savolainen's 2009 article uses a content analysis of the shoppers' think-aloud responses to printed and Internet house listings, as they identified those most relevant to their search. Grounded in earlier studies of information processing and consumer choice, his analysis examines the cognitive mechanisms used to interpret cues about dwelling places (identification of key attributes of importance, specification of more particular details, comparison of attributes across houses, evaluations of dwellings, and explanations for their judgments). The liberal use of quotations from the respondents makes this study interesting reading.

The findings of consumer behavior now range far afield and are increasingly particular. The phenomenological study of three Danish brothers (Mick & Buhl, 1992), described in a previous chapter, is another example of how diverse this literature has become.

12.2.3. Hobbyist

Due perhaps to the influence of Savolainen's (1995) Everyday Life Information Seeking (ELIS) framework, along with Stebbins' (2001, 2009) Serious Leisure research agenda, more attention has been paid to nonwork information behavior, including such voluntary activities as hobbies, games and sports. These are preoccupations that are not paid work, yet may be work-like in the intensity with which they are pursued. Hartel (2003, 2005) reviews much of the general literature on serious leisure, while individual studies (e.g., Adams, 2009; Case, 2009a; Chang, 2009; Duff & Johnson, 2003; Fulton, 2005b, 2009; Hartel, 2010, 2011; Otto, Metz, & Ensmenger, 2011; Yakel, 2004) contain some overview of past research in a particular domain (e.g., collecting, cooking, genealogy, and games or sports).

My own study of coin collectors (Case, 2009a, 2010) could serve as an example of the hobbyist aspect of serious leisure; other studies will illustrate the gaming and sports sides of this category. It has been estimated by scholars in various nations that perhaps 30% of the public collects *something*. The question has always remained "why?" In starting my investigation I reviewed the voluminous literature on collecting and its psychological motivations. I chose a framework developed by Ruth Formanek (1991) of five common themes of collecting to structure my observations.

Over a period of four years I made participant observations of coin collectors in various venues: five coin shows in two countries, visits to five local meetings of a group of coin enthusiasts, spoke with 53 collectors about their interests and interviewed two in greater depth, read through hundreds of postings on various numismatic electronic bulletin boards, and bought and sold several dozen coins over eBay. My notes, transcripts, photos, and memories were sorted according to four of Formanek's five themes: extension of the self, financial investment, addiction and social; the fifth theme, preservation, appeared to have little relevance, perhaps because coins may last for millennia without human intervention. My 2009 article illustrates these themes with quotations from collectors. It also contains a review of works about collecting as a broader topic, and particularly its psychological motivations. In a 2010 article I narrowed my focus to the dilemma of detecting counterfeit coins in online auctions, and developed a flow-chart of collector information gathering and decision making, based on my observations and experiences.

Lee and Trace (2009) is another study of collecting, in this case of rubber ducks. The investigators spotlight the importance of information sharing among members of a community, downplaying the centrality of individual information seeking and formal sources. This pattern is certainly true of the next leisure pursuit we will examine: amateur genealogy.

According to Bishop (2005) we could see genealogy as the collecting of people. Whether that is so or not, it is the case that assembling family histories is one of the most popular hobbies, particularly in the immigrant-formed nations of the Americas. It has also been the single most popular topic in the hobbyist genre of studies, undoubtedly because amateur genealogists are frequent users of libraries, archives, and the Internet. Yet genealogy is another lesser pursuit with deep psychological motivations, particularly the quest for self-identity.

While there is a fairly long history (across several disciplines) of examining the sources, motivations, and satisfactions of preparing family histories, the practice has been so changed by the advent of the Internet that the earlier studies are not worth reviewing; descriptions of that literature are found in some of the publications mentioned here. Duff and Johnson's (2003) study was perhaps the first to focus on information seeking, examining patterns of use of libraries, archives, librarians, archivists, and other family historians. Yakel (2004) interviewed 29 genealogists and family historians, finding that the activity was a form of seeking meaning and led to the formation and use of strong social networks. In particular, information sharing via the Internet and genealogical societies was very common. The most prolific researcher on this topic has been Fulton (2005b, 2009a, 2009b). Her publications report interviews with 24 amateur genealogists from multiple nations, again with emphasis on the reciprocal sharing of information and the social and psychological benefits of this pastime. A final example (Case, 2009b) explores the links between genealogy and various health issues.

Family historians often join local genealogical societies, yet it is not clear whether club membership itself represents a hobby. Cox et al. (2008) say that the photo-sharing Web site Flickr promotes the hobby of amateur photography without the complications of local photography clubs. Their interviews with 11 users suggest high satisfaction with the service, yet possible problems with reciprocal tagging, along with the potential for commercial colonization. Prigoda and McKenzie (2007) examine a group of knitters who meet in a public library, exploring this situation as a ground for both sharing of information and the development of caring and meaning.

Cooking and traveling are two other hobbyist interests. Hartel's (2010, 2011) study of gourmet cooks shows the degree to which information is critical in support of this hobby; they are also good illustrations of the value of photography in conducting such studies. An investigation of travelers' sharing of information online (Lueg, 2008) shows how their interactions create communities of knowledge production. Little, Williams, and Yost (2011) write about the historical evolution of information sources and habits of airline passengers.

Investing is a hobby for some people. O'Connor characterized some of the 16 female investors she studied as hobbyists in their activities and attitudes. Like almost a half-million people in the United States, these women had joined one of the 30,000 investment clubs in the nation. O'Connor examines their sources, motivations, cognitive biases, and interactions with one another. Another study of the information behavior of investors, although not explicitly hobby oriented, is Williamson and Smith (2010).

Games and sports are also common leisure activities that we could consider under this category (even though "hobbies" has somewhat different connotations). Adams (2009) investigates how players in virtual games find the information they need to succeed, and how they form meanings about their activities. Chang (2009) turns her attention to the sport of backpacking, which could also be seen as a form of travel or tourism. She focuses on how those travelers gather information, finding that their use of sources varies by task, and tends to occur over three stages. Otto et al. (2011) offer a review of what is known about the information gathering of players of fantasy football and baseball.

The volume of *Library Trends* in which the studies by Adams, Case, and Chang appear contain additional studies that fall into a broader category of voluntary activities.

12.2.4. Gatekeeper

The noted sociologist Robert Merton (1973, p. 521) credits psychologist Kurt Lewin (1943) for introducing "the notion of the gatekeeper role ... into social science." Although Lewin used the term in a very specific context — to discuss how housewives influence the eating habits of their household — it has since been applied widely to many types of organizations and institutions.

"Gatekeeping" has been invoked particularly in the study of scientists (e.g., Crane, 1967, 1972), with a defining aspect being the "two-step flow" of information: that a single person receives the information first, then passes it on to other members of his or her group. Rogers (1994) suggests that the concept (although not the term) goes much further back in time to Robert Parks' (1922) discussion of the power exercised by newspaper editors (a concern that has not diminished — see Donohue, Olien, & Tichenor, 1989). It was subsequently used to characterize the behavior of community "opinion leaders" who mold the knowledge and attitudes of their neighbors.

A gatekeeper is one who controls the flow of information over a channel: shaping, emphasizing, or withholding it (Barzilai-Nahon, 2005; Shoemaker, 1991). Gatekeepers provide a key link between their organization, audience, or community and the outside environment. Merton and Crane believed that the gatekeeping role was critical in the development and evaluation of junior scientists. Baldwin and Rice (1997) characterized gatekeepers in research organizations in this way:

> Gatekeepers read more journals, have more external contacts, generate more ideas, and engage in more problem solving than non-gatekeepers. Gatekeepers not only provide information, but they also give practical and political advice. (p. 675)

A comprehensive review by Metoyer-Duran (1993) found 803 publications on gatekeepers appearing between 1977 and the end of 1992. Her review focuses on their role in the health sciences, education, science and technology, communication studies, journalism, and information studies. A complete explication of "gatekeeping" is found in Shoemaker (1991); as she notes, it has proved to be a robust concept, despite its age.

Gatekeeping continues to be the focus of investigation in information seeking. A 1999 study by John Agada featured in-depth interviews with 20 gatekeepers in an African American neighborhood of inner-city Milwaukee, WI. In this study of "information use environments," gatekeepers were described as individuals able to move between cultures and link their communities with resources. Agada identified his 20 informants through community organizations and interviewed them about their information needs regarding race relations, crime, and family. As he found, "interpersonal sources were preferred over all other sources because of concerns about trustworthiness and credibility" (p. 74).

The most frequently cited needs had to do with discrimination and race relations, followed by crime and safety, and family planning and birth control. After those three categories of need, there was a sharp drop in frequency; the most common among the remaining 16 categories were child care and family relationships, recreation and culture, health, housekeeping and household maintenance, and employment. Some categories that were ranked highly in earlier studies ranked much lower in this one: finance and housing (Dervin, 1976b) and public affairs and education (Metoyer-Duran, 1993). Agada concludes that this is due to the short-term orientation of the urban poor, which leads them to "seek coping information rather than information and activities that would transform their socioeconomic conditions" (p. 79). By far the top strategies were to ask a neighbor/friend/ acquaintance and/or the relevant agency. Thirteen other sources for information, including other gatekeeper/opinion leaders, telephone directory, newspapers, family member, libraries, acquaintances working at agencies, and politicians, in that order. Agada provides some interesting examples of how people describe their needs, and the ways that they might be resolved, based on Robert Taylor's (1991) categories of information use.

Baldwin and Rice (1997) also invoked the concept of gatekeeper in their telephone survey of 100 randomly selected securities analysts, who they note "think of themselves as gatekeepers in their organizations" (p. 688). A sophisticated statistical analysis of data on individual characteristics (e.g., years of experience, gender, and age), use of different information sources (e.g., magazines and communication with management and other analysts), and their institutional resources (e.g., having an assistant and having a budget for travel) led to their conclusion that "individual characteristics have little influence on the information sources and communication channels used by analysts, and thereby do not have a significant influence on the outcomes of analysts' information activities" (p. 674). Rather, the degree of *institutional resources* available was found to have a strong influence on both the analysts' use of source and channels, and the outcomes of their work (e.g., income, ranking in polls of analysts, and number of research reports published). Baldwin and Rice discuss the implications of their study for improving the gatekeeping role within organizations.

Abrahamson et al. (2008) liken gatekeeping to the behaviors of lay intermediaries who search for health information on behalf of others. This kind of proxy searching and translation is similar to that discussed by Stavri (2001) in her review of personal health information seeking. Sturges (2001) is another review that discusses intermediaries as gatekeepers.

A review by Lu (2007) suggest that the concept of gatekeeping needs to be further studied, analyzed as to its contingent and contextual nature, and better connected to the literature on social networks and social capital.

12.2.5. *Patient*

A number of factors have contributed to a continual growth in the seeking of medical information by *patients* (or "health care consumers"): an increased concern with health in general and with preventive medicine in particular; a growing number of "self-help" and homeopathic medicine texts; and the proliferation of consumer health information sites on the Internet. Anker, Reinhart, and Feeley (2011) identified 648 studies relevant to patient information seeking, published between 1978 and 2010 — about 20 publications per year. Clearly this literature has grown too large to review comprehensively, although a forthcoming book by Johnson and Case (2012) will consider a larger portion of it than I can here.

The growth and easy accessibility of health Web sites continues to shape patient behavior. The Pew Internet Project (Fox, 2011) finds that 59% of all U.S. adults are using the Internet to look for health/medical information, and that overall 80% of Internet users have done this — making it the third-most popular type of usage (after e-mail and search engines). Use of the Internet for health will be considered here only in the context of alternative sources of information (e.g., doctors, friends, print publications, and broadcast media).

Although the dissemination of health advice to the general public has always been important, where the layperson is concerned the more critical question is increasingly "why don't people *act* on the information they have?" Making useful (and potentially life-saving) information available to patients is the easier part of the equation; getting them to apply it is much harder. At the core of this problem are the issues raised in Chapter 5 of this book under the headings of "avoidance" and "overload." As analyses by Pálsdóttir (2008, 2010) demonstrate, a proportion of a population may treat health information passively, discussing and acting on it much less frequently than other people.

An excellent review of the problem of nonuse of health information — dubbed the "knowledge–behavior gap" — is found in the background to a study by Sligo and Jameson (2000), which is the featured example here of health information seeking and use among the general public. I draw extensively upon their discussion in the paragraphs that follow.

The issue of how behaviors may be purposefully changed has long been of central concern among scholars of attitude, persuasion, compliance, propaganda, diffusion, and like topics. Hyman and Sheatsley's (1947) discussion of "why information campaigns fail" is usually cited as the earliest explanation of why information does not always change behavior, although the roots of this line of thinking go back to at least to Gabriel Tarde's (1903) treatise on "imitation" and the diffusion of ideas and behaviors.

Sligo and Jameson (2000) examined the issue of information seeking and use from the perspective of populations at risk from disease. One aspect of what they call "the knowledge-behavior gap in use of health information" is whether individuals receive relevant information in the first place — the "information poverty" problem discussed in Chapter 5. The related "knowledge gap hypothesis," that segments of the population may acquire information at differential rates, originated over 30 years ago with Tichenor et al. (1970) and continues to attract scholarly attention (e.g., Gaziano, 1997; Viswanath & Finnegan, 1996).

Yet even when knowledge gaps are overcome, we cannot be sure it will make a difference for the individual. Gaziano (1997) noted that "barriers" to the gain (and subsequent application) of information have both internal and external origins. The internal barriers are both social and psychological, having to do with personality, motivation, interest, and involvement with others. Barriers considered external are social and situational, including socialization and identity issues, membership in socioeconomic and ethnic groups, and access to information sources. Sligo and Jameson point out that internal and external barriers overlap in various ways; they review, for example, literature emphasizing that learning from others is highly sensitized to local social norms (external) and the internal perception that another is similar to oneself (an "insider").

Sligo and Jameson's empirical study concerned information about cervical cancer, screening, and related topics among Pacific Island immigrants living in a small New Zealand city. They conducted lengthy interviews with a snowball sample of 20 women from Fiji, Samoa, Tonga, and other islands — a group that could be considered comparable to the urban, lower socioeconomic level groups in North American studies of knowledge gaps. However, Sligo and Jameson found less isolation and more learning than did investigations by Chatman (1996) and Greenberg, Bowes, and Dervin (1970). Perhaps the most interesting aspect of their findings is the way in which cultural norms (e.g., taboos about discussing sexual matters) differentially influenced getting information versus acting on that information: participants preferred learning about cervical health through their own cultural networks, yet preferred (for reasons of privacy) to have health care provided by practitioners outside their ethnic group.

Sligo and Jameson suggest that attention is shifting away from the internal and psychological reasons that people fail to acquire and act on information, and toward "structural" explanations for lack of behavior change: do factors in the environment (e.g., the economic and social consequences of change) *support* the actions implied by the acquired information? To put this in terms of some of Sligo and Jameson's findings: information is hard to absorb when a local vocabulary is lacking for it (some Pacific languages have no word for "cervix," for example); culture is a filter for health information (e.g., "not all cultures believe that disease can exist in the absence of adverse symptoms," p. 866); information from "outsiders" will be accepted as long as it is sanctioned by passage through local channels (e.g., ethnic community organizations).

The investigation by Sligo and Jameson was strictly limited in the size, uniqueness, and composition of its sample (i.e., small numbers of diverse women from various islands, living in one New Zealand city), but it raises fascinating questions about the role of both culture and interpersonal networks in the diffusion of health information, while offering practical advice for health-care providers in that context. Best of all, it asks us to question the generalizations of past research regarding urban minorities and their "gaps" in knowledge regarding medicine.

There have been a number of other studies and reviews focused on women. Ankem (2007) interviewed 28 women seeking treatment of fibroids, finding that the Internet was especially important for learning about treatment options; friends, magazines, and television were also important sources of information. Warner and Procaccino (2004) surveyed a broad sample (by age and education) of 119 women regarding their seeking of health-related information. They found that physicians, medical or health books, people with similar medical conditions, family or friends, nurses or pharmacists, Web sites and public libraries were the most common sources of health information, in that order. A similar investigation was conducted among Somali women living in the UK, by Davies and Bath (2003). McKenzie (2002a, 2002b, 2003a, 2003b) and Carey, McKechnie, and McKenzie (2001) studied the information behavior of pregnant women, in some cases along with those of their midwives (McKenzie, 2004). Baker (1996) has considered the information needs of women suffering from multiple sclerosis.

Rees and Bath (2001) conducted a study of the information needs and seeking of women with breast cancer, utilizing the Monitoring/Blunting Style Scale (MBSS, also called the Miller Behavioral Style Scale). The eight-item MBSS is the most widely used instrument for measuring how people react to threatening information; a "monitoring" response is to scan the environment for potential threats, while a "blunting" behavior (e.g., going to the movies) ignores threatening information or distracts the person from it. A later investigation by Williamson and Manaszewicz (2002) reviewed additional literature on the use of the MBSS and conducted interviews with 34 women to aid in the design of a Web portal; Williamson and Manaszewicz cast doubt on the utility and validity of the MBSS in this particular context.

Marton's (2003) examination of health information seeking by 265 women ranked Web information high on relevance but only moderately on perceived reliability; in contrast, health-care providers, books, and pamphlets received high ratings on both of those attributes. However, other studies (Wikgren, 2001, 2003) of Internet health discussion groups emphasize the Internet as a source of interpersonal communication and emotional support, as well as medical information. Wikgren (2003) found that 80% of references to sources in these discussions were to Web pages and that 60% of all references referred to a source with scientific medical contents — suggesting a considerable degree of reliability.

Men have been less frequently examined in the health information behavior literature. One publication singling out males is Wellstead's (2011) interview study of 15 men undergoing psychological stress; he concludes that men were reluctant to seek help and often unaware of counseling services available to them. Feltwell and Rees (2004) studied the partners of men with prostrate cancer.

Often health-related information behavior investigations concern a particular medical condition or the potential for it, most typically some form of cancer. Among the reviews and analysis of the cancer information-seeking literature, Ankem (2006a, 2006b), Johnson (1997), and Rees and Bath (2000b) cover the literature that has to do with cancer information, reflecting the largest proportion of serious health problems that can precipitate information seeking. McCaughan and McKenna (2007), in a study of 27 newly diagnosed cancer patients, describe the stages they go through as "never-ending sense-making," in which only latter stages show a readiness to accept and act upon relevant treatment information.

Abrahamson et al. (2008) studied how people without medical training sought cancer information on behalf of others. Using both a Web-based survey and phone interviews (with a subsample), they documented a pattern familiar from other studies: the majority of mediary searchers are women, searching on behalf of family and friends. However, Harris et al. (2006) point out that their study and others find that women tend not to discuss with medical professionals the health information they discover on their own.

A reanalysis of U.S. National Cancer Institute data by Kwon and Kim (2009) that libraries rank fifth as a "first-choice" source of cancer information, with the first four sources being the Internet, followed distantly by books, health-care providers, then magazines. They discovered that those who seek cancer information from libraries first tend to have less online experience and trust in that source. Some good commentaries on health information for the public, including the role of various library types, are found in the special issue edited by Mays (2005).

Johnson, Andrews, and Allard (2001) offered a model for studying cancer genetics information seeking, drawing upon research on cancer patients. Johnson et al. (2005) argue that issues surrounding genomics makes the topic a "perfect information seeking research problem." Andrews, Johnson, Case, Allard, and Kelly (2005) and Case et al. (2004) reported on a telephone survey of 882 adults regarding the public's sources of information regarding genetic screening and the genetic bases for cancer. The respondents said they would be more likely to access the Internet first before turning to health-care providers or relatives — both of which are better sources of information about a person's actual, genetic basis for disease. Johnson, Case, Andrews, Allard, and Johnson (2006) presented contrasting ways of considering survey data about health information sources, as either "fields" or "pathways"; the former approach is the traditional view of individuals choosing among one or more information sources, while the latter instead sees the search for an answer as a serial chain of sources that continues until the seeker is satisfied or exhausted. Relatedly, Taylor, Alman, David, and Manchester (2001) focused on genetics-related information available through the Internet.

HIV/AIDS has been another condition addressed in health information behavior research. Veinot (2010) analyzed past studies and used responses from AIDS sufferers to develop her model of HIV/AIDS help networks. Her model depicts resources (e.g., medical treatment, information, emotional support, and social networks) available to patients, and their potential responses to the stresses brought on by their condition. Hogan and Palmer (2005) conducted a nationwide survey of people living with HIV/AIDS and their use of information sources. They found doctors to be the most used, useful, understandable, trustworthy, and available source; HIV-positive peer educators, nurses, and case managers also ranked highly on these dimensions. Interestingly, the Internet did not rank very highly, except for availability; in most respects, it was considered little better than ads or brochures from pharmaceutical companies. The information seeking of spinal surgery patients, both before and after the procedure, were examined by Holmes and Lenz (2002). Tuominen (2004) analyzed accounts of information behavior produced in interviews with 20 heart surgery patients and their spouses. Cases in which patients sought information about a potentially risky medicine were studied by Lion and Meertens (2001). Pettigrew (1999) conducted an ethnographic study of visitors to a chiropody clinic, noting that it was a venue for gathering a variety of complementary information.

Studies by Hepworth, Harrison, and James (2003a, 2003b), Box, Hepworth, and Harrison (2003), and Hepworth and Harrison (2004) used a variety of methods (focus group interviews, audio diaries, and questionnaires) to investigate the information needs of people with multiple sclerosis. The thousands of responses they gathered indicated a need for information to be tailored to various audiences (including the patients, the public, and health-care providers) regarding the disease, its symptoms, and treatment.

A number of studies have addressed social, age, and economic factors in the use of health information. Matthews, Sellergren, Manfredi, and Williams (2002) employed focus group interviews to explore factors affecting medical information seeking among African American cancer patients. They identified several cultural and socioeconomic barriers, including limited knowledge and misinformation about cancer, mistrust of the medical community, privacy concerns, religious beliefs, fear, and stigma associated with seeking help. In a survey of the Finnish population, Ek and Widén-Wulff (2008) demonstrate that a "sense of coherence" is strongly related to both social factors and perceptions of health. They believe that this represents a "meta-literacy" that could be useful in studying and intervening in health-related behaviors. Studies by Eriksson-Backa (2008, 2010) uncovered barriers that the elderly face in finding and using health information.

Marshall (1993), Muha, Smith, Baum, Ter Maat, and Ward (1998), and Pifalo et al. (1997) describe the extent of use of patient libraries and other health information services by several hundred consumers, most of whom used the telephone to contact the services. These studies emphasize the role of information in helping patients to "cope" with health problems as much as in aiding them to talk with health-care providers and make decisions about treatment. Kwon and Kim (2009) discuss the public library as an alternate source of health information.

By way of a review of the health-care literature, Donat and Pettigrew (2002) addressed the topic of the terminally ill patient, pointing out that the patient as well as caregivers may have many motivations to seek information during the dying process. Baker (2004b) carried out empirical research on terminal illness through a content analysis of conversations between a husband who was dying and his wife (a grief counselor). Baker concluded that a person near death may need a variety of information to help her or him cope with dying and death. Their needs reflected physical, emotional, spiritual, and financial dimensions of the patient's situation. Finally, Fourie's (2008) study of patients, their family members, and caregivers in a palliative care center demonstrates how illness and dying affect others in addition to the patient.

A lengthy review of literature on information seeking and communication among health-care providers and patients is due to appear shortly after publication of this book (Johnson & Case, 2012).

12.2.6. Students

One of the most widely studied roles of all (given the voluminous research literatures on education and learning) is that of "student" — a category that virtually everyone inhabits at some point during their lives. Julien et al. (2011) found that students constitute a minimum of 19% of the participants in information behavior studies, and probably a greater percentage than that. Because most studies involving students are actually focused on some other phenomenon (e.g., task performance), and because being a student coincides with other categories discussed here (see the age-based findings, below), research on that role will be noted here much more selectively.

Gross (2001) and Gross and Saxton (2001) are reports of two investigations of "imposed" information seeking — queries developed by one person (usually a teacher) but given to someone else to resolve — in public and school libraries. Gross' first study took place in three elementary school libraries and found that between 32% and 43% of all circulation transactions involved imposed queries. The second survey, undertaken in 13 public libraries among 1107 older users, also indicates that instructors' assignments are still a major source of imposed queries, along with requests from spouses and children of library users. Additional studies by Gross (2004a, 2004b) also concern imposed queries and information seeking in schools. Beautyman and Shenton (2009) examined the way that elementary school assignments sometimes lead to stimulation of students' curiosity and information seeking — a topic explored with adolescents by Bowler (2010). A related review by Hultgren and Limberg (2003) of the learning and information behavior literature suggested a strong relationship between the nature of school assignments and the ways in which students seek and use information.

Whitmire (2003) examined the information-seeking behavior of 20 senior undergraduates as they researched a major paper. Whitmire based her investigation on Kuhlthau's Information Search Process model and four other research models from educational psychology. She found that students' epistemological beliefs (e.g., the belief that "right and wrong answers exist for everything," versus the belief that "all knowledge is contextual") affected their choice of topic, the ways they looked for information, how they evaluated it, and their ability to recognize cognitive authority.

Foster and Ford (2003) examined the role of serendipity in the information behavior of 45 university students and faculty, particularly how they accidentally or incidentally acquired information of interest to them. Foster (2004) identifies three "core processes" (p. 232) and three levels of interaction with the context of the information — likening chosen behaviors to selections from an artist's "palette" (p. 235).

Given (2002a, 2002b) undertook qualitative interviews with 25 "mature" university undergraduates. Based on Savolainen's (see Kari & Savolainen, 2003) framework for the study of everyday life information seeking, Given explored how the academic and nonacademic information needs of these students relate to one another, including the role of social and cultural capital. Interviews and observations by Jeong (2004) revealed gaps in the knowledge of Korean graduate students in the United States regarding American culture; he documented language and financial barriers that inhibited these students from learning more about their surroundings. Seldén (2001) employed interviews, observation, and textual analysis to investigate the information seeking, career, identity, and independence of 10 doctoral students in business administration.

Heinström (2003) tested the personality attributes of 305 master's degree students in a variety of disciplines. Her quantitative analysis finds that five personality dimensions — neuroticism, extraversion, openness to experience, competitiveness, and conscientiousness — interact with contextual factors to affect students' information behavior. Toms and Duff (2002) studied 11 history students, mostly at the doctoral stage of study. In addition to interviews, respondents kept diaries describing their visits to six different archives. Toms and Duff note that diaries are strong evidence which complements that from interviews, yet which depends heavily on the commitment of respondents to complete the diary.

As described in an earlier chapter, Constance Mellon (1986) studied a large sample of university students to explore the role of anxiety in the search for information in libraries, a theme also explored in other studies of college (e.g., Jiao & Onwuegbuzie, 1997) and high school (Kuhlthau, 1988a, 1991) students. The information seeking of doctoral students was studied by Cole (1998), Mehra (2007), and Seldén (2001). Additional studies of university students were conducted by Cole et al. (2005), Hyldegard (2009), Kerins et al. (2004), and Thórsteinsdóttir (2000), among many others. Connaway et al. (2011) also include some students in their study of information source convenience, and Heinström's (2006) studies of incidental information acquisition included respondents ranging from grade six to master's degree level. As featured under "age," Julien (1999) examined the information seeking of high-school age students, a group also featured in Lilley (2008) and Haras (2011), which focus more on the potential influence of ethnicity on information behaviors.

12.2.7. Other Roles

Beyond the categories listed above, other studies of "roles" tend to be narrowly defined groups. These other roles for which I have found a minimum of five examples in the information behavior literature include newcomer (e.g., Gundry & Rousseau, 1994; Louis, 1980; Miller & Jablin, 1991; Morrison, 1993, 2002; Ostroff & Kozlowski, 1992), immigrant (Caidi & Allard, 2005; Caidi et al., 2010; Courtright, 2005, Fisher et al., 2004; Fisher, Marcoux et al., 2004; Mason and Lamain, 2007; Silvio, 2006), parent (e.g., Hersberger, 2001; McKenzie, 2006; Naumer, 2005; Walker, 2009; Walter, 1994), victim of discrimination or violence (e.g., Agada, 1999; Dunne, 2002; Harris, 1988; Harris & Dewdney, 1994; Westbrook, 2009; Whitt, 1993; Williamson, Schauder, & Bow, 2000), and of course, the ubiquitous "user," the abstract object of thousands of studies.

12.3. By Demographic Group

As already mentioned, demographic breakdowns figure prominently in studies of roles that people take on in their lives. As in most social research, the factors most commonly examined have been age, gender, and racial or ethnic (or, in the language of Metoyer-Duran, 1993, "ethnolinguistic") membership. Gender has been less likely to be the central focus of information-seeking investigations, and gender differences are treated sparingly at the end of this section. Geographic categories, such as "rural" and "urban," likewise tend to be secondary considerations, although they have been implicitly examined in some studies of "citizen information needs."

Age has been the focus of several investigations, particularly the ends of the continuum: children and the elderly. I begin by reviewing recent studies of children and teenagers, then move on to the elderly. Children and adolescents are under-studied groups (considering their numbers and importance) according to Todd (2003). Those studies that have appeared tend to look at aspects of library or Internet usage, but with the broader intent of understanding the child's thinking, learning, and social interactions (Table 12.2).

12.3.1. Age

Among the broader studies of children is that of Virginia Walter (1994). Walter declared (p. 111) that "very little is known" about the information needs of children. Her investigation interviewed 25 adults — school nurses, social workers, probation workers, child care providers or administrators, police officers, recreation center directors, and others — who worked with children in two California counties. Walter asked these informants what they thought were the primary information needs of children, where and how children found that information, and what the information gaps were and how they occurred. Her findings are summarized in terms of Abraham Maslow's (1970) "hierarchy of needs": self-actualization, esteem, love/belonging, safety, and physiological, with the latter being the most basic.

Walter found that physiological and safety needs — knowing how to avoid risky behaviors, understanding basic health and nutrition, and knowing what to do in an emergency — were the categories mentioned most often, considered the most important, and also as most often cited as unmet. The need for sex education was found in all but the top category of the hierarchy, while the need to instill children with ethics and values to guide them emerged in all but the bottom two categories. Informants saw children as having many potential information sources, such as parents and teachers,

Table 12.2: Works reviewed, and related works cited, for group.

Group	Works reviewed to illustrate findings	Some other relevant works cited
Age	Agosto, 2005, 2006; Asla, 2006; Beautyman, 2009; Cooper, 2002; Hamer, 2003; Julien, 1998, 1999, 2004; Shenton, 2003, 2004; van der Rijt, 1996; Walter, 1994; Williamson, 1997, 2009	Alexandersson, 2003; Biesecker, 1990; Bilal, 2007; Chatman, 1992; Chelton, 2004; Detlefsen, 2004; Dresang, 1999; Enochsson, 2000; Eriksson-Backa, 2008, 2010; Getz, 2010; Hirsh, 1997; Jansen, 2011; Johnson, 1997; Kafai, 1997; Laplante, 2011; Large, 1998, 2008; Lu, 2010; Mata, 2010; Meyers, 2007, 2009; Tinker, 1993; Todd, 2003, 2004; Turk-Charles, 1997; Wicks, 2004; Xie, 2008
Racial or ethnic	Fisher, 2004; Kelly, 2009; Newhagen, 1994; Spink, 1999, 2001	Agada, 1999; Atwood, 1982; Chatman, 1987, 1996; Chouhan, 2004; Courtright, 2005; Freimuth, 1993; Haras, 2011; Jeong, 2004; Lilley, 2008; Matthews, 2002; Morey, 2007
Socioeconomic status	Hersberger, 2001, 2003; Niederdeppe, 2008; Savolainen, 1995, 2008	Chatman, 1985, 1991, 1995; Childers, 1975; Courtright, 2005; Dervin, 1972; Fisher, 2004; Freimuth, 1990
Other groups: Gender, urban/rural	Dunne, 2002; Williamson, 2000	Anwar, 1998; Baker, 1996; Case, 1987; Creelman, 1990; Freimuth, 1989, 1993; Hamer, 2003; Harris, 1988, 1994, 2006, 2010; Ikoja-Odongo, 2002; Jiyane, 2004; Mooko, 2002; Westbrook, 2009; Whitt, 1993; Yeh, 2008

Note: Studies are listed by first author only, plus year. See the references for clarification.

but they were prone to receiving misinformation from peers and the media. They saw children's barriers to information as stemming from their low status in society, ineffective parental communication, and competition from the media.

Cooper (2002) observed seven-year-old children browsing in a library to understand how people who are still learning to read are able to search through printed material. Cooper found that children often picked books on the basis of their covers rather than a closer examination of the contents. Using much different approaches and research questions, Alexandersson and Limberg (2003) performed an ethnographic study in which 11-year-olds were observed, interviewed, and surveyed regarding how they construct meaning from books, films, CD-ROMs, and the Internet.

Children's use of electronic information sources (as a sole source) will not be reviewed here, but nevertheless it has been the subject of a number of reports and commentaries, including Bilal (2007), Chelton and Cool (2004), Dresang (1999), Enochsson (2000), Hirsh (1997), Kafai and Bates (1997), Large, Beheshti, and Breuleux (1998), Large, Nesset, and Beheshti (2008), and Massey et al. (2007). A conclusion of some of these studies is that children and youth will increasingly turn to the World Wide Web for reading, and for answers to their questions.

In between children and teenagers are the "tweens," aged nine through thirteen years. Two articles by Meyers et al. (2007, 2009) have examined this population through interviews and focus groups with 34 tweens in three settings. Their interest is in youth information seeking outside of school, its sources, barriers, and emotional components. Their 2009 article offers some principles for services to tweens, while the 2007 piece concerns methodological considerations in studying this group. Lu's (2010) study of coping is also concerned with this age group.

The information-seeking behavior of young people was the subject of a series of articles by Shenton and Dixon (2003a, 2003b, 2004a, 2004b). Rather than studying sources or habits, their qualitative investigation among English children examined characteristics that correlate with the use of a range of information sources. Shenton and Dixon (2003a) offered a model of the information behavior of the young. How youngsters obtain information from other people, particularly friends, was the focus of Shenton and Dixon (2003b). In a later article (Shenton & Dixon, 2004a) they emphasize that some seeking patterns reflect personal problems faced by the youngsters in their study, while others are attempts to simplify information seeking. Shenton and Dixon (2004b) discuss approaches to studying the information behavior of the young. As mentioned earlier, Beautyman and Shenton (2009) consider how elementary school work may spark curiosity about related topics. And Carey et al. (2001) included some preschool children among their sample of informants about everyday life information seeking.

Children's use of electronic information sources (as a single source) will not be reviewed here, but certainly it has been the subject of a number of recent reports and commentaries, including Chelton and Cool (2004), Dresang (1999), Enochsson (2000), Hirsh (1997), Kafai and Bates (1997), Large et al. (1998), and Large et al. (2008). A conclusion of some of these studies is that children and youth will increasingly turn to the World Wide Web for answers to their questions.

Information-seeking behaviors of teenagers have been studied by several researchers. Julien (1998, 1999) studied their decisions about future careers through a two-part study. First, she surveyed 399 male and female teenagers in one Canadian city, and then followed up with interviews of 30 of them, evenly divided by gender. Julien found that a majority of the adolescents had questions about careers. Some had very general questions ("What should I do?"), while others wanted more specific facts (what school to attend to pursue their goal). Their information needs are described as "wondering ... what jobs are like ... what they would enjoy ... what they would be good at" (1998, p. 377). There was a narrow difference in the frequency of the top information sources, which in order were self (own thinking), books/pamphlets, guidance counselor, friends, worker, mother, and father — each used by 35% or more of the teenagers. The least-used sources were public libraries and work experiences, even though 88% had work experience. Books and counselors were seen as less helpful than friends, workers, or family members. According to Julien, 40% of those surveyed did "not know where to go for help in making decisions, and a similar proportion feel that there are too many places to go for help in their information seeking." Most career information was found incidentally, rather than purposefully, and teenagers' decision making "does not follow the logical pattern suggested in the career development literature" (1998, p. 379). She concludes that emotional support may be more important than instrumental help (e.g., with understanding choices) in making decisions about careers at such ages. A later publication by Julien (2004) categorized the 30 informants into five types of decision-making styles, based on locus of control and degree of active information seeking.

Agosto and Hughes-Hassell (2005, 2006) investigated the everyday life information seeking of urban young adults through group interviews, surveys, audio journals, "photo tours," and activity logs. The informants were 27 Philadelphia teenagers, ages 14–17, nearly all of whom were racial minorities. Agosto and Hughes-Hassell found that friends and family members were preferred sources, cell phones were the favorite medium, and schoolwork, social life, and the time or date of events were the most common topics of interest. Their 2006 article creates a model based on 7 variables and 28 topics.

Information sharing and social networks among young people have been receiving additional attention. Jansen, Sobel, and Cook (2011) analyze over 34,000 responses to examine use of social networking sites. Todd and Edwards (2004) reviewed investigations of how teenage girls find out about drug usage, drawing on the work of Chatman, Dervin, and Kuhlthau. Not surprisingly, the main informants were other teenagers.

An older group of young people (ages 18–29) were the respondents in Laplante and Downie's (2011) study of music information seeking. Ending our examination of younger people, Hamer (2003) adopted a social constructivist perspective in a study of young men's information needs related to coming out and to forming a gay identity. Their information seeking most often took place through online forums. Hamer relates his findings to Chatman's Theory of Information Poverty (Chatman, 1996).

On the other end of the age distribution, Williamson (1997) and her colleagues interviewed 202 elderly (age 60 and older) Australian residents to understand how their physical, social, and cultural environments shaped their information seeking. In three focused interviews, respondents related episodes in which they "had needed to 'find out, understand, or clarify' something for their everyday lives" (p. 340). Participants were later prompted with a series of topics commonly found to come up at community information centers, and with potential sources of information found to be relevant in the Chen and Hernon (1982) and Warner et al. (1973) community studies. In addition, each respondent completed telephone diaries over a two-week period. The diaries asked the participants to record, in their own words, why they made each telephone call and what it was about.

Williamson found that health and financial topics came up in every interview, reflecting not only the typical ailments of the aged but also the fact that over 60% were on a fixed retirement income. Recreation or leisure activities, along with volunteering, were also frequent areas of interest. The telephone conversations reflected in the diaries were much more likely to be about personal events than information of a more common type. The most frequent sources of information were, in order, family, newspapers, friends, television, other printed information (e.g., pension newsletters and "junk mail"), and radio. Information was obtained both purposefully and incidentally from all sources; however, there were definite patterns in regard to these. Incidental information gathering was more likely to take place from mass media, such as newspapers, radio, and television. Less frequently used sources of information included professionals, organizations such as stores and self-help groups, magazines, government departments, and information agencies such as libraries; these were used to seek information purposefully. No information was sought from digital sources even though a few respondents had both computers and modems at home. Professionals were the top choice for information as far as health, drugs, and the law were concerned.

Williamson (1997) offers a good discussion of the importance of unconscious information needs and incidental information seeking, as opposed to information purposefully sought in reaction to a well-defined, conscious need. However, distinguishing between purposeful and incidental information seeking turned out to be difficult in many cases. Williamson gives the example of happening across a listing for a television program on cancer and then deciding to watch it; such incidents were coded as incidental if they were not part of a regular pattern of viewing. Williamson acknowledges the arbitrariness of deciding when watching, reading, or listening passes from incidental to purposeful. She concludes her study by proposing an "ecological model of use" for everyday information.

Williamson has continued to study the elderly as an important yet vulnerable population. Asla, Williamson, and Mills (2006) spotlight the "oldest old" (85 years and up) as demographic that should be investigated. They see a role for information provision in contributing to successful aging. Williamson and Asla (2009) describe a "fourth age," beyond retirement years (the third age), in which increasing illness and dependence make a marked difference in life. They believe improved information literacy skills will play a key role in helping this growing demographic.

A rather different investigation, but with some parallel results, is reported by van der Rijt (1996), who conducted a secondary analysis of a survey of 319 elderly (age 65 and older) Dutch citizens. This time there was more of an emphasis on health information and the measures were exclusively quantitative. Van der Rijt found that by far the highest interest item on a list of 27 topics was "provision for elderly living independently" (52% indicated interest in this), followed by information about a healthy diet (43%), physical symptoms of aging (38%), and social benefits/compensation (35%). About half of the remaining 23 items (e.g., housing, crime, safety, and leisure) were of interest to between 20% and 31% of respondents, while the bottom four topics (e.g., information about drinking problems, employment, and handicaps) were of interest to only 5% or fewer.

Van der Rijt's main focus was the factor analysis of these data and a multiple regression of the resulting factors. He concludes that having experienced a health problem (e.g., "I become tired quickly") was the most powerful influence in seeking information. He expected to find associations by gender (e.g., that women would be more interested in health and safety while men would be more concerned about finances), but these did not emerge, except in a great interest in leisure information by younger men. Four general "orientations" to health emerged, including Preventative (avoiding harm), Fatalism (seeing health as a matter of luck), Internal Control (believing one was in complete control over health), and Unconcern (simply not worrying about it). The Preventative orientation was found to be particularly influential in information seeking; if an individual was intent upon staying healthy through positive diet and exercises habits while avoiding unhealthy practices, they were more likely to seek information than individuals of other orientations. The study of 29 older adults by Wicks (2004) also demonstrates how information sources vary by role, retirement status, and living situation.

Other studies involving the elderly include those by Getz and Weissman (2010), Eriksson-Backa (2008, 2010 — described under "patients"), Mata and Nunes (2010), Niemelä and Huotari (2008), Tinker, McCreadie, and Salvage (1993), Wicks (2004), and Xie (2008).

In between teenagers and the elderly, age-focused studies of the information seeking of general populations do not appear to be common. However, "adult" populations — which include the elderly but not children and teenagers — have been widely studied. Age-based differences are noted in the statistical analyses of the studies of "citizens."

The health information-seeking literature includes a number of observations about age, which are summarized by Johnson (1997). For example, Biesecker and Biesecker (1990) find that the elderly are less likely to question physicians themselves and more likely to bring someone along to do so on their behalf. Turk-Charles, Meyerowitz, and Gatz (1997) found no difference among age cohorts of cancer patients in terms of learning from friends and mass media. The elderly still rely on their doctors and other human sources for information, but they are beginning to use the Internet in greater numbers, according to Detlefsen (2004).

12.3.2. Racial and Ethnolinguistic Minorities

The assumption that membership in an ethnic or racial minority predicts attitudes, beliefs, and behaviors seems to underlie many studies. Along with age and gender (the two most commonly measured variables), the racial and/or ethnic background is usually recorded even when it is not particularly important to the investigation, as it is commonly regarded as "potentially useful" information for analysis.

Likewise, in studies of information needs and uses, such demographic information tends to be collected when it is available, either through self-report (on questionnaires) or through observation by an investigator. It is not certain that racial or ethnic minority status predicts information seeking in most cases. Since at least the publication of "Challenges to Sociocultural Predictors of Information Seeking" (Atwood & Dervin, 1982), Brenda Dervin has argued that the *situation* (or context) in which information seeking takes place is a much more powerful predictor of thoughts and behavior in that regard than is personal background. In other words, Dervin's research, as well as her sense-making paradigm, says that people have much in common in the way that they react to the kinds of problematic situations that prompt a search for information or other "help."

Dervin's research *does* demonstrate associations between racial/ethnic groups and certain types of problems. For example, Dervin et al. (1984) show African Americans more likely to experience "gap situations" and problems related to transportation, housing, and safety or crime, while Hispanics were more likely to face issues of caring for children. Underlying factors — having more time, money, opportunities, and other resources — are the source of these situations.

When information consumption is habitual, rather than situational, a better argument can be made for racial (as well as ethnic and class) differences. Among the investigations that have featured race in regard to information consumption is John Newhagen's (1994) study of "media use and political efficacy." A journalism professor Newhagen conducted a telephone survey of 356 randomly selected residents of Maryland in 1992. The study tested racial and class differences in perceived *self-efficacy* (Bandura, 1977) in regard to politics. Newhagen wanted to know if amount and type of media use predicted how politically involved and effective respondents felt they were, and if they believed that the political system included them. For example, someone who agreed strongly with statements like "I consider myself well-qualified to participate in politics" would be said to feel effective on a personal level, where as agreeing with items like "the people have the final say in how the country is run" indicates a judgment that the political *system* is effective.

The knowledge gap hypothesis (see Chapters 4 and 5), along with previous research on social class membership, would predict that African-Americans would have a different belief structure than their white counterparts, including feeling less powerful and less involved in politics. What was the role of media use and social class (middle-class versus poor neighborhood) in political efficacy? Newhagen's results suggest several interesting conclusions. Paying attention to news and opinion (whether newspaper, radio, or TV) results in higher feelings of self-efficacy, regardless of race, economic status, or even education; listening to talk radio was even more highly correlated with feelings of political effectiveness. However, racial differences became apparent in watching of primetime TV: the more entertainment programming that African Americans watched, the more they felt that the political system was ineffective, and that they were powerless to change it. Newhagen concluded that political efficacy is neither race nor class driven, yet he is unable to explain the correlation of low efficacy with entertainment. Is it the case that people who feel powerless watch entertainment programs, or that a heavy diet of entertainment programming makes one feel ineffective? Whichever the direction of causation, it seems that one's choice of source for information about political realities shapes one's belief system, and hence a person's degree of participation in the world — including whether one seeks further information about a particular issue.

Spink, Bray, Jaeckel, and Sidberry (1999; also reported in Spink & Cole, 2001) investigated "everyday life information seeking by low-income African-American households" in Dallas, Texas, describing it as the largest such study ever conducted. They interviewed 300 heads of households in a low-income housing development, asking questions about their needs for services and information, as well as their activities (including use of media) and demographic background data. In-depth follow-up interviews have since been conducted with a subsample of residents. What these residents most wanted to know about were local news (e.g., local activities and family events), followed by information relevant to personal security and health. Education and employment information was judged less important, while state, national, and international events were "of little direct interest" (p. 380). Respondents ranked family and school as the most important sources of news events, followed by television, newspapers, and radio. Friends and neighbors were the least important source for general news; they were the second- and third-ranked sources (preceded by newspapers — by far the best source) for information on employment. Spink *et al.* discuss these findings in the context of the "information environment" for these families, and how they relate to theories regarding *habitus* — ways of seeing and thinking that guide choices in life (Bourdieu, 1984).

Fisher, Marcoux et al. (2004) examined the role of interpersonal sources and information grounds among 51 Hispanic farm workers at community technology centers. Most of them learned useful information through churches, schools, and their workplace — although other locales mentioned medical clinics, hair salons, barber shops, a day-care center, a car garage, a radio station, a bookstore, and a restaurant. The informants valued their information grounds for offering easy, face-to-face communication and reliable sources.

A review by Johnson (1997) pointed out studies indicating that health information-seeking practices may be influenced by membership in racial and ethnic groups. Kelly, Sturm, Kemp, Holland, and Ferketich (2009), in a comparison of samples of African American versus "other" groups, found just a few significant differences in their information behavior. The African Americans were much more likely to report receiving information about cancer genetics from local clergy or church members, or thorough their child's school; they were also much less likely to have Internet access at home. Freimuth, Edgar, and Fitzpatrick's (1993) results suggest that African Americans are more likely to be fatalistic about health problems and therefore less likely to do something about them, including learning more about prevention. Matthews et al. (2002) found African Americans less likely than European-Americans to seek help or information. That 22% of African Americans may conduct proxy searching of health information was one finding of the study by Morey (2007).

Other studies with a racial or ethnic emphasis include Agada (1999, discussed under "gatekeepers"), Chatman (1991, 1996), Chouhan and Miles (2004), Courtright (2005, discussed under "patients"), Jeong (2004), Lilley (2008), and Metoyer-Duran (1991).

12.3.3. Socioeconomic Status

I use the term "socioeconomic status" to characterize any comparisons of information seekers by income group (e.g., "the poor"), or social or economic "class."

Childers and Post (1975) were among the earliest to associate demographic factors with a "culture of information poverty," associating it primarily with low-income groups, such as public housing tenants. An earlier review by Dervin and Greenberg (1972) claimed that about 200 studies relevant to the "communication environment of the poor" existed at that time; they examined 30 of the most relevant, mostly from 1967 to 1972. Their summary suggested that the poor in America did not lack in access to information channels, and depended heavily on television as a source. Greenberg et al.'s (1970) research in Cleveland showed that low-income African American adults used TV for both escape and learning (e.g., what life is like and how others solve problems). Many investigations since that time have explored the degree to which TV viewing can lead to misconceptions about the "real" world (Morgan & Shanahan, 1997). Among all poor populations, newspaper readership was low, with most attention being paid to headlines and advertising. In the Cleveland study, Greenberg et al. found that professionals, lawyers, relatives, neighbors, and health-care providers had been common sources of "help or information" in the past.

Later, Dervin et al. (1984) found that higher-income respondents were more likely to report problematic situations overall, and more gaps that involved recreation, learning something new, and concerns about jobs, government, and current events. These same situations were of concern to those respondents with more years of education than the others. However, their data also demonstrated that demographic factors are less effective for predicting the questions that people have, the barriers they face, and the kind of help they need, than are situational factors (e.g., whether they feel "stopped" because they need to make a decision, or because they feel lost, out of control, or in need of a guide).

Several studies by Chatman (1985, 1987, 1991), described in previous chapters, along with Chatman and Pendleton (1995) are also relevant to this theme. These ethnographic studies of the working poor, like earlier studies, found a preference for interpersonal sources and a heavy use of television for escape and for surveillance.

In the health context, Niederdeppe (2008) considered the knowledge gap hypothesis in terms of differential levels of education. Using the timing of five media announcements of cancer among celebrities, and data from the U.S. Health Information National Trends Survey, Niederdeppe demonstrates that such news correlated with higher information seeking among those with higher education. He suggests that at least part of the explanation lies in greater health knowledge and community involvement among those with more education.

Savolainen's (1995) study of 22 Finns found relatively few class differences in terms of their lifestyles. Where they existed, differences involved priorities for the use of free time, including the greater consumption of literature and "facts" by the middle-class teachers when compared to the workers he interviewed, who emphasized entertainment (p. 274). After collecting data on both preferences for media content, and how much time was spent with individual media, Savolainen classified each respondent as being primarily oriented to media in a manner that was either *Cognitive* (preferring cultural, social, political, and science content, more inclined to reading and to "serious" broadcasting programs), *Affective* (inclined to entertainment, crime, and accident reports, more inclined to watch television than read), or *Balanced* (making use of both types of elements). These three classifications were mapped across three other categories: light, medium, or heavy use of media. In this way, each respondent was located on two nine-cell matrices, one for print media and a second for electronic media. Reflecting on the distribution of the 22 respondents on these two charts, Savolainen noted that

> social class will not solely determine the type of media orientation. Although all teachers were not cognitively oriented and all workers not affectively oriented, way of life based on social class seems to play its own role in the direction of media use ... Teachers tend to prefer more markedly "serious" programs, devoting less time to entertainment and to electronic media in general .... In contrast, watching television, chiefly entertainment, all evening long with minor interruptions is not very unusual among workers ... affective elements tend to be emphasized in industrial worker's [sic] media orientation. (p. 279)

For an example of a study of this demographic segment, consider Julie Hersberger's (2001) "everyday information needs and information sources of homeless parents." While "parent" could also be considered a social role, the homeless are by definition also "poor"; in fact, they are, at least temporarily, the very poorest in our society. Hersberger spent a year as participant observer in six homeless shelters in Indianapolis, Indiana. In addition to her other observations, she conducted interviews with 28 informants, generating over 800 pages of transcripts. Obviously, financial needs were the most pressing issue among this sample, followed by child care, then housing, health, employment, education, transportation, public assistance, and problems associated with living in the shelter. Altogether, Hersberger identified 16 major problem categories and 145 specific needs within them. Social service staff were the most frequently mentioned information sources in nearly all major categories of need, with friends and family, personal experience, and other shelter residents also common sources of help. For some problems, additional sources were prominent: newspapers and signs (in the case of housing and employment), television talk shows (child behavior problems), and health-care professionals (health problems). A second study by Hersberger (2003) was a social network analysis based on interviews with 21 homeless parents in shelters in the American states of North Carolina and Washington. Hersberger found the social networks of these informants were small and sometimes unconnected and that they used secrecy and deception at times to protect themselves.

In her conclusions, Hersberger discussed the "complex and messy" nature of everyday life for the homeless, relating it to Chatman's characterizations of the poor and "insiders." Some informants, experienced at being homeless, knew how to find out what they needed to know. Others "often failed to seek information when required or recommended to by others" — reinforcing the insider pattern of ignoring sources of information from "outside." Hersberger found that it was rare for homeless parents to consider public libraries or the electronic sources they offered, preferring instead interpersonal sources.

Savolainen (2008c) investigated a sample of 18 unemployed persons. The focus of the study was their motivation for seeking work, and how they talked about those motivations. The unemployed are a fairly consistent minority, even in developed economies (Perttilä & Ek, 2010) who are also a low-income group.

Poverty is also a major factor in health information seeking. Freimuth (1990) says that the poor not only know less about cancer than the affluent, but also have a greater need for information due to risk factors. She noted that they are more likely to rely on television and folk tales for medical information, and are less likely to read about it.

Other studies mentioned above (Caidi & Allard, 2005; Caidi et al., 2010; Courtright, 2005, Fisher et al., 2004; Fisher, Marcoux et al., 2004; Mason & Lamain, 2007; Silvio, 2006) include immigrants who are highly likely to have low incomes, as well.

12.3.4. Other Demographic Groups

Gender has not been a primary focus of many information-seeking studies, although it appears frequently in analyses of results. More commonly, it emerges in combination with some other variable or situation, such as health (see above). Typically the focus is on women. Roma Harris (1988) and Harris and Dewdney (1994), for example, write about "the information needs of battered women"; a study of shelters for domestic violence victims also includes predominately women informants. Baker (1996) studies "the nature of information needed by women with Multiple Sclerosis." Dunne (2002) examined the information behavior of battered women. She advanced a "person-in-progressive-situations" model charting stages in information seeking and explains three types of barriers that battered women face in finding information. Ikoja-Odongo (2002), Jiyane and

Ocholla (2004), and Mooko (2002) each studied samples of South African women using interviews and questionnaires; all three studies stress a reliance on personal experience and the dominance of information obtained by word of mouth. Freimuth, Stein, and Kean (1989) and Freimuth et al. (1993) note that women are more likely to be information seekers than are men in the context of health matters in general and cancer in particular. Urquhart (2011) is a meta-synthesis of research on women's information behavior. The investigations mentioned above by Hamer (2003) and Wellstead (2011) are among the few in which males are singled out for study on their own.

Another category that has received some attention is that of the urban/ rural divide. Some aspects of this were mentioned in the context of surveys of "citizen" information needs. Most studies have been implicitly urban, or at least suburban — after all, that is where most people live. A few studies have explicitly sampled rural populations. Anwar and Supaat (1998) examined the "information needs of rural Malaysians" in a survey of 108 people living in three villages. Vavrek (1995), in a discussion of rural public libraries, provided some data on the information needs and seeking of rural residents. Case and Rogers (1987) described the information environment of small farm operators.

A common concern with rural areas is access to health information and services, for both patients and providers. Harris et al. (2006) examine where rural Canadians find health information. Harris et al. (2010) put a spotlight on provision of HIV/AIDS information in rural areas. Dee (1993) examined how rural physicians may differ in their use of sources from their urban counterparts; this was also a concern of Ely et al. (1992). Salasin and Cedar (1985) surveyed a large sample of rural mental health-care workers about their communication patterns.

Gay, lesbian, bisexual, or transgendered individuals are featured in a few studies, including Creelman and Harris (1990), Hamer (2003), Whitt (1993), and Yeh (2008).

Some demographic groups studied are relatively small, and may be the subject of few investigations. Williamson et al. (2000) and Beverley, Bath, and Barber (2007) studied the blind and sight impaired. Based on their figures, this group (in which membership is a matter of degree) may constitute only about 1.5% of a nation's population. Undoubtedly, many other differently abled groups and other population segments have never been examined from the perspective of information needs. Partly this may be a question of resources (do we have the time and money to study every group?) and partly a factor of utility (would the study result in useful knowledge?).

The uneven pattern of demographic-focused studies is an issue of overlap. It is important to remember that people are members of several groups at once. A French-Canadian lawyer who is a member of the Green Party, practices Catholicism, and is an environmental activist and an urban dweller could be studied from a number of perspectives. She could be a respondent in a study of the information needs of Canadian citizens, urban residents, attorneys, or political, religious, or ethnic minorities, to name just a few possibilities. Who is sampled, and from what perspective, is up to the motivations of the investigators and their sponsors.

Dervin (1989) raised challenging questions about the value and validity of demographic-based investigations. However, when a background characteristic such as having a disability results in *persistent* situational differences, a study of that small segment of the population makes more sense.

12.4. Summary

It can be seen that there is great variety in the kinds of populations and activities that have been examined. In recent years, more attention has been paid to contextual, situational, or role variables, rather than the usual demographic variables. Relatively small populations (e.g., the sight-impaired, Canadian literary critics, or homeless parents) have been sampled for investigation. Investigations concerned with health information seeking have become a prominent genre, rivaled mainly by the ever-constant attention to students of all types and ages.

One thing that these studies have in common, however, is a concern with sources and channels, typically interpersonal channels versus mass and/or specialized media. A frequent finding is that people still turn to other people for information. Despite an effort to examine the process of information seeking, much of it still comes down to "who or what do people consult for information?" This is an old question within the information needs, uses, and seeking literature, and it continues to dominate the discussion of findings.

In the final chapter, I will summarize a few of the things we have learned from nearly a century of studying information seeking by occupation, role, and demographic category. I point out some trends and gaps in this vast literature and suggest some directions for the future.

Recommended for Further Reading

Baldwin, N. S., & Rice, R. E. (1997). Information-seeking behavior of securities analysts: Individual and institutional influences, information sources and channels, and outcomes. *Journal of the American Society for Information Science, 48,* 674–693.

This is an example of a quantitative, source- and channel-oriented study. Baldwin and Rice offer a model depicting individual characteristics, institutional resources, channels used, and the effect of these on "outcomes," such as the incomes and satisfactions of the 100 securities analysts they study. Baldwin and Rice demonstrate that the resources available to an analyst — such as the size of firm, staff, and budget — both directly and indirectly affect information seeking. More importantly for this chapter, they also discuss the way in which these analysts were gatekeepers in their organizations.

Fisher, K., Naumer, C., Durrance, J., Stromski, L. & Christiansen, T. (2005). Something old, something new: Preliminary findings from an exploratory study about people's information habits and information grounds. *Information Research, 10*(2) paper 223. Retrieved from http:// InformationR.net/ir/10-2/paper223.html
   An ambitious, large-scale study of a broad segment of the urban population. Fisher and her colleagues find empirical support for her notion of "information grounds" — fertile places in which people may gather information about many daily concerns.

Kuhlthau, C. C. (1991). Inside the search process: Information seeking from the user's perspective. *Journal of the American Society for Information Science, 42*, 361–371.
   A seminal discussion of how information seeking looks (and feels!) to high school and college students. This piece nicely brings together theory and empirical observations to chart the psychological stages of information seeking.

Newhagen, J. (1994). Media use and political efficacy: The suburbanization of race and class. *Journal of the American Society for Information Science, 45*, 386–394.
   An investigation that considers both race and social class in regard to patterns of information consumption. Based on a telephone survey of 356 people, Newhagen's investigation explored perceived self-efficacy regarding politics, finding that neither race nor class predicted feelings of low efficacy as much as did watching television entertainment programming. Newhagen's results suggest that one's main source of information about politics largely determines whether one seeks further information from other sources, and whether one becomes more involved (e.g., by voting).

Savolainen, R. (1995). Everyday life information seeking: Approaching information seeking in the context of "way of life." *Library and Information Science Research, 17*, 259–294.

Savolainen's study of the lifestyles and media habits of 22 ordinary people makes fascinating reading. A highly original piece of research, it describes theories and methods not previously used in studies of this type. It also sheds some light on class differences in media usage.

Sligo, F. X., & Jameson, A. M. (2000). The knowledge-behavior gap in use of health information. *Journal of the American Society for Information Science, 51*(9), 858–869.

An interesting discussion of both the "knowledge-behavior gap" and studies of ethic minorities.

Chapter 13

Reviewing, Critiquing, Concluding

> Studies have moved from an orientation that is primarily system-centered ... to an orientation that is also user-centered.
>
> — Choo (1998, p. 39)

> There is a need for an integrative model of information need, information-seeking behaviour and information use. That integrative model is already almost complete: it is a person-centred model, based largely on Dervin's "sense-making" approach ...
>
> — Wilson (1994, p. 42)

Chapter Outline

13.1. Reviewing

This book has described the ways in which people look for information and how that phenomenon has been studied. Let us first consider what we have read, then I will make eight conclusions about the changing emphasis of information behavior research, and end by discussing some recent and future trends.

Chapter 1 briefly considered the history and scope of information seeking, emphasizing the changing nature of the research conducted over about eight decades of scholarly interest in the topic. I introduced 10 myths about information that Brenda Dervin highlighted in 1976, and suggested that these were useful for understanding why research on information behavior has taken the path that it has. We will take a fresh look at those myths in a few pages.

In Chapter 2, we considered five "scenarios" of information seeking to look at the process from the individual's point of view. We cannot learn any "facts" from such hypothetical examples, but they serve to sensitize us to the wide range of thoughts and actions that might be included under the label of *information seeking*. It also shows the effects of such variables as time pressure, types of motivations and sources, and the scope of relevant information. Taken as a whole, the five scenarios may illustrate why it is that some investigators are now more focused on the phenomenology of sensemaking than on the ways that a particular source (or channel) of information is used by its intended audience.

In Chapter 3, we explored the central concept of *information*. We learned that attempting to define information in a rigorous way runs headlong into difficult problems of scope. For starters, is information distinct from its associated terms, such as data, fact, and knowledge, or does it subsume them? For the purposes of this book, I have chosen a broad definition of information as "any difference that makes a difference" to a human being, an inclusive concept that allows us to go beyond the narrow limits of source-oriented and system-oriented information research.

In contrast, other writers have made difficult choices regarding other issues surrounding the definition of information. Some have argued that information must be defined as something factually *true*, while I consider "misinformation" to be a subset of a more general concept of information. Must information be communicated to us intentionally to be information? I do not believe so. I hold that it could also be a mere difference that we perceive in our environment. Does information always reduce uncertainty? No, sometimes it increases uncertainty, as when learning a fact raises further questions and concerns about it. Must information be "useful" for some practical purpose, such as for solving a problem or making a decision? No, sometimes information, while noticed, has no immediate application. Can entertainment itself be considered to be information? Yes. I made the case that the artificial distinction between cognitive input that is "useful" and input that is "hedonistic" is unnecessarily judgmental and restrictive.

In Chapter 4, we examined definitions of two derivative concepts (e.g., information need and information seeking) that are central to this book. "Information needs" are not directly observable, but are inferred from actions or cognitions. I described various characterizations of how information needs are thought to arise. The concept of "information seeking" was explored as it has been discussed by various authors. I made a case that the term "information behavior" is better suited for characterizing the many types of human behaviors that concern information.

Chapter 5 considered many other concepts relevant to information-seeking literature — including relevance itself — along with decision making, problem solving, browsing, foraging, encountering, selective exposure, avoidance, overload, information anxiety, knowledge gaps, information poverty, pertinence, relevance, salience, entertainment, situation, context and colla- boration. In that chapter I pointed out that most writers assume that information seeking arises out of a sense of uncertainty — an anomaly, gap, or problem. Attempts to define and address the feeling of uncertainty give rise to a "need" that might later be expressed as a question or action. Issues of relevance and pertinence arise when information is considered as a potential response to the need. Several conditions may be invoked in this process, including at times anxiety, creativity, play, and entertainment. Context determines much of a person's perceptions throughout this process, and it affects one's choice of sources and meanings.

It is difficult to summarize Chapters 6 through 12 in just a few words, so I will merely remind the reader of their sequence and content. For readers who are new to research in general, these were undoubtedly complex. Chapters 6 and 7 examined first some of the more prominent models used to study information behavior, and then the various paradigms and theories that have been applied to do so. Chapter 8 discussed methods in a general way, and Chapter 9 offered examples of investigations of information seeking that used each method.

In Chapter 10, I reviewed the origins and growth of the information needs, seeking, and uses of literature, highlighting its character and topics, and offering evidence that the corpus of studies could easily stretch into the five-digit range, even if narrowly construed. Chapter 10 also built a justification for the sampling scheme I used in Chapters 11 and 12. Chapter 11 reviewed individual studies of information seeking to illustrate the research findings by *occupation*, and Chapter 12 considered the *social roles* and *demographic* segmentations that are sometimes the focus of such investigations. I pointed out trends toward more study of contexts and roles, and of smaller populations. However, it is still apparent that many studies continue to be concerned with long-standing questions of which sources and channels are used in which situations. "Other people" remain a chief source of answers to many common questions.

Now that I have, in the traditional fashion, "told you what I told you," I will move on to a critique of information behavior research. I will start with the complaints of four decades ago, and then move on to some criticisms that are more current.

13.2. Critiquing

13.2.1. A History of Complaint

In 1966, Herbert Menzel of New York University published what was to become the first among the series of the *Annual Review of Information Science and Technology (ARIST)* chapters on "information needs and uses." Menzel, whose concern was strictly limited to reviewing the burgeoning number of studies on scientists and engineers, opined that "all is not well with the quality of work performed in the field during the past few years" in which "sometimes excellent ideas lead to results that are either of dubious reliability and validity, or else of a barren superficiality" (1966b, p. 42). Menzel alluded to "poorly designed opinion polls," "primitive data-gathering instruments," and "categories too much tied to specific situations to make generalizations and extrapolations plausible" in his list of the faults of studies of "communication gathering behavior" (1966b, pp. 42–44). Menzel's suggested corrective was that researchers should draw upon "methods and techniques ... in communication behavior research and other branches of sociology and psychology," among other disciplines (p. 42).

Thus, began a steady stream of complaints and remedies directed at the study of information needs and seeking. Just a year after Menzel's review, another one by Herner and Herner (1967) lambasted studies of information users for seven alleged faults: using a narrow range of research techniques, studying too many disparate groups of users, failing to use consistent language, failing to innovate, failing to build on past findings, failing to learn from mistakes, and not using experimental designs.

In 1968 William Paisley pointed out the "defective methodology" and "shallow conceptualization" apparent in this research, expressing his

> concern over the field's failure to adopt the sound methods of its own best work. Mistakes of the 1950s are repeated in the 1960s. Inconclusive studies are conducted to fill gaps left by previous inconclusive studies. (p. 2)

Paisley also regretted that "the field has almost no theory" (p. 26), yet was able to conclude that it was "growing in size and maturing in quality .... More adequate theories of information-processing behavior will follow" (p. 23).

Two years later, Tom Allen griped about "the sort of trivia that many authors submit as research reports," particularly those "so involved with local circumstances that any generalization is questionable"; still, Allen thought there was "a strong corpus of good research in the field" (1969, p. 3).

This pattern of criticism represented by Paisley and Allen — disparaging remarks about the state of findings and methodology, coupled with optimistic comments about recent and future improvements — has persisted for more than three decades. In 1970, Lipetz's *ARIST* chapter observed that "the study of information needs and uses is still in its infancy, yet it exhibits considerable vigor" (p. 25). Diana Crane (1971) of Johns Hopkins University praised advances in methodology while acknowledging weaknesses in theory. Lin and Garvey (1972) declared that the literature lacked a conceptual framework.

The 1974 *ARIST* chapter by John Martyn spoke of a literature "cluttered with the results of an enormous number of surveys of indifferent quality ... what this reviewer classes as 'Gee Whiz' research" (p. 4). Martyn suggested that progress could be made by focusing more on "communication" and less on "information" (p. 21), a point that Brenda Dervin reinforced in 1976 and that Tom Wilson later argued had yet to be fully realized even by 1994.

The fault-finding intensified in the 1980s. The problem was not so much with a general definition for information, wrote Tom Wilson in 1981, "as with a failure to use a definition appropriate to the ... investigation" (p. 3). Four years later, Wersig and Windel (1985) objected to a lack of "empirically supported theoretical basis," particularly that which would explain "the subjective and nonrational aspects of information behavior" (p. 12). The *ARIST* review by Dervin and Nilan in 1986 cited several of the complaints mentioned above, characterizing them as a "concern for conceptual impoverishment" that had impeded the development of definitions and theories. And yet they still concluded that "a quantum and revolutionary conceptual leap in this area has been made since 1978" (p. 24).

Eight years later, a 50-year perspective by Wilson (1994) agreed with Dervin and Nilan about those "leaps" forward. Wilson believed that there *had* been discernible progress accomplished in five decades of research on information needs and uses, although "much time has been wasted." In particular, Wilson concluded that "a firmer theoretical base now exists than was the case fifty (or even twenty) years ago" (p. 43).

What is there about this topic of study that leads to both pessimism and optimism? Has any other literature generated so many complaints of low quality, or exhibited so many signs of being overstudied? Katzer et al. (1998) suggest that several social science and professional literatures also contain more chaff than wheat. Katzer et al. single out research on education for particular criticism, citing one finding that about half of it should not have been published at all. So investigations of information behaviors are at least not alone in exhibiting an uneven quality. And on the positive side of the ledger, it is evident that information behavior research is no longer lacking in theory or depth of description — two frequent criticisms that have been lodged against it.

13.2.2. Other Considerations

At this point the reader might well ask, are we making progress toward better understanding of information behaviors? Or is "progress" in research simply an illusion? The received view among many information-seeking researchers has been that more meaningful research — if not actual progress — can be attained through shifts in theoretical and methodological orientation (toward the more phenomenological, contextual, and hermeneutic) and by a more qualitative emphasis (which typically involves studying fewer people but in greater depth). It is as though repeated criticisms of quantitative survey methodologies during the 1960s and 1970s lead inevitably to the embrace of the phenomenological and hermeneutic in the 1990s. Despite that trend, many investigations (particularly in the very active area of health information) still use the same kinds of questionnaires, interviews, and first-hand observations that have been used for decades.

Diversity of method is undoubtedly a good thing. It leads to more varied perspectives on the same phenomena. As I emphasize in Chapters 11 and 12, there is certainly a great deal of diversity in the kind of people and behaviors that are being studied, and in the methods that are being used to study them. However, that also means that there is more *fragmentation* than ever before among the thousands of diverse examples of human information seeking.

After decades of "de-contextualized" studies that tried to make generalizations about large groups (e.g., "engineers"), are we now facing the other extreme: tinier and tinier samples of smaller and smaller groups? In information-seeking studies, it is not unusual to encounter samples of fewer than 10, or even of a single individual. Even the anthropological studies that are so often emulated these days often typically tried to capture the cultural world of some hundreds or thousands of individuals through interaction with at least a few dozen members. The populations that are studied are sometimes rather small in themselves ("social science faculty studying the Kurds," or "collectors of rubber ducks"), although we hope that the basic processes uncovered in such investigations might be generalizable. The trend toward studies of smaller and smaller groups recalls Fischer's (1970) "prodigious fallacy": the idea that uniqueness makes for significance that an unusual event is, by definition, important. The objects of information-seeking research have become, likewise, increasingly "unusual."

And what of the *utility* of information behavior studies? The origins of today's investigations lie in earlier "information needs and uses" research aimed at improving the performance of an institution's operations. Those studies were conducted by librarians to know what books to buy; by journalism instructors to understand which news had the most impact; and by social workers to learn how to better serve their clients. Yet to read some of today's information-seeking research it would seem that we have now reached the point where the scholarliness of the studies correlates with their degree of *uselessness* for institutional purposes. Certainly, we could say that information behavior research has become more "scholarly," but perhaps less applicable as well. Vakkari (2008), Järvelin and Ingwersen (2004), and others have advised that information-seeking research would be more useful and rigorous if it were to focus on discrete tasks and tools, rather than trying to capture the full range of information behavior by a person or group; this advice is worth heeding.

It is also hard to resist the conclusion that the information behavior literature is somewhat faddish. Certain themes and sources are cited by one study that are picked up in later studies, but without necessarily leading either to an advancement of theory or to an accumulation of comparable findings. As Pettigrew and McKechnie (2001) and Rosenbaum (2010) have noted, theories are sometimes cited with little explanation. And the results are rarely cumulative: it is often difficult to summarize a genre of studies, or even a single study, when its main result is merely a "thick description" of what the investigator observed rather than a clearly stated conclusion or theme. Types of occupations, roles, and other variables are sometimes studied in ways that make the various results difficult to relate to one another.

Finally, there is the issue of widening scope. The widespread influence of the Internet and World Wide Web on human behavior has spawned a vast number of investigations in itself. The appearance of a plethora of "Web searching" studies has unfortunately tended to blur the identity of the "traditional" information behavior literature. In decades past, investigations that focused on searching electronic resources were not typically called "information seeking" studies; they were, rather, a subtopic within other research areas: information retrieval, online searching, system evaluation, or human–computer interaction. Now, searching the Web is increasingly characterized as "information seeking." Has information behavior, then, subsumed all of what used to be called "online searching"? It would appear so (e.g., see the definitions provided by Wilson, 2000).

There is a problem with this broadening of scope: As "information behavior" takes in more territory, it weakens its distinctiveness as a concept. In a world in which everything is described as "short," height ceases to be a useful construct. Is there *any* topic in information studies that has nothing to do with "information behavior"? This question recalls Fairthorne's (1969, p. 26) comments of nearly four decades past, regarding the scope of "information science":

> [There is] a dangerous tendency to bring in every and any science or technique or phenomenon under the 'information' heading. Certainly hitherto distinct activities and interests should be unified, if indeed

> they have common principles. However, one does not create common
> principles by giving different things the same name.

If information behavior includes all aspects of searching, seeking and use, then it is even more important for authors to exercise precision in their titles and abstracts. Too many evaluations of searching skills or system features are now labeled "information seeking" or "information behavior"; these terms have simply become too popular to be descriptive. As Fairthorne says, we need to be looking for the underlying principles, and highlighting those in our research projects and titles.

A possibly related issue, discussed in Chapter 7, has to do with "theoretical sprawl." That chapter listed 23 groups of theories (more than 30 individual theories) that have been popular in information behavior research. Perhaps two-thirds of them continue to be cited with some regularity in the last few years. For an area of inquiry with just a few hundred active researchers, this is quite a bit of theoretical diversity. Undoubtedly one of the reasons for this wide choice of theory has to do with the diversity of the investigators themselves, with a mixture of backgrounds in the humanities, social sciences, and sciences. We tend to cite that literature we first encountered, early in our schooling. Colleagues educated in humanistic traditions may lack common ground with those whose background lies in the social sciences.

Theories form communities of discourse, around which individual investigations are discussed and compared. When we employ perhaps two dozen different sets of philosophical assumptions and methods, it is difficult to meaningfully critique, and expand on, each others' studies. This problem is confounded when researchers use theory lightly, as may be the case in about half of our research studies (Rosenbaum, 2010). This "shallow" use of theory may be why, as an unidentified commentator noted in the fascinating "behaviour/practice debate" recorded in the journal *Information Research* (Wilson & Savolainen, 2009), "... much of the research conducted within the two [camps of theories] doesn't differ in any significant way (ontologically, epistemologically or methodologically)." One would think that theory would make a wide difference in the kinds of evidence examined, its analysis, and interpretation; however, many information behavior research reports look surprisingly similar in these respects, even while citing quite different theories and assumptions.

This is not to argue that we must all use the same theory, merely to point out that the literature would be more coherent if it were an active debate over the utility of six theories, instead of two or three dozen, and if the reports of research conducted under various theories reached conclusions that were distinct from one another. Let's consider how a more restricted use of theory might evolve.

As mentioned in Chapter 7, certain theories have become more popular over the most recent decade, while others have declined in popularity. The aforementioned debate about characterizing our research as a study of "practices" rather than "behavior" might indicate a possible convergence in some senses, rather than a divergence. For one thing, it seems that the debating parties agree on common concepts and literature, and perhaps even methods. They disagree on what "umbrella term" should be used, and on which specific theorists should be followed most closely.

Should the practice umbrella continue to attract more researchers (as seems likely), it is possible to imagine a long-term split in the field, with the minority group (mostly outside of the United States) pursuing a coherent agenda centered on just two or three theories, originating mainly in the work of perhaps five theorists (e.g., Bourdieu, de Certeau, Lave, Wenger, and Giddens — all of whom are concerned with "practices" in some sense). The majority of behavior researchers would continue to be conduct their research as before, based on the work of dozens of different theories and theorists. This would not necessarily be a bad outcome, as the practice scholars at least would be producing a more comprehensive body of work. The possibility that a majority of current behavior researchers would become genuine followers of practice theories seems unlikely, for reasons outlined by Wilson and Savolainen (2009). It is also the case that many competing theories will dominate in the growing corpus of work on health-related information seeking (see my comments below).

This may be useless speculation, as it is more likely that patterns of influence and citation will continue more or less as they are. Yet, it is worth reflecting on the increased coherence (and with it, rigor) that a smaller set of theories might bring to information behavior research. We might develop a more meaningful dialogue about our research results and their import for each theory. We might actually influence scholars in other disciplines from which those theories originated. We might develop a better explanation for our research agenda.

13.3. Conclusions and Trends

Despite the concerns of the past, information behavior research has grown in many respects. The overuse of survey research and the lack of theory that so concerned critics in the 1960s and 1970s have been addressed. More research on information behavior is being conducted than ever before, and the research community is increasingly international. Fifty years ago the majority of information-seeking research was conducted in the United Kingdom and North America. Now the research community has become global, with leading investigators found in other parts of Europe (especially the Nordic countries), along with Australia, Asia, and Africa. The field has many talented scholars, some of them highly influential and productive even though in relatively early stages of their careers. This development is partly due to the success of the Information Seeking in Context (ISIC) conferences, the ninth of which will take place in Japan in September 2012; these meetings have provided a fertile ground for the exchange of ideas and findings about information behavior.

That the journal *Information Research* has made relevant research freely available in electronic form has made information behavior scholarship highly accessible to the world. Various other journals (e.g., *JASIS&T*, *Library & Information Science Research*, *Library Quarterly*, and the *Journal of Documentation*) have published quite a bit of information behavior research. And several collections have appeared in book form that provide comprehensive frameworks for information behavior researchers. Among these are *Theories of Information Behavior* (Fisher, Erdelez, & McKechnie, 2005), *New Directions in Human Information Behavior* (Spink & Cole, 2006), *Information and Emotion* (Nahl & Bilal, 2007), *Everyday Information Practices* (Savolainen, 2008a), *Critical Theory for Library and Information Science* (Leckie et al., 2010), and the first volume of *New Directions in Information Behavior* (Spink & Heinström, 2011).

Information behavior research has matured, bringing the seeker into focus, through more attention to the search process and to the thoughts and emotions of the seeker. Now the dynamic, personal, and context-laden nature of information behavior seems to be taken as a given by all investigators. This paradigmatic shift has resulted in greater use of theory, as well as more diversity in methods. While some resulting research has not been rigorous, the rest has added a new dimension to what was once merely a collection of shallow surveys of large, heterogeneous populations like "engineers."

The shift in conceptualization has been major, although slow to emerge, starting nearly 40 years ago, as Brenda Dervin questioned the static ways in which "needs and uses" had been characterized. Dervin's 1972 book chapter with Bradley Greenberg raised important questions about the information-seeking habits of the urban poor. Four years later, Dervin published an article that clearly stated her rethinking of the then-current tendency to characterize use of informal sources of information as "least effort" and "irrational" behavior. Her 1976 *Journal of Broadcasting* article described a case of "disciplinary schizophrenia" among researchers studying information needs and uses. According to Dervin,

> our research data and our practitioner experiences say "relativism" loud and clear. Meanings are in people. People construct their own reality. No knowledge is absolute. Messages sent do not equal those received. The same person is different across time and space. On the

other hand, we commit ourselves to research and action efforts which seek deterministic answers. We continue to look for normative, nonvariant rules. We seek enduring personality variables that persist across time and space. (1976a, p. 324)

Dervin's counter assumptions took some time to have an effect — Wilson (1994) believes that it took at least a decade. For his part, Wilson (1981) and Wilson and Streatfield (1977) made similar arguments during the same time frame, as did a few of the review authors mentioned earlier. Their concerns are still ignored in investigations that try to generalize about what kind of people use what kinds of information. But the movement to pay more attention to context and meaning has had a lasting effect; many more investigators are trying to study the aspects of time, space, and situation that make a difference in the ways that people create, encounter, perceive, ignore, seek, and use information.

13.3.1. *Eight Lessons of Information Behavior Research*

I will conclude this book by reinterpreting Dervin's 10 myths in light of what has happened since they were introduced. In the list below I have merged several of Dervin's related assumptions together into six main points, and restated them in terms of the lessons I think we can take away from them. I have also added two conclusions of my own, in consideration of what has been said in this book.

1. *Formal sources and rationalized searches reflect only one side of human information behavior.* Empirical research tells us that many people use formal sources rarely, relying instead on informal sources such as friends and family, or knowledgeable colleagues at work, along with what they learn from mass media and other elements of their environment. Some investigators complain that *least effort seeking* is too common. Yet there are inherent efficiencies in least effort behavior — for instance, searching takes no longer than is necessary to produce, on average, a satisfactory result. Thus, it is wrong to interpret least effort information seeking as "irrational." Such behavior can be both satisfying and successful.
2. *More information is not always better.* We have seen that a major preoccupation of humans is filtering, interpreting, and understanding the overload of information with which they are faced. There is justification for consciously ignoring or filtering relevant information in situations in which there is not enough time or energy to consider all of it. Ignoring or avoiding information is at times a reasonable strategy for living

and working, especially when it promotes psychological coping. The ever-evolving number of channels and sources bombarding us with information only makes this point more obvious with the passage of time.

3. *Context is central to the transfer of information.* Information-seeking research demonstrates that people strive toward a holistic view of their world. Sometimes they do not connect external information to their internal reality because of anxiety, or because they do not see the relevance of it. Partly for this reason, humans are prone to ignoring isolated bits of information — sometimes at great cost to their goals and lives. The individual's definition of the situation will shape his or her needs as much as does the "real" situation itself. Much of what we bring to bear on information in creating meaning from it is not only "outside" of the package (as has been frequently pointed out) but also outside of the information itself: our accumulated personal experiences and secondhand experiences, including our understanding of the world and of language.

4. *Sometimes information — particularly generalized packages of information — doesn't help.* "Information" on its own does not satisfy many human needs. Humans want to "understand," but they more often need information to pursue more basic needs such as food, shelter, and clothing. It is not clear that there is a basic "need for information," although some scholars believe this to be true. Often people facing problems are looking for a customized solution, rather than the standardized response of an information system or agency. Even when individuals really do need information, the "chunks" of it encompassed by books, articles, and Websites may not provide the instructions or answers that they need.

5. *Sometimes it is not possible to make information available or accessible.* Institutions and their formal information systems often are not able to keep up with the unique and unpredictable demands they face. Formal systems will never be able to satisfy most information needs. Yet we often act as if we expect them to do so. The continuing discussion of the importance of the "digital divide" (e.g., Hilbert, 2011) illustrates how information systems are thought to address basic human needs.

6. *Information seeking is a dynamic process.* Information needs may quickly arise and either be satisfied or fade away. The nature of one's "question" may change at various points in a search. Satisfying one information need may simply give rise to yet another question or problem. But the difficulty of studying such a shifting scenario leads to a tendency to look at an information-seeking episode as something rather simple, linear, and complete. The usual script assumes that a need arises, a person conducts a

search of a single source in a particular channel, and finds an answer — end of search! But human information seeking simply is not so simple. It is neither straightforward nor typically complete; it is more like a series of interruptions, punctuated by other interruptions. In keeping with this realization, more recent models of information seeking (e.g., ASK) have emphasized the dynamic, iterative nature of needs and searches.

7. *Information seeking is not always about a "problem" or "problematic situation."* Some information-related behavior is creative in its origins — it is not driven by the need to provide a response to a situation. Traditional information-seeking research, even the more recent versions of it, implicitly assumes that people react to a problem state. In most cases, this is true enough: people often *do* seek information to solve problems or even to find explicit answers to specific questions. However, the oft-stated inadequacies of information-seeking research (e.g., its inability to explain why people act as they do) indicate that information seeking is much more than solving problems, finding facts, or making decisions. Sometimes it is a quest for entertainment or distraction; sometimes it is an act of serendipity.

8. *Information behavior is not always about "sense-making" either.* Despite the recent emphasis on sense-making rather than "usage," the study of information seeking is still largely the study of channels and *sources.* Perhaps in part this is due to the popularity of the World Wide Web, the latest "channel" to be widely studied. It has encouraged both investigation and speculation on the inner desires of the public for information, entertainment, and transactions. It is certainly true that the steady stream of health-related research still emphasizes formal information; "making sense of one's situation" can only be of limited usefulness or comfort when faced with a potentially fatal illness, for example.

Over the last two decades many information behavior researchers have embraced the sense-making paradigm, which has done the invaluable service of revitalizing research on information seeking. But life is not entirely about uncertainty, gaps, or discontinuities. And questions raised about the assumptions of sense-making (e.g., Davenport, 2010; Heap, 1975) cannot be ignored. The sense-making approach does not capture all aspects of information behavior, and indeed tends to limit what can be addressed using its unique methodology. Other theories and methods offer valid and (potentially more reliable) ways of studying the topic. This may be why there has been a slow decline in the number of sense-making studies in recent years.

13.3.2.   Trends and Final Thoughts

It is a dangerous thing to try to predict the future. For one thing, larger or unseen trends may swamp the particular phenomena upon which one is focusing — consider, for example, the potential effects of global warming on almost any human endeavor. As I write this final chapter most of the developed economies in the world are struggling with fundamental economic and structural issues that seem to resist any short-term solution. In the United States, many of the major state-supported universities now receive only 10% or 20% of their budget from the states that control them, leading those institutions ever deeper into large, externally funded research, along with the distraction of having to raise additional money in other ways. It is not hard to imagine some of the likely consequences: downsizing or elimination of some departments, an insistence that all research be externally funded (or useful in other ways, such as its impact on a profession or local community), an increase in faculty teaching loads, and gradual privatization of some universities. All of these overarching trends will have some effect on the future of academic research, including that in information behavior.

I have some observations of my own, but first I will turn to a recent article by Wilson (2010b) who was brave enough to make predictions based on his long career in information behavior research. Among the trends that Wilson identifies are technological developments (particularly as regards social media) will continue to drive research; the digital divide will continue to persist within nations and between them, and that this will attract policy-related research efforts that might involve information behavior researchers; negative effects of the Internet on children, and its positive use in education, also means opportunities for applied and policy research; and that

> the present focus on small-scale studies ... will decline as investigators discover that there is little new that can be said, and that there will be a growth in policy-related large-scale projects ... This may result in a decline in academic research in the field ...

It is hard to argue with most of these predictions. For example, it seems obvious that technological change affects the behaviors and habits of people, and that in turn affects their seeking and use of information. I will simply comment on Wilson's final point, and add a prediction of my own: There will be an increase in health-related information behavior research. The rise in the importance of health as an area of application goes hand-in-hand with advances in medical research, efforts to make health care more efficient, and an aging population, as well as a relative shortage of health professionals available to focus on issues of information and communication. The increased attention to health can already be seen in recent projects in some Canadian and U.S. information studies departments, as well as those in Finland, the United Kingdom, and Australia, among other nations.

Whichever trends prove to be true, it can be seen that information behavior research has continued to develop along multiple lines, and to maintain its popularity. The field still retains themes, theories, and methodologies from half a century past, and some of these older approaches remain useful. At the same time, it has embraced new perspectives, theories, and methods that would have been considered highly unusual in 1970. The vigor it has shown over the last three decades — with many productive researchers still in the early stages of their careers — bodes well for the future.

Recommended for Further Reading

Davenport, E. (2010). Confessional methods and everyday life information seeking. In B. Cronin (Ed.), *Annual review of information science and technology* (Vol. 44, pp. 533–562). Medford, NJ: Information Today.

Davenport's critique of certain methods often used in information behavior research cannot be ignored. Her examples include the use of focus groups, the critical incident technique, and the micro-moment time-line interview method employed in sense-making research. Her analysis discusses how some researchers have violated the original assumptions and reliability safeguards of these methods.

Rosenbaum, H. (2010). Anthony Giddens' influence on library and information science. In G. J. Leckie, L. M. Given, & J. E. Buschman (Eds.), *Critical theory for library and information science* (pp. 119–130). Santa Barbara, CA: Libraries Unlimited.

A synopsis of the work of perhaps the most influential living social theorist; this chapter also contains an analysis of how superficially some studies have treated theory. While not focused on information behavior, several of the examples studied are from that research tradition. The volume from which the chapter comes also contains good explanations of the work of several other theorists influential in information behavior research, including Bourdieu, de Certeau, Foucault, and Lave.

Savolainen, R. (2007). Information behavior and information practice: Reviewing the 'umbrella concepts' of information-seeking studies. *Library Quarterly, 77*, 109–132.

A thoughtful analysis of the epistemological divide between two labels for research on human seeking and use of information.

Wilson, T. D. (2010). Fifty years of information behavior research. *Bulletin of the American Society for Information Science and Technology, 36*(3). Retrieved from http://www.asis.org/Bulletin/Feb-10/FebMar10_Wilson.html
While one could quibble with some of the trends Tom Wilson identifies, his article is a fascinating, first-person account of the changes in the field over five decades. Among the trends he discusses are the rise of social media, the persistence of digital divides within and among nations, and the growth of policy and applied research at the expense of small-scale and unfunded studies.

Appendix A: Glossary

This glossary features key terms from the text. In each case the short definition refers to the chapter in which the word (or phrase) is discussed, and often a citation to one or more of the best commentaries on the term.

Action theory: A research tradition with origins in the psychological work of Leont'ev (1978) and Vygotsky (1978). The theory is concerned with both internal reasoning and external actions, which work together in the formation of human consciousness. This approach has been more frequently used to study computer-related tasks than information behavior *per se* (see Chapter 7; Wilson, 2008b).

ASK (Anomalous State of Knowledge): A recognized gap or uncertainty (i.e., an anomaly) in an individual's state of knowledge regarding a situation or topic. Faced with an ASK, the individual may attempt to address their uncertainty by requesting or consulting information; in that case, the person will then judge whether the anomaly has been resolved; if it is not resolved, another ASK may be generated, or the motivation to address it may be exhausted (see Chapter 5; Belkin, 2005).

Avoidance (of Information): The tendency for humans to avoid exposure to information that conflicts with their prior knowledge, beliefs and attitudes, and/or which causes them anxiety (see "Blunting"; see also Chapter 5; Sairanen & Savolainen, 2010).

Blunting: A hypothesized style of processing information — both cognitively and emotionally. "Blunting" refers to a style in which a person responds to unpleasant realities or threatening information by blocking it from their attention, perhaps by distracting themselves with other stimuli. Blunters tend not to seek information that might be disturbing. Blunting tendencies are measured with a scale, called either the Monitoring-Blunting Style Scale, or the Miller Behavioral Style Scale (see "Avoidance," "Coping," and "Monitoring"; see also Baker, 2005; Case et al., 2005; Miller, 1987).

Browsing: The common behavior of scanning the environment, prompted by interest or expectation, but without a clearly defined goal or plan. Definitions and treatments of browsing may vary depending upon the context in which it occurs, for example, browsing is typically characterized in terms of a purposive interaction with some kind of source or channel of information, for example, browsing goods in a department store, books in a library, or electronic text on a computer screen (see Chapter 5; Bates, 2007; Chang & Rice, 1993).

Channel: A medium utilized to convey information; the means by which a message travels from a source to a receiver. In information-seeking research, channels have been operationalized in a variety of overlapping ways, including as print, human (e.g., an individual), or electronic. Channel is closely related (and sometimes conflated with) the concept of a source (see "Source" in this Glossary); however, many different sources can inhabit one type of channel. If one reads about something, the channel is print media while the source is the particular author of the document. Likewise, when someone tells us something (whether through writing, speaking or bodily movement), the channel is interpersonal while the source is the particular person who originated the message (see Chapter 3; Berlo, 1960).

Constructivist: A research tradition having its roots in educational psychology (e.g., Dewey, 1933; Kelly, 1963; Leont'ev, 1978; Vygotsky, 1978). This mix of theories and methodologies emphasizes the ways in which individuals construct an understanding of their world. This approach is related to sense making and to action theory. Within information behavior research, constructivism has been especially influential in the works of Brenda Dervin and Carol Kuhlthau (see Chapter 7; Bates, 2005a; Dervin, 2005; Talja, Tuominen, & Savolainen, 2005; Wilson, 2008b).

Constructionism: A metatheory for understanding knowledge formation and its social and power relationships. Practitioners of constructionism analyze human discourse (e.g., conversations and writings) to show how meanings and self-concepts are formed (see Chapter 7; Bates, 2005a; Savolainen, 2007a; Talja et al., 2005).

Context: "A spatial and temporal background which affects all thinking" (Dewey, 1960, p. 90). Among the many factors that could be contextual are individuals, their attributes and behaviors; the characteristics, rules and structure of an organization; or the attributes, norms and beliefs of a given culture. What is identified as a contextual factor depends on what is being studied (see Chapter 7; Cool, 2001; Courtright, 2007; Dervin, 1997; Johnson, 2003).

Coping: A response to psychological stress that may involve a variety of cognitive and physical behaviors intended to avoid or alleviate distress (see Chapter 5; Case et al., 2005; Savolainen, 2007b; Tuominen, 2004).

Critical incident technique: A type of question used in an interview in which the interviewee is asked to describe an incident that sticks out as particularly important in some way — perhaps because it signaled a change in the environment, brought their attention to bear on a problem, or caused them to see a situation in a new light (see Chapter 9; Davenport, 2010; Urquhart et al., 2003).

Curiosity: According to Webster's New World Dictionary, curiosity is a word that is used to indicate a general "desire to know," sometimes about "things that do not necessarily concern one." When curiosity is habitual in a person, they are said to be inquisitive (see Chapter 5; Bates, 2007; Bowler, 2010).

Data: In Latin, "the givens," data are typically thought of by information behavior researchers as a "raw" form of information — numbers or words or observations or measurements or facts — before being "digested" via human cognition or use. In this way they are often thought of as the "base" of a hierarchy that includes information in the middle, then knowledge on top (although many disagree with this view, see Chapter 3; Bates, 2005b; Frické, 2009).

Demand: A request for information, whether given to a person or information system. A term used to distinguish between an action taken in response to an information need, and the concept of "information need" itself (see Chapter 4; Beautyman & Shenton, 2009; Cole, 2012).

Decision-making: Evaluating and choosing among alternative actions to take in response to a perceived problem. The final stages that follow problem-solving activities (see Chapter 5; Berryman, 2008; March, 1994).

Diffusion (of Innovation): Over time, the growth in knowledge or acceptance of an idea, object or practice among members of a social system. Also known as "adoption of innovations." Diffusion operates within the context of a social structure and through channels of communication (see Chapter 3; Lajoie-Paquette, 2005; Rogers, 2003).

Domain analysis: The analysis of the formation of knowledge and its categories within academic disciplines or other discourse communities. Although the idea of studying domains has earlier versions (e.g., Spradley, 1980), within information behavior research it is most identified with Birger Hjørland (2002a) (Hjørland & Albrechtsen; 1995). Domain analysis can also be applied to non-academic communities such as hobbyists (see Hartel, 2003; Talja, 2005).

Encountering (of Information): The accidental or serendipitous exposure to information that turns out of be relevant to a preexisting information need, or which sparks curiosity about an emerging topic of interest (see Chapter 5; Awamura, 2006; Erdelez, 2005).

Entertainment: Any activity designed to delight (Zillman & Bryant, 1986). Entertainment is little discussed in the context of information seeking, which tends toward a utilitarian view of any kind of search, in keeping with its original concerns with facts and non-fiction documents. However, recognizing that people often seek a mix of satisfactions and outcomes helps to explain some of the non-optimal search strategies and outcomes that have been observed, even among scientists and scholars. The notion of entertainment seeking is addressed in "uses and gratifications" research and in various theories of entertainment, enjoyment and persuasion (see Chapters 5 and 7; Vorderer, Klimmt, & Ritterfeld, 2004; Miron & Bryant, 2002).

Entropy: A measure of the degree of disorganization in a system — reflecting a tendency for any state of affairs to lose order and become more random. A concept from physics employed by Claude Shannon to define his measure of information (see Chapter 3; Morowitz, 1991; Ritchie, 1991).

Epistemology: Epistemology is a branch of philosophy concerned with the nature, sources, and limits of knowledge (see Hjørland, 2002b, 2005b).

Everyday Life Information Seeking (ELIS): Reijo Savolainen's label for the study of information-seeking behavior outside formal contexts. ELIS is based on Bourdieu's concept of "habitus" (one's habits and "way of life") and Savolainen's notion of "mastery of life." ELIS is a departure from the majority of information behavior research that tends to focus on work tasks and occupations (or roles, such as "student"); instead ELIS focuses on ordinary people as they structure their time, consume goods and services, and practice their hobbies or sports (see Chapter 12; Savolainen, 1995, 2008a).

Flow: A concept popularized by the psychologist Mihalyi Csikszentmihalyi, "flow" is a pleasant state of mind in which the present experience is so totally involving that the passage of time is not noticed. Not to be confused with "two-step flow" (see Csikszentmihalyi, 1990; Heinström, 2010; Naumer, 2005).

Focus group: Properly a "focused group interview," this is a technique whereby a small group (typically 6–12 persons) is interviewed together. Because members of the group hear each other's responses to the questions (or other stimuli, such as an advertisement), synergies may result that elicit more information and emotional responses than would normally take place in an interview with just one respondent. The practice was pioneered by the sociologist Robert Merton (Merton et al., 1956) and subsequently became popular in marketing research and later in information behavior studies (see Chapter 9; Davenport, 2010; Lunt & Livingstone, 1996).

Gap (or Information Gap): At the individual level, an encounter with a discrepancy or lack of "sense" in a person's environment. As defined by Dervin (1983b, p. 156), a gap is a state that arises within a person that might be filled by "information" or by some other kind of "help" or "bridge." On the societal level of analysis, gaps may be differential across human groups. That is, when one human group (whether defined by income, education, location, or other variable) is systematically deficient in what they know, we say that a "knowledge gap" exists (see Chapter 5; Chatman & Pendleton, 1995; Dervin, 1983b, 1992; Niederdeppe, 2008).

Gatekeeper: A person who controls, influences and/or shapes the flow of information over a channel or within a group. A gatekeeper may or may not be an "opinion leader" (see Chapter 12; Barzilai-Nahon, 2005; Shoemaker, 1991).

Hypothesis: A hypothesis is a conjecture to be researched. For example, an experiment may confirm or disconfirm a hypothesis (see Chapter 9).

Ideographic: One of two fundamental approaches to conducting research. An ideographic orientation to research is concerned with unique circumstances, facts and processes. In contrast, a nomothetic orientation aims to discover general laws underlying a phenomenon. The natural sciences have a nomothetic orientation, while the humanities tend to take an ideographic approach to knowledge (see Bates, 2005a).

Information ground: According to Pettigrew (1999, p. 811), this is an "environment temporarily created by the behavior of people who have come together to perform a task, but from which emerges a social atmosphere that fosters the spontaneous and serendipitous sharing of information." Thus, a medical clinic, bar or Laundromat might create an opportunity for encountering of information (see Fisher, 2005).

Information literacy: According to Julien (2001, p. 1054), "the ability to make efficient and effective use of information sources (see also Julien & Given, 2003; Lowe & Eisenberg, 2005; Thompson, 2007).

Information need: A hypothesized state brought about when an individual realizes that they are not comfortable with their current state of knowledge. According to Taylor (1968), an information need may go through the following four stages on the way to being articulated: visceral, unconscious, formalized, and compromised (see Chapter 4; Cole, 2012; Lundh, 2010).

Information overload: A state in which too much information leads to a generalized state of anxiety and/or confusion, or an inability to make a decision regarding a specific problem (see Chapter 5; Allen & Wilson, 2003; Bawden & Robinson, 2009; Eppler & Mengis, 2004).

Information poverty: A state thought to exist in a person, or among members of a demographic group, when they are not only devoid of useful information but tend to lack the necessary skills to information themselves (see Chapter 5; Haider & Bawden, 2007; Hersberger, 2005).

Information quality: The perceived attributes of information that make it of value to a potential user in a specific context. Some components of quality include relevance, timeliness, accuracy, specificity, comprehensiveness, and authoritativeness (see Chapter 3; Paisley, 1980; Dervin, 1989).

Information retrieval (IR): According to Wikipedia, IR is "the art and science of searching for information in documents, searching for documents themselves, searching for metadata which describe documents, or searching within databases ... ." IR systems respond to formal queries with a "best match" of documents most likely to be relevant to the query. Most of the IR literature has been defined as out of scope in this volume, with certain exceptions — for example, commentaries on the nature of "relevance" (see Ingwersen & Järvelin, 2005; Marchionini, 2008).

Information seeking: Information seeking is behavior that occurs when an individual senses a problematic situation or information gap, in which his or her internal knowledge and beliefs, and model of the environment, fail to suggest a path toward satisfaction of his or her goals. "Information seeking" has become a catchall phrase encompassing behaviors of interest to a variety of researchers and practitioners: librarians, communication theorists, cognitive psychologists, health care professionals, information scientists, and marketing specialists, to name a few (see Chapter 5; Savolainen, 2008a; Wilson, 2008a).

Intentionality (of information): The assumption that information must involve an intention to communicate something to another entity. Under this assumption, signs or data "out there" in the environment are not considered to be information, rather information is created by the organism that perceives the signs or data (see Chapter 3; Bowers & Bradac, 1982).

Knowledge: According to Webster's New World Dictionary, the term can indicate one of four related notions "the act, fact or state of knowing"; "acquaintance with facts; range of information, awareness, or under-standing"; "all that has been perceived or grasped by the mind; learning; enlightenment"; or "the body of facts accumulated by mankind." Usage in studies of information seeking tends toward the first three of these definitions, since it is usually individuals who are being studied, rather than all humans throughout history. A distinction is often made between internal knowledge of and external information about a topic, even though at times these could be the same (see Chapter 3; Frické, 2009).

Knowledge domain: A body of knowledge (e.g., medicine) composed of an array of representations, such as text documents, audiovisual recordings, and human memory (see Chapter 8; Hjørland, 2002a).

Meta-analysis: A procedure for synthesizing and interpreting the findings of several studies at once. Most commonly meta-analysis is applied to multiple experiments of surveys that used the same, or similar, measures (see Chapter 9; Ankem, 2005; Haug, 1997; Hunt, 1997).

Metatheory: Theory about theory, or in other words, the assumptions we make about a phenomenon and the proper way to study it (see Bates, 2005a; Dervin, 1999, 2005).

Methods (of research): A systematic way of studying something, typically in a series of prescribed steps. The procedures and techniques used by researchers to provide knowledge of the phenomena being investigated in a given discipline (see Chapter 8).

Methodology: The study of methods of investigation, including the branch of philosophy that considers the principles of inquiry (see Chapter 8).

Model: A simplified version of reality, often reflecting a theory about how some part of the world operates. Models are typically expressed as diagrams depicting variables and their connections; causal models use arrows to depict the direction of time and influence among the variables. Theories and models are necessary because our bounded rationality does not permit us to take into account all possible variables (see Chapter 7; Bates, 2005a; Wilson, 1999, 2005).

Monitoring: A hypothesized style of processing information — both cognitively and emotionally. "Monitoring" refers to the tendency of a person to actively scan the environment for information relevant to their concerns, even at the risk of provoking anxiety; this kind of information seeking may, in fact, be motivated by worry about something, such as a potentially threatening medical condition. Monitoring tendencies are measured with a scale, called either the Monitoring-Blunting Style Scale, or the Miller Behavioral Style Scale (MBSS) (see "Avoidance." See also Baker, 2005; Case, et al., 2005; Miller, 1987).

Motivation: A mental and/or emotional state that causes a person to act. An unobservable variable thought to account for individual differences in thought to account for individual differences in information seeking (see Chapter 5; Pysczynski, Greenberg, & Solomon, 1999).

Noise: The effect of entropy on a message, as when electromagnetic static interferes with a radio broadcast or telephone conversation (see Chapter 3; Shannon, 1949; Ritchie, 1991).

Nomothetic: One of two fundamental approaches to conducting research. A nomothetic orientation aims to discover general laws underlying a phenomenon. It stands in contrast to an ideographic orientation to research, which is concerned with unique circumstances, facts, and processes. The natural sciences have a nomothetic orientation, while the humanities tend to take an ideographic approach to knowledge (see Bates, 2005a).

Ontology: The philosophical investigation of existence, or being. Ontology is concerned with questions of what actually exists in the world, and with the meaning of "existence." Computer scientists sometimes use the term to refer to a specification of the concepts and relationships that can exist for an agent or community (see Hjørland, 2004).

Operational definition: The definition of the phenomena in terms of the operations (i.e., procedures and categories) by which observations will be categorized. For example, an instance of a behavior called "reading" might be defined and recognized as "staring at a printed page for a period of at least 5 seconds" (see Chapter 8).

Operationalization: The process of developing operational definitions, which in terms specify the way that measurements are to be taken (see Chapter 8).

Opinion leader: An individual who is able to influence other members of a social group in regards to their knowledge of, and attitudes toward, developments. According to Rogers (2003), opinion leaders are typically more informed than those who turn to them for information, and occupy a more central position in an interpersonal communication network.

Paradigm: A term popularized by historian of science Thomas Kuhn in his book, *The Structure of Scientific Revolutions* (1962). A paradigm is an overarching perspective or tradition that guides the perception and selection of research problems, and determines the choice of methods and perhaps even whether research is funded; it is the set of beliefs shared by a community of scholars or scientists (see Kuhn, 1962; Masterman, 1970).

Pertinence: A property that assigns an answer to an information need; that is, a searcher's judgment regarding the relationship between their need and the information received; sometimes called "situational relevance" to distinguish it from the technical use of the term "relevance" to refer to an evaluation of the match between a question (or search statement) and the usefulness of information (see Chapter 5; Belkin & Vickery, 1985; Froehlich, 1994).

Physicality (of information): The assumption that information must take on some physical form, that is, be resident in the printed characters of a book, the electrical signals of a human brain, the sound waves of human speech, or some other physical manifestation (see Chapter 3).

Principle of Least Effort (PLE): According to Zipf (1949), people naturally adopt a course of action that keeps their usage of resources in harmony, that is, managing their behavior in such a way that they will expend the least average amount of effort as they accomplish their tasks. This idea has been extended into the realms of information seeking and problem solving as a form of "satisficing" (see Chapters 1 and 7; Case, 2005; Jansen & Rieh, 2010).

Problem solving: Identifying issues worthy of attention, then setting goals and designing suitable courses of action. Some authors regard problem solving as encompassing decision- and choice-making as well, but the most notable students of problem solving regard it as a precursor to decision-making (see Chapter 5; March, 1994).

Relevance: In information search and retrieval, an evaluation of the match between a question (or search statement) and the answer (or text) retrieved by that statement (see Chapter 5; Froehlich, 1994).

Reliability: A quality of a measurement or method that leads us to trust it in repeated application. Specifically, the judgment that the measure would, under the exact same circumstances, lead to highly similar outcomes. For example, guessing the age of respondents based on their physical appearance is likely to be an unreliable measure, while measuring age by checking birth records is likely to be highly reliable.

Salience: An aspect of an event or object that a viewer perceives as relevant to his or her personal situation and needs. Salience has been characterized as an antecedent factor in motivating a person to seek information (see Chapter 5; Johnson, 1996, 1997).

Satisficing: The tendency for humans to seek a solution with an acceptable range of quality or completeness, rather than to strive to obtain an ideal or perfect outcome; that is, humans do not normally put forth enough effort to optimize their choices in life, but rather they tend to accept the first satisfactory solution to a problem that they encounter instead of continuing to examine alternatives (see Chapter 5; Hardy, 1982; Poole, 1985; Prabha, Connaway et al., 2007).

Selective exposure: The tendency for humans to seek information that is congruent with their prior knowledge, beliefs and attitudes. In addition, a high level of interest regarding a certain topic will tend to increase exposure — interested people are motivated to acquire more information (see Chapter 5; Hyman & Sheatsley, 1947).

Sense making: An approach to studying human use of information and information systems, using distinctive assumptions and methods. The focus is how a person makes sense of their situation and chooses a response when they are met by a discontinuity — a gap or barrier — in their life. Sense making assumes that discontinuities are a common and fundamental aspect of reality, that human communication is central to the process of bridging gaps, and that feelings are an important component of information seeking (see Chapters 5 and 7; Dervin, 1992; Dervin, Foreman-Wernet, & Lauterbach, 2003; Tidline, 2005; Weick, 1995).

Sensitizing concept: A general label for phenomena of interest that serves to draw our attention to it for investigation, yet lacks precise definition. Examples from Herbert Blumer (1986, p. 148) include concepts like culture, social structure, or personality — which "are not definitive concepts but are sensitizing in nature. They lack precise reference ... Instead, they rest on a general sense of what is relevant." We might consider "information" to be a such a sensitizing concept for information behavior research.

Serendipity: The action of, or an aptitude for, encountering relevant information by accident (see Chapter 5; Foster & Ford, 2003; Rioux, 2005).

Situation: A context bounded in time and space. According to Cool (2001, p. 7), one definition of situation is "a general term that refers to people, places and events. For example, a stressful situation is one in which these factors combine to make participants feel uncomfortable" (see Cool, 2001; Johnson, 2003).

Snowball sample: A type of sampling sometimes employed in interviewing in which a person interviewed is asked to provide the names of other people who fit the researcher's criteria for study, and whom might also agree to be interviewed (see Spradley, 1979, 1980).

Source: An individual or institution that originates the information (Rogers, 2003). In much information-seeking research, documents are commonly described as being "sources" but properly speaking they are "channels" (see "Channel" in this Glossary); the source is/are the individual(s) who authored the document. Thus, when we read a book, the channel is "print" but the source is the author of the book (see Chapter 3; Berlo, 1960).

Theory: A set of abstract statements that provide an explanation for an area of inquiry; a set of propositions that describe causal processes (see Chapter 7; Glaser & Strauss, 1967; Reynolds, 1971).

Two-step flow: A model of diffusion suggesting that much information from mass media reaches people via other people — particularly opinion leaders, who filter and pass on news to their acquaintances. This view, developed in the 1940s, was a departure from an earlier "hypodermic needle" or "bullet" theory stressing the direct effects of print and audiovisual messages on the knowledge and opinions of an audience (see Case, et al., 2005; Rogers, 2003).

Uncertainty: In human terms, the condition of not having certain knowledge or of not knowing beyond a doubt; a lack of understanding or a gap in meaning that can lead to information seeking (see Kuhlthau, 1993a, p. 111; Kuhlthau, 2004a). Uncertainty may be brought about when an individual realizes that they are not comfortable with their current level of certainty about an environmental object or topic (see Atkin, 1973). In engineering terms, Claude Shannon defined uncertainty in terms of a receiver's expectations regarding a finite and known set of symbols that were being transmitted to him or her (see Chapters 3 and 4).

Utility (of information): The assumption that information must be useful. The most common utility is thought to be uncertainty reduction, however information may have other utilities, such as stimulation or entertainment. The utility of information is presumed to be the main motivation for information seeking, that is, it is used to satisfy a need to know, or to help achieve a goal (see Chapter 3; Atkin, 1973; Johnson, 1997).

Uses and Gratifications: A broad research approach, originating in 1940s studies of radio listeners, that has enjoyed renewed popularity since the 1970s. According to Katz et al. (1974), this research tradition is concerned with psychological and social origins of needs, which generate expectations of available sources for entertainment and information. These expectations lead to differing patterns of usage of these sources (of which mass media are the most often studied), which result in need gratifications and perhaps other outcomes. A key tenet of the "uses and grats" approach is that the audience is active and goal directed, rather than the passive recipient of messages that cause "effects" among them (see Chapter 7; Katz et al., 1974, Palmgreen, 1984).

Validity: A quality of a measurement or method such that it accurately captures what we are trying to measure. For example, observing a person entering a school building is a relevant yet very weak (we might argue, invalid) indicator of the concept of "learning"; asking the person specific questions about content learned (perhaps both before an after a learning activity, such as reading a book or listening to a lecture), seems to be a better way of judging whether learning has taken place. Such "face validity" is a more common and superficial judgment, however there are more complex and technical aspects to judgments of validity. Valid measures resist counter explanations — for example, "Well that person merely entered the school building in order to pick up their child" (see Chapter 8).

Appendix B: Questions for Discussion and Application

Chapter 1
(Introduction)

1. How much information do you encounter in a day? Leaving aside the difficult issue of how to assess images (i.e., what you see around you or on television screens), let's just think about amounts simply in terms of *words*. If you could count up all the words that you hear or read in a typical day, about how many thousands would there be?

Assume that most half-hour television or radio broadcasts contain about 3000 words, that newspaper articles are about 1000 words long, that there are about 500 words on a typical book page, and that people speak (conversationally) at roughly 100 words per minute. Consider what you hear, see or read in the course of a typical work day, starting with any news you may read or listen to in the morning and continuing through to the last things you hear or read before falling asleep. Don't forget to consider the following: conversations you have with others, announcements or conversations that you overhear, signs and billboards that you pass along the way, and of course, conscious watching, listening, or reading of news and entertainment.

2. Have you ever read a research study that aimed to understand how people are affected by information? Relate what you remember from it. Did the study reach any conclusions? If so, did the conclusions make sense? Did the topic of the study itself seem important enough to be worthy of investigation? If not, what kind of topic *would* be worthy of a study?

3. Some people believe that information can never be "objective" — that is, the "truth" and meaning of the information is always open to interpretation. Among other implications, this stance suggests that any advice from "experts" is always open to doubt.

Consider the common (and difficult) case in which a medical doctor recommends a surgical procedure based on a diagnosis of cancer. If you were the patient, which of the following choice(s) seem(s) most comfortable to you: (1) Agree to the treatment without question. (2) Agree only after some thought and discussion with loved ones. (3) Agree only after much reading of medical literature on the topic. (4) Agree only if a second doctor renders the same opinion. (5) Agree only if you think there is a "fair" balance between the degree of risk and pain involved (on one hand), and the goodness of the possible outcome of the procedure (e.g., What are my chances of a permanent "cure"?). For each of these choices of action, how much weight is being given to the expert's opinion versus your own thoughts and feelings?

Chapter 2
(Scenarios)

1. Which of the scenarios described in this chapter seemed most familiar to you? Are they familiar because you have done the kind of seeking depicted, because you are interested in the topic of the search, because you identified with the character, or for another reason?
2. Invent your own scenario and describe it in 100–300 words. Base your story on a situation with which you are familiar enough to describe the kinds of results that might be found by a person actively seeking information. If are not sure where to begin, modify the following scenario according to your knowledge, interests and circumstances: You have just received news that a close friend or relative has been reported to be "missing" from a hiking trip in a remote location in Chile. What would you do to find out more? Who would you call or email and what would you ask? Would you search the Internet for a map and/or travel information? Would you contact an embassy? Would you make airline reservations to go to Chile? In what order would you proceed and what would you do in response to each "answer" you receive to your queries.
3. Do you vary your level of attention and selectiveness depending on the *context* in which you seek information? For example, does the setting, your purpose, and the type of people involved affect how you acquire information? Consider these three scenarios:
   a. You are in a large bookstore looking for several books to take on vacation with you.
   b. You are sitting at a computer in a public place while you search the Internet to find some information on a topic for a report you are writing.
   c. You are at a conference interviewing several people to find out their reactions to the meeting content, hotel services, choice of conference location, etc.

In each case, consider how easy (or hard) it is to obtain the result you are seeking; the nature of your motivation; how thorough you think you would need to be; the time or social pressure you may feel (e.g., are other persons waiting to look at what you are browsing?); and the specificity, reliability and believability of the information you are likely to encounter.

Chapter 3
(The Concept of Information)

1. Information can be a commodity but does not always "behave" in the same way as other commodities. For one thing, if I give (or sell) information to you, I still retain it myself rather than giving it up, as in the case of a normal commodity. Another difference is the way that giving away valuable information may actually increase its value. Two examples are: (1) Broadcast television programs provide their programs for "free" (actually, in exchange for audience attention to advertising); the more people who take advantage of this free programming, the more valuable it becomes as both a topic of conversation among audience members and as a source of revenue for broadcasters and advertisers. (2) Although musicians sometimes give away their music on the Internet, in some cases their revenues have increased as a larger audience is exposed to their music and is more willing to buy the albums from which the songs came — since they have had an opportunity to preview what they will be getting when they buy the album. And then there is always the income from touring.

   Can you think of other examples in which information differs from other potential commodities — and changes human behavior as a result? How about ways in which information is treated as *similar* to other commodities — for example, carrots, cars, clothing, or condos?
2. Advertisers are often willing to pay a lot to place their message on a billboard along a busy highway. But how much information can actually be conveyed in a glimpse that lasts only a few seconds? And how likely is it to result in the viewer purchasing or using the advertised product or concept? For each of the following signs, answer these three questions: (1) How much information — in terms of distinct concepts — would you say is actually conveyed by the sign? (2) How likely are people to take in the information — can it be easily (and perhaps, amusingly) absorbed and understood in a few seconds? (3) How likely are people to respond in the way the advertiser wants — how soon can they respond, and how costly will it be to do so?
3. The content of the highway billboards:
   a. "Radio WXYZ, 109.9 FM. It's all you need to have on." (Background: Picture of several naked men and women, taken from the back.)
   b. "Vista Del Basura Estates — if you lived here, you would already be home!" (Background: Outline of a palatial home.)
   c. "Wouldn't you like to see your grandchildren grow up? Quit smoking. You'll live to see that, and more." (Background: No picture, but a

second message below it, in smaller type: "The National Council of Health Maintenance Organizations urges you to stop smoking — for your children's sake, and yours.")

    d. "Drink Vishnu Cola." (Background: Image of a smiling young man, holding a bottle near his face.)

4. Is a picture *typically* "worth a thousand words"? Or is it closer to either 100 or 10,000 words? Imagine a few of the photographs you've taken in the last year; about how many words would it take to describe their content? If, instead of photographs, each had been one minute of video, how many more words would be needed to describe them?

5. The groundbreaking work of Claude Shannon at Bell Laboratories led to his so-called "Information Theory," sometimes summarized in a model showing a source that creates a message, sent over a channel to a receiver. Along the way the message may be acted on by "noise," which degrades, weakens or confuses the strength of the signal carrying the message. Before reading this chapter had you heard of this theory, or seen a similar model? If so, where was it described, and in what kind of context was it used? Give an example of the creation, sending and reception of a message, and describe what kind of noise might disrupt the fidelity of the signal.

Chapter 4
(Needs and Seeking)

1. Do people really "need" information, or is it just a by-product of other things we need? Consider the type of subjects and outcomes that are typical of primary education (i.e., what school systems try to teach children from ages 5 through 12). Are all of them directly related to another, more basic need, such as making a living? Are all of them really necessary, in your view?

2. Recollect and describe two episodes in your life in which learning some information led to more uncertainty in your life. This could be, for example, a doctor's comment that you needed a certain medical test, the realization that you could not locate your keys, or incomplete news about an event.

3. Have you ever been aware that you *should* know something, but don't? How did you recognize that state of mind? Did you have a feeling of "anxiety," or a sense of "nagging doubt"? Or was it that somebody reminded you that you were "ignorant of the facts"? What were the circumstances that led to your realization that you lacked useful knowledge, and how did you resolve the situation?

4. Rober Taylor described a process that he called "question negotiation," in which one person described a question or need that they had, while the

second person tried to understand the query and match it to a source of information. Describe an experience that you had that contained two or more of the following elements: A person with a need or question that they found difficult to put into words; a resulting statement that needed to be rephrased at least once in order to make it "right"; a second person who tried to clarify what the first person was telling them, by asking questions about what the meant about what they said; a resulting search for information that imperfectly matched the original need, due to the unavailability or different organization of the material in the channel (e.g., the Internet) or source (e.g., a particular book). Finally, describe how the situation turned out: Did the first person have their question(s) answered?

Chapter 5
(Related Concepts)

1. Consider how the spoken phrase "that's the thing that is causing the problem" might be interpreted in these different cases:
   a. A discussion of how Palestinians have expressed their grievances in Israel;
   b. A mechanic pointing under the hood of a car;
   c. One of two friends, referring to a continuing misunderstanding between them.

   What could the statement possibly *mean* in each case? That is, how does the *context* of the statement change the potential range of *meanings* that an observer might attribute to it?
2. Look at one of Richard Saul Wurman's "Access" guides — bookstores and public libraries often have several in the series (e.g., "New York/ Access" or "Hawaii/Access"). Ask yourself whether you would find it easier (or harder) to locate what you want within an unfamiliar city using an Access guide versus a more typical guidebook. What information do you most value in a tourist guide, and in what formats do you find it most useful?
3. Do you believe that "knowledge gaps" exist between different segments of society? For instance, is there a "digital divide" that separates people who have access to Internet resources from those who do not have access? If you believe that some groups have considerably less *information* than others, then which of these factors are most responsible for (or at least correlated with) such gaps: wealth, class, gender, age, race, ethnicity, or geography?
4. For examples, consider the following questions: Do "the rich get richer" mainly because of who they know? Do men tend to know more than

women in such a way that consistently maintains their power differential? Are the elderly usually wiser than the rest of us? Does being a minority (in any sense — racial, ethnic, religious, or simply being left-handed) mean that some doors are often closed? Are rural people always "the last to know" about trends in society? If you find some kernel of truth in these questions, then how would you go about gathering evidence to demonstrate the truth of each statement?

5. Think back on your schooling. Can you recall an incident in which something you learned about in a classroom led to a search for information beyond the course assignments? For example, did reading or hearing about an event in history, a famous person, or scientific discovery, lead you to seek out additional information to satisfy your own curiosity? Identify such an incident and describe how you pursued additional information on the topic.

**Chapter 6
(Models)**

1. Models are often said to precede theories — which is why this chapter appears before the chapter describing theories. Other than Wilson's second model, which explicitly mentions several possible theories, would you say that any of the other models embody any theories or assumptions about that way that people perceive, seek and/or use information? For instance, one possible assumption is that information resides in people (i.e., in terms of meanings) rather than in things ("containers" like books or films). For each model, then, would you say that the information seeking it describes is more of a search for meaning, or more about finding and examining the contents of information containers? Can you identify other basic assumptions behind these models?

2. Which of the models depicted in this chapter makes the most sense to you? Which factors are most influential in your choice: The level of detail? The particular words chosen to describe the process? The emphasis — for example, written information, or everyday life information?

3. The models described in this chapter appear to vary the most in regards to the "outcomes" — the explicit actions or other behaviors that come about as a result of the factors highlighted in the earlier stages of the model. Outcomes are variously characterized in terms of words like demands, success, satisfaction, attention, search, seeking, gathering, giving, interpersonal contact, and various kinds of "information use." Why do models differ so much in the way that they describe human behavior that results from information seeking situations? Why isn't there more agreement on a standard vocabulary for describing these things? Consider the main factors identified by each model and how that

limits or proscribes what kinds of outcomes are likely in the case of each model.
4. What do you believe about the nature of reality? Does it exist completely outside of human consciousness, or do are some aspects of reality "constructed" by our minds and/or through social interaction? What do you take as evidence for your views, that is, what experiences or knowledge persuades you that your view of reality is probably accurate?

Chapter 7
(Paradigms and Theories)

1. Which of the theories presented in this chapter makes the most sense to you? Why? Is it due to the level of detail? The words chosen to describe the process? The emphasis — for example, formal written information versus everyday life information? The ease with which you can think of human behavior that seems to fit the theory? Make a case for why the particular theory you chose is the most useful of those described in this chapter.
2. Information seeking researchers are divided regarding the importance and suitability of Zipf's Principle of Least Effort for investigating information seeking. Some critics say it is purely descriptive of overall tendencies, rather than an adequate explanation of specific behaviors. Others complain that it tends to be used to blame people for not searching rigorously enough — instead of focusing on the barriers that discourage us from being systematic in our searches for information.

   Does the Principle of Least Effort seem valid to you? What evidence (examples of your behavior or that of others) can you offer that either support or contradict this Principle?
3. Forty years ago it was fair to say that most theories applied in information seeking studies tended to come from the disciplines of psychology, sociology, or communication. In your view, is that still chiefly true? In recent years we have had a few examples of theory coming from anthropology and ecology (foraging theory), and from the study of literature (reader response theory). Based on your own familiarity with academic disciplines, are there other sources of theory that might be useful in studying information behavior? For instance, do the humanities disciplines offer alternative views of information seeking?
4. Are there any theories described in this chapter that seem far-removed from the usual concerns of information behavior research? Pick a theory that seems unusual and find a description of it on the Internet or in print. After reading the description, explain why you think it may or may not be applicable for the study of information seeking, use, or related topics.

Chapter 8
(Methods)

1. If you were to begin a study of information seeking today, which methodological approach would you be most comfortable with, and why? Consider a group with which you are familiar — students in a particular discipline, members of an organization you belong to, or people who share your interest in a particular sport or hobby. How would you go about investigating their information needs and behaviors?

2. Qualitative approaches to studying information behavior — for example, participant observation, ethnographic interviews — have been on the increase over the last three decades. Why might they be? In your view do such approaches to studying people hold more promise than methods more commonly used in decades past — especially surveys and experiments?

3. If you were studying the workings of an organization and you overheard the following statements from an employee, what could you assume about the meaning and implications of the word "murp," given the context in which it is used?

   a. "Bill has been murping the development committee meetings again. It's so hard to reach consensus in a group that size, and his behavior doesn't help matters."

   b. "The murp in the computer room needs to be replaced again. It seems to be randomly deleting email messages."

   c. "If we could just agree on how to evaluate the murp, we could move ahead with the study. Some of the staff think that there's no way to measure it directly."

   In each case imagine yourself to be a *participant observer* who needs to understand if the statement has any implications for information flows within the organization. Other than the obvious question ("Excuse me, but what is a 'murp'?"), *what would you ask* to understand the problem implied in each case? *How else would you observe* (through watching, interviewing or reading relevant documents) such that you could understand whether "murp" has an important (or trivial) effect on information transfer within the organization?

4. For many types of topics it is better to use two or three distinct methods of investigation (e.g., observation plus interview plus examination of artifacts), rather than one (e.g., a web survey). Which methods might you use to study the following topics and situations: (1) The process, information sources and channels used by two couples as they plan their summer vacation together, starting six months in advance of travel. (2) Decision-making among a department of seven marketing specialists in the consumer products division of a manufacturing company. (3) The

information sources and channels used by a physician's Assistant as she examines and screens 50 patients over the course of a week in which they appear in a family medicine clinic. (4) The information sources and channels used by two parents as they choose a school for their six-year-old child. In each case be mindful of issues related to privacy and reactivity of those observed, and to issues of access to data, noting these as you describe the methods used.

Chapter 9
(Methodological Examples)

1. Choose one of the empirical studies cited in this chapter and locate the original article or chapter in which it was reported. Read it carefully and develop responses to the following questions:
   a. What kind of phenomenon or problem is being studied? In your view, does the researcher make good arguments as to *why* it is being studied? Does it seem important to *you*?
   b. Are definitions offered for the key terms and concepts used in the study? Is there any indication of how those words relate to one another? Does it explain how we know that the concepts really exist, and how to recognize and/or measure them?
   c. What has been left out of any literature review that precedes the study? What other literature might have been reviewed that you are aware of as being somewhat relevant to the subject of the study?
   d. Consider the choice of words used by the author to report the study. Is the language biased in any way — that is, slanted towards a particular view of people or the phenomenon being studied? An example would be words that suggest that the persons studied are "lazy" in seeking information, or that assume that the only valid information is that from an institutional source.
2. Choose one of the empirical studies cited in this chapter and locate the original article or chapter in which it was reported. Read it carefully and develop responses to the following questions:
   a. Do you see any weaknesses in the design of the study? Are you convinced by the researcher's reasons for designing the investigation in the way that s/he did?
   b. When and where were the observations made? Who made them? What might have been left out of the observations? Consider other evidence that might have been gathered in this investigation. For example, what other kinds of behaviors might have been examined, and what other kinds of people might have been sampled, that would provide examples of the phenomenon of interest?

    c. Do you agree with the interpretations and conclusions suggested in the article? Do you see any weaknesses in the arguments that accompany it? Can you suggest another interpretation of the results that the author conveys?

3. The next time that you are in a bookstore or library watch for any outward signs of uncertainty, frustration and similar cognitive and emotional states. Is anyone moving quickly from place to place? Do you hear expressions of uncertainty like "It should be around here somewhere" or direct questions to others, such as "Do you know where X is?" Are there any overt signs of frustration, such as shaking of head or throwing up of hands? How do people respond to a failure to find something to satisfy a cognitive need? How would you study uncertainty, or frustration?

4. Think of a domain of knowledge (e.g., a sport, hobby, or job) with which you are very familiar. Draw an "information horizon" picture of the various channels and sources that inform you about your interests in that area. For example, the people, websites, mass media, events and so forth through which you learn about this topic. Model your diagram after those found in one of these studies: Huvila (2009), Savolainen (2007c), or Sonnenwald et al. (2001).

Chapter 10
(Reviewing Research: Size and History)

1. Are you surprised by what is said about the history and size of the information behavior literature? Would you agree that the study of this topic actually began in the early 20th century, or would you choose a later date for when serious investigation really began? Do you agree with the way that I have defined the scope of "information behavior," for example, by relying on published reviews of "information needs and uses" studies? What other means could we use to define and measure this literature? If you think that the scope of the topic could be defined differently (i.e., including or excluding certain topics), would you revise my estimate of the size of the relevant literature upwards or downwards?

2. This chapter suggests that there seems to have been a slow-down in the number of information behavior studies conducted during the 1980s when compared to the 1970s and the period from 1990 to 2012. Can you think of reasons why this would have been so? Consider changes in technology, education, the economy, and personal habits.

3. Which of the following research methods seems most fruitful to you for the goal of understanding basic aspects of information behavior? Try

ranking the usefulness of each approach, considering their relative reliability and validity.

    a. Case studies

    b. Ethnography interviews

    c. Discourse analysis

    d. Discourse analysis

    e. Questionnaires (via a website)

    f. Laboratory experiments

    g. Field experiments

4. Write a 2000 words wiki article like those found on Wikipedia, or on some sites internal to organizations. Pick a topic discussed in this book, and identify (or inventing) at least 10 sources of information about the subject of the article. Be creative in how you discuss the topic, for example, describing the contrasting results of hypothetical investigations, or citing fictional interviews with authors or respondents. Display the result as it might appear on a website.

Chapter 11
(Reviewing Research: By Occupation)

1. A great many investigations have been conducted of a relatively small number of occupations — especially scientists, engineers, medical doctors and managers. Is this degree of research attention deserved, compared to other possible occupations (e.g., lawyers, historians or journalists)? Why or why not? Which occupation(s) do you believe have not received enough research attention, and why?

2. In your view is it still worthwhile to conduct investigations of the information behavior of "metadisciplines" such as the humanities, sciences or social sciences? Why or why not? If you believe that studies of "scientists" or "humanists" are too broad to be of much use, then how narrow should information behavior investigations be? That is, should they attempt to generalize about entire disciplines (e.g., psychologists) or focus on much smaller occupational groups (e.g., cognitive psychologists studying "the role of mental models in learning" at Cambridge University)?

3. Is it a problem that medical doctors so often choose not to pursue questions they have regarding diseases and treatments? Or is this just an unavoidable circumstance of being a busy professional whose time is highly valuable? How might a hospital or clinic make it easier for doctors to find the answers to questions that come up in the course of examining patients?

4. Make an argument for studying an occupation that has not yet been studied (or at least not so identified in this book). How common and

widespread is the occupation? What kind of training or experience does it require? What makes it different from other jobs, and worthy of study? What would be a good way of sampling that population? How would you go about studying it?

Chapter 12
(Reviewing Research: By Role and Demographic Group)

1. Why do you think it is that few studies have focused on differences between men and women in their information seeking? Is it because there are no systematic differences between them? Or is it that such differences are overshadowed by (i.e., better predicted by) other variables, such as education, age, interests, personal situations, health issues, etc.?

2. One common role is not comprehensively reviewed in this chapter: that of "student." What might we be able to learn from investigations of student use of print and electronic materials? In what ways might the role of student differ from the others reviewed in this chapter? For example, can we assume that most students are fairly competent at seeking and using information, given their frequent exposure to instruction and assignments?

3. A common finding of studies of general populations (e.g., "citizens") has been that they rely first on their own experience and second on family and friends before ever turning to formal sources (e.g., professionals or books). Are there situations (e.g., health problems) or topics (e.g., financial security) for which this pattern is possibly dysfunctional or cause for public concern?

4. Make an argument for studying social role or type of person that has not yet been studied (or at least not so identified in this book). How common and widespread is the role or group? What special challenges does that type of role, or person, face? What makes it worthy of study? What would be a good way of sampling that population? How would you go about studying it?

Chapter 13
(Reviewing, Critiquing, Concluding)

1. How would you compare information behavior research to other disciplines with which you are familiar (e.g., education, history, psychology)? In comparing disciplines, comment on their subject matter, methods and standards.

2. Do you disagree with any of the "eight lessons of information behavior research"? For example, do you accept the conclusions that "sometimes

information doesn't help," or "information seeking is not always about "sense making"? Why or why not?

3. Now that you have read this book, how would you rate the importance of information behavior research? That is, how important is this line of research, compared to other topics with which you are familiar? Make some explicit comparisons to research agendas in other fields.

References

Abbott, R. (2004). Subjectivity as a concern for information science: A Popperian perspective. *Journal of Information Science, 30*, 95–106.

Abrahamson, J. A., Fisher, K. E., Turner, A. G., Durrance, J. C., & Turner, T. C. (2008). Lay information mediary behavior uncovered: Exploring how nonprofessionals seek health information for themselves and others online. *Journal of the Medical Library Association, 96*(4), 310–323.

Adams, S. S. (2009). What games have to offer: Information behavior and meaning-making in virtual play spaces. *Library Trends, 57*(4), 676–693.

Afifi, T. D., & Afifi, W. A. (2009). Introduction. In T. D. Afifi & W. A. Afifi (Eds.), *Uncertainty, information management, and disclosure decisions: Theories and applications* (pp. 1–5). New York, NY: Routledge.

Afifi, W. A., & Weiner, J. L. (2004). Toward a theory a motivated information management. *Communication Theory, 14*, 167–190.

Afifi, W. A., & Weiner, J. L. (2006). Seeking information about sexual health: Applying the theory of motivated information management. *Human Communication Research, 32*, 35–57.

Agada, J. (1999). Inner-city gatekeepers: An exploratory survey of their information use environment. *Journal of the American Society for Information Science, 50*, 74–85.

Agarwal, N., Xu, Y., & Poo, D. (2011). A context-based investigation into source use by information seekers. *Journal of the American Society for Information Science and Technology, 62*(6), 1087–1104.

Agosto, D. E., & Hughes-Hassell, S. (2005). People, places, and questions: An investigation of the everyday life information-seeking behaviors of urban young adults. *Library & Information Science Research, 27.*

Agosto, D. E., & Hughes-Hassell, S. (2006). Toward a model of the everyday life information needs of urban teenagers, part 2: Empirical model. *Journal of the American Society for Information Science and Technology, 57*(11), 1418–1426.

Aguilar, F. (1967). *Scanning the business environment.* New York, NY: Macmillan.

Ainslie, T. (1986). *Ainslie's complete guide to thoroughbred racing* (3rd ed.). New York, NY: Simon & Schuster.

Alexandersson, M., & Limberg, L. (2003). Constructing meaning through information artefacts. *The New Review of Information Behaviour Research: Studies of Information Seeking in Context (Proceedings of ISIC 2002), 4*, 17–30.

Allard, S., Levine, K. J., & Tenopir, C. (2009). Design engineers and technical professionals at work: Observing information usage in the workplace. *Journal of the American Society for Information Science and Technology, 60*(3), 443–454.

Allen, B. L. (1996). *Information tasks: Toward a user-centered approach to information systems*. New York, NY: Academic Press.

Allen, D., Karanasios, S., & Slavova, M. (2011). Working with activity theory: Context, technology, and information behavior. *Journal of American Society for Information Science and Technology, 62*(4), 776–788.

Allen, D., & Wilson, T. D. (2003). Information overload: Context and causes. *The New Review of Information Behaviour Research: Studies of Information Seeking in Context (Proceedings of ISIC 2002), 4,* 31–44.

Allen, D. K., Wilson, T. D., Norman, A., & Knight, C. (2008). Information on the move: The use of mobile information systems by UK police forces. *Information Research, 13*(4). Retrieved from http://InformationR.net/ir/13-4/paper378.html

Allen, T. J. (1969). Information needs and uses. In C. Cuadra (Ed.), *Annual review of information science and technology* (Vol. 4, pp. 3–29). Chicago, IL: Encyclopaedia Britannica.

Allen, T. J. (1977). *Managing the flow of information*. Cambridge, MA: MIT Press.

Allen, T. J., & Cohen, S. I. (1969). Information flow in research and development laboratories. *Administrative Science Quarterly, 14,* 12–19.

Allport, G. W., & Postman, L. (1947). *The psychology of rumor*. New York, NY: Holt.

Altheide, D. (1987). Ethnographic content analysis. *Qualitative Sociology, 10,* 65–77.

Altheide, D. (1996). *Qualitative media analysis* (Vol. 38). Thousand Oaks, CA: Sage Publications.

Andrews, J. E., Johnson, J. D., Case, D. O., Allard, S. L., & Kelly, K. (2005). Intention to seek information on cancer genetics. *Information Research, 10*(4). Retrieved from http://informationr.net/ir/10-4/paper238.html

Ankem, K. (2005). Approaches to meta-analysis: A guide for LIS researchers. *Library & Information Science Research, 27,* 164–176.

Ankem, K. (2006a). Factors influencing information needs among cancer patients: A meta-analysis. *Library & Information Science Research, 28*(1), 7–23.

Ankem, K. (2006b). Use of information sources by cancer patients: Results of a systematic review of the research literature. *Information Research, 11*(3). Retrieved from http://informationr.net/ir/11-3/paper254.html

Ankem, K. (2007). Information-seeking behavior of women in their path to an innovative alternate treatment for symptomatic uterine fibroids. *Journal of the Medical Library Association, 95*(2), 164–172.

Anker, A., Reinhart, A., & Feeley, T. (2011). Health information seeking: A review of measures and methods. *Patient Education and Counseling, 82,* 346–354.

Ansari, M., & Zuberi, N. (2010). Information seeking behaviour of media professionals in Karachi. *Malaysian Journal of Library & Information Science, 15*(2), 71–84.

Anwar, M., & Asghar, M. (2009). Information seeking behavior of Pakistani newspaper journalists. *Pakistan Journal of Library & Information Science, 10,* 57–79.

Anwar, M., & Supaat, H. (1998). Information needs of rural Malaysians: An exploratory study of a cluster of three villages with no library service. *International Information & Library Review, 30,* 23–37.

Apted, S. (1971). General purposive browsing. *Library Association Record, 73,* 66–78.

Artandi, S. (1973). Information concepts and their utility. *Journal of the American Society for Information Science, 24*(4), 42–245.

Asla, T., Williamson, K., & Mills, J. (2006). The role of information in successful aging: The case for a research focus on the oldest old. *Library & Information Science Research, 28*(1), 49–63.

Aspray, W., & Hayes, B. (Eds.). (2011). *Everyday information: The evolution of information seeking in America.* Cambridge, MA: MIT Press.

Associated Press. (2007). *AP-Ipsos-books and reading.* Retrieved from http://surveys.ap.org/

Atkin, C. (1972). Anticipated communication and mass media information-seeking. *Public Opinion Quarterly, 36,* 188–199.

Atkin, C. (1973). Instrumental utilities and information-seeking. In P. Clarke (Ed.), *New models for mass communication research* (pp. 205–242). Beverly Hills, CA: Sage Publications.

Atkin, C. (1985). Informational utility and selective exposure to entertainment media. In D. Zillmann & J. Bryant (Eds.), *Selective exposure to communication* (pp. 63–91). Hillsdale, NJ: Lawrence Erlbaum Associates.

Attfield, S., Blandford, A., & Dowell, J. (2003). Information seeking in the context of writing: A design psychology interpretation of the 'problematic situation'. *Journal of Documentation, 59,* 430–453.

Attfield, S., & Dowell, J. (2003). Information seeking and use by newspaper journalists. *Journal of Documentation, 59,* 187–204.

Atwood, R., & Dervin, B. (1982). Challenges to sociocultural predictors of information seeking: A test of race vs situation movement state. In M. Burgoon (Ed.), *Communication yearbook* (Vol. 5, pp. 549–569). New Brunswick, NJ: Transaction Books.

Auerbach. (1965). *DOD user needs study, phase I: Final technical report 1151-TR3.* Philadelphia, PA: Auerbach Corporation.

Auster, E., & Choo, C. (1993). Environmental scanning by CEOs in two Canadian industries. *Journal of the American Society for Information Science, 44,* 194–203.

Awamura, N. (2006). Rethinking the information behavior model of information encountering: An analysis of the interviews on information encountering on the web. *Library and Information Science, 55,* 47–69.

Ayres, L. P., & McKinnie, A. (1916). *The public library and the public schools* (Vol. XXI). Cleveland, OH: Survey Committee of the Cleveland Foundation.

Ayris, P. (1986). *The stimulation of creativity: A review of the literature concerning the concept of browsing, 1970–1985.* CRUS Working Paper No. 5. Center for Research on User Studies (CRUS), University of Sheffield, Sheffield, UK.

Babbie, E. (2009). *The practice of social research* (12th ed.). Belmont, CA: Wadsworth Publishing.

Babrow, A. S. (1992). Communication and problematic integration: Understanding diverging probability and value, ambiguity, ambivalence, and impossibility. *Communication Theory, 2,* 95–130.

Babrow, A. S., Kasch, C. R., & Ford, L. A. (1998). The many meanings of uncertainty in illness: Toward a systematic accounting. *Health Communication, 10,* 1–23.

Baker, L. M. (1996). The nature of the information needed by women with multiple sclerosis. *Library & Information Science Research, 18,* 67–81.

Baker, L. M. (2004a). The information needs of female police officers involved in undercover prostitution work. *Information Research, 10*(1). Retrieved from http://InformationR.net/ir/10-1/paper209.html

Baker, L. M. (2004b). Information needs at the end of life: A content analysis of one person's story. *Journal of the Medical Libraries Association, 92,* 78–82.

Baker, L. M. (2005). Monitoring and blunting. In K. E. Fisher, S. Erdelez & E. F. McKechnie (Eds.), *Theories of information behavior* (pp. 239–241). Medford, NJ: Information Today.

Baker, L. M., Case, P., & Policicchio, D. L. (2003). General health problems of inner-city sex workers: A pilot study. *Journal of the Medical Library Association, 91,* 67–71.

Baker, L. M., & Pettigrew, K. E. (1999). Theories for practitioners: Two frameworks for studying consumer health information seeking behavior. *Bulletin of the Medical Library Association, 87,* 444–450.

Baker, L. M., Wilson, F. L., Nordstrom, C. K., & Legwand, C. (2007). Mothers' knowledge and information needs relating to childhood immunizations. *Issues in Comprehensive Pediatric Nursing, 30*(1/2), 39–53.

Baker, S. (1986). Overload, browsers, and selections. *Library & Information Science Research, 8,* 315–329.

Baker, T. L. (1999). *Doing social research* (3rd ed.). New York, NY: McGraw-Hill.

Bakhtin, M. M. (1981). *The dialogic imagination.* Austin, TX: University of Texas Press.

Baldwin, N. S., & Rice, R. E. (1997). Information-seeking behavior of securities analysts: Individual and institutional influences, information sources and channels, and outcomes. *Journal of the American Society for Information Science, 48,* 674–693.

Bandura, A. (1977). *Social learning theory.* Englewood Cliffs, NJ: Prentice Hall.

Bandura, A. (1986). *Social foundations of thought and action.* Englewood Cliffs, NJ: Prentice Hall.

Bandura, A. (2001). Social cognitive theory: An agentic perspective. *Annual review of psychology* (Vol. 52, pp. 1–26). Palo Alto, CA: Annual Reviews, Inc.

Barry, C. (1994). User-defined relevance criteria: An exploratory study. *Journal of the American Society for Information Science, 45,* 149–159.

Barry, C. (1995). Critical issues in evaluating the the impact of IT on information activity in academic research: Developing a qualitative research solution. *Library & Information Science Research, 17,* 107–134.

Barzilai-Nahon, K. (2005). Network gatekeeping. In K. E. Fisher, S. Erdelez & E. F. McKechnie (Eds.), *Theories of information behavior* (pp. 247–253). Medford, NJ: Information Today.

Bates, J. A. (2004). Use of narrative interviewing in everyday information behavior research. *Library & Information Science Research, 26,* 15–28.

Bates, M. J. (1989). The design of browsing and berrypicking techniques for the online search interface. *Online Review, 13*(5), 407–424.

Bates, M. J. (1996). Learning about the information seeking of interdisciplinary scholars and students. *Library Trends, 45*(2), 155–164.

Bates, M. J. (2002). Toward an integrated model of information seeking and searching. *The New Review of Information Behaviour Research: Studies of Information Seeking in Context (Proceedings of ISIC 2002), 3*, 1–16.

Bates, M. J. (2005a). An introduction to metatheories, theories, and models. In K. E. Fisher, S. Erdelez & E. F. McKechnie (Eds.), *Theories of information behavior* (pp. 1–24). Medford, NJ: Information Today.

Bates, M. J. (2005b). Information and knowledge: An evolutionary framework for information science. *Information Research, 10*(4). Retrieved from http://informationr.net/ir/10-4/paper239.html

Bates, M. J. (2005c). Berrypicking. In K. E. Fisher, S. Erdelez & E. F. McKechnie (Eds.), *Theories of information behavior* (pp. 58–62). Medford, NJ: Information Today.

Bates, M. J. (2007). What is browsing – Really? A model drawing from behavioural science research. *Information Research, 12*(4). Retrieved from http://InformationR.net/ir/12-4/paper330.html

Bateson, G. (1972). *Steps to an ecology of mind.* New York, NY: Ballantine Books.

Bateson, G. (1978). The pattern which connects. *Co-Evolution Quarterly, 18*, 4–15.

Batson, C., Coke, J., Chard, F., Smith, D., & Taliaferro, A. (1979). Generality of the 'glow of goodwill': Effects of mood on helping and information acquisition. *Social Psychology Quarterly, 42*, 176–179.

Bawden, D., & Robinson, L. (2009). The dark side of information: Overload, anxiety and other paradoxes and pathologies. *Journal of Information Science, 35*(2), 180–191.

Baxter, G., Marcella, R., & Illingworth, L. (2010). Organizational information behaviour in the public consultation process in Scotland. *Information Research, 15*(4). Retrieved from http://InformationR.net/ir/15-4/paper442.html

Beautyman, W., & Shenton, A. (2009). When does an academic information need stimulate a school-inspired information want? *Journal of Librarianship & Information Science, 41*(2), 67–80.

Bebout, L., Davis, J., & Oehlerts, D. (1975). User studies in the humanities: A survey and a proposal. *RQ, 15*(1), 40–44.

Beer, S. (2004). Information flow and peripherality in remote island areas of Scotland. *Libri, 54*(3), 148–157.

Belefant-Miller, H., & King, D. W. (2001). How, what and why science faculty read. *Science and Technology Libraries, 19*, 91–112.

Belefant-Miller, H., & King, D. W. (2003). A profile of faculty reading and information-use behaviors on the cusp of the electronic age. *Journal of the American Society for Information Science and Technology, 54*, 179–181.

Belk, R. W. (1975). Situational variables and consumer behavior. *Journal of Consumer Research, 2*, 157–167.

Belk, R. W. (1995). *Collecting in a consumer society.* London: Routledge.

Belk, R. W., Sherry, Jr., J., & Wallendorf, M. (1988). Naturalistic inquiry into buyer-seller behavior at a swap meet. *Journal of Consumer Research, 14*, 449–469.

Belkin, N. J. (1978). Information concepts for information science. *Journal of Documentation, 34*, 55–85.

Belkin, N. J. (2005). Anomalous state of knowledge. In K. E. Fisher, S. Erdelez & E. F. McKechnie (Eds.), *Theories of information behavior* (pp. 44–48). Medford, NJ: Information Today.

Belkin, N. J., Oddy, R., & Brooks, H. (1982). ASK for information retrieval. *Journal of Documentation, 38*(2), 61–71.

Belkin, N. J., & Robertson, S. (1976). Information science and the phenomenon of information. *Journal of the American Society for Information Science, 27*, 197–204.

Belkin, N. J., & Vickery, A. (1985). *Interaction in information systems: A review of research from document retrieval to knowledge-based systems*. Boston Spa, UK: British Library.

Bennett, N., Casebeer, L., Zheng, S., & Kristofco, R. (2006). Information-seeking behaviors and reflective practice. *Journal of Continuing Education in the Health Professions, 26*(2), 120–127.

Benoit, G. (2000). Critical theory as a foundation for pragmatic information systems design. *Information Research, 6*(2). Retrieved from http://InformationR.net/ir/6-2/paper98.html

Benoit, G. (2005). Communicative action. In K. E. Fisher, S. Erdelez & E. F. McKechnie (Eds.), *Theories of information behavior* (pp. 99–103). Medford, NJ: Information Today.

Berelson, B. (1949). *The library's public*. New York, NY: Columbia University Press.

Berger, C. R. (1987). Communicating under uncertainty. In M. Roloff & G. Miller (Eds.), *Interpersonal processes: New directions in communication research* (pp. 39–62). Newbury Park, CA: Sage Publications.

Berger, C. R. (1997). Message production under uncertainty. In G. Philipsen & T. Albrecht (Eds.), *Developing communication theories* (pp. 29–56). Albany, NY: State University of New York Press.

Berger, C. R. (2002). Strategic and nonstrategic information acquisition. *Human Communication Research, 28*, 287–297.

Berger, C. R., & Bradac, J. J. (1982). *Language and social knowledge: Uncertainty in interpersonal relations*. London: Edward Arnold Publishers Ltd.

Berger, C. R., & Calabrese, R. (1975). Some explorations in initial interaction and beyond: Toward a developmental theory of interpersonal communication. *Human Communication Research, 1*, 99–112.

Berger, P., & Luckmann, T. (1967). *The social construction of reality*. New York, NY: Doubleday.

Berlo, D. (1960). *The process of communication: An introduction to theory and practice*. New York, NY: Holt, Rinehart and Winston.

Berlo, D. (1977). Communication as process: Review and commentary. In B. Ruben (Ed.), *Communication yearbook* (Vol. 1, pp. 11–28). New Brunswick, NJ: Transaction Books.

Berlyne, D. E. (1960). *Conflict, arousal, and curiosity*. New York, NY: McGraw-Hill.

Berryman, J. M. (2008). Judgements during information seeking: A naturalistic approach to understanding the assessment of enough information. *Journal of Information Science, 34*(2), 196–206.

Beverley, C. A., Bath, P. A., & Barber, R. (2007). Can two established information models explain the information behaviour of visually impaired people seeking health and social care information? *Journal of Documentation, 63*(1), 9–32.

Bianchi, M. (Ed.) (1997a). *The active consumer: Novelty and surprise in consumer choice.* London: Routledge.

Bianchi, M. (1997b). Collecting as a paradigm of consumption. *Journal of Cultural Economics, 21,* 275–289.

Bichteler, J., & Ward, D. (1989). Information-seeking behavior of geoscientists. *Special Libraries, 79*(3), 169–178.

Bierbaum, E. (1990). A paradigm for the 90s. *American Libraries, 21,* 18–19.

Biesecker, A. E., & Biesecker, T. D. (1990). Patient information-seeking behaviors when communicating with doctors. *Medical Care, 28,* 19–28.

Bijker, W. E., Hughes, T. P., & Pinch, T. J. (Eds.). (1984). *The social construction of technological systems.* Cambridge, MA: MIT Press.

Bilal, D. (2007). Grounding children's information behavior and system design in child development theories. In D. Nahl & D. Bilal (Eds.), *Information and emotion: The emergent affective paradigm in information behavior research and theory* (pp. 39–50). Medford, NJ: Information Today.

Bishop, R. (2005). 'The essential force of the clan': Developing a collecting-inspired ideology of genealogy through textual analysis. *The Journal of Popular Culture, 8,* 990–1010.

Björneborn, L. (2005). Small-world network exploration. In K. E. Fisher, S. Erdelez & E. F. McKechnie (Eds.), *Theories of information behavior* (pp. 230–234, 318–322). Medford, NJ: Information Today.

Black, A. (2006). Information history. In B. Cronin (Ed.), *Annual review of information science and technology* (Vol. 40, pp. 441–473). Medford, NJ: Information Today.

Bloch, P., Ridgway, N., & Sherrell, D. (1989). Extending the concept of shopping: An investigation of browsing activity. *Journal of the Academy of Marketing Science, 17,* 13–21.

Bloch, P., Sherrell, D., & Ridgway, N. (1986). Consumer search: An extended framework. *Journal of Consumer Research, 13,* 119–126.

Blythe, J., & Royle, J. (1993). Assessing nurses' information needs in the work environment. *Bulletin of the Medical Library Association, 81*(4), 189–196.

Blumer, H. (1986). *Symbolic interactionism: Perspective and method.* Englewood Cliffs, NJ: Prentice Hall.

Bogart, L. (1983). Mass media: Knowledge as entertainment. In K. Boulding & L. Senesh (Eds.), *The optimum utilization of knowledge: Making knowledge serve human betterment* (pp. 216–231). Boulder, CO: Westview Press.

Borgatti, S., Mehra, A., Brass, D., & Labianca, G. (2009). Network analysis in the social sciences. *Science, 323,* 892–895.

Borgman, C. L. (Ed.) (1990). *Scholarly communication and bibliometrics.* Newbury Park, CA: Sage Publications.

Borgman, C. L. (1996). Why are online catalogs still hard to use? *Journal of the American Society for Information Science, 47*, 493–503.

Borgman, C. L. (2000). *From Gutenberg to the global information infrastructure: Access to information in the networked world.* Cambridge, MA: MIT Press.

Borgman, C. L., & Furner, J. (2002). Scholarly communication and bibliometrics. In B. Cronin (Ed.), *Annual review of information science and technology* (Vol. 36, pp. 3–72). Medford, NJ: Information Today.

Bosman, J., & Renckstorf, K. (1996). Information needs: Problems, interests and consumption. In K. Renckstorf (Ed.), *Media use as social action* (pp. 43–52). London: John Libbey.

Bouazza, A. (1989). Information user studies. In *Encyclopedia of library and information science* (Vol. 44, Suppl. 9, pp. 144–164). New York, NY: M. Dekker.

Boulding, K. (1956). *The image: Knowledge in life and society.* Ann Arbor, MI: University of Michigan Press.

Bourdieu, P. (1984). *Distinction: A social critique of the judgement of taste* (R. Nice, Trans.). London: Routledge.

Bourdieu, P. (1990). *The logic of practice* (R. Nice, Trans.). Cambridge: Polity Press.

Bowers, J. W., & Bradac, J. J. (1982). Issues in communication theory: A metatheoretical analysis. In M. Burgoon (Ed.), *Communication yearbook* (Vol. 5). New Brunswick, NJ: Transaction Books.

Bowler, L. (2010). The self-regulation of curiosity and interest during the information search process of adolescent students. *Journal of the American Society for Information Science and Technology, 61*(7), 1332–1344.

Bowler, S., Donovan, T., & Snipp, J. (1993). Local sources of information and voter choice in state elections: Microlevel foundations of the "friends and neighbors" effect. *American Politics Quarterly, 21*, 473–489.

Box, V., Hepworth, M., & Harrison, J. (2003). Identifying information needs of people with multiple sclerosis. *Nursing Times, 99*(49), 32–36.

Boyce, B., Meadow, C., & Kraft, D. (1994). *Measurement in information science.* San Diego, CA: Academic Press.

Bradac, J. J. (2001). Theory comparison: Uncertainty reduction, problematic integration, uncertainty management, and other curious constructs. *Journal of Communication, 51*, 456–476.

Braman, S. (1989). Defining information: An approach for policy-makers. *Telecommunications Policy, 13*, 233–242.

Braman, S. (2006). The micro- and macroeconomics of information. In B. Cronin (Ed.), *Annual review of information science and technology* (Vol. 40, pp. 3–52). Medford, NJ: Information Today.

Brashers, D. E. (2001). Communication and uncertainty management. *Journal of Communication, 51*, 456–476.

Brashers, D. E., Goldsmith, D. J., & Hsieh, E. (2002). Information seeking and avoiding in health contexts. *Human Communication Research, 28*, 258–271.

Brashers, D. E., Neidig, J. L., Haas, S. M., Dobbs, L. K., Cardillo, L. W., & Russell, J. A. (2000). Communication in the management of uncertainty: The case of persons living with HIV or AIDS. *Communication Monographs, 67*(1), 63–84.

Brier, S. (1992). Information and consciousness: A critique of the mechanistic concept of information. *Cybernetics and Human Knowing, 1*(2–3), 71–94.

Brine, A., & Feather, J. (2010). The information needs of UK historic houses: Mapping the ground. *Journal of Documentation, 66*(1), 28–45.

Brittain, J. M. (1970). *Information and its users: A review with special reference to the social sciences.* New York, NY: Wiley.

Broder, A., Kumar, R., Maghoul, F., Raghavan, P., Rajagopalan, S., Stata, R., Tomkins, A., & Wienr, J. (2000). *Graph structure in the web.* Retrieved from http://www.almaden.ibm.com/cs/k53/www9.final/

Bronstein, J. (2007). The role of the research phase in information seeking behaviour of Jewish studies scholars: A modification of Ellis's behavioural characteristics. *Information Research, 12*(3). Retrieved from http://informationr.net/ir/12-3/paper318.html

Bronstein, J., & Baruchson-Arbib, S. (2008). The application of cost-benefit and least effort theories in studies of information seeking behavior of humanities scholars: The case of Jewish studies scholars in Israel. *Journal of Information Science, 34*(2), 131–144.

Brown, C. D. (2001). The role of computer-mediated communication in the research process of music scholars: An exploratory investigation. *Information Research, 6*(2). Retrieved from http://InformationR.net/ir/6-2/paper99.html

Brown, C. D. (2002). Straddling the humanities and social sciences: The research process of music scholars. *Library & Information Science Research, 24*, 73–94.

Brown, C. D. (2010). Communication in the sciences. In B. Cronin (Ed.), *Annual review of information science and technology* (Vol. 44, pp. 287–316). Medford, NJ: Information Today.

Brown, C. M. (1999). Information seeking behavior of scientists in the electronic information age: Astronomers, chemists, mathematicians, and physicists. *Journal of the American Society for Information Science, 50*, 929–943.

Brown, J., & Duguid, P. (2000). *The social life of information.* Boston, MA: Harvard Business School Press.

Brown, J. D., & Childers, K. (2002). Effects of media on personal and public health. In J. Bryant & D. Zillman (Eds.), *Media effects: Advances in theory and research* (pp. 453–488). Mahwah, NJ: Lawrence Erlbaum Associates.

Bruce, H. (1994). A cognitive view of the situational dynamism of user-centered relevance estimation. *Journal of the American Society for Information Science, 45*, 142–149.

Bruce, H. (1998). User satisfaction with information seeking on the Internet. *Journal of the American Society for Information Science, 49*(6), 541–556.

Bruce, H. (2005). The pain hypothesis. In K. E. Fisher, S. Erdelez & E. F. McKechnie (Eds.), *Theories of information behavior* (pp. 270–274). Medford, NJ: Information Today.

Bruce, H., Fidel, R., Pejtersen, A. M., Dumais, S., Grudin, J., & Poltrock, S. (2003). A comparison of the collaborative information retrieval behaviour of two design teams. *The New Review of Information Behaviour Research: Studies of Information Seeking in Context (Proceedings of ISIC 2002), 4*, 139–153.

Brucks, M. (1985). The effects of product class knowledge on information search behavior. *Journal of Consumer Research, 12*, 1–16.

Bruner, J. S. (1973). *Beyond the information given: Studies in the psychology of knowing*. New York, NY: W. W. Norton & Company.

Bruner, J. S. (1990). *Acts of meaning*. Cambridge, MA: Harvard University Press.

Bryant, J., & Miron, D. (2002). Entertainment as media effect. In J. Bryant & D. Zillman (Eds.), *Media effects: Advances in theory and research* (pp. 549–582). Mahwah, NJ: Lawrence Erlbaum Associates.

Bryant, J., & Vorderer, P. (2006). *Psychology of entertainment*. Mahwah, NJ: Lawrence Erlbaum Associates.

Buckland, M. K. (1991a). Information as thing. *Journal of the American Society for Information Science, 42,* 351–360.

Buckland, M. K. (1991b). *Information and information systems*. New York, NY: Greenwood Press.

Buckland, M. K. (1998). What is a 'document'? In T. Hahn & M. Buckland (Eds.), *Historical studies in information science* (pp. 215–220). Medford, NJ: Information Today.

Budd, J. M. (1995). An epistemological foundation for library and information science. *Library Quarterly, 65*(3), 295–318.

Budd, J. M., & Raber, D. (1996). Discourse analysis: Method and application in the study of information. *Information Processing & Management, 32,* 217–226.

Budd, J. M. (2011). Meaning, truth, and information: Prolegomena to a theory. *Journal of Documentation, 67*(1), 56–74.

Burnett, G., Besant, M., & Chatman, E. A. (2001). Small worlds: Normative behavior in virtual communities and feminist bookselling. *Journal of the American Society for Information Science and Technology, 52,* 536–547.

Burnett, G., & Jaeger, P. T. (2008). Small worlds, life worlds, and information: The ramifications of the information behaviour of social groups in public policy and the public sphere. *Information Research, 13*(2). Retrieved from http://InformationR.net/ir/13-2/paper346.html

Burrell, G., & Morgan, G. (1988). *Sociological paradigms and organizational analysis*. Portsmouth, NH: Heinemann.

Byström, K. (2005). Information activities in work tasks. In K. E. Fisher, S. Erdelez & E. F. McKechnie (Eds.), *Theories of information behavior* (pp. 174–178). Medford, NJ: Information Today.

Byström, K., & Järvelin, K. (1995). Task complexity affects information seeking and use. *Information Processing & Management, 31,* 191–213.

Cacioppo, J. T., & Petty, R. E. (1982). The need for cognition. *Journal of Personality and Social Psychology, 42,* 116–131.

Caidi, N. (2001). Interdisciplinarity: What is it and what are its implications for information seeking? *Humanities Collections, 1*(4), 35–46.

Caidi, N., & Allard, D. (2005). Social inclusion of newcomers to Canada: An information problem? *Library & Information Science Research, 27*(3), 302–324.

Caidi, N., Allard, D., & Quirke, L. (2010). The information practices of immigrants. In B. Cronin (Ed.), *Annual review of information science and technology* (Vol. 44, pp. 493–531). Medford, NJ: Information Today.

Campbell, D. K. (2006). The context of the information behavior of prison inmates. *Progressive Librarian, 26,* 18–32.

Campbell, D. T., & Stanley, J. C. (1963). *Experimental and quasi-experimental designs for research*. Chicago, IL: Rand McNally.

Campbell, F. (1997). Journalistic construction of news: information gathering. *New Library World, 98*(1133), 60–64.

Campbell, J. (1982). *Grammatical man: Information, entropy, language, and life*. New York, NY: Touchstone.

Cappella, J. (1977). Research methodology in communication: Review and methodology. In B. Ruben (Ed.), *Communication yearbook* (Vol. 1, pp. 37–53) New Brunswick, NJ: Transaction Books.

Capurro, R., & Hjørland, B. (2002). The concept of information. In B. Cronin (Ed.), *Annual review of information science and technology* (Vol. 37, pp. 343–411). Medford, NJ: Information Today.

Carey, R. F., McKechnie, L., & McKenzie, P. (2001). Gaining access to everyday life information seeking. *Library & Information Science Research, 23*, 319–334.

Carter, R. (1965). Communication and affective relations. *Journalism Quarterly, 42*, 203–212.

Carter, R. (1973). Communication as behavior. Paper presented at the annual meeting of the Association for Education in Journalism, Fort Collins, CO.

Carter, R. (1978). A very peculiar horse race. In G. Bishop, R. Meadow & M. Jackson-Beeck (Eds.), *The presidential debates*. New York, NY: Praeger.

Case, D. O. (1986). Collection and organization of written information by social scientists and humanists: A review and exploratory study. *Journal of Information Science, 11*(3), 97–104.

Case, D. O. (1991). The collection and use of information by some American historians: A study of motives and methods. *The Library Quarterly, 61*(1), 61–82.

Case, D. (1994). The social shaping of videotex: How information services for the public have evolved. *Journal of the American Society for Information Science, 45*, 483–497.

Case, D. O. (1998). Enthusiasts, deregulators, guardians and skeptics: Contrasting policy views of the national information infrastructure. *Library & Information Science Research, 20*, 377–413.

Case, D. O. (2000). *What information seeking research can learn from studies of consumers*. Unpublished paper. Third International Conference on Information Seeking in Context (ISIC) 2000, University College of Borås, Sweden.

Case, D. O. (2005). Principle of least effort. In K. E. Fisher, S. Erdelez & E. F. McKechnie (Eds.), *Theories of information behavior* (pp. 289–292). Medford, NJ: Information Today.

Case, D. O. (2006). Information behavior. In B. Cronin (Ed.), *Annual review of information science and technology* (Vol. 40, pp. 293–328). Medford, NJ: Information Today.

Case, D. O. (2009a). Serial collecting as leisure, and coin collecting in particular. *Library Trends, 57*(4), 729–752.

Case, D. O. (2009b). Collection of family health histories: The link between genealogy and public health. *Journal of the American Society for Information Science and Technology, 59*(14), 2312–2319.

Case, D. O. (2010). A model of the information seeking and decision making of online coin buyers. *Information Research, 15*(4). Retrieved from http://InformationR.net/ir/15-4/paper448.html

Case, D. O., Borgman, C. B., & Meadow, C. T. (1986). End-user information-seeking in the energy field: Implications for end-user access to DOE RECON databases. *Information Processing & Management, 22*, 299–308.

Case, D., & Higgins, G. (2000). How can we investigate citation behavior? A study of reasons for citing literature in communication. *Journal of the American Society for Information Science, 51*(7), 635–645.

Case, D. O., Johnson, J. D., Andrews, J. E., & Allard, S. L. (2005). Avoiding versus seeking: The relationship of information seeking to avoidance, blunting, coping, dissonance and related concepts. *Journal of the Medical Libraries Association, 93*, 353–362.

Case, D. O., Johnson, J. D., Andrews, J. E., Allard, S., & Kelly, K. M. (2004). From two-step flow to the internet: The changing array of sources for genetics information seeking. *Journal of the American Society for Information Science and Technology, 55*, 660–669.

Case, D. O., & Rogers, E. M. (1987). The adoption and social impacts of information technology in U.S. agriculture. *The Information Society, 5*(2), 57–66.

Cermak, G. W. (1996). An approach to mapping entertainment alternatives. In R. R. Dohlakia, N. Mundorf & N. Dohlakia (Eds.), *New infotainment technologies in the home: Demand-side perspectives* (pp. 115–134). Mahwah, NJ: Lawrence Erlbaum Associates.

Chaffee, S. (1991). *Communication concepts 1: Explication*. Newbury Park, CA: Sage Publications.

Chang, S.-J. L. (2005). Chang's browsing. In K. E. Fisher, S. Erdelez & E. F. McKechnie (Eds.), *Theories of information behavior* (pp. 69–74). Medford, NJ: Information Today.

Chang, S.-J. L. (2006). An investigation into information needs and information seeking behavior of elementary and middle school teachers teaching indigenous courses. *Journal of Library & Information Studies, 4*(1/2), 49–76.

Chang, S., & Rice, R. (1993). Browsing: A multidimensional framework. In M. Williams (Ed.), *Annual review of information science and technology* (Vol. 28, pp. 231–276). Medford, NJ: Learned Information.

Chang, S.-J. L. (2009). Information research in leisure: Implications from an empirical study of backpackers. *Library Trends, 57*(4), 711–768.

Chatman, E. A. (1985). Information, mass media use, and the working poor. *Library & Information Science Research, 7*, 97–113.

Chatman, E. A. (1986). Diffusion theory: A review and test of a conceptual model in information diffusion. *Journal of the American Society for Information Science, 37*, 377–386.

Chatman, E. A. (1987). The information world of low-skilled workers. *Library & Information Science Research, 9*, 265–283.

Chatman, E. A. (1990). Alienation theory: Application of a conceptual framework to a study of information among janitors. *RQ, 29*, 355–368.

Chatman, E. A. (1991). Life in a small world: Applicability of gratification theory to information-seeking behavior. *Journal of the American Society for Information Science, 42*, 438–449.

Chatman, E. A. (1992). *The information world of retired women.* Westport, CT: Greenwood Press.

Chatman, E. A. (1996). The impoverished life-world of outsiders. *Journal of the American Society for Information Science, 47*, 193–206.

Chatman, E. A. (1999). A theory of life in the round. *Journal of the American Society for Information Science, 50*, 207–217.

Chatman, E. A. (2000). Framing social life in theory and research. *The New Review of Information Behaviour Research, 1*, 3–17.

Chatman, E. A., & Pendleton, V. (1995). Knowledge gap, information seeking and the poor. *The Reference Librarian, 49/50*, 135–145.

Cheatle, E. (1992). *Information needs of solicitors.* Unpublished Masters of Science, City University, London.

Chelton, M. K. (2001). Young adults as problems: How the social construction of a marginalized user category occurs. *Journal of Education for Library and Information Science, 42*(1), 4–11.

Chelton, M. K., & Cool, C. (Eds.). (2004). *Youth information-seeking behavior: Theories, models and approaches.* Metuchen, NJ: Scarecrow Press.

Chen, C., & Hernon, P. (1982). *Information-seeking: Assessing and anticipating user needs.* New York, NY: Neal-Schuman.

Cherwitz, R., & Hikins, J. (1986). *Communication and knowledge: An investigation in rhetorical epistemology.* Columbia, SC: University of South Carolina Press.

Chew, F. (1994). The relationship of information needs to issue relevance and media use. *Journalism Quarterly, 71*, 676–688.

Chew, F., & Palmer, S. (1994). Interest, the knowledge gap, and television programming. *Journal of Broadcasting and Electronic Media, 38*, 271–287.

Childers, T., & Post, J. (1975). *The information-poor in America.* Metuchen, NJ: Scarecrow.

Cho, H., & LaRose, R. (1999). Privacy issues in Internet surveys. *Social Science Computer Review, 17*, 421–434.

Choo, C. W. (1998). *The knowing organization: How organizations use information to construct meaning, create knowledge, and make decisions.* New York, NY: Oxford University Press.

Choo, C. W. (2001a). Environmental scanning as information seeking and organizational learning. *Information Research, 7*(1). Retrieved from http://InformationR.net/ir/7-1/paper112.html

Choo, C. W. (2001b). *Information management for the intelligent organization: the art of scanning the environment.* Medford, NJ: Information Today.

Choo, C. W. (2007). Information seeking in organizations: Epistemic contexts and contests. *Information Research, 12*(2). Retrieved from http://InformationR.net/ir/12-2/paper298.html

Choo, C. W., & Auster, E. (1993). Environmental scanning: Acquisition and use of information by managers. In M. Williams (Ed.), *Annual review of information science and technology* (Vol. 28, pp. 279–314). Medford, NJ: Learned Information.

Choo, C. W., Bergeron, P., Detlor, B., & Heaton, L. (2008). Information culture and information use: An exploratory study of three organizations. *Journal of the American Society for Information Science and Technology, 59*(5), 792–804.

Chouhan, K., & Miles, B. (2004). Information flows and the black community. *Library & Information Update, 3*(7/8), 50–51.

Chu, C. (1999). Literary critics at work and their information needs: A research phases model. *Library & Information Science Research, 21*(2), 247–273.

Cicourel, A. V. (1964). *Method and measurement in sociology*. New York, NY: Free Press.

Clements, J. (1999). Investors' game: 'The price is right'. *Wall Street Journal, 235*(June), C1.

Cobbledick, S. (1996). The information-seeking behavior of artists: Exploratory interviews. *Library Quarterly, 66*, 343–372.

Cogdill, K. W. (2003). Information needs and information seeking in primary care: A study of nurse practitioners. *Journal of the Medical Libraries Association, 91*, 203–215.

Cohen, A. R., Stotland, E., & Wolfe, D. M. (1955). An experimental investigation of need for cognition. *Journal of Abnormal and Social Psychology, 51*, 291–294.

Cole, C. (1993). Shannon revisited: Information in terms of uncertainty. *Journal of the American Society for Information Science, 44*, 204–211.

Cole, C. (1994). Operationalizing the notion of information as a subjective construct. *Journal of the American Society for Information Science, 45*, 465–476.

Cole, C. (1998). Information acquisition in history Ph.D. students: Inferencing and the formation of knowledge structures. *The Library Quarterly, 68*(1), 33–54.

Cole, C. (2012). *Information need: A theory connecting information search to knowledge formation*. Medford, NJ: Information Today Inc.

Cole, C., & Balasubramanian, S. (1993). Age differences in consumers' search for information: Public policy implications. *Journal of Consumer Research, 20*, 157–169.

Cole, C., & Kuhlthau, C. (2000, August 16–18). Information and information seeking of novice versus expert lawyers: how experts add value. Paper presented at the Information Seeking in Context, Göteborg, Sweden.

Cole, C., Leide, J., Beheshti, J., Large, A., & Brooks, M. (2005). Investigating the anomalous states of knowledge hypothesis in a real-life problem situation: A study of history and psychology undergraduates seeking information for a course essay. *Journal of the American Society for Information Science and Technology, 56*, 1544–1554.

Coleman, J. (1988). Social capital in the creation of human capital. *American Journal of Sociology, 94*(Suppl.), 95–120.

Connaway, L. S., Dickey, T. J., & Radford, M. L. (2011). 'If it is too inconvenient I'm not going after it:' Convenience as a critical factor in information-seeking behaviors. *Library & Information Science Research, 33*(3), 179–190.

Connelly, D., Rich, E., Curley, S., & Kelly, J. (1990). Knowledge resource preference of family physicians. *The Journal of Family Practice, 30*(3), 353–359.

Cook, T., & Campbell, D. (1979). *Experimental and quasi-experimental designs for research*. Chicago, IL: Rand McNally.

Cook, T., & Leviton, L. (1980). Reviewing the literature: A comparison of traditional methods with meta-analysis. *Journal of Personality, 48*, 449–472.

Cool, C. (2001). The concept of situation in information science. In M. E. Williams (Ed.), *Annual review of information science and technology* (Vol. 35, pp. 5–42). Medford, NJ: Information Today.

Cooper, L. Z. (2002). A case study of information-seeking behavior in 7-year-old children in a semistructured situation. *Journal of the American Society for Information Science and Technology, 53*, 904–922.

Corcoran-Perry, S., & Graves, J. (1990). Supplemental-information-seeking behavior of cardiovascular nurses. *Research in Nursing & Health, 13*, 119–127.

Cornelius, I. (2002). Theorizing information. In B. Cronin (Ed.), *Annual review of information science and technology* (Vol. 36, pp. 393–425). Medford, NJ: Information Today.

Cornelius, I. V. (1996). *Meaning and method in information studies.* Norwood, NJ: Ablex Publishing Corporation.

Correia, Z., & Wilson, T. D. (2001). Factors influencing environmental scanning in the organizational context. *Information Research, 7*(1). Retrieved from http://InformationR.net/ir/7-1/paper121.html

Courtright, C. (2005). Health information-seeking among Latino newcomers: An exploratory study. *Information Research, 10*(2). Retrieved from http://InformationR.net/ir/10-2/paper224.html

Courtright, C. (2007). The problem of context in information behavior research. In B. Cronin (Ed.), *Annual review of information science and technology* (Vol. 41, pp. 273–306). Medford, NJ: Information Today.

Covell, D., Uman, G., & Manning, P. (1985). Information needs in office practice: Are they being met? *Annals of Internal Medicine, 103*, 596–599.

Cowan, S. (2004). Informing visual poetry: Information needs and sources of artists. *Art Documentation, 23*(2), 14–20.

Cox, A. M., Clough, P. D., & Marlow, J. (2008). Flickr: A first look at user behaviour in the context of photography as serious leisure. *Information Research, 13*(1). Retrieved from http://InformationR.net/ir/13-1/paper336.html

Crane, D. (1967). The gatekeepers of science: Some factors affecting the selection of articles for scientific journals. *American Sociologist, 2*(4), 195–201.

Crane, D. (1971). Information needs and uses. In C. A. Cuadra & A. W. Luke (Eds.), *Annual review of information science and technology* (Vol. 6, pp. 3–39). Chicago, IL: Encyclopaedia Britannica.

Crane, D. (1972). *Invisible colleges: Diffusion of knowledge in scientific communities.* Chicago, IL: University of Chicago Press.

Crawford, S. (1978). Information needs and uses. In M. E. Williams (Ed.), *Annual review of information science and technology* (Vol. 13, pp. 61–81). White Plains, NY: Knowledge Industry.

Creelman, J., & Harris, R. M. (1990). Coming out: The information needs of lesbians. *Collection Building, 10*(3/4), 37–41.

Creswell, J. W., & Clark, V. (2011). *Designing and conducting mixed methods research.* Los Angeles, CA: Sage Publications.

Cronin, B. (1984). *The citation process.* London: Taylor Graham.

Cronin, B., & Hert, C. A. (1995). Scholarly foraging and network discovery tools. *Journal of Documentation, 51*(4), 388–403.

Crowley, B. (2005). *Spanning the theory-practice divide in library and information science.* Lanham, MD: Scarecrow Press.

Csikszentmihalyi, M. (1990). *Flow: The psychology of optimal experience.* New York, NY: Harper and Row.

Culnan, M. J. (1983). Environmental scanning: The effects of task complexity and sources accessibility on information gathering behavior. *Decision Sciences, 14*(2), 194–206.

Curry, A. (1994). American Psycho: A collection management survey in Canadian public libraries. *Library & Information Science Research, 16*, 201–217.

Cyert, R., Simon, H., & Trow, D. (1956). Observation of a business decision. *Journal of Business, 29*, 237–248.

Czaja, R., Manfredi, C., & Price, J. (2003). The determinants and consequences of information seeking among cancer patients. *Journal of Health Communication, 8*, 529–562.

Daft, R. D., & Lengel, R. H. (1986). Organizational information requirements, media richness and structural design. *Management Science, 32*, 207–224.

Daft, R. D., Sormunen, J., & Parks, D. (1988). Chief executive scanning, environmental characteristics, and company performance: An empirical study. *Strategic Management Journal, 9*, 123–139.

Dalton, M. S., & Charnigo, L. (2004). Historians and their information sources. *College & Research Libraries, 65*, 400–425.

Darnton, R. (2000). Paris: The early Internet. *The New York Review of Books, 97*(12), 42–49.

Davenport, E. (2010). Confessional methods and everyday life information seeking. In B. Cronin (Ed.), *Annual review of information science and technology* (Vol. 44, pp. 533–562). Medford, NJ: Information Today.

Davenport, E., & Hall, H. (2002). Organizational knowledge and communities of practice. In B. Cronin (Ed.), *Annual review of information science and technology* (Vol. 36, pp. 171–219). Medford, NJ: Information Today.

Davenport, E., Higgins, M., & Somerville, I. (2000). Narratives of new media in Scottish households: The evolution of a framework of inquiry. *Journal of the American Society for Information Science, 51*, 900–912.

Davies, E., & McKenzie, P. J. (2004). Preparing for opening night: Temporal boundary objects in textually-mediated professional practice. *Information Research, 10*(1), Retrieved from http://InformationR.net/ir/10-1/paper211.html

Davies, K. (2009). Quantifying the information needs of doctors in the UK using clinical librarians. *Health Information and Libraries Journal, 26*(4), 289–297.

Davies, M. M., & Bath, P. A. (2003). Interpersonal sources of health and maternity information for Somali women living in the UK: Information seeking and evaluation. *Journal of Documentation, 58*, 302–318.

Davis, D. A., Thomson, M. A., Oxman, A. D., & Haynes, R. B. (1995). Changing physician performance: A systematic review of the effect of continuing medical education strategies. *Journal of the American Medical Association, 274*(9), 700–705.

Davis, M. (1986). 'That's classic! The phenomenology and rhetoric of successful social theories. *Philosophy of the Social Sciences, 16*, 285–301.

Davis, R., & Bailey, C. (1964). *Bibliography of use studies* (Project No. 195). Philadelphia, PA: Drexel Institute of Technology.

Dawson, M., & Chatman, E. A. (2001). Reference group theory with implications for information studies: A theoretical essay. *Information Research, 6*(3). Retrieved from http://Informationr.net/ir/6-3/paper105.html

Day, R. (2005). Clearing up 'implicit knowledge': Implications for knowledge management, information science, psychology and social epistemology. *Journal of the American Society for Information Science and Technology, 56,* 630–635.

de Alwis, G., Majid, S., & Chaudhry, A. (2006). Transformation in managers' information seeking behaviour: A review of the literature. *Journal of Information Science, 32*(4), 362–377.

de Certeau, M. (1984). *The practice of everyday life.* Berkeley, CA: University of California Press.

Dee, C. (1993). Information needs of the rural physician: A descriptive study. *Bulletin of the American Medical Association, 81*(3), 259–264.

Derr, R. L. (1983). A conceptual analysis of information need. *Information Processing & Management, 19,* 273–278.

Derr, R. L. (1985). The concept of information in ordinary discourse. *Information Processing & Management, 21*(6), 489–499.

Dervin, B. (1976a). Strategies for dealing with human information needs: Information or communication? *Journal of Broadcasting, 20*(3), 324–351.

Dervin, B. (1976b). The everyday information needs of the average citizen: A taxonomy for analysis. In M. Kochen & J. Donahue (Eds.), *Information for the community* (pp. 23–35). Chicago, IL: American Library Association.

Dervin, B. (1977). Useful theory for librarianship: Communication not information. *Drexel Library Quarterly, 13,* 16–32.

Dervin, B. (1983a). More will be less unless: The scientific humanization of information systems. *National Forum, 63*(3), 25–27.

Dervin, B. (1983b). Information as a user construct: The relevance of perceived information needs to synthesis and interpretation. In S. A. Ward & L. J. Reed (Eds.), *Knowledge structure and use: Implications for synthesis and interpretation* (pp. 153–184). Philadelphia, PA: Temple University Press.

Dervin, B. (1989). Users as research inventions: How research categories perpetuate inequities. *Journal of Communication, 39*(3), 216–232.

Dervin, B. (1991). Comparative theory reconceptulized: From entities and states to processes and dynamics. *Communication Theory, 1,* 59–69.

Dervin, B. (1992). From the mind's eye of the user: The sense-making qualitative-quantitative methodology. In J. Glazier & R. Powell (Eds.), *Qualitative research in information management* (pp. 61–84). Englewood, CO: Libraries Unlimited.

Dervin, B. (1997). Given a context by any other name: Methodological tools for taming the unruly beast. In P. Vakkari, R. Savolainen, & B. Dervin (Eds.), *Information seeking in context: Proceedings of a meeting in Finland 14-16 August 1996* (pp. 13–38). London: Taylor Graham.

Dervin, B. (1999). On studying information seeking methodologically: The implications of connecting metatheory to method. *Information Processing & Management, 35,* 727–750.

Dervin, B. (2003). Human studies and user studies: A call for methodological interdisciplinarity. *Information Research*, 9(1). Retrieved from http://InformationR.net/ir/9-1/paper166.html

Dervin, B. (2005). What methodology does to theory: Sense-making methodology as exemplar. In K. E. Fisher, S. Erdelez & E. F. McKechnie (Eds.), *Theories of information behavior* (pp. 25–30). Medford, NJ: Information Today.

Dervin, B., & Dewdney, P. (1986). Neutral questioning: A new approach to the reference interview. *RQ, 25*, 506–513.

Dervin, B., Ellyson, S., Hawkes, G., Guagnano, G., & White, N. (1984). *Information needs of California – 1984*. Davis, CA: Institute of Governmental Affairs, University of California.

Dervin, B., Foreman-Wernet, L., & Lauterbach, E. (Eds.). (2003). *Sense-making methodology reader: Selected writings of Brenda Dervin*. Cresskill, NJ: Hampton Press.

Dervin, B., & Greenberg, B. S. (1972). The communication environment of the urban poor. In F. Kline & P. Titchenor (Eds.), *Current perspectives in mass communication research* (pp. 195–235). Beverly Hills, CA: Sage Publications.

Dervin, B., Jacobson, T., & Nilan, M. (1982). Measuring aspects of information seeking: A test of a quantitative/qualitative methodology. In M. Burgoon (Ed.), *Communication yearbook* (Vol. 6, pp. 419–445). Beverly Hills, CA: Sage Publications.

Dervin, B., & Nilan, M. (1986). Information needs and uses. In M. Williams (Ed.), *Annual review of information science and technology* (Vol. 21, pp. 1–25). White Plains, NY: Knowledge Industry.

Dervin, B., Nilan, M., & Jacobson, T. (1982). Improving predictions of information use: A comparison of predictor types in a health communication setting. In M. Burgoon (Ed.), *Communication yearbook* (Vol. 5, pp. 807–830). Beverly Hills, CA: Sage Publications.

Desouza, K., Awazu, Y., & Wan, Y. (2006). Factors governing the consumption of explicit knowledge. *Journal of the American Society for Information Science and Technology, 57*(1), 36–43.

Detlefsen, E. G. (2004). Where am I to go? Use of the internet for consumer health information by two vulnerable communities. *Library Trends, 53*, 283–300.

Deutsch, K. W. (1963). *The nerves of government: Models of political communication and control*. New York, NY: Free Press.

DeWeese, L. (1967). A bibliography of use studies: A supplement to Davis, R. A. and Bailey, C. A. "Bibliography of use studies," Drexel Institute of Technology, 1964. Lafayette, IN: Purdue University.

Dewey, J. (1910/1933). *How we think*. Boston, MA: D.C. Heath.

Dewey, J. (1960). *On experience, nature, and freedom*. New York, NY: The Liberal Arts Press.

Dick, A. (1999). Epistemological positions and library and information science. *Library Quarterly, 69*, 305–323.

Diener, E., & Crandall, R. (1978). *Ethics in social and behavioral research*. Chicago, IL: University of Chicago Press.

Dillman, D., Smyth, J., & Christian, L. (2008). *Internet, mail and mixed-mode surveys: The tailored design method* (3rd ed.). New York, NY: Wiley.

Dimmick, J., Kline, S., & Stafford, L. (2000). The gratification niches of personal e-mail and the telephone. *Communication Research, 27*, 227–248.

Dixon, C. M. (2005). Strength of weak ties. In K. E. Fisher, S. Erdelez & E. F. McKechnie (Eds.), *Theories of information behavior* (pp. 344–348). Medford, NJ: Information Today.

Donat, J. F., & Pettigrew, K. E. (2002). The final context: Information behaviour surrounding the dying patient. *The New Review of Information Behaviour Research: Studies of Information Seeking in Context (Proceedings of ISIC 2002), 3*, 175–186.

Donnelly, W. (1986). *The confetti generation: How the new communications technology is fragmenting America.* New York, NY: Henry Holt & Company.

Donohew, L., Nair, M., & Finn, S. (1984). Automaticity, arousal, and information exposure. In R. Bostrom & B. Westley (Eds.), *Communication yearbook* (Vol. 8, pp. 267–284). Beverly Hills, CA: Sage Publications.

Donohew, L., & Tipton, L. (1973). A conceptual model of information seeking, avoiding and processing. In P. Clarke (Ed.), *New models for mass communication research* (pp. 243–269). Beverly Hills, CA: Sage Publications.

Donohew, L., Tipton, L., & Haney, R. (1978). Analysis of information-seeking strategies. *Journalism Quarterly, 55*, 25–31.

Donohue, G. A., Olien, C. N., & Tichenor, P. J. (1989). Structure and constraints on community newspaper gatekeepers. *Journalism Quarterly, 66*, 807–812.

Dorsch, J. L., & Pifalo, V. (1997). Information needs of rural health professionals: A retrospective study. *Bulletin of the Medical Library Association, 85*, 341–347.

Downey, G. (2007). Human geography and information studies. In B. Cronin (Ed.), *Annual Review of Information Science and Technology* (Vol. 41, pp. 683–727). Medford, NJ: Information Today, Inc.

Doyal, L., & Gough, I. (1984). A theory of human needs. *Critical Social Policy, 11*, 147–150.

Dozier, D., & Rice, R. (1984). Rival theories of electronic newsreading. In R. Rice (Ed.), *The new media* (pp. 103–128). Beverly Hills, CA: Sage Publications.

Dresang, E. (1999). More research needed: Informal information-seeking behavior of youth on the internet. *Journal of the American Society for Information Science, 50*, 1123–1124.

Dretske, F. (1990). Putting information to work. In P. Hanson (Ed.), *Information, language, and cognition* (pp. 112–124). Vancouver: University of British Columbia Press.

Dretske, F. I. (1981). *Knowledge and the flow of information.* Cambridge: MIT Press.

Dretske, F. I. (1983). Précis of 'Knowledge & the flow of information'. *Behavioral and Brain Sciences, 6*, 55–90.

Driscoll, J. M., & Lanzetta, J. T. (1965). Effects of two sources of uncertainty in decision making. *Psychological Reports, 17*, 635–648.

du Preez, M., & Fourie, I. (2009). The information behaviour of consulting engineers in South Africa. *Mousaion, 27*(1), 137–158.

Duff, W. M., & Johnson, C. A. (2002). Accidentally found on purpose: Information seeking behavior of historians in archives. *Library Quarterly*, *72*, 475–499.

Duff, W. M., & Johnson, C. A. (2003). Where is the list with all the names? Information-seeking behavior of genealogists. *American Archivist*, *66*(1), 79–95.

Duncan, R. (1972). Characteristics of organizational environments and perceived environmental uncertainty. *Administrative Science Quarterly*, *17*, 313–327.

Dunne, J. E. (2002). Information seeking and use by battered women: A "person-in-progressive-situations" approach. *Library & Information Science Research*, *24*, 343–355.

Dupagne, M., & Garrison, B. (2006). The meaning and influence of convergence: A qualitative case study of newsroom work at the Tampa News Center. *Journalism Studies*, *7*, 237–255.

Dupuit, J. (1952). On the measurement of the utility of public works. *International Economic Papers*, *2*, 83–110.

Durkheim, E. (1951). *Suicide*. Glencoe, IL: The Free Press.

Durlak, J. (1987). A typology of interactive media. In M. McLaughlin (Ed.), *Communication yearbook* (Vol. 10, pp. 743–757). Beverly Hills, CA: Sage Publications.

Durrance, J. C. (1984). *Armed for action – Library response to citizen information needs*. New York, NY: Neal-Schuman Publishers.

Durrance, J. C. (1988). Information needs: Old song, new tune. *Rethinking the library* (pp. 159–178). Washington, DC: United States Government Printing Office.

Edwards, P. M. (2005). Taylor's question negotiation. In K. E. Fisher, S. Erdelez & E. F. McKechnie (Eds.), *Theories of information behavior* (pp. 358–362). Medford, NJ: Information Today.

Eisenberg, M. B. (1988). Measuring relevance judgments. *Information Processing & Management*, *24*, 373–389.

Ek, S., & Heinström, J. (2011). Monitoring or avoiding health information – The relation to inner inclination and health status. *Health Information and Libraries Journal*, *28*(3), 200–209.

Ek, S., & Widén-Wulff, G. (2008). Information mastering, perceived health and societal status: An empirical study of the Finnish population. *Libri*, *58*, 74–81.

Ekoja, I. I. (2004). Sensitising users for increased information use: The case of Nigerian farmers. *African Journal of Library, Archives & Information Science*, *14*, 193–204.

Ekström, M. (2000). Information, storytelling and attractions: TV journalism in three modes of communication. *Media, Culture & Society*, *22*, 465–492.

Eliot, C. W. (1902). The divisions of a library into books in use, and books not in use. *Library Journal*, *27*(July), 51–56.

Ellis, B. E. (1985). *Less than zero*. New York, NY: Simon & Schuster.

Ellis, B. E. (1991). *American psycho*. New York, NY: Vintage Books.

Ellis, B. E. (2010). *Imperial bedrooms*. New York, NY: Random House.

Ellis, D. (1989). A behavioural approach to information retrieval design. *Journal of Documentation*, *45*, 171–212.

Ellis, D. (1993). Modeling the information seeking patterns of academic researchers: A grounded theory approach. *Library Quarterly*, *6*(3), 469–486.

Ellis, D. (2005). Ellis's model of information-seeking behavior. In K. E. Fisher, S. Erdelez & E. F. McKechnie (Eds.), *Theories of information behavior* (pp. 138–142). Medford, NJ: Information Today.

Ellis, D., Cox, D., & Hall, K. (1993). A comparison of the information seeking patterns of researchers in the physical and social sciences. *Journal of Documentation, 49*, 356–369.

Ellis, D., & Haugan, M. (1997). Modelling the information seeking patterns of engineers and research scientists in an industrial environment. *Journal of Documentation, 53*(4), 384–403.

Elsweiler, D., Wilson, M., & Kirkegaard-Lunn, B. (2011). Understanding casual-leisure information behaviour. In A. Spink & J. Heinström (Eds.), *New directions in information behaviour* (Vol. 1, pp. 211–241). Bingley, UK: Emerald Group Publishing Limited.

Ely, J., Burch, R., & Vinson, D. (1992). The information needs of family physicians: Case-specific clinical questions. *The Journal of Family Practice, 35*(3), 265–269.

Enochsson, A. (2000, August 16–18). Children choosing web pages. Paper presented at the Information Seeking in Context, Göteborg, Sweden.

Eppler, M. J., & Mengis, J. (2004). The concept of information overload: A review of literature from organization science, accounting, marketing, MIS, and related disciplines. *The Information Society, 30*, 325–344.

Erdelez, S. (1997). Information encountering: A conceptual framework for accidental information discovery. In P. Vakkari, R. Savolainen & B. Dervin (Eds.), *Information seeking in context: Proceedings of a meeting in Finland 14–16 August 1996* (pp. 412–421). London: Taylor Graham.

Erdelez, S. (1999). Information encountering: It's more than bumping into information. *Bulletin of the American Society for Information Science, 25*(3), 25–29.

Erdelez, S. (2004). Investigation of information encountering in the controlled research environment. *Information Processing & Management, 40*(6), 1013–1025.

Erdelez, S. (2005). Information encountering. In K. E. Fisher, S. Erdelez & E. F. McKechnie (Eds.), *Theories of information behavior* (pp. 179–184). Medford, NJ: Information Today.

Erdelez, S., & Rioux, K. (2000, August 16–18). Sharing information encountered for others on the web. Paper presented at the Information Seeking in Context, Göteborg, Sweden.

Eriksson-Backa, K. (2008). Access to health information: Perceptions of barriers among elderly in a language minority. *Information Research, 13*(4). Retrieved from http://InformationR.net/ir/13-4/paper368.html

Eriksson-Backa, K. (2010). Elderly people, health information, and libraries: A small-scale study on seniors in a language minority. *Libri, 60*(2), 181–194.

Fabritius, H. (1999). Triangulation as a multi-perspective strategy in a qualitative study of information seeking behaviour of journalists. In T. D. Wilson & D. K. Allen (Eds.), *Information behaviour: Proceedings of the second international conference on research in information needs, seeking and use in different contexts, 13/15 August 1998, Sheffield, UK* (pp. 406–419). London: Taylor Graham.

Fairthorne, R. A. (1969). The scope and aims of the information sciences and technologies. In International Federation for Documentation, Committee on

Research on the Theoretical Basis of Information, *On theoretical problems of informatics*, FID 435 (pp. 25–31). Moscow: All-Union Institute for Scientific and Technological Information.

Fairthorne, R. (1975). Information: One label, several bottles. In A. Debons & W. Cameron (Eds.), *Perspectives in information science* (pp. 65–73). Leyden: Noordhof.

Farhoomand, A. F., & Drury, D. H. (2002). Managerial information overload. *Communications of the ACM, 45*(10), 127–131.

Feltwell, A. K., & Rees, C. E. (2004). The information-seeking behavior of partners of men with prostrate cancer: A qualitative study. *Patient Education and Counseling, 54*, 179–185.

Ferguson, D. A., & Perse, E. M. (2000). The world wide web as a functional alternative to television. *Journal of Broadcasting and Electronic Media, 44*, 155–174.

Fidel, R. (2008). Are we there yet? Mixed methods research in library and information science. *Library & Information Science Research, 30*(4), 265–272.

Fidel, R., & Green, M. (2004). The many faces of accessibility: Engineers' perception of information sources. *Information Processing & Management, 40*, 563–581.

Fidel, R., Pejtersen, A. M., Cleal, B., & Bruce, H. (2004). A multidimensional approach to the study of human-information interaction: A case study of collaborative information retrieval. *Journal of the American Society for Information Science and Technology, 55*, 939–953.

Finholt, T. A. (2002). Collaboratories. In B. Cronin (Ed.), *Annual review of information science and technology* (Vol. 36, pp. 73–107). Medford, NJ: Information Today.

Finn, S. (1985). Information-theoretic measures of reader enjoyment. *Written Communication, 2*(4), 358–376.

Finn, S. (1986). Unpredictability as a correlate of reader enjoyment of news articles. *Journalism Quarterly, 62*, 334–339.

Fischer, D. H. (1970). *Historians' fallacies*. New York, NY: Harper & Row.

Fish, S. (1987). *Is there a text in this class? The authority of interpretive communities* (2nd ed.). Cambridge, MA: Harvard University Press.

Fishbein, M., & Ajzen, I. (1975). *Belief, attitude, intention and behavior: An introduction to theory and research*. Reding, MA: Addison-Wesley.

Fisher, K. E. (2005). Information grounds. In K. E. Fisher, S. Erdelez & E. F. McKechnie (Eds.), *Theories of information behavior* (pp. 185–190). Medford, NJ: Information Today.

Fisher, K. E., Durrance, J. C., & Hinton, M. B. (2004). Information grounds and the use of need-based services by immigrants in Queens, New York: A context-based, outcome evaluation approach. *Journal of the American Society for Information Science and Technology, 55*, 754–766.

Fisher, K. E., Erdelez, S., & McKechnie, E. F. (Eds.). (2005). *Theories of information behavior*. Medford, NJ: Information Today.

Fisher, K. E., & Julien, H. (2009). Information behavior. In B. Cronin (Ed.), *Annual review of information science and technology* (Vol. 43). Medford, NJ: Information Today.

Fisher, K. E., & Landry, C. F. (2007). Understanding the information behavior of stay-at-home mothers through affect. In D. Nahl & D. Bilal (Eds.), *Information and emotion: The emergent affective paradigm in information behavior research and theory* (pp. 211–233). Medford, NJ: Information Today.

Fisher, K. E., Marcoux, E., Miller, L. S., Sánchez, A., & Cunningham, E. R. (2004). Information behaviour of migrant Hispanic farm workers and their families in the Pacific Northwest. *Information Research, 10*(1). Retrieved from InformationR.net/ir/10-1/paper199.html

Fisher, K. E., Naumer, C., Durrance, J. C., Stromski, L., & Christiansen, T. (2005). Something old, something new: Preliminary findings from an exploratory study about people's information habits and information grounds. *Information Research, 10*(2). Retrieved from http://InformationR.net/ir/10-2/paper223.html

Flanagin, A. J., & Metzger, M. J. (2001). Internet use in the contemporary media environment. *Human Communication Research, 27*, 153–181.

Flaxbart, D. (2001). Conversations with chemists: Information-seeking behavior of chemistry faculty in the electronic age. *Science and Technology Libraries, 21*(3/4), 5–26.

Floridi, L. (2005). Is information meaningful data? *Philosophy and Phenomenological Research, 70*, 351–370.

Florio, E., & DeMartini, J. (1993). The use of information by policymakers at the local community level. *Knowledge: Creation, diffusion, utilization, 15*, 106–123.

Folkman, S. (1984). Personal control and stress and coping processes: A theoretical analysis. *Journal of Personality and Social Psychology, 46*, 839–852.

Ford, L. A., Babrow, A. S., & Stohl, C. (1996). Social support and the management of uncertainty: An application of problematic integration theory. *Communication Monographs, 63*, 189–207.

Ford, N. (2003). Towards a model of learning for educational informatics. *Journal of Documentation, 60*(2), 183–225.

Ford, N. (2004a). Modeling cognitive processes in information seeking: From Popper to Pask. *Journal of the American Society for Information Science and Technology, 55*, 769–782.

Ford, N. (2004b). Creativity and convergence in information science research: The roles of objectivity and subjectivity, constraint, and control. *Journal of the American Society for Information Science and Technology, 55*, 1169–1182.

Formanek, R. (1991). Why they collect: Collectors reveal their motivations. *Journal of Social Behavior and Personality, 6*(6), 275–286.

Forsythe, D., Buchanan, B., Osheroff, J., & Miller, R. (1992). Expanding the concept of medical information: An observational study of physicians' information needs. *Computers and Biomedical Research, 25*, 181–200.

Foster, A. (2004). A nonlinear model of information-seeking behavior. *Journal of the American Society for Information Science and Technology, 55*, 228–237.

Foster, A., & Ford, N. (2003). Serendipity and information seeking: An empirical study. *Journal of Documentation, 59*, 321–343.

Foster, A., Urquhart, C., & Turner, J. (2008). Validating coding for a theoretical model of information behaviour. *Information Research, 13*(4). Retrieved from http://InformationR.net/ir/13-4/paper358.html

Foster, J. (2009). Understanding interaction in information seeking and use as a discourse: A dialogic approach. *Journal of Documentation, 65*(1), 83–105.

Foucault, M. (1972). *The order of things: An archaeology of the human sciences.* London: Tavistock.

Foucault, M. (1980). *Power/knowledge: Selected interviews and writings, 1972–1977.* London: Harvester Press.

Fourie, I. (2008). Information needs and information behaviour of patients and their family members in a cancer palliative care setting: An exploratory study of an existential context from different perspectives. *Information Research, 13*(4). Retrieved from http://InformationR.net/ir/13-4/paper360.html

Fourie, I. (2009). Learning from research on the information behaviour of healthcare professionals: A review of the literature 2004–2008 with a focus on emotion. *Health Information & Libraries Journal, 26*(3), 171–186.

Fox, C. J. (1983). *Information and misinformation.* Westport, CT: Greenwood Press.

Fox, S. (2011). *Health Topics: 80% of internet users look for health information online.* Washington, DC: Pew Research Center.

Foxall, G. R. (1983). *Consumer choice.* New York, NY: St. Martin's Press.

Friedson, E. (1986). *Professional powers: A Study of the institutionalization of formal knowledge.* Chicago, IL: University of Chicago Press.

Freimuth, V. (1990). The chronically uninformed: Closing the knowledge gap in health. In E. Ray & L. Donohew (Eds.), *Communication and health: Systems and applications* (pp. 171–186). Hillsdale, NJ: Lawrence Erlbaum Associates.

Freimuth, V., Edgar, T., & Fitzpatrick, M. (1993). Introduction: The role of communication in health promotion. *Communication Research, 20,* 509–516.

Freimuth, V. S., Stein, J. A., & Kean, T. J. (1989). *Searching for health information: The Cancer Information Service model.* Philadelphia, PA: University of Pennsylvania Press.

Freud, S. (1922). *Beyond the pleasure principle* (C. Hubback, Trans.). London: International Psycho-Analytic Press.

Freud, S. (1905/1960). *Jokes and their relation to the unconscious.* New York, NY: W. W. Norton & Company.

Freund, L., Toms, E. G., & Waterhouse, J. (2005). Modeling the information behaviour of software engineers using a work-task framework. In A. Grove (Ed.), *ASIS&T'05: Proceedings of the annual meeting of the American Society for Information Science and Technology* (Vol. 42, pp. 187–214). Silver Spring, MD: American Society for Information Science and Technology.

Frey, D. (1982). Different levels of cognitive dissonance, information seeking, and information avoidance. *Journal of Personality and Social Psychology, 43,* 1175–1183.

Frey, D., & Rosch, M. (1984). Information seeking after decisions: The roles of novelty of information and decision reversibility. *Personality and Social Psychology Bulletin, 10,* 91–98.

Frické, M. (1997). Information using likeness measures. *Journal of the American Society for Information Science, 48,* 882–892.

Frické, M. (2009). The knowledge pyramid: A critique of the DIKW hierarchy. *Journal of Information Science, 35*(2), 131–142.

Friestad, M., & Wright, P. (1994). The persuasion knowledge model: How people cope with persuasion attempts. *Journal of Consumer Research, 21,* 1–27.

Froehlich, T. J. (1991). Towards a better conceptual framework for understanding relevance for information science research. *Proceedings of the 54th annual meeting of the American Society for Information Science,* Learned Information, Medford, NJ (Vol. 28, pp. 118–125).

Froehlich, T. J. (1994). Relevance reconsidered – Towards an agenda for the 21st century: Introduction to special topic issue on relevance research. *Journal of the American Society for Information Science, 45,* 124–134.

Frohmann, B. P. (2004). *Deflating information: From science studies to documentation.* Toronto: University of Toronto Press.

Fry, J. (2006). Scholarly research and information practices: A domain analytic approach. *Information Processing & Management, 42,* 299–316.

Fulton, C. (2005a). Chatman's life in the round. In K. E. Fisher, S. Erdelez & E. F. McKechnie (Eds.), *Theories of information behavior* (pp. 79–82). Medford, NJ: Information Today.

Fulton, C. (2005b). Finding pleasure in information seeking: Leisure and amateur genealogists exploring their Irish ancestry. In A. Grove (Ed.), *ASIS&T'05: Proceedings of the annual meeting of the American Society for Information Science and Technology* (Vol. 42, pp. 1292–1303). Silver Spring, MD: American Society for Information Science and Technology.

Fulton, C. (2009a). Quid pro quo: Information sharing in leisure activities. *Library Trends, 57*(4), 753–768.

Fulton, C. (2009b). The pleasure principle: The power of positive affect in information seeking. *Aslib Proceedings, 61*(3), 245–261.

Furner, J. (2004). Information studies without information. *Library Trends, 52,* 427–446.

Furse, D., Punj, G., & Stewart, D. (1984). A typology of individual search strategies among purchasers of new automobiles. *Journal of Consumer Research, 10,* 417–431.

Gadamer, H. G. (1976). *Philosophical hermeneutics* (D. Linge, Trans.). Berkeley, CA: University of California Press.

Gantz, W., Fitzmaurice, M., & Fink, E. (1991). Assessing the active component of information-seeking. *Journalism Quarterly, 68,* 630–637.

Gardner, H. (1985). *The mind's new science: A history of the cognitive revolution.* New York, NY: Basic Books.

Garfinkel, H. (1967). *Studies in ethnomethodology.* Englewood Cliffs, NJ: Prentice Hall.

Garner, W. R. (1962). *Uncertainty and structure as psychological concepts.* New York, NY: Wiley.

Garvey, W. D. (1979). *Communication: The essence of science.* Oxford: Pergamon.

Gaziano, C. (1997). Forecast 2000: Widening knowledge gaps. *Journalism and Mass Communication Quarterly, 74*(2), 237–264.

Geertz, C. (1973). *The interpretation of culture.* New York, NY: Basic Books.

Gelder, A. (1981). *A study of information needs and habits of different groups of users of employment law.* Unpublished Masters of Science, City University, London.

Gerrig, R. J., & Prentice, D. A. (1991). The representation of fictional information. *Psychological Science, 2,* 336–340.

Gerstberger, P., & Allen, T. (1968). Criteria used by research and development engineers in the selection of an information source. *Journal of Applied Psychology, 52,* 272–279.

Gettier, Jr., E. (1963). Is justified true belief knowledge? *Analysis, 23,* 121–123.

Getz, I., & Weissman, G. (2010). An information needs profile of Israeli older adults, regarding the law and services. *Journal of Librarianship & Information Science, 42*(2), 136–146.

Giddens, A. (1984). *The constitution of society: Outline of the theory of structuration.* Cambridge, UK: Polity Press.

Giddens, A. (1989). The orthodox consensus and the emerging synthesis. In B. Dervin, L. Grossberg, B. O'Keefe & E. Wartella (Eds.), *Rethinking communication: Paradigm issues* (Vol. 1, pp. 53–65). Newbury Park, CA: Sage Publications.

Given, L. (2002a). Discursive constructions in the university context: Social positioning theory and mature undergraduates' information behaviours. *The New Review of Information Behaviour Research: Studies of Information Seeking in Context (Proceedings of ISIC 2002), 3,* 127–142.

Given, L. (2002b). The academic and the everyday: Investigating the overlap in mature undergraduates' information-seeking behaviors. *Library & Information Science Research, 24,* 17–29.

Given, L. (2005). Social positioning. In K. E. Fisher, S. Erdelez & E. F. McKechnie (Eds.), *Theories of information behavior* (pp. 334–338). Medford, NJ: Information Today.

Glaser, B., & Strauss, A. (1967). *The discovery of grounded theory: Strategies for qualitative research.* Chicago, IL: Aldine Publishing Co.

Glass, A., Holyoak, K., & Santa, J. (1979). *Cognition.* Reading, MA: Addison-Wesley.

Godbold, N. (2006). Beyond information seeking: Towards a general model of information behaviour. *Information Research, 11*(4). Retrieved from http://InformationR.net/ir/11-4/paper269.html

Goffman, E. (1959). *The presentation of self in everyday life.* New York, NY: Doubleday.

Goffman, E. (1974). *Frame analysis: An essay on the organization of experience.* New York, NY: Macmillan.

Goffman, E. (1983). Interaction order. *American Sociological Review, 48,* 1–17.

Goldman, A. I. (1970). *A theory of human action.* Princeton, NJ: Princeton University Press.

Goldstein, W. M., & Hogarth, R. M. (1997). *Research on judgment and decision-making: Currents, connections and controversies.* New York, NY: Cambridge University Press.

González-Teruel, A., & Abad-García, M. F. (2007). Information needs and uses: An analysis of the literature published in Spain, 1990–2004. *Library & Information Science Research, 29*(1), 30–46.

Goren, D. (1989). Journalists as scientists or prophets? Comments on Katz. *American Behavioral Scientist, 33*, 251–254.

Gorman, P. (1995). Information needs of physicians. *Journal of the American Society for Information Science, 46*, 737–742.

Gorman, P. (1999). Information seeking of primary care physicians: Conceptual models and empirical studies. In T. D. Wilson & D. K. Allen (Eds.), *Information behaviour: Proceedings of the second international conference on research in information needs, seeking and use in different contexts, 13/15 August 1998, Sheffield, UK* (pp. 226–240). London: Taylor Graham.

Gorman, P., & Helfand, M. (1995). Information seeking in primary care: How physicians choose which clinical questions to pursue and which to leave unanswered. *Medical Decision Making, 15*, 113–119.

Gorman, P., Lavelle, M., Delcambre, L., & Maier, D. (2002). Following experts at work in their own information spaces: Using observational methods to develop tolls for the digital library. *Journal of the American Society for Information Science and Technology, 53*, 1245–1250.

Gould, C. (1988). *Information needs in the humanities: An assessment*. Stanford, CA: Research Libraries Group.

Gould, C., & Handler, G. (1989). *Information needs in the social sciences: An assessment*. Stanford, CA: Research Libraries Group.

Gould, C., & Pearce, K. (1991). *Information needs in the sciences: An assessment*. Mountain View, CA: Research Libraries Group.

Goulding, A. (2001). Information poverty or overload? *Journal of Librarianship and Information Science, 33*, 109–111.

Graber, D. (1984). *Processing the news: How people tame the information tide*. New York, NY: Longman.

Graber, D. (1989). Content and meaning: What's it all about? *American Behavioral Scientist, 33*, 144–151.

Gralewska-Vickery, A. (1973). Communication and information needs of earth science engineers. *Information Processing and Management, 12*(4), 251–282.

Granovetter, M. S. (1973). The strength of weak ties. *American Journal of Sociology, 78*, 1360–1380.

Granovetter, M. S. (1982). The strength of weak ties: A network theory revisited. In P. Marsden & N. Lin (Eds.), *Social structure and network analysis* (pp. 105–130). Beverly Hills, CA: Sage Publications.

Gratch, B. (1990). Exploring the principle of least effort and its value to research. *C&RL News, 51*, 727–728.

Green, A. (1990). What do we mean by user needs? *British Journal of Academic Librarianship, 5*, 65–78.

Greenberg, B., Bowes, J., & Dervin, B. (1970). *Communication and related behaviors of a sample of Cleveland Black adults*. Project CUP, Report No. 13, Communication among the urban poor. Michigan State University, East Lansing, MI.

Griffin, R. J., Dunwoody, S., & Neuwirth, K. (1999). Proposed model of the relationship of risk information seeking and processing to the development of preventive behaviors. *Environmental Research Section A, 80*, S230–S245.

Gross, M. (2001). Imposed information seeking in public libraries and school library media centers: A common behaviour? *Information Research*, 6(2). Retrieved from http://InformationR.net/ir/6-2/paper100.html

Gross, M. (2004a). Children's information seeking at school: Findings from a qualitative study. In M. K. Chelton & C. Cool (Eds.), *Youth information-seeking behavior: Theories, models and issues* (pp. 211–240). Lanham, MD: Scarecrow Press.

Gross, M. (2004b). *Children's questions: Information seeking behavior in school.* Lanham, MD: Scarecrow Press.

Gross, M., & Saxton, M. (2001). Who wants to know? Imposed queries in the public library. *Public Libraries*, 40(3), 170–176.

Grunig, J. (1989). Publics, audience and market segments: Segmentation principles for campaigns. In C. Salmon (Ed.), *Information campaigns: Balancing social values and social change* (pp. 199–228). Beverly Hills, CA: Sage Publications.

Guba, E. G., & Lincoln, Y. S. (2005). Paradigmatic controversies, contradictions, and emerging influences. In N. K. Denzin & Y. S. Lincoln (Eds.), *The Sage handbook of qualitative research* (pp. 191–215). Thousand Oaks, CA: Sage.

Gundry, L. K., & Rousseau, D. M. (1994). Critical incidents in communicating culture to newcomers. *Human Relations*, 47, 1063–1087.

Guo, B. (2009). Moderating effects of task characteristics on information source use: An individual-level analysis of R&D professionals in new product development. *Journal of Information Science*, 35(5), 527–547.

Habermas, J. (1979). *Communication and the evolution of society* (T. McCarthy, Trans.). Boston, MA: Beacon Press.

Habermas, J. (1984). *Theory of communicative action. Reason and rationalization of society* (T. McCarthy, Trans., Vol. 1). Boston, MA: Beacon Press.

Habermas, J. (1987). *Theory of communicative action. Lifeworld and system: A critique of functionalist reason* (Vol. 2). New York, NY: Polity Press.

Hacking, I. (1999). *The social construction of what?* Cambridge, MA: Harvard University Press.

Haider, J., & Bawden, D. (2007). Conceptions of 'information poverty' in LIS: A discourse analysis. *Journal of Documentation*, 63, 534–557.

Haig, P. (1993). Nursing journals: Are nurses using them? *Nursing Standard*, 8(1), 22–25.

Hainsworth, M.M. (1992). *Information seeking behavior of judges.* Unpublished doctoral. Florida State University, Tallahassee, FL.

Hall, H. (2003). Borrowed theory: Applying exchange theories in information science research. *Library & Information Science Research*, 25, 287–305.

Hall, H., & Widén, G. (2008). Social exchange, social capital and information sharing in line environments: Lessons from three case studies. Paper presented at the conference, "From information provision to knowledge production," Oulu, Finland.

Hallmark, J. (2001). Information-seeking behavior of academic meteorologists and the role of information specialists. *Science and Technology Libraries*, 21(1/2), 53–64.

Hamer, J. S. (2003). Coming-out: Gay males' information seeking. *School Libraries Worldwide*, 9(2), 73–89.

Hampshire, S. (1982). *Thought and action.* Notre Dame: University of Notre Dame Press.

Haras, C. (2011). Information behaviors of Latinos attending high school in East Los Angeles. *Library & Information Science Research, 33*(1), 34–40.

Hardy, A. (1982). The selection of channels when seeking information: Cost/benefit vs. least effort. *Information Processing & Management, 18,* 289–293.

Harré, R. (1984). *Personal being: A theory for individual psychology.* Cambridge, MA: Harvard University Press.

Harré, R. (1994). *The discursive mind.* Thousand Oaks, CA: Sage Publications.

Harris, R. M. (1988). The information needs of battered women. *RQ, 27,* 62–70.

Harris, R. M., & Dewdney, P. (1994). *Barriers to information: how formal help systems fail battered women.* Westport, CT: Greenwood Press.

Harris, R. M., Veinot, T. C., & Bella, L. (2010). A relational perspective on HIV/AIDS information behaviour in rural Canada. *Libri, 60*(2), 129–141.

Harris, R.M., Wathen, C.N., & Fear, J. M. (2006). Searching for health information in rural Canada. Where do residents look for health information and what do they do when they find it? *Information Research, 12*(1). Retrieved from http://InformationR.net/ir/12-1/paper274.html

Harrison, J., Hepworth, M., & de Chazal, P. (2004). NHS and social care interface: A study of social workers' library and information needs. *Journal of Librarianship and Information Science, 36*(1), 27–35.

Hartel, J. (2003). The serious leisure frontier in library and information studies: Hobby domains (Special Issue: Domain Analysis). *Knowledge Organization, 3,* 228–238.

Hartel, J. (2005). Serious leisure. In K. E. Fisher, S. Erdelez & E. F. McKechnie (Eds.), *Theories of information behavior* (pp. 313–317). Medford, NJ: Information Today.

Hartel, J. (2010). Managing documents at home for serious leisure: A case study of the hobby of gourmet cooking. *Journal of Documentation, 66*(6), 847–874.

Hartel, J. (2011). Information in the hobby of gourmet cooking: Four contexts. In W. Aspray & B. Hayes (Eds.), *Everyday information: The evolution of information seeking in America* (pp. 217–248). Cambridge, MA: MIT Press.

Harter, S. P. (1992). Psychological relevance and information science. *Journal of the American Society for Information Science, 43,* 602–615.

Haruna, I., & Mabawonku, I. (2001). Information needs and seeking behaviour of legal practitioners and the challenges to law libraries in Lagos, Nigeria. *International Information and Library Review, 33*(1), 69–87.

Haug, J. D. (1997). Physicians' preferences for information sources: A meta analytic study. *Bulletin of the Medical Library Association, 85*(3), 223–232.

Hauser, J., Urban, G., & Weinberg, B. (1993). How consumers allocate their time when searching for information. *Journal of Marketing Research, 30,* 452–466.

Hayes, R. (1993). Measurement of information. *Information Processing & Management, 29,* 1–11.

Hayter, S. (2007). The affective dimensions of information behaviour: A small world perspective. In D. Nahl & D. Bilal (Eds.), *Information and emotion: The emergent affective paradigm in information behavior research and theory* (pp. 255–266). Medford, NJ: Information Today.

Haythornthwaite, C. (1996). Social network analysis: An approach and technique for the study of information exchange. *Library & Information Science Research, 18*(4), 323–342.

Heap, J. (1975). What are sense making practices? *Sociological Inquiry, 46*, 107–115.

Heffernan, M. (2011). *Willful blindness.* New York, NY: Walker Publishing.

Heinström, J. (2003). Five personality dimensions and their influence on information behaviour. *Information Research, 9*(1). Retrieved from http://InformationR.net/ir/9-1/paper165.html

Heinström, J. (2006). Psychological factors behind incidental information acquisition. *Library & Information Science Research, 28*(4), 579–594.

Heinström, J. (2010). *From fear to flow: Personality and information interaction.* Oxford: Chandos Publishing.

Hektor, A. (2003). Information activities on the internet in everyday life. *The New Review of Information Behaviour Research: Studies of Information Seeking in Context (Proceedings of ISIC 2002), 4*, 127–138.

Held, D. (1980). *Introduction to critical theory: Horkheimer to Habermas.* Berkeley, CA: University of California Press.

Hemmig, W. (2009). An empirical study of the information-seeking behavior of practicing visual artists. *Journal of Documentation, 65*(4), 682–703.

Hemminger, B. M., Lu, D., Vaughan, K. T. L., & Adams, S. J. (2007). Information seeking behavior of academic scientists. *Journal of the American Society for Information Science and Technology, 58*(14), 2205–2225.

Hempel, C. (1952). Fundamentals of concept formation in empirical science. *International encyclopedia of unified science* (Vol. 2, No. 7). Chicago, IL: University of Chicago Press.

Henefer, J., & Fulton, C. (2005). Krikelas's model of information seeking. In K. E. Fisher, S. Erdelez & E. F. McKechnie (Eds.), *Theories of information behavior* (pp. 225–229). Medford, NJ: Information Today.

Henning, B., & Vorderer, P. (2001). Psychological escapism: Predicting the amount of television viewing by need for cognition. *Journal of Communication, 51*(1), 100–120.

Hepworth, M. (2004). A framework for understanding user requirements for an information service: Defining the needs of informal carriers. *Journal of the American Society for Information Science and Technology, 55*, 695–708.

Hepworth, M., & Harrison, J. (2004). A Survey of the information needs of people with Multiple Sclerosis. *Health Informatics Journal, 10*(1), 49–69.

Hepworth, M., Harrison, J., & James, N. (2003a). Information needs of people with MS. *Library & Information Update, 2*(3), 38–39.

Hepworth, M., Harrison, J., & James, N. (2003b). Information needs of people with multiple sclerosis and the implications for information provision based on a national UK survey. *Aslib Proceedings, 55*, 290–303.

Herman, E. (2004a). Research in progress: Some preliminary and key insights into the information needs of the contemporary academic researcher: Part 1. *Aslib Proceedings, 56*, 34–47.

Herman, E. (2004b). Research in progress: Some preliminary insights into the information needs of the contemporary academic researcher: Part 2. *Aslib Proceedings, 56*, 118–131.

Herner, S. (1970). Browsing. In A. Kent & H. Lancour (Eds.), *Encyclopedia of library and information science* (Vol. 3, pp. 408–415). New York, NY: Marcel Dekker.

Herner, S., & Herner, M. (1967). Information needs and uses in science and technology. In C. A. Cuadra (Ed.), *Annual review of information science and technology* (Vol. 2, pp. 1–34). Chicago, IL: Encyclopaedia Britannica.

Hernon, P. (1984). Information needs and gathering patterns of academic social scientists, with special emphasis given to historians and their use of U.S. government publications. *Government Information Quarterly, 1*, 401–429.

Hersberger, J. (2001). Everyday information needs and information sources of homeless parents. *The New Review of Information Behaviour Research: Studies of Information Seeking in Context (Proceedings of ISIC 2000), 2*, 119–134.

Hersberger, J. (2003). A qualitative approach to examining information transfer via social networks among homeless populations. *The New Review of Information Behaviour Research: Studies of Information Seeking in Context (Proceedings of ISIC 2002), 4*, 95–108.

Hersberger, J. (2005). Chatman's information poverty. In K. E. Fisher, S. Erdelez & E. F. McKechnie (Eds.), *Theories of information behavior* (pp. 75–78). Medford, NJ: Information Today.

Hertzum, M. (2002). The importance of trust in software engineers' assessment and choice of information sources. *Information and Organization, 12*(1), 1–18.

Hertzum, M. (2008). Collaborative information seeking: The combined activity of information seeking and collaborative grounding. *Information Processing & Management, 44*(2), 957–962.

Hertzum, M., & Pejtersen, A. M. (2000). The information-seeking practices of engineers: Searching for documents as well as people. *Information Processing & Management, 36*, 761–778.

Hewins, E. T. (1990). Information need and use studies. In M. E. Williams (Ed.), *Annual review of information science and technology* (Vol. 25, pp. 145–172). New York, NY: Elsevier.

Higgins, M. (1999). Meta-information, and time: Factors in human decision making. *Journal of the American Society for Information Science, 50*, 132–139.

Hilbert, M. (2011). The end justifies the definition: The manifold outlooks on the digital divide and their practical usefulness for policy-making. *Telecommunications Policy, 35*(8), 715–736.

Hirschman, E. C., & Holbrook, M. B. (1986). Expanding the ontology and methodology of research on the consumption experience. In D. Brinberg & R. Lutz (Eds.), *Perspectives on methodology in consumer research* (pp. 213–252). New York, NY: Springer-Verlag.

Hirsh, S. (1997). How do children find information on different types of tasks? Children's use of the science library catalog. *Library Trends, 45*, 725–746.

Hirsh, S., & Dinkelacker, J. (2004). Seeking information in order to produce information: An empirical study at Hewlett Packard Labs. *Journal of the American Society for Information Science and Technology, 55*(9), 807–817.

Hirshleifer, J. (1973). Economics of information: Where are we in the theory of information? *American Economic Association, 63*(2), 31–39.

Hjørland, B. (2002a). Domain analysis in information science: Eleven approaches – Traditional as well as innovative. *Journal of Documentation, 58,* 422–462.

Hjørland, B. (2002b). Epistemology and the socio-cognitive perspective in information science. *Journal of the American Society for Information Science and Technology, 53,* 257–270.

Hjørland, B. (2004). Arguments for philosophical realism in library and information science. *Library Trends, 52,* 488–506.

Hjørland, B. (2005a). Introduction to the special issue: Library and information science and the philosophy of science. *Journal of Documentation 61,* 5–10.

Hjørland, B. (2005b). Empiricism, rationalism and positivism in library and information science. *Journal of Documentation, 61,* 130–155.

Hjørland, B. (2005c). Afterword: Comments on the articles and proposals for further work. *Journal of Documentation, 61,* 5–10.

Hjørland, B. (2005d). The socio-cognitive theory of users situated in specific contexts and domains. In K. E. Fisher, S. Erdelez & E. F. McKechnie (Eds.), *Theories of information behavior* (pp. 339–343). Medford, NJ: Information Today.

Hjørland, B., & Albrechtsen, H. (1995). Toward a new horizon in information science: Domain analysis. *Journal of the American Society for Information Science, 46,* 400–425.

Hjørland, B., & Christensen, F. S. (2002). Work tasks and socio-cognitive relevance: A specific example. *Journal of the American Society for Information Science and Technology, 53*(11), 960–965.

Hogan, T. P., & Palmer, C. L. (2005). 'Information work' and chronic illness: Interpreting results from a nationwide survey of people living with HIV/AIDS. In A. Grove (Ed.), *ASIS&T'05: Proceedings of the annual meeting of the American Society for Information Science and Technology,* The American Society for Information Science and Technology, Silver Spring, MD (Vol. 42, pp. 1098–1122).

Hogeweg de Haart, H. P. (1981). *Characteristics of social science information.* Budapest: Hungarian Academy of Sciences.

Holland, M. P., & Powell, C. K. (1995). A longitudinal survey of the information seeking and use habits of some engineers. *College and Research Libraries, 55*(1), 7–15.

Holmes, K. L., & Lenz, E. R. (2002). Perceived self-care information needs and information-seeking behaviors before and after elective spinal procedures. *Journal of Neuroscience Nursing, 29,* 79–85.

Holmöv, P. (1982). Motivation for reading different context domains. *Communication Research, 9,* 314–320.

Holt, D. (1995). How consumers consume: A typology of consumption practices. *Journal of Consumer Research, 22,* 1–16.

Hörz, H. (1996). Reflections on a philosophical notion of information. In K. Kornwachs & K. Jacoby (Eds.), *Information: New questions to a multidisciplinary concept* (pp. 229–244). Berlin: Akademie Verlag.

Houston, R. (2011). CNI: Compelled nonuse of information. *Information Processing & Management, 47*(3), 363–375.

Howard, D. L. (1994). Pertinence as reflected in personal constructs. *Journal of the American Society for Information Science, 45*, 172–185.

Huber, G., & Sorrentino, R. (1996). Uncertainty in interpersonal and intergroup relations. In R. Sorrentino & E. T. Higgins (Eds.), *Handbook of motivation and cognition* (Vol. 3, pp. 591–619). New York, NY: Guilford.

Huberman, B., Pirollis, P., Pitkow, J., & Lukose, R. (1998). Strong regularities in world wide web surfing. *Science, 280*, 95–97.

Hultgren, F., & Limberg, L. (2003). A study of research on children's information behaviour in a school context. *The New Review of Information Behaviour Research: Studies of Information Seeking in Context (Proceedings of ISIC 2002), 4*, 1–15.

Hunt, M. (1997). *How science takes stock: The story of meta-analysis.* New York, NY: Russell Sage Foundation.

Huotari, M.-L., & Chatman, E. A. (2001). Using everyday life information seeking to explain organizational behavior. *Library & Information Science Research, 23*, 351–366.

Huotari, M.-L., & Wilson, T.D. (2001). Determining organizational information needs: The critical success factors approach. *Information Research, 6*(3). Retrieved from http://InformationR.net/ir/6-3/paper108.html

Hussey, L. (2010). Social capital, symbolic violence, and fields of cultural production: Pierre Bourdieu and Library and Information Science. In G. Leckie, L. Given & J. Buschman (Eds.), *Critical theory for library and information science: Exploring the social from across the disciplines* (pp. 41–52). Santa Barbara, CA: Libraries Unlimited.

Huvila, I. (2008a). Information work analysis: An approach to research on information interactions and information behaviour in context. *Information Research, 13*(3). Retrieved from http://InformationR.net/ir/13-3/paper349.html

Huvila, I. (2008b). The information condition: information use by archaeologists in labour, work and action. *Information Research, 13*(4) paper 369. Retrieved from http://InformationR.net/ir/13-4/paper369.html

Huvila, I. (2009). Analytical information horizon maps. *Library & Information Science Research, 31*(1), 18–28.

Huvila, I. (2010). Information sources and perceived success in corporate finance. *Journal of the American Society for Information Science and Technology, 61*(11), 2219–2229.

Hyldegard, J. (2009). Beyond the search process-Exploring group members' information behavior in context. *Information Processing & Management, 45*(1), 142–158.

Hyman, H. H., & Sheatsley, P. B. (1947). Some reasons why information campaigns fail. *Public Opinion Quarterly, 11*, 412–423.

Ignatieff, M. (1984). *The needs of strangers.* London: Chatto and Windus.

Ikoja-Odongo, R. (2002). Insights into the information needs of women in the informal sector of Uganda. *South African Journal of Library & Information Science, 68*(1), 39–52.

Ikoja-Odongo, R., & Mostert, J. (2006). Information seeking behaviour: A conceptual framework. *South African Journal of Library & Information Science, 72*(3), 145–158.

Ikoja-Odongo, R., & Ocholla, D. N. (2003). Information needs and information-seeking behavior of artisan fisher folk of Uganda. *Library & Information Science Research, 25,* 89–105.

Ikoja-Odongo, R., & Ocholla, D. N. (2004). Information seeking behaviour of the informal sector entrepreneurs: The Uganda experience. *Libri, 11*(1), 54–66.

Ingwersen, P. (1996). Cognitive perspectives of information retrieval interaction: Elements of a cognitive IR theory. *Journal of Documentation, 52,* 3–50.

Ingwersen, P., & Järvelin, K. (2005). *The turn: Integration of information seeking and retrieval in context.* Dordrecht: Springer.

Ipe, M. (2003). Knowledge sharing in organizations: A conceptual framework. *Human Resources Development Review, 2*(4), 337–359.

Iser, W. (1978). *The act of reading.* Baltimore, MD: Johns Hopkins University.

Israel, M., & Hay, I. (2006). *Research ethics for social scientists: Between ethical conduct and regulatory compliance.* London: Sage Publications.

Jacoby, J. (2005). Optimal foraging. In K. E. Fisher, S. Erdelez & E. F. McKechnie (Eds.), *Theories of information behavior* (pp. 259–264). Medford, NJ: Information Today.

Jacoby, J., Speller, D. D., & Berning, C. A. (1974). Brand choice behavior as a function of information load: Replication and extension. *Journal of Consumer Research, 1,* 33–42.

Jaeger, P. T., & Burnett, G. (2010). *Information worlds: Social context, technology, and information behavior in the age of the internet.* New York, NY: Routledge.

Jaeger, P. T., & Thompson, K. M. (2004). Social information behavior and the democratic process: Information poverty, normative behavior, and electronic government in the United States. *Library & Information Science Research, 26,* 94–107.

Jamali, H. R., & Nicholas, D. (2010). Interdisciplinarity and the information-seeking behavior of scientists. *Information Processing & Management, 46*(2), 233–243.

Janes, J., & McKinney, R. (1992). Relevance judgments of actual users and secondary judges: A comparative study. *Library Quarterly, 62*(2), 150–168.

Janesick, V. J. (1998). The dance of qualitative research design: Metaphor, methodolatry, and meaning. In N. Denzin & Y. Lincoln (Eds.), *Strategies of qualitative inquiry* (pp. 35–55). Thousand Oaks, CA: Sage Publications.

Jansen, B. J., & Rieh, S. Y. (2010). The seventeen theoretical constructs of information searching and information retrieval. *Journal of the American Society for Information Science and Technology, 61*(8), 1517–1534.

Jansen, B. J., Sobel, K., & Cook, G. (2011). Classifying ecommerce information sharing behaviour by youths on social networking sites. *Journal of Information Science, 37*(2), 120–136.

Järvelin, K., & Ingwersen, P. (2004). Information seeking research needs extension towards tasks and technology. *Information Research, 10*(1). Retrieved from http://InformationR.net/ir/10-1/paper212.html

Järvelin, K., & Wilson, T.D. (2003). On conceptual models for information seeking and retrieval research. *Information Research, 9*(1). Retrieved from http://InformationR.net/ir/9-1/paper163.html

Jeong, W. (2004). Unbreakable ethnic bonds: Information-seeking behavior of Korean graduate students in the United States. *Library & Information Science Research, 26,* 384–400.

Jiao, Q., & Onwuegbuzie, A. (1997). Antecedents of library anxiety. *The Library Quarterly, 67*, 372–389.

Jiyane, V., & Ocholla, D. N. (2004). Media accessibility and exploitation by rural women in Melmoth, KwaZulu-Natal. *South African Journal of Libraries and information Science, 70*(1), 1–8.

Johannisson, J., & Sundin, O. (2007). Putting discourse to work: Information practices and the professional project of nurses. *Library Quarterly, 77*(2), 199–218.

Johnson, C. A. (2005). Nan Lin's theory of social capital. In K. E. Fisher, S. Erdelez & E. F. McKechnie (Eds.), *Theories of information behavior* (pp. 323–327). Medford, NJ: Information Today.

Johnson, C. A. (2007). Social capital and the search for information: Examining the role of social capital in information seeking behavior in Mongolia. *Journal of the American Society for Information Science and Technology, 58*, 883–894.

Johnson, J. D. (1996). *Information seeking: An organizational dilemma*. Westport, CT: Quorum Books.

Johnson, J. D. (1997). *Cancer-related information seeking*. Cresskill, NJ: Hampton Press.

Johnson, J. D. (2003). On contexts of information seeking. *Information Processing & Management, 39*, 735–760.

Johnson, J. D., Andrews, J. E., & Allard, S. (2001). A model of understanding and affecting cancer genetics information seeking. *Library & Information Science Research, 23*, 335–349.

Johnson, J. D., Andrews, J. E., Case, D. O., & Allard, S. L. (2005). Genomics: The perfect information seeking research problem. *Journal of Health Communication, 10*(4), 323–329.

Johnson, J. D., Case, D., Andrews, J. E., Allard, S. L., & Johnson, N. E. (2006). Fields and pathways: Contrasting or complementary views of information seeking. *Information Processing & Management, 42*, 569–582.

Johnson, J. D., & Case, D. O. (2012). *Health information seeking*. New York, NY: Peter Lang Publishing.

Johnson, J. D., & Meischke, H. (1993). A comprehensive model of cancer-related information seeking applied to magazines. *Human Communication Research, 19*, 343–367.

Jones, S. G. (Ed.) (1999). *Doing Internet research. Critical issues and methods for examining the net*. Thousand Oaks, CA: Sage Publications.

Josefsson, U. (2006). Patients' online information seeking behavior. In M. Murero & R. E. Rice (Eds.), *The internet and health care: Theory, research, and practice (in press)*. Mahwah, NJ: Lawrence Erlbaum Associates.

Joyce, S. (2005). Symbolic violence. In K. E. Fisher, S. Erdelez & E. F. McKechnie (Eds.), *Theories of information behavior* (pp. 349–353). Medford, NJ: Information Today.

Julien, H. (1996). A content analysis of the recent information needs and uses literature. *Library & Information Science Research, 18*, 53–65.

Julien, H. (1998). Adolescent career decision making and the potential role of the public library. *Public Libraries, 37*(6), 376–381.

Julien, H. (1999). Barriers to adolescent information seeking for career decision making. *Journal of the American Society for Information Science, 50*, 38–48.

Julien, H. (2001). Use of information. In J. S. Schement (Ed.), *Encyclopedia of communication and information* (Vol. 3, pp. 1051–1056). New York, NY: Macmillan.

Julien, H. (2004). Adolescent decision-making for careers: An exploration of information behavior. In M. K. Chelton & C. Cool (Eds.), *Youth information-seeking behavior: Theories, models and issues* (pp. 321–352). Lanham, MD: Scarecrow Press.

Julien, H., & Duggan, L. (2000). A longitudinal analysis of the information needs and uses literature. *Library & Information Science Research, 22,* 291–309.

Julien, H., & Given, L. M. (2003). Faculty-librarian relationship in the information literacy context: A content analysis of librarians' expressed attitudes and experiences. *Canadian Journal of Information and Library Science, 27,* 65–87.

Julien, H., & Michels, D. (2004). Intra-individual information behaviour. *Information Processing & Management, 40*(3), 547–562.

Julien, H., Pecoskie, J. L., & Reed, K. (2011). Trends in information behavior research, 1999–2008: A content analysis. *Library & Information Science Research, 33*(1), 19–24.

Kafai, Y. B., & Bates, M. J. (1997). Internet web-searching in the elementary classroom: Building a foundation for information literacy. *School Library Media Quarterly, 25,* 103–111.

Kahlor, L. (2010). PRISM: A planned risk information seeking model. *Health Communication, 25*(4), 345–356.

Kalms, B. (2008). Household information practices: How and why householders process and manage information. *Information Research, 13*(1). Retrieved from http://InformationR.net/ir/13-1/paper339.html

Kaplowitz, M. D., Hadlock, T. D., & Levine, R. (2004). A comparison of web and mail survey response rates. *Public Opinion Quarterly, 68,* 94–101.

Kari, J. (2007). Conceptualizing the personal outcomes of information. *Information Research, 12*(2). Retrieved from http://InformationR.net/ir/12-2/paper292.html

Kari, J. (2010). Diversity in the conceptions of information use. *Information Research, 15*(3). Retrieved from http://InformationR.net/ir/15-13/colis7/colis709.htm

Kari, J., & Savolainen, R. (2003). Towards a contextual model of information seeking on the web. *The New Review of Information Behaviour Research: Studies of Information Seeking in Context (Proceedings of ISIC 2002), 4,* 155–175.

Katopol, P. (2005). Library anxiety. In K. E. Fisher, S. Erdelez & E. F. McKechnie (Eds.), *Theories of information behavior* (pp. 235–238). Medford, NJ: Information Today.

Katopol, P. F. (2007). "Just enough" information: Information behaviour, organizational culture, and decision making in municipal government. *Canadian Journal of Information and Library Science, 31*(3/4), 233–247.

Katz, D., & Kahn, R. (1978). *The social psychology of organizations* (2nd ed.). New York, NY: Wiley.

Katz, E. (1989). Journalists as scientists. *American Behavioral Scientist, 33,* 238–246.

Katz, E., Blumler, J., & Gurevitch, M. (1974). Utilization of mass communication by the individual. In J. Blumler & E. Katz (Eds.), *The uses of mass communication:*

Current perspectives on uses and gratifications research. Beverly Hills, CA: Sage Publications.

Katzer, J., Cook, K., & Crouch, W. (1998). *Evaluating information: A guide for users of social science research* (4th ed.). Boston, MA: McGraw-Hill.

Kaye, B. K., & Johnson, T. J. (2003). From here to obscurity? Media substitution theory and traditional media in an on-line world. *Journal of the American Society for Information Science and Technology, 54*, 260–273.

Kellermann, K., & Reynolds, R. (1990). When ignorance is bliss: The role of motivation to reduce uncertainty in uncertainty reduction theory. *Human Communication Research, 17*, 5–75.

Kelly, D. (2005). Implicit feedback: Using behavior to infer relevance. In A. Spink & C. Cole (Eds.), *New directions in cognitive information retrieval* (pp. 169–186). New York, NY: Springer.

Kelly, G. (1963). *A theory of personality: The psychology of personal constructs*. New York, NY: W. W. Norton & Company.

Kelly, K., Sturm, A., Kemp, K., Holland, J., & Ferketich, A. (2009). How can we reach them? Information seeking and preferences for a cancer family history campaign in underserved communities. *Journal of Health Communication, 14*(6), 573–589.

Kemp, D. (1974). Relevance, pertinence and information system development. *Information Storage and Retrieval, 10*, 37–47.

Kenner, H. (1986). Neatness doesn't count after all. *Discover, 7*(4), 86–93.

Kerins, G., Madden, R., & Fulton, C. (2004). Information seeking and students studying for professional careers: The cases of engineering and law students in Ireland. *Information Research, 10*(1). Retrieved from http://informationr.net/ir/10-1/paper208.html

Kerlinger, F. (1973). *Foundations of behavioral research*. New York, NY: Holt, Rinehart and Winston.

Kiesler, S., & Sproull, L. (1982). Managerial response to changing environments: Perspectives on problem sensing from social cognition. *Administrative Science Quarterly, 27*, 548–570.

Kim, J.-N., & Grunig, J. E. (2011). Problem solving and communicative action: A situational theory of problem solving. *Journal of Communication, 61*, 120–149.

King, D. W., Casto, J., & Jones, H. (1994). *Communication by engineers: A literature review of engineer's information needs, seeking processes, and use*. Washington, DC: Council on Library Resources.

King, D. W., & Tenopir, C. (2001). Using and reading scholarly literature. In M. E. Williams (Ed.), *Annual review of information science and technology* (Vol. 34, pp. 423–477). Medford, NJ: Information Today.

Kitchens, J. T., Powell, L., & Williams, G. (2003). Information, please? Information seeking, mass media, and the undecided voter. *Communication Research Reports, 20*, 73–80.

Kitchin, H. A. (2003). The tri-council policy statement and research in cyberspace: Research ethics, the Internet, and revising a living document. *Journal of Academic Ethics, 1*, 397–418.

Klapp, O. (1982). Meaning lag in the information society. *Journal of Communication, 32*(2), 56–66.

Klapper, J. (1960). *The effects of mass communication.* Glencoe, IL: Free Press.

Klein, G. (2009). *Streetlights and shadows: Searching for the keys to adaptive decision making.* Cambridge, MA: MIT Press.

Klir, G. J. (1996). Foreword. In K. Kornwachs & K. Jacoby (Eds.), *Information: New questions to a multidisciplinary concept* (pp. VII–VIII). Berlin: Akademie Verlag.

Knaus, C. S., Pinkleton, B. E., & Austin, E. W. (2000). The ability of the AIDS quilt to motivate information seeking, personal discussion, and preventative behavior as a health communication intervention. *Health Communication, 12*, 301–316.

Knorr-Cetina, K. D. (1981). *The manufacture of knowledge: A essay on the constructivist and contextual nature of science.* Oxford: Pergamon Press.

Knorr-Cetina, K. D., & Mulkay, M. J. (Eds.). (1983). *Science observed: Perspectives on the social study of science.* London: Sage Publications.

Kormos, J. (2005). On the methods by which we acquire information, and the effectiveness of libraries in supporting these behaviors. *LIBRI: International journal of libraries and information services, 55*(2–3), 67–168.

Krampen, G., Fell, C., & Schui, G. (2011). Psychologists' research activities and professional information-seeking behavior: Empirical analyses with reference to the theory of the intellectual and social organization of the sciences. *Journal of Information Science, 37*(4), 439–450.

Kremer, J. (2011). *Using statistics to plan new editorial.* Retrieved from http://www.bookmarket.com/statistics

Krikelas, J. (1983). Information-seeking behavior: Patterns and concepts. *Drexel Library Quarterly, 19*, 5–20.

Krippendorff, K. (1980). *Content analysis: An introduction to its methodology.* Beverly Hills, CA: Sage Publications.

Krippendorff, K. (1984). Paradox and information. In B. Dervin & M. Voigt (Eds.), *Progress in communication sciences* (Vol. 5, pp. 45–72). Norwood, NJ: Ablex.

Krippendorff, K. (2009). *On communicating: Otherness, meaning, and information.* New York, NY: Routledge.

Krueger, R., & Casey, M. A. (2000). *Focus groups: A practical guide for applied research* (3rd ed.). Thousand Oaks, CA: Sage Publications.

Kubey, R., & Csikszentmihalyi, M. (1990). *Television and the quality of life: How viewing shapes everyday experience.* Hillsdale, NJ: Erlbaum.

Kubey, R., Larson, R., & Csikszentmihalyi, M. (1996). Experience sampling method applications to communication research questions. *Journal of Communication, 46*(2), 99–120.

Kuhlthau, C. C. (1988a). Developing a model of the library search process: Cognitive and affective aspects. *Reference Quarterly, 28*, 232–242.

Kuhlthau, C. C. (1988b). Longitudinal case studies of the information search process of users in libraries. *Library & Information Science Research, 10*, 251–304.

Kuhlthau, C. C. (1991). Inside the search process: Information seeking from the user's perspective. *Journal of the American Society for Information Science, 42*, 361–371.

Kuhlthau, C. C. (1993a). *Seeking meaning: A process approach to library and Information services.* Norwood, NJ: Ablex.

Kuhlthau, C. C. (1993b). A principle of uncertainty for information seeking. *Journal of Documentation, 49*, 339–355.

Kuhlthau, C. C. (1997). The influence of uncertainty on the information seeking behavior of a securities analyst. In P. Vakkari, R. Savolainen & B. Dervin (Eds.), *Information seeking in context: Proceedings of a meeting in Finland, August 14–16, 1996*. London: Taylor Graham.

Kuhlthau, C. C. (1999). The role of experience in the information search process of an early career information worker: Perceptions of uncertainty, complexity, construction, and sources. *Journal of the American Society for Information Science, 50*, 399–412.

Kuhlthau, C. C. (2004a). *Seeking meaning: A process approach to library and information services* (2nd ed.). Westport, CT: Libraries Unlimited.

Kuhlthau, C. C. (2004b). Student learning in the library: What library power librarians say. In M. Chelton & C. Cool (Eds.), *Youth information-seeking behavior: Theories, models and issues* (pp. 37–64). Lanham, MD: Scarecrow Press.

Kuhlthau, C. C. (2005). Kuhlthau's information search process. In K. E. Fisher, S. Erdelez & E. F. McKechnie (Eds.), *Theories of information behavior* (pp. 230–234). Medford, NJ: Information Today.

Kuhlthau, C. C., & Tama, S. L. (2001). Information search process of lawyers, a call for 'just for me' information services. *Journal of Documentation, 57*, 25–43.

Kuhn, T. (1962). *The structure of scientific revolutions*. Chicago, IL: University of Chicago Press.

Kuruppu, P. U., & Gruber, A. M. (2006). Understanding the information needs of academic scholars in agricultural and biological sciences. *Journal of Academic Librarianship, 32*(6), 609–623.

Kwak, N. (1999). Revisiting the knowledge gap hypothesis. *Communication Research, 26*, 385–414.

Kwasitsu, L. (2003). Information-seeking behavior of design, process, and manufacturing engineers. *Library & Information Science Research, 25*, 459–476.

Kwasnik, B. H. (1992, August 10–14). A descriptive study of the functional components of browsing. In J. Larson and C. Unger (Eds.), *Engineering for Human-Computer Interaction: Proceedings of the IFIP TC2/WG2.7 Working Conference on Engineering for Human-Computer Interaction, IFIP Transactions, A-18*, Ellivuori, Finland (pp. 191–203).

Kwon, N. (2008). A mixed methods investigation of the relationship between critical thinking and library anxiety among undergraduate students in their information search process. *College & Research Libraries, 69*(2), 117–131.

Kwon, N., & Kim, K. (2009). Who goes to a library for cancer information in the e-health era? A secondary data analysis of the Health Information National Trends Survey (HINTS). *Library & Information Science Research, 31*(3), 192–200.

Lachman, R., Lachman, J. L., & Butterfield, E. C. (1979). *Cognitive psychology and information processing: An introduction*. Hillsdale, NJ: Lawrence Erlbaum Associates.

Lajoie-Paquette, D. (2005). Diffusion theory. In K. E. Fisher, S. Erdelez & E. F. McKechnie (Eds.), *Theories of information behavior* (pp. 118–122). Medford, NJ: Information Today.

Lakshminarayanan, B. (2010). *Towards developing an integrated model of information behaviour*. Unpublished Ph.D. Queensland University of Technology, Sydney, Australia.

Lambert, J. D. (2010). The information-seeking habits of Baptist ministers. *Journal of Religious & Theological Information, 9*(1/2), 1–19.

Lambert, S. D., & Loiselle, C. G. (2007). Health information-seeking behavior. *Qualitative Health Research, 17*(8), 1006–1019.

Lan, X. (2010). An examination of consumer browsing behaviors. *Qualitative Market Research: An International Journal, 13*(2), 154–173.

Landry, C. F. (2006). Work roles, tasks, and the information behavior of dentists. *Journal of the American Society for Information Science and Technology, 57*(14), 1896–1908.

Lang, A., Newhagen, J., & Reeves, B. (1996). Negative video as structure: Emotion, attention, capacity, and memory. *Journal of Broadcasting and Electronic Media, 40*, 460–477.

Laplante, A., & Downie, J. S. (2011). The utilitarian and hedonic outcomes of music information-seeking in everyday life. *Library & Information Science Research, 33*(3), 202–210.

Large, A., Beheshti, J., & Breuleux, A. (1998). Information seeking in a multimedia environment by primary school students. *Library & Information Science Research, 20*, 343–376.

Large, A., Nesset, V., & Beheshti, J. (2008). Children as information seekers: What researchers tell us. *New Review of Children's Literature & Librarianship, 14*(2), 121–140.

Larkin, C. (2010). Looking toward the future while learning from the past: Information retrieval in the visual arts. *Art Documentation, 29*(1), 49–60.

Lasch, C. (1995). *The revolt of the elites and the betrayal of democracy*. New York, NY: W. W. Norton & Company.

Latour, B., & Woolgar, S. (1979). *Laboratory life: The social construction of scientific facts*. Beverly Hills, CA: Sage Publications.

Lave, J., & Wenger, E. (1991). *Situated learning: Legitimate peripheral participation*. Cambridge, UK: Cambridge University Press.

Layne, S. S. (1994). Artists, art historians, and visual art information. *Reference Librarian, 47*, 23–36.

Lechte, J. (1994). *Fifty key contemporary thinkers: From structuralism to postmodernity*. London: Routledge.

Leckie, G. J. (1996). Female farmers and the social construction of access to agricultural information. *Library & Information Science Research, 18*, 297–321.

Leckie, G. J. (2005). General model of the information seeking of professionals. In K. E. Fisher, S. Erdelez & E. F. McKechnie (Eds.), *Theories of information behavior* (pp. 158–163). Medford, NJ: Information Today.

Leckie, G. J., Given, L. M., & Buschman, J. E. (Eds.). (2010). *Critical theory for library and information science: Exploring the social from across the disciplines*. Santa Barbara, CA: Libraries Unlimited.

Leckie, G. J., Pettigrew, K. E., & Sylvain, C. (1996). Modeling the information seeking of professionals: A general model derived from research on engineers, health care professionals and lawyers. *Library Quarterly, 66*, 161–193.

Lederer, K., Galtung, J., & Antal, D. (Eds.). (1980). *Human needs, a contribution to the current debate*. Cambridge, MA: Oelgeschlagen, Gunn & Hain.

Lee, C. P., & Trace, C. B. (2009). The role of information in a community of hobbyist collectors. *Journal of the American Society for Information Science and Technology, 60*(3), 621–637.

Lehmann, D. (1999). Introduction: Consumer behavior and Y2K. *Journal of Marketing, 63*, 14–18.

Leont'ev, A. N. (1978). *Activity, consciousness and personality*. Englewood Cliffs, NJ: Prentice Hall.

Leung, L., & Wei, R. (1999a). The gratifications of pager use: Sociability, information-seeking, entertainment, utility, and fashion and status. *Telematics and Informatics, 15*(4), 253–264.

Leung, L., & Wei, R. (1999b). Seeking news via the pager: An expectancy-value study. *Journal of Broadcasting and Electronic Media, 43*, 299–315.

Levine, M. (1969). An essay on browsing. *RQ, 9*(1), 35–36, 93.

Levitan, K. B. (1980). Applying a holistic framework to synthesize information science research. In B. Dervin & M. Voigt (Eds.), *Progress in communication science* (Vol. 2, pp. 241–273). Norwood, NJ: Ablex.

Levy, M., & Windahl, S. (1984). Audience activity and gratifications: A conceptual clarification and exploration. *Communication Research, 11*, 51–78.

Lewin, K. (1943). Forces behind food habits and methods of change. *Bulletin of the National Research Council, 108*, 65.

Leydesdorff, L. (1998). Theories of citation? *Scientometrics, 43*, 5–25.

Liebnau, J., & Backhouse, J. (1990). *Understanding information*. London: Macmillan.

Liehr, P., & Smith, M. (1999). Middle range theory: Spinning research and practice to create knowledge for the new millennium. *Advances in Nursing Science, 21*(4), 81–91.

Liew, C. L., & Ng, S. N. (2006). Beyond the notes: A qualitative study of the information-seeking behavior of ethnomusicologists. *Journal of Academic Librarianship, 32*(1), 60–68.

Lilley, S. C. (2008). Information barriers and Māori secondary school students. *Information Research, 13*(4). Retrieved from http://InformationR.net/ir/13-4/paper373.html

Lin, N. (2002). *Social capital: A theory of social structure and action*. Cambridge: Cambridge University Press.

Lin, N., & Garvey, W. D. (1972). Information needs and uses. In C. Cuadra & A. W. Luke (Eds.), *Annual review of information science and technology* (Vol. 7, pp. 5–37). Washington, DC: American Society for Information Science.

Lincoln, Y. S., & Guba, E. G. (1985). *Naturalistic inquiry*. Newbury Park, CA: Sage Publications.

Line, M. B. (1974). Draft definitions: Information and library needs, wants, demands and uses. *Aslib Proceedings, 27*(7), 87–97.

Lion, R., & Meertens, R. M. (2001). Seeking information about a risky medicine: Effects of risk-taking tendency and accountability. *Journal of Applied Psychology, 31*, 778–795.

Lipetz, B.-A. (1970). Information needs and uses. In C. A. Cuadra & A. W. Luke (Eds.), *Annual review of information science and technology* (Vol. 5, pp. 3–32). Chicago, IL: Encyclopaedia Britannica.

Little, R., Williams, C., & Yost, J. (2011). Airline travel: A history of information-seeking behavior by leisure and business passengers. In W. Aspray & B. Hayes (Eds.), *Everyday information: The evolution of information seeking in America* (pp. 121–156). Cambridge, MA: MIT Press.

Littlejohn, S. W. (1983). *Theories of human communication*. Belmont, CA: Wadsworth.

Livingstone, S. (2006). The influence of Personal Influence on the study of audiences. *The Annals of the American Academy of Political and Social Science, 608*(1), 233–250.

Longo, D. R. (2005). Understanding health information, communication, and information seeking of patients and consumers: A comprehensive and integrated model. *Health Expectations, 8*, 189–194.

Losee, R. (1997). A discipline independent definition of information. *Journal of the American Society for Information Science, 48*, 254–269.

Louis, M. (1980). Surprise and sensemaking: What newcomers experience in entering unfamiliar organizational settings. *Administrative Science Quarterly, 25*, 226–251.

Lowe, C. A., & Eisenberg, M. B. (2005). Big6 skills for information literacy. In K. E. Fisher, S. Erdelez & E. F. McKechnie (Eds.), *Theories of information behavior* (pp. 63–68). Medford, NJ: Information Today.

Lu, L., & Yuan, Y. (2011). Shall I google it or ask the competent villain down the hall? The moderating role of information need in information source selection. *Journal of the American Society for Information Science and Technology, 62*(1), 133–145.

Lu, Y. L. (2007). The human in human information acquisition: Understanding gatekeeping and proposing new directions in scholarship. *Library & Information Science Research, 29*(1), 103–123.

Lu, Y. L. (2010). Children's information seeking in coping with daily-life problems: An investigation of fifth- and sixth-grade students. *Library & Information Science Research, 32*(1), 77–88.

Lueg, C. P. (2008). Beyond FAQs: From information sharing to knowledge generation in online travel communities. Paper presented at the conference, "From information provision to knowledge production," Oulu, Finland.

Luhmann, N. (2000). *The reality of the mass media*. Stanford, CA: Stanford University Press.

Lundh, A. (2010). Studying information needs as question-negotiations in an educational context: A methodological comment. *Information Research, 15*(4). Retrieved from http://InformationR.net/ir/15-4/colis722.html

Lunt, P., & Livingstone, S. (1996). Rethinking the focus group in media and communications research. *Journal of Communication, 46*(2), 79–98.

Machlup, F. (1983). Semantic quirks in studies of information. In F. Machlup & U. Mansfield (Eds.), *The study of information: Interdisciplinary messages* (pp. 641–672). New York, NY: Wiley.

Machlup, F., & Mansfield, U. (1983). Cultural diversity in studies of information. In F. Machlup & U. Mansfield (Eds.), *The study of information: Interdisciplinary messages*. New York, NY: Wiley.

MacIntosh-Murray, A. (2001). Scanning and vicarious learning from adverse events in health care. *Information Research, 7*(1). Retrieved from http://InformationR.net/ir/7-1/paper113.html

MacIntosh-Murray, A., & Choo, C. W. (2005). Information behavior in the context of improving patient safety. *Journal of the American Society for Information Science and Technology, 56,* 1332–1345.

MacIntosh-Murray, A., & Choo, C. W. (2006). Information failures in health care. In B. Cronin (Ed.), *Annual review of information science and technology* (Vol. 40, pp. 357–392). Medford, NJ: Information Today.

MacKay, D. (1969). *Information, mechanism and meaning*. Cambridge, MA: MIT Press.

Mackenzie, M. L. (2002, November 18–21). Information gathering: The information behaviors of line-managers within a business environment. *Proceedings of the 65th annual meeting of the American Society for Information Science and Technology* (pp. 164–170). Medford, NJ: Information Today.

Mackenzie, M. L. (2003a). An exploratory study investigating the information behaviour of line managers within a business environment. *The New Review of Information Behaviour Research: Studies of Information Seeking in Context (Proceedings of ISIC 2002), 4,* 63–78.

Mackenzie, M. L. (2003b, October 19–22). Information gathering revealed within the social network of line-managers. In R. Todd (Ed.), *Proceedings of the 66th annual meeting of the American Society for Information Science and Technology* (Vol. 40, pp. 85–94). Medford, NJ: Information Today.

Mackenzie, M. L. (2004, November 12–17). The cultural influences of information flow at work: Manager information behavior documented. In L. Schamber and C. Barry (Eds.), *Proceedings of the 67th annual meeting of the American Society for Information Science and Technology* (Vol. 41, pp. 184–190). Medford, NJ: Information Today.

Mackenzie, M. L. (2005). Managers look to the social network to seek information. *Information Research, 10*(2). Retrieved from http://informationr.net/ir/10-2/paper216.html

Majid, S., Anwar, M., & Eisenschitz, T. (2000). Information needs and information seeking behavior of agricultural scientists in Malaysia. *Library & Information Science Research, 22,* 145–163.

Makri, S., & Warwick, C. (2010). Information for inspiration: Understanding architects' information seeking and use behaviors to inform design. *Journal of the American Society for Information Science and Technology, 61*(9), 1745–1770.

Manicas, P. T. (1998). *A history and philosophy of the social sciences*. London: Basil Blackwell.

Mann, T. (1993). The principle of least effort. In *Library research models: A guide to classification, cataloging and computers* (pp. 91–101). New York, NY: Oxford University Press.

Marcella, R., & Baxter, G. (2000). Information need, information seeking behaviour and participation, with special reference to needs related to citizenship: Results of a national survey. *Journal of Documentation, 56,* 136–160.

Marcella, R., & Baxter, G. (2001). A random walk around Britain: A critical assessment of the random walk sample as a method of collecting data on the public's citizenship information needs. *The New Review of Information Behaviour Research: Studies of Information Seeking in Context (Proceedings of ISIC 2000)*, *2*, 87–103.

Marcella, R., & Baxter, G. (2005). Information interchange. In K. E. Fisher, S. Erdelez & E. F. McKechnie (Eds.), *Theories of information behavior* (pp. 204–209). Medford, NJ: Information Today.

March, J. (1994). *A primer on decision making: How decisions happen.* New York, NY: The Free Press.

March, J., & Shapira, Z. (1992). Behavioral decision theory and organizational decision theory. In M. Zey (Ed.), *Decision making: Alternatives to rational choice models* (pp. 273–303). Newbury Park, CA: Sage Publications.

Marchionini, G. (1995). *Information seeking in electronic environments.* New York, NY: Cambridge University Press.

Marchionini, G. (2008). Human – Information interaction research and development. *Library & Information Science Research*, *30*(3), 165–174.

Marshall, J. (1993). Issues in clinical information delivery. *Library Trends*, *42*(1), 83–107.

Marton, C. (2003). Quality of health information on the Web: User perceptions of relevance and reliability. *The New Review of Information Behaviour Research: Studies of Information Seeking in Context (Proceedings of ISIC 2002)*, *4*, 195–206.

Martyn, J. (1974). Information needs and uses. In M. Williams (Ed.), *Annual review of information science and technology* (Vol. 9, pp. 3–23). Washington, DC: American Society for Information Science.

Martzoukou, K. (2005). A review of Web information seeking research: Considerations of method and foci of interest. *Information Research*, *10*(2). Retrieved from http://informationr.net/ir/10-2/paper215.html.

Maslow, A. H. (1963). The need to know and the fear of knowing. *The Journal of General Psychology*, *68*, 111–125.

Maslow, A. H. (1970). *Motivation and personality* (2nd ed.). New York, NY: Harper & Row.

Mason, D., & Lamain, C. (2007). *Nau mai haere mai ki Aotearoa: Information seeking behaviour of New Zealand immigrants.* Wellington: The Centre for Applied Cross-cultural Research, Victoria University of Wellington.

Mason, H., & Robinson, L. (2011). The information-related behaviour of emerging artists and designers: Inspiration and guidance for new practitioners. *Journal of Documentation*, *67*(1), 159–180.

Massey, S., Druin, A., & Weeks, A. (2007). Emotion, response, and recommendation: The role of affect in children's book reviews in a digital library. In D. Nahl & D. Bilal (Eds.), *Information and emotion: The emergent affective paradigm in information behavior research and theory* (pp. 135–160). Medford, NJ: Information Today.

Massey, S., Weeks, A., & Druin, A. (2005). Initial findings from a three-year international case study exploring children's responses to literature in a digital library. *Library Trends*, *54*(3), 245–265.

Masterman, M. (1970). The nature of a paradigm. In I. Lakatos & A. Musgrave (Eds.), *Criticism and the growth of knowledge: Proceedings of the international colloquium in the philosophy of science, London, 1965* (Vol. 4, pp. 59–90). Cambridge, UK: Cambridge University Press.

Mata, R., & Nunes, L. (2010). When less is enough: Cognitive aging, information search, and decision quality in consumer choice. *Psychology and Aging, 25*(2), 289–298.

Matthews, A. K., Sellergren, S. A., Manfredi, C., & Williams, M. (2002). Factors influencing medical information seeking among African American cancer patients. *Journal of Health Communication, 7*, 205–219.

Mays, T. L. (2005). Consumer health issues, trends, and research. *Library Trends, 53*(2/3), 395–518.

Max-Neef, M. (1992). *From the outside looking in: Experiences in barefoot economics.* Uppsala, Sweden: Dag Hammarskjöld Foundation.

McCaughan, E., & McKenna, H. (2007). Never-ending making sense: Towards a substantive theory of the information-seeking behaviour of newly diagnosed cancer patients. *Journal of Clinical Nursing, 16*, 2096–2104.

McCombs, M. (1972). Mass communication in political campaigns: Information, gratification, and persuasion. In F. Kline & P. Tichenor (Eds.), *Current perspectives in mass communication research.* Beverly Hills, CA: Sage Publications.

McCracken, G. (1987). Advertising: Meaning or information? In M. Wallendorf & P. Anderson (Eds.), *Advances in consumer research* (Vol. 14, pp. 121–124). Provo, UT: Association for Consumer Research.

McCreadie, M., & Rice, R. (1999). Trends in analyzing access to information. Part I: Cross-disciplinary conceptualizations of access. *Information Processing and Management, 35*, 45–76.

McKechnie, L. M., Baker, L., Greenwood, M., & Julien, H. (2002). Research method trends in human information behaviour literature. *The New Review of Information Behaviour Research: Studies of Information Seeking in Context (Proceedings of ISIC 2002), 3*, 113–126.

McKechnie, L. M., & Pettigrew, K. E. (2002). Surveying the use of theory in library and information science research: A disciplinary perspective. *Library Trends, 50*, 406–417.

McKenzie, P. J. (2002a). Communication barriers and information-seeking counter-strategies in accounts of practitioner-patient encounters. *Library & Information Science Research, 24*, 31–47.

McKenzie, P. J. (2002b). Connecting with information sources: How accounts of information seeking take discursive action. *The New Review of Information Behaviour Research: Studies of Information Seeking in Context (Proceedings of ISIC 2002), 3*, 161–174.

McKenzie, P. J. (2003a). A model of information practices in accounts of everyday-life information seeking. *Journal of Documentation, 59*, 19–40.

McKenzie, P. J. (2003b). Justifying cognitive authority decisions: Discursive strategies of information seekers. *Library Quarterly, 73*, 261–288.

McKenzie, P. J. (2004). Positioning theory and the negotiation of information needs in a clinical midwifery setting. *Journal of the American Society for Information Science and Technology, 55*, 685–694.

McKenzie, P. J. (2005). Interpretive repertoires. In K. E. Fisher, S. Erdelez & E. F. McKechnie (Eds.), *Theories of information behavior* (pp. 221–224). Medford, NJ: Information Today.

McKenzie, P. J. (2006). The seeking of baby-feeding information by Canadian women pregnant with twins. *Midwifery, 22*(3), 218–227.

McKenzie, P. J. (2009). Informing choice: The organization of institutional interaction in clinical midwifery care. *Library & Information Science Research, 31*(3), 163–173.

McKenzie, P. J. (2010). Informing relationships: Small talk, informing and relationship building in midwife-woman interaction. *Information Research, 15*(1). Retrieved from http://InformationR.net/ir/15-1/paper423.html

McKnight, M. (2006). The information seeking of on-duty critical care nurses: Evidence from participant observation and in-context interviews RMP. *Journal of the Medical Library Association, 94*(2), 145–151.

McKnight, M. (2007). A grounded theory model of on-duty critical care nurses' information behavior – The patient-chart cycle of informative interactions. *Journal of Documentation, 63*(1), 57–73.

McQuail, D., & Gurevitch, M. (1974). Explaining audience behavior: Three approaches considered. In J. Blumler & E. Katz (Eds.), *The uses of mass communication: Current perspectives on uses and gratifications research* (pp. 287–302). Beverly Hills, CA: Sage Publications.

McQuail, D., & Windahl, S. (1993). *Communication models for the study of mass communications* (2nd ed.). New York, NY: Longman Publishing.

Medaille, A. (2010). Creativity and craft: The information-seeking behavior of theatre artists. *Journal of Documentation, 66*(3), 327–347.

Meho, L. I., & Haas, S. W. (2001). Information-seeking behavior and use of social science faculty studying stateless nations: A case study. *Library & Information Science Research, 23*, 5–25.

Meho, L. I., & Tibbo, H. R. (2003). Modeling the information-seeking behavior of social scientists: Ellis's study revisited. *Journal of the American Society for Information Science and Technology, 54*, 570–587.

Mehra, B. (2007). Affective factors in information seeking during the cross-cultural learning process of international doctoral students in library and information science education. In D. Nahl & D. Bilal (Eds.), *Information and emotion: The emergent affective paradigm in information behavior research and theory* (pp. 279–301). Medford, NJ: Information Today.

Meier, R. (1963). Communication overload: Proposals from the study of a university library. *Administrative Science Quarterly, 7*, 521–544.

Mellon, C. (1986). Library anxiety: A grounded theory and its development. *College and Research Libraries, 47*, 160–165.

Mendelsohn, H. (1966). *Mass entertainment.* New Haven, CT: College and University Press.

Mendelsohn, H. (1973). Some reasons why information campaigns can succeed. *Public Opinion Quarterly, 37*, 50–61.

Menzel, H. (1960). *Review of studies in the flow of information among scientists.* New York, NY: Columbia University Bureau of Applied Social Research.

Menzel, H. (1964). The information needs of current scientific research. *Library Quarterly, 34*, 4–19.

Menzel, H. (1966a). Can science information needs be ascertained empirically? In L. Thayer (Ed.), *Communications: Concepts and perspectives* (pp. 279–295). Washington, DC: Spartan Books.

Menzel, H. (1966b). Information needs and uses in science and technology. In C. A. Cuadra & A. W. Luke (Eds.), *Annual review of information science and technology* (Vol. 1, pp. 41–69). Chicago, IL: Encyclopaedia Britannica.

Merton, R. (1968). *Social theory and social structure* (2nd ed.). New York, NY: Free Press.

Merton, R. K. (1972). Insiders and outsiders: A chapter in the sociology of knowledge. *American Journal of Sociology*, *78*, 9–47.

Merton, R. K. (1973). *The sociolology of science: Theoretical and empirical investigations*. Chicago, IL: University of Chicago Press.

Merton, R. K., Fiske, M., & Kendall, P. (1956). *The focused interview*. New York, NY: The Free Press.

Metoyer-Duran, C. (1991). Information seeking behavior of gatekeepers in ethnolinguistic communities: Overview of a taxonomy. *Library & Information Science Research*, *13*, 319–346.

Metoyer-Duran, C. (1993). Information gatekeepers. In M. Williams (Ed.), *Annual review of information science and technology* (Vol. 28, pp. 111–150). Medford, NJ: Learned Information.

Meyer, H. W. J. (2003). Information use in rural development. *The New Review of Information Behaviour Research: Studies of Information Seeking in Context (Proceedings of ISIC 2002)*, *4*, 109–125.

Meyers, E. M., Fisher, K. E., & Marcoux, E. (2007). Studying the everyday information behavior of tweens: Notes from the field. *Library & Information Science Research*, *29*(3), 310–331.

Meyers, E. M., Fisher, K. E., & Marcoux, E. (2009). Making sense of an information world: The everyday-life information behavior of preteens. *Library Quarterly*, *79*(3), 301–341.

Mick, C. K., Lindsey, G. N., & Callahan, D. (1980). Toward usable user studies. *Journal of the American Society for Information Science*, *31*, 347–356.

Mick, D., & Buhl, C. (1992). A meaning-based model of advertising experiences. *Journal of Consumer Research*, *19*, 317–338.

Mick, D., & DeMoss, M. (1990). Self-gifts: Phenomenological insights from four contexts. *Journal of Consumer Research*, *17*, 322–332.

Miller, G. A. (1968). Psychology and information. *American Documentation*, *19*, 286–289.

Miller, G. A. (1983a). Information theory in psychology. In M. Machlup & U. Mansfield (Eds.), *The study of information: Interdisciplinary messages* (pp. 493–496). New York, NY: Wiley.

Miller, G. A. (1983b). Informavores. In F. Machlup & U. Mansfield (Eds.), *The study of information: Interdisciplinary messages* (pp. 111–113). New York, NY: Wiley.

Miller, G. A., Galanter, E., & Pribram, K. H. (1960). *Plans and the structure of behavior*. New York, NY: Holt.

Miller, G. R. (1969). Human information processing: Some research guidelines. In R. J. Kibler & L. L. Barker (Eds.), *Conceptual frontiers in speech communication* (pp. 51–68). New York, NY: Speech Communication Association.

Miller, J. G. (1960). Information input overload and psychopathology. *American Journal of Psychiatry, 116*, 695–704.

Miller, J. G. (1978). *Living systems*. New York, NY: McGraw-Hill.

Miller, S. (1987). Monitoring and blunting: Validation of a questionnaire to assess styles of information seeking under threat. *Journal of Personality and Social Psychology, 52*, 345–353.

Miller, V. D., & Jablin, F. M. (1991). Information seeking during organizational entry: Influences, tactics, and a model of the process. *Academy of Management Review, 16*, 92–120.

Mintzberg, H. (1975). *Impediments to the use of management information*. New York, NY: National Association of Accountants.

Miranda, S. V., & Tarapanoff, K. (2008). Information needs and information competencies: A case study of the off-site supervision of financial institutions in Brazil. *Information Research, 13*(2). Retrieved from http://InformationR.net/ir/13-2/paper344.html

Miwa, M. (2005). Bandura's social cognition. In K. E. Fisher, S. Erdelez & E. F. McKechnie (Eds.), *Theories of information behavior* (pp. 54–57). Medford, NJ: Information Today.

Mizzaro, S. (1998). Relevance: The whole history. In T. Hahn & M. Buckland (Eds.), *Historical studies in information science* (pp. 221–243). Medford, NJ: Information Today.

Mnubi-Mchombu, C., Mostert, J., & Ocholla, D. (2009). Information needs and information-seeking behavior of orphans and vulnerable children and their caregivers in Okahandja, Namibia. *African Journal of Library, Archives & Information Science, 19*(1), 39–52.

Mokros, H., Mullins, L., & Saracevic, T. (1995). Practice and personhood in professional interaction: Social identities and information needs. *Library & Information Science Research, 17*, 237–257.

Mon, L. (2005). Face threat. In K. E. Fisher, S. Erdelez & E. F. McKechnie (Eds.), *Theories of information behavior* (pp. 149–152). Medford, NJ: Information Today.

Mooers, C. N. (1960). Mooers' law, or why some information systems are used and others are not (unpaged editorial). *American Documentation* (Vol. 11, No. 3).

Mooko, N. P. (2002). The use and awareness of women's groups as sources of information in three small villages in Botswana. *South African Journal of Library & Information Science, 68*, 104–111.

Morey, O. (2007). Health information ties: Preliminary findings on the health information seeking behaviour of an African–American community. *Information Research, 12*(2). Retrieved from http://InformationR.net/ir/12-2/paper297.html

Morgan, M., & Shanahan, J. (1997). Two decades of cultivation research: An appraisal and meta-analysis. In B. Burleson (Ed.), *Communication yearbook* (Vol. 20, pp. 1–45). Thousand Oaks, CA: Sage Publications.

Morowitz, H. (1991). *The thermodynamics of pizza*. New Brunswick, NJ: Rutgers University Press.

Morrison, E. W. (1993). Newcomer information seeking: Exploring types, modes, sources, and outcomes. *Academy of Management Journal, 36*, 557–589.

Morrison, E. W. (2002). Information seeking within organizations. *Human Communication Research, 28*, 229–242.

Moyer-Gusé, E. (2008). Toward a theory of entertainment persuasion: Explaining the persuasive effects of entertainment-education messages. *Communication Theory, 18*, 407–425.

Muha, C., Smith, K., Baum, S., Ter Maat, J., & Ward, J. (1998). The use and selection of sources in information seeking: The Cancer Information Service experience. Part 8. *Journal of Health Communication, 3*(suppl.), 109–120.

Mullaly-Quijas, P., Ward, D., & Woefl, N. (1994). Using focus groups to discover health professionals' information needs: A regional marketing study. *Bulletin of the Medical Library Association, 82*(3), 305–311.

Murphy, J. (2003). Information-seeking habits of environmental scientists: A study of interdisciplinary scientists at the Environmental Protection Agency in Research Triangle Park, North Carolina. *Issues in Science and Technology Librarianship.* Retrieved from http://www.istl.org/03-summer/refereed.html

Murray, H. A. (1938). *Explorations in personality.* New York, NY: Oxford University Press.

Nahl, D. (2005). Affective load. In K. E. Fisher, S. Erdelez & E. F. McKechnie (Eds.), *Theories of information behavior* (pp. 39–44). Medford, NJ: Information Today.

Nahl, D. (2007). A discourse analysis technique for charting the flow of micro-information behavior. *Journal of Documentation, 63*(3), 323–339.

Nahl, D., & Bilal, D. (Eds.). (2007). *Information and emotion: The emergent affective paradigm in information behavior research and theory.* Medford, NJ: Information Today.

Nardi, B. (Ed.) (1996). *Context and consciousness: Activity theory and human-computer interaction.* Cambridge, MA: MIT Press.

Naumer, C. (2005). Flow theory. In K. E. Fisher, S. Erdelez & E. F. McKechnie (Eds.), *Theories of information behavior* (pp. 153–157). Medford, NJ: Information Today.

Nauta, D. (1972). *The meaning of information.* The Hague: Mouton.

Neill, S. (1992). *Dilemmas in the Study of Information: Exploring the Boundaries of Information Science.* Westport, CT: Greenwood Press.

Nelson, C. E., & Pollock, D. K. (1970). *Communication among scientists and engineers.* Lexington, MA: Heath Lexington Books.

Newhagen, J. (1994). Media use and political efficacy: The suburbanization of race and class. *Journal of the American Society for Information Science, 45*, 386–394.

Newhagen, J. (1997). The role of feedback in the assessment of news. *Information Processing & Management, 33*, 583–594.

Nicholas, D., & Williams, P. (1999). The changing information environment: The impact of the Internet on information seeking behavior in the media. In T. D. Wilson & D. K. Allen (Eds.), *Information behaviour: Proceedings of the second international conference on research in information needs, seeking and use in different contexts, 13/15 August 1998, Sheffield, UK*, Taylor Graham, London (pp. 451–462).

Nicholas, D., Williams, P., Cole, P., & Martin, H. (2000). The impact of internet on information seeking in the media. *Aslib Proceedings, 52*(3), 98–114.

Nicholas, D., Williams, P., Smith, A., & Longbottom, P. (2005). The information needs of perioperative staff: A preparatory study for a proposed specialist library for theatres (NeLH). *Health Information and Libraries Journal, 22*(1), 35–43.

Niederdeppe, J. (2008). Beyond knowledge gaps: Examining socioeconomic differences in response to cancer news. *Human Communication Research, 34*(3), 423–447.

Niedwiedzka, B. (2003). A proposed general model of information behaviour. *Information Research, 9*(1). Retrieved from http://InformationR.net/ir/9-1/paper164.html

Niemelä, R., & Huotari, M.-L. (2008). Information use and enactment: The perspective of senior citizens' everyday life information behavior. Paper presented at the conference, "From information provision to knowledge production," Oulu, Finland.

Noar, S. M., Benac, C. N., & Harris, M. S. (2007). Does tailoring matter? Metaanalytic review of tailored print health behavior change interventions. *Psychological Bulletin, 133*, 673–693.

Noble, R., & Coughlin, C. (1997). Information-seeking practices of Canadian academic chemists: A study of information needs and use of resources in chemistry. *Canadian Journal of Communication, 20*(3/4), 49–60.

Nørretranders, T. (1998). *The user illusion: cutting consciousness down to size.* New York, NY: Viking.

Norris, P. (2001). *Digital divide: Civic engagement, information poverty, and the Internet worldwide.* Cambridge: Cambridge University Press.

North American Aviation. (1966). *Final report DOD user-needs study, phase II: Flow of scientific and technical information within the defense industry. Volumes I-III.* Anaheim, CA: North American Aviation.

Nunberg, G. (1996). Farewell to the information age. In G. Nunberg (Ed.), *The future of the book* (pp. 103–138). Berkeley, CA: University of California Press.

Oatley, K. (1999). Why fiction may be twice as true as facts: Fiction as cognitive and emotional stimulation. *Review of General Psychology, 3*, 101–117.

O'Connor, B. C., Copeland, J. H., & Kearns, J. L. (2003). *Hunting and gathering on the information savanna.* Lanham, MD: Scarecrow Press.

O'Connor, J. (1968). Some questions concerning "information need". *American Documentation, 19*(2), 200–203.

O'Connor, L. G. (2011). Duct tape and WD-40: The information worlds of female investors. *Library & Information Science Research, 33*, 228–235.

Olsson, M. (2005). Beyond 'needy' individuals: Conceptualizing information behavior. In A. Grove (Ed.), *ASIS&T'05: Proceedings of the annual meeting of the American Society for Information Science and Technology*, American Society for Information Science and Technology, Silver Spring, MD (Vol. 42, pp. 43–55).

Olsson, M. R. (2009). Re-thinking our concept of users. *Australian Academic & Research Libraries, 40*(1), 22–35.

Olsson, M. R. (2010a). All the world's a stage-the information practices and sense-making of theatre professionals. *Libri, 60*(3), 241–252.

Olsson, M. R. (2010b). Michel Foucault: Discourse, power/knowledge, and the battle for truth. In G. Leckie, L. Given & J. Buschman (Eds.), *Critical theory for library and information science: Exploring the social from across the disciplines* (pp. 63–74). Santa Barbara, CA: Libraries Unlimited.

O'Meara, J. (1989). Anthropology as empirical science. *American Anthropologist, 91*, 354–369.

Onwuegbuzie, A. J., Johnson, R. B., & Collins, K. (2009). Call for mixed analysis: A philosophical framework for combining qualitative and quantitative approaches. *International Journal of Multiple Research Approaches, 3*(2), 114–139.

Ooi, K. (2011). Selecting fiction as part of everyday life information seeking. *Journal of Documentation, 67*(5), 748–772.

O'Reilly, Jr., C. (1980). Individuals and information overload: Is more necessarily better? *Academy of Management Journal, 23*(4), 684–696.

Orr, R. (1970). The scientist as information processor: A conceptual model illustrated with data on variables related to library utilization. In C. Nelson & D. Pollock (Eds.), *Communication among scientists and engineers* (pp. 143–189). Lexington, MA: D.C. Heath.

Osheroff, J., Forsythe, D., Buchanan, B., Bankowitz, R., Blumenfeld, B., & Miller, R. (1991). Physicians' information needs: An analysis of questions posed during clinical teaching. *Annals of Internal Medicine, 114*, 576–581.

Ostroff, C., & Kozlowski, S. W. (1992). Organizational socialization as a learning process: The role of information acquisition. *Personnel Psychology, 45*, 849–874.

Otike, J. (1999). The information needs and seeking habits of lawyers in England: A pilot study. *International Information & Library Review, 31*, 19–39.

Otto, J., Metz, S., & Ensmenger, N. (2011). Sports fans and their information-gathering habits: How media technologies have brought fans closer to their teams over time. In W. Aspray & B. Hayes (Eds.), *Everyday information: The evolution of information seeking in America* (pp. 185–216). Cambridge, MA: MIT Press.

Overhage, C. F., & Harman, R. J. (1965). *Intrex: Report of a planning conference on information transfer experiments.* Cambridge, MA: MIT Press.

Owen, D. J., & Fang, M. L.-E. (2003). Information-seeking behavior in complementary and alternative medicine (CAM): An online survey of faculty at a health sciences campus. *Journal of the Medical Libraries Association, 91*(3), 311–321.

Owen, R. S. (1992). Clarifying the simple assumption of the information load paradigm. In J. John, F. Sherry & B. Sternthal (Eds.), *Advances in consumer research* (Vol. 19, pp. 770–776). Provo, UT: Association for Consumer Research.

Ozanne, J. L., Brucks, M., & Grewal, D. (1992). A study of information search behavior during the categorization of new products. *Journal of Consumer Research, 18*, 452–463.

Paisley, W. J. (1965). *The flow of (behavioral) science information – A review of the research literature.* Stanford, CA: Institute for Communication Research, Stanford University.

Paisley, W. J. (1968). Information needs and uses. In C. Cuadra (Ed.), *Annual review of information science and technology* (Vol. 3, pp. 1–30). Chicago, IL: Encyclopaedia Britannica.

Paisley, W. J. (1980). Information and work. In B. Dervin & M. Voigt (Eds.), *Progress in communication sciences* (Vol. 2, pp. 114–165). Norwood, NJ: Ablex.

Paisley, W. J. (1986). The convergence of communication and information science. In H. Edelman (Ed.), *Libraries and information science in the electronic age* (pp. 122–153). Philadelphia, PA: ISI Press.

Paisley, W. J. (1990). Information science as a multidiscipline. In J. Pemberton & A. Prentice (Eds.), *Information science: The interdisciplinary context* (pp. 3–24). New York, NY: Neal-Schuman Publishers.

Paisley, W. J. (1993). Knowledge utilization: The role of new communication technologies. *Journal of the American Society for Information Science, 44*, 222–234.

Palmer, C. L. (1996). Information work at the boundaries of science: Linking information services to research practices. *Library Trends, 45*, 165–191.

Palmer, C. L. (1999). Structures and strategies of interdisciplinary science. *Journal of the American Society for Information Science, 50*, 242–253.

Palmer, C. L., & Neumann, L. J. (2002). The information work of interdisciplinary humanities scholars: Exploration and translation. *Library Quarterly, 72*, 85–117.

Palmer, J. (1991). Scientists and information: I. Using cluster analysis to identify information style. *Journal of Documentation, 47*, 105–129.

Palmgreen, P. (1984). Uses and gratifications: A theoretical perspective. In R. Bostrom (Ed.), *Communication yearbook* (Vol. 8, pp. 20–55). Beverly Hills, CA: Sage Publications.

Palmour, V., Rathbun, P., Brown, W., Dervin, B., & Dowd, P. (1979). *Information needs of Californians*. Rockville, MD: King Research, Inc.

Palmquist, R. A. (2005). Taylor's information use environments. In K. E. Fisher, S. Erdelez & E. F. McKechnie (Eds.), *Theories of information behavior* (pp. 354–357). Medford, NJ: Information Today.

Pálsdóttir, A. (2008). Information behaviour, health self-efficacy beliefs and health behaviour in Icelanders' everyday life. *Information Research, 13*(1). Retrieved from http://informationr.net/ir/13-1/paper334.html

Pálsdóttir, A. (2010). The connection between purposive information seeking and information encountering: A study of Icelanders' health and lifestyle information seeking. *Journal of Documentation, 66*(2), 224–244.

Park, T. (1994). Toward a theory of user-based relevance: A call for a new paradigm of inquiry. *Journal of the American Society for Information Science, 45*, 135–141.

Parks, R. E. (1922). *The immigrant press and its control*. New York, NY: Harper.

Pascal, B. (1670/1940). *Pensées* (W. Trotter, Trans.). New York, NY: The Modern Library.

Pavitt, C. (1999). The third way: Scientific realism and communication theory. *Communication Theory, 9*, 162–188.

Pearlin, L. I. (1959). Social and personal stress and escape television viewing. *Public Opinion Quarterly, 23*, 255–259.

Perrow, C. (1989). On not using libraries. In B. P. Lynch (Ed.), *Humanists at work: Disciplinary perspectives and personal reflections* (pp. 29–42). Chicago, IL: University of Illinois at Chicago.

Perttilä, R., & Ek, S. (2010). Information behaviour and coping functions of long-term unemployed people in Finland. *Libri, 60*(2), 107–116.

Pettigrew, K. E. (1999). Waiting for chiropody: Contextual results from an ethnographic study of information behaviour among attendees at community clinics. *Information Processing and Management, 35*, 801–817.

Pettigrew, K. E. (2000). Lay information provision in community settings: How community health nurses disseminate human services information to the elderly. *Library Quarterly, 70*, 47–85.

Pettigrew, K. E., Durrance, J. C., & Unruh, K. T. (2002). Facilitating community information seeking using the Internet: Findings from three public library-community network systems. *Journal of the American Society for Information Science and Technology, 53*, 894–903.

Pettigrew, K. E., Fidel, R., & Bruce, H. (2001). Conceptual frameworks in information behavior. In M. E. Williams (Ed.), *Annual review of information science and technology* (Vol. 35, pp. 43–78). Medford, NJ: Information Today.

Pettigrew, K. E., & McKechnie, L. (2001). The use of theory in information science research. *Journal of the American Society for Information Science and Technology, 52*, 62–73.

Piaget, J. (1952). *The language and thought of the child.* London: Routledge.

Pifalo, V., Hollander, S., Henderson, C., DeSalvo, P., & Gill, G. (1997). The impact of consumer health information provided by libraries: The Delaware experience. *Bulletin of the Medical Library Association, 85*(1), 16–22.

Pinelli, T., Barclay, R., Glassman, N., Kennedy, J., & Demerath, L. (1991). The relationship between seven variables and the use of U.S. government technical reports by U.S. aerospace engineers and scientists. In J. Griffiths (Ed.), *ASIS'91: Proceedings of the 54th ASIS annual meeting, Washington, DC, October 27–31, 1991*, Learned Information, Medford, NJ (Vol. 28, pp. 313–321).

Pinelli, T. E. (1991). The information-seeking habits and practices of engineers. *Science and Technology Libraries, 11*(3), 5–25.

Pirolli, P. (2009). *Information foraging theory: Adaptive interaction with information.* New York, NY: Oxford University Press.

Pirolli, P., & Card, S. (1999). Information foraging. *Psychological Review, 106*, 643–675.

Poole, H. (1985). *Theories of the middle range.* Norwood, NJ: Ablex.

Poole, M. S., & McPhee, R. D. (1994). Methodology in interpersonal communication research. In M. L. Knapp, G. R. Miller (Eds.) *Handbook of interpersonal communication.* (2nd ed., pp. 42–99). Thousand Oaks, CA: Sage Publications.

Popkin, S. L. (1993). Information shortcuts and the reasoning voter. In B. Grofman (Ed.), *Information, participation and choice: An economic theory of democracy in perspective* (pp. 17–35). Ann Arbor, MI: University of Michigan Press.

Popper, K. (1972). *Objective knowledge: An evolutionary approach.* London: Oxford University Press.

Potter, J. (1996). *Representing reality: Discourse, rhetoric and social construction.* London: Sage Publications.

Prabha, C., Connaway, L. S., Olszewski, L., & Jenkins, L. R. (2007). What is enough? Satisficing information needs. *Journal of Documentation, 63*(1), 74–89.

Pratt, A. D. (1977). The information of the image. *Libri, 27*(3), 204–220.

Prekop, P. (2002). A qualitative study of collaborative information seeking. *Journal of Documentation, 58*(5), 533–562.

Price, D. (1965). Is technology historically independent of science? *Technology and Culture, 6,* 553–568.

Price, I. D. S. (1963). *Little science, big science.* New York, NY: Columbia University Press.

Prigoda, E., & McKenzie, P. J. (2007). Purls of wisdom: A collectivist study of human information behaviour in a public library knitting group. *Journal of Documentation, 63*(1), 90–114.

Proper, H., & Bruza, P. (1999). What is information discovery about? *Journal of the American Society for Information Science, 50,* 737–750.

Pysczynski, T., Greenberg, J., & Solomon, S. (1999). A dual-process model of defense against conscious and unconscious death-related thoughts: An extension of terror management theory. *Psychological Review, 106,* 835–845.

Raber, D. (2003). *The problem of information: An introduction to information science.* Lanham, MD: Scarecrow Press.

Radford, M. L. (2001). Encountering users, encountering images. *Journal of Education for Library and Information Science, 42*(1), 27–41.

Radway, J. (1985). *Reading the romance: Women, patriarchy, and popular literature.* Chapel Hill, NC: University of North Carolina Press.

Rayburn, J. D., II., & Palmgreen, P. (1984). Merging uses and gratifications and expectancy-value theory. *Communication Research, 11,* 537–562.

Reagan, J. (1996). The 'repertoire' of information sources. *Journal of Broadcasting & Electronic Media, 40,* 112–121.

Reddy, M. C., & Jansen, B. J. (2008). A model for understanding collaborative information behavior in context: A study of two healthcare teams. *Information Processing & Management, 44*(1), 256–273.

Reddy, M. C., & Spence, P. R. (2008). Collaborative information seeking: A field study of a multidisciplinary patient care team. *Information Processing & Management, 44*(1), 242–255.

Rees, A., & Saracevic, T. (1966). The measurability of relevance. *Proceedings of the American Documentation Institute, 3,* 225–234.

Rees, C. E., & Bath, P. A. (2000a). The psychometric properties of the Miller behavioural style scale with adult daughters of women with early breast cancer: A literature review and empirical study. *Journal of Advances in Nursing, 32,* 366–374.

Rees, C. E., & Bath, P. A. (2000b). Mass media sources for breast cancer information: Their advantages and disadvantages for women with the disease. *Journal of Documentation, 56,* 235–249.

Rees, C. E., & Bath, P. A. (2001). Information seeking behaviors of women with breast cancer. *Oncology Nursing Forum, 28*(5), 899–907.

Reeves, B. (1989). Theories about news and theories about cognition. *American Behavioral Scientist, 33*(2), 191–198.

Reneker, M. (1993). A qualitative study of information seeking among members of an academic community: Methodological issues and problems. *Library Quarterly, 63*, 487–507.

Reuter, K. (2007). Assessing aesthetic relevance: Children's book selection behavior in a digital library. *Journal of the American Society for Information Science and Technology, 58*(12), 1745–1763.

Reynolds, P. D. (1971). *A primer in theory construction.* New York, NY: Bobbs-Merrill Company.

Rice, R. E., & Atkin, C. (Eds.). (1989). *Public communication campaigns.* Newbury Park, CA: Sage Publications.

Rice, R. E., & Atkin, C. (1994). Principles of successful public communication campaigns. In J. Bryant & D. Zillmann (Eds.), *Media effects: Advances in theory and research* (pp. 365–387). Hillsdale, NJ: Lawrence Erlbaum Associates.

Rice, R. E., & Borgman, C. L. (1983). The use of computer-monitored data in information science and communication research. *Journal of the American Society for Information Science, 34*, 247–256.

Richmond, C. (1988). Hand and mouth: Information gathering and use in England in the later middle ages. *Journal of Historical Sociology, 1*, 233–252.

Rioux, K. (2005). Information acquiring-and-sharing. In K. E. Fisher, S. Erdelez & E. F. McKechnie (Eds.), *Theories of information behavior* (pp. 169–173). Medford, NJ: Information Today.

Ritchie, L. D. (1986). Shannon and Weaver: Unraveling the paradox of information. *Communication Research, 13*, 278–298.

Ritchie, L. D. (1991). *Information* (Vol. 2). Newbury Park, CA: Sage Publications.

Ritchie, L. D. (2003). Statistical probability as a metaphor for epistemological probability. *Metaphor and Symbol, 1*, 1–11.

Ritzer, G. (2008). *Classical sociological theory* (5th ed.). New York, NY: McGraw-Hill.

Roberts, N. (1975). Draft definitions: Information and library needs, wants, demands and uses: A comment. *Aslib Proceedings, 27*(7), 308–313.

Roberts, R. M. (1989). *Serendipity: Accidental discoveries in science.* New York, NY: Wiley.

Robertson, R. D. (1980). Small group decision making: The uncertain role of information in reducing uncertainty. *Political Behavior, 2*, 163–188.

Roeh, I. (1989). Journalism as storytelling, coverage as narrative. *American Behavioral Scientist, 33*(2), 162–168.

Robinson, M. A. (2010). An empirical analysis of engineers' information behaviors. *Journal of the American Society for Information Science and Technology, 61*(4), 640–658.

Rogers, E. M. (1986). *Communication technology: The new media in society.* New York, NY: The Free Press.

Rogers, E. M. (1994). *A history of communication study: A biographical approach.* New York, NY: The Free Press.

Rogers, E. M. (2003). *Diffusion of innovations* (5th ed.). New York, NY: The Free Press.

Rohde, N. F. (1986). Information needs. *Advances in Librarianship, 14*, 49–73.

Rokeach, M. (1960). *The open and closed mind.* New York, NY: Basic Books.

Rosch, E., & Lloyd, B. (Eds.). (1978). *Cognition and categorization.* Hillsdale, NJ: Lawrence Erlbaum Associates.

Rose, T. (2003). Technology's impact on the information-seeking behavior of art historians. *Art Documentation, 21*(2), 35–42.

Rosen, N. O., & Knäuper, B. (2009). A little uncertainty goes a long way: State and trait differences in uncertainty interact to increase information seeking but also increase worry. *Health Communication, 24*, 228–238.

Rosenbaum, H. (1993). Information use environments and structuration: Towards an integration of Taylor and Giddens. In S. Bonzi (Ed.), ASIS '93: *Proceedings of the 56th annual meeting of the American Society for Information Science, 30*, 235–245. Medford, NJ: Learned Information, Inc.

Rosenbaum, H. (2010). Anthony Giddens' influence on library and information science. In G. Leckie, L. Given & J. Buschman (Eds.), *Critical theory for library and information science: Exploring the social from across the disciplines* (pp. 119–130). Santa Barbara, CA: Libraries Unlimited.

Rosenberg, V. (1967). Factors affecting the preferences of industrial personnel for information gathering methods. *Information Storage and Retrieval, 3*, 119–127.

Rosenblatt, L. (1994). *The reader, the text, the poem: The transactional theory of the literary work* (2nd ed.). Carbondale, IL: Southern Illinois Press.

Rosengren, K. (1974). Uses and gratifications: A paradigm outlined. In J. Blumler & E. Katz (Eds.), *The uses of mass communication: Current perspectives on uses and gratifications research.* Beverly Hills, CA: Sage Publications.

Rosengren, K. (1989). Paradigms lost and regained. In B. Dervin, L. Grossberg, B. O'Keefe & E. Wartella (Eds.), *Rethinking communication: Paradigm issues* (Vol. 1, pp. 21–39). Newbury Park, CA: Sage Publications.

Ross, C. S. (1999). Finding without seeking: the information encounter in the context of reading for pleasure. *Information Processing and Management, 35*, 783–799.

Ross, C. S. (2005). Reader response theory. In K. E. Fisher, S. Erdelez & E. F. McKechnie (Eds.), *Theories of information behavior* (pp. 303–307). Medford, NJ: Information Today.

Ross, C. S. (2009). Reader on top: Public libraries, pleasure reading, and models of reading. *Library Trends, 57*(4), 632–656.

Ross, S. S., & Middleberg, D. (2001). *The seventh annual Middleberg/Ross survey of media in the wired world.* Retrieved from http://www.writenews.com/2001/041301_journalists_internet.htm

Rothbauer, P. (2005). Practice of everyday life. In K. E. Fisher, S. Erdelez & E. F. McKechnie (Eds.), *Theories of information behavior* (pp. 284–288). Medford, NJ: Information Today.

Rothbauer, P. M. (2010). Beyond a signpost for resistance: The promise of Michel de Certeau's practice of everyday life for LIS scholarship. In G. Leckie, L. Given & J. Buschman (Eds.), *Critical theory for library and information science: Exploring the social from across the disciplines* (pp. 53–62). Santa Barbara, CA: Libraries Unlimited.

Rowley, J. (2007). The wisdom hierarchy: Representations of the DIKW hierarchy. *Journal of Information Science, 33*(2), 163–180.

Ruben, B. D. (1992). The communication-information relationship in system-theoretic perspective. *Journal of the American Society for Information Science, 43*, 15–27.

Rubin, A. M. (1983). Television uses and gratifications: The interactions of viewing patterns and motivations. *Journal of Broadcasting, 27*, 37–51.

Rubin, A. M. (1994). Media uses and effects: A uses-and-gratifications perspective. In J. Bryant & D. Zillmann (Eds.), *Media effects: Advances in theory and research* (pp. 417–436). Hillsdale, NJ: Lawrence Erlbaum Associates.

Rubin, R. (2010). *Foundations of library and information science* (3rd ed.). New York, NY: Neal-Schuman Publishers.

Ruggiero, T. E. (2000). Uses and gratifications theory in the 21st century. *Mass Communications & Society, 3*, 3–37.

Ruvane, M. B. (2005). Annotation as process: A vital information seeking activity in historical geographic research. In A. Grove (Ed.), *ASIS&T'05: Proceedings of the annual meeting of the American Society for Information Science and Technology* (Vol. 42, pp. 506–522). Silver Spring, MD: American Society for Information Science and Technology.

Saab, D. J., & Riss, U. V. (2011). Information as ontologization. *Journal of the American Society for Information Science and Technology, 62*(11), 2236–2246.

Sairanen, A., & Savolainen, R. (2010). Avoiding health information in the context of uncertainty management. *Information Research, 15*(4).

Salasin, J., & Cedar, T. (1985). Information-seeking behavior in an applied research/ special delivery setting. *Journal of the American Society for Information Science, 36*, 94–102.

Salomon, L., & Koppelman, F. (1992). Teleshopping or going shopping? An information acquisition perspective. *Behaviour and Information Technology, 11*, 189–198.

Salton, G., & McGill, M. (1983). *Introduction to modern information retrieval.* New York, NY: McGraw-Hill.

Sandstrom, A., & Sandstrom, P. E. (1995). The use and misuse of anthropological methods in library and information science research. *Library Quarterly, 65*, 161–199.

Sandstrom, P. E. (1994). An optimal foraging approach to information seeking and use. *Library Quarterly, 64*, 414–449.

Sandstrom, P. E. (2001). Scholarly communication as a socioecological system. *Scientometrics, 51*, 573–605.

Saunders, C., & Jones, J. (1990). Temporal sequences in information acquisition for decision making. *Academy of Management Review, 15*, 29–46.

Savolainen, R. (1993). The sense-making theory: Reviewing the interests of a user-centered approach to information seeking and use. *Information Processing & Management, 29*, 13–28.

Savolainen, R. (1995). Everyday life information seeking: Approaching information seeking in the context of "way of life". *Library & Information Science Research, 17*, 259–294.

Savolainen, R. (1999). Seeking and using information from the Internet: The context of non-work use. In T. D. Wilson & D. K. Allen (Eds.), *Information behaviour: Proceedings of the second international conference on research in information needs, seeking and use in different contexts, 13/15 August 1998, Sheffield, UK* (pp. 356–370). London: Taylor Graham.

Savolainen, R. (2001). 'Living encyclopedia' or idle talk? Seeking and providing consumer information in an Internet newsgroup. *Library & Information Science Research, 23,* 67–90.

Savolainen, R. (2004). Enthusiastic, realistic and critical: Discourses of Internet use in the context of everyday life information seeking. *Information Research, 10*(1). Retrieved from http://informationr.net/ir/10-1/paper198.html

Savolainen, R. (2005). Everyday life information seeking. In K. E. Fisher, S. Erdelez & E. F. McKechnie (Eds.), *Theories of information behavior* (pp. 143–148). Medford, NJ: Information Today.

Savolainen, R. (2006). Spatial factors as contextual qualifiers of information seeking. *Information Research, 11*(4). Retrieved from http://InformationR.net/ir/11-4/paper261.html

Savolainen, R. (2007a). Information behavior and information practice: Reviewing the "umbrella concepts" of information-seeking studies. *Library Quarterly, 77,* 109–132.

Savolainen, R. (2007b). Filtering and withdrawing: Strategies for coping with information overload in everyday contexts. *Journal of Information Science, 33*(2006)5, 611–621.

Savolainen, R. (2007c). Information source horizons and source preferences of environmental activists: A social phenomenological approach. *Journal of the American Society for Information Science and Technology, 58*(12), 1709–1719.

Savolainen, R. (2007d). Media credibility and cognitive authority: The case of seeking orienting information. *Information Research, 12*(3). Retrieved from http://InformationR.net/ir/12-3/paper319.html

Savolainen, R. (2008a). *Everyday information practices: A social phenomenological perspective.* Lanham, MD: Scarecrow Press.

Savolainen, R. (2008b). Source preferences in the context of seeking problem-specific information. *Information Processing & Management, 44*(1), 274–293.

Savolainen, R. (2008c). Autonomous, controlled and half-hearted: Unemployed people's motivations to seek information about jobs. *Information Research, 13*(4). Retrieved from http://informationr.net/ir/13-4/paper362.html

Savolainen, R. (2009a). Epistemic work and knowing in practice as conceptualizations of information use. *Information Research, 14*(1). Retrieved from http://InformationR.net/ir/14-1/paper392.html

Savolainen, R. (2009b). Information use and information processing: Comparison of conceptualizations. *Journal of Documentation, 65*(2), 187–207.

Savolainen, R. (2009c). Small world and information grounds as contexts of information seeking and sharing. *Library & Information Science Research, 31*(1), 38–45.

Savolainen, R. (2009d). Interpreting informational cues: An exploratorative study on information use among prospective homebuyers. *Journal of the American Society for Information Science and Technology, 60*(11), 2244–2254.

Savolainen, R. (2010). Source preference criteria in the context of everyday projects: Relevance judgments made by prospective homebuyers. *Journal of Documentation*, *66*(2), 70–92.

Savolainen, R., & Kari, J. (2004a). Placing the internet in information source horizons: A study of information seeking by internet users in the context of self-development. *Library & Information Science Research*, *26*, 415–433.

Savolainen, R., & Kari, J. (2004b). Conceptions of the Internet in everyday life information seeking. *Journal of Information Science*, *30*, 219–226.

Savolainen, R., & Kari, J. (2004c). Enthusiastic, realistic and critical: Discourses of Internet use in the context of everyday life information seeking. *Information Research*, *10*(1). Retrieved from http://informationr.net/ir/10-1/paper198.html

Schement, J. R. (1993a). An etymological exploration of the links between information and communication. In J. R. Schement & B. Ruben (Eds.), *Information and behavior* (Vol. 4, pp. 173–187). New Brunswick, NJ: Transaction Publishers.

Schement, J. R. (1993b). Communication and information. In J. R. Schement & B. Ruben (Eds.), *Information and behavior* (Vol. 4, pp. 3–33). New Brunswick, NJ: Transaction Publishers.

Schiller, H. (1996). *Information inequality: The deepening social crisis in America*. New York, NY: Routledge.

Schmidt, J., & Spreng, R. (1996). A proposed model of external consumer information search. *Journal of the Academy of Marketing Science*, *24*(3), 246–256.

Schrader, A. (1983). *Toward a theory of library and information science*. Unpublished doctoral dissertation, Indiana University, Bloomington, IN.

Schramm, W. (1973). Channels and audiences. In I. Pool, W. Schramm, N. Maccoby & E. Parker (Eds.), *Handbook of communication* (pp. 116–140). Chicago, IL: Rand McNally.

Schutt, R. (2008). *Investigating the social world: The process and practice of research* (6th ed.). Thousand Oaks, CA: Pine Forge Press.

Schutz, A. (1962). *Collected papers, I: The problem of social reality*. The Hague: Martinus Nijhoff.

Schutz, A. (1964). *Collected papers, II: Studies in social theory*. The Hague: Martinus Nijhoff.

Schutz, A. (1967). *The phenomenology of the social world*. Evanston, IL: Northwestern University.

Schwartz, B. (2004). *The paradox of choice: Why more is less*. New York, NY: ECCO.

Schwarzer, R. (2011). Health behavior change. In H. S. Friedman (Ed.), *Oxford handbook of health psychology* (pp. 591–611). New York, NY: Oxford University Press.

Scott, J. (2000). *Social network analysis: A handbook* (6th ed.). Thousand Oaks, CA: Sage Publications.

Scott, L. (1994). The bridge from text to mind: Adapting reader-response theory to consumer research. *Journal of Consumer Research*, *21*, 461–480.

Searle, J. (1983). *Intentionality: Essays in the philosophy of mind*. Cambridge, UK: Cambridge University Press.

Sears, D., & Freedman, J. (1967). Selective exposure to information: A critical review. *Public Opinion Quarterly, 31,* 194–213.

Seldén, L. (2001). Academic information seeking – Careers and capital types. *The New Review of Information Behaviour Research: Studies of Information Seeking in Context (Proceedings of ISIC 2000), 2,* 195–216.

Seldén, L. (2005). On Grounded Theory – With some malice. *Journal of Documentation, 61,* 114–129.

Serema, B. C. (2002). *Community information structures in Botswana: A challenge for librarians.* IFLA. Retrieved from http://www.ifla.org/IV/ifla68/papers/029-114e.pdf

Shah, C. (2010). Collaborative information seeking: A literature review. In W. A. (Ed.), *Advances in librarianship* (Vol. 32, pp. 3–33). Bingley, UK: Emerald Group Publishing Limited.

Shannon, C. (1949). The mathematical theory of communication. In C. Shannon & W. Weaver (Eds.), *The mathematical theory of communication* (pp. 31–125). Urbana, IL: University of Illinois Press.

Shapiro, G. (1986). *A skeleton in the darkroom: Stories of serendipity in science.* San Francisco, CA: Harper & Row.

Shenton, A. K., & Dixon, P. (2003a). Models of young people's information seeking. *Journal of Librarianship and Information Science, 35,* 5–22.

Shenton, A. K., & Dixon, P. (2003b). Youngsters' use of other people as an information-seeking method. *Journal of Librarianship and Information Science, 35,* 219–233.

Shenton, A. K., & Dixon, P. (2004a). Issues arising from youngsters' information-seeking behavior. *Library & Information Science Research, 26,* 177–200.

Shenton, A. K., & Dixon, P. (2004b). The nature of information needs and strategies for their investigation in youngsters. *Library & Information Science Research, 26,* 296–310.

Shenton, A. K., & Hayter, S. (2006). Terminology deconstructed: Phenomenographic approaches to investigating the term "information". *Library & Information Science Research, 28*(4), 563–578.

Shera, J. H., & Cleveland, D. B. (1977). History and foundations of information science. In M. E. Williams (Ed.), *Annual review of information science and technology* (Vol. 12, pp. 249–275). White Plains, NY: Knowledge Industry.

Sherry, Jr., J. L. (1990). A sociocultural analysis of a midwestern American flea market. *Journal of Consumer Research, 17,* 13–30.

Shim, W. (2003). Using handheld computers in information seeking research. *Journal of Education for Library and Information Science, 44,* 258–265.

Shoemaker, P. J. (1991). *Gatekeeping* (Vol. 3). Newbury Park, CA: Sage Publications.

Shuchman, H. L. (1981). *Information transfer in engineering.* Glastonbury, CT: The Futures Group.

Shugan, S. (1980). The cost of thinking. *Journal of Consumer Research, 7,* 99–111.

Sievert, D., & Sievert, M. (1989). Philosophical research: Report from the field. *Humanists at work: disciplinary perspectives and personal reflections* (pp. 95–99).

Chicago, IL: University of Illinois at Chicago, Institute for the Humanities and the University Library.

Silvio, D. H. (2006). The information needs and information seeking behaviour of immigrant southern Sudanese youth in the city of London, Ontario: An exploratory study. *Library Review*, *55*(4), 259–266.

Simon, H. (1992). Decision making and problem solving. In M. Zey (Ed.), *Decision making: Alternatives to rational choice models* (pp. 32–53). Newbury Park, CA: Sage Publications.

Simon, J., & Burstein, P. (1985). *Basic research methods in social science* (3rd ed.). New York, NY: Random House.

Sin, S.-C. (2011). Towards agency–structure integration: A person-in-environment (PIE) framework for modelling individual-level information behaviours and outcomes. In A. Spink & J. Heinström (Eds.), *New directions in information behaviour* (pp. 181–209). Bingley, UK: Emerald Group Publishing Limited.

Skinner, Q. (Ed.) (1985). *The return of grand theory in the human sciences*. Cambridge, UK: Cambridge University Press.

Slater, M. (1988). Social scientists' information needs in the 1980's. *Journal of Documentation*, *44*, 226–237.

Slife, B., & Williams, R. N. (1995). *What's behind the research? Discovering hidden assumptions in the behavioral sciences*. Thousand Oaks, CA: Sage Publications.

Sligo, F. X., & Jameson, A. M. (2000). The knowledge-behavior gap in use of health information. *Journal of the American Society for Information Science*, *51*(9), 858–869.

Smith, E. A., & Winterhalder, B. (Eds.). (1992). *Evolutionary ecology and human behavior*. New York, NY: Aldine de Gruyter.

Solomon, P. (1997a). Conversation in information-seeking contexts: A test of an analytical framework. *Library & Information Science Research*, *19*, 217–248.

Solomon, P. (1997b). Discovering information behavior in sense making: I. Time and timing. II. The social. III. The person. *Journal of the American Society for Information Science*, *48*(12), 1097–1138.

Solomon, P. (2002). Discovering information in context. In B. Cronin (Ed.), *Annual review of information science and technology* (Vol. 36, pp. 229–264). Medford, NJ: Information Today.

Sonnenwald, D. H. (2006). Challenges in sharing information effectively: Examples from command and control. *Information Research*, *11*(3). Retrieved from http://InformationR.net/ir/11-3/paper251.html

Sonnenwald, D. H., & Iivonen, M. (1999). An integrated human information behavior research framework for information studies. *Library & Information Science Research*, *21*, 429–457.

Sonnenwald, D. H., & Pierce, L. G. (2000). Information behavior in dynamic groups work contexts: Interwoven situational awareness, dense social networks and contested collaboration in command and control. *Information Processing & Management*, *36*(3), 461–479.

Sonnenwald, D. H., Wildemuth, B. M., & Harmon, G. L. (2001). A research method to investigate information seeking using the concept of information horizons: An example from a study of lower socio-economic student's information seeking behaviour. *The New Review of Information Behaviour Research*, *2*, 65–86.

Sorrentino, R. M., & Roney, C. J. R. (2000). *The uncertain mind: Individual differences in facing the unknown.* Philadelphia, PA: Psychology Press.

Spacks, P. (1985). *Gossip.* New York, NY: Knopf.

Spasser, M. A. (1999). Informing information science: the case for activity theory. *Journal of the American Society for Information Science, 50*(12), 1136–1138.

Spencer, C. C. (1971). Random time sampling with self-observation for library cost studies: Unit costs of interlibrary loans and photocopies at a regional medical library. *Journal of the American Society for Information Science, 22,* 153–160.

Sperber, D., & Wilson, D. (1995). *Relevance: Communication and cognition* (2nd ed.). Cambridge, MA: Harvard University Press.

Spink, A. (1997). Information science: A third feedback framework. *Journal of the American Society for Information Science, 48,* 728–740.

Spink, A., Bray, K. E., Jaeckel, M., & Sidberry, G. (1999). Everyday life information-seeking by low-income African American households: Wynnewood healthy neighborhood project. In T. D. Wilson & D. K. Allen (Eds.), *Information behaviour: Proceedings of the second international conference on research in information needs, seeking and use in different contexts, 13/15 August 1998, Sheffield, UK* (pp. 371–383). London: Taylor Graham.

Spink, A., & Cole, C. (2001). Information and poverty: Information-seeking channels used by African American low-income households. *Library & Information Science Research, 23,* 1–22.

Spink, A., & Cole, C. (2004). A human information behavior approach to a philosophy of information. *Library Trends, 52,* 617–628.

Spink, A., & Cole, C. (Eds.). (2005). *New directions in cognitive information retrieval.* New York, NY: Springer.

Spink, A., & Cole, C. (Eds.). (2006). *New directions in human information behavior.* New York, NY: Springer.

Spink, A., & Heinström, J. (Eds.). (2011). *New directions in information behaviour* (Vol. 1). Bingley, UK: Emerald Group Publishing Limited.

Spink, A., Ozmutlu, H. C., & Lorence, D. P. (2004). Web searching for sexual information: An exploratory study. *Information Processing & Management, 40,* 113–124.

Spradley, J. P. (1979). *The ethnographic interview.* New York, NY: Holt, Rinehart and Winston.

Spradley, J. P. (1980). *Participant observation.* New York, NY: Holt, Rinehart & Winston.

Stake, R.E. (2008). Case studies. In N. Denzin & Y. Lincoln (Eds.), *Strategies of qualitative inquiry* (3rd ed., pp. 119–150). Thousand Oaks, CA: Sage Publications.

Stam, D. C. (1984). How art historians look for information. *Art Documentation, 3*(1), 117–119.

Stam, D. C. (1995). Artists and art libraries. *Art Libraries Journal, 20*(2), 21–24.

Stavri, Z. (2001). Personal health information-seeking: A qualitative review of the literature. *MEDINFO Proceedings,* 1484–1488.

Stebbins, R. A. (2001). *New directions in the theory and research of serious leisure, Mellen studies in sociology* (Vol. 28). Lewiston, NY: Edwin Mellen Press.

Stebbins, R. A. (2009). Introduction: Pleasurable pursuits: Leisure and LIS research. *Library Trends, 57*(4), 618–631.

Stefl-Mabry, J. (2003). A social judgment analysis of information source preference profiles: An exploratory study to empirically represent media selection patterns. *Journal of the American Society for Information Science and Technology, 54*, 879–904.

Stefl-Mabry, J. (2005). The reality of media preferences: Do professional groups vary in awareness? *Journal of the American Society for Information Science and Technology, 56*, 1419–1426.

Stephens, D. W., & Krebs, J. R. (1986). *Foraging theory.* Princeton, NJ: Princeton University Press.

Stern, B. B. (1989). Literary explication: A methodology for consumer research. In E. C. Hirschman (Ed.), *Interpretive consumer research* (pp. 48–59). Provo, UT: Association for Consumer Research.

Stern, B. B. (1992). Crafty advertisers: Literary versus literal deceptiveness. *Journal of Public Policy and Marketing, 11*, 72–81.

Stewart, J. (1997). Developing communication theories. In G. Philipsen & T. Albrecht (Eds.), *Developing communication theories* (pp. 157–192). Albany, NY: State University of New York Press.

Stieg, M. F. (1981). The information needs of historians. *College & Research Libraries, 42*, 549–560.

Stilwell, C. (2002). The case for informationally based social inclusion for sex workers: A South African exploratory study. *Libri, 52*(2), 67–77.

Stocking, S. H., & Gross, P. H. (1989). *How do journalists think? A proposal for the study of cognitive bias in newsmaking.* Bloomington, IN: ERIC Clearinghouse on Reading and Communication Skills.

Stone, A., & Shiffman, S. (1992). Reflections on the intensive measurement of stress, coping, and mood, with an emphasis on daily measures. *Psychology and Health, 7*, 115–129.

Stone, S. (1980). CRUS humanities research programme. In S. Stone (Ed.), *Humanities information research: Proceedings of a seminar; Sheffield, 1980.* BLR&DD Report No. 5588 (pp. 15–26). Sheffield, UK: University of Sheffield.

Stone, S. (1982). Humanities scholars: Information needs and uses. *Journal of Documentation, 38*(4), 292–313.

Stonier, T. (1990). *Information and the internal structure of the universe.* Berlin: Springer.

Stooke, R. (2005). Institutional ethnography. In K. E. Fisher, S. Erdelez & E. F. McKechnie (Eds.), *Theories of information behavior* (pp. 210–214). Medford, NJ: Information Today.

Strother, E., Lancaster, D., & Gardiner, J. (1986). Information needs of practising dentists. *Bulletin of the Medical Library Association, 74*(3), 227–230.

Sturges, P. (2001). Gatekeepers and other intermediaries. *Aslib Proceedings, 53*(2), 62–67.

Suleiman, S., & Crosman, I. (Eds.). (1980). *The reader in the text.* Princeton, NJ: Princeton University Press.

Sundin, O. (2002). Nurses' information seeking and use as participation in occupational communities. *The New Review of Information Behaviour Research: Studies of Information Seeking in Context (Proceedings of ISIC 2002)*, *3*, 187–202.

Sundin, O. (2003). Towards an understanding of symbolic aspects of professional information: An analysis of the nursing knowledge domain. *Knowledge Organization*, *30*, 170–181.

Sundin, O., & Hedman, J. (2005). Professions and occupational identities. In K. E. Fisher, S. Erdelez & E. F. McKechnie (Eds.), *Theories of information behavior* (pp. 293–297). Medford, NJ: Information Today.

Sutton, S. (1994). The role of attorney mental models of law in case relevance determinations: An exploratory analysis. *Journal of the American Society for Information Science*, *45*, 186–200.

Swanson, E. (1987). Information channel disposition and use. *Decision Sciences*, *18*, 131–145.

Sweeny, K., Melnyk, D., Miller, W., & Shepperd, J. (2010). Information avoidance: Who, what, when, and why. *Review of General Psychology*, *14*, 340–353.

Talja, S. (1997). Constituting 'information' and 'user' as research objects: A theory of knowledge formations as an alternative to the information man-theory. In P. Vakkari, R. Savolainen, & B. Dervin (Eds.), *Information seeking in context: Proceedings of a meeting in Finland 14–16 August 1996* (pp. 67–80). London: Taylor Graham.

Talja, S. (2002). Information sharing in academic communities: Types and levels of collaboration in information seeking and use. *The New Review of Information Behaviour Research: Studies of Information Seeking in Context (Proceedings of ISIC 2002)*, *3*, 143–160.

Talja, S. (2005). The domain analytic approach to scholars' information practices. In K. E. Fisher, S. Erdelez & E. F. McKechnie (Eds.), *Theories of information behavior* (pp. 123–127). Medford, NJ: Information Today.

Talja, S. (2010). Jean Lave's practice theory. In G. J. Leckie, L. M. Given & J. E. Buschman (Eds.), *Critical theory for library and information science: Exploring the social from across the disciplines* (pp. 205–220). Santa Barbara, CA: Libraries Unlimited.

Talja, S., & Hansen, P. (2006). Information sharing. In A. Spink & C. Cole (Eds.), *New directions in human information behavior* (pp. 113–134). Dordrecht: Springer.

Talja, S., Keso, H., & Pietiläinen, T. (1999). The production of 'context' in information seeking research: A metatheoretical view. *Information Processing & Management*, *35*, 751–763.

Talja, S., & Maula, H. (2003). Reasons for the use and non-use of electronic journals and databases: A domain analytic study in four scholarly disciplines. *Journal of Documentation*, *59*, 673–691.

Talja, S., Tuominen, K., & Savolainen, R. (2005). "Isms" in information science. *Journal of Documentation*, *61*, 79–101.

Tannenbaum, S. J. (1994). Knowing and acting in medical practice: The epidemiological politics of outcomes practice. *Journal of Health Politics*, *19*(1), 27–44.

Tarde, G. (1903). *The laws of imitation* (E. C. Parsons, Trans.). New York, NY: Holt.

Tardy, R. W., & Hale, C. (1998). Getting 'plugged in': A network analysis of health-information seeking among 'stay-at-home moms'. *Communication Monographs*, *65*, 336–357.

Taylor, M., Alman, A., David, A., & Manchester, D. (2001). Use of the internet by patients and their families to obtain genetics-related information. *Mayo Clinic Proceedings*, *76*, 772–776.

Taylor, R. S. (1962). The process of asking questions. *Journal of the American Society for Information Science*, *13*, 391–396.

Taylor, R. S. (1968). Question-negotiation and information seeking in libraries. *College and Research Libraries*, *29*, 178–194.

Taylor, R. S. (1991). Information use environments. In B. Dervin & M. Voigt (Eds.), *Progress in communication sciences* (Vol. 10). Norwood, NJ: Ablex.

Tenopir, C., & King, D. W. (2004). *Communication patterns of engineers*. New York, NY: Wiley.

Tenopir, C., King, D. W., Spencer, J., & Wu, L. (2009). Variations in article seeking and reading patterns of academics: What makes a difference? *Library & Information Science Research*, *31*(3), 139–148.

ter Huurne, E. F. J., Griffen, R. J., & Gutteling, J. M. (2009). Risk information seeking among U.S. and Dutch residents: An application of the model of risk information seeking and processing. *Science Communication*, *31*(2), 215–237.

Tewksbury, D. (2003). What do Americans really want to know? Tracking the behavior of news readers on the Internet. *Journal of Communication*, *53*, 694–710.

Thayer, L. (1987). How does information "inform"? In B. D. Ruben (Ed.), *Information and behavior* (Vol. 2, pp. 13–26). New Brunswick, NJ: Transaction Publishers.

Thivant, E. (2005). Information seeking and use behaviour of economists and business analysts. *Information Research*, *10*(4). Retrieved from http://informationr.net/ir/10-4/paper234.html

Thomas, N. P., & Nyce, J. M. (2001). Context as category: Opportunities for ethnographic analysis in library and information science research. *The New Review of Information Behaviour Research*, *2*, 105–118.

Thompson, F. (1968). The organization is the information. *American Documentation*, *19*, 305–308.

Thompson, K. M. (2007). Furthering understanding of information literacy through the social study of information poverty. *The Canadian Journal of Information and Library Science*, *31*, 87–115.

Thompson, R., & Croft, B. (1989). Support for browsing in an intelligent text retrieval system. *International Journal of Man-Machine Studies*, *30*, 639–668.

Thompson, S., & O'Hair, H. (2008). Advice-giving and the management of uncertainty for cancer survivors. *Health Communication*, *23*(4), 340–348.

Thórsteinsdóttir, G. (2000). Information seeking behaviour of distance-learning students. *Information Research*, *6*(2).

Tibbo, H. (1991). Information systems, services, and technology for the humanities. In M. Williams (Ed.), *Annual review of information science and technology* (Vol. 26, pp. 287–346). Medford, NJ: Learned Information.

Tichenor, P. J., Donohue, G. A., & Olien, C. N. (1970). Mass media flow and differential growth of knowledge. *Public Opinion Quarterly, 34*, 159–170.

Tidline, T. J. (2005). Dervin's sense-making. In K. E. Fisher, S. Erdelez & E. F. McKechnie (Eds.), *Theories of information behavior* (pp. 113–117). Medford, NJ: Information Today.

Timko, M., & Loynes, R. M. A. (1989). Market information needs for prairie farmers. *Canadian Journal of Agricultural Economics, 37*, 609–627.

Timmers, C. F., & Glas, C. A. W. (2008). Developing scales for information-seeking behaviour. *Journal of Documentation, 66*(1), 44–69.

Timpka, T., & Arborelius, E. (1990). The GP's dilemmas: A study of knowledge need and use during health care consultations. *Methods of information in medicine, 29*, 23–29.

Tinker, A., McCreadie, C., & Salvage, A. (1993). *The information needs of elderly people – An exploratory study*. London: Age Concern Institute of Gerontology.

Todd, R. J. (2003). Adolescents of the information age: Patterns of information seeking and use, and implications for information professionals. *School Libraries Worldwide, 9*(2), 27–46.

Todd, R. J., & Edwards, S. (2004). Adolescent's information seeking and utilization in relation to drugs. In M. K. Chelton & C. Cool (Eds.), *Youth information-seeking behavior: Theories, models and issues* (pp. 353–386). Lanham, MD: Scarecrow Press.

Toms, E. G. (1999). What motivates the browser? In T. D. Wilson & D. K. Allen (Eds.), *Information behaviour: Proceedings of the second international conference on research in information needs, seeking and use in different contexts, 13/15 August 1998, Sheffield, UK* (pp. 191–208). London: Taylor Graham.

Toms, E. G., & Duff, W. (2002). "I spent 1 1/2 hours sifting through one large box ...". Diaries as information behavior of the archives user: Lessons learned. *Journal of the American Society for Information Science and Technology, 53*, 1232–1238.

Törnudd, E. (1959). *Study on the use of scientific literature and references services by Scandinavian scientists and engineers engaged in research and development: Proceedings of the International Conference on Scientific Information, Washington, DC, November 16–21, 1958, Volume I*. Washington, DC: National Academy of Sciences – National Research Council.

Trochim, W., & Donnelly, J. (2007). *The research methods knowledge base* (3rd ed.). Mason, OH: Atomic Dog Publishing.

Tufte, E. (1983). *The visual display of quantitative information*. Cheshire, CT: Graphics Press.

Tuominen, K. (2004). 'Whoever increases his knowledge merely increases his heartache.' Moral tensions in heart surgery patients' and their spouses' talk about information seeking. *Information Research, 10*(1). Retrieved from http://InformationR.net/ir/10-1/paper202.html

Tuominen, K., & Savolainen, R. (1997). A social constructionist approach to the study of information use as discursive action. In P. Vakkari, R. Savolainen, & B. Dervin (Eds.), *Information seeking in context: Proceedings of a meeting in Finland 14–16 August 1996* (pp. 81–96). London: Taylor Graham.

Tuominen, K., Talja, S., Savolainen, R. (2002). Discourse, cognition, and reality: Toward a social constructionist metatheory for library and information science. In H. Bruce, R. Fidel, P. Ingwersen, & P. Vakkari (Eds.), *Emerging frameworks and methods: Proceedings of the Fourth International Conference on Conceptions of Library and Information Science, CoLIS 4* (pp. 271–283). Greenwood Village, CO: Libraries Unlimited.

Tuominen, K., Talja, S., & Savolainen, R. (2005). The social constructionist viewpoint on information practices. In K. E. Fisher, S. Erdelez & E. F. McKechnie (Eds.), *Theories of information behavior* (pp. 328–333). Medford, NJ: Information Today.

Turk-Charles, S., Meyerowitz, B., & Gatz, M. (1997). Age differences in information seeking among cancer patients. *International Journal of Aging and Human Development, 45*(2), 85–98.

Turner, A. M., Stavri, Z., Revere, D., & Altamore, R. (2008). From the ground up: information needs of nurses in a rural public health department in Oregon. *Journal of the Medical Library Association, 96*(4), 335–342.

Turner, D. (2010). Orally-based information. *Journal of Documentation, 66*(3), 370–383.

Urbany, J., Dickson, P., & Wilkie, W. (1989). Buyer uncertainty and information search. *Journal of Consumer Research, 16*, 208–215.

Urquhart, C. (1998). Personal knowledge: A clinical perspective from the Value and EVINCE projects in health library and information services. *Journal of Documentation, 54*(4), 420–442.

Urquhart, C. (1999). Using vignettes to diagnose information seeking strategies: opportunities and possible problems for information use studies of health professionals. In T. D. Wilson, & D. K. Allen (Eds.), *Information behaviour: Proceedings of the second international conference on research in information needs, seeking and use in different contexts, 13/15 August 1998, Sheffield, UK* (pp. 277–289). London: Taylor Graham.

Urquhart, C. (2001). Bridging information requirements and information needs assessment: Do scenarios and vignettes provide a link? *Information Research, 6*(2). Retrieved from http://InformationR.net/ir/6-2/paper102.html

Urquhart, C. (2011). Meta-synthesis of research on information seeking behaviour. *Information Research, 16*(1). Retrieved from http://InformationR.net/ir/16-1/paper455.html

Urquhart, C., Light, A., Thomas, R., Barker, A., Yeoman, A., Cooper, J., ... Spink, A. (2003). Critical incident technique and explication interviewing in studies of information behavior. *Library & Information Science Research, 25*, 63–88.

Vakkari, P. (1997). Information seeking in context: A challenging metatheory. In P. Vakkari, R. Savolainen, & B. Dervin (Eds.), *Information seeking in context: Proceedings of a meeting in Finland 14–16 August 1996* (pp. 451–463). London: Taylor Graham.

Vakkari, P. (1999). Task complexity, problem structure and information actions: Integrating studies on information seeking and retrieval. *Information Processing and Management, 35*, 819–837.

Vakkari, P. (2008). Trends and approaches in information behaviour research. *Information Research, 13*(4). Retrieved from http://InformationR.net/ir/13-4/paper361.html

Vale, M. (1988). *Information structure and information seeking behavior of lawyers.* Unpublished doctoral, Stanford University, Stanford, CA.

van de Wijngaert, L. (1999). A policy capturing study of media choice: The effect information [sic] of needs and user characteristics on media choice. In T. D. Wilson & D. K. Allen (Eds.), *Information behaviour: Proceedings of the second international conference on research in information needs, seeking and use in different contexts, 13/15 August 1998, Sheffield, UK* (pp. 463–478). London: Taylor Graham.

van der Rijt, G. (1996). Information needs of the elderly. In K. Renckstorf (Ed.), *Media use as social action: European approach to audience studies* (pp. 163–178). London: John Libbey & Company Ltd.

van Dijk, T. A., & Kintsch, W. (1983). *Strategies of discourse comprehension.* Orlando, FL: Academic Press.

Van Snippenburg, L. (1996). Viewership of information-oriented TV programmes. In K. Renckstorf (Ed.), *Media use as social action: European approach to audience studies* (pp. 113–125). London: John Libbey & Company Ltd.

Varlejs, J. (1987). Information seeking: Changing perspectives. In J. Varlejs (Ed.), *Information seeking: Basing services on users' behaviors. Proceedings of the twenty-fourth annual symposium of the graduate alumni and faculty of the Rutgers School of Communication, Information, and Library Studies, 10, April 1986* (pp. 67–82). Jefferson, NC: McFarland.

Vavrek, B. (1995). Rural information needs and the role of the public library. *Library Trends, 44*(3), 21–48.

Veinot, T. C. (2009). Interactive acquisition and sharing: Understanding the dynamics of HIV/AIDS information networks. *Journal of the American Society for Information Science and Technology, 60*(11), 2313–2332.

Veinot, T. C. (2010). A multilevel model of HIV/AIDS information/help network development. *Journal of Documentation, 66*(6), 875–905.

Veinot, T. C., & Williams, K. (in press). Following the 'community' thread from sociology to information behavior and informatics: Uncovering theoretical continuities and research opportunities. *Journal of the American Society for Information Science and Technology.* Retrieved from: http://onlinelibrary.wiley.com/doi/10.1002/asi.21653/abstract

Viswanath, K., & Finnegan, J. (1996). The knowledge gap hypothesis: 25 years later. In B. Burleson (Ed.), *Communication yearbook* (Vol. 19, pp. 187–227). Thousand Oaks, CA: Sage Publications.

Voigt, M. (1961). *Scientists' approaches to information.* Chicago, IL: American Library Association.

von Thaden, T. L. (2008). Distributed information behavior: A study of dynamic practice in a safety critical environment. *Journal of the American Society for Information Science and Technology, 59*(10), 1555–1569.

Vorderer, P., Klimmt, C., & Ritterfeld, U. (2004). Enjoyment: At the heart of media entertainment. *Communication Theory, 14*, 388–408.

Vygotsky, L. (1978). *Mind in society: The development of higher psychological processes.* Cambridge, MA: Harvard University Press.

Wakeham, M. (1992). The information seeking behavior of nurses in the UK. *Information Service and Use, 12*, 131–140.

Waldhart, T. J., & Waldhart, E. S. (1975). *Communication research in library and information science: A bibliography on communication in the sciences, social sciences, and technology.* Littleton, CO: Libraries Unlimited, Inc.

Walker, C. G. (2009). Seeking Information: A study of the use and understanding of information by parents of young children. *Journal of Information Literacy*, *3*(2), 53–63.

Walsh, R. L. (1994). *Lawyers' attitude toward information*. Unpublished Masters of Science, City University, London.

Walter, V. A. (1994). The information needs of children. In I. Godden (Ed.), *Advances in librarianship* (Vol. 18, pp. 111–129). San Diego, CA: Academic Press.

Walters, C. (1974). *Consumer behavior: Theory and practice*. London: Irwin.

Wang, P. (2001). Methodologies and methods for user behavioral research. In M. E. Williams (Ed.), *Annual review of information science and technology* (Vol. 34, pp. 53–100). Medford, NJ: Information Today.

Warner, D., & Procaccino, J. D. (2004). Toward wellness: Women seeking health information. *Journal of the American Society for Information Science and Technology*, *55*, 709–730.

Warner, E., Murray, A. D., & Palmour, V. E. (1973). *Information needs of urban citizens, final report*. Washington, DC: U.S. Department of Health, Education and Welfare, Office of Education, Bureau of Libraries and Learning Resources.

Warwick, C., Rimmer, J., Blandford, A., Gow, J., & Buchanan, G. (2009). Cognitive economy and satisficing in information seeking: A longitudinal study of undergraduate information behavior. *Journal of the American Society for Information Science and Technology*, *60*(12), 2402–2415.

Watson-Boone, R. (1994). The information needs and habits of humanities scholars. *RQ*, *34*, 203–216.

Watt, Jr., J., & Krull, R. (1974). An information theory measure for television programming. *Communication Research*, *1*, 44–68.

Watts, D. (2004). *Six degrees: The science of a connected age*. New York, NY: W. W. Norton & Company.

Weaver, W. (1949). Recent contributions to the mathematical theory of communication. In C. Shann & W. Weaver (Eds.), *The mathematical theory of communication* (pp. 1–28). Urbana, IL: University of Illinois Press.

Webb, E., Campbell, D., Schwartz, R., Sechrest, L., & Grove, J. (1981). *Nonreactive measures in the social sciences*. Boston, MA: Houghton Mifflin.

Weick, K. (1970). The twigging of overload. In H. Pepinsky (Ed.), *People and information* (pp. 67–129). New York, NY: Pergamon.

Weick, K. (1995). *Sensemaking in organizations*. Thousand Oaks, CA: Sage Publications.

Wellisch, H. (1972). From information science to informatics: A terminological investigation. *Journal of Librarianship*, *4*, 157–187.

Wellstead, P. (2011). Information behaviour of Australian men experiencing stressful life events: the role of social networks and confidants. *Information Research*, *16*(2). Retrieved from http://informationr.net/ir/16-2/paper474.html

Wenger, E. (1998). *Communities of practice: Learning, meaning, and identity*. Cambridge, UK: Cambridge University Press.

Wersig, G., & Neveling, U. (1975). The phenomena of interest to information science. *Information Scientist*, *9*, 127–140.

Wersig, G., & Windel, G. (1985). Information science needs a theory of 'information actions'. *Social Science Information Studies*, *5*, 11–23.

Westbrook, L. (2003). Information needs and experiences of scholars in women's studies: Problems and solutions. *College & Research Libraries*, *64*, 192–209.

Westbrook, L. (2008). E-government support for people in crisis: An evaluation of police department website support for domestic violence survivors using 'person-in-situation' information needs analysis. *Library & Information Science Research*, *30*(1), 22–38.

Westbrook, L. (2009). Crisis information concerns: Information needs of domestic violence survivors. *Information Processing & Management*, *45*(1), 98–114.

Westley, B. H., & Barrow, L. C. (1959). An investigation of news-seeking behavior. *Journalism Quarterly*, *36*, 431–438.

Westley, B. H., & Maclean, Jr., M. (1957). A conceptual model for communications research. *Journalism Quarterly*, *34*(1), 31–38.

Wheeler, L., & Reis, H. (1991). Self-recording of everyday life events: Origins, types and uses. *Journal of Personality*, *59*(3), 339–354.

White, H. D. (2001). Authors as citers over time. *Journal of the American Society for Information Science and Technology*, *52*, 87–108.

White, M. D. (1975). The communications behavior of academic economists in research phases. *Library Quarterly*, *45*, 337–354.

White, M. D. (2000). Questioning behavior on a consumer health electronic list. *Library Quarterly*, *70*, 302–334.

White, M. D., & Marsh, E. E. (2006). Content analysis: A flexible methodology. *Library Trends*, *55*(1), 22–45.

White, M. D., Matteson, M., & Abels, E. G. (2008). Beyond dictionaries – Understanding information behavior of professional translators. *Journal of Documentation*, *64*(4), 576–601.

Whitmire, E. (2003). Epistemological beliefs and the information-seeking behavior of undergraduates. *Library & Information Science Research*, *25*, 127–142.

Whitt, A. J. (1993). The information needs of lesbians. *Library & Information Science Research*, *15*, 275–288.

Whittaker, S. (2011). Personal information management: From information consumption to curation. In B. Cronin (Ed.), *Annual review of information science and technology* (Vol. 45, pp. 3–62). Medford, NJ: Information Today.

Wiberley, S. E., & Jones, W. G. (1989). Patterns of information seeking in the humanities. *College & Research Libraries*, *50*, 638–645.

Wiberley, S. E., & Jones, W. G. (1994). Humanists revisited: A longitudinal look at the adoption of information technology. *College and Research Libraries*, *55*, 499–509.

Wiberley, S. E., & Jones, W. G. (2000). Time and technology: A decade-long look at humanists' use of electronic information technology. *College and Research Libraries*, *61*, 421–431.

Wicks, D. A. (1999). The information-seeking behavior of pastoral clergy: A study of the interaction of their work worlds and work roles. *Library & Information Science Research*, *21*, 202–226.

Wicks, D. A. (2004). Older adults and their information seeking. *Behavioral & Social Sciences Librarian*, *22*(2), 1–26.

Widén-Wulff, G. (2003). Information as a resource in the insurance business: The impact of structures and processes on organization information behaviour. *The*

New Review of Information Behaviour Research: Studies of Information Seeking in Context (Proceedings of ISIC 2002), *4*, 79–94.

Widén-Wulff, G. (2007). *Challenges of knowledge sharing in practice: A social approach*. Oxford, UK: Chandos.

Widén-Wulff, G., & Davenport, E. (2007). Activity systems, information sharing and the development of organizational knowledge in two Finnish firms: An exploratory study using Activity Theory. *Information Research*, *12*(3). Retrieved from http://InformationR.net/ir/12-3/paper310.html

Widén-Wulff, G., & Ginman, M. (2004). Explaining knowledge sharing in organizations through the dimensions of social capital. *Journal of Information Science*, *30*(5), 448–458.

Wiering, L. (2005). Uncertainty in the face of illness: Factors influencing patients' knowledge-related confidence. Paper presented at the conference, Tailoring health messages: Bridging the gap between social and humanistic perspectives on health communication, Mone Veritá, Switzerland, July 6–10, 2005.

Wikgren, M. (2001). Health discussions on the Internet: A study of knowledge communication through citations. *Library & Information Science Research*, *23*, 305–317.

Wikgren, M. (2003). Everyday health information exchange and citation behaviour in Internet discussion groups. *The New Review of Information Behaviour Research: Studies of Information Seeking in Context (Proceedings of ISIC 2002)*, *4*, 225–239.

Wildemuth, B. M. (2009). *Applications of social research methods to questions in information and library science*. Aurora, CO: Libraries Unlimited.

Wilkinson, M. A. (2001). Information sources used by lawyers in problem solving: an empirical exploration. *Library & Information Science Research*, *23*, 257–276.

Williams, F. (Ed.) (1987). *Technology and communication behavior*. Belmont, CA: Wadsworth Publishing Company.

Williams, F., Dordick, H., & Horstmann, F. (1977). Where citizens go for information. *Journal of Communication*, *27*, 95–100.

Williamson, K. (1997). The information needs and information-seeking behaviour of older adults: An Australian study. In P. Vakkari, R. Savolainen, B. Dervin (Eds.), *Information seeking in context: Proceedings of a meeting in Finland 14–16 August 1996* (pp. 337–350). London: Taylor Graham.

Williamson, K. (1998). Discovered by chance: The role of incidental information acquisition in an ecological model of information use. *Library & Information Science Research*, *20*, 23–40.

Williamson, K. (2005). Ecological theory of human information behavior. In K. E. Fisher, S. Erdelez & E. F. McKechnie (Eds.), *Theories of information behavior* (pp. 128–132). Medford, NJ: Information Today.

Williamson, K., & Asla, T. (2009). Information behavior of people in the fourth age: Implications for the conceptualization of information literacy. *Library & Information Science Research*, *31*(2), 76–83.

Williamson, K., & Manaszewicz, R. (2002). Breast cancer information needs and seeking: Towards an intelligent, user sensitive portal to breast cancer knowledge online. *The New Review of Information Behaviour Research: Studies of Information Seeking in Context (Proceedings of ISIC 2002)*, *3*, 203–219.

Williamson, K., Schauder, D., & Bow, A. (2000). Information seeking by blind and sight impaired citizens: an ecological study. *Information Research*. Retrieved from http://informationr.net/ir/5-4/paper79.html

Williamson, K., & Smith, D. K. (2010). Empowered or vulnerable? The role of information for Australian online investors. *Canadian Journal of Information and Library Science, 34*(1), 39–81.

Wilson, P. (1973). Situational relevance. *Information Storage and Retrieval, 9*, 457–471.

Wilson, P. (1983). *Second-hand knowledge: An inquiry into cognitive authority.* Westport, CT: Greenwood Press.

Wilson, P. (1995). Unused relevant information in research and development. *Journal of the American Society for Information Science, 46*, 45–51.

Wilson, P. (1996). Research and information overload. *Library Trends, 45*, 194–203.

Wilson, T. D. (1981). On user studies and information needs. *Journal of Documentation, 37*, 3–15.

Wilson, T. D. (1984). The cognitive approach to information seeking behavior and information use. *Social Science Information Studies, 4*, 197–204.

Wilson, T. D. (1994). Information needs and uses: Fifty years of progress? In B. Vickery (Ed.), *Fifty years of progress: A Journal of Documentation Review* (pp. 15–52). London: Aslib.

Wilson, T. D. (1997). Information behaviour: An interdisciplinary perspective. In P. Vakkari, R. Savolainen, B. Dervin (Eds.), *Information seeking in context: Proceedings of a meeting in Finland 14–16 August 1996* (pp. 39–49). London: Taylor Graham.

Wilson, T. D. (1999a). Models in information behaviour research. *Journal of Documentation, 55*(3), 249–270.

Wilson, T. D. (1999b, December 14). *Re: Information behaviour*. Retrieved from http://listserv.utk.edu/cgi-bin/wa?A2=ind9912&L=jesse&F=&S=&P=5004

Wilson, T. D. (2000). Human information behavior. *Informing Science, 3*(2), 49–55.

Wilson, T. D. (2002). Alfred Schutz, phenomenology and research methodology for information behaviour research. *The New Review of Information Behaviour Research: Studies of Information Seeking in Context (Proceedings of ISIC 2002), 3*, 71–82.

Wilson, T. D. (2003). Alfred Schutz, phenomenology and research methodology for information behaviour research. *New Review of Information Behaviour Research, 3*, 71–81.

Wilson, T. D. (2005). Evolution in information behavior modeling: Wilson's model. In K. E. Fisher, S. Erdelez & E. F. McKechnie (Eds.), *Theories of information behavior* (pp. 31–36). Medford, NJ: Information Today.

Wilson, T. D. (2006). A re-examination of information seeking behaviour in the context of activity theory. *Information Research, 11*(4). Retrieved from http://InformationR.net/ir/11-4/paper260.html

Wilson, T. D. (2008a). The information user: Past, present and future. *Journal of Information Science, 34*(4), 457–464.

Wilson, T. D. (2008b). Activity theory and information seeking. *Annual Review of Information Science and Technology, 42*, 119–161.

Wilson, T. D. (2010a). Information sharing: An exploration of the literature and some propositions. *Information Research*, *15*(4). Retrieved from http://InformationR. net/ir/15-4/paper440.html

Wilson, T. D. (2010b). Fifty years of information behavior research. *Bulletin of the American Society for Information Science and Technology*, *36*(3). Retrieved from http://www.asis.org/Bulletin/Feb-10/FebMar10_Wilson.html

Wilson, T. D., Ford, N., Ellis, D., Foster, A., & Spink, A. (2002). Information seeking and mediated searching, Part 2: Uncertainty and its correlates. *Journal of the American Society for Information Science and Technology*, *53*, 704–715.

Wilson, T. D., & Savolainen, R. (2009). The behaviour/practice debate: A discussion prompted by Tom Wilson's review of Reijo Savolainen's Everyday information practices: a social phenomenological perspective. Lanham, MD: Scarecrow Press, 2008. *Information Research*, *14*(2). Retrieved from http://InformationR.net/ir/14-2/paper403.html

Wilson, T. D., & Streatfield, D. R. (1977). Information needs in local authority social services departments: An interim report on Project INISS. *Journal of Documentation*, *33*, 277–293.

Wise, K., Alhabash, S., & Park, H. (2010). Emotional responses during social information seeking on Facebook. *Cyberpsychology, Behavior, and Social Networking*, *13*(5), 555–562.

Wolf, F. M. (1986). *Meta-analysis: Quantitative methods for research scientists.* Newbury Park, CA: Sage Publications.

Wolton, D. (1989). Rationality and subjectivity in applied science, social science, and journalism; Comments on Katz. *American Behavioral Scientist*, *33*(2), 247–250.

Woudstra, L., & van den Hooff, B. (2008). Inside the source selection process: Selection criteria for human information sources. *Information Processing & Management*, *44*(3), 1267–1278.

Wurman, R. (1989). *Information anxiety.* New York, NY: Doubleday.

Xie, B. (2008). The mutual shaping of online and offline social relationships. *Information Research*, *13*(3). Retrieved from http://InformationR.net/ir/13-3/paper350.html

Xu, Y. J., Tan, C. Y., & Yang, L. (2006). Who will you ask? An empirical study of interpersonal task information seeking. *Journal of the American Society for Information Science and Technology*, *57*(12), 1666–1677.

Yakel, E. (2004). Seeking information, seeking connections, seeking meaning: Genealogists and family historians. *Information Research*, *10*(1). Retrieved from http://informationr.net/ir/10-1/paper205.html

Yakel, E. (2005). Archival intelligence. In K. E. Fisher, S. Erdelez & E. F. McKechnie (Eds.), *Theories of information behavior* (pp. 49–53). Medford, NJ: Information Today.

Yeh, N.-C. (2008). The social constructionist viewpoint on gays and lesbians, and their information behaviour *Information Research*, *13*(4), paper 364. Retrieved from http://InformationR.net/ir/13-4/paper364.html

Yin, R. (2011). *Applications of case study research.* Thousand Oaks, CA: Sage Publications.

Yitzhaki, M., & Hammershlag, G. (2004). Accessibility and use of information sources among computer scientists and software engineers in Israel: Academy versus industry. *Journal of the American Society for Information Science and Technology*, *55*, 832–842.

Yoo, C. Y. (2011). Modeling audience interactivity as the gratification-seeking process in online newspapers. *Communication Theory*, *21*, 67–89.

Yoon, K., & Nilan, M. S. (1999). Toward a reconceptualization of information seeking research: Focus on the exchange of meaning. *Information Processing & Management*, *35*, 871–890.

Younger, P. (2010). Internet-based information-seeking behaviour amongst doctors and nurses: A short review of the literature. *Health Information and Libraries Journal*, *27*(1), 2–10.

Yovits, M., & Foulk, C. (1985). Experiments and analysis of information use and value in a decision making context. *Journal of the American Society for Information Science*, *36*, 63–81.

Zach, L. (2006). Using a multiple-case studies design to investigate the information-seeking behavior of arts administrators. *Library Trends*, *55*(1), 4–21.

Zelizer, B. (1993). Journalists as interpretive communities. *Critical Studies in Mass Communication*, *10*, 219–237.

Zerbinos, E. (1990). Information seeking and information processing: Newspapers versus videotext. *Journalism Quarterly*, *67*, 920–929.

Zey, M. (Ed.) (1992). *Decision making: Alternatives to rational choice models*. Newbury Park, CA: Sage Publications.

Zhang, Y. (2000). Using the Internet for survey research: A case study. *Journal of the American Society for Information Science*, *51*, 57–68.

Zhao, Y., Zhang, R., & Klein, K. K. (2009). Perceived information needs and availability: Results of a survey of small dairy farmers in Inner Mongolia. *Information Research*, *14*(3). Retrieved from http://InformationR.net/ir/14-3/paper411.html

Zillmann, D., & Bryant, J. (Eds.). (1985). *Selective exposure to communication*. Hillsdale, NJ: Lawrence Erlbaum Associates.

Zillmann, D., & Bryant, J. (1986). Exploring the entertainment experience. In J. Bryant & D. Zillmann (Eds.), *Perspectives on media effects* (pp. 303–324). Hillsdale, NJ: Lawrence Erlbaum Associates.

Zillmann, D., & Bryant, J. (1994). Entertainment as media effect. In J. Bryant & D. Zillmann (Eds.), *Media effects: Advances in theory and research* (pp. 437–461). Hillsdale, NJ: Lawrence Erlbaum Associates.

Ziman, J. (1976). *The force of knowledge: The scientific dimension of society*. Cambridge, UK: Cambridge University Press.

Zipf, G. (1949). *Human behavior and the principle of least effort: An introduction to human ecology*. New York, NY: Addison-Wesley.

Zubek, J. (Ed.) (1969). *Sensory deprivation: Fifteen years of research*. New York, NY: Appleton Century Crofts.

Zuckerman, H. (1987). Citation analysis and the complex problem of intellectual influence. *Scientometrics*, *12*, 329–338.

Zunde, P. (1984). Selected bibliography on information theory applications to information science and related subject areas. *Information Processing and Management*, *20*, 417–497.

Zweizig, D. (1977). Measuring library use. *Drexel Library Quarterly*, *13*, 2–15.

Subject Index